MW00817003

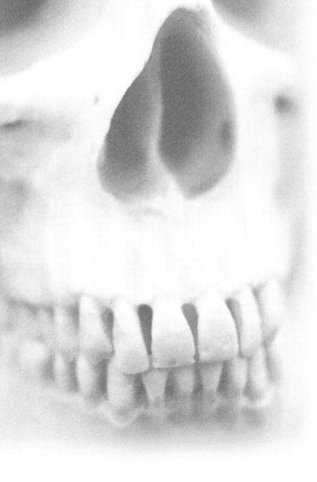

UNFORGETTABLE

GHOST STORY INTERVIEWS

Praises

"These stories will send shivers up your spine, and rightly so—they all really took place! If you've ever wanted to experience something paranormal, let this book be your guide."

— Dennis William Hauck,
"Haunted Places—The National Directory"

"If you're a lover of the supernatural, get cozy in an easy chair and prepare yourself for the inevitable. Eyewitness accounts told in a straightforward manner!"

— Tim Palmieri,
Western Outlaw-Lawman History Association

"Mr. Garcez book is a compendium of firsthand encounters with the paranormal, and run the gamut from sweet and poignant to hair-raising. It's a delightful read."

— Richard Wagner,
Author, Sex Therapist & Advice Columnist

"The reader is transported into the world of the supernatural, by a great storyteller who weaves history and personal interviews into a series of riveting tales, sure to make your skin crawl!"

— Rob & Anne Wlodarski

"Antonio has a rare talent for telling detail; he paints unforgettably creepy images that linger long after the book is done."

— Chris Woodyard,
"Ghost Stories of Canada"

"Antonio shows respect for the tales, and those who tell them, and understands that history and culture are inextricably bound to all folklore."

— Jo-Anne Christensen,
"Haunted Hotels"

©2024 by ANTONIO R. GARCEZ
1st Print edition—2024

ISBN 978-0-9898985-6-0
New Mexico, USA

All rights reserved. Published by Red Rabbit Press LLC

No part of this book may be reproduced in any form or by any
electronic or mechanical means including information storage and
retrieval systems, without permission in writing from the publisher,
except by a reviewer who may quote brief passages in a review.

Historical documentation and photos from archival resources listed at
end of book in References.

Present day photos taken by the author at the time of his research
investigations and interviews.

Author's website: GhostBooks.biz

DEDICATION

To all loving ancestors who remain present in our lives,
and are closer than we realize.

CONTENTS

ABOUT THE AUTHOR

ACKNOWLEDGEMENTS

REFERENCES

OTHER BOOKS BY ANTONIO R. GARCEZ

FOREWORD

Please do come in. Have a seat someplace comfortable, and be welcomed. You're about to experience something profound. You're going to gain the type of insight one can only glean from truly communicating with a fellow human being. As Charles Dickens noted, we're all fellow travelers to the grave, none of us is above or below anyone else. We're all heading toward that dark abyss... yet some of us may have gotten a glimpse of what lies just beyond. Folks don't share something like that with just anyone. That requires trust.

Thankfully, Antonio Garcez built that trust over a lifetime of chronicling accounts of the unexplained. He talked to people... he saw them and reached them, which will become evident as you turn these pages. That type of connection with all kinds of people from all walks of life isn't easy to form. Add in the strange subject matter: the supernatural, ghost encounters, and other events that not everyone believes exists, and that ability to connect on a deeper level becomes a rare gift. Thankfully, Antonio was born with it.

When it comes to personal accounts of encounters with ghosts, angels, and things that bump in the night, it's tempting to pontificate as to the cause. We want to find some reason, or at least a theory. Maybe even take up electronic equipment to seek it out to prove or disprove its existence. The short answer is: we don't know why or how these things happen. But we do know that millions of people the world over have had such encounters. There's a word for "ghost" in every language. There's a cultural understanding of what a ghost represents. And of course, our religious texts and even some of our history books give a nod to specters and spooks.

Ghosts are with us whether you choose to believe or not.

I've spent my own lifetime chasing these enigmas wherever they led me for my own books, podcasts, live programs, and television productions I've worked on. I understand the draw of wanting to wrap my hands and head around what they mean, even if the answers I find apply only to myself. We chase these stories and long to hear them from others who have had a brush with the supernatural because we are indeed fellow passengers to the grave. We're all going to pass on one day, and what comes next is one of the greatest mysteries humans have ever pondered.

Sadly, we lost Antonio in 2023 to Parkinson's. For him, the mystery is finally solved. I've thought since his passing: if only he could come back and tell us there truly is something more. But the more I thought about it, the more I figured: Perhaps he already did. Maybe he even had the good sense to document it while he was still alive. What you're holding in your hands right now is not only the testimony of dozens of people who have witnessed the profound nature of ghosts and spirits, but the life's work of a man who earned the trust of these people enough to share something deeply personal. That in itself is the mark of an extraordinary person. Because of the trust earned by Antonio, I give serious credence to the accounts and stories you're about to experience in the coming pages.

Believe. Don't believe. The choice is yours. But don't step to these pages lightly. There's wisdom here. Insight. There are people sharing some of their most vulnerable moments with someone they trust for no other reason than to speak it out loud and relive an incredible moment.

Antonio Garcez will forever be remembered as a person who gave a voice to the ghosts and the people who experienced them.

— Jeff Belanger
Author of The World's Most Haunted Places,
and Our Haunted Lives

INTRODUCTION

The stories contained within these pages, are not your typical ghost stories. They are real and told to me in an interview format. The people I interviewed for this book are from all walks of life who have had first-hand encounters with ghosts. These individuals have seen, in some cases spoken to, and have even been physically touched by spirit(s).

My interviews required a considerable amount of editing. As anyone knows who has conducted interviews by transcribing from tape recording session to the written page, the process is not as simple as it might first appear. Careful attention must be paid in order to keep the right "feeling" of the interview. Staying true to the emphasis presented by the interviewee, keeping the subject matter in context, and attempting to represent in words facial expressions and hand gestures can be challenging, but is not impossible. I also attempted to keep the narrative flow and the patois of the interviewee as close to genuine as possible, arranging sentences in an orderly manner for the story to proceed smoothly and be understood clearly. While this editing was necessary, it does not detract from the story's principal subject matter. The stories speak for themselves.

Undoubtedly, some of them will arouse curiosity, speculation, fear, and even cause a few of you to probe further into the subject of the paranormal. I am content to leave you with more questions than answers. I never have an idea where all this research of eyewitness accounts will lead. Frankly, like you, I am just along for the ride, and thus far it has been a ride of extraordinary wonder and unexpected amazement. Ghost stories engage me.

I am aware that it is simplistic to overemphasize the negative aspects of ghosts as evil or scary. However, focusing on these points alone promotes neither a positive nor hopeful view of our own end result. The best definitions of the existence of ghosts must be viewed through our own personal traditions of cultural and spiritual beliefs. This being said, I know that ghosts and spirits do exist and are manifest among us.

Lastly, I know one day I'll cease to record personal interviews of ghost sightings and encounters, many that push us to consider a very active life-after-death existence. One day I'll feel the ethereal presence of a soft touch on my shoulder, followed by familiar, spoken voices stating in unison, "Come on Antonio, it's now YOUR time to join us. Let's go, there is so much to catch up with!" I am most fortunate and grateful to have been given such a tremendously rewarding life of, and love for, storytelling.

— Antonio R. Garcez

PRIVATE HOMES

ALGODONES, NM

Located north of the Village of Bernalillo, Algodones has approximately 700 inhabitants. To the east is the north end of the Sandia mountain range; to its north and west is the Santa Ana Indian pueblo land. The Village of Algodones, dotted with farmland, is primarily a sleepy, quiet town of families, a few artists, and one general store.

VINCENT T. MARTINEZ'S STORY

"I sure don't want my fellow neighbors to know where I live. Algodones is a very small community and even though I believe that most of the people here would not condemn me for disclosing my experiences, there are some who would definitely not appreciate me talking about this. Let's just say my house is located west of the interstate and not far from a few new homes that have been built in the neighborhood. That's all I'll say.

Before all the new construction began next to my parents' home, I experienced very unusual activity there. This activity was so terrible I even moved about 40 miles south to Los Lunas, New Mexico to live with my brother and his family for a time. The ghost experience I had really scared me to my core.

In the summer of 1998 my parents, both in their eighties and experiencing advancing physical disabilities, accepted the recommendations to move into a skilled nursing facility. My father had been battling terrible blood clots in his legs and my mother was going blind due to macular degeneration. My brother and I had been observing the slow, cautious movements around their house and decided the time had come to help them find a safer living environment. We visited several assisted living facilities in nearby Albuquerque and chose one located not far from the State Fairgrounds.

Their move from Algodones to their new residence went smoothly and since I was a bachelor, living in Florida at the time, I decided to return to New Mexico and into their now vacant home. This unexpected opportunity had fallen into my lap and at the absolute right time for me to return to New Mexico.

When I arrived to the house, I was surprised at how tidy and clean my parents had managed to keep the inside, but due to their advanced ages, they were not able to maintain the exterior and yard. They also owned an old, German shepherd named Baby. Baby had both the front and back yards all to himself.

Because of the father's walking problems, he rarely walked outside in the yard. It was left up to my mother to water the plants and feed Baby. I was a shocked to see what appeared to be years of trash and junk littering the yard. I immediately cleaned up what I could and planned to trim Baby's fur. One look at Baby confirmed she hadn't been groomed in months.

It didn't take me long to get projects organized and prioritized. I was also glad to know that all this work was good for my own mental health. I had been divorced from my wife for less than a year and moving back to New Mexico was definitely what I needed to keep my mind occupied.

After several days of clearing the yard and clipping Baby's fur, I started focusing on other areas of the house including the front porch. From there I planned to eventually make my way into the kitchen and living rooms. I knew my parents were not going to return to live in this house, so along with my brother, we planned to clean it up and when upgrades were completed, decide if I was going to continue to live in the house or we'd sell it.

During days prior to my parents move, we'd phoned and spoke to each other. I remember that my mother telling me, "Vicente, I keep hearing strange things coming from the ceiling. I hear people laughing and sometimes when I walk to other rooms, I'll hear the sound of footsteps over my head in the ceiling, following me around the house." Another time, my mother phoned me in Florida and informed me that she was seeing the figure of a small bearded man standing in the doorway just staring at her. The man would raise his tiny hands to his face and cover his mouth and giggle like a child.

Whenever I heard these stories, I just conclude that my mother's vision was getting worse and that the blindness was advancing and causing her to see things. I assured my mother that these visions were simply due to her macular degeneration, but she would insist this was not the case. "How about the laughing, that's not due to my eyes!" And she'd further say, "There are spirits in this house and Vicente, even your father has mentioned seeing them." At these times in our conversation I would agree with her then change the subject to something else, but her statements would always leave me feeling uncomfortable and concerned.

I had never encountered anything that might be considered to be from the world of ghosts. The time I spent at the house as a young boy, was free of any such things or so I thought. After I finished re-doing the back rooms, I did begin to hear and have a few unexplained things happen to me.

One afternoon, while removing old carpet in the hallway, holding a carpet knife in my left hand and pulling with my right, I happened to look up and noticed what appeared to be a shadow of a tiny man. This small figure stood about two or three feet tall and stood at the end of the hall just staring at me. Understand that I'm not making an effort to stretch the truth; it was a human figure resembling a dwarf size person, perhaps even smaller than that.

Reacting with fear, I instinctively threw the knife at it and watched as the knife went flying directly through the figure and hit the wall! The little man, I'll call it a man, raised his small arms to its face then disappeared. In that instant, I ran after him, down the hall and into the living room. I didn't see one shred of evidence whatsoever that this "thing" was anywhere in the house. This encounter took place about three weeks after I moved into the house.

Because of what my parents had informed me before, regarding their experiences with what they termed "spirits" in the house, I was now very open to the possibility of agreeing with them. But not wanting to surrender totally to such a crazy imagination, I convinced myself that perhaps I was stressed out and not aware to what degree. After all, I had gone through – a divorce, a recent cross-country move of many miles, relocating to New Mexico, moving my parents into a facility and now in the middle of remodeling my boyhood home – this did seem like a lot to take on all at once and could be causing my imagination to work over time—so I thought.

I went back to work in the hallway and didn't have another sighting like that one for about a week. One evening about five o'clock, as I was in the kitchen making dinner, my back was facing the hallway when suddenly I heard an unusual noise in the ceiling, directly above my head.

It sounded like two wood boards being loudly "slapped" together! I instantly stopped what I was doing, I listened and then heard a high-pitched voice of someone, or something, speaking. At first it was difficult to make out, then the words became clearer and all at once I understood them. I heard "You didn't hurt me and you think you can hurt me—I'll hurt you!" coming down from the ceiling.

I grabbed a metal serving spoon with a long handle that was sitting in the sink and used it to tap three times at the ceiling. I pounded the ceiling directly above me several times! Then I listened for a response. I kept silent attempting to listen for further sounds, but all was still. All of a sudden, my whole body was shaken by the sound of three loud "thuds" hitting back. You should have seen me jump!

After this point, I knew something was in the house. If not in the house, then up between the ceiling and the roof—somewhere in the attic!

I reached for the phone and called my brother, I described everything. He told me to be careful because both my parents had always mentioned hearing and seeing similar things as well. My brother was well aware that I never took our parents unusual descriptions seriously but advised me to just be careful.

I told my brother that I was going to get a flashlight from my car and climb up into the attic through the crawlspace. The entrance to the attic was through a small door in the ceiling of the bathroom. He said, "Please Vicente, be careful. There might be nests of spiders and who knows what else is living in that attic." I told him I would phone him as soon as I finish so he would not have to worry.

I grabbed a ladder from the garage and a flashlight from the car, when into the bathroom. I could tell by the small square panel of plywood door that it had not been opened for many years. The whole ceiling had been painted over and no one had taken the time to remove the door, so the paint had adhered the door to the ceiling.

With some effort, I was able to push in the door and detach it. What a mess. Bits of newspaper and paper pulp used years ago for insulation fell over me like grey flakes of snow. I switched on the flashlight and cautiously peered into the dark attic.

I could see that a delicate shower of dust covered all the electrical wires along with crisscrossing spider webs. The air was stifling hot. I move the light beam over to the area above the kitchen ceiling, and spotted something strange. It was a doll or something resembling one. I thought, why would someone place a doll in the attic? I decided not to crawl over to that area without first changing my clothes. I returned to the garage and found a pair of old Levis I used earlier to paint the bedrooms and an old dirty blue shirt. After I changed into these dirty clothes, I returned to the opening and slowly climbed up into the attic.

I carefully crawled around to most areas of the attic expecting to encounter a live mouse or rat, but there was no sign of anything alive, not even dead critters. I looked to my left and saw a small envelope that was lying against a ceiling beam. I picked it up and tossed it down through the attic opening.

As I mentioned earlier, initially I spotted what I thought was a doll at one end of the attic. I decided to crawl over to that "thing" and find out what it was. As soon as I did, I noticed it was an old stuffed toy animal. It looked like a teddy bear. Well, in the darkness it looked like a teddy bear. As I picked it up in one hand I felt how strangely stiff it was. I crawled back to the opening and before heading out feet first, I placed the doll to the side of the opening. Using my dangling foot, I felt for the ladder step and moved most of my body down and out of the attic. I reached back for the stuffed toy animal and brought it down with me.

In the safety and brightly lit area of the bathroom, I saw what I was holding in my hands. This "stuffed toy" was not a child's toy but an actual mummified cat! Strangely, whoever placed this dead cat in the attic had taken the time to also dress it in a baby boy's suit. Let me describe it.

It was a dark suit with a tie and infant shoes. The front legs of the dead cat were covered in a red shirt, while the rear legs went through the small trousers ending with shoes. I'd imagine these were kept in place using glue. The cat's face was shaved of its fur in order to give it a more human like appearance with painted eyebrows and lips. It was a disgusting thing to see, creepy and evil looking.

I clumsily dropped the hideous doll and as it hit the floor, its head detached from the body exposing the cat's neck bones. As soon as I could, I pulled myself together, collected the parts and took it outside. As I was walking through the house carrying this "thing" toward the front door, directly above me in the ceiling I heard the sound of footsteps following my every step throughout the house. I had chills!

Once outside the house, I walked over to one of the trashcans I used to burn household trash. I removed the wire mesh covering the can and placed the mummified cat down inside. I covered it with newspaper and cardboard trash and used my cigarette lighter to start a fire. I watched as it made popping sounds, blew out thick black smoked and waiting until everything burned into smoldering ashes.

Then I remembered the envelope I found in the attic and threw out

The bearded man photo.

the attic door before stepping down the ladder. I ran inside, opened it and discovered an old photo of a scary bearded man, similarly staring back at me. I decided to keep it and show it to my brother. Could this possibly be the ghost of the little bearded figure my parents and now me, have seen?

I don't have answers as to who placed these things in my parents' attic or the reason for the noises, the voices and what appeared to me to be a bearded dwarf. All I can say is that with my destruction of the mummified cat, removing the bearded man's photo from the property, disturbing activity stopped and I've lived in the house without any further episodes.

My brother and I have thought about selling the house and dividing the money between us, but I kind of like living here. I'm just sad when imagining what terrifying sounds and apparitions our parents went through over the years, trying to get us to believe them and not ever getting help or protection from either of us. I'll always regret this."

ANTONITO, NM

Situated north of the New Mexico state line, in the San Luis Valley, is the small town of Antonito. The area has a rich cultural heritage and history provided by the colonial settlements of the Spanish and Anglo, also etched deeply in its pre-European contact is the area's heritage of the Native American. The Cumbres & Toltec Railroad, which leaves daily from Antonito's old train station, is a big draw for visitors. Antonito is composed primarily of a friendly, working class residential community, surrounded by an expanse of high desert plains. It was built by the railroad as a community whose primary function was to house Anglos who wanted to distance themselves from the pre-established Hispanic town of Conejos, which lies just a few miles north of town. As Interstate 285 traverses its central core, in the distance to the east can be seen the Culebra Range of spectacular mountains which remain as sentinels, eye witnesses to Antonito's agrarian history.

EDWARD H. SAUNDER S' STORY

Edward is a character of sorts. He's wheelchair bound, but that has not put a damper on his lively attitude to life. As we talked at his kitchen table, we were interrupted with phone calls from two friends; one being a woman who he stated was a girlfriend. My interview lasted for just about two hours, but the impression this jovial man left with me will linger for definitely much longer.

— Antonio

"I was born in Columbus, Ohio, 88 years ago. In 1967, my wife, Vivian, and I moved to Denver and 14 years later, after her death, I decided to move to Antonito, NM. I've been living here ever since.

I lost the use of both legs in a truck accident while driving for a freight company. That accident happened about four years after my wife and I had moved to Denver. The odd thing about this accident was that I was not even driving the truck at the time. I was getting ready to enter the truck cab, when another truck came by and struck me. I was holding on to my truck's door handle, pulling myself up about to get into the cab when the other driver misjudged his turn and scraped me off my truck. I dropped to the ground immediately with injuries to my lower legs. The accident happened so quickly all I can remember of the accident is a loud noise and nothing else. The bones in both legs were crushed. Since that time, I've never been able to fully walk on my own, and have been dependent on this wheelchair most of the time.

I did receive insurance settlement money, but not much of it is left. The rents are low here in Antonito and I don't need much in the way of entertainment or fancy food, so I do all right here. Now it's just me and my dog Blacky, that misses me like the dickens whenever I leave her at home for any short length of time.

So, you'd like to know about my ghost story? Well, I haven't told anyone except for a few close friends at the senior center. And as you told me, one of them gals told you about the old man in the wheelchair who's seen ghosts, and that's how you found out about me. Once I tell you my story, you'll only be one of the few who'll know of it.

Well, approximately five years ago, one evening, about 6 or 7 p.m., I was in my backyard watering plants and filling a birdbath by a nearby tree. Blacky was alone inside the house. It was an uneventful day for the most part. Suddenly, I heard Blacky begin to bark, as if he were in danger, or alerting me to some kind of danger. I turned my wheelchair around to face the back door and I saw the large figure of a man standing at the door, staring back at me from inside my house!

I didn't recognize this guy, but I was able to clearly make out his features. He was about 50 years old or so, with a very thick and dark moustache. His face was big and round, and his shoulders were very broad.

His overall appearance gave me the impression that his intentions were not very positive. He didn't move a muscle when I asked, "Who are you, what are you doing in my house?" Blacky was barking uncontrollably.

I shouted out to him again, "Who are you?" I began to feel uneasy because he refused to respond to my questions. I felt helpless but determined to find out who this man was, and what he was doing inside my house.

He and I both stood looking at each other, not making any movements. I'll admit I was confused as to what to do next. Something inside of me urged me to stand my ground and make the first move toward him. I dropped the water hose and began to push the wheels of my wheelchair towards the house. Just then I saw this man turn away from the door, and move back within the darkened house. Blacky, still in the house, abruptly stopped barking. I was paralyzed with a gripping fear that something happened to Blacky.

I was sure shaken up! I just knew that this man had hurt or even killed my dog. My spirit sank, I felt so helpless. In my soul, I knew that something awful had just taken place. As I rolled up the short ramp that led up to my back door, pulled open the door and entered my house.

As soon as I entered the kitchen and turned on the light, I felt a heaviness to the atmosphere and my body instantly surrounded in a freezing temperature. It was unlike anything I had ever felt before or since. It felt as if I had just been wrapped in a large invisible blanket of intense darkness. Even though the kitchen light was on, and I could clearly see, it did nothing to remove the overwhelming terror I felt. I knew that something evil was very close to me.

My entire body began to shake from the cold and shiver from the freezing dead air. The whole house felt over taken by this bitter cold. I knew that something had happened to my Blacky because normally he would come running directly to me when I'd come through the door into the house. In a nervous, shaky voice I yelled out, "Whoever you are, you better get running or else!" There was only silence.

I managed to roll my wheelchair down the hallway leading into the living room and when I entered the room I spotted Blacky cowering under one of the chairs. I wanted to search every room of my small home for this stranger to see if he was still in the house. I remembered I was in no shape to physically confront any intruder or risk being hurt so I stayed put. I called Blacky to come to me, but he would not budge.

I grabbed the phone, called my neighbor, who lived one house away from mine. He answered and said that he would be right over. In just a few minutes I heard him call to me from the outside, he was at my front door and tried opening the door but the door was locked! Given all that had happened, I had forgotten to unlock the front door and quickly opened it.

When my neighbor came inside, I described the strange man I had seen inside my house while I was outside watering. Then, without any urging from me, my neighbor searched all the rooms of the house, including both bedroom closets. Not wanting to miss a thing, he even looked under my bed. As soon as my neighbor was done inspecting the house, Blacky overcame his terrified state, came over to me and jumped up on my lap.

Nothing was found out of the ordinary or looked as if anything had been disturbed. All my windows were closed, the back and front entry doors to the outside were also both secure. I was unable to understand what had just happened or who the strange man was. I know I was not imagining it, because even my dog had responded to him. It was a hell of a thing to think that I had seen a ghost, but what else could it have been? I thanked my neighbor and after we had talked for a few minutes more, he left us. As nightfall came, I slowly began to feel more comfortable and watching television for a few hours. I felt that everything was getting back to normal, and decided to go to bed sooner than I normally would. I kept wondering if I might have imagined it all and ended up sleeping with most of the house lights on for added security, just in case. I quickly discovered that I was not prepared for what would become a constant series of bad nightmares that took me months to overcome. These would repeatedly awaken me from sleeping and each dream scenario included that man with the moustache. In my dreams, he would yell at me for no reason, just yell at me.

As the yelling got louder, to the point of madness, I would wake up. It was the intensity of anger in his voice that upset me the most. I could not understand the things he was yelling at me, but I knew that this was not good or positive.

These terrible nightmares continued nightly, often causing me to awaken myself due to my moans and sometimes screams. But one night in particular was the scariest. After I woke up from one of these nightmares while still laying in my bed, I suddenly heard the insane laughter of this man's voice coming from within the room!

I was overwhelmed with a gripping terror. I'll never forget that wicked laugh, followed by the words, "Why did you do this to me, why did you do it!" My body trembled with fear as I looked everywhere for who this was. Then immediately after he stopped speaking I heard the sound of wood snapping, or cracking. The cracking sounded like a two by four board being snapped in half! It was so loud directly above my head, coming from the ceiling. I was afraid that the ceiling was breaking apart and sat frozen with fear in bed.

Suddenly, just as fast as it started, the atmosphere of the room became quiet and still. The terrifying voice and laughter of the man was gone, the cracking stopped. The feeling of dread left and a comforting sense of relief came over me. I turned on the lamp on my bedside, and left it on until morning daylight appeared.

During this entire night, I didn't dare get out of bed to use the bathroom. I had the feeling that if this thing was capable of speaking and making loud sounds then, who knows what I might have seen looking back at me in the bathroom mirror! I tried to go back to sleep and eventually I did. The next morning, when I finally got out of bed, I saw nothing different in the room at all. But just a few days later, another totally unexpected thing happened.

I left my house to visit my sister in Durango, Colorado. I was gone for two long weeks; she was in the hospital being treated for pancreatic cancer. I was unable to take Blacky with me, so I left him at home with a neighbor. I kept in touch with my neighbor by telephone, and would call every few days. One day my neighbor informed me that someone came to the house and left a note with a name and phone number. When

I returned home, he handed me my mail and the note.

I did not recognize the name on the note, but did call the number. I asked the man who answered what he wanted to talk to me about. It so happened that he, his older brother and father had lived in my house before me. He told me about his family's history, but most importantly was the terrible fact that when they lived in the house, both he and his brother, were relentlessly physically abused by their father. He said their father was a raging alcoholic and extremely abusive when he drank.

He then told me about one particular tragic episode that happened between them. One evening, after the father had been drinking and began physically assaulting him, his older brother took matters into his own hands, and shot his father with a gun. The bullet severed a large vein in the father's chest and he died a few hours later. This was disturbing to hear but the exact reason for this man's visit to my home remained unclear. Everything began to make sense as he continued speaking.

He told me he had been having dreams of his father in recent months and his therapist convinced him that part of his recovery might involve returning to his childhood home, and confront those traumatic memories head on. Eventually he found the courage and decided to make the long drive from Nevada to my home, his boyhood home, hoping to conquer his reoccurring nightmares.

I informed him of my own recent nightmares, and about the man I saw standing inside the house, yelling at me. He couldn't believe the details and similarities of my nightmares with his own. As I described the ghost's features, and the words this spirit had spoken to me this man said that I had just described his father! I was stunned, and accepted that this ghostly presence was this man's father! I have no doubt about it.

This visitor thanked me for speaking with him and most of all, listening without judgment for all that he had shared. He began to apologize for the experiences and nightmares I had been having but I told him he was not the cause. I was grateful to know the previous history and traumatic event that took place because it helped provide a very good explanation for what had been causing it all.

Since we met, there have not been further disturbances', nightmares or cracking sounds in the ceiling. I truly believe that because of our mutual nightmares, the intimate details shared about surviving a terrible childhood, our discussion that day, has all somehow resulted in ending everything negative in the house. I have not had another frightening nightmare or sightings since.

I believe that the spirit of the murdered man may have needed to communicate something with both myself, and his only living son. I can't think of a reason why, but maybe after all is said and done, some of the dead do not really rest, especially if they treated others so badly while they were alive."

BELEN, NM

Belen is Spanish for Bethlehem and over time has gained the nickname "Hub City" because of the Belen Cutoff of the Atchison, Topeka, and Santa Fe Railway. The Cutoff made it possible for many more trains to traverse east and west across the United States. Prior to the Belen Cutoff, train traffic came through the steep Raton Pass on the Colorado and New Mexico border. To this day, an average of 110 trains travel through Belen in a 24-hour period on the Southern Transcon including the New Mexico's new commuter Rail Runner train. Belen also has the only Harvey House Museum in the State.

MARY J. ROGER'S STORY

"I've lived in the town of Belen since the fall of 1966, when my husband Larry and I first arrived in New Mexico. Originally, we're from the state of Illinois. Joliet, Illinois to be exact. Joliet is located just to the south of Chicago. As I said, we arrived in New Mexico in the fall and my dear God I didn't know I was in for such a change. The culture and the people of this state were so different than what I was used to in Joliet. I tell you, my taste buds were quickly burned and reborn with New Mexico's chile. I'm not complaining. Today I'll bet you that I'm one of the greatest consumers of red chile in the state. My daughter and her husband will vow to this! I really do love living here and I've made so many lifelong friends. I've been very happy living here and don't have to suffer the humidity of Joliet either. I know Larry feels the same.

My story is about my little granddaughter, Florinda. She died at the age of eleven and both my husband and I miss her so much. I hope I can make it through his interview without crying like a fool, but to this very day I do miss her so very much.

In Joliet, my son and his new wife were living in a small apartment above our retail store. My husband, Larry and I had our own living space on the ground level at the back of the store. Our store was located on East Jackson Street. For those readers who might be familiar, our store was located between Clay and Benton Streets. We sold everything from milk to mouse traps.

My fondest memory of that time was when the great blues singer, Ethel Waters walked into the store one evening looking for Juicy Fruit chewing gum. I noticed her immediately as she stepped into my store. There was something different about this strikingly beautiful black woman. She was dressed in a long blue coat with a black fur collar and wearing high-heeled shoes covered with glass beads. I tell you it was like gazing upon royalty!

I had just finished having dinner when I heard the store's front door swing open and in walked Miss Waters. I was shocked! She purchased two packs of gum and two whole cases, forty-eight soda pops of Canada Dry Ginger Ale, for her friends who were waiting in a car outside. She paid with a five-dollar bill, way more than what was the total. She handed me the money and said, "Go ahead girl, you keep the rest."

Ethel Waters.

After she left, I held onto her five-dollar bill and I never spent it. I framed the bill and hung it on the wall behind the register with a handwritten sign that said, "If Ethel Waters shops at this store, so should you." I still have that five-dollar bill. It's packed away with all my other things in the garage, but I've proudly held onto it all these years!

My son and his wife were so happy when their baby Florinda arrived, and Larry and I were the proudest of grandparents. I would position my little granddaughter's bassinette next to the counter, right next to my chair, where I would sit. I practically raised her because both her parents worked during the day and sometimes into the night. They worked for a factory that made metal cans and not ever having owned a car, they depended on friends to get them to and from work. But this Grandma was not inconvenienced in the least to baby-sit her granddaughter.

Strange things started to happen. Sometimes I'd find Florinda laughing and giggling for no apparent reason. While at other times, like during her afternoon naps, and after making sure she was asleep, I'd walk away to the rear of the store and I would suddenly hear her start to laugh. As I'd return and peek inside her bassinette, she would have the most joyful look. I didn't think much of this, so I'd just pick her up and hold her until she'd fall asleep in my arms. Then I'd return her back to her bassinette and covered her with her blanket.

Other unusual occurrences surrounding the baby would be common, for example, I'd hear her make "baby talk" sounds. It was nothing that I could make sense of, just typical baby vocalizing sounds. But one day when I was alone with her in the store, I walked over to unpack a case of oatmeal to display on a shelf. I was only two aisles away when I heard a woman's voice say, "My, what a pretty girl you are. Your grandma's girl, aren't you?"

I turned around, kicked the boxes out of my way, and I yelled out, "Who's there. Can I help you? Is anyone there?" I knew I was the only adult in the store and remember rushing over to Flornida side but, of course, there was only myself and my granddaughter. No woman, absolutely no one else.

Florinda.

Mary in her youth.

The sound of the woman's voice took me by surprise and, interestingly enough, so very familiar. Then it hit me, the voice belonged to my grandmother, Luella Carla Thompson. Grandmother Thompson had long since died and I was just twenty years old. I knew my grandmother very well. She was a wonderful woman, an ex-slave in fact. She did domestic work for a white family in Chicago for many years until her death. I recognized her voice so true and clear, just as I remember hearing it.

I spoke out saying, "Granny, isn't your baby beautiful? Take care of her, please take care of her." I reached down to pick up Florinda and that's when I received the loveliest gesture from heaven. I felt, really felt, my granny's hand gently stroke the left side of my cheek. It felt as if she was standing right beside me and lovingly placed hand on my face to signify that she heard me and would always be with my granddaughter. I was so happy that I cried and cried knowing that I had just communicated with my own granny. It was the sweetest touch of warmth. Her hand on my cheek felt amazing and very real. If you've ever had the opportunity to communicate with a spirit, the spirit of someone so close to you, you'd know what I mean. It's a gesture of love in its purest sense.

I won't go into the details of my granddaughter's death, but even though it was a terrible ordeal to go through for all of us, I felt comforted knowing that Granny Thompson had taken care of my granddaughter as she lived and is now with my little baby's spirit. My Granny made her presence known to me; with perhaps an insight warning that Florinda would be with her soon. I have no problem describing just how special Granny's visit to me was that evening. It was truly a gift of comfort from

God and Granny knowing they are together. And I have been blessed."

CAÑON CITY, CO

Cañon City rests within south central Colorado and is situated on state highway 50, northwest of Pueblo, CO. To the north of town is the Rampart range of mountains, and to the south, the Wet Mountains. Many visitors regard Cañon City as the gateway to the Royal Gorge State Park, which has the world's highest suspension bridge at more than 1,000 feet.

In town, you'll discover an exhibit of local archeological examples of dinosaur bones—the Dinosaur Depot. The museum also offers directions to a self-guided dinosaur hike that is not far from town. What is unusual about this town is that there are nine state penitentiaries within its location. Within one of these properties is the Colorado Territorial Prison Museum. It's an excellent opportunity to view jail cells, historical criminal documents, and see an actual gas chamber! Just east of town is located The Benedictine Holy Cross Abbey and vineyard. Prior to its closing the Abbey offered a good taste sampling of its award-winning vintages.

MARTHA MUNROE'S STORY

My meeting with Martha was a joy I'll not soon forget. Her eagerness to make me feel welcome in her house and her genuine nature was something I'll always remember. Our interview was held in her living room, surrounded by numerous framed family photos she had arranged with care. During the interview, whenever she would speak of a particular family member, she would get up off her chair and return with one of their photos, saying "Here, this is him, oh, he was such a handsome man," etc.

Martha's story is a winding story of secrets, travels, and heartfelt sincerity, and it is so very telling in its moralistic description. I admittedly was emotionally moved.

— Antonio

"Originally I was born in Colorado, then moved to Seattle, Washington, in the late 1960s. In 1984, I returned to Colorado, and remain to this day in Cañon City. My story is about an aunt of mine who lived most all her life in Cañon City. She was my favorite aunt, Aunt Billie. Both she and I kept in close contact with each other throughout her life. There was a similarity in our lives, which we were both very proud of, in that we never married, and remained comfortably independent spinsters.

Aunt Billie was born in 1904 and was the oldest of three children, a boy and two girls. My mother was the youngest. For as long as I could remember my Aunt Billie always wore her hair in a tight bun in the back of her hair. She like this look and never change her hairstyle. From the start, my mother told me that my aunt was a very strong-willed girl and had her own way of doing things. From time to time when the question would arise as to why she had never married, Aunt Billie simply responded, "Men are too complicated. I like my life to be simple. I don't need a man hanging around me like a lost calf."

In her later years, Aunt Billie suffered from rheumatoid arthritis in her spine and joints. This condition worsened as the years pasted. Because of this chronic disease she was never able to visit me in Seattle. When I'd ask her to visit she would answer, "Oh, it's too wet and cold. Opossum, you know my back can't take the wet rain." 'Opossum' was an endearing name she would call me. Having been a premature new-born, Aunt Billie said that when she had first laid her eyes on me, I resembled a tiny baby opossum. So, from an early age, as soon as I was able to understand people and my surroundings, I always associated my aunt's face with the special endearing name she'd call me. Over the years, our bond as aunt and niece grew stronger. I often attempted to visit my aunt at least once a year, or once every other year. I always remembered special days in her life, like birthdays and holidays until the day Aunt Billie abruptly died.

Aunt Billie wearing hair bow.

It was a fall day. Her death was due to the rupture of an abdominal aortic aneurysm. Up until the end of her life in 1984, we both remained very close.

Within the week of her death, a few close friends from her church had cleaned her house and boxed up all her personal items, then placed everything in her garage. After selling my own house in, I decided to move into my aunt's house in Cañon City. I made the long move from Washington State in the fall of 1984, and as I've said before, have made Cañyon City my home ever since.

Aunt Billie's personality was that of a very quiet, private person. To those who did not know her well, at times she would appear to be a bit of a secretive individual. Overall, she was friendly and filled with compassion for those who knew her at church. She never gave me any reason to believe that she would hide any secrets from me—ever. But as the months went by, I would, in fact, discover a tragic secret that she kept well hidden from me and everyone who loved her, for her entire life.

There was a period in her life, about two years, when she left Colorado to work for a water faucet manufacturing company in Kansas City, Missouri. This was what she told my family. She never did say much about her move, except, "I'll never want to visit that town again." There are very few further details provided except to say that the weather was too humid, the people were not friendly, and she could not wait to pick up her final employment paycheck and return to Colorado. This was the extent of the story she had told my mother regarding the two years she spent in Missouri. On rare occasions, my aunt was known to display a bit of anger, my family never pressed the issue with her. My mother always sensed there was something "not right" about her explanation, so in-

Aunt Billie with dog Freddie in 1941.

stead of asking the question of what really happened during those two years, we just never asked.

After I moved into my aunt's house, there was nothing unusual that happened that I could identify as being haunted. Everything seemed to be going well, and I spent the entire fall at the house in peace. I kept the majority of my aunt's furnishings, but purchased a new mattress for the bed. The garage still contained the taped and sealed cardboard boxes of her personal items that her church friends had stored for me. I didn't even think of going through any of the boxes until the weather turned warmer in the late spring. During my first month at the house, my aunt's friends would occasionally drop by to say hello and to reminisce about my aunt and the times they had spent together.

I had not experienced anything unusual but in late November, I began to notice something very curious was repeatedly taking place with unusual regularity.

This began one morning on November 15 at about 10:30 am, while I was seated at my chair in the kitchen. I was finishing up my breakfast and I had just poured myself coffee. As soon as I sat down, I began to hear the sound of a kitten crying. I love cats, although I hadn't owned one for more than three years after my last cat had died. The cries stopped briefly so I was listening carefully, when the crying started up again and began to get progressively louder. I was really concerned for the kitten, got up and off my chair, and walked a few steps to the backdoor that leads outside to the backyard. I opened the door and looked everywhere, but didn't see a kitten or a cat.

I understand that this in itself is not unusual, but while I was standing at the backdoor, I heard the crying once more but this time it appeared to be coming from inside the house, actually from the living room. I walked over to the living room and now heard, very clearly the distinct, muffled sounds of a baby crying. The crying sound was not a very loud sound, but was more muted and repressed. I must have stood in my living room for a good five minutes, listening and waiting for something—anything— else to happen.

The cries were definitely not those of a kitten's, this was the sound that a very tiny infant. Most importantly, the cries were coming from somewhere in the house. I looked out the front window several times, and never saw a baby in the yard or on the sidewalk. No, these cries were coming from within my house! As the seconds passed, the crying also disappeared, and I was left with more questions than answers.

Throughout the day the crying would start then stop. For the coming days, this is how things continued for me. I knew this was not something that I could, or would, tolerate for very long. Sometimes, I would be awakened at night by the sounds, and sometimes I would be lulled to sleep by them. I can't explain why, but I knew that the child's crying was of a spiritual nature. The crying was such a distant and soft sound, that I was not really bothered by it, however it did cause me some concern. This continued for three or four days, then I decided to put an end to it.

While living in Seattle, I once attended a book signing at a local bookstore for an author who wrote about the paranormal. I remember she responded to a question from the audience that pertained to the subject of spirits in her presentation. In her response, the author offered a few spiritual, countermeasures for eliminating unwanted entities. One that I distinctly remember was her instruction to speak directly to spirits. In addition, she also mentioned that lighting a candle and blessing affected areas with holy water from a Catholic church could help intensified the communication process. She described in detail a bit more of the process, but the only portion I could recall was those two simple rules. Talk to the spirits and light a candle. So, the next time I heard the crying, I lit a candle and began addressing the spirit of the baby that resided in my aunt's house directly.

I was sitting in the living room watching television when suddenly, once more the crying started up. I turned off the television, and got up off my chair and lit the candle I placed on my coffee table. I was anticipating the opportunity to do this, so I was ready. I was eager to communicate with the spirit. Surprisingly, I was not the least bit scared. After all, it was only a baby.

After lighting the candle, I said, "Please, whoever you are, I want you to leave this house and be at peace. I don't want you to stay around and cry like you have been doing. So, please go and find the peace you need. I do not like hearing your crying, please leave my house, and find your mother." I also said a few more things that I can't remember, but these statements were what I attempted to express. The crying seemed to end right after I stopped speaking. I settled into bed for the night and left the candle to burn completely out overnight.

From my bedroom, I could see small shadows dancing on the wall in the hallway that were created by the flickering flame. I did not hear any further crying since I addressed the spirit earlier in the day. Personally, I felt a peace and calm come over me and throughout the house. I slept soundly that same night. Early that next morning I remembered a vivid and very detailed dream that I found difficult to accept it was just a dream.

In this dream, I found myself walking into a large white painted room so brightly bathed in light that I had to squint. As I entered the room I spotted a woman seated in a chair with her back to me. As I approached her, I immediately saw that it was my Aunt Billie! Her head was bowed down, looking at a newborn baby in her arms. My aunt's hair was long and draped around her shoulders. It was not at all as I remembered her customarily wearing it, in a tight bun. She seemed relaxed and had a loving smile on her face. She also looked to be so very, very young. I would guess her to be in her mid-20s. There were no words exchanged between us. I tried to speak, but I was unable to form a sentence, not even a single word. We just looked into each other's eyes, and that seemed to be enough.

Within a minute, my aunt stood up off her chair and turned to her side, displaying the newborn to me proudly. This act indicated to me how much love there was between her and the baby. I instinctively reached out to hold the baby in my arms, but somehow I understood that I could not, so I returned my arms to my sides. As soon as I did this, I awoke from my dream. It was all that quick.

After I awoke that morning, the crying baby sounds never returned. I knew that my attempt to communicate with the spirit, and lighting the candle triggered some sort of cleansing that cleared my house of that poor innocent baby's anguished soul. My dream sealed these thoughts for me, and I was so happy to know that my aunt's spirit was also helping me get through this. I was very happy to have experienced this beautiful dream about my aunt and the baby in her arms.

A few months later, as the weather started warming up, I decided to bring one of Aunt Billie's cardboard boxes from the garage into the house. I wanted to finally search through her personal papers, and whatever else she chose to keep stored. There were about 10 boxes and two big, old trunks. I decided to leave the trunks for another time.

In the boxes that I opened, I discovered a few surprises such as photos of relatives, old photos of my aunt, my uncle and my mother, which were taken in 1910. I also found a hand-beaded necklace, and two pewter spoons that belonged to my great-grandmother. There were linens, Christmas cards and a collection of small hats, and other non-valuables, but that was about it. It was not until I decided to open the remaining locked trunks that things got very interesting indeed.

Because they were so heavy, and I was not able to carry them into the house, I used a folding chair in the garage and seated myself before the first trunk. I looked all over for the keys, but was unable to find them. I asked an older gentleman friend of my aunts who lived nearby to help me open both the trunks. He used a large screwdriver and hammer, and after spending a few minutes, he successfully opened both trunks.

While my friend was attempting to open the second trunk, he missed hitting the screwdriver and struck his hand, and broke through skin, causing a really nasty cut. Because he was taking a prescribed blood thinner, he bled quite a bit all over the cement floor.

It wasn't a serious wound, but it did need some disinfecting careful and attention. So, he left me in the garage, and went to his home to dress the wound. After I cleaned up the spots of blood on the floor, I sat by the first trunk and continued my exploration of what other treasures my aunt had stored.

The first trunk contained papers, mostly stuffed envelopes with cancelled bank checks and a once beautiful handmade quilt. Unfortunately, the quilt was both unsalvageable and unusable because of heavy concentrations of rodent urine and black mold from exposure to moisture. The trunk also contained a large tin box filled with antique Christmas ornaments. That was the extent of the contents in the first trunk. Now the other trunk was next in line.

As soon as I opened its lid, I knew that this trunk's purpose was for much more important items. The small boxes it contained were stacked neatly and my aunt had taken great care by stuffing wadded newspaper between each box, in order to secure them from moving about. Slowly, I opened the first box and discovered letters that were typewritten from a hospital in Kansas City, detailing its cost for services rendered. The invoices were made out to my aunt, and were marked "paid in full."

One box contained a baby rattle and blanket. Another box contained the most surprising in terms of all. As I opened its lid, I found placed on top of it a small stack of invoices, a four-by-five-inch photo of an infant who appeared to be asleep on a large white pillow. I picked the photo up and turned it over. On the back of the photo, my aunt had written in pencil the words, "My precious, Elizabeth Lavender Owen. Age 11 days. Mother's dove and life." My jaw dropped and I was in total shock.

The papers scattered on top of the photo were paid invoices describing funeral and cemetery services rendered from businesses in Kansas City. My heart was broken for both my aunt and the loss of her beautiful baby girl. I cried for over an hour and was emotionally on the verge of physically collapsing. Everything was now making so much sad sense to me. My dear aunt got pregnant, then moved out of state to Kansas

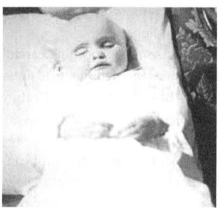

City to give birth to a child she would eventually lose to a very unexpected, early death. I was devastated for my aunt's tragic experience. Although I was shocked beyond words at this discovery, I could only imagine how terrible a time it must have been for Aunt Billie, to have dealt with this all by herself, so many years ago and in secret. It must have been devastating for her.

Then, as I was trying to process it all, the realization of hearing the crying sounds, and the dream I dreamt, hit me like a ton of bricks. I now know the meaning of my experiences at my aunt's house. There was a reason for it all and believe it was a divine reason. That reason being that when, and only when, I had discovered aunt's secret past, would there be the moment she, her daughter could truly achieve together, their final state of peace. Although I felt that I had been given the honor of this family discovery, more than that, I wanted to believe that there was a divine hand that played a major role in the whole experience, mine, my aunt Billie's and cousin.

Several days after this discovery, I would look at the picture of my deceased cousin, laying on that white pillow and it made me cry all over again. It was a long time before I was able to just look at the photo and smile knowing that Elizabeth Lavender Owen, and her mother, my Aunt Billie, were together forever in love and peace.

Today, I keep both my aunt and my little cousin's picture by my bed and I light a candle in both their memories and especially on their birthdays. On Christmas, I decorate a tree and place two custom made holiday photo ornaments within the branches of my tree. Aside from all of my other holiday decorations, to me, these are my most cherished and proudly displayed each year."

CERRILLOS, NM

The Tano Indians were the first people in the Cerrillos, New Mexico area. Their pueblos, large and small, were spread out randomly throughout the Galisteo Basin. Archaeologists believe that the Tano's occupied these sites with no more than a few thousand people at one time. Some of the pueblos may have been abandoned when the farmlands wore out. Evidence has shown that the farmland (Burnt Corn Ruin) five miles east of Cerrillos was destroyed in battle. Tumbled stones, broken potshards and discarded tools of rock were discovered in records of excavations.

The film Young Guns is a fictionalized retelling of the adventures of Billy the Kid during the Lincoln County War, which took place in New

Mexico during 1877–1878. It was filmed in and around Cerrillos, New Mexico and a sequel, Young Guns II was released in 1990.

Cerrillos is thought to be the location of the state's oldest turquoise mines. Prior to the 1920s, the state was the country's largest producer of turquoise, though it is more or less exhausted today.

MARGARET P. GARCIA'S STORY

"I remember exactly when I began to experience a haunting in my house. It was three days after the terrorist attack on the World Trade Center in New York in 2001. It was September 14th. I was in my kitchen that morning watching the television broadcasts from New York, as I'm sure most of my neighbors in Cerrillos, and the rest of the world, were doing.

I remember waking up that morning from a strong internal sense that I was not alone, and someone was in the room with me. It was around seven in the morning, I lived alone and owned no animals. I have a history of being sensitive when it comes to having a "feeling" of spirits and can also pick up certain vibes from people.

I opened my eyes and was already facing the bedroom door, when I watched the door slowly start to close all on its own. It was September so the weather was getting quite chilly. I had the house sealed up tight to keep the cold out. As the door came to a close, I heard the door's locking mechanism click shut! Immediately I thought that a burglar was in my house so I yelled, "You S.O.B., get the hell out of my house. I'll shoot you in the ass!" I wasn't kidding. I kept a loaded pistol on the floor between my bed and my nightstand and I wasn't afraid to use it! I didn't bother with dressing. I reached for the pistol, opened the door, and walked into the hall ready to shoot!

Years before my husband Felipe passed, he gave me lessons on how to handle and shoot a gun. Felipe always said that I learned quickly. I knew that if I owned a gun, I better be prepared to use it. So, that morning as I walked out into my short hallway, I was prepared to shoot whoever had broken into my home.

I looked everywhere inside, under tables, and even in the closets. I checked all the front and rear doors and windows. They were all locked! As soon as I realized that no one was in my house, that's when the real fear set in. I knew I had not imagined the door closing on its own, I actually saw it close then heard it lock! I immediately made the sign of the cross, sat on my sofa praying and asking whatever, whoever was here, to leave or to somehow let me know what it wants.

I waited for a few seconds for a sign or response but nothing happened. I then went into my kitchen, made some coffee, and started washing apples for the empanadas (turnovers) I planned to make. As I was at my sink, I heard the voice of a small girl behind me say, "Margaret, don't cry." I was startled and instantly turned around. No one was there and I knew something was up.

I thought about the terrible events taking place in New York and that perhaps were now affecting my state of mind. I wondered if I might be depressed on some level. I questioned my sanity and tried to rationalize what I had experienced. I pulled out a chair and sat at the dining table. I sobbed and sobbed like a child. For some unknown reason, emotions of grief were overwhelming me.

After composing myself, I thought more about what I heard, and what the voice said about not crying. I phoned my friend, Araceli, who lives in Santa Fe. I explained everything to her and all that was going on that morning; she asked me if I wanted her to come over. I told her, yes, I definitely needed you here as soon as you can get here. She said ok and that she should be at my house within two hours, but first she would need to stop at the bank. "Not a problem," I said.

While waiting for Araceli's visit, I busied myself with kneading dough and started cooking the apples to make the empanada filling. After two hours, Araceli hadn't shown up, but decided to wait a bit more before calling her. After four hours passed, and still no Araceli, I was worried and called her home.

Her older daughter answered the phone and was surprised to hear my voice. I asked, "Patsy, are you alright, is everything alright?"

She was clearly crying and said, "No Margaret, my mother died!" I broke down and we both cried. Araceli's daughter, a schoolteacher, told me that she had received a phone call at her work informing her that her mother was in a car accident and taken to a hospital. The surgeons attempted to save her from a terrible injury to her head, but Araceli's brain had absorbed the direct trauma hit of the impact. She died on the operating table. I was a complete and total emotional wreck.

In the following days, I don't remember details but somehow made it through my best friend's funeral. I missed her so much, and became obsessed with chores, cleaning, and anything that would take my mind away from any thoughts about her death. This was a near impossibility between her death, but also hearing so much about the September 11th attacks. That was a rough time for all of us, but an especially overwhelming time for me to manage all at once.

I remember waking up some mornings with my pillow soaked with my perspiration and tears. Eventually I sought help from my doctor and with medication, I was able to better cope and function. I was diagnosed with debilitating anxiety and depression, but after a couple of months of good healthcare, I discovered ways to live in the moment and keep moving forward.

I hadn't visited Araceli's grave several months after her funeral, but one day, I decided I needed to go to reconfirm the reality that she was, in fact, no longer physically present in this world. I drove my car to the cemetery and purchased a bouquet of flowers before heading to her gravesite.

When I arrived at the gravesite, I parked and waited a few minutes before getting out of the car. I then noticed the figure of a small girl sitting on the ground near Araceli's grave. The girl was dressed in a long dark coat. It was only when I focused on her coat that I realized the style of coat was very dated. No child I knew today wore that style of coat. Not since the 1950's have I seen this style of coat or do I even know if it's still available to purchase anywhere.

There was no one else in the general area, so I decided to get out of the car and approach the girl. Before I got out of my car, I turned away to tucked my purse under the front passenger seat, then grabbed the flower bouquet on the seat next to me. As I reached for the car's handle, I glanced out the window and noticed that the girl was gone! I thought this was really strange. I thought, "Where did she go and how did she get away so quickly?"

I got out of my car, walked over to Araceli's grave, and offered my prayers. I expected to get emotionally upset and sad but surprisingly, I did not. I kept looking around for that little girl but she was nowhere to been found.

I returned to my car and drove to visit Araceli's daughter. When I arrived, I knew that this visit would be much more emotionally difficult for me than visiting the cemetery. Her daughter had taken the death very hard and was devastated beyond words. I was hoping I'd be able to be of support and get through the visit without breaking down.

Her daughter was in the process of cleaning out her mother's closet and separating clothes, shoes, and other personal items. As she brought out a dress or sweater, I'd share with her just how much her mother enjoyed each article of clothing. "Oh, Araceli wore that dress to the mall. I remember the time when your mother wore that other dress to the restaurant. She dropped red chile on that one"—things like that.

Then her daughter reached behind one of the dresses hanging in the closet and brought out a blue child's coat. I instantly froze as I felt my heart stop. Then I asked, "Whose coat is that?!"

Her daughter answered, "That's mom's. She held on to it since she was ten years old." I responded, "That's the same coat I noticed a little girl wearing earlier at your mother's gravesite!"

After describing to Araceli's daughter, the details of my experience, we cried and held each other. We were shocked and bewildered by my explanation of having heard the little girl's voice months before, pleading for me to not cry, then seeing a little girl in this coat, just vanish at the cemetery, and now I was holding that same coat in my hands—Araceli's coat!

We couldn't make sense of any of this, but Araceli's daughter shared her explanation. She said what if it's possible for our spirit to somehow revert back in time. That our spirits, knowing we will soon be leaving this earth, can somehow reach back in time and come forward to the present. As in her mother's case, her spirit was attempting to prepare me for her

Araceli's coat.

approaching death; she manifested signs to me three times—twice in my home and once at the cemetery. Each time, Araceli chose to appear in the form of a child, in her coat, so as not to alarm me. It's as good an explanation as any and I'm comfortable sharing it.

So, that's my story of my being visited by a spirit. I'm not afraid of spirit energy or anything to do with them. I welcome visits and whatever messages they can pass along. I truly believe that Araceli left me with so much to think about and so much to learn from.

I hope I offered someone reading my story a bit of support or a sense of peace if they are going through a rough time in their lives. I know we are never alone. We always have our friends and family who have passed still with us, guiding us, and showing us right from wrong."

CHINO VALLEY, AZ

Chino Valley is the site of the first territorial capital of Arizona. The capital moved to Prescott, 15 miles away, in 1864. U.S. Army Cavalry Lt. Amiel W. Whipple, while traveling through the area in 1854, gave the community its name. "Chino" is the Mexican name for the abundant curly grama grass growing in the area.

In 1895, a narrow-gauge branch of the United Verde and Pacific Railroad to Jerome, joining the Prescott and Arizona Central, was completed, and Jerome Junction was established. Between 1900 and 1925, the activities of Jerome Junction were absorbed by Chino Valley.

The town is in north central Arizona, on Arizona 89, 15 miles north of Prescott and 35 miles south of Ash Fork, which is on Interstate 40. It was incorporated in 1970 and is at an elevation of 4,750 feet.

The economy of Chino Valley is based on a mixture of retail, commercial, and government activities. With the significant growth in Chino Valley, employment has been created in construction, service, and supplies. Agriculture is also a viable business.

LISA AND GERI'S STORY

My interview with Lisa and Geri, her partner of 33 years, took place in their home 20 miles south of Chino Valley in the nearby town of Prescott. The women purchased the house and 15 acres in Chino Valley in 1962 from a woman who had lived in the house for only three months. Lisa and Geri were attending a party in Phoenix, and by chance, happened to meet the seller of the property. As their conversation progressed, the seller informed Lisa and Geri about the home. That night Lisa and Geri made arrangements to meet her at the property the next day. They drove 150 miles north to Chino Valley and immediately fell in love with the old two story house and surrounding land.

What now follows is both women's story of an incredible ghostly experience. I don't believe many people would choose to remain in such a negatively active house unless they had to. What happened to Lisa and Geri in their home is a testament to their strong will to conquer what evil existed in the house. Did they eventually overcome this evil presence? Read on.

—Antonio

LISA'S EXPLANATION

After buying the property, Geri and I immediately went to work. With sledge hammers in hand, we set our goal to make a home out of this real fixer-upper and started demolishing the two most important rooms: the kitchen and bathroom. The bedrooms would be next, followed by the living and dining rooms. We decided to leave the outside of the house until the entire inside was finished. The roof had been patched six years before with hot tar, so we felt it could withstand the elements for another year or two.

We spent several days removing walls, windows and other debris from each living space. It was really hard work. Our evenings were spent resting in a beat-up old travel trailer we bought and parked on the property. It was nice to have the trailer to shower and relax in after a hard day of dust and sweat. Eventually, the kitchen was completed, and a week later, so was the bathroom. We started on the two upstairs bedrooms but strange things began as we began.

One morning, after breakfast, I left Geri at the kitchen table reading the newspaper and walked up the short flight of stairs to the second floor. As soon as I got to the top of the floor landing, a door in one of the bedrooms slammed shut with a loud bang. The noise was loud enough to startle one of our small dogs who immediately came running up the stairs to investigate. He stood directly facing the door that had slammed shut and frantically began barking.

Geri, called out to me from downstairs, "Hey, what's going on up there?"

I answered, "Nothing, the wind just blew the door shut." Geri called our dog, and as he ran back downstairs, I approached the door and reached for the door knob. I turned the knob and pushed on the door to open it. I heard the lock click on the opposite side of the door, as though someone turned the lock, and the door would not open. I thought the lock might have gotten stuck from the force of the slam, so I played with it for a few seconds. I managed to open the door about an inch but it slammed closed tight again. I immediately felt that something was not right. I called to Geri, "You need to get up here right now!" I told her that I thought someone was in the bedroom. We readied ourselves for the possibility of encountering an intruder. Again, I turned the knob and pushed on the door. This time it gave a little and with Geri also pressing against the door, it opened wide.

We entered the bedroom, expecting to encounter someone, but it was empty and we both felt a bone chilling cold surround us. An oppressive sense of heaviness, or thickness hung in the atmosphere throughout the room. Geri said, "Let's get the hell out of here!" We rushed down the stairs and back into the kitchen. Neither one of us could speak or could think of anything to say. Needless to say, we decided to leave the clearing of the bedrooms for another day and retreated our trailer. The memory of what had happened that morning stayed with us throughout that day.

The next evening, we were sitting at the kitchen table having dinner. Our only form of entertainment at the time was small radio, which was plugged into a living room outlet, one of the few working outlets in the entire house. Suddenly, the dogs began barking. Above our heads on the second floor, Geri and I heard the hurried footsteps of someone suddenly running from one end of the bedroom to the other. We sat frozen with terror staring at each other. Between the footsteps, the barking dogs and the music on the radio, our senses were overloaded. We were terrified and again concerned that someone might be in the house. Geri stayed in the kitchen while I ran out to the trailer. I loaded our shotgun, returned into the kitchen ready to confront the intruder.

With the dogs leading the way, Geri and I cautiously walked up the stairs. Geri reached for the light switch, and flipped the on switch to the single light bulb hanging from wires at the top of the stairs. The dogs dashed into that same bedroom where we had experienced the negative vibes earlier in the day, then instantly ran out crying as if someone had hit them. I immediately thought, no S.O.B. was going to hit our dogs. I yelled out, "Hey, we've got a gun—get out here now!" The only sound we heard was the sound of our dogs barking behind us. Then I yelled out, "I said, I've got a gun; show yourself!" There was no answer. We decided to enter the room anyway.

Once again we were dumbfounded that there was no one else in that bedroom. We checked the closet and opened the closed window and looked outside. No one. We also checked the adjacent bedroom, and again the window was closed shut and the room also empty. We were at a loss to explain what was going on.

We sat at the top of the stairs trying to make sense of something that made no sense. Geri began to cry, and I placed my arm around her. She was really frightened. Just then we heard a hideous laugh, followed once again by the bedroom door slamming right next to us! I got up and pointed the gun at the door, "Get out here!" I said, "Get out now!"

The laughter began again and with a courage that even surprised me, I walked to the door and turned the knob and kicked it open. The room was empty! That was enough for us. We flew out of the house and spent the most nerve-racking night huddled together in our trailer. Needless to say, we could not sleep and held watch all night until the rays of the sun filled the trailer.

In the comforting light of the morning, we walked out of the trailer and whistled for our dogs. The dogs were nowhere to be seen. They were probably out among the desert brush chasing a skunk or something. I grabbed my gun once again, and we cautiously re-entered the house. It was strange to be stepping quietly inside the house, as though we were visitors not wanting to disturb the occupants, but we did not want to take any chances. Upstairs nothing seemed out of place. The feeling was a totally different from the frightful night before; everything seemed calm and peaceful.

As the morning progressed into the afternoon, we returned to our established working routine. When only one of our dogs reappeared, Geri was concerned for the whereabouts of the other one.

After searching for a few minutes, Geri came running over to where I was mixing paint. She cried out, "Come look. I found her, and she's dead!" I followed her inside the house to the living room. There in the corner, where a water pipe was exposed next to the wall, was our Mitzy. Her head was wedged at an angle, lodged tightly between the wall and the pipe! There was no rational reason for how this happened—none at all.

We had to forcefully pull the pipe away from the wall in order to dislodge Mitzy's head. We buried her in the yard and of course, cried for days. Things had turned dangerously frightening to us—the footsteps, the laughter, the slamming doors, the eerie feelings in the bedroom, and now the shocking death of Mitzy.

Weeks passed, and the unexplainable occurrences had stopped. The physical energy and care that we had put into the house renovations were beginning to show. It looked great! We then progressed to the second floor. We started with the farthest bedroom from the stair landing. After that one was completed, we entered the bedroom where we had experienced the disturbing phenomenon.

The walls were covered in old floral print wallpaper, which we wanted to immediately remove. High on the walls were faded square outlines on the wallpaper that showed where picture frames had hung for many years. Geri was going to tackle the removal of the wallpaper, while I scraped the paint off the window frames and door. Now Geri can tell you what she discovered.

GERI'S EXPLANATION

As I was stripping away the old wallpaper, I reached a section of wall about two feet above the floor. I pulled the paper away from the wall and underneath I discovered what appeared to be bloodstains! I called Lisa to come look and asked her to tell me what she thought these spots looked like. She also agreed that it appeared to be old, dried blood. We felt goose bumps break out all over our bodies. I quickly removed the rest of the paper while Lisa finished mixing the paint. We decided that I would painted over the stains with two coats and hope for the best. The following day we brought in a bed, dresser, small table, and a lamp. The room was done at last!

We had invited friends over one day that had traveled from Phoenix, and greeted us with house-warming gifts. They loved the house and the decorating we spent so much effort on. Five of our visitors chose not to make the long return drive home that evening, and decided to spend the night. We stayed up late that night eating, drinking, and enjoying each other's company in the living room.

During the evening, we suddenly heard a loud crashing noise from an upstairs bedroom. We ran up the stairs, and I tried to open the door, but found that, once again, it would not open. With our friends as witnesses, I pushed and pushed. But I knew that just as before, there was someone or something inside the bedroom blocking me from opening the door. I could feel the strength of the spirit energy blocking and pressing up against the door. A friend standing near me, came to my rescue, and together we pushed the door open.

We were, however, not ready for the scene of destruction the bedroom was in. A lamp lay broken on the floor, and blankets had been removed off the bed and thrown all about the room. Strangest of all was the wall, by the bed—the bloodstains had reappeared! They had come through the newly painted wall!

The sight was unbelievable and really scary. One friend said nervously, "Girls, you've got ghosts in this house!" Lisa and I kept quiet because in our hearts, we knew she was right. With the help of our friends, we cleaned the mess in the bedroom and returned to the living room. Lisa and I felt comfortable informing our friends of the other happenings we had been experiencing. As we expected everyone was shocked to hear details of our terrifying encounters.

As the discussion continued, suddenly from the upstairs came that horrible laugh! Everyone heard it! Our friend Yolanda let out a scream! We pleaded with everyone to help us solve this thing once and for all. There was strength in our numbers, so we decided to walk back upstairs to confront the ghost. We needed to demand it to leave the house.

This time the bedroom door was wide open. And on the bed, we had just remade, lay clothes. The various items of clothes were shockingly arranged on the bed in the form of a body! The only thing missing was the actual body. Various items of clothing were neatly placed on the bed as to give us the impression that a body was lying in a coffin! The arms of the shirt were folded at the elbows and crossed over the chest. I grabbed the clothes and threw them back into the closet.

We decided to join hold hands, form a circle and pray. We prayed to Jesus to remove this ghost, or ghosts, and forever cleanse our house of all evil energy. Suddenly, in the middle of our prayers, we heard the quick footsteps of someone rushing downstairs, followed by the sound of breaking glass! It was so loud and each of us heard it. Together, we ran downstairs to see what glass had shattered but when we entered the kitchen, found absolutely no broken glass anywhere. We held on to each other's hands tightly and all let out a sigh of relief. I cried and thanked Jesus for getting rid of this unnerving spirit energy.

We could feel the air in the house was lighter and energy surrounding us much calmer than ever. I felt confident that by joining all our positive energies and combined prayers, we had successfully cleared the house of whatever was haunting it. We felt wonderfully empowered after this and are grateful that we now live in this beautiful, loving and peaceful living environment.

CLAYTON, NM

VALENTINA BALDERAMO'S STORY

"I was raised in Oklahoma in the town of Guthrie, located northwest of Oklahoma City. My parents Amelia and Edwardo Padilla were both born in the Texas town of San Antonio. They moved to Oklahoma in 1941. Mother was a surgical nurse and father was a personal pilot for a single family. He earned his flying license when they lived in Texas. I was born in Oklahoma the same year they moved to Guthrie. I moved to Clayton, New Mexico in 1959 three years after marring my first husband, Shawn. Today I'm a 68-year-old widow and live with my daughter Sophia in Clayton. My first daughter, Gracie, died of bone cancer at the age of eleven.

My story is about the unusual circumstances that took place during my daughter Gracie's short childhood. Both my parents and my husband were raised Catholic. My parents were not at all hesitant to speak of such things as ghosts and they even had a few personal stories of their own. Shawn's parents were immigrants from Ireland and being Irish, ghost stories were very much a tradition to their folklore.

Our house in Guthrie was located on Cooksey Road, just a block or so west of the local town cemetery. I'd visit the cemetery during sad occasions such as funerals of neighbors and business acquaintances, but never at any other times. I am the type of person who always keeps her distance from such hallowed grounds. I'm telling you this so you understand from the beginning that I'm not drawn to spooky things or experiences. I'm not necessarily afraid per se, but I don't enjoy being reminded of death.

Well, as I recall one spring day, I was calling out for my daughter Gracie. Strangely, she did not answer me. Gracie was eight years old at the time. Gracie was a headstrong girl often prone to getting into mischief. To give you an idea as to how spunky and daring she was, there were times she would bring home live snakes she'd caught and kept them as pets in her room! She was fearless! That girl often made me a nervous wreck!

I'd be cautious when entering her bedroom, afraid of who-knows-what could be slithering or crawling about. In as many times as I'd reprimand her, eventually she would win me over by saying that she needed to know all about animals and study them because she wanted to be a veterinarian when she grew up. I would relent, but always insisted that she tell me what animal she'd have at any given day stashed away in a box in her room—especially if it was a snake!

One day as I was getting ready to head into town, I called out to invite her to accompany me. I walked through the house and couldn't find her. I decided to walk outside to see if she was in the front or back yard. As I walked out the front door I spotted Cora, a girlfriend of Gracie's, on her bicycle coming toward our house from down the street. I asked Cora if she knew where Gracie was. She stopped near me, pointed her finger in one direction and said, "Yes, Gracie is over there playing with her friend in the cemetery."

"What?" I said, "The cemetery, what is she doing there?"

Cora answered, "She's talking to her friend and playing with her doll." Then Cora quickly stated, "I'm sorry, but I need to go to the bathroom, I have to hurry home." I smiled to myself and Cora road away. I knew I needed to get in the car and drive over to get Gracie. I kept thinking, "What on earth would she be doing playing in the cemetery?"

I got in my car and drove the short distance up to the gates of the Summit View Cemetery. From where I was seated, I spotted Gracie's in her brown dress. She was seated below one of many small statues of an angel, I believe in the children's section of the cemetery. "Gracie" I yelled, "What are you doing? Come over here now!" Gracie turned her head, waved at me then calmly walked out to where I was parked.

Opening the car door and sitting beside me I asked her, "What in heaven's name where you doing here?"

"Just playing with my friend," she answered.

I responded, "What—what friend? I didn't see anyone. Where's your friend, what's her name?"

"Oh, she already left. Her name is Irene and when she noticed you drive up, she just left," she answered.

Not totally understanding her answer, I said, "Well then why didn't I see her? Tell me Gracie, why didn't I see her? Was she scared of getting caught in the cemetery? How about her mother, I bet she knew her mother wouldn't want her to be here in the cemetery!"

Gracie looked directly at me and said, "Mother, she saw the car coming when you came up to the street corner, then she ran home."

"Well, Gracie" I said, "I don't want you or Cora to ever be in this place again. This place is holy and is a place for people who have gone back to heaven to live with God. Little girls like you and your friend don't have any reason to ever be here, especially by themselves. Do you understand me?"

Gracie answered, "Mommy, we were just playing with her doll, we were having a party. This is a nice place and the grass is soft. It's perfect for a party." Given the detailed descriptions and after giving a little further thought to this explanation, I realized I might have overreacted by speaking harsh to my daughter. The cemetery was, after all, a quiet place with lots of shade trees and the caretaker, Mr. Bondini, a friend of my husbands, was often there. In fact, Gracie and I spotted Mr. Bondini just a short distance away on the grounds. He waved to us and walked right over to the car.

"Hello," I said. "How are you doing?"

"Just taking care of things," he said.

Before I said another word, Gracie asked, "Mr. Bondini, would it be alright with you if Cora and I have a party by that tree?"

"A party?" He responded.

Gracie answered, "Yes, just with our doll and a friend."

"Sure, you can do that anytime you like." Then looking in my direction he said, "I'll make sure to watch over them."

"Okay," I said, "I just don't want the neighbors to start thinking my daughter's odd for playing in the cemetery."

Mr. Bondini answered, "Well if that were the case, you can imagine all the stories they tell about me. I'm here, alone, most days and nights."

I responded, "I would be very grateful if you could check up on the girls whenever you see them out here."

"Not to worry, I'll keep a close eye on them for you."

The last thing I remember saying to Mr. Bondini was, "And right now over there is a girl hiding in those bushes. Isn't that right Gracie?" Gracie kept quiet and after I repeated my question, she answered, "I don't know, I think she already went home."

Because of the short walking distance from our house to the cemetery, the safety of being in such a private secure place, free from traffic, I thought it really might not be such a bad idea to have the girls meet and play here.

I don't want to give you the impression that Gracie would go to the cemetery each day—not at all. She would go with Cora once a week, sometimes once every two weeks to the cemetery until these visits became less and less. Eventually Cora decided to spend more of her free time with her friends at school. About that time, Gracie also became more of a library bookworm. She mentioned to me that she wanted to visit the library and read books about animals. That's all she ever wanted to do was to read books about animals.

Well, a few days later, as I was in her room folding Gracie's clothes and putting them away in her dresser drawer, I spotted a small unfamiliar doll. The doll was not very unusual, but it did seem a bit old fashioned. The doll's clothes were yellowed and its head was made of porcelain. It's arms and legs were made of stitched cloth and it had a very musty scent—an earthy, moldy smell.

I picked up the dirty doll and inspected it further. I noticed a slip of paper tucked between the doll's undergarment and dress. I carefully removed it, unfolded the paper and placed the doll on top of the dresser. The paper read, "We love you Irene. Mommy and Papa." I thought, what was Gracie doing with this little girl's personal doll. Surely Irene, the owner of the doll, couldn't have given away such a personal item. That afternoon, as soon as Gracie returned from school, I made it a point to asked her about it.

As I confronted my daughter she said, "Irene told me I could take the doll home for a few days as long as I'd remember to return it to her when I was done."

"But why would you want to play with such a dirty toy? I asked. "And where do Irene and her parents live? I've never seen her." I responded. "They live in town. But Irene and I play with our dolls at the cemetery."

Startled, I said, "Gracie, you mean that that doll's clothes are dirty because of playing with it in the dirt from the cemetery"

Gracie responded. "Yes, Mommy, I guess so."

I said, "Well, that's all I need to hear. You take that doll back to your friend and don't bring anymore dirty dolls into this house again. Do you understand me Gracie? No more!"

Gracie said she was going to the cemetery to return the doll to Irene. When I asked her how did she know her friend would be at the cemetery since she hadn't been there in over a week, Gracie said, "I'll just leave it by the stone."

Immediately the words came out of my mouth, "The stone, what do you mean? That's a grave!" Without taking another breath I said, "Gracie you get in the car with me now, we're going to the cemetery and you show me where this grave is."

When we arrived at the cemetery Gracie pointed out the grave, we both got out of the car and walked over to the stone marker. I didn't know what to expect. The name written on the stone was of a man who died many years ago. I asked Gracie, "So this is the grave—right?"

Gracie responded, "Yes, here is where we play."

"Okay," I said, "Leave the doll here and let's go home." Gracie placed the doll on the stone and on our drive home I told her, "That's the last time you're going to be in that place. I don't ever want you to enter those gates again. Do you hear what I'm telling you Gracie—do you?"

I knew something was not right. I'd never seen Gracie's friend Irene, and although even Cora mentioned playing with Irene, I never actually saw her. I didn't feel well about this. And now with the doll and the grave, these negative disturbing feelings just intensified.

Gracie never return to the cemetery until her death three years later. As I said earlier in my story, my daughter died of bone cancer. Gracie was buried on July 21, 1962. So, you may be thinking to yourself, "What does this have to do with a ghost?" Well, when Gracie was admitted for the last time at the hospital, a few nights before her death, I entered her room early one morning and sitting on top of her bedside table I spotted that same dirty doll she and I had returned to the cemetery three years before! This time the dirty doll appeared to have been cleaned, perhaps washed. When Gracie woke from her sleep, I asked my daughter what the doll was doing in her room. She answered, "Irene came by and said she wanted to leave her doll with me."

I asked, "Where are her parents. Did she say anything else?"

Gracie answered, "No, she just walked out of the room."

Irene's doll remained in Gracie's hospital room until her death on the morning of July 16th. When it came time to remove her little belongings from the hospital room, I asked the nursing staff for the whereabouts of the doll. No one had removed it and didn't have any idea as to where it might be. My husband spoke to the two night nurses. They adamantly stated, "We were the only ones here last night, Mr. Balderamo. None of us saw anyone come in or leave your daughter's room."

This might seem odd to anyone who doesn't believe in ghosts, but both my husband and I feel confident that three years before her death, at the cemetery, the spirit of a little girl named Irene appeared to Gracie. We believe Irene was "sent" to befriend our daughter. Gracie only knew that she had a "new friend" and this little girl's spirit must have known what was to take place, what the future held for Gracie. We believe the spirit that visited Gracie for the last few hours of her life, was a child angel, and angel sent to comfort her, and gave her the doll as a symbol of friendship, something that would offer her peace of mind. I believe with all my heart this little girl angel helped my daughter "cross over" from this life to the next.

Gracie was in a lot of pain during her last hospital stay, but Shawn and I noticed that she was asleep for much of the time. On her last full day of

life, a beautiful smile seemed frozen on her face. All her visible pain was gone, and in its place, a look of complete peace could be felt. I spent the last few hours with her, stroking her hair as her father and I kept telling her over and over how much she meant to us. Then she passed.

Shawn and I chose a burial plot for Gracie at Summit View Cemetery. The plot was a short distance from the statue of the angel where Gracie used to play three years before with her friend Irene. I know I'll never have my daughter with me in her physical form, but I know she's in good hands. And one day I know I'll get to see and hold both she and my husband in my arms again."

COLORADO SPRINGS, CO

In its early history, Colorado Springs was known as Little London. The city was founded by Gen. William J. Palmer in 1872, and given the town's cultured and urbane atmosphere—having fine hotels and opera houses— Palmer chose to make the town his home. Palmer was a Civil War hero and railroad magnate, who had a great influence on much of Colorado's settlement process.

Today, Colorado Springs, the state's second largest city, continues its level of artistic endeavor by possessing a performing arts center, a symphony, and the Pioneers Museum. The city is also home to one of the nation's three U.S. Olympic Training Centers.

Several major Colorado attractions surround Colorado Springs. Some of the more well-known are Pikes Peak, a grand 14,000 ft. mountain, the U.S. Air Force Academy that includes the Cadet Chapel and the Honor Court, and Garden of the Gods, a spectacular city park of immense red rock formations.

PAUL R. GREEN'S STORY

I interviewed Paul at his sister's home in Denver. She mentioned that her brother was on his way to her home from Colorado Springs, and that his story was a fascinating one. Paul, and his partner's, haunting experiences might be the best account of a ghost I'd ever heard. With an obvious smile on my face, I assured her that after we finished up with the interview, I would decide if his story would be one that I'd consider including in this book. As it so happened, Paul's story is one of those, which in my estimation is quite fasci-nating, and gives potential home buyers good reason to seriously think about investing in any property which might cause one to feel the least bit uneasy.

— Antonio

"Originally I'm from Denver, I was born there. After graduating from college, I was hired as a school teacher and spent four years working in this profession. I retired early from the school system for health reasons. One day a student with whom I had a disagreement with, decided he would take revenge for my recommendation to expel him. He dropped a chair on me as I was walking down a flight of stairs. My doctor later informed me that I might have been easily killed by that assault. The injuries I sustained were to my upper spine, and one neck bone that was fractured when I fell and rolled down the stairs. Because the student was a minor, not much in the way of punishment was handed to him, at least not to my satisfaction. So today I'm forcibly retired and making the best of a situation that could have ended a lot worst.

Two years after the incident, and after completing the mandatory reha-bilitation program, my partner Rodney and I decided to move to Colora-do Springs, we purchased a home and invest in our future by purchasing two other properties that also needed upgrading. These two investment properties would need improvements to bring them up to a level where we could rent them, but with a little hard work and of course money, we were confident we could accomplish this.

At the time, real estate was a good investment, refurbishing neglected properties and putting them back on the market was proving to be a very good way to go. Before I met Rodney, he had already been buying, refurbishing and selling properties and had set up a nice personal, financial nest egg. When I came into the picture, as a couple, we decided to pull our resources together and jointly work towards better financial freedom and security. Anyone who has ever been a teacher knows, the time, personal expense and extra social activities required are rarely reflected in our pay-checks. This unexpected assault, put a strain on us, and delayed our future plans, but together we found our way and got back on track.

So, as for my story, I'll begin by telling you that I was never so scared as when I experienced spirits at one of our properties. I never, ever thought that I would have such an encounter, I didn't even believe in such things as ghosts, but I certainly do now.

The property where this ghost experience took place was on the east side of town, on a street off of Palmer Park Boulevard. Before Rodney and I purchased this house, I was hesitant to consider it because of the terrible state it was in. It definitely needed so much work to bring it back to an appropriate livable condition that I thought, no way was I going to be a part of this money pit. But Rodney convinced me in the end, and within a few days, I signed the real estate contract and became its new, hesitant owner with unexpressed reservations.

We decided to do most of the demolition work ourselves, which meant removing trash, a non-load bearing wall, cabinets, doors and a few broken windows. For the major construction work, we hired a licensed contractor. I remember the first morning I entered the house, alone, without Rodney because he was working at his home office.

As I entered the house, the first thing that struck me was its putrid scent. The odor hung heavy in the air and smelt like damp, moldy carpet. I also felt an overall eeriness throughout the house. It was a weightiness that pushed on me from all sides. I immediately had the unreasonable thought that a serious illness was eminent and about to come on. I knew this was absurd, but that is what I felt at this moment while standing in the foyer. It was an irrational, weird, and alarming sensation, to say the least.

I immediately opened wide the front door and throughout the entire house opened all the windows to draw in clean, fresh air. When I walked toward one of the bedroom windows, I noticed there was a person's shadowy outline on the curtain, standing right outside. I took hold of the window frame and pulled the shear curtains aside, but the figure was gone! I opened the window and looked for whoever that was, but he was nowhere to be seen! I never actually saw the person, just his shadow. Even after searching outside around the yard and checking the door locks on the gates, he just 'poof' vanished!

I was concerned that perhaps this might have been a burglary in progress, that perhaps I unknowingly had disrupted or stopped. So, I cautiously went back into the house and continued investigating. That's when I noticed the drawings—crayon marks on the walls in one of the bedrooms. I did not expect to see them. A child had chosen a small section of the wall, about six-by-four feet area, to draw a series of pictures. There were eight of them, about four feet high from the floor. As far as subject matter, they were what a child would draw, clouds, houses, animals, etc. I didn't pay them any further attention, and chose that bedroom to begin the cleaning.

I began removing the carpet at one of the room's corner. As I was cutting into sections before carrying it out to the front yard, I pulled up a three-by-three section of carpet by the wall where the child's drawings were. Suddenly, I was hit on the back of my head with a small roll of toilet paper! I dropped what I was doing and spotted the roll of paper, rolling along the floor, until it stopped against the wall. I didn't hear footsteps or any other sound.

I called out, "Rodney, what are you doing here?" I waited for his voice to answer, and when it didn't, I jumped up and walked to the living room calling his name, but he was nowhere. I walked out to the front yard and didn't see a car, or any signs of anyone else on the street. I immediately got so upset, that I didn't want to return inside the house. At this point, I was genuinely to afraid to return inside the house alone again.

I threw my carpet knife just inside front door, shut and locked the door, got into my car and drove home. Keep in mind that the time of this incident was early morning, the sun was out, and people were already busy with activities. When I arrived home, I called Rodney on his cell phone and described my experience. He said he would come home on his lunch break so I could give him a more detailed description and explanation.

When he finished hearing my story, he said he would not return to his office and would accompany me to the house. He quickly changed out his office clothes and into his grubby workshop clothes. When we got to the house, we entered the front door together and were hit with the reeking stench of urine. "What's that!" Rodney said, "What died in here!" Because the windows were still opened, I surmised that whatever was causing the stench must have come in from the outside. Both of us walked all around the outside of the house, and didn't see or smell anything close to what we smelled when we walked in the house.

Things were getting stranger and stranger. Rodney was first one to say that the house might possibility be haunted. I didn't want to even speak the words, but when he said that, I looked at him and said, "Yeah, well what else could have tossed that paper roll at me? And how about that figure I saw outside the window?"

We simply could not understand why these strange ghostly things were happening. I felt seriously reluctant to go back inside the house. As we were standing on the driveway, discussing the predicament, Rodney turned to face the house, raised his pointed finger at the small kitchen window and said, "Who's that?" I turned and spotted, just as he was disappearing, the same shadow figure I had seen earlier, but now it was from inside the kitchen looking out!

We both ran to the sidewalk and didn't need any further evidence to convince us that what we had both seen was a ghost! The house was as haunted as any house could be, and so we decided to put it back on the market as is, without attempting any further repairs or upgrades!

We swore not to tell anyone of our experience, but we couldn't keep such an experience to ourselves. That same Saturday, we pre-planned a dinner party with two other male couples at our home, and described to share with them what had happened at the new property. The response from our friends was predictable; they didn't believe us and laughed at our expense. Rodney and I looked at each other and without saying a word, decided to drop the subject, go along with the fun and act as if we had been caught spinning a scary tale.

Since that get-together, and unfortunate experience of our friends not believing us, we wondered if anyone would accept us speaking our truth? In an attempt to avoid any further responses like this, we've not shared or discussed this with anyone else, until my interview with you today. My advice to potential home buyers is to pay attention to what "vibes" you might sense while inspecting properties because ghost energies may also be part of the deal.

We sold the house and have not had any further contact with the new owners after signing the closing papers. I don't venture out to that area of town if I can help it, and definitely not to the street where the house still stands. I'm not quite sure why we experienced the ghost at the house, what it wanted, or why it was hanging out at the property, but that's for someone else to discover. Rodney and I don't want to ever again experience anything "supernatural" again. I believe it's best to leave ghost energies to qualified paranormal professionals and God!"

CORTEZ, CO

In the southwestern area of Colorado lies the town of Cortez. Many historically fascinating sites of the area's first ancient inhabitants—the Anasazi— are easily reached, including the entrance to world-famous Mesa Verde National Park, a World Heritage Cultural Site. At the park, you'll be able to explore the landscape where these ancestral Puebloan people constructed 1,000 years ago, cliff dwellings that they carved out of the red sandstone walls of the canyons.

Cortez has numerous parks and trails. The colorfully decorated Cortez Cultural Center offers among other things, a forum for Native cultural arts, educational programs, interpretive exhibits, out-door dramas, and Native American Dances.

The two nearby independent learning centers, Crow Canyon Archeological Center and Anasazi Heritage Center, provide the visitor with a grand display of southwest ancient cultural history. The Four Corners area where Cortez is located is a community that is contemporarily diverse and proud of its ancient cultural legacy.

ALEJANDRO MAESTA'S STORY

I interviewed Alejandro at his Cortez home at 7 o'clock. The interview ended at around 9:30 that night. We discussed his story at length, and after recording all the information that I needed, he informed me of another property he was aware of, that had a reputation of being haunted. Due to my time constraints, I was unable to follow-up with that lead. In the meantime, I know you'll find Alejandro's story to be quite interesting and thought provoking.

— Antonio

"I've lived in Cortez with my wife and son for close to six years. My wife, Adelia, and I moved to Colorado in the spring of 2000. I'm originally from Tucson, Arizona, and Adelia is from Santa Fe, New Mexico.

My wife and I experienced the ghost in the house we used to share with another couple, in Cortez, in 1999. The house belonged to our best friend Jimmy's family. Jimmy and his girlfriend, Rita, lived in the house after they graduated from college. Soon after Adelia and I married, Jimmy and Rita invited us to stay at the three-story house for as long as we needed. The arrangement we had with our friends was to share the utility bills 50/50, and any maintenance to the property that might come up.

The large house had five bedrooms and a huge attic. Jimmy and Rita took over the first floor and Adelia and I used the third floor as our living space. The second floor was pretty much kept empty but occasionally used for temporary storage. Using the attic for storage, having to carry boxes up the long flight of stairs took too much effort, so the second floor served as the best storage option at the time. This also gave both couples the necessary privacy sound buffer between floors.

Before Jimmy and Rita moved into the house, Jimmy's parents had rented it to a couple with three children. This couple moved out of the house soon after their eldest son committed suicide in the attic by hanging himself. Adelia and I knew about the house's terrible history but chose to ignore any negative thoughts or concerns we may have had. Our friends, Jimmy and Rita, had after all been living in the house for one year and hadn't experienced anything unusual during their time.

53

Adelia and I decided to move in, even if it meant having to live directly below the attic where the suicide happened. Our initial move went well, but after our first week, we did begin to experience strange things.

We started hearing footsteps on the stairs that led from the third floor to the attic. They weren't heavy sounds, just the sound of the stair boards creaking as if someone was walking on them. We heard these sounds during the day as well as at night. This was all we heard for the first couple of weeks. At first, the sounds did not bother or scare us. We weren't even sure if they were in fact footsteps, maybe it was just the old house foundation settling, or maybe the noise was due to temperature changes. But whatever the reason, they definitely did sound like someone's footsteps.

This went on for a few weeks, until one evening, as Adelia and I were getting ready for bed, we heard a loud sound that came from the direction of the stairs. Adelia and I stopped what we were doing and looked at each other. Startled, I said, "What the hell was that?" Then I walked over to where the stairs were located outside the largest room we used as a living room. I turned on the light and saw one of my baseball trophy's and several other nick-knacks were all scattered on the floor—broken! Adelia had previously placed these on the stairs to display.

Interestingly enough, this heavy metal trophy had to have been somehow lifted off the stairs and tossed over the four-foot tall railing onto the floor. It seemed impossible for to us to imagine how this happened without someone actually making the effort to physically do this. This became the starting point for more unusual things that were about to take place in the house.

Both Adelia and I began to feel a sensation of uneasiness, and even tinges of fear from time to time. Sometimes we would sense that when alone in the house, we were being watched. I know this might sound crazy, but we each felt that someone was following us from room to room. Adelia also started sometimes noticing unexplainable darting red lights. There was one time when we were lying in bed, Adelia poked me and said, "Alejandro, did you see that. When I looked by the door that she was pointing to, I saw a single red dot of light move from on the wall down to the floor!" It was strange things like this that were taking place more and more.

Another time when I was standing in front of the bathroom mirror, I spotted a shadow move behind me from one side of the bathroom to the other. This startled me and I even let out a little scream. I told Adelia about this and she confirmed that she had also experienced the same thing when she was in our bedroom standing in front of the dresser mirror.

I described to Jimmy about what Adelia and I had been hearing, and now seeing, on the third floor. Jimmy said that he had moved the dresser mirror in our bedroom from the attic. But neither he nor Rita ever said if they have experienced anything ghost-like in the house before. We thought how could they have not?

Given all that we had experienced, we were soon to experience something very convincing. One evening, at about 9 p.m., while Adelia and I were watching television in the living room, we actually saw a chair with rollers totally move on its own! The chair was placed against the desk where it had been for weeks, but that night it moved away from the desk and rolled across the room by itself! Adelia and I got up off the couch and stood staring at the chair. We were of course shaken by what we had just seen. Apprehensively, I walked over to the chair, grabbed it with one hand and returned it to where we had placed it up to the desk.

My wife and I tried to rationalize that it was not a ghost that had moved it, that it must have been something we were unaware of, something with the rollers, or something in the legs. Whatever it was did unnerve us.

The most obvious evidence that we had a ghost living with us took place when I was getting ready for work one morning. Adelia had already left, and I was finishing drinking my coffee. As I was thinking about the routine of my day, I thought I heard a voice or voices coming from the stairwell. I walked over and yelled down the stairs, "Jimmy, are you calling me?" When I didn't get a response, I got a strange feeling to turn my head upward facing the attic door. Something was drawing my attention.

Curiosity got the better of me, and not having a rational reason, I decided to walk up the short flight of stairs and take a look inside the attic.

When I reached the door in the ceiling, I unlocked it, and cautiously peered inside. At first, I didn't see much except for the window that was allowing the sunlight to fill half of the attic with light. As I took a few more steps inside, I noticed that it was empty except for a broom that had been laid across the top of a white, plastic trash can.

Suddenly, I heard a boy's voice say softly, "It's so cold here, it's so dark." I instantly froze! I was both questioning what I "thought" I heard and also knew what I "did" just hear a disembodied voice of a ghost! All I remember saying was "God help you, God forgive you!" Then I slammed the attic door and didn't even bother to lock it. I just ran down the stairs, knocking over my half-filled cup of coffee.

When I got to my job later that morning, I called Adelia and told her all about what happened and what I heard. Right then and there we decided to move out for good. Both of us had never experienced anything so terrifying as this before. In the span of a few short months the ghost experiences convinced us that they do exist and can move things. The bigger question became why would we continue to live in a house with the ghost of a teenager who hung himself and refuses to leave? It would have been clearly asking for further contact to unexplained activity that we did not want to ever experience again.

After Adelia and I informed Jimmy we decided to move out and nervously told him why, Jimmy opened up to us and shared his own experiences with ghosts in the house. Remember, Jimmy initially refused to admit to us that the house was haunted. Jimmy said that he had actually seen the shadows that Adelia and I had seen. Even Jimmy's wife Rita had seen them and heard the voice of the boy on two separate occasions while she was alone. Jimmy apologized for not telling us about the spirits but thought that having new people and "positive" energies in the house would put an end to the hauntings. I couldn't follow his screwy logic but we remain friends to this day. He and Rita have also moved out of that house and said it was a long time coming but the best decision they've made in years.

The house was sold and I don't know if the new owners have experienced anything like we did, but I sure hope not. I also hope that the teen boy has been able to move on to a more peaceful dimension, wherever that might be. It must be terrible to be stuck in this world when you don't even have a physical body to inhabit. Anyway, those are my thoughts and experiences with ghosts.

DOUGLAS, AZ

Douglas, on the Mexican border, is 118 miles southeast of Tucson, and can be reached via Interstate 10 to U.S. 80. Across the border from Douglas is Agua Prieta in Sonora, Mexico. The Janos Highway, the shortest route to Mexico City and Guadalajara by paved roads from the western United States, begins in Douglas.

Douglas, at an elevation of 3,990 feet, was founded in 1901 as a site for a copper smelter and incorporated in 1905. Originally, it was an annual round-up spot for ranchers. Agriculture and ranching are still important segments of the area's economy.

NANDY AND VICTORIA RYAN'S STORY

Our interview took place in the Ryan's wonderfully restored, one-hundred-year-old adobe house, which they purchased over 40 years ago. Victoria and her husband, Nandy, currently occupy the house. They have a son, who was raised in the house, but unlike his parents, he did not personally experience any of the ghostly events. Their son currently lives in California and teaches at a state university.

The Ryan's, now retired, have furnished their house throughout the years with antique pieces of furniture and folk art from old Mexico. Very early on in their marriage, the "travel bug" bit them. Subsequently, through their travels and purchases, they've come to know and make many friends on both sides of the border.

The house has the appearance of a folk museum, with a wonderful display of very old hand-made wooden furniture and many other works of Mexican folk art—masks, dolls, weavings, etc.

The massive wooden "vigas," or beams, that support the ceiling of the house were also brought over from Mexico when the Ryan's remodeled their house. The vigas were taken from a church built in the late 1700s in the Mexican state of Chihuahua. The church was abandoned on land that Mexican friends of the Ryan's had purchased. Knowing the Ryan's might want the hand-carved vigas for their home, the friends in Mexico had the 50 or so vigas trucked to Douglas as a gift to the Ryan's. The old vigas can now be viewed in their entire antique splendor as they decorate the ceiling overhead. Aside from the already mentioned vigas and decorations, the whole house has most of the original plank flooring, including the many scratches, knots, and imperfections that add so much to the character of the house. I couldn't help but mention the loud snapping, and creaking sounds the floor made when I walked over it. Victoria responded, "Yes, it takes a little getting used to, doesn't it?"

Aside from the annoying floor noises, Victoria and Nandy have experienced quite a lot of other "disturbances" in their home. I arrived at their house at 4 p.m. and I finished the interview at 10 p.m. Aside from their story of the paranormal, they had many other stories regarding their travels that kept me wide-eyed and hanging on each word they spoke, stories that were incredibly interesting, filled with their unforgettable adventures.

—Antonio

As you can see, the house has a lot of special things that we enjoy collecting. It can make some visitors feel overwhelmed. We use that old red trastero (dish cabinet) over there against the living room wall to display Victoria's doll collection. It has an interesting story in itself.

When we first noticed, weird occurrences taking place in the house, we knew it had to be a ghost. My wife's art supplies began to do some strange things. This might sound crazy, but her brushes moved on their own. One afternoon we both stood watching as the brushes lifted themselves out of the metal can and fell onto the table and floor! The brushes rolled a few feet and then came to a stop. We knew that this had to be the work of a ghost. What else could it be? This happened only twice, and Victoria joked that if she could train the ghost to paint on canvas, we would be rich indeed.

The next experience we had took place one November morning, about two months later, in the early morning hours. We were awakened from our sound sleep by the noise of the floorboards in the living room creaking, as if someone were walking about the house. Thinking it might be a burglar after our collections, I got out of bed and carefully walked to the living room to see, only to discover that there was not a soul in the house: so to speak.

Victoria also got out of bed, and we inspected every drawer, showcase, and cabinet for missing items. Everything was in its place, except for her paintbrushes, that were tossed about the living room floor! We immediately thought that maybe an opossum or some other animal might have entered the house and caused all the noise and mess. Our theory soon changed when we began to hear soft laughter and whispering voice. We both were able to hear this voice and it frightened us. After a few seconds, the laughter slowly went away. "Well," I said to Victoria, "our ghost is back!"

Just three days later, at about 4 p.m., I was in the kitchen making a sandwich when I heard someone say, "Nandy, you stupid man, you're a stupid man, why are you so stupid?" I turned around expecting to see someone, but I was alone, and Victoria was in the front yard watering her apricot tree. I walked out to ask Victoria if she had called me stupid. When I saw, her sitting beside the tree pulling out the weeds, I knew she could not have been the one to call me such names. I told her about what I had heard in the kitchen. With a surprised expression on her face, she told me that the same thing had happened to her earlier that same morning! Not wanting to worry me, she had decided it would be best not to mention it to me.

We had a strong suspicion that things were not going to go very well from then on, especially since the ghost was now speaking to us with unkind words. We decided to give the ghost no further attention, hoping that perhaps by ignoring it, it would find some other house to haunt.

That same night, we heard a whispering voice that seemed to be coming from the ceiling above our heads. Try as we could, we were unable to make sense out what the whispering voice was saying. This last episode made us feel annoyed and a little fearful.

The sound of someone walking about the house was now becoming a regular day-and-night experience for us. Then things really started to take off. We began to predict when the ghost would want to start trouble, because we would feel a chilling-cold temperature change in the house, even in the month of June when the weather is already quite hot. Once the noises began, the living room always stayed the coldest room in our house. The doors on the old red trastero would also quickly open and then slam shut by an unseen hand. It was truly disturbing to witness.

The ghost next chose my wife's doll collection to vent its anger on. Apparently, the ghost did not like the dolls because we found them tossed about the living room. One morning we discovered one doll in the toilet, head first!

Another very scary experience with the ghost was when our religious items began to be attacked. In our collection, we have several religious statues from old Mexico, New Mexico, and Guatemala. The statues are placed throughout the house, and we would find them turned to face the wall! We have a small crucifix that I had placed above our bed, which had also been turned to face the wall. Once we saw this side of the ghost's activity, we said enough is enough and decided to call a local priest for help.

It so happened that the Catholic priest was out of town for a week, so we instead contacted an Episcopalian priest who agreed to bless our house. We were surprised when the priest informed us that given his busy schedule, he would make an exception and conduct the house blessing the following morning. This was good news for us, but when we returned home our ghost must have known something was about to change, because of what happened next.

As soon as we returned home from our visit with the priest and turned on the lights, I saw a dark shadow-like figure quickly dash from the living room into the kitchen! Victoria and I had never seen anything like this in our home ever. About an hour later, as we were both seated in the living room watching television, a small clay vase on a side table fell to the floor. Luckily, due to the thick carpet, it didn't break. I picked up the vase and placed it in a box inside a closet.

We felt that it would be a good idea to light a few white candles and place them in each room of the house. After doing this, we again sat in the living room and watched television until we felt sleepy. We snuffed out all the candles in the house except for the one in our bedroom. We didn't want to risk having the ghost get so angry that it would want to start a fire.

Throughout the night, we kept hearing footsteps pacing across the floors of the house. The ghost was apparently upset and was making sure we were well aware of its distress. At one point, we heard a loud "thud" followed by the sound of rocks being dropped on the floor. I got out of bed and walked to each room and saw nothing out of place. I then shouted, "Knock it off, you'll soon be gone from this house, so be still!" After that, I went to bed, and we didn't hear any more noise.

At 9 a.m. the following morning, there was a knock on the front door. It was the priest. He entered, and I offered him some coffee. Being in a bit of a hurry, he declined my offer and got to the business of ridding the house of our unwelcome ghost. The ritual of a house blessing did not take longer than a half hour or so. During the ritual, nothing unusual happened, except that we smelled a strong odor of what I can only describe as iron or sulfur. We didn't know where this smell came from.

The priest left our home and all appeared to be well. Victoria and I decided that it would be a good idea to thoroughly clean the house, so we gathered together a mop, broom, and dust pan and got to work. As we carefully moved furniture and rugs, it came time to move the red trastero. When I looked underneath the trastero, I noticed the floor had a thick layer of wall plaster that must have come loose from the adobe wall behind it. As we each took hold of one end the trastero to slide away from the wall, an even larger portion of plaster fell from the wall directly behind it. The thought then hit me: "So this must have been the noise I had heard the night before of dirt or rocks hitting the wooden floor."

In the light of day, we could see that the fallen plaster had been covering a small, wooden-door frame that had been built into the living room wall many years before we owned the house. We were at a loss to guess why someone would have built such a thing and place it in a wall, and then cover it all up with plaster? We concluded that the ghostly noises must have been due to whatever this little door represented. I located a small picture of the Virgin of Guadalupe and a small metal crucifix and secured them to the small door. I then mixed some new plaster and carefully re-plastered the entire area, sealing the religious articles within the completed new wall also covering the door. We chose not to pry open the door because whatever sealed in there before us, was sealed in there permanently and should not ever be disturbed.

Since then, we have had no further disturbances. Why the ghost was upset, we have no clue. Why it waited all these years to show its anger remains a mystery to us. We are sure glad to have it gone and hope it stays gone.

DURANGO, CO

The town is located in the Animas River Valley of Colorado, where the glistening lure of gold enticed non-Native Americans to move into this fertile valley by the thousands. Following this influx, came the usual trains, supply wagons and eager homesteaders.

Today, as in its past, the Durango & Silverton Narrow Gauge Railroad transports people on a 45-mile trip through the San Juan Mountains, in route to the high elevation town of Silverton. Many locals still strongly believe that the mountains that surround Durango continue to hold a wealth of undiscovered gold ore.

Due to the three rushing whitewater rivers that are located nearby— the Animas, Dolores, and Piedras—recreational water and other outdoor activities abound in Durango. Each summer the Iron Horse Classic bicycle race draws cyclists from all over the country.

There is much to see and do in Durango's historic center. The town has not one, but two, National Historic Districts. Thankfully it has managed to preserve many of its historic buildings and landmarks. Downtown is delightfully peppered with espresso bars, art galleries, and boutiques. The town also boasts of it being one of the world's premiere mountain biking centers!

And if you choose to spend a night in any one of Durango's 1,800 historic Victorian period hotels, or bed-and-breakfasts, do ask the proprietors if you can have the haunted room for the night. That is, if you dare.

FELINA KLINE'S STORY

I met Feline for coffee one Friday morning at a local coffee house, The Steaming Bean, on Main Avenue. My immediate impression of Felina was that she was going to be a somewhat difficult person to interview, given her unusually nervous and fidgeting manner. Throughout the interview she would take written notes, and on several occasions, she stopped to ask me questions regarding my research, my own experiences with spirits, and if I truly did believe what I was writing about.

After an hour of answering my questions and two double espressos, hers—not mine—she presented me with her story. After our interview, her face appeared to have a desire to ask me something. I asked, "Is there something else you'd like to say?" Felina replied, "Yes, my husband Dan has been having the strangest thing take place within the last month. This only happens when Dan's in the attic of our house. I've seen the scratches that appear on his neck and back. He doesn't go up to the attic unless he absolutely has to, otherwise, we just leave the voices we sometimes hear in the attic alone."

— Antonio

My husband, son, and I are originally from Glenwood Springs, Colorado. At the time of our initial arrival in Durango, about 15 years ago, we were renting a house in the west side of town. Not long after, we purchased a home in a subdivision on the east side. The community where that home was located was up on a large expanse of farmable acreage, with streams that ran through the area. When we first moved into what we now refer to as, "the haunted house," we had no idea as to the tragic history regarding the death of a little girl in a hot tub. We lived in that home until strange things began to take place. That's when I put my foot down and said to my husband, "I'm taking the kids and getting the hell out of this place. So, I told him, you better decide real quick if you want to come with us or not!" Needless to say, we put the house on the market, sold it, and bought another one in town.

Initially, nothing unusual took place when we first moved in. We remodeled most of the bedrooms, the kitchen and bathrooms, leaving the remodeling of the living and dining rooms for the following year. The house had two patios, one that led out to the side of the house, which offered a great vista to the pasture, and the other that had an arbor with climbing vines that sheltered a large hot tub. Both patios had double sliding glass doors that opened out to the yard.

Our first indication that something ghostly was amiss took place one day when I noticed a pair of small handprints on the glass of the sliding doors that led out to the hot tub. I tried to wipe then off with glass cleaner and a paper towel, but they would not come off. I really did put a lot of 'elbow grease' into removing them, but the glass would not come clean. So, I imagined that a previous child had had some type of solvent on their hands when they placed them on the glass, and the marks had become permanent. I didn't think any more about this because of all the other, more important chores that had to be done around the property. I could live with these little prints for a while. But little did I know what strange things were to follow.

I would say that it would have been about a month later that my husband, Dan, began to hear the sound of a child playing in the living room and kitchen. At the time, our son, Andrew, was four years old, and we kept a close eye on his whereabouts. Dan kept asking me if I had left Andrew in the kitchen by himself. When I would tell him that Andrew was in his bedroom, Dan would actually get up off his chair and check for himself.

What I didn't know was that Dan had been hearing such noises about a week after we moved into the house. He didn't want to alarm me, so he convinced himself that it was his imagination playing tricks. It was not until about a month later that he confided in me about the sounds he was hearing. He told me that sometimes the sounds of a child's laughter would awaken him from sleep. I never heard any sounds he described hearing in the house. But I would find some of Andrew's toys in unusually odd places throughout the house.

I began to suspect that something weird was going on when one day I discovered one of Andrew's plastic dinosaurs on top of the refrigerator. I asked Dan if Andrew had misbehaved, and caused Dan to put the toy up away from our son's grasp. Dan said, "No, I didn't put it there." I left Dan more confused than before. The next unexplainable thing to happen was when I found a framed picture of my parents under my bed! I took the picture and held it up to Andrew and asked him if he moved the photo. All Andrew did was to gently hit it with his fingers as if he wanted to play. At four-years old, I couldn't imagine how he could have taken the picture off the table without breaking it and then toss it under the bed.

Not long after that last incident, I started hearing the voice of another child in the house. I only heard the voice coming from our bedroom, and not from the kitchen or living room as Dan was experiencing. The voice was faint and distant at first then it got louder but didn't last very long. It would be a chuckle, and sometimes a long playful scream of delight, exactly sound that a young child would produce.

This went on for about two days before I began to get an over whelming creepy feeling. Dan and I did not believe in ghosts, spirits, or what have you, although we did have a run in with a relative of Dan's who supposedly did experience such manifestations while on a trip to the Bahamas one year. We just laughed at his story and attributed it all to him being on vacation with too much alcohol and partying. But these weirdly, recently occurring instances were far too strange to just brush off as something we both could have imagined.

Another example that something was off about our home was what took place just a week after I started hearing the child's voice. As Dan and I were already in bed for the night, we were startled to hear a loud noise coming from our closet. I jumped out of bed, quickly opened the closet doors and saw that all my shoes (which I had carefully placed on the shelves) were now scattered all over the floor! There was no way that they could have fallen without the direct physical effort of someone tossing then to the floor—no way!

As I turned to face Dan, and was about to tell him what had just happened, he motioned to me be silent by holding his finger to his mouth. After a few seconds, Dan said that right at the moment that I opened the closet doors, he spotted the small shadowy figure of a young girl standing at our bedroom door.

I was definitely scared now. Dan just refused to believe. Instead he wanted us to just get to sleep and discuss the matter in the morning, but I would have none of that. I immediately walked over to our Andrew's bed, picked him up in my arms and brought him back to our bed. I was taking no chances with my son.

The following day, and weeks after, we noticed that the ghostly events pretty much ended. But one Saturday morning as I was attending a local garage sale, I met two women who were selling framed, embroidered flower art that they both had made. During our conversation, I informed them that I had recently moved to my home and spoke to them of the location. They both grew silent, soon one woman spoke, "Are you aware of the child who died at your home?" Shocked and very taken aback by her question, I answered, "No, I'm not aware of anyone dying. Where and how did she die?"

"It's so sad, it was a little girl. She somehow made her way out to the hot tub, fell in and drowned. You mean no one has told you about her? The realtor didn't tell you about the girl?" I answered, "No, no, no!" The woman answered, "Well, the family moved out not long after their daughter's tragic accident. I'm sorry, but someone should have told you about that tragedy."

My mind was a big whirlwind of thoughts. But now everything started to come together for me. I immediately drove into town to meet Dan at a restaurant for lunch, and informed him of what the women had shared with me that morning. Without any hesitation, Dan said, "Well, when do you want to move out?" I was surprised but relieved by his quick response, and responded, "As soon as we can!"

We listed the house with a realtor, and within a few weeks, sold the property and moved to our new location in town. All the renovations we had made to the house were a great selling feature, so we did well with the sale. We decided not to include the tragic death history about that property because it was never officially told to us.

Today, in our new home we have made it a point to ask the real estate agent if he was aware of anyone dying in the home, he answered, none that he could confirm. Except for a few unusual things like the scratches that Dan gets on his shoulders each time he's in the attic, and a mysterious deep low growl we sometimes hear but can't figure out from where it originates. Dan and I have a new respect for things like hauntings and spirits. I'm not totally convinced yet but I do strongly suspect our new house might also be haunted too! Thankfully, my son Andrew does not remember anything frightening from the previous house."

EAGLE, CO

Surrounded by Bureau of Land Management and National Forest lands, Eagle is nestled within the Vail Valley mountain area. The town is also just 30 miles west of Vail. Eagle is a small community that has within its historic district quaint shops, a bakery, and restaurant, and all without the big city attractions.

If the wondrous solitude of hiking a grand Colorado mountain or two intrigues you, then the town of Eagle would be worth a visit. And for the anglers, the Eagle River meanders along the town. Eagle is close to both Vail and Copper Mountain ski resorts, and lies just east on I-70 from Glenwood Canyon. Operated by its local historical society, Eagle also has a museum and visitors' center.

RICHARD ORTEGA'S STORY

Richard and I were seated in his kitchen when I conducted the interview. When appropriate to the context of the story, a portion of the interview was conducted in Spanish. Richard has led a very interesting life, and aside from ghost stories, he has other equally dramatic, personal stories to tell, which he shared with me. One of these accounts took place on a visit to England. He and his wife were given a personal tour of the Queen's botanical nursery. Con-

cluding their visit, they were each given a souvenir packet of radish seeds, which at his return to the United States, he planted. This is Richard's story.

— Antonio

"I'm originally from Carbondale, about an hour and a half south of Eagle. My father and I were born in Mexico. I was brought to the United States at the age of three. My father married my mother, who is Ute Indian from the Ute Mountain Indian Reservation, near the Four Corners area. She left the United States, moved to Mexico, and lived with my father's parents two years before I was born. Five years later, they returned to my mother's homeland in Colorado. When I began working at the Eagle County building in the early 1990s, a fellow worker informed me that he had witnessed a few strange things at one end of the building. Things like hearing footsteps while being alone inside, doors closing on their own and lights that would turn on and off by themselves. I was skeptical and even made fun of the guy. But that stopped when I had my own experiences about a month later.

One winter night, during my first week of employment, as I was working on the second floor, I happened to look out of one window and spotted an older man walking about the grounds. Nothing unusual about that, except this man was pushing a wheelchair, and the ground was covered in about two inches of snow.

The next day I mentioned this to a co-worker and he seemed stunned. He said, "You mean you saw the ghost?" I said, "Ghost, what do you mean a ghost? I just saw an older man with a wheel chair. I didn't see a ghost. It was just a man pushing a wheelchair." My co-worker, who had worked for the county a few years before I was hired said, "Yeah, that's the ghost of the guy who died here before the building was built. He's always seen pushing a wheelchair!"

The story goes like this: No one knows who this older man was, but he came into the town of Eagle one day and wandered onto the grounds of the county offices. Some think he might have been a homeless man who was dropped off at the highway 70 exit into town.

He was in pretty poor shape given the way he was dressed and that he was pushing his wheelchair. A few locals noticed him because of the snowstorm taking place at the time. The cops were called to investigate this stranger, but they find him and failed to make contact. They thought he must have left town by hitching a ride near the highway. Perhaps a passing motorist took pity on him and gave him a lift, they just didn't know. After the snowstorm, his body was discovered along with his wheelchair, near the frontage road, a short distance from town. He didn't have any personal identification or documents with him, which would have helped authorities. Besides the wheelchair, all he had with him were the dirty clothes he was wearing, a torn, plaid blanket covering his lower body, a small plastic bottle of orange juice, and a brown paper bag of uneaten fried chicken. That's all.

My co-worker Andy, also told me that a few other employees had seen this ghost inside the building, as far back as a year before I started my employment. "Wow, so you've seen this guy's ghost?" He said. Again, I responded, "I don't think it was a ghost, just an old man pushing a wheelchair. He seemed very much alive to me, nothing like what I'd imagine a ghost to look like. If this was a ghost, he sure looked alive and real!"

A month later, at around 1 a.m., I was working in the south side of the building and decided to walk over to the utility room for supplies. As I was taking something off the shelf, I heard the sound of footsteps just out in the hallway, coming in my direction. I felt that somehow, someone had found a way into the locked building. I turned to face the closed door and noticed that the hall light coming from underneath the door, was being blocked by someone standing in front of the door! As I was about to ask, "Who's there?" I saw the door's knob began to slowly turn. I asked, "Who's there? Andy, is that you?" No response. This time I said, "Andy, stop playing around!" But still no response. Then I noticed that the shadow on the other side of the door had moved passed and away from the door.

I opened the door expecting to see Andy, but there was no one there! I knew that something strange was going on. I thought I was going crazy. But seeing the door knob turn was not imagined. I saw it move. I couldn't believe it, but who or what could have turned it? As much as I tried to ignore and forget about this, I couldn't. I was completely alone in the building and knew this had to be some ghostly thing.

I spent the rest of the night expecting to see something materialize in front of me. Every little noise would send my heart racing. I'm not ashamed to say that I was terrified—because I really was. But nothing further like this happened that night, and I was so relieved to see the morning sunlight come through the large windows of the building that morning.

A few weeks later, as I was getting over that first, and hoping last experience, another thing happen. I was on the first floor alone and heard the sound of furniture being roughly moved around a room. The sound was coming from down the hall. Only this morning, I was alone in the building because my co-worker was absent due to a heavy snowstorm. The sounds I was hearing were making my stomach twist nervously!

I don't remember how but I got up the courage to walk over to the room and open the door. It was empty, but I immediately heard the rasping sound of a male voice saying something that sounded like, "I don't care no more, I don't care nothing, nothing." The voice slowly faded away and moved to the next room where it repeated once more, and faded away for good. I could hear my heart pounding inside my chest and decided to quit my job that morning.

I immediately packed up my stuff, walked outside into the chilly dark night, got into my car, and drove away for good. I honestly did do that. I

Eagle County building.

didn't believe that having a ghost confront me while I'm working was the best thing in the long run for my nerves, heart or health, so I quit.

I have never, ever or since, had such a scary encounter as the ones I experienced in the Eagle County building. I've returned twice to the county building. First to collect my personal belongings, and the last was to discuss requesting a letter of recommendation from my supervisor. That was a few years ago, and I almost never mentioned the ghost in that building. I'm willing to bet anything that others working there today still continue to experience ghost activity in that building. I bet you!"

ESPAÑOLA, NM

Española is quickly becoming the city at the center of it all in northern New Mexico. Rich in culture and history (Española was the first Capitol City in America), the city is also leading the way into the future on major issues including transportation, water planning, and more. Seated in the beautiful Española Valley between the Sangre de Cristo Mountains and Jemez Mountains, Española is a wonderful place to work, play, and to call home.

PORTER MITCHELL'S STORY

"My wife Pauline and I moved to Española in 1993. Prior to our move we lived in Grand Junction, Colorado. Pauline's mother was a Mandan Indian of Canada and her father was Portuguese. Pauline was also raised in Provincetown, Massachusetts. I, on the other hand, am a regular white boy, born and raised in Grand Junction. Pauline and I met while we were both separately vacationing in Cancun, Mexico. Within three months of our relationship, we decided to live together, so she moved to South Dakota, within the year we married, and a year after, our daughter Paula was born.

A year after the birth of our daughter, an old friend of mine from high school asked me to apply for a job as an illustrator with his New Mexico-based magazine. The job fit in perfectly with our financial needs. Not having any pressing reason to remain in South Dakota, we decided to make the move south. As long as I had a computer, I'd have no problems continuing with my design work. So as soon as we made the decision to move to New Mexico, I got on the phone and located a realtor in Santa Fe.

Within two months, the three of us drove to Santa Fe, New Mexico to meet with the realtor. We blocked out three days—Tuesday, Wednesday and Thursday—for viewing potential properties to purchase around the Santa Fe area.

We left early Saturday morning from Grand Junction, spent two nights on the road, stopped for gas in the town of Taos before making the two-hour drive into Santa Fe. When we approached the town of Española, Pauline suggested we stop for a restroom break.

While stopped in Española, Pauline noticed a Home-For-Sale sign at an intersection and encouraged me to call for details. I called the number using my cell phone. A woman, Mrs. Santiago, answered and I asked her about the property. Pauline was listening and motioned to me that we should take a look. I gave the woman our location, where we were parked, and she met up with us, and soon we were following behind her to the property.

As we drove a few miles eastward, the house and property lay before us in a cottonwood tree-covered parcel. The house's appearance was not uniquely special, but the beautiful expansive view of rolling hills against the powder blue sky was so inviting, the total panorama hooked us right then and there. Everything about the property was what we were looking for. The barn, the well-house, the fruit trees, all of it was what we imagined to be out of a Western novel. The asking price was also very much in our price range. In fact, if we purchased it, we'd still have extra money to use towards improvements on the property. As soon as we walked inside the house, I could see in Pauline's eyes that she was totally taken over by its quaint and well-kept appearance. We thanked Mrs. Santiago and told her we were very interested, but had to get back on the road. I was honest with her and informed her that we were also looking to buy a house in Santa Fe. She was very understanding and bid us, "Good-luck!"

After spending two days with the realtor, and looking over fourteen potential houses, we decided not to settle in Santa Fe and instead looked into the very real possibility of purchasing the property we looked at earlier in Española. So, we returned to the property and after weeks waiting for the inspection report then the financing process, we purchased the house from Mrs. Santiago.

Everything was going well for us after moving in, all except for a little reoccurring incident. Pauline kept mentioning to me that she kept seeing a young boy outside on the property. When she walked by a window that faced the backyard, she would sometimes see him in the corner area where two of the coyote fences met. It's an area of the yard were three apple trees and a very tall cottonwood tree had grown. When Pauline left the house, walking out the back door to greet the little boy, he would vanish. The little boy was becoming a problem after she spotted him one afternoon peering into the kitchen window! Pauline said, "I yelled at him to get away, and when I ran out the door, as usual, he was gone!"

I mentioned to Pauline that we should go around to all the neighbors and ask about this little "Peeping Tom." That evening we asked the neighbors and without exception, each one stated they didn't know of any little boy fitting this description. So, while walking home, we decided to always keep a watchful eye for this kid. Apparently, the walk throughout the neighborhood did the trick because for the next few months we didn't have any further "visits" from this boy—so we thought.

It was approximately six months later, and Pauline and I were in the kitchen talking. Paula was also with us sitting in her highchair. Pauline and I had discussed and decided to purchase a baby monitor for Paula's bedroom. That week we purchased the monitor and placed one speaker in the kitchen and one in our bedroom. The device was a nice safety addition and surprisingly gave us much comfort, until one evening.

As I was driving home from visiting a friend in Santa Fe, I received a call on my phone from Pauline asking me to come home right away, "It's not an emergency, but I need you to come home as soon as you can." I asked her what was going on, and she answered, "Porter, I think we have a ghost!"

"A ghost?" I said, "What do you mean a ghost?" Then I started to laugh. Pauline said, "Okay, laugh but we have a ghost, so get yourself home."

As I walked through the front door, I found Pauline sitting in the living room on the couch with Paula asleep beside her. Pauline explained that after she laid our daughter in her crib, Pauline walked to the kitchen to prepare a small sack of green beans for dinner. About halfway into her work, she heard the strange voice of a young boy coming from the monitor's speaker that was on the kitchen table. She said she stopped her food prepping, walked over to the table, took a seat and paused to listen.

The unmistakable voice of a boy was saying something in Spanish, Paula was giggling and responding in baby talk. Pauline immediately got off her chair and rushed into the bedroom. She hit the light switch, turned on the light and found Paula standing up on her mattress, holding on to the crib rails, and laughing! Not knowing what was happening, Pauline lifted Paula into her arms and walked over to the living room sofa and sat down. When I walked into the house that is where they had been for the past forty minutes. I asked Pauline, "Are you sure what you heard was real?"

Pauline answered, "Porter, I grew up with spiritual stuff going on all the time in my house in Canada, I know what this is! My mother was into spirits and I know what I heard is what I heard and I have no doubt there is a little boy's spirit on this property! Why he's here is a mystery to me, but I don't want him playing with my baby!"

"Okay, okay," I said, "We'll take care of it. But is Paula alright?" "Oh, she's fine," my wife answered. "She was having a great time laughing, but it's not right to have a spirit hanging out with our daughter in her bedroom. Paula is sleeping with us from now on. Can you move her crib into our bedroom, please?"

I move the crib into our bedroom to keep things calm in our home and spent the next few nights in our daughter's room. I never experienced anything strange, but we did hear dishes being moved about in the kitchen and twice the television turned on by its self in the middle of the night. After the second time of being abruptly awakened by this, I pulled the television's electrical plug out from the outlet and as I draped the plug and cord over the T.V. I felt sure it would be silenced once and for all.

In the morning Pauline called me from the living room. She said, "Well, look here Porter. It appears our ghost wants to play games with you." The television cord was no longer draped over the T.V. set; it was on the floor and I counted ten knots along its length!

With a shocked look on my face I said to Pauline, "Oh boy we've got ourselves some problems here, don't we?"

Pauline said, "I'm going to phone Mrs. Santiago and ask her if she knows anything about this." Pauline spoke for less than ten minutes with Mrs. Santiago and after hanging up she told me she would be paying us a visit as soon as she could. Within the hour Mrs. Santiago drove up our driveway, parked and walked up to our front door. When Pauline opened the door, Mrs. Santiago took hold of Pauline and appeared to have been crying. Pauline lead her into the living room where we all sat across from each other. Mrs. Santiago began to tell us an amazing heartbreaking personal story.

Early on, when Mrs. Santiago and her since deceased husband, Edward lived in the house, they had four children, two boys and two girls. One of the young boys, Cipriano climbed the large cottonwood tree in the backyard and fell, breaking his neck just where the spine meets the shoulders. He lived for ten days. After Mrs. Santiago told her story, she asked Pauline for a description of the little boy she had seen in the yard and house. Pauline described the boy she had been seeing and Mrs. Santiago showed us a photo of her little boy. Pauline, said, "Yes, that's him. I'm so very sorry for your loss."

Mrs. Santiago was smiling as she was crying, "That's my little Cipriano, he was so happy living in this house. He loved his baby sister, Amalia. He was always playing with her. I think he's now watching over your little girl. I know he won't hurt her; he's just playing with her. You don't have to be afraid, he was a good boy."

Needless to say, Pauline and I were numb from shock and speechless. After a few silent moments, I said, "Well, now we know what we're up against. The spirit is just curious and wanting attention. Can we ask you to ask him to go home with you or to heaven? I don't think his spirit needs to hang around at this house any longer, do you?"

Mrs. Santiago answered, "Oh no, he needs to go to heaven to be with his father." I'll go to the church today and pray for him to leave you and your family alone."

That's all it took. We never again had another incident with Cipriano's spirit in our house. It helped that we were able to identify Cipriano, and having his mother instruct him to join his father, he apparently obeyed like any child should. Our daughter Paula is now seventeen and she doesn't remember anything about the little boy visiting her. Although our story is not a scary one, it did leave us with a few sleepless nights. Well, so much for the idea that ghosts don't exist because they did for us!"

FLAGSTAFF, AZ

Flagstaff, located at the intersection of Interstates 17 and 40, is the largest city and regional center of northern Arizona. It is county seat for Coconino, the second largest U.S. County with 12 million acres. Flagstaff, at 7,000 feet, is one of the highest U.S. cities and its breathtaking backdrop is even higher. The community sits at the base of San Francisco Peaks, Arizona's highest point at 12,633 feet. Flagstaff is a year-round mecca for visitors.

Many Arizonans maintain second homes here. Summer temperatures average 20 degrees cooler than Phoenix. In Winter, there is skiing, ice skating, and hunting. Flagstaff has long been a transportation hub. Located along an old wagon road to California, Flagstaff was established after the railroad arrived in 1881.Today the town links Interstate 40 to Interstate 17, Arizona 89 to Page and Utah, and Arizona 180 to the Grand Canyon. Historic Route 66 passes through Flagstaff.

Flagstaff's name comes from a tall pine tree that was made into a flagpole in 1876 to celebrate the Declaration of Independence Centennial. Flagstaff is a governmental, educational, transportation, cultural, and commercial center. Tourism is a major source of employment. Traditional economic activities continue to employ people.

MARCUS AND GINGER LA PORTE'S STORY

I interviewed husband and wife, Marcus and Ginger, at their home one evening. The La Portes' are a couple in their late 40s who have lived in Flagstaff since 1977. They met and married in New Orleans, Louisiana. Today, they live in a large two-story log home, six miles north of Flagstaff's central district. We sat down for a long comfortable conversation in their living room. The living room has three very large, floor-to-ceiling picture windows, which allowed me to view the beautiful night sky. As their story developed, I began to feel a little bit nervous. Needless to say, it was a scary one.

Their story will make the reader pause, and think twice about ever again purchasing "bargain items" at yard sales. What follows is a story that can happen in any state to anyone. The La Portes' simply were a couple that happened to be unaware of anything related to ghosts in their personal lives. As you will now read, such an attitude does not necessarily prevent ghosts from reaching out to touch the world of the living.

—Antonio

Marcus and I decided one July weekend to clean out our garage and basement. It was incredible the see how much "junk" we had stored away throughout all the years. We decided that the best thing to do with all the used clothes and odds and ends was to hold a yard sale. We decided on a sale date, placed an advertisement in the local paper and got to work cleaning out the house. We informed some of our neighbors about the upcoming sale, and word quickly spread around. Marcus also spoke to his mother, who had moved to Flagstaff two years ago. He convinced her that the yard sale would be a great way to sell some of the antiques she had brought from her hometown of New Orleans. Although at first she was reluctant to even think of parting with her cherished antiques, she thought more about it and changed her mind.

The Saturday sale took place as planned and in preparation we found more "junk" and treasures than we had ever realized we owned and Marcus's mother's antiques were a huge hit.

A neighbor came by before the 8 a.m. starting time and bought a dresser of mother's. This dresser was not a very pretty piece of furniture at all. It needed refinishing and the mirror was particularly in need of restoring. However, our neighbor said she "loved it" and she had a perfect space in her guestroom for it!

I could tell that Mother La Porte was very eager to part with this piece of furniture. I asked her why she was so eager to sell the dresser, when just a few days ago she would not even have considered selling any of her antiques. She answered, "Well, I should have gotten rid of that evil thing a long time ago." Her words made me ask what she meant by referring to the dresser as "evil." She responded, "Oh, it's nothing dear, just nothing." I could tell by her voice that she wanted to drop the subject, so I didn't ask any further questions. Over all, the sale was a big success, and most of mother's antiques did sell. We donated what remained of the unsold items to a local thrift shop. Not only did we make money but we increased our living and storage spaces as a bonus benefit.

About a month later, the neighbor who bought the dresser phoned and described a very strange thing that had happened to their family. She said that she had removed the dresser from the guest room, and put it in their garage with a carpet draped over it for protection. She shared and describe the trouble she and her family had been experiencing. I was so curious and interested in hearing more in the little she already said that I invited her right over to our house. I wanted her to tell her story in the presence of Marcus and his mother. I informed Mother of some of the story which our neighbor had shared with me over the phone. Mother responded, "Let's just wait to hear what she has to say." Soon there was a knock on the door and I invited the neighbor inside. We sat around the kitchen table and she told the most incredible, scary story I have ever heard.

Our neighbor, Beverly, started her story by saying that after purchasing the antique dresser from our yard sale, she dusted it off and placed the dresser in her guestroom. "I loved it," she said "I even bought a blue flower vase and a brass brush-and-comb set to display, that I knew would enhance its look. I placed these things on top of a white doily on the dresser. It looked beautiful. I also went out and purchased a cute little embroidered boudoir stool and placed it in front of the dresser. It was perfect."

The following weekend, her daughter had come to visit from Phoenix and spent the night in the guestroom with the dresser. During the night Beverly's daughter, Lisa, said that she was awakened by a noise in the room. She opened her eyes and saw a strange blonde-haired woman seated by the dresser. This spirit woman was busy brushing her hair then noticed Lisa watching her and turned to face Lisa directly. In a split second, the blonde woman disappeared from where she was seated and was now standing right next to the side of the bed!

Lisa was shocked by this and wondered what was happening and who this stranger in her room was. She watched as this ghostly woman forcefully waved her arms above her head. Lisa noticed the ghost woman opening her mouth wide and making extreme facial gestures, which gave Lisa the impression that, the ghost was upset and screaming at her but strangely, made no actual sounds.

Soon Lisa found the courage to grab her pillow, and threw it at the ghost. Instantly, the image of the ghost woman seemed to dissolve and completely vanished before her eyes. With tear-filled eyes, Lisa turned on the lights and sat up on the side of the bed trying to compose herself. She was not sure what had just happened or why. Did she dream it, or did an actual ghost visit her? After pondering what she had just witnessed, Lisa grew sleepy, crawled under the covers and fell back to sleep. Lisa also left the bedroom light on, just in case anything else was to appear.

In the morning, Lisa told her mother about what she had experienced, even describing it as a nightmare. Beverly told us that she was fascinated by her daughter's story, but skeptical. However, our Beverly's skepticism soon ended when they both went up to the dresser and discovered that on the new brush-and-comb set were several strands of blond hair! Since they are of Chinese descent, Beverly, her husband, and daughter Lisa each have dark black hair. Whose hair was this on the brush? Beverly presented the brush with the blonde hair strands to Lisa. Lisa, very apprehensively stated, "You see, now you have actual physical evidence right there! I told you there was a blonde-haired woman in the room with me brushing her hair with a brush."

Beverly needed no further explanations. Immediately, she and her daughter removed the dresser from the house and placed it in the garage and immediately covered it with an old piece of carpet. The brush with the blond hair was wrapped in newspapers, placed in a plastic bag, and disposed of in the trash.

Since that night the ghost has not returned or shown itself. Beverly wanted to know if Mother La Porte would buy back her antique dresser. Marcus's mother said she would, and arrangements were made to place the dresser back in storage. Not once did Mother La Porte add anything to the neighbor's story. In fact, Mother just sat quietly in her chair listening to the stories.

After the Beverly left our house that evening, Marcus's mother surprised us by telling us that she had had a similar visit from the strange blond woman, when the dresser was in her own bedroom, back in New Orleans. She had purchased the dresser from an elderly African-American gentleman. He explained to her that the dresser, among other furniture he was selling, was from an estate sale. Apparently, the furniture and other items he was selling were all that remained of a disastrous house fire. Several family members had been burned to death in that fire.

Marcus's mother then explained that one night she heard a voice coming from her bedroom. As she walked into the bedroom to investigate, she was surprised to see a strange woman standing by the dresser. The blonde-haired woman stood with her hands raised and clutched together in front of her. She was dressed in a light blue nightgown and had an expression of dread on her face. Marcus's mother asked the woman, "Who are you? How did you get here?" Incredibly, the woman's image immediately disappeared. Marcus's mother had never experienced anything like this before. It was only after she had brought the dresser into the bedroom that this ghost appeared. The dresser must somehow be mysteriously connected with this woman ghost. "I know it's the dresser," she said "I could feel it in my soul that that dresser had something to do with the ghost."

Mother La Porte wasted no time in removing the dresser from her own bedroom and out to the porch at the rear of the house, where it remained for several years. The ghost of the blonde woman was not seen again until this most recent time in Flagstaff.

The dresser now sits in a Flagstaff storage unit. Who knows where it will eventually end up? For now, the ghost will have to just wait until she can reappear to someone else. Maybe by then there will be a new way for her to tell her story instead of just scaring people.

FLORENCE, AZ

Florence is in Pinal County, midway between Phoenix and Tucson. Colonel Levi Ruggles, an Indian agent, staked and plotted the town in 1866. Sources cite different origins for the town's name, but all agree it was someone's sister or daughter. By the 1920s, the area had become the agricultural center of the county.

The Florence business district is still on Main Street, and aside from the obvious improvements, downtown looks much as it must have in the 1880s. Both visitors and residents appreciate the diversity of the community. Florence offers the convenience and small western community lifestyle, yet it is only 45 minutes away from the Phoenix and Tucson metropolitan areas. Incorporated in 1908, Florence, at an elevation of 1,493 feet, has been the county seat since its formation in 1875.

NANCY L. CORRALES'S STORY

I interviewed Nancy at her home, located on the far-east portion of the city. Nancy is a 50-year-old divorced woman with two teenage boys. Nancy's family is originally from the state of Texas; her parents moved to Florence in the 1930s to work as farm workers in the cotton fields. Her story is about a peculiar uncle named Edward, or as she referred to him, Uncle Eddie. Uncle Eddie was Nancy's mother's older brother who lived with the Corrales family until his death in 1954.

After divorcing her husband in 1979, Nancy returned to Florence, to the home where she had spent her youth. The house is an old one-story adobe brick building, with a large rusted sheet metal roof. These days Nancy spends her days tending to her rose and vegetable gardens, and some evenings she can be found at the lo-cal church bingo. "I live a peaceful life here in Florence. I love my neighbors very much. Everyone is so kind to each other," she said.

Nancy also stated, "My uncle was a really 'special' man. Once you hear my story about him, you'll know why." What follows is my interview with Nancy and her experience with the ghost of Uncle Eddie.

—Antonio

Growing up in a small town like Florence was really fortunate for a young girl like me. I enjoyed the freedom and safety of being able to go to the grocery store and not worry about being assaulted. Even though I carried no money, all I had to do was sign my name on a receipt and at the end of each month my parents would total up the charges and pay their bill. What bothered me was not being allowed to buy candy only milk, eggs, and bread.

Sometimes, after returning from work, my Uncle Eddie would accompany me to the store. His favorite gesture was to treat me to a candy bar. He would also buy two bottles of beer, which he would take to his friend's house. Uncle Eddie and his friend would drink their beers while listening to the radio. I know that today this might not seem a very exciting thing to do, but when I was younger, we enjoyed the simple things in life.

Uncle Eddie had diabetes, and since we did not have much money at the time, he seldom ever visited a doctor. He ate and drank anything he wanted and eventually it all caught up with him.

One evening, as we were all sitting at the kitchen table, he complained about something clouding his vision. Within a few days he began to see less and less in his right eye, until he totally lost his sight. When he eventually visited the doctor, the news was bad. He was told that his loss of sight was due to his diabetes.

After losing his sight, Uncle Eddie's personality began to change. He became depressed and spent nights lying awake in his bed. He knew that things could only get worse as the days progressed. He was unable to properly care for his disease, and the result was that his body was seriously suffering. His family and friends attempted many times to help him with his depression, but he knew that his life would be cut short.

I remember the few times I caught him sitting at the side of his bed, and just staring into space. I felt so very sad for him and helpless to do anything for him. Soon his right foot became infected, and the infection rapidly spread. He was taken to a Phoenix hospital and when the doctor saw the condition of his foot, the decision to amputate was made that same day. So now my uncle was without sight in one eye, and without a right foot. When we returned home with Uncle Eddie, his depression got a lot worse. He was fully aware of the seriousness of his condition and began to talk about death more and more.

Uncle Eddie called two of his friends over to the house one day, and informed them and my parents what he wanted done for his funeral, when that time came. Thinking back, I know this was a healthy way to look at death and to prepare for it, but I was so very upset to think that my uncle would soon not be with us for much longer. Everyone present said that they would do as he wished to fulfill his desires, but one of his wishes really scared us.

He said that he always had had a great fear of being buried alive. He wanted to make sure that he was completely dead when his coffin was lowered into the earth. To make sure of this he wanted to personally speak to the undertaker in Florence and to tell him about his unusual request. Uncle Eddie wrote a letter, which he and the undertaker signed. In the letter, Uncle Eddie had requested that right before his body was to be placed in the coffin, his heart would be pierced with a long, sewing needle to make sure he was completely dead. This unusual agreement was signed and given to the local doctor, who placed the letter in his medical file.

As the months came and went, we saw my uncle grow worse, until one morning he did not wake up from his sleep. Uncle Eddie had died peacefully that night in his sleep. The funeral arrangements were followed, just as he had requested, the undertaker pierced his heart with a needle. The doctor was called to witness and sign his name, thereby stating that the procedure had been completed.

When the funeral and eventual burial took place, it was attended by all of my uncle's friends and relatives. We all deeply grieved for uncle Eddie. His death affected me the most, and I fell into a pattern of crying myself to sleep with his image on my mind. It was terrible. I really truly missed him.

About a month after my uncle's death, my family began experiencing strange, unusual things in our house. My mother was the first person to hear her brother's presence in the house. Early one morning, as she was sitting in the living room, she heard his familiar coughing and sneezing! As she tells it, "I felt that someone was in the living room with me." Then I heard the coughing sound coming from his room. I made the sign of the cross and walked towards my brother's bedroom and right before I entered, I heard him sneeze! As I opened the door I could see that the room was empty. I sat down on his bed and cried and cried." After my mother's experience, I also had my own encounter with my uncle's spirit.

The following night, as I lay asleep in my bed, I suddenly awoke with a feeling of overwhelming urgency. I don't know what this feeling was about, but I lay there in bed for a few minutes just staring up at the ceiling. Eventually, I decided to go to the bathroom. As I returned to my bedroom, I walked past the living room and froze in my steps.

There, sitting on the couch, was my uncle! In the darkness, I clearly saw him as he slipped on one boot and then another. He must have sensed me watching him because he turned and waved of his hand at me. At first I was filled with fear, but then my eyes filled with tears. I stood frozen in place, as I watched him dissolve into thin air. I screamed out, "Uncle Eddie don't go, please don't go!" My parents came to me, and through my tears I tried to tell them what I had just seen. We all broke down and cried that night wishing we could see him just one more time. Since that night, we have not seen Uncle Eddie until the following year.

On the first anniversary of my uncle's death we held a remembrance rosary prayer ceremony at the local church. That evening when we returned home from church, we witnessed the strangest thing. As my family and I were seated at the kitchen table, we noticed that the single light bulb, hanging from an electrical cord in the middle of the kitchen ceiling, began to move! First it swung back and forth, and then it began swirling in small circles. We stopped our conversation and stared with open mouths at this light bulb moving on its own. All of a sudden I said, "It's my uncle, I know it's my uncle doing this!" Then the bulb began to making even larger circles. The shadows caused by the spinning bulb were spinning all around us. We instinctively took hold of each other's hands and began to pray.

The bulb began to spin even faster until we could hear it hit against the ceiling with a 'thump' with each hit. I was afraid that any second it was going to break. Then just as suddenly as it began spinning, the bulb came to a complete stop. We looked at each other in total disbelief as my mother prayed even louder. Each of us believed that this was the spirit of my uncle and he had caused this. When my mother ended her prayer, she said out loud, "Eddie, we know it's you, please be at peace and go to heaven. We are scared and want you to have peace. Please go now, please." The room fell still and no one said anything more. Grandma invited us to pray the Our Father and we did. Nothing like this ever happened again in the house after this mysterious ghostly episode.

I personally believe that my uncle wanted to just let us know that he was still around. After mother asked him to leave, I felt that he heard our prayers and did move on. I don't know what else to think about all of this. I know that my Uncle Eddie did not want to scare us like he did. I just hope he has finally found peace and knows he is never forgotten.

GLOBE, AZ

Globe, in east central Arizona, has been an important copper mining center for more than a century. Located in a steep canyon, at 3,500 feet, in the Pinal Mountains, Globe is the county seat of Gila County.

Globe was founded as a mining town in 1876 because of its ample water supply and its attractive location for distribution of mining products. The city was incorporated twice prior to its present incorporation in 1907. More than 20 percent of the employment in Globe is related to mining and the production of copper. Over half of Gila County's sizable manufacturing sector employment is in copper smelting, refining, or rod production. In the area, there are three copper mines, several concentrators, a smelter, and a rod mill. All of Gila County is a designated Enterprise Zone.

The local tourism industry has been enhanced by a $50-million investment from the federal government to provide recreational campgrounds and amenities at nearby Roosevelt Lake.

ROXANNE MOSES'S STORY

I interviewed Roxanne, or "Roxy," at her ranch, located in a small canyon not far from Roosevelt Lake. Roxanne, her husband, and 46-year-old son have lived in this home all their lives. The house and land belonged to Roxanne's grandparents. Because of the distant location of their home, the Moses family rarely ventures out into town these days. Today, the family farms a few acres of cotton and ranches cattle.

The geography of the land is very dry, with a few groves of trees dotting the landscape. Roxanne's grandparents planted some of the trees, and a partially standing wooden fence that meanders near the base of each tree can usually which ones. Years ago, the purpose of this fencing was to discourage the cattle from eating the sapling trees.

On the property are two large barns, several small sheds for tools and supplies, a chicken coop, two corrals, an outhouse (no longer in use), the remains of a collapsed small house that was built at the turn of the century, and the main house.

Roxy has plenty of stories to tell about years past, but it is her story of ghostly encounters that she and her family have experienced on the ranch that is most interesting indeed.

—Antonio

Like my own grandparents, homesteaders came to this part of the state to work in the copper mines and ranch. Many years ago, my grandparents moved to this area to ranch and raise a family, Globe was then a small developing town. It turned out that fortune was on their side, because on our particular piece of land, they located two natural springs on the property. While the property was remote, the availability of water was most important at the time.

To the east of the main house that grandfather built are the remains of the original house of the previous family that had lived here. I don't know anything about those folks except that I've heard they had a very hard time making a living. In the rubble of that house, my grandmother found a broken sewing machine, a small box of odds and ends, and pictures of people she believed were the original owners of the property. Grandfather won the property from the original owner in two card games.

I was told that during the first poker game, the owner of the property lost all his money. After losing the first game, grandfather gave the man the opportunity to win back his loss with another game. This time the stakes were higher, it was for the property!

Having run out of money, the man put up his homestead as a wager against grandfather's wealth of silver and Mexican gold coins. It was with the loss of this last card game that grandfather won the property. That's how things used to be done in those years.

You could walk into a saloon and walk out a rich man or poor man; it all depended on who held the lucky cards. Grandfather now had a ranch and a bag of money he used to develop the land. My grandparents built the new house and barns, and soon my father was born. During 1917, the first year of my own life, my grandmother died. Grandfather died two years after. I was the only child my parents had. I was quite lucky to have been born; my mother had three miscarriages before me.

As an only child, I was spoiled rotten. I didn't have any friends to play with because of the distance between the houses. However, we did go to church every Sunday, and that's when I would get to meet and play with the other children of my own age. The earliest memory I have of ghosts took place when I was a little girl.

I remember one night looking out my window, I spotted mysterious small balls of light that bounced and danced in the distant hills. My parents also saw the lights. Mother and Father told me that the spirits of the

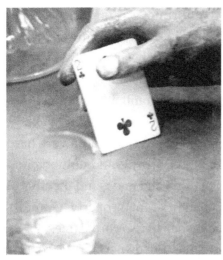

Apaches who used to inhabit the hills and canyons around here caused the lights. The lights appeared and disappeared at all times of the year. I was never afraid of these lights; we all just accepted them as something normal. To this day the lights can still be seen.

Aside from these lights, there's another, more frightening thing I have seen several times on the ranch. One day, when I was about 19 years old, I was moving three horses from one corral to another. This was during the late morning, just before noon. Suddenly the animals began to erratically move around. Something was spooking them. I thought that there might be a rattlesnake nearby, or a cougar or something. These hills were filled with snakes, and it is not unusual for them to be found close to the house. One evening I had even spotted five of them coiled up next to our front door!

I walked over to the barn and looked everywhere. There wasn't a snake or anything else anywhere. Still, when I tried to corral the horses by moving them through the area, they once again put their ears back— as scared horses do—and refused to pass by the barn. This time, when I glanced over to the opened barn door, I spotted a strange man standing beside the door holding on to a horse's harnesses. I was not familiar with either this man or his horse.

I immediately got a weird feeling about them. The man was dressed in a peculiar manner, wearing waist high dark brown trousers, which were held up with thick black leather suspenders. His shirt was grayish in color, and he sported a long thick moustache. I waved to him. He ignored me. Then he and the horse turned around and walked into the barn. I was annoyed by his lack of manners, and walked over to speak to him.

As I entered the barn, the man and horse were nowhere to be found! I thought, "What happened? Where did they go? Was I going crazy?" Then it hit me. I had just seen a ghost! I ran out of that barn so fast, I ran faster than a scared mouse! I tell you I was so afraid!

When I got inside the house, I told my mother about the ghost. I was so excited and went on and on about the ghost. Mother just sat in her chair and listened. Soon, I got a little upset with her calm attitude and asked her why wasn't she as excited as I was? She told me to calm down and to listen to what she had to say. She said, "I've also actually seen ghosts here several times before. I just haven't told you about them because I didn't want to scare you."

I was so surprised to hear my mother's responses. I said to her, "Why, why didn't you trust me enough to tell me about them?" My mother responded, "Well, just look at how you are reacting to what you just saw! Now how do you think you would have reacted if I had told you about my and your father's experiences?" I answered, "You mean father has also seen these ghosts?" "Oh, yes, honey. Several times!" she said. I just couldn't believe what I was hearing.

After a few minutes, we went into the living room, and mother began to tell me her story about her encounter with the ghosts. "You know those old pictures that grandmother found in the old house? Well, I've seen the woman in one of those pictures, and so has your father!"

She said that about the time that I was five years of age, she had her first encounter with a ghost in the house. We had all gone to sleep for the night, and sometime after midnight, a noise awoke her from her sleep. She opened her eyes and saw a light coming from the living room. Thinking that my father had left a lamp on, she got out of bed to investigate. As she entered the living room, she stopped dead in her steps. There standing at the door that led to my bedroom, was a woman whom my mother did not immediately recognize. The woman must have been about 60 years old and was wearing a long black Victorian style dress. Mother noticed that the woman's hair was parted in the middle, and pulled back tightly into a large bun.

Suddenly, something within mother told her that this woman was a ghost. Even more surprising was when mother recognized the woman from photos she had seen among those discovered in the collapsed house years before!

Mother said that as soon as she realized who this ghost was, she raised her hands to her bosom and calmly spoke to the ghost saying, "I know you are a ghost. Why did you come to our house?" The ghost woman reached for the long silver chain that hung around her neck, at the end of which was a black, flat shiny stone. The ghost did not respond to my mother's question. Instead, the ghost slowly turned her head to one side and gradually faded from view. She disappeared completely into thin air!

Mother said that instead of being frightened, she was mostly fascinated by actually having seen a real ghost! You would have to know my mother to know why she would have such a reaction. She was by nature not a very timid woman by any definition!

After the ghost disappeared, mother went into my bedroom and made sure that I was asleep and that no harm had come to me. Satisfied, knowing I was safe she went back to bed. The following morning, she informed my father about her experience. Dad's reaction was disbelief, mother said, "I don't care what you think. I saw what I saw, and that's good enough for me!" Little did my father know that very soon his disbelief would change.

A few nights after my mother's experience, father was in the barn finishing up with the day's work. It was late, and there was no electricity in the barn, so kerosene lamps were used for light. Father had two lamps lit in the area where he was rubbing a saddle with oil. He said that he heard the sound of footsteps crunching down upon small stones on the dirt floor. The footsteps got closer as they made their way towards him in the darkness.

Thinking it was my mother; he turned to look in the direction of the footsteps. Standing directly a few yards in front of my father was the same woman whom my mother had described to him just a few nights before! The woman was holding a lit candle. My father—being the brave man that he is—let out a scream and threw the small can of oil he was holding at the ghost! He ran to the house and told my mother about the ghost woman in the barn. But when they both returned to the barn to investigate, she was gone.

The next morning my father discovered, on the dirt floor in the barn, drops of beeswax, which had dripped in the same area where the woman had been standing with her lit candle! To be sure, this made a quick believer of my father. No more would he doubt the existence of ghosts!

Sadly, both my parents have since died. My son has been the only other person who has had an encounter with a ghost on the property. His experience took place after he had returned home from the army in the late 1970s. One day as he sat under one of the large trees by the house writing a letter he said that he heard a noise in the tree's branches above him. As soon as he looked up, a flock of birds came down from the tree and began to fly all around him. This was definitely unusual behavior for birds. The birds flew down in a flock. They did not hurt him in any way; they were just flying all about him.

Being concerned about the birds' reaction he got up and moved under another tree. The birds flew away towards the hills. Apparently, that was not the end of it, because whatever invisible force had directed the birds, the same force followed my son to this new location.

As he picked up his pen, and again tried to write, suddenly he felt an invisible hand slap the side of his face, and knocked off his glasses! He was stunned and couldn't believe this had just happened. At the same time, he heard the sound of a woman's laughter! He looked all around and saw no one. That was enough for him. He walked over to pick up his glasses, and ran quickly over to the center of the yard. His arms were covered in goose bumps! He wanted to get as far away from the trees as possible. He knew there was no rational explanation for what he had just experienced, except to believe that it had to have been a ghost.

To this day we have not had any further experiences with the ghosts of the man and his horse, or with the woman. We believe that the ghosts must be of the family who lived here before us. It is clear to my husband and I that the woman we saw is the same woman in the old picture. Aside from my own son's experience with the ghost and being slapped, no one else has been attacked. Now that my husband and I are much older. I don't think the ghosts want to be bothering with us seniors. I guess they think that we'll soon be joining them, so why bother.

GRASS VALLEY, CA

Between 1848 and 1849 prospectors in search of gold from Oregon, along with emigrants from the east coast in search of fertile land, settled in Grass Valley. To this day, many believe that millions of dollars of unmined gold ore lies still undiscovered in and around the pleasant town of Grass Valley. Because of its abundance, gold played a key role in the areas population explosion.

Locals often tell the story of a miner who one day, was searching the area for his lost cow. As he walked about the fields, he stubbed his toe upon a rock, dislodging it. As he picked up the rock, he noticed the unique, and unmistakable sparkle of gold that capped itself to the rock. This accidental result of fortune, soon gave way to another fortuitous encounter by a man who was searching for stones to fashion a chimney for his new home. Among the stones in his collection, were several covered in gold. Soon a staggeringly rich vein of gold ore was discovered, causing even more of a frenzy.

As like other towns in the area, in 1855 a devastating fire swept the town, and destroyed the 300 plus structures of Grass Valley. The town's people rallied together, and rebuilt the town. By the 1860's over 150 million dollars in gold was extracted from the two major mines, North Star, and Empire. In 1956, both mines were closed, and today remain as a city park and museum.

Today, Grass Valley is renowned as a living museum, filled with early gold rush period architecture, and thrives as a modern business center.

LEO OTT'S STORY

I was born and raised in Fresno California. During my childhood, my parents enjoyed taking the family on visits throughout the Gold Rush Country. As I got older and able to drive a car, I found myself taking frequent trips on my own into this historic area of northern California. I enjoyed the history and architecture of the area and knew that when the opportunity presented itself, I would one day make it my home. Nine years ago, after a major turn of events in my personal life, I decided to make the move from Fresno and settle in this area.

At the time of my move, I had a wonderful relationship with a man who unfortunately died in a motorcycle accident. I was devastated by the loss, and was going through a bout of depression, and needed to find a new focus for my life again. John and I were together for two years, but I've never really gotten over the pain of losing him. I don't know if I'll ever fully recover from this loss. I imagine I might sound as if I want people to feel sorry for me, but on the contrary, I just want to let you know what I was going through at the time. Surprisingly for me, I've grown to enjoy the privacy and ease of doing things on my own.

Before moving out of Fresno, I studied yoga for five years and became interested in following a healthy lifestyle, eating only vegetarian based foods, and eliminating milk and egg products from my diet. This change also prompted me to look at the direction my life was headed. I decided to make the move out of a large city and, when the time came, to begin searching for a property. My plan was to locate a house, and land that would allow me the peace and quiet I needed. I searched around the area for weeks, looking to purchase a home and small acreage to start a business growing organic vegetables and flowers.

In Fresno one morning, I was having coffee at a local bakery. As I read through a listing of available properties in a local paper, a description of a house in the gold rush town of Grass Valley caught my attention. Grass Valley was not my first choice, but after reading the property's description, I knew I had to at least take a look.

After driving the long highway and arriving at the property, I was not disappointed. The house was just what I was looking for, and the sloping four acres of land was perfect for growing plants. I purchased the property, moved in two months later and soon felt very comfortable in my new home. Living alone was at first difficult for me, but gradually I got into the routine of doing life on my own and the daily routine of household chores.

As for my ghost experiences, that started during my first winter in the house. At first I rationalized that it was just my imagination, but it didn't take long for me to finally realize that there was something much more complex going on.

I remember the first time I noticed something I was in the bedroom. It was one afternoon in November, I was typing an email to a friend on the computer, when I heard footsteps in the hallway. I had no doubt that there was someone in the house because the footsteps were loud, and distinctly 'footsteps.' I wondered who could have just walked into my house and got out of my chair to have a look. I took a few cautious steps toward the bedroom door. I wanted to call out and ask who was there, but I thought it would be best to surprise whoever it was. Perhaps it was a visiting friend, or the real estate agent who sold me the house. I opened the bedroom door and stepped out into the hallway. Nobody was there and I was all by myself.

I searched the whole house and didn't find anyone, or any evidence of anyone being in the house. The front and rear screen doors were still locked from the inside. At that moment, an inner voice said that things were not going to remain the same for me. I was convinced that what I had heard was not my imagination. As the day progressed, I kept listening for any further 'footsteps.' Nothing happened until a few hours later, when the footsteps in the hallway started again!

This time I sat perfectly still in my chair. My hands frozen in position over the computer keyboard as I held my breath. With each step, the footsteps made the old wooden plank floor creaked. Slowly the steps came up to the room where I was seated. I heard them stop at my door. I turned apprehensively to face who ever, or whatever would be standing at the door. I saw the smoky grey figure of a person. It was not a white form, as most people might imagine a ghost to appear, this ghost was a hazy, grey in color. I quickly stood up, out of the chair I was sitting on, and remember saying out loud, "Oh, God!"

I'm not ashamed to admit that I was terrified! I took a few steps back and screamed! I sensed that this spirit was not friendly, or familiar. It was dark and ominous. Without thinking I screamed

again, but this time I yelled, "Get out, get out of my house!" Immediately I saw this ghostly grey smoke began to shrink in mass until it became a tiny spot of black. It was a quarter size of darkness that hung in the air for about 30 seconds, until it simply ceased to be visible. It faded into completely into nothingness and I couldn't believe my eyes!

Slowly I walk towards the door and out into the hallway. I didn't know what this was, how it appeared or what made it shrink. After searching the entire house, nothing was out of place. Nothing had been disturbed or moved. I looked at the clock on my wall, and the time was 4 pm. The day was sunny, I do not drink, or do drugs. The only medication I use is for seasonal allergies, and that's it. I swear I saw this thing come into my house and appear to me in broad daylight!

The next incident took place a couple of days after this one. I was outside hammering a garden hose holder to the side of the house. I was coiling the hose around the holder, when I noticed movement in the yard. I glanced over to the porch and saw a man sitting on my porch chair! I was only about twenty feet away, and there was a leafless rose vine covering most of the porch, but I could see this man in his mid-forties, sitting on the porch staring straight ahead. I dropped the hose I was holding and with command in my voice I spoke in his direction, "Can I help you?"

He turned his head towards me then disappeared! This all happened within the span of about 5 seconds. I had had enough. I was convinced that my house was haunted. There were ghosts not only in the house, but also outside around the property! I didn't know what to do about this. What was I supposed to do? I walked back into the house, grabbed a few clothes, my car keys, and drove to Fresno for the night. No way was I going to stay alone in the house. Imagine looking at the face of the ghost of the old man, just a few feet away. I was not going to go through that experience alone again.

When I got to Fresno, I spent the night at my cousin Duke's apartment. The next day I asked Duke, who was unemployed at the time, to come spend a few days with me. Duke was intrigued with my ghost story, and he accepted my invitation. His curiosity was definitely aroused and he excitedly said, "I'd enjoy having an encounter with a real ghost. After all, how many times does an opportunity come up to spend a night at a haunted house? Not often or ever!"

I spent one more day in Fresno, then the next morning Duke and I drove back to Grass Valley. Everything seemed normal and ordinary when we reached the house. No evidence of any ghost activity that I could see. The front door to the house was locked as I had left it. I started up the furnace and we both found our own comfortable positions in front of the television. I thought to myself, no more ghosts, please, no more ghosts.

We were watching the evening news when suddenly from the kitchen we heard the sound of a dish fall into the porcelain sink. The sound startled me so much, I jumped straight out of my chair! We stood still looking at each other, waiting for something further to happen. But nothing did. I cautiously walked to the kitchen and saw that a small serving dish was lying in the sink. I picked it up and retuned it back on to the dish rack. Nothing unusual that couldn't be explained I thought. Just a dish that had slipped off the dish rack. That's all.

I turned around to walk back to the living room, saying to Duke "No ghost, just a dish." Not more than a few seconds after I sat back down on my chair, once again the sound of the dish being moved broke the silence. I knew this was not normal. You had to be there in the room with us to see the terrified look that came over both our faces.

Duke said "Let me go take a look." As he walked to the sink, he reached inside and pulled out the same dish I had just placed back on the dish rack! "That's impossible" I said. "You know I placed it on the rack myself, just a second ago. That dish could not have jumped back in the sink like that on its own." I tried to make light of the situation, Duke said "We've got a little 'Linda Blair' thing going on here." He picked up the dish, gave it a quick inspection, then placed it back in the sink saying "Well, Mr. Ghost if you want to play house, go ahead and enjoy yourself."

Duke came back to the living room and we continued to watch the television. I remained nervous, but Duke did not seem to be bothered at all by the kitchen incident. His lack of concerned must have transferred over to me because I soon began to feel more at ease. I started to get sleepy and said "Duke, I'm going to call it a night, you know where the blankets are, see you in the morning."

That night I slept very lightly. Twice, I heard Duke walk down the hall and into the bathroom. I thought it was odd that he didn't flush the toilet, but thought he didn't want to wake me by making noise. Nothing I could call strange, or paranormal took place during the night. However, the next morning something did.

I was the first to wake up, and walked into the bathroom. I noticed that Duke had not used the bathroom. When I went into the living room, I found him asleep on the sofa. The television was turned on but the volume was off, and it appeared that he left the lamp by the front door on all night. I spoke, "Duke, wake up what are you doing asleep here in the living room?"

He explained that not long after I had gone to bed, he had turned all the lights off except for the television. At about 11:30 pm, he heard a noise in the kitchen. He turned to look and saw some guy leaning against the sink! He could tell it was a ghost because of the transparency of the figure. Speaking in a shaky voice, Duke said "What do you want? Don't hurt me." Duke said the ghost then smiled at him and disappeared! Duke was shaken by the apparition, but did not want to bother me. Instead Duke decided to turn on the lights, and sleep with the television on for the rest of the night.

I asked Duke why didn't he just come over to my bedroom and wake me. He could have told me about the ghost that appeared to him when he got up twice to use the bathroom during the night. Duke looked at me and said "What do you mean? I didn't use the bathroom at all last night. To get to the bathroom, I would have had to walk through the kitchen. I wasn't going to get up and take a chance of meeting up with that ghost again! Your house is haunted Leo, I believe you. This house is definitely haunted!

We both were deciding what to do next. Duke described the ghost in detail, but neither he nor I could identify who it might be. Finally, I made the decision to remain strong, and I told Duke that I was not going to leave and give up my house over to a ghost. I was planning on staying for good. I made sure to speak loudly, directing my words to the ghost "One of us is going to have to leave the house, and it's not going to be me, so who every you are, you better leave now!"

Duke spent another night with me, and neither of us experienced another disturbance. Although we were both a little shaken up, things seemed to be going alright. I drove Duke back to his home in Fresno, all the while I was apprehensive about returning to my home alone. But I drew strength from my conviction of knowing it was my home, and after all, I did not want to let the ghost get the better of me. I had been through

too much in my life to give all up to some wayward ghost!

When I got home, I walked into the darkened living room, turned on the light and said "Look, I want to be at peace with my house, I hope you can understand this. I don't want to have to be on the lookout for you. I don't know what you want but please, leave me alone to live my life. You've already lived yours, so you should go on and live your own life doing whatever you need to do, do it somewhere else and leave me alone." I must have said something that the ghost understood, because as soon as I had finished saying the last word, I heard a loud "crack" sound. It was a sound of a board snapping in half. It was sudden and loud. It startled the heck out of me, but I knew this must be the answer to my firm declaration. The ghost heard me and respected my stand. I immediately felt the heavy atmosphere in the room change. Difficult as it is to try to explain, I felt that the ghost had left my house.

I know I took a chance of angering the ghost, but it was after all my house. I couldn't keep spending further nights in other people's homes. It was my house and I was willing to fight to keep it!

It's now been a few years since all those occurrences took place, and nothing ghostly has appeared to me at the house. I don't hear noises at night, see shadows or dishes flying in the air. I am finally living a normal life, the life I always wanted.

One re-occurring question people ask me when I tell them my story is, "Do you think the spirit you saw was your partner who died, and wanted to make contact with you?" My answer is that this ghost was definitely not anything like John would have behaved. I don't believe that loved ones want to come back and scare us. The ghost I experienced was a dark and mischievous one.

As I said before, I was frightened and could sense the negative energy of this ghost. Love gives a very different presence, very different from what this ghost was manifesting to me. I haven't had and more incidences and I don't want any. So far it has stayed away.

JEMEZ SPRINGS PUEBLO, NM

The Pueblo of Jemez located 27 miles northwest of Bernalillo is the only remaining Towa-speaking pueblo. Beautifully surrounded by colorful red sandstone mesas, the pueblo is situated within an awe inspiring natural setting of wonder. In the 1830s, survivors of nearby Pecos (Cicúye) Pueblo, a once-mighty trading center

Jemez Pueblo 1850.

which now lies in ruins, joined Jemez. Many Pecos Pueblo warriors at first resisted the invading Spanish forces under conquistador Diego de Vargas 12 years after the Pueblo Revolt in 1680 but later allied with the conquerors.

Due to the popularity of all things American Indian, which increased in the 70's and 80's, the potters of Jemez refined the quality of their clay art form searching for a distinctive style of their own. Today Jemez pottery stands alone and recognized for its matte-on-gloss designs, having stylized feathers and geometric designs. The Pueblo of Jemez has generally closed its village to all non-Indians and chose this policy for not having adequate tourism facilities and for issues that arose regarding the privacy of its inhabitants. However, the pueblo village is only open to the public on special Feast Days, but the pueblo chooses not to openly publicize these observances, so ask around if you wish to attend.

MARCUS D. PACHECO'S STORY

While visiting the Taos pueblo, I made a pre-arranged date (my third) for my interview with Marcus. Marcus is an interesting guy in that he's always on the go and very difficult to pin down. I was fortunate to eventually rope him in and sit him down for what would become another unique personal story. His particular story takes place both here in the United States and Europe.

Breaking a sincere personal contract between two men has in the past, but sadly lacking in the present, been accepted as a serious breach of personal integrity and not to be treated lightly.

As you'll soon come to read, this not only pertains to the living, but also upheld as well by those who have passed. Marcus' story reminds us to hold true when giving our "word," and in doing so, we will be judged by our peers, both living and dead.

—Antonio

"My family has lived on the pueblo land for generations and I was born and raised in the Jemez Pueblo. I was the only one of my siblings in my family to enlist in the armed forces. I chose the army. My father, a carefree kind of guy, married and remarried three times and I'm his oldest son from his first marriage. Today I live in Taos with my wife's people and our two daughters. The story I'm going to tell you took place at Jemez Pueblo—my pueblo.

I was about nineteen years old at the time of my experience. That spring I headed out of New Mexico to Texas for military training before being deployed to Germany. A few years later, after returning home from Germany, I met and married my wife. At this time, we didn't get along with my father's then wife, so we chose to move off the Jemez Reservation and into my wife's reservation in Taos. This is where we have lived ever since.

My story begins during my military deployment. It all began with a loan of money. Just a couple of months before leaving for Texas, I ask a few friends for financial support to repair my car. As it turned out, my car gave out on me as I was heading back home one evening while in New Mexico. First the oil light came on the dash, I saw some smoke seep out from under the hood, the car shook and just shut off.

Eventually, I learned that somehow all the motor oil had leaked out leaving me with an engine empty of oil! If you know anything about a car's engine, oil is a car's lifeblood. Well, I was unaware of any oil leak problem and burned the engine out. The only way to repair it would be to remove the damaged engine and replace it with a rebuilt one. But this of course would cost money, money I didn't have.

I started asking around for financial help but all I kept getting were excuses. I did eventually, get some money from my father and an older friend of the family name Andy. Andy lent me $1,500.00 with the understanding that I would repay him within two a month period. I agreed but foolishly managed to spend the money on other things instead of fixing my car.

So now I was not only left without a car but without Andy's money as well! As the promised two-month payment deadline approached, I kept avoiding Andy whenever possible. I even moved off the pueblo and in with my sister's family in Albuquerque. I was holding out for my paperwork from the army, ordering me to ship out to Texas, just until I could getaway.

I know this was not right, or the honorable thing to do, but it was where my head was and I'd made plenty of poor choices then. I know for sure that if the pueblo governors ever hear about this, they would intervene and not in my favor. My behavior over this loan also hurt my father's very good reputation among our pueblo, but I was young, irresponsible and frankly stupid.

My father was so upset, angry and hurt with me and informed me that Andy had been saving the loan money for several years. He was planning to use it as a down payment to purchase a newer house. I asked my father to tell Andy that I would make good on the loan once I returned from Germany. But my father refused to relay my message, and told me to take responsibility and speak to him myself, man to man. Unbeknownst to either of us, Andy had been struggling with health issues and died unexpectedly from a stroke before I could get to him.

While I was doing my army base service in Augsburg, Germany, I started having a series of strange dreams. In the dreams, I was back home in Jemez, and I'd be awakened by the sensation of a presence of someone in the room with me. A few times I would hear a male voice yell out, 'Marcus, Marcus!' I didn't know where this voice was coming from and I was so confused because there was nothing subtle about hearing my name.

Being American Indian, I knew that there was something going on that went beyond me having nightmares; no, there was much more to this. The voice was familiar, but not distinct enough for me to recognize whom it might be. Then, a few days later the thought hit me and I realized who that familiar voice was. The voice calling me in those dreams was Andy – its Andy's voice!

Dwelling on my newfound discovery didn't help me. I became nervous and obsessed with trying to make sense of these dreams. There was no way to deny the fact that Andy wanted me to make things right. I knew I had to do everything in my power to appease him. I thought, if today he's choosing to contact me through my dreams, how far would his spirit go to make his intentions known? I started worrying would the next step be for Andy to actually appear to me? I definitely didn't want that to happen. I decide that I had to make everything right with him. The wrong that I had committed by breaking our agreement had now become too real for me to ignore. Andy's spirit had even follow me to Germany!

As soon as I had the appropriate opportunity, I contacted my father by phone and informed him of my dreams and especially hearing Andy's strong, emotional voice awaken me. My father stated to me, "You know our people don't hurt each other or break agreements between us like you did to Andy. Andy was a good man; he trusted you and you must do what's right. I didn't raise you like that. I'll need to contact someone here at the pueblo to pray for Andy's soul, but you'll have to repay him by helping out his family when you get back to the U.S. When he calls out your name again, you be sure to tell him that you'll keep the promise and make it all right!" I promised my father that I would honor his words and do as he instructed me to.

The next time I had a dream and heard Andy's voice calling me, I sat up in my bed and told him, "I promise I'll repay you. Andy please don't keep waking me up, I'll help your family when I return. I promise." As soon as I said this, I felt a comforting relief come over me. I felt a peace replace all the fear and anxiety I had been carrying totally away. From that night forward, I didn't hear Andy's voice or wake up from any more nightmares.

Two nights before I was to return back to the states, I was awakened by Andy's voice, only this time I actually saw him standing at the foot of my bed, a dark misty outline of Andy, just feet away! I remember saying, 'I'm so sorry. Please, please don't visit me anymore. I'll return your money to your family. Don't visit me anymore, please!' As soon as I stopped speaking, I noticed a few tiny white twinkling light flash from the mist as Andy's figure slowly disappeared. Within a second or two his image totally vanished before my eyes! As you might imagine, I didn't get much sleep for the remainder of that night.

When I arrived in the States a few days later and headed over to the pueblo where I made it a point to stop in to see my father. After exchanging hugs and greetings, I spoke further with my father about all my dream and actual encounter with Andy's spirit.

My father was not surprised by what I described. He said, 'As long as you keep your promise to Andy and offer prayers to his spirit, I'm sure things will begin to get better for you.' I assured my father of my intentions and showed him the cash I had saved and was carrying in my wallet. The cash I was going to return to Andy's family. My father said, 'Andy was a good friend of mine and I've been offering him prayers while you were away. Give the money to Andy's daughter; she is all that remains of his family.' Later that same day, while visiting with my friends and relatives, I slipped as everyone was watching a baseball game on television and drove over to the pueblo's cemetery.

I found Andy's gravesite, and sincerely offered my prayers to him. I also thought ahead and brought one of the army caps I wore while in Germany as an offering of peace and respect. I placed the cap on top of an ornate iron cross attached to his headstone, stood at attention and saluted him.

By coincidence, or maybe not, as I was driving back to my father's home, I happened to notice Andy's daughter walking along the road with her young daughter. I stopped and called her over to my car. I did not mention anything about my contact experiences with her father while in Germany, or the events that led up to them. I presented her with the loan payment I owed her father. She seemed very surprised but grateful. We spoke a short while longer and ended with a shared hug between us.

I drove to my father's house and told him what I had done. That I returned Andy's loan to his daughter as I promised. He patted me on the back and said, 'Son, that will take care of any more contact from Andy. By making good on your promise you've restored balance to our lives, thank you.'

My father was correct. Andy's spirit is at rest, there are no more nightmares or voices waking me up at night and most of all, I'm confident I never will again.

Many years have since passed and my father has also died. Today I sit here before you with a diagnosis of stage three cancer, but I'm not afraid of the ultimate outcome. My only concern is for my family. I know that I don't have much time left here in this life, but leave it for God to decide when. But you know, I am inspired and encouraged by my experience with Andy's spirit. I know we don't stop existing totally when our bodies die; we can and do continue on and somehow might have the chance to make contact again with the living. This was proven to me all those years ago when Andy's spirit made contact with me in Germany."

JICARILLA APACHE RESERVATION, NM

The Jicarilla people currently live in the northern portion of New Mexico and speak a Southern Athabaskan language. They were one of the six southern bands that migrated south from Canada between 1300 and 1500 A.D. The term Jicarilla comes from Mexican Spanish meaning "little basket." The Jicarilla reservation has a land area of 1,364 square miles and a population of roughly 3,403.

The capital Dulce, with most of the tribal offices comprises over 95 percent of the reservation's population. The tribe owns the Apache Nugget Casino, located on the reservation and the Best Western Jicarilla Inn and Casino, both located in Dulce.

TOWN OF DULCE

Located in the northern area of New Mexico in Rio Arriba County, I toured the little village and spoke to various persons in town regarding possible paranormal experiences. I was surprised to have encountered at least five persons who instead offered me reports of weird legends that they say have persisted in the area for centuries. These stories are about the unusual and secretive caverns and the world of celestial beings that inhabit these underground caverns. Apparently, from these accounts the alien beings and their caverns are centered in the mountains of Dulce.

These individuals further informed me that UFO aliens are using these bases to carry out missions involving humans and the earth's weather system. I found this information intriguing, but not totally surprising. After all, New Mexico does have an undeniable reputation for firsthand UFO sightings and recalling the southern town of Roswell, even crashes.

— Antonio

NANETTE PANCITA'S STORY

Nanette and I met for her interview at the Jicarilla Inn and Casino located on the reservation. After our initial greetings, we entered the casino and located a quiet spot at a table within the restaurant. What I had imagined would be a simple story turned out to be a real eye opener for me. I in for a surprise and I know you will be too.

At the end of our interview, Nanette suggested I interview a friend with a similar story of encountering a ghost. She said "A guy I know named Rudy Lebeck who lives just north of Albuquerque in the village of Placitas who also had an unforgettable encounter with spirits. You should interview him as well. I'll give you his phone number. He'll be more than happy to discuss his experiences with you!" I interviewed Rudy and his interview and story are included in this book as well.

— Antonio

"I was born and lived on the Jicarilla reservation for most of my forty-eight years of life. I am an artist, and early in my life chose to make my living creating and producing photographs that I've taken in and around the southwestern region of the U.S. In addition to this, I'm also a bead worker. My proudest accomplishment with my photography, was an international showing, which featured my prints in Norway. How that show was developed and put together by my gallery representative is a long and interesting story in itself; but as it turned out was for me, a great honor and accomplishment.

Today I travel around the U.S. attending numerous art and trade shows; events that I need to attend for marketing my photography and beadwork. These events have afforded me the opportunity to cross paths with other native individuals, who are also considered prominent artists in their chosen fields of expression.

One very significant, upcoming, life event that I know will impact my career, is my plan to marry an oil painter from the Central American country of Belize. Rodrigo is a descendant of the Mayan people of Belize. After we marry, I plan to relocate south with Rodrigo for who knows how long. Oh, I'll still continue my photography, and I'm hoping this change of location will open up new doors of opportunity for me. At least that's Rodrigo's and my plan.

Rodrigo expressed to me that he finds our Apache people to be friendly, but also 'very American' in our dress and attitudes. Of course, this opinion is coming from a person whose immediate family still lives in the jungle highlands, speak only in their native language and practice ancient forms of spirituality. Rodrigo's culture is fascinating to me. Each moment with him affords me the opportunity to learn about his culture and to hear his spoken language.

Obviously, I don't know a word of the Mayan language, but every now and then he'll speak a word or sentence and I become totally amazed by its beauty. Because I also have a very strong pride in my own Apache people's distinct customs and language, I know he and I will get along fine. We might have a few disagreements, but after all we're artists!

I know you want to know about the spiritual things that I personally had happen to me, so before anything else, first let me say that as a Jicarilla Apache woman, we rarely speak of ghosts or supernatural occurrences. This is especially true when other Jicarilla's are in hearing range. Within our tribe there is a lot of superstitions and fear surrounding the mentioning of ghosts and spirits, even to speak of simple things as 'butterflies' in regards to art. I believe this is due to a strong cultural belief in our traditional ways of respecting all forms of life's energy, including those who have passed over to the spirit form. Personally, I'm glad we still carry this respect within our tribe. I know many other native tribes do as well. It is an important cultural understanding to respect, maintain and is a healthy one.

That being said, I'll now tell you about my experience with spirits that took place in the Spring of 1998. I had planned on taking a horseback ride deep within our reservation's forested mountains to take photographs of our beautiful, natural surroundings. I was going to gather as much photographic images as possible for a native women's show my agent was organizing for me in Chicago. I made sure to pack enough food, water and digital memory cards to last at least a week or more. Taking a trip like this was not unusual for me. I've taken many successful photography trips before, and knew how to prepare. I even packed my pistol just in case I ran into any problems with crazy animals of the 'two-legged' human kind.

It was one early Saturday morning when a friend of mine help load my horse, Star Child, and packing gear into his horse trailer. He hitched the trailer to his pick-up truck and he drove us to a trailhead not far from my house. After unloading Star Child, and all my gear, we said our goodbyes, and I began my ride into the mountains. The morning was uneventful, except for the small heard of elk that I spotted on a hill beyond the hill I was on. The trail was a good one, clearly marked and free of any debris so Star Child and I had no problem navigating it. I'd been on this trail a few years past, so I knew from memory the valleys and uphill climbs we'd be traversing. I figured that we'd arrive at camp by four that afternoon if not earlier.

I'd been on the trail for about five hours when suddenly from my left I spotted the movement of a shadowy dark figure between the trees. The shadow figure seemed to float from one tree to another, like it was gliding on invisible wheels or something. I blinked and rubbed my eyes to make sure I wasn't imagining this. As I kept my eyes closely focused on the figure, the next movement went behind a tree and disappeared altogether. I waited for a few minutes then continued riding ahead.

A while later, closer to a half hour, once more I noticed the same dark figure moving nearby among the tree trunks. The difference between the first sighting and this one was that before noticing the dark figure, I distinctly heard the sound of a woman's voice speaking in our Apache tongue. The voice said, 'Use the feather. Use the feather.' Star Child came to a sudden stop without my pulling on his reins. I noticed his ears perked up high, and if anyone reading this knows anything about horses, when a horse perks his ears up in this manner, it's a warning, it means watch out, something is not right!

I immediately felt a surge of electricity shoot up my left leg, starting at the foot, followed by the uncomfortable awareness that something unusual and of a 'spiritual' nature was near us. Due to my innate sense of caution, I was now on alert, especially to the possibility of an attack of a spiritual nature. Native people know that forest spirits do exist, so it's best to be ready and always on the alert.

I took my right hand and gently patted Star Child on the base of his neck in order to comfort him. Visually scanning the forest before me, I responded to the voice within the trees in Apache, 'If you are a good spirit, I honor you and ask for your protection, if not I ask that you leave me alone and go away!' As soon as I finished speaking, I heard the distinct voice of a woman again state in our apache tongue, 'The feather. The feather.' All I could think of was that the eagle feather I had placed on my hat had something to do with this, so I removed it from my hat, hopped off my horse and attached it to Star Child's leather rein, just below his left eye. Eagle feathers are highly respected and considered sacred to native people. This particular feather was given to me by my Aunt, so its meaning significance is doubly important to me.

The remainder of my journey into the mountains went without any further distractions, however I was well aware that something was actively about. At the end of each day, as soon as the setting sun transitioned into evening, I always offered my prayers to the Creator and asked for my protections from my loving ancestors. This definitely gave me the confidence and courage to continue on with my work and journey. And because of my deep spiritual belief regarding the power that comes from such faith, I had no doubt that I was being protected against any negative things or situation I might encounter.

After spending six days in the mountains finishing up with all my photography work, I was glad to finally make the return trip back to my home. And regarding the darting spirit figure I saw within the trees; I felt that I had made a positive connection with that spirit acknowledging its presence and offering prayer. This to me was positive and on some level – felt protective. I knew I had been moved to attach the eagle feather to my horse for some good reason. Even though at the time, I didn't realize why. I just instinctively knew I was contacted by spirit and I needed to change something. It pays to remain calm and focused on moments we're not sure what we've observed and heard, most people miss these attempts and opportunities, when they happen, from loving ancestors who have passed.

My second experience happened three days after returning to home. Paul, my aunt Annie's husband, asked me to help him construct a wheel-chair ramp for Annie. She had uncontrolled diabetes for years and unfortunately, had her right leg amputated below the knee as a result of complications. Annie would need the ramp built as soon as possible to assist with her moving in, out and throughout their mobile home. I was eager to begin and offered to Paul that I would happy to pick up the lumber and other necessary supplies the following day so we could start as soon as possible.

The day we decided to start, I took measurement for the area where the ramp was to be constructed, which actually did not take up too much front yard footage. Paul and I headed out to purchase the lumber, screws and metal braces. The first thing left to do when we returned was to dig the four by four support post holes and prepare for casting in cement the next morning.

I arrived at my aunt's home with two shovels; one for me, the other for Paul. I began digging into the soft soil, while Paul dug another just opposite from where I stood. We needed to dig a hole roughly ten inches in diameter and two feet deep. After completing the first two holes we continued on to the next two, then we'd have two left for a total of six holes.

As I was digging a third hole, and after going down about a foot, my shovel hit what I thought was a cream-colored broken piece of ceramics. After pressing down into another shovel-full of dirt, I heard another click of the shovel hitting something solid. As I looked closer, again thought it was something made of ceramic material, or maybe even a chunk of white limestone. I carefully dug around this object and brought it up in a shovel full of moist soil. I dropped the clump of soil next to the hole and with my bare hands began to dislodge the compacted dirt from the cream-colored material.

I froze when I realized what this was, and shouted for Paul to come quick. As he came over to where I was standing, I held out my open hand with the object in my palm and asked him to tell me what he thought I was holding. He didn't hesitate, 'Nanette, that's a human jawbone!' I dropped it onto the ground and repeatedly wiped my hands off.

What I had uncovered from my digging was a human jawbone! I felt ill and so really frightened. Paul was speechless. All sort of thoughts raced through my mind. Above all else was the knowledge that there most likely could be an entire human skeleton buried just below the surface of my aunt's house—in her front yard!

I took a cautious closer look at the jawbone lying on the ground and felt nauseous. I called to Paul to quickly bring me the water hose. I rinsed off my hands and ask Paul to return the jawbone with the teeth back into the hole. I kept scrubbing my hands so hard I thought my hands would bleed, I didn't want one speck of that soil left on my hands. A feeling of such abhorrence came over me, knowing I had just touched the remains of a dead person. I was so upset and truly disturbed by this I wanted to run away, far away. As Paul watched my reaction, he stood back and made the sign of the cross over his chest, and began recited out loud the Lord's Prayer in Apache. Then we both sat down and discussed the situation.

Now with the discovery of a skeleton on the property, my Aunt Annie and Paul would need to ask for the assistance of one of our medicine people to come and take care of this in the Apache manner. We mentioned to my aunt what we had uncovered and as I expected, without hesitation she chose to move into her sister's home several miles away that very day.

Without getting into the details of what transpired the weeks following this discovery, all I'll say is that the tribal police were called. They conducted an appropriate investigation followed by a blessing ceremony performed by a respected tribal elder. It was revealed that the bones were centuries old and most importantly, not involved in a murder or crime. My aunt and Paul relocated their mobile home to a new location on the reservation and Paul and I constructed Annie's wheelchair ramp in no time.

I do believe that the woman's voice I heard weeks before during my trip into the woods, had something to do with this experience at my aunt's house. After all, the voice referenced the sacred eagle feather; urging me to be careful, and to guard myself from the unknown forces that could cause me harm. I'm grateful for that. Since that day I carry a small eagle feather's fluff with me everywhere. It's our keen sense of spiritual connectedness and guidance from ancestors to stay aware, take precautions and remain open to messages from ancestors that may appear in many unexpected forms. I do believe this is the right way for all of us to practice and live."

MANCOS, CO

Situated in the Four Corners area of Colorado, Mancos is located

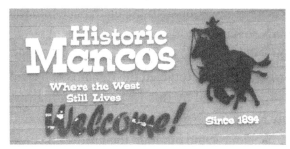

roughly half-way between the towns of Durango and Cortez. The basis of Mancos's revenue is tourism. Due to its close proximity to nearby Mesa Verde National Park, Mancos—as well as the town of Cortez—has become a home base for visitors to this important area of ancient Anasazi culture.

A few restaurants and bed-and-breakfast inns can be found in the area. Mancos has also partnered for the area's annual Mesa Verde Indian Arts and Western Culture Festival, and hosts the festival's fiddling contest. The town also offers tourists the services of its new Mancos Visitors' Center and the Pioneer Museum.

JOSH KAHN'S STORY

I conducted the interview with Josh in the living room of his home. Josh's right leg was in a cast due to an accidental fall he had taken two weeks prior to my visit. Given the great weather, we decided that the best area of his home to do the interview would be in his back yard, where a nice set of patio chairs and a relaxing couch were located. I sat on one of the chairs while Josh lay on the couch resting his fractured leg upon two pillows.

Josh presented me with his unusually intriguing story of love, loss and eventually a level of remarkable peace. As Josh stated "I found a level of mental satisfaction where the monster of the "unknown" is vanquished, and where my world has transformed into one where I can now recognize the beauty that lies beyond death."

Josh's story can offer us all a great deal more than an ordinary ghost story. His story as you will read, is thought provoking and will enlighten your heart. To communicate with those who have passed on to the afterlife can be psychologically inhibiting, but in Josh's case, the experience was comforting.

— Antonio

"I've lived in Mancos since November of 1989, and moved here from Seattle, Washington with my two-year-old cat, Buddy. I was originally going to relocate to Durango, but was surprisingly unaware of Durango's expensive real estate market, so I choose Mancos, Colorado—I have not regretted it. I bought a two-bedroom house on the north side of town, which I still live in today.

I decided to move away from Seattle after two close friends died of AIDS. The first was my friend, Edward, who I knew from high school. At first, he and I were best friends, and after dating for a few months he moved into my house and we became partners. We lived together for six years. I was aware beforehand that Edward was infected with the HIV virus. He disclosed this to me early on before we began our romance. We were in love and AIDS was not going to prevent us from enjoying a full and loving relationship, as long as we were careful and took the necessary precautions.

Sadly, I went through the whole ordeal of seeing Edward slowly succumb to the disease until he eventually, and peacefully, died. I was devastated beyond words. During this stressful time, I had a true friend who was my support and shoulder to lean on. Her name was Jennifer, a woman who also had the HIV virus. She was a true friend who I had met one afternoon at a support meeting for partners and friends of persons living with the disease. As I said, Jennifer had the disease, and suffered with it for several years before she herself succumbed to its complications, and died in 1989.

Given all my recent past history of sadness and memories, I decided to leave Seattle for my own peace of mind and relocate to the southwest. I had visited the state of Colorado years ago, and definitely believed that I would return as a permanent resident one day. This became a reality for me in the spring of 1989.

My story takes place in September of 1993. I had been living in Mancos for a few years; one day, I took a drive to Durango, intending to spend most of the day shopping and enjoy a meal at a favorite restaurant. I did the typical visit to Walmart and eventually purchased a vacuum cleaner. While strolling up and down the aisles, I noticed that there was an older gentleman, who I'd guessed to be about the age of 65 or so, who was obviously following me. I was 51 at the time. In my opinion, he was not a bad looking man, and given my need for companionship and loneliness, I eventually found the courage to approach and speak to him.

He told me his name was Michael Elbaum. A Jew, like myself, I thought. If this works out between us, it would be wonderful to share our cultural similarities. As you can tell by my thoughts and eagerness, I was already making plans for our future together, all this after just a simple chance meeting in Wal-Mart of all places.

Michael turned out to be a very friendly and intellectually stimulating man. After talking briefly, he asked me if I would be open to continuing our conversation over coffee. I eagerly agreed, and we drove in separate cars to a nearby Denny's restaurant.

We sat in the non-smoking area, at the opposite side of the entrance. Michael told me a little about himself. That he was staying with a group of young seminarians in Durango, but was visiting from Delaware. He was Jewish by birth, but raised Catholic. In fact, as it turned out, he was a missionary brother—not a priest—in a Catholic religious order of priests and nuns, devoted exclusively to the service of the poor or, as he explained, pastoral work, particularly in the cities. Their work had an emphasis on the study of theology as well. He was not in the least attracted to me romantically, but instead wanted to share with me what made him follow me. I was thinking to myself, "What have I gotten myself into? This guy is not at all what I hoped for, and is now sounding really odd."

I asked him, "I'm not sure what you're getting at. Can you tell me what's exactly is going on?" Michael answered, "I hope you don't think I'm crazy, but because of my spiritual studies and intense work experience, I've become sensitive to spirits and have discovered the ability to sense and see things most people don't. In your case for example, I see a man who is very, very much devoted to you. His image, or spirit, stands close to you and I can tell by his 'light' that he shared a close relationship with you. He's actually with you here, right now, as I am speaking to you. Before you ask me where he is, I'll tell you that he is standing to your left, and is extending his left arm, and in his opened hand he is holding two rings. I'm assuming he was your partner. Is any of this making any sense to you?"

As you might imagine, I was totally amazed and somewhat taken aback by Michael's insight, and without thinking, just answered "Yes, his name is Edward and we were indeed life partners. He died after a long illness." I slowly glanced over to my left, hoping to see Edward, his image or ghost, something but I didn't see anything. I returned my attention to Michael and asked, "How did you know this, I mean, are you psychic, or what?"

Michael answered, "No, I'm not a full-fledged psychic, but I am able to see spirits but before I go any further, Edward is now gesturing for me to tell you not to worry about him, and he's holding up a record album. I don't know what this means but it's an older album and on the cover, is a picture of 'Donovan'. He's also singing a song you might remember. He's singing, 'Jennifer, Juniper.' Does this mean anything to you?"

I instantly made the connection between the song title and my friend, Jennifer, who had passed away. I was totally blown away at Michael's description and at the same time, really uncomfortable with all the details he was telling me about my private life. I took a deep breath and asked him, "Who told you about all these private details about my life? Honestly, I don't know what you're up to but with all due respect, I think you're setting me up for something." Michael apologized for upsetting me, and before he finished his explanation, I interrupted him and said, "I can't believe what is happening, I'm so sorry I need to go!" I got up off my chair, gave Michael my phone number, and thanked him. I left the restaurant, got in my car and drove away.

I drove back to Mancos, crying and shaking most of the way. After arriving home, and feeding my cat, I took off my shoes, sat down in my living room, and turned on the television hoping to distract my thoughts. I watched only a few minutes of television before my emotions resurfaced, I pressed the mute button, turning off the sound and began to cry. Within a few seconds, I heard two distinct taps coming from the ceiling over the front door. I was startled by the sound, and immediately stopped crying. As I sat staring towards the front door, I noticed something slowly float down from near the ceiling. A small white feather came floating down from the ceiling, and I watched as it landed on top of my shoes.

I was stunned. It did not take me long to realize what this was. I felt in my heart that Edward was giving me a sign, and with it, trying to show how he was still with me. As soon as I came to this conclusion, an unexplainable peace came over me. I was so happy and comforted by this that I spoke out loud, "Thank you babe, I'll always love you too!"

I took the feather and placed it in front of Edward's photo that I had placed on a nightstand in the second bedroom. I closed the bedroom door and returned to the living room, thinking about all that had taken place that day. I felt totally blessed that Michael and I had connected that day at Wal-Mart, and he provided me beautifully with messages from Edward that I never expected. We've kept in contact by phone and through emails ever since. I know that Edward connected Michael and I and our friendship from the other side."

MURPHY, CA

The year was 1848 when brothers Daniel and John Murphy came to the area. Rumor has it that the brothers were clever to a shrewd end, as they sold supplies, and traded goods to the local miners at inflated prices. Their double-dealing trading practices did not end with their fellow miners, but instead gained further malice as they exploited local Native Americans as cheap labor. The brothers owned joint mining claims in the area, and in no time, became very wealthy as a result of the millions of gold ore extracted from their mines.

Many notable names in history have visited Murphy's, e.g. President Ulysses S. Grant, Horatio Alger, Charles Bolton, aka Black Bart, and Mark Twain. Unusually unique, Murphy's is celebrated for its climate that closely duplicates the wine growing regions of France. As a result, there are several wineries located within a four-mile radius of Murphy's' main street, that have established themselves as superb and spectacular facilities.

Today, Murphy's offers many natural attractions and unique shopping. Art galleries and beautiful rolling hills are a visual feast for all. Events not to be overlooked are the annual Irish Days and Christmas Open House celebrations.

MEGAN WENTWORTH'S STORY

I've lived in Murphy, since the age of nine months, and I've heard that there are many homes and businesses that are haunted in the area. I was told that the Murphy Hotel has some ghostly activity that continues to this very day. This particular haunting is due to the murder of a man who was killed many years ago. Apparently, his body is buried somewhere on the hotel grounds, but this is just one of the many stories I've heard growing up. One property that I know for a fact is haunted is my own home on French Gulch Road.

The property on which our home is built,

Megan Wentworh.

Mr. Stanton is buried somewhere in the old town cemetery.

is without a doubt, an activity hub of ghostly occurrences. The name of the original owner of our property was Oliver Stanton. Mr. Stanton was known locally by the strange name of "The Goat Man." My family was told that this nick-name was given to him because of the hundreds of goats he owned, and let run lose on the property. Interestingly, when my family moved into the property, there was an actual old goat still living on the property. It stayed on our property for about three years, until one day it just disappeared.

People who knew The Goat Man have told us that he was a very private person, always kept to himself. Some have hinted he was also somewhat insane. Another rumor we've heard, is that he had a cache of gold buried somewhere on the property, in a location known only to him. I know that Mr. Stanton is also buried somewhere in the old town cemetery. I have visited the cemetery trying to locate his grave, but I've not been able to find it. My parents have asked some of the neighbors if they have a photo of Mr. Stanton, but no one has come forward with one yet.

After moving onto the property, we found numerous personal items that belonged to Mr. Stanton. An old barn was filled with antique farming tools, personal papers, tools, etc. Prior to our purchase, the property had been abandoned for many years. People just stayed away from it, and I imagine this was due to the Goat Man's strange reputation.

Before our main house was built, for several months my family lived in the original, smaller cabin fronting the road. During our stay at this cabin is where, as a child, I experienced my first encounter with a ghost.

I remember one evening, as I entered the living room, I saw an old man sitting on our couch looking right at me. He was rather tall, and lanky. His face had a very weathered look. He was wearing a long shirt, buttoned to the neck, and old jeans, and didn't speak a word to me. The really strange thing was the overwhelming scent of pine wood shavings that immediately filled the room. I've never understood why, but I got the strong scent of cut pine.

After we stared at each other and nothing was said between us, I turned around and walked away not caring to ask who he even was. Sometime later I mentioned the man to my mother, who told me she was unaware of any visitor in our house. She changed the subject by asking

This cabin is where I experienced my first encounter.

me if I had completed some tasks she asked me to do for her. I had not and proceeded to do as she requested. I forgot about the whole encounter, and never brought it up again.

As the months went by, we eventually moved into the completed main house up on the hill, where I experienced even more ghostly activity. One night, at about 11pm, my best friend Rachel and I got into our separate beds, and something caught our attention. This will sound crazy, but we spotted a circular green, soft-yellow tinted light glowing and beginning to form off the floor of the room. We were amazed, scared and speechless. The light moved up and around on the wall, and then it moved toward the closet where it just vanished in the blink of an eye. We kept this sight to ourselves and never told anyone for fear they might think we were crazy. We weren't crazy but that sighting sure was! To this day, we have no explanation or understand of what that light was, where it came from or what it meant. Just glad I've never seen anything like this since and never hope to ever see something like this ever again.

The next thing Rachel and I experienced was when we were sitting on the couch watching television. The blinds on the windows in the room were pulled half way down from the ceiling. There was no wind outside or ceiling fan turned on. Suddenly, one of the blinds began to shake back and forth with enough force to hit hard against the window. All the windows in the room were securely closed and locked, so as I said before,

The main house.

there was no wind causing this activity. None of the other blinds were shaking, just this one particular one directly in front of where we were seated. The blind continued swaying on its own for a few seconds. My friend and I were totally fascinated. Once more, I mentioned what I had seen to my mother. This time she said that she could appreciate what I was describing, because she had also experienced unusual activity, and had even seen shadows of people moving about the house, even walking up the stairs.

My boyfriend once saw the shadow of a man walking outside the house. My boyfriend is 6'5", 250 lbs., and a mechanic by trade. He described a time while sitting at our kitchen table, when something caught his eye. He saw a dark figure slowly walking past the windows. He said the figure immediately left him sensing an ominous impression of power around it. Since then, my boyfriend doesn't like being at the house by himself. He tells me the property gives him the creeps.

On another evening two friends, who had been staying at the property, were standing in the front yard waiting for a car to pick them up and take them home. In the distance, they noticed the figure of a man walking up the road, towards the house. They kept their eyes fixed on this stranger, as he slowly made his way towards them. When he got to about 15 feet from them, he stopped, stood facing them, then without saying a word he simply faded into thin air! That was it, he completely vanished. The men ran back into the house, and hysterically told me their story. I just got all freaked out. I knew they had just had an encounter with our ghost. Interestingly, whenever a ghost is seen on the property, it's always been a male figure.

Other examples of the ghost inhabiting the house include noisy footsteps and shaking door knobs. These, together with the unexpected sighting of a shadowy figure, are very common. We tend to hear footsteps walking throughout the house, both day or night and at all hours. My father confessed that he used to hear the same footsteps in the cabin, before we moved, and now he also hears them in the new house. The doors in the house will also make noise on their own as if someone is grabbing hold of the knob and shaking it. We'll watch the knob as it slowly turns, then shakes stronger and faster, until it rattles very loudly. It's as if someone on the other side of the door is angry, or trying to break out but we know there is no one there.

Visitors to our house have reported hearing faint almost muffled voices in the kitchen, when no one is around. One day my girlfriend was alone in the house, sitting in the living room. Suddenly she heard someone's voice speaking out loud, and noisily moving things around dishes and silverware in the kitchen. Then, she heard the refrigerator door being opened and closed. She got up and walked into the kitchen to investigate. Upon entering the kitchen, she saw nothing but the refrigerator door left wide open. She had heard about other ghost activity and simply told whoever this was, to stop disturbing her and to get out. She said the remainder of the afternoon and evening all she heard was what came out of the television set, that she had turned on.

I own a pit bull who is a very mellow and sweet dog. She also exhibits strange behavior at the house. On many occasions, something seems to grab her attention, and she'll sit and stare for hours at one spot on the wall. This odd behavior really scares me. She'll just sit at the foot of the stairs, and seems to focus for long periods of time at something invisible. I know that she sees the ghost of someone. I've heard that animals have the extra sense to see ghosts. Her behavior scares the "you know what" out of me! One time I was seated at the living room couch, watching television. My dog was lying on my lap. When suddenly, she turned her head, and once again began to stare at something near the stairs. As I caressed her head, I noticed that whatever she was looking at, was threating her to the point where she began to growl and bark. She jumped off my lap,

We hear them following us around in our orchard.

ran to the stairs and growled at something that I couldn't see. Suddenly she ran up the stairs still barking some more, then ran back downstairs and continued to bark at whatever remained at the top of the stairs. She didn't stop until I walked up to the top of the stairs, turned and casually walked back down.

My dog's behavior is not something that only happens once in a while. This goes on all the time. There's something that likes to hang around those stairs that only she is able to see. It drives her crazy. These are the stairs where my mother said she has actually seen the ghost of a man who walked up those same stairs.

The footsteps are not isolated to just the inside of the house, we hear them following us around in our orchard. We hear the footsteps of someone stepping on the fallen leaves between the trees, and with each step we can hear them crunching with every step. The sounds are very obvious, and surprisingly most often heard during the daylight hours. The orchard is kept free of weeds, and the trees are regularly pruned, so it's easy to see between the rows. It always gives us a creepy feeling to hear these ghostly footsteps following us throughout the orchard, especially in broad daylight!

For whatever reason, the ghost has chosen to linger on the property. I don't think he wants to hurt us. He likes hanging around our house—his old property. I know I've never done anything to cause the ghost of this man to come after me, but I can't believe I'm going to say this but, I'd like to actually see him. I think it might be interesting to know what he looks like and if could somehow communicate. That might be really cool but then again, it might not!"

OROVILLE, CA

Oroville's non-Native American history begins with Gabriel Moraga, who visited the area in 1808. Gabriel Moraga was followed by Spanish explorer Captain Luis Arguello, who in 1820, noticing the many wild pigeon feathers floating on the river, immediately named the river "Rio de las Plumas," or the River of Feathers. Ultimately, the river was lastingly named, The Feather River. In 1848, Anglo settler John Bidwell, discovered gold along the river bank, thus beginning a massive gold rush of fortune seekers. The birth of "Ophir City", a tent town, soon changed its name in 1856 to Oroville, which is Spanish for "City of Gold," and remains today, the official city name.

Oroville is filled with many historical sites and landmarks. Of particular note is the Ishi Monument dedicated to the memory of Ishi, the last known member of the Yahi Indian nation. The monument reads: The Last Yahi Indian, "For thousands of years the Yahi Indians roamed the foothills between Mt. Lassen and the Sacramento Valley, settlement of this region by the white man brought death to the Yahi by gun, by disease, and by hunger. By the turn of the century only a few remained. Ishi, the last known survivor of these people, was discovered at this site in 1911. His death in 1916 brought an end to Stone Age California."

IRENE LOBAIN'S STORY

Peter and I have lived in Oroville for 28 years. Our ghost experiences began fifteen years ago, a few weeks after my husband mother passed. Peter's mother, Mary, came to live with us in June of 1986, and died in September of that same year. Mary was diagnosed with cancer of the sinuses which developed into a very inva-

Mary Lobain.

sive cancer. It was not long before the doctors changed her prognosis to terminal.

Peter and I were devastated by the news, however Mary's overall attitude was surprisingly realistic and tranquil. Mary, the daughter of a Methodist minister, was born in Jamaica, and raised in West Virginia where she lived most her life. When she was diagnosed with cancer, most of her family and friends had preceded her in death. She had no family to care for her in West Virginia, so we decided to move her to Oroville.

Not long after Mary's death and burial, Peter began experiencing unexplained activity in our home, hearing voices, seeing unusual shadows, and images in mirrors, to name a few. On one occasion, I also encountered my own ghost experience, which left me terrified and speechless.

Two weeks after Mary's funeral, one early afternoon, Peter was on the phone speaking to our banker when he happened to glanced out the dining room window and saw the image of his mother standing next to our car. Peter explained that his mother's ghost was dressed in her favorite green dress, holding her white purse. Peter's impression on the visitation was that his mother's spirit was waiting to be driven into nearby Chico to do her shopping. Mary always enjoyed, and looked forward to, her Friday shopping trip with her son.

Peter told me he was surprised and moved by this image. Our banker sensed that something was had distracted Peter and asked, "Are you alright, is everything okay?" Peter politely ended his phone call with the banker saying "I need to take care of something, I'll call you later."

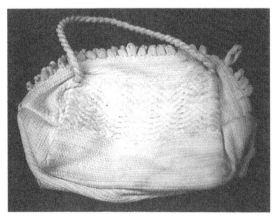
The ghost was holding her white purse.

Peter looked at me and nervously described what he had just seen standing at the driveway. I was not convinced and told him that his imagination was at work. He insisted that he had just seen Mary standing by the car, but also admitted that he wasn't actually sure. Later that night, before going to bed, we talked more about it. I was concerned about his mental state, whether he was overwhelmingly stressed, or depressed. I carefully suggested Peter call his doctor to discuss what he had thought he'd seen. Peter assured me he would do this sometime within the following week.

Early the next morning, about 4 am, I was awakened by the pressure of a hand on my forehead. I opened my eyes and suddenly I was smelling my mother-in-law's favorite perfume. I was shocked and could feel my heart pounding in my chest! I sat up, looked over at Peter but he was sound asleep. As I leaned back on my pillow, I sensed Mary's presence in the room, she was there in that moment with us, I just knew it! I kept my eyes opened and slowly scanned the darkened bedroom. Sure enough, an elongated white light formed in front of the closet door, the same, full height of the door. The light hovered a few inches off the floor. It was a dim light that alternatively glowed bright then dim, bright again, then dim. It seemed for a second, like it was like a pumping heartbeat, except totally silent.

With my eyes fixed on the pulsating light, I got the courage to whisper, "Mary everything is ok, you can go now. Peter and I will be ok." The light kept glowing and the perfume scent grew stronger. Peter suddenly awoke and asked me what was going on. I told him to look over toward the closet, "See that light over there?" I said. Peter's fumbling hand reached over to the night stand, to grab his glasses but by the time Peter placed his glasses over his eyes, the mysterious light was gone.

Although the light had disappeared, I remained convinced that Mary was still in the house. For the remainder of that morning, I was unable to go back to sleep. Peter kept insisting that I repeat word for word, what exactly I had seen. I knew he was trying to make sense of what had appeared to me, but his intense questioning was upsetting me. I told him I needed to go to the kitchen and think about things. A few hours later, as the sun was coming up, I explained to Peter that I would have a much clearer mind to discuss everything over breakfast. Peter agreed and remained in bed until 8 am.

At breakfast, we discussed what I had seen and what it all might have meant. Could the glowing light that I had seen, actually be Mary's ghost? Could there possibly be another explanation for the lights, perhaps the headlights from a passing car outside? Or, do I have an overactive imagination? So many possibilities crossed my mind, but in my heart, I knew what I had seen was not something that could be explained in normal terms. And what about my smelling Mary's perfume? I couldn't think of a 100% explanation that made any sense to me. I'm convinced it was Mary's spirit that had visited us, and oddly enough, we were actually both individually hoping to have more.

For the rest of the day, Peter and I went about our daily routines. But try as I might, Mary's visit the night before, was impossible for me to erase from my mind so I decided to take a drive into town and do some shopping. When I returned to the house, I walked into the kitchen, placed my purchases on top of the kitchen island. As I turned to open the pantry door, I noticed something on the counter by the sink. It was Mary's favorite coffee cup, and set next to it was a small teaspoon.

I called to Peter, in the living room watching television, "Hey, were you going to use your mother's coffee cup for something?" He said, "No, why?" I asked him to come into the kitchen immediately! We both stood staring silently with our eyes fixed on Mary's cup and spoon. He swore he didn't take it out of the cupboard, and I know I didn't. All the tiny hairs on my neck and arms stood on end. I believed Peter and he believed me, neither of us would have ever thought to play such a trick on the other, at least not at this serious time of grieving.

Without hesitation, I said to Peter, "Because of everything you and I have experienced, I think your mother wants to tell us something. I think she wants to hear you're ok and that we'll be ok. I think you should tell her out loud that it's okay to leave the house, that you and I will be fine." Peter gave me a funny look, but thought I might be making total sense. He reached out and too hold of my hand and said, "Mom, everything will be okay. You can go now, go be with dad. We love you." The next thing that happened might sound crazy, but it did happen, I swear it did!

Right after my husband spoke, we heard Mary's soft voice respond out of thin air directly between us, "Love you too son." I nervously let go of Peter's hand and we embraced. He began to cry and we both felt comforted hearing Mary's response and that everything would be fine from now on. I absolutely knew Mary was happy and satisfied in our responses to her.

Nothing more has taken place to indicate Mary is still active in the house. The experience left me a with unexpected courage and a new be-

We both stood, our eyes fixed at the cup and spoon.

lief about the future existence of some form of life-after-death existence for us. I was a non-believer, but no longer.

My husband Peter passed away on April 12, 1997 from a sudden heart attack. I miss him very much, but because of our experience with Mary's spirit, I truly believe and know that Peter and his mother are together. This gives me so much comfort especially during the times when I miss him. I've hoped for a sighting or visit from Peter, but so far, I haven't. I believe we somehow continue living after we die, but will just have to wait and see for myself when my time comes. Thank you for allowing me to share my ghost experiences. I hope my story will bring peace to someone trying to live with grief.

PECOS, NM

Pecos is small village perched on the edge of the Pecos Wilderness and Santa Fe National Forest. The Pecos Wilderness is a protected wilderness area within the Santa Fe National Forest and Carson National Forest, and represents over 220,000 acres of pristine wilderness.

At midpoint in a passage through the southern Sangre de Cristo Mountains, the ruins of a Pecos pueblo and Spanish mission share a small ridge. Long before Spaniards arrived, this village commanded the trade path between Pueblo farmers of the Rio Grande and tribes who hunted the buffalo plains. Its 2,000 residents could marshal 500 fighting men. Its frontier location brought both war and trade. At trade fairs Plains tribes—mostly nomadic Apaches—brought slaves, buffalo hides, flint, and shells to trade for pottery, crops, textiles and turquoise with the river Pueblos. Pecos Indians were middlemen, traders, and consumers of the goods and cultures of the very different people on either side of the mountains. They became economically powerful and practiced in the art and custom of two worlds.

Pecos Indians remained Puebloan in culture—despite cultural blending's—practicing an ancient agricultural tradition born north from Mexico by the seeds of sacred corn. By the late Pueblo period, the last few centuries before the Spaniards arrived in the Southwest, people in this valley had congregated in multi-storied towns overlooking the streams and fields that nourished their crops. In the 1400s these groups gathered into Pecos pueblo, which became a regional power.

A Spanish conquistador described the pueblo in 1584 set on a "high and narrow hill, enclosed on both sides by two streams and many trees." The hill was cleared of trees. "It has the greatest and best buildings of these provinces and is most thickly settled." The people had "quantities of maize, cotton, beans, and squash," and the pueblo was "enclosed and protected by a wall and large houses, and by tiers of walkways which look out over the countryside. On these they keep their offensive and defensive arms: bows, arrows, shields, spears, and war clubs." Like other Pueblo groups, the Pecos enjoyed a rich culture with inventive architecture and beautiful crafts. Their elaborate religious life, evidenced by many ceremonial kivas, reached out to the nurturing spirits of all things, animate and inanimate.

Fine-tuned adjustments to their natural and cultivated world rested on practical science infused with spirituality. Through story and dance tradition, knowledge and wisdom of centuries past was conveyed. Individual, family and social life were regulated via a religion binding all things together and holding balance, harmony, and fitness as the highest ideals. But ideals did not always prevail. Warfare between Pueblo groups was common. The frontier people of Pecos had to be vigilant with nomadic Plains Indians whose intent—trade or war—could be unpredictable. Neighboring pueblos saw the Pecos as dominant. The Spaniards soon learned that the Pecos could be determined enemies or powerful allies.

First to settle here were pre-pueblo people who lived in pit houses along drainages about 800 A.D. Around 1100, the first Puebloans began building their rock-and-mud villages in the valley. Two-dozen villages rose here over the next two centuries, including one where Pecos pueblo stands today. Sometime in the 14th century, the settlement patterns changed dramatically. Within one generation, small villages were abandoned and Pecos pueblo grew larger. By 1450, it had become a well-planned frontier fortress five stories high with a population over 2,000.

The land around the pueblo was a storehouse of natural products the Pecos knew intimately. They used virtually every plant for food, clothing, shelter, or medicine and turned every part of the game they hunted into something useful.

Farming supplied most of their diet. The staple crops were the usual trio of corn, beans, and squash cultivated along Glorieta Creek and the area's many drainages. Water was as important to the Pecos as to us. They built check dams to slow the runoff of rain and grew their crops where topsoil collected. Yields were apparently considerable. In 1541, Coronado found the Pueblo storerooms piled high with corn with a three-year supply by one estimate.

Location, power, and the ability to supply needed goods made Pecos a major trade center on the eastern flank of the Puebloan world. Pecos Indians bartered crops, clothing, pottery with the Apaches and later the Spaniards and Comanche's for buffalo products, Alibates flint for cutting tools and slaves. These Plains goods were in turn swapped west to other pueblos for pottery, parrot feathers, turquoise, and other items. Trading could go quickly or take weeks. Rings left by tipis set up for long spells of bartering are still visible in the area. Uneasy relationships between Pueblos and the Plains tribes made hostilities a continual threat. The rock wall circling the pueblo, a relic from trading days, was too low to serve a defensive purpose. It was probably a boundary other tribes were not allowed to cross."

ROXANA A. WILLIAM'S STORY

"I presently live in the village of Pecos, a short driving distance from the Pecos monument. I've lived in the area for most of my life. Today, my 79-year old mother lives at my home with me along with my two dogs, Lucy and Desi. My husband died eleven years ago from a long battle with cancer, and a few days after his funeral, I chose to add my two dogs into my home. I needed some companions to help me through the grieving process and these two dogs, just puppies, littermates at the time, have provided me with the companionship I needed at that difficult time in my life.

After my husband's funeral, I would take long walks up to Rowe mesa. I'd often take the puppies with me to provide them with exercise. On these hikes, I'd have lots of time to think about my life and my future. As I'd be hiking, lost in my thoughts, I started noticing the puppies yelping, barking at a squirrel, or when something would get their attention. I'd be instantly snap away from my contemplating and my attention turned to what the puppies were reacting to. This is how I spent my first few weeks, alone with my dogs. I'm informing you of this pattern because one early afternoon, all this would change.

One day as I was taking my usual hike up on the mesa, my dogs began to bark at something near a grouping of shrubs and trees. This area was a few feet from where we were and as I carefully approached, I noticed a foggy, white mist slowly forming before us. It was a about five by six feet in total size. This misty fog seemed to come through the shrubs and became more solid within just a matter of seconds.

As the dogs continued barking loudly with their little voices, I was in awe trying to figure out just what was happening. The mist stopped in mid-air, then slowly floated down onto the ground. It floated up and passed through the shrubs, then floated high up into the air and then landed on the ground again. All this took place in, in broad daylight and within a few seconds

This is not going to make any sense, but I was not in the least scared. I wondered if this was because of my state of mind at the time, feeling emotionally and psychologically numb with grief. So, I continued watching as this suspicious mist floated about and eventually transformed before my eyes.

Immediately after it landed on the ground, the mist's composition became cloudier and visibly much denser. I could see an outline forming within the mist, a distinct outline of a human figure, a man actually! The figure was about my height, thin, very short hair, almost bald, and totally naked. I was sure that I was witnessing a spirit manifesting. All the time this was happening, I realized that the dogs were silent. I looked to see where they were and saw them comfortably lying in the shadow of one of the trees.

This spirit figure was not an adult but younger and somewhere between the ages of nine and thirteen. Upon closer observation, I noticed that he was wearing a necklace, a shell type necklace that pueblo people sometimes wear today. As I continued focusing on this boy figure, it became clear to me that he was of Native American decent.

This spirit figure was not fully formed or clearly defined, his features and the outline of his body seemed to be dissolving and reforming. There was no doubt in my mind that this was a true spirit manifestation, happening right in front of me. His image lasted for about few seconds, then as the wind became strong enough to move the tree branches, the image slowly dissolved and faded away.

The reality of what I had just seen hit and I began to tremble. I rubbed both my arms and just wept. I was suddenly scared, but not enough to run away. I soon gathered my thoughts and began accepting what I had seen as a spirit who had appeared to me for some reason I was unable to understand. I chose to sit on the ground and somehow try to think about all the possible reasons why this appeared to me. I kept coming up with empty answers. But I could not forget the little native boy's image or about what the significance to me might be. After a few minutes, I called to my dogs and we hiked back to the car and drove home.

When I arrived home, I described to my mother my experience with this spirit. She got very quiet, then asked me to promise that I would not go hiking anywhere near that part of the woods alone again or from now on. I agreed and told her that I didn't feel comfortable doing this either.

And as of that date, I've not gone up to the mesa since.

About a month after that experience, my friend Martin and I went to visit the Pecos Monument. Martin was an established artist; an oil painter and he had an appointment with the monument's site supervisor. Martin wanted to set up his easel and paints in one of the areas of the monument using a large canvas and needed permission from the park service. I was left to busy myself within the museum portion of the Visitors center. A collection of pottery and other artifacts were displayed and I had no problem spending the time looking over everything.

I remember gazing at a diorama display about daily life of a pueblo community, when I heard a familiar voice call out my name. I turned around and saw Elaine, a girlfriend who moved away from Pecos a few years ago and was now living in the northern town of Chama.

"Roxie, is that you?" she said. We hugged and she told me all about her home and husband. She also mentioned that she was in town visiting her mother and brother. She was at the monument because of an old pot her brother had recently purchased from an friend of his. The pot was wrapped in a bath towel and placed in a cardboard box she was holding. Elaine's brother, Hector was at home with the flu and asked her if she could do him a favor and ask any monument personal what type of pot it was, it's age, etc.

I asked Elaine if I could take a look at it. "Sure Roxie," she said. The pot looked old, it could have even been an ancient pot. I'm not very knowledgeable about pots, but to me it looked authentically old.

Elaine and I talked about several things in our lives, but during our conversation, she asked me, "Roxie, you don't seem right, what's up?" I mentioned to her how difficult it's been for me to get along with life after my husband's death. And then I mentioned to her my experience with the spirit. "Are you serious, I need to know everything about what you saw, Roxie."

After describing what I experienced, she placed the cardboard box down and said, "Roxie, my brother had the same experience with a young man's spirit up there on that mesa. He and his friend, Diego were hunting elk when a young boy's spirit appeared to him. Right there in the open, an Indian boy's spirit wearing the necklace you described appeared to him. Diego was several yards away at the time, so he was unable to verify the story, but Hector swears he saw this spirit come right up to him." "Do you think Hector would talk to me about the spirit?" I asked. Elaine answered, "He doesn't speak to anyone about it. He mentioned it to me years ago and has never spoken about it since. I don't think he would, but you never know, you'll just have to ask him."

After Martin was done with his appointment, we drove to my home and had dinner. The following day I decided to drive to Elaine's mother's house and speak with her brother. She did not have a phone, so I was unable to call in advance. When I arrived at their house, Elaine's mother answered the door and invited me to enter. She told me that Elaine was in Santa Fe. When I asked for Hector, she stated he was in bed with the flu. I walked to his bedroom door and when I asked him if he would mind discussing his experience with me, adding that I had my own encounter with the spirit, he flatly stated, "No, I don't want to talk about it. Don't ever bring it up again—okay!"

I was surprised by his stern reaction and response. I said, "Sure, hope you feel better." I left the house with mixed emotions. Knowing that I would never be able to share our joint experiences with Hector, I drove away thinking how terrible his encounter must have been. Mine was quite pleasant, not at all upsetting. A little bit startling, yes, but nothing to make me react in the negative way Hector had.

I'll never know what the spirit's intent was—to give me a message, a warning or perhaps a sign, I'll never know. I just know that I was not the only person to have seen this particular spirit and believe there must be others who have also seen it besides Hector and myself. Maybe someone reading my story will come forward and validate all this by sharing their own account; but then again, maybe not."

PLACITAS, NM

Placitas, located in Sandoval County New Mexico lies northeast of Albuquerque and south of Santa Fe. Begun as the original settlement of 1765 - San Jose de Las Huertas inception was in an area located in the lower Las Huertas Canyon and inhabited by twenty-one original settlers. Not exactly a city nor town although it has somewhat of a village center, Placitas remains but a series of small communities of homes that have found themselves nestled in the northern foothills of the Sandia Mountain range. Paved and dirt roads are common in the area as are a few spring-fed creeks that offer life to box elder, willows and native evergreens.

RUDY LEBECK'S STORY

Rudy and I sat outside his Placitas home on comfortable chairs overlooking the Sandia mountain range to the distant south. The visual panorama was stunning and awe inspiring. On a small garden table placed between us was Rudy's personal collection of found objects from the area such as rusted bullet casings, small animal bones, a dried foot -long snakeskin and various vintage, faded colored, medicine bottles.

As I observed this collection I located a small area on the table where I placed my tape recorder. Rudy's story will lend credence to the fact that if you ever knowingly disturb a burial site, it would be best to make amends to the spirit from that gravesite and praying for protection from any potential negative attachments. However, if reverence and a respectful attitude are paid to the deceased, there just might be an acknowledgment or token of affection somehow presented in return to the living for their respectful offering and gesture. Here's Rudy's story to back-up this recommendation.

— Antonio

"I'm a recent arrival to the Placitas area. I'm originally born and raised in Buffalo, New York and at the age of twenty-two, I married my girlfriend and we moved to Tucson, Arizona. I got a job well paying job at a local radio station and within three years, we had saved up enough to move away from the extreme heat of Arizona and relocate to a milder temperature. We scouted the southwest and decided on the mountain community of Placitas, New Mexico.

Five months after making our move out to Placitas, I landed another job at a radio station, a 40-minute drive north in Santa Fe. My daily drive north every day, to and from my house wasn't so bad at first, considering the pleasant views, but eventually it started to become a drag. So, I began looking for a new job closer to home. At the time my wife, Maria was a nurse at Presbyterian Hospital in Rio Rancho, a suburb of Albuquerque. She thoroughly enjoys her job.

After submitting my notice to quit the Santa Fe radio station, I was out of work for almost ten months. I've always been an outdoors kind of guy, hiking, and camping in the wilderness whenever possible. Maria on the other hand, was perfectly happy staying at home and watching television. It was during this period of lack of work that I chose to occupy my days of unemployment by taking our dog, Hobo with me hiking the back hills of our Placitas community.

One early morning Hobo and I headed out to the distant northeastern hills and came upon three small Cairns, or mounds of rocks. These rock piles were not a natural formation, but clearly humans had constructed them, they were so uniquely stacked. I had seen two examples of such small structures much closer to Placitas, but never formations out here in the hills and in such isolation. The mounds were circular, about six to seven feet in width, and close to three or four feet high. I knew they had to be older than ten or more years because of their appearance. My dog and I walked around the mounds but I didn't think much more about them. I decided to continue on our hike and headed further northeast.

We had left the mounds, not more, twenty minutes or so, when Hobo started to sniff at something off to the side a sloping area. I approached and saw what looked like animal bones together with a dark grey colored clay pot! Although filled in with reddish colored earth, after removing this hardened mud, the pot's unmistakable form was very much recognizable. I had the feeling that we had come across a very, old Indian site, perhaps even a burial site. I know that it had to be ancient because to the pot did not have any familiar pueblo designs, it was simply a dark colored clay pot. When I tried to separate some of the dirt from the bones, a large portion of dirt gave way, and the bones broke in two! No doubt, these bones were not of a recently buried animal or even a person. These bones were, in my estimation, from an ancient period.

I decided to rebury these items and place handfuls of dirt back on top of the small bones and the pot. I covered as much of these with soil as I possibly could. My dog went off and clearly wasn't interested in what I was doing. Within about an hour I finished reburying the items and gathered rocks and made a border around the grave.

As I was about to leave, I decided to place a large rock in the middle of this circle of rocks as a symbol of respect to whomever these artifacts might have belonged to. Obviously, many years ago someone took the time and effort to respectfully bury these, so I thought I'd make a similar effort in helping to preserve the intentions of the family or tribe. When I finished, I decided to head back home.

About a week past when I strangely had a dream about the pot and bones. It was a summer evening and the rain was coming down hard. That night I found it difficult to sleep. I kept thinking over and over in my mind about the bones I had come across the week before. Mary felt my body turning uncomfortable in bed next to hers so she urged me to get out of bed and go into the living room to watch some television. Usually watching a few minutes of television with the volume turned off is enough to lull me into a semi-conscious state, thereby clearing my mind and causing me to drift into sleep.

I took Mary's suggestion; got out of bed and walked down the hall to the living room. After switching on the T.V., I sat in my large leather chair and began to change the channels until I found a nature program about the life of deep-water crabs. Just what I needed, to take my mind off of things and bore me to sleep. As I sat in the chair, with each minute that passed, my eyelids grew heavier and eventually, I fell into a deep sleep.

I don't know how long I was asleep, but I suddenly felt the need to open my eyes. I remember slowly opening my eyes and spotting a young man, about fifteen or so years old, standing in the living room ten feet from my chair. My face was cradled in the bend of my elbow, but I could still see and my eyes stayed focused on the figure standing before me. I more interested and curious than afraid! The figure didn't speak, or even move. I could vaguely make out any physical features but knew it was a male energy.

Eventually I saw this figure slightly raise its head up in a kind of greeting way, then nodded yes a few times in a gesture I understood to say 'thank you.' This thought occurred to me because of all the mental energy I had spent thinking about the bones and items that I discovered way out in that remote area of land. This spirit figure was acknowledging my actions and now letting me know, I offered respect to the items and did something positive, and appropriate by reburying them. So here was this ghostly apparition gesturing and clearly communicating its gratitude.

I never felt the need to speak or to get up from the chair. Mainly because I was so exhausted and sleepy. The total experience at that moment was one of complete peace and calm. Time ceased to exist, and words were not necessary in this brief but intense moment. We were communicating through thoughts and that was plenty.

Once this thought of thankfulness was conveyed to me, the figure opened its right fist, which had been closed, and let something drop to the floor. The object looked like a small round ball, but when the ball hit the floor, it made absolutely no sound. The figure then slowly began to fade into the darkest corner of the room. I sat up in the chair and I stared into that pitch-black corner, trying to see the figure but with only the glowing light of the television I couldn't see the figure any more. My eyes

caught the site of the round item he dropped lying on the floor, and I got out of the chair and walked over to pick it up—it was a rock.

I held the grey colored, walnut size rock in my hand. It was unusually light in weight, and left me with more questions than answers. I switched off the television and walked to the bedroom. As soon as I got under the covers I fell into a deep sleep. The next morning, I decided to return to the gravesite area. All I can say at this point is that I was 'driven' to return to the grave as soon as I could with no rhyme or reason. I just felt a strong need to return.

When I arrived at the gravesite, I didn't see anything that looked immediately out of place. All the stones I had left before were still arranged in the circle, just as I left them. The large stone I had placed within the middle of the circle was still upright and nothing at all seemed disturbed. However, on closer inspection I notice that a small round stone, similar to the one the spirit visitor had presented me with, was now resting on top of the largest of the stones! Without hesitating, I reached into my pocket, felt for the stone and brought it out of my pants pocket.

While standing next to the grave and holding the small stone in my right hand, a feeling came over me. An unexplainable urged to place that stone I received, right next to the other stone sitting on top of the large stone. After rubbing the sides of the large stone with my two hands, I felt it was time to place the stone I had, together with, and next to the other stone already on top of the larger one.

As you might have expected, nothing unusual took place. I said a prayer to the spirit of the buried person, and return to my home. I was about

fifty feet away from the grave when I heard the cawing sounds of a raven. I turned to see a very large, black raven circling above and watched as it quickly descended to the ground, hopped towards the grave and leaped up upon the large stone.

As the raven stood onto the stone, I watched from a distance as it picked up one of the smaller round stones in its beak and, without hesitation, took flight! Up and into the west it flew. At the time, not understanding what all this meant, I was confident to simply hope it was a positive sign from the 'other side.'

About two years later, I was speaking to a woman friend of mine from the Jicarilla Apache tribe, and a photography artist from the Dulce area of New Mexico. Her name is Nanette Pancita. After hearing my story, she stated, 'I don't know how to advise you Rudy, you were visited by a spirit and you followed through with your instincts. You did what any respectful Apache person might have done in a similar situation. Your actions were correct and respectful.

The fact that you also witnessed the raven come down and retrieve the gift that was given to you, shows it was accepted and taken to the west, which is the area we Apache people believe is the spiritual gate to the next world. You were given an experience few people, even us Natives, rarely ever claim to have had.'

So, this was my first and only direct contact experience to date that I've ever had with a spirit. I don't talk too much at all about it. My hope in telling you my story is that others can relate on some level, and if they ever come across a grave, artifacts, no matter how old, they should be respectful and leave them alone. Grave robbing continues today and often, all over the southwest. Indian pottery, old stone beads and artifacts, many removed from gravesites, turn up in antique stores all the time. I know that these objects can bring in lots of money. My question then becomes, is the hope and ultimate intent of individual collectors to just make money regardless of where or how invaluable artifacts might be obtained? There are unknown consequences for those who disturb or remove human remains from any gravesite, not just in this life but also in the next. For personal safety, well-being and dignity I ask everyone to seriously beware and show more respect!"

SONORA, CA

Sonora has been the center for county, government and business since the mid-1800's. It is one of the most prominent towns in the Mother Lode, preserving its rich history while acting as the commercial hub for a three-county area.

St. James Episcopal Church is located at the corner of Washington and Snells Streets, dates from the 1850's. Better known as the Red Church, it is one of Tuolumne County's most photographed buildings.

Many Washington Street business buildings date back to Gold Rush days and a few of the businesses, including the Union Democrat, have been serving the public since the 1850's. The side streets have a number of Victorian era homes built around the turn of the century for Sonora's elite.

The Miwok Native American nation prospered in Sonora until the arrival of gold seekers. Today's Washington Street is believed to follow the long-established Miwok trail. The Miwok welcomed and traded with the first onslaught of miners in 1848, but they were soon displaced as work spread around the world that the hills were rich with gold.

Miners from Sonora, Mexico were the first to settle in what they called Sonorian Camp. Then came men from the Eastern United States, Europe, South American, the Caribbean, Canada, the South Pacific and China. Traders followed and Sonora became the commercial center of the southern Mother Lode.

The City of Sonora was incorporated in 1851 and was named the county seat the same year. Life became quieter as easily gotten gold disappeared, however, today Sonora remains the commercial and governmental center of the area.

Today, the city of Sonora's population hovers in the 5,000 plus count. There is an additional "shadow" population of vacationers, shoppers and downtown employees of from 12,000 to 20,000. One of the historic downtown sites which has been recently restored is the Opera Hall. In its previous lives the building has been a stable, a garage and a storage building. Today the Opera Hall which is a picture of its past, is the location for many community events, private parties and art exhibits.

GERALD AND LEE'S STORY

I moved to Sonora about 15 years ago from San Francisco. Searching for a more peaceful and less stressful life, I had contemplated making a move out of the city for several months. The daily grind of living in such a large city as San Francisco had become more and more of an effort. I wanted a stress-less quality of life that a smaller community like Sonora could offer.

Prior to my move, I was employed as a juvenile probation officer. My caseload of kids was between 38 to 45, a ridiculous number, and as much a stress producing job as any could be.

In theory, I was supposed to make contact with each 'client' once or twice a month, make contact with their parents, school, social worker, write reports that were submitted to the juvenile court, attended meetings, chart in the client's file, be called into court by deposition, attend to numerous emergencies, the list went on and on. And all this was to be done within a month's time. I became psychologically numb, or as is commonly termed within the department for a worker who has reached his limit—a 'burn-out!'

So, 15 years ago I made the decision to leave my job, move and settle into the more relaxed community of Sonora. I purchased a small two-bedroom bungalow on the south side of town, a short walking distance to main street. I wasn't necessarily much into making new friends immediately. I wasn't anti-social, I just wanted to take things easy for a time, and did some fixing up and landscaping around the house. One of the renovations to my home I accomplished, was to turn a bedroom into a computer room/home office. Soon after, I started my own design and marketing consulting business out of this room.

Friends still living in San Francisco, and new acquaintances in Sonora began to use my skills and services. Quickly word got around about the new advertising guy in town, and within a week, I acquired four local accounts!

One of these new accounts was with a gentleman named Lee who like myself, moved away from a big city to seek the sanity of a smaller town. Like myself, Lee also started a small, home based business. He responded to a newspaper ad I placed, and when he stopped in to describe his advertising needs, we really 'hit it off.' Unknowingly to either one of us, our business relationship, lead us in time to a great friendship, and eventually developed into a romantic partnership.

At the time, Lee's business interest was raising local organic herbs and flowers. He singularly handled the full duties of the business from planting seeds, harvesting, and eventually distributing his organic produce to restaurants in the Sacramento area. Twice a week he would load up his Nissan pickup, and attend the popular Farmer's Market in San Francisco. The town of Sonora also has a wonderful Farmer's Market located at the fairgrounds, that Lee occasionally still attends to this day.

One day during one of Lee's initial visits to my home, as we were seated in my living room discussing the direction that he wished to go with his advertisements, he mentioned an experience he had, just one week earlier.

Lee began by first telling me, "I know we don't know each other very well yet, so I hope you don't think I'm crazy, or some kind of a new age looney. I don't know how else to share this, except to just say that I've had an encounter with a ghost." I was of course taken aback by his announcement, but reassured him I'd listen without judgements and as long as I could ask follow up questions. He accepted and began telling me the story of his encounter with a spirit. Little did I know at the time, but I would also share this 'experience.'

Lee began by telling me that one early Friday morning, while on a 'produce run' to Sacramento, he decided to visit his 78-year-old female friend, Lillian. Lillian lived alone on Sonora's north end, and had recently been released from the hospital. She suffered from diabetic complications, and a long battle with congestive heart disease. Lillian and Lee became good friends over the years, and because of her ill health, Lee had become Lillian's transportation to, and from, many of her medical appointments and follow up visits.

On Thursday, the day before he was to drive to Sacramento, Lee spoke to Lillian on the phone. Lee told her he would be visiting her early Friday, the next morning. Lee said that she sounded well, and was in good spirits. On Friday, Lee drove up to Lillian's house, walked up to her front door and turned the knob but the door was locked. She usually left the door unlocked and he would always walk in. This time he gave a few extra loud knocks but still there was no answer. Since Lillian did not respond to his knocks, Lee thought that Lillian must have forgotten about his visit, and had over-slept. Lee told me that he immediately became concerned that something was not right. He called out her name, then heard Lillian softly answer, "Lee, oh Lee come inside honey."

At this point in Lee's story, for an unknown reason, I became covered in goose-bumps. I felt the hair on the back of my neck stand on end! Not wanting to interrupt his story, I kept these sensations to myself, and allowed Lee to continue.

Lee continued, responding to Lillian's invitation to come inside, "Lillian the door is locked. You need to unlock the door." When Lillian did not respond, Lee took a peek through the window and saw a darkened living room.

Lee called out again and repeated, "Lillian, unlock the door." Still not getting a response, Lee walked around back to Lillian's backyard, and up the few stairs leading to the back porch door. He found the door unlocked, and went inside.

Upon stepping into the hallway from the kitchen, Lee could see light coming from Lillian's bedroom. The bedroom door was opened, and the lamp on the nightstand next to her bed was on. Lee stood in the hallway, so as not to startle her, and called out her name. When she did not answer, he cautiously walked into her bedroom where he found her lifeless body in bed. Lee said he reached to touch her round face, and when he held it in his hands, it was as cold as a block of ice. Lillian had no doubt been dead for a several hours. Unable to hold back his tears, he said a few prayers, then used her phone to notify the authorities.

I asked Lee the obvious question; what

Lee took a peek through window and saw a dark living room.

he thought about Lillian's disembodied voice answering him from inside the house, a few minutes before he entered? He said, "I was sad and upset, how could I not be, but because I was shocked to find her dead, somehow some of my senses stopped functioning normally."

Lee then looked at me and asked, "Gerald, are you alright, you don't look so good." I nervously said, "You don't know this Lee, but I also had something strange happen to me regarding Lillian." I began my story by reaching for one of my files, then asking him to confirm Lillian's physical address and phone number. After confirming each of the details I had just read to Lee, he looked at me in total shock and amazement." Yes, yes Gerald that's Lillian. Did you also know her?" He asked.

I told Lee that I had called and spoken to Lillian on the phone the FOLLOWING Monday! She had asked me to design an inexpensive business card and letter head logo for her, the month before. Because of personal issues, she assured me she was in no rush, and asked me to take all the time I needed. I called her on Monday at 3 pm to inform her that the work was completed, and she needed to give a final approval on the job before it could be printed. Lillian said, "I'll have to first take care of some 'lose ends.' I'll be by your office sometime before the week is up." How could

Photo captures more than just Lillian's backdoor stairs. Do you see it?!

Lillian have died on Friday morning, and three days later, we spoke by phone? This was absolutely impossible and just blew my mind. It was however true. I called, she answered, we spoke about the project and planned to meet up later that week.

Lee and I were speechless. At the time, there was nothing either of us could say explain this, other than to acknowledge that somehow Lillian's spirit was strong enough to communicate by phone AFTER she passed, and just not ready to crossover to the "other side".

Lillian was scheduled to be buried in two days. I decided to attend the funeral with

Lee. After the funeral, when we arrived at my home, I told Lee that I was going to get rid of the work I had completed for Lillian. I needed to clear my mind. I gathered all the paperwork, walked to the backyard, and put everything into the trash dumpster in the alley. I spoke privately asking Lillian that I hope she was satisfied with the logo I had designed for her, and that she did not need to pay me a "home visit" because as far as I was concerned, her account was paid in full!

Thankfully, I've not heard or seen any spooky ghost around my house, and never hope to!" I must admit that from time to time when my office phone rings, I hesitate a little before I answer. Now I wonder if a living person is calling, or could it ever again be a voice from beyond the grave? Now, this second type of call would be absolutely and unforgettably spooky, for sure!

SPRINGFIELD, MA

HARLEN RUSSELL'S STORY

The paranormal experience that I went through took place outside of Springfield, Massachusetts in the winter of 1996, and it left me a changed man forever. I worked as an agent for the Donaldson Jason S – Mulberry Real Estate Group LLC. Additionally, since that day I no longer view strangers, or the homeless as being so distant from my life that they have no direct impact on me, because they absolutely do. I'll explain.

On the early winter morning of my ghostly encounter I had driven to a potential commercial real estate property, from my home a distance of approximately 16 miles. It was a particularly cold and icy morning with a thick snow covering everything. The temperature was in the low teens, very windy and bone chilling cold.

As I approached the store parking lot, I noticed a snow-covered shopping cart that someone had placed directly in front of the main entrance door. I parked my truck, walked up the seven stairs to the cart and pulling back a small carpet, loaded with about three or four inches of snow.

No sooner had I let the carpet and snow fall to the floor, a nearby pile of snow next to the cart moved. I watched in shock as an older man, who looked to be in his late eighties, rolled out from under the snow pile and said, "Hello."

I returned his greeting then asked, "Did you spend the night here?" "Yes sir, I did and I hope that was alright?" He answered. "Yes, yes of course, but don't you have a warmer place to stay. You can't be sleeping outside in this weather!" I said. He said he didn't have any place and would soon be leaving the property entrance.

I told him to be careful, turned around and slipped my key into unlock the lock the door. A few minutes after walking inside the building, I began to think more and more about this man's terrible situation. I thought that the least I should do, was to contact the local sheriff's office and have an officer check on the man's wellbeing. I placed a call to the sheriff and within a few minutes a black and white drove up to the front of the entrance.

From the window, I observed the officer converse with the homeless man. When finished, the officer entered the store and informed me that the old man would be leaving as soon as he got his things together. I said that would be fine. Then the officer drove off.

I began to think about the man's homeless predicament and how he was having to cope with this deadly outdoor weather. I noticed he was just wearing dirty jeans, a light jacket, worn sneakers, a pair of light cotton gloves and a single, dirty wet blanket he used as a shield against the cold. That was it.

As I looked at his face I couldn't help but notice how white his teeth were and although he was covered in dirty and torn clothes, he did not reek of an unpleasant odor. Quite the contrary, he smelled of a mixture that I can only describe as baby powder and oranges, which was indeed pleasant.

I began to think, what more could I do for this person. Then I thought he must be hungry, so I searched around in a refrigerator in the back room of the store where I found a half-filled jug of orange juice and a two-day old bag of fried chicken. I thought, this would have to do.

I heated up the 5 pieces of chicken in the microwave the walked outside to where he was sitting and gave him the food and drink. He thanked me as his hands eagerly accepted the gifts. I left him to eat in private as snow was falling all around.

Within two minutes the snow stopped and I once more walked outside this time with the intention of asking him to come inside to warm up for a few minutes before venturing off, but when I opened the front door he was gone!

When I say he was gone, I mean he had vanished! Just two minutes before, if that, both he and his shopping cart were at my front door and now they were gone. I scanned the stairs in order to spot his tracks, using the freshly fallen snow to track which way he had headed, but there were none!

Immediately I knew what I had just experienced was not of this world, but of the spiritual world. I was so moved by the whole experience that I began to tear up, especially because I had no doubt that I had been visited by a divine spirit.

I'm not a Bible thumper or heavy into any religion at all, but if nothing else I know that at the least, an angel visited me that winter morning in 1996.

The lesson that I carry with me from that blessed morning is that, each one of us is much more responsible for the welfare of all of us as the family of man. We need to understand that every small gesture of caring and compassion is priceless. That is in itself truly divine. I can only hope that this unexpected encounter was a test of compassion and humanity that I passed. I sincerely hope my story will inspire others to reflect on how they might respond if they ever found themselves, face to face, with someone experiencing similar desperate circumstances.

TRUTH OR CONSEQUENCES, NM

KATHY C. ALMENDRO'S STORY

"I'm originally from Eugene, Oregon. My husband and I had been thinking of moving to the southwest for several years prior to our retirement from our carpet and flooring business. We have owned our business for over 19 years and due to our decreasing physical health, we thought it best to south to Tucson, Arizona or New Mexico. Thankfully we chose New Mexico. Arizona's temperature, we quickly found out, was way too hot. Although it does get hot here in Truth or Consequences, aka T or C, the summers are distinctly milder.

In 1992, we found, purchased and moved into a property on a street that fronts the river to the south of town. Our house is not unlike our neighbors' homes; we own a trailer and have a wood deck that is built directly outside our back door. Living next to the river is a fortunate location to have because I'm sensitive to the heat and, even though the summers are mild, it helps cool the air. The close proximity to the river allows cool air to flow over the water and onto the properties, like ours, that borders its banks.

During the period that the realtor showed us the property, we visited at least ten houses before settling on this one, which appealed to us the most. The doublewide trailer was a fairly new one, but strangely when we did the walk-through, it was not difficult to notice that all the windows that faced the river had a doll positioned in such a manner that it looked out. Each window, without exception, had a doll sitting on its sill.

I immediately thought to ask the obvious question to the realtor, "Why are these dolls at only these windows and not anywhere else throughout the house?"

The realtor had no idea, and jokingly responded, "Well, the elderly woman who owns the home must like to have them keep an eye on her whenever she's sitting outside on the deck. You can never have too much company!" My husband Ralph and I looked at each other, but aside from thinking this strangely weird behavior to be the workings of a senior mind gone crazy, we dropped the issue and a few hours later purchased the property.

My husband, Ralph and I never did get the opportunity to meet with the seller, so after closing the deal, we moved in sometime in October. Fortunately, the seller did not own a cat or dog, she kept a clean house that was in move in condition.

Two days following our move, Ralph came up to where I was sitting in the living room and said, "Kathy, you've got to come outside and see what I found." We walked out the back door and down and around to the front of the wood deck.

Attached to all the wood framing of the deck that faced the river was a large collection of crucifixes, religious charms and actual bible pages attached to the wood frame with push pins! Now, all this stuff was haphazardly done, giving the impression that it had been worked on within a few minutes, and no doubt, just a few hours prior to our actual move into the house.

Ralph and I had no idea what to make of this bazaar discovery. Ralph spoke first saying, "This is the work of the seller and this is really weird behavior. She's the one behind all those dolls propped up facing the window!"

I responded, "Yep, I think you're right. This can only be a direct connection to her. What a crazy old broad."

We had no use for these items, so I walked over to our laundry area grabbed an empty cardboard box, went back to the deck and quickly removed all the paraphernalia. It was clear that this old woman worked so hard to attach all this to the deck. After removing and collecting everything, I drove to the center of town and deposited the contents into a charity collection and donation bin.

About three or four weeks later, I was in the front of the house, the side closest to the street, sitting in the living room. Suddenly I distinctly heard the back door open then slam shut! The door slammed with such a force that I physically jumped a little off my chair. I called out, "Ralph, what's wrong with you? You're going to slam that door off its hinges!" Expecting to hear my husband's voice answer me, I only heard footsteps coming towards me. As I heard Ralph entering the room, I turned around in my chair expecting to see him, but instead I didn't see anyone. I didn't know what to think but I know what I heard, solid footsteps coming towards me.

The following day, I was returning from grocery shopping and approaching the house from the back door. It was noon and a beautiful bright day. I parked the car on the side of the house and walked up the stairs that led up to the back door. I was attempting to walk holding two

149

full bags of groceries, place the key in the lock and open the door all at once but it was not easy.

As I opened the door, I spotted the back of Ralph's head protruding at the top of his chair, rocking back and forth in the living room. I yelled out to Ralph, "Hey, can you please help me? Didn't you hear me drive up just now?" When there was no response from Ralph, I asked again, "Ralph, what's the matter with you? Didn't you hear me? I said, could you give me a hand with these sacks?"

I placed the grocery sacks haphazardly on top of the kitchen table turned to confront Ralph in the living room but Ralph was nowhere to be seen. His rocking chair slowly came to a stop, as if my husband had just risen off it! I didn't hear him get up, walk away or even move. I was speechless. Without waiting another minute, I ran out the back door, got into the car and drove away thinking that wasn't Ralph but perhaps an intruder. I called Ralph on his cell phone and found out that he was not even in the house but visiting with a friend in town. I explained what I had seen and then called the police.

The police investigated the house, the closets and anywhere else that a person might hide. The house was empty and no one was found to be anywhere inside or around the outside of the property. My jewelry and personal items of value were still where I had placed them. Absolutely nothing was out of place. With Ralph accompanying me through the back door and into the house, we talked about what I had seen and then together we chose to explain it as having imagined it all. Without any rational reason to totally satisfy me, this decision was the easiest and best at the time.

The next time something weird happened in the house, was exactly two days later. It was a Saturday evening; I was at the kitchen sink, rinsing a pot of beets that I was preparing for our early dinner. As I was bent over the sink, I immediately felt a cold sensation move from my two shoulders and up my head! The sensation followed along through my neck and wrapped around the whole upper half of my body! I let out a scream knowing something had just touched me. I dropped the beets into the sink, and ran into the living room looking for Ralph.

Ralph heard me and came running inside through the back door. My heart was beating so fast I thought I was going to have an attack or faint right on the spot! As Ralph took hold of me, I shaking and started crying uncontrollably like a baby. I told Ralph what had happened and he held onto me. "I know baby, I know," he said. "I also had something happen to me in the kitchen right after that day you thought you saw me rocking in my chair. I didn't want to tell you about it because I knew you'd react like this."

Ralph said, "I was outside at the carport when my eyes caught the image of a man standing inside the house at the kitchen window. I looked at him for a few seconds and he instantly disappeared. I grabbed the iron bar I had placed at the side of the house, ran into the house and was expecting to confront the intruder you said you saw in our living room. When I entered the house, I looked everywhere and there was nobody. I believe you, baby. I think we have a ghost in the house." I was shocked! There is not another word to describe my terror; I was shocked by what Ralph had just said.

After wiping my tears, I felt so enraged by this news that I sternly spoke to Ralph, "God damn it Ralph, do you know how much I've struggled with all this? I've been thinking one minute I'm going nuts then I think I'm not well and I maybe having a nervous breakdown! What are we going to do about this? How are we going to get rid of it?" Ralph answered, "I'm sorry I didn't tell you about this. I didn't want to upset you more than I already knew you were. In answer to your question, what are we going to do? I don't know. I just don't know."

Even after all that Ralph and I had experienced, I dug my heels in and shouted out, "Damn you ghost man, you're not going to get to us, I won't let you!" And with that both Ralph and I resolved to stay put and fight this thing! Our courage and strength to fight on lasted for only about another week until the ultimate example of the ghost's anger caused us to seriously regret our home purchase.

Like I said, this last encounter took place about a week later. Ralph and I were in bed when the phone rang at 11:05 p.m. I was reading my magazine when the cell phone's ring startled me. I answered the phone and heard my neighbor's voice from across the street say she was calling to find out if we were all right. "What do you mean, June? We're fine. Why?" I said.

June responded in a very distressed voice, "Kathy, there's a fire in your living room! I just looked out the window and your living room is on fire!"

I jumped out of bed and yelled to Ralph, "Quick Ralph, our house is on fire!" We both ran into the living room expecting to see flames shooting every which way, but saw nothing. Not a single flame or even the slightest scent of smoke. While still holding the phone in my hand, I said, "June, I'm standing right in the living room and everything is fine." At this very moment, as soon as I paused to take a breath, both Ralph and I heard the deep laugh of a man's voice over our heads, in the living room. Not something you'd expect to hear or want to hear in the middle of the night!

Suddenly, a hard knock came at the front door. I opened the door with much apprehension. Standing outside in the darkness was our neighbor June. I invited her inside and turned on the lights. The look on June's face was total shock. "How on earth? she asked "I saw your living room all blazing with flames! she continued, I just can't believe this!"

I tried to calm her by saying, "I don't understand what's happening, but thank you for calling me. You don't know how much I appreciate your call." After a few minutes, June left and Ralph and I were sitting in the living room. At that moment, we decided we had no choice but to move out for our peace of mind and now safety.

We listed the house and within three months, the house sold to a couple that owned three dogs. We never mentioned the ghostly sightings that we experienced at the house to the real estate agent or new owners. We didn't want anyone to think Ralph and I were mentally unstable. We've kept these haunting episodes to ourselves and never even mentioned them to our former neighbor, June. We couldn't help but wonder if she might have had some information about former owners and the history of any unexplained activity she may have observed, such as the night she called to alert us about a fire in our living room that she insisted she saw.

As it stands today, we've now lived in T or C for several years and are living in a beautiful, property free from any supernatural surprises or ghosts of any kind. Good riddance is all I can say. In our case, the ghost was successful in removing us from that property; we sold the house but who knows what the new owners have experienced. I see them in town and usually exchange a friendly wave, but I never have found the courage to ask them anything other than, "How are you?" They don't show any external signs of stress or fatigue so I'm just going to assume they're comfortable with the property."

TUOLUMNE, CA

In 1848 the Reverend James Wood discovered gold in Tuolumne County near present day Jamestown. Just one year later, thousands of miners invaded the numerous county's streams and gulches, setting up camps and seeking their fortunes in the hard-rock mine business. Soon permanent stone, brick and wood buildings began to replace the miners canvas tents. The established new town of Sonora sprang from this wealth of venture seekers, and in no-time became the county seat, as it remains to this day.

As the first world war broke out, newcomers settled in the area, and tired their luck at the more stable logging and ranching business. Tuolumne soon became the center of California's timber industry. In 1897 the railroad came into Tuolumne County and began another definite boon, which benefitted both the mining and timber industries.

In its recent history, the Hollywood film industry discovered Tuolumne County, and used its scenic beauty for various movie and television productions. From the 1960's to the present, many visitors have discovered the area as a beautiful, and somewhat affordable area in which to retire.

ROBERT AND NANCE BELL'S STORY

When the actual day arrived for my wife Nance and I to make the move out of Fresno, we thought long and hard of retiring to Kingman Arizona, where our daughter and her family had moved a few years before. However, the more we thought about this possibility, it just didn't make much sense for us to pick-up, and move several hundred miles away to an unfamiliar town. Having both lived and worked all our lives up to that point in California, it was difficult to imagine moving out of the state and starting over in Arizona. Being both in our mid-sixties, our options were limited to a great extent. When we did sell our home, we looked for a nice, quiet, rural community not far from Fresno, in the gold rush area of northern California.

Well, the day arrived, and the three of us, Nance, myself and our small dog Cindy, got in our RV and traveled into the Sierra Nevada mountain range of the state. We located a realtor, and searched for about two weeks investigating all the small towns in the area. Our real estate agent in Sonora, California eventually located a quaint little three bed room house, on 4 acres in the southeastern area of Calaveras county, not far from Tuolumne. Nance and I knew immediately this was where we would make our new home.

Because of its age, the house was in need of a few upgrades, but nothing that would take any major construction. On the property was a detached garage, a workshop and a chicken coop made of wood and rusted wire and hinges. Over the years, from lack of use and neglect, half the chicken house had fallen to the ground. I was drawn to it from the start. I guess it's strangely familiar design brought back old memories of my childhood in Nebraska. My family raised a breed of chicken, named Barred Rock. My

grandmother was very fond of a particular coop that grandfather constructed similar to the one on this property. The uniqueness of the wire-enclosed run, the nesting boxes stacked four levels, and where the door was located on the east side rekindled wonderful childhood memories for me.

While Nance got busy with

The chicken coop was almost an exact replica. decorating the house, general landscaping and replanting the garden with new bulbs, I got busy updating the other three buildings, included the chicken house. We wanted to keep a few chickens for fresh organic eggs, so I knew I would soon have to get to fixing up that old chicken house sooner than later.

When we moved unto the property, I didn't notice anything strange, or out of the ordinary that I could label ghostly, or paranormal. Nance, on the other hand, did have an experience. She mentioned hearing someone's footsteps waking in the middle of the night throughout the house. She didn't place much importance to this, until the frightening experience we both had one early evening, while seated in our living room.

At that time, we had been living in the house for about three weeks. It was about 6 or 7pm, I was writing a letter to my sister, and Nance was reading a new gardening book she had borrowed from a neighbor. Suddenly, we heard something moving about in the kitchen. I stopped my writing and paused to listen. Nance glanced up from her book and softly asked, "Robert, did you hear that?" I answered, "Stay still, it might be a mouse, I'll go see where it is." As soon as got up and off my chair, we both heard a male voice coming from the kitchen, whispering unintelligible words.

"Don't panic," I said, "Just stay where you are." I walked to the kitchen and because there was still enough sun light coming into the room to make things visible, I didn't bother to switch on the light. But when I entered the kitchen, my nose was immediately hit by the overpowering odor of sweat, human perspiration!

As I searched around our small kitchen looking for a source or evidence, I checked the door leading out to the back yard. It was locked. I looked up and glanced out through the small window built into the door, I noticed nothing unusual in the yard. Suddenly, I heard the sound of a cabinet door open to my right, and as I turned around towards the sink, I spotted Nance standing by the entrance to the kitchen. Nance was pointing at the kitchen cabinet and for me to take notice of something.

The cabinet door began to slowly open on its own, and then quickly opened all the way! This was followed by the door next to it, which also quickly opened. Without realizing it, I ran over to Nance's side. The tension and energy in the room was intense. Something was definitely not right. Call it a ghost or spirit, I became a believer that very instant. At the time, I never believed in the paranormal, but at the same time I really didn't disbelieve in such things as ghosts or spirits, it's just that I've never seen any. Like most people, I needed proof.

I knew Nance felt the same as I did about ghosts. From time to time, we've both had friends come to us with crazy stories about things they've read, or what they heard on the television but overall we just were not the type of people who believed in such things. But what my wife and I both experienced that day caused us to rethink the whole ghost 'thing."

I quickly moved over in front of the cabinet, and thinking I might spot a small animal, I carefully looked inside but saw nothing. I closed the doors and turned to Nance. "What the hell was that?" I said. Nance answered, "Robert we have a ghost. What are we going to do?" Immediately, a small glass vase with flowers that Nance had set on the window sill, moved off the sill and came crashing to the floor, sending glass shards everywhere! Instinctively I yelled, "Okay, you can leave us alone now. Do you hear, we want you to leave us alone!"

As soon as I finished talking, we heard the same whispering man's ghostly voice speak, "Damn you Robert, damn you Robert." Just as before, the atmosphere in the kitchen was thick with the odor of sweat. Nance looked at me, then walked out towards the living room and sat motionless in her chair.

I asked, "What just happened in there? Nance, you heard the voice too, didn't you?" Nance responded, "Yes, and I think we have a big problem Robert. I don't think it was smart of you to anger the spirit like you did." I attempted to convince Nance that I was not wanting to argue with any ghost, but seeing that Nance was under a lot of stress, I let it go.

After that first encounter with the spirit, I had another unusual occurrence. One morning, after breakfast, I took a short walk out to the chicken house. I loaded up the wheel barrow with screws, nails, hammer, wire and a saw. Whoever built the chicken house must have been a very precise woodworker, because on closer inspection, I noticed the expertly made clean-cut notches, and framing the builder had made. This was not just a regular chicken house it was crafted to be a very nice work to be proud of. Having worked on a few wood projects myself, I could totally appreciate this.

Over the years, and through many seasons of snow and summer sun, the structure had weathered well through the seasons. A few rotted boards and hinges were in need of replacement, as was the roof, but except for this and some new galvanized wire, not much more would be needed—just the chickens. I got busy with the needed repair work and because of my intense focus, I didn't even notice the hours pass by. I glanced at my watch, it was 1:30 pm and I was expected Nance to call me to the house for lunch.

I decided to leave what I was doing to get some food in me, and walked back to the house. I placed my saw on top of an old wood box, and noticed a piece of red cloth a few feet away, protruding out from underneath a fallen nest box. It caught my interest, and decided to pull it out. At first, I thought it was just an old piece of shirt. I held one corner of the box, and as I reached down, I spotted a rattlesnake!

I must have jumped about three feet off the ground! It gave me quite a scare. I dropped the box, but soon regained my senses and watched as the snake harmlessly slithered away, disappearing into some brush. I made quite sure the snake had moved on. I used a long stick to tap the nest box, then reached in for the red cloth.

As I pulled on one corner of the cloth, I discovered it was a handkerchief. This handkerchief had been used to wrapped some small square object. As I gave a stronger tug on the handkerchief, it tore away from my hand, over time the cloth had mildewed and rotted. Using my stick, I moved the wrapped object away from the box, then rolled it out onto the ground. I picked it up and began to unwrap the rotted handkerchief.

It didn't take much to remove the cloth and soil from what I could now see was a small leather wallet. I carefully opened the wallet, and could tell by its condition that it was very old. It was made up of just one compartment, or pocket, not a wallet of the modern-day type with slots for credit cards, and a plastic view window for a driver's license, this was for its time, a practical man's wallet for carrying bill currency and not much

A small leather wallet!

else.

I carried the wallet out into the bright sunlight, away from the shaded canopy of black oak trees where the chicken house was located, and leaned my back against a tree. I opened the wallet and found three things that the mold had not completely rotted away. There was a short personal letter with the words written in pencil, "Tom, you need to meet the cart from Sacramento on the 14th. Iron straps. The office will pay your fee at the gate. Don't be late." This letter was dated August 6, 1943 and was signed, "Howard." The second thing I found tucked in the wallet's pocket was a $1.00 U.S. bill. The last item that was a tucked into one corner pocket was a small metal crucifix. That was all. I discovered nothing to identify the owner's name or address.

Upon entering the house a few minutes later, I showed Nance what I had found. She looked at the wallet and said, "I bet someone might have stolen it, then forgot where they placed it, otherwise why would it be inside of a chicken's nest box?" Nance held the wallet in her hand, then lifted it to her nose, "Robert, have you taken a good sniff at this. Doesn't it remind you of something?" She said. Her words jarred my memory. I took it from her and sure enough the wallet's musty odor scent was exactly the same odor that we had both smelled when we had our ghostly visit in the kitchen a few days earlier. I have to say that I was a bit unnerved at that point.

I decided then and there, that the best place to take the wallet would be outside, away from the house. Without wasting any time, I got up from the table and walked straight outside to the garage. I placed the wallet inside a small cardboard box, and placed the box on a shelf, where it has stayed to this day.

One evening about a week or so later, we were both in the front yard. Nance was watering her new flower beds, and I was sitting on the stairs. We were talking about what we would next focus on as far as improving the property. I suggested we remove a large tree that over the years, was now more than 50% rotted away. Instead of describing to Nance how I would go about sawing away certain branches, I asked her to follow me to the back yard so I could specifically show her. Nance turned off the water, and as we began to walk to the back yard, our dog Cindy ran up ahead of us and began to bark uncontrollably.

As we neared the tree, Cindy came running back to us, and ceased her barking. Immediately we thought a cat or squirrel had frightened her. As I reached down to comfort Cindy, I noticed she nervously jumped away from my hand and focused her attention to the area where the clump of trees, and chicken house was. Both Nance and I also turned our attention to where our dog was focused, and what we saw scared the hell out of us!

Standing there by the chicken house was the ghostly image of a man walking very slowly around the shrubbery! The image had a phosphorescent glow to it. Not a very bright light, just enough for us to make out its form, and to know this was a man. At one point, he bent down straightened up, continuing walking. He didn't wear a hat, or any other identifying clothing, it was just the outline of a man's figure.

Nance and I spoke in whispered voices. I said, "Can this be true. Nance we're actually seeing a ghost!" Nance said, "I knew something was not right. And I bet this might have something to do with the wallet."

Somehow I worked up the nerve to yell out to the ghost, "Hey, hey there, what are you doing? What are you doing over there?" The ghost gave no indication that it heard me, it just continued to walk about the area in an aimless manner. We continued to watch it, more like mesmerized by it for about two minutes. I had no need to walk on over and confront it. Our dog Cindy with an occasional whimper now and then, laid on the grass next to Nance, and stared at the ghostly figure, we all did.

I told Nance I was going to phone a neighbor and have them come over to watched the ghost with us. Obviously, the ghost was not going away, so we might as well have more witnesses. As I walked into the house, I switched on a light and reached for the phone. I heard Nance yell out, "Robert, it disappeared!" Just at that moment, the strong odor of sweat came into the room!

What would a ghost want with a wallet that only has $1.00 in it?

I decided not to "tempt" the ghost any further. I said, "Okay, no problem, we're not going to bother you, just please go back outside!" Nance came into the house and without me saying anything, she said, "Robert, the smell is back, can you smell it?" I said, "Yes, I can. Then told Nance to hurry and turn on all the lights in the house."

The odor lingered in the house for about ten minutes, all the time giving us an unsettling feeling of knowing the ghost was in the house with us. Happily, nothing was moved or broken. Eventually the odor left, and we had no further sightings or activity since that night.

I don't know why or how we managed to stop this but as of today, the odor and apparition has not come back. We've lived on the property for close to six years now. Nance and I have discussed the possibility that maybe the wallet has something to do with the ghost. But what would a ghost want with a wallet that only had a note and a $1.00 bill? We have spoken to our daughter and a neighbor about the ghost, but they just listened to our story, and had nothing significant to add to this experience.

We've discovered that it's not too difficult for us to live with a ghost. I have fourteen laying hens in the chicken house now, and like I said, since the last incident, my wife and I have not had any more visits from the ghost. I just make sure to feed and care for the chickens during the daylight hours. No way am I going to venture out there when the sun goes down. I don't want any more encounters with spirits, or rattlesnakes. No way!

I'm a little concerned that now that we've shared my story, this doesn't somehow cause things to start up again. I'm not sure how I would react if this spirit or smell returns just because I've talked about it. I do hope my storing the wallet away keeps that spirit outside and away from entering the house. Beyond this, there is not much more to say.

PET HAUNTINGS

AMADOR CITY, CA

Amador City and County are both named for a wealthy California rancher, Jose Maria Amador. The major creek he mined for gold was named after him, "Amadores's Creek." Out cropping's of gold ore were numerous along Amador's Creek and were extensively worked for the precious metal. In the summer of 1851 Amador City was established. Amador's first mines were the "Original" or "Little" to the north, and the "Spring Hill" located to the south of town. The town's most productive mine of all was the "Keystone" which produced close to $24 million in the yellow ore.

Today Amador County covers an area of 568 square miles of grassy, delicate rolling hills on its western edge, and a craggy, rough mountainous landscape to its eastern boundary. The county was established in 1854, with the town of Jackson as its county seat.

In 1878, a devastating fire consumed most every building on Amador's main street, sparing only two, the Fleehart, and the facade of the Amador Hotel. Because of its susceptibility to fire, building with wood became quite dangerous, and was replaced with brick and stone. Tin roofs also were incorporated into new buildings, and attics were lined with sand and bricks, in the hope of preventing dangerous wayward sparks from taking hold. Safety measures such as these, helped to preserve the majority of Amador's buildings for over 120 years.

IVAN THOMAS'S STORY

I've lived in Amador all my life. My parents, were both were raised in Stockton, California. In 1924 they moved to Amador City right after getting married. My father was soon offered a better paying job with the state forest service at Lake Tahoe, and once again, they moved. In less than one year, my father was injured on the job when a large tree limb fell, and broke his right leg and hip. He was disabled from that day on.

With what little money my parents had saved, and with the money from his disability check, they moved south and purchased a small ranch house on ten acres just outside Amador City. A few months after, I was born. My birth was followed by my sister Sandra, and my youngest sister Helen. Of all my family, today the only ones left living are Sandra and myself. Sandra currently lives in a rest home in Sacramento.

Sandra lived at the house until she had to be moved to Sacramento. I couldn't take care of her, so it was decided the best thing was for her to move to Sacramento. Her son lives in Sacramento, and is now able to visit with her more often. I don't think she'll be living much longer, the last time I visited her, she didn't recognize me.

So now it's just me, and my small dog Colonel. I raised Colonel since he was a puppy. His mother was kicked by a neighbor's horse, and the litter of puppies was left without a mother. I bottle fed Colonel for about a month before he could eat on his own. He's my little guy. He lets me know when anyone comes on to the property—living or dead!

About three years ago, before Sandra moved away, Colonel was asleep out on the front porch. That's where I have his bed, you can go see it, its right over there, under the bench. As a puppy, he took to liking that cardboard box so much, that even after he got older, he would walk inside it and fall asleep. He's never been happier. I guess it makes the little guy feel safe.

Well, one afternoon, while my sister and I were seated at the kitchen table, we heard Colonel barking in the front yard. We walked outside on the porch and saw him barking, and barking at nothing in particular. He was just barking at the thin air.

I turned to Sandra and asked her, "What's going on here." We didn't have any explanation for Colonel's weird behavior. He kept barking, then suddenly we saw all the hair on his back began to rise, and he started to growl in a low 'throaty' sound. We could see that his eyes were focused on an invisible "thing" and he was not about to look away or be distracted. Suddenly, he ran back as if something lunged at him, then he quickly ran back and tried to snap at whatever it was that had attacked him. This went on for a short time before we saw him recoil in pain, as if he were hit by something or someone.

I had had enough and intervened by placing myself between my dog and whatever was attacking him. As soon as I positioned myself in front of the dog, whatever it was made its way around me, and went directly into the house with Colonel bolting right behind it! My sister and I were suddenly scared, and as Sandra stood holding the front door open with one hand, and then with the other hand she made the sign of the cross over her chest. Goosebumps sprang up all over my neck and arms.

My sister and I went into the house and found Colonel barking madly at one corner of the living room. It appeared as if whatever this was, a spirit or ghost, was somehow in the wall! Colonel was going nuts. In just a few seconds Colonel stopped barking and indicated that he wanted to be let outside. When I opened the door for him, he went straight for his water bowl and drinking.

That day we were both left with many unanswered questions. Luckily, we both felt comforted by our dog's protective nature. We knew that if there were any future 'visits' by a spirit or ghost, Colonel would not let them get the upper hand. Or so we thought.

A friend of Sandra's came over that evening, and invited both Sandra and Colonel to her home for the weekend. I decided not to let my fear get the better of me, so I chose to stay home.

Later that night I was awakened by a loud noise in the kitchen, that sounded like a dish crashing to the floor. It startled me to the point where I stood sitting upright in bed! After I listened for a few minutes and heard nothing else. Thinking I was dreaming, I decided to lie back in bed and try to fall asleep.

As I began to close my eyes, I first heard the sound of a soft mumbling voice. A coldness came over me because I immediately knew the ghost had returned. I kept quiet, and could only make out that it was a male voice, but the words were not at all clear. There was also a tone of anger in the voice. A rapid muttering, mixed with anger is how I would put it. So much was racing in my mind at that moment. I found it difficult to move. I decided to just lie in bed and hope it would go away. The voice stopped abruptly but I didn't have time to breathe a sigh of relief because

I heard the doorknob begin to slowly turn.

something else started happening. I began to hear the sound of footsteps coming down the hall from the kitchen, and they were making their way towards my room! I was completely, and fully awake at that moment. I'm not ashamed to admit that I was terrified.

As the footsteps came closer, I braced myself for what I might see. My imagination went wild with the thought of seeing a bloody face, a skull, or even something worst. As I said, my imagination was going crazy. As the footsteps reached my closed bedroom door, I heard the door knob begin to slowly turn. I couldn't take any more. I jumped out of bed and turned on the lights. I grabbed the door knob and swung it opened. There was no ghost, or anything visible at all. I was relieved but also unnerved by the experience.

The next morning, I phoned Sandra and described what I had experienced. She said that because of what we had both experienced with our dog the day before, the thing must have returned. I didn't want to allow my imagination take the better of me. So, I decided not to talk or think about it any further.

Later that evening, around the same time as before, I was awakened by a dish breaking in the kitchen, and the footsteps started up again. This time, I knew I was not imaging any of this. This was real, and it was in my house!

I was even more scared then the night before. As the footsteps came closer and closer towards my bedroom door, I began to pray out loud. As the footsteps stopped outside my door, once again I heard the door knob begin to turn. I kept quiet and opened my eyes wide. Keeping still, the door slowly opened and the sound of the footsteps walked into my room. I was shaking by that point, frozen with fear. I tried hard not to make any sudden move, and to pretended I was asleep.

The footsteps came right up to the side of the bed and stopped. In a few seconds, I felt the side of my mattress compress as if someone had sat on it. No kidding, I actually felt the side of the mattress move. At that moment, the word 'fear' cannot even begin to describe how I felt. Not knowing what to next expect, I felt the absolute sensation of a cold face brush against mine. I knew it was a face because I could hear its heavy breathing in my ear! I was shaking.

The next thing that the ghost did was to laugh directly in my ear! It was a menacing laugh, a devilish and very evil kind of laugh. It wasn't very loud, but it was eerie alright. Something stirred in me right at that moment! I called the name of 'Jesus' to help me as I sat upright in bed! Directly at the foot of my bed I saw the ghost! He was a short, round-type of man, wearing a French brown beret, a white shirt buttoned to the neck, and wearing a brown suit. No tie, or jewelry. With both hands, he held on to the belt at his side as he gazed at me with a glaring smile.

I don't know how or why, but my fear subsided and I got the courage to ask," Why are you here?" He looked at me with an inquisitive face, slowly and slightly bending a little towards me. He paused and then quickly leaned back and without making any noise, appeared to let out a huge laugh! Whatever he must have made of my question, gave him a lot humor. He closed his eyes, and opened his mouth as he laughed, and laughed.

I couldn't take my eyes off him. This whole experience took place in under a minute, definitely not any longer. Then this short fat ghost began to disappear. Just slowly into nothingness. He laughed himself into thin air. I began to see the bedroom wall behind him as he started to vanish, until he quickly and totally vanished from the room!

I was left with a feeling of freedom. Somehow, I knew that he would not be returning ever again. I knew there would never be anymore footsteps, breaking glass and teasing of my dog. He was gone for good!

Why was he visiting our house, did he have a message to deliver? Who knows, perhaps he didn't want to do anything more than have some fun before moving on to who knows where? Nothing paranormal has taken place in this house since that time. Nothing at all. I can't explain why this man would want to be in our house.

Strange to admit that I'm glad it happened to me. It scared the 'you know what' out of me, but I'm better for the experience. Now I know for sure that this life is not the end of us. We go on further after we die to somewhere else, and I truly believe this.

SILVERTHORNE, CO

In 1859, the Breckenridge gold rush ushered in the influx of Summit County's first settlements. The town of Silverthorne is situated within Summit County on Interstate 70, lying roughly between Denver and Vail. Silverthorne offers the visitor a more affordable alternative to the more costlier choices available in the surrounding major ski-area towns.

Jointly sharing its delightful mountain location with other, more well known, lively, skiing destinations within Summit County, Silverthorne is considered the ski area's gateway town. One beautiful aspect of Silverthorne is the Blue River that flows right through town, attracting fly fishermen from beyond the town's boundaries.

Of note are the Silverthorne Factory Stores, encompassing over 70 name-brand outlets with offer bargain prices. Also, a well- known, regular routine followed by skiers, due to its better value for money, is to rent skis in Silverthorne, then venture out to Vail mountain.

ARTHUR PATTERSON'S STORY

Arthur, his wife Della, and I met together in their living room for the interview. Throughout the interview Della wept as Arthur was moved to a few tears. Their story pertains to their beloved dog, Georgie, and their strong, spiritual bond. Sad as it ultimately ends, their story is beautiful in its emotional impact, as it outlines the strong bond they shared between themselves and their pet.

Throughout the years of many interviews I've conducted with individuals for their personal stories, I've come across a few that have involved animals. This particular story is one of my favorites, due to its raw degree of emotion and psychic perception.

After reading this story, the question may be pondered; do animals possess the ability to communicate with us in a manner that is consistent with our own abilities? Who can say, but after reading this story, it might not be that difficult to gain an insight into the possibility that it may be so.

— Antonio

"I've lived in Silverthorne for only about nine years, not much time, but plenty enough to know the town and area well enough to be happy with my retirement. It's interesting that you happened to come across me at this time, because what I experienced just happened two weeks ago, right in this house.

My wife and I had left for a week's vacation to Denver to relax and just take in the city. Our children live out of state, so our only responsibility is Georgie, a German shepherd dog we've owned for 11 years. We had asked a neighbor to look after the house and property, and to feed and care for our dog in our absence.

It was early morning and I was driving my wife and I home on Interstate 70. We were returning back home, coming down from the mountain at about 7 a.m., when the strangest thought came to my mind. I had an image that flashed before me like the picture frames of a movie. I saw a mental movie of our dog, barking and yelping uncontrollably. She was in obvious pain and I felt as if I needed to hurry and get home as soon as possible. I turned to my wife and told her of my unusual thoughts, and she said, "Oh Arthur, you're missing that dog as if it were one of your kids. Georgie is fine, you know she's in good hands." But I could not get the thought out of my head. It was very real to me, and my thoughts were compelling me to hurry home—quickly. I kept hearing my dog's barking in my ears. Never have I had such thoughts that were so vivid as this.

My wife kept telling me to slow down, and reminding me about the posted speed limit, but as soon as I'd slow down, I'd very soon start to speed up again, until I was ultimately stopped, and given a ticket by a highway patrolman. In the process of the officer writing the ticket, my wife was reminding me of how dangerous I was driving. But through it all, my mind was preoccupied with my mental picture of Georgie's howling and yelping. Eventually, we were off again and this time I was driving a lot more cautiously.

As soon as we drove up to our house and into the driveway, I told my wife that I was going to first check on our dog. I walked to the door that leads to the backyard, but it was locked from the inside. I whistled for Georgie, but there was silence. Thinking that the neighbor had taken her for a morning walk, I went next door and knocked on his front door. He answered. I had obviously awakened him from sleep.

I asked him how things went during our absence, he said fine except for the night before. He said, "Georgie must have seen an animal of some sort that she wanted to run after. She was barking and making a lot of noise. I went to see what was going on, but didn't spot anything unusual. Just in case, I decided to put her on her long yard chain to be sure she would not run off. I did check on her before going to bed and noticed that she had been digging in a few areas along the base of the backyard's tall, chain link fence. Aside from that, I haven't checked on her since, but as far as I'm aware, she's fine."

I told him that I had whistled for Georgie, but had not got a response. He said, "I hope she didn't get loose. I hooked the clasp on her collar, and made sure it was pretty secure." Then he added, "I'll come over and see you in a few minutes, just let me get dressed."

I walked over to our house's front door and immediately walked through the house, towards the kitchen, to the back door. As I entered the kitchen, I found my wife crying. I asked her what was wrong. She said, "Go take a look." She pointed to the backyard. I opened the door and was shocked to see my dog hanging from a portion of the backyard's six-foot high fence—obviously dead!

I walked to the fence and could tell that Georgie had attempted, and succeeded in, climbing her way up and over the fence, but the chain that had kept her from running off had caused her death. The collar and chain functioned as a noose. Due to its short length, Georgie had jumped over the fence, but was unsuccessful in reaching the ground. She had hung herself in the process of climbing over the fence. Georgie was suspended about two feet off the ground, in mid-fall against the fence. By her body's condition, stiff with death, it was clear that she had died within hours of our return.

Was our dog's spirit somehow attempting to spiritually contact me? Do animals have this ability as I've heard humans supposedly do? After I personally experienced this with my dog, I've been left a changed person. I do believe that we, and all living things, have the ability to communicate after death. Georgie had indeed been communicating with great urgency and mental images racing through my mind. I said in the beginning, this just happened two weeks ago, so it's all still fresh in my memory."

STEAMBOAT SPRINGS, CO

JOANNE PARENTI'S STORY

I conducted the interview with Joanne at her neighbor Olivia's home. During the interview, Olivia kept Joanne and I well hydrated and fed with her frequent visits, by refilling our glasses with fresh tea and placing a plate stacked high with homemade raisin cookies.

I could easily tell that both these women were very close friends and were so happy to host a visiting writer. When the time came for me to move on to my other appointments, it was difficult to bid farewell to these two accommodating ladies.

Joanne's personal story is quite unusual in that it includes an animal spirit. However, such stories as these offer us all just another unique, spiritual avenue to contemplate—animals and the after-life.

— Antonio

"I was born in Denver and at the age of three, my parents moved us to Tacoma, Washington, where I spent the remainder of my youth and young adult years. Many years later my husband, a 19-year-old daughter and I decided to move back to Colorado and settled in Steamboat Springs. My story involves several very active ghosts, and one that took the form of an animal.

I began working at Steamboat Lake State Park soon after moving to the area when a park ranger and I happened to meet one evening at a mutual friend's home. After introducing him to my husband we discovered that the ranger was related to my father's family. He told me about a job opening coming up at the Dutch Hill Campground. The job was caretaker of the laundry and shower facilities. I applied for the job and was hired a few weeks later.

My responsibilities involved not much more than physical work, work I was happy to do. The job was physically demanding, but gave me the opportunity to meet and talk with visitors from all over Colorado and the nation. One visitor to the campground, a woman of about 60 years of age named Pamela Dover, asked me after talking with her for some time, if I would also be interested in caring for her elderly mother who lived in town. The job would start at the beginning of the winter, which would fit perfectly into my schedule, as the park 's campground closes for the season then.

I started as caretaker for Pamela's elderly mother, with whom I immediately felt so relaxed and comfortable with. She reminded me of an aunt that I had been close to and who died when I was only 16 years old. The elder Mrs. Dover was born and raised in Colorado, and was, at the time, facing the inevitable end of her life from a severe, chronic life-long disease. My time with Mrs. Dover did not last very long because within just a few months of being hired, she died unexpectedly.

After Mrs. Dover's death, her daughter, Pamela, asked me to stay on as a housekeeper. Given the fact that my family needed the extra money, and we both lived nearby, I agreed and was soon balancing two jobs, which once again, I found fitted into my schedule perfectly. But, the unforeseen, unusual events were not expected, planned for, or welcomed by any stretch of my imagination.

One Saturday morning about 7 am, I was at the Dover house alone, trying to remove the vacuum from the broom closet in the upstairs hallway. I suddenly heard the sound of a cat meowing in the bedroom down the hall. I knew from working at the home for many months that the owners did not own a cat, or even like cats. I walked over to the bedroom, opened the door and was surprised to see a light gray cat sitting on the window's sill, inside the bedroom. Carefully, I move towards the cat, it immediately glared and hissed at me, then jumped off the sill, and ran out the open bedroom door.

I spent a long time searching throughout the entire house for that cat, until I decided to give up the search and inform Pamela about it later that day. After telling her about the cat, Pamela said that she had no idea at all whom the cat belonged to, or how it could have gotten into the house. The cat's presence was a complete mystery and I kept hearing it meowing from different parts of the house. To this day I can't explain what happened to this cat or if it was even real. It is a total mystery but also spooky when I hear it crying.

The following day, another unexplainable thing happened to me. As I was in the kitchen, Pamela had gone to visit family in Florida. My daughter came to help me with some chores that needed to be taken care of. Each Sunday evening, I would prepare meals for Pamela, package and freeze them for her use throughout the week. I was doing this when I asked my daughter to open a cupboard and grab me a spice that I needed. As she opened the cupboard door above the kitchen counter, she screamed! The cat I had seen the day before suddenly jumped out of the cupboard and dashed right into the living room! I rushed after it, the door on the opposite side was closed and the cat couldn't get passed me if it wanted to. When I stood in the doorway and looked everywhere for the cat, it was nowhere to be found. I knew something was very strange when this cat totally disappeared! We also could not account for its unusual presence in the cupboard, since there were no other access spaces for it to enter except directly from the front of the cupboard.

There was nowhere that cat could have been hiding, my daughter and I searched high and low for that cat. It simply, and suddenly, disappeared as quick as it had appeared. I knew that there had to be some explanation, but could only come up with-this cat was not real and had to be a spirit. The cat made one other appearance to me after that as I was climbing the stairs it quickly ran across the landing from one side to the other, right through a solid wall. I knew then this was a ghost cat!

A week later, a roofer that I phoned to repair a damaged seam running above a portion of the kitchen and service porch was busy on the job at the house, when out of the blue he asked me, "Who was that young man tapping on the second story window, trying to get my attention?" I responded that there was no young man living in the house, only an elderly woman who was currently away. I asked him to explain.

He stated that he moved his ladder over to the closed window where he spotted the young man. As he was standing on his ladder, he peered inside the window where the young man was tapping from, but the room was empty. However, he did notice a small cat sitting inside near the doorway, which kept meowing and meowing. A stream of shivers went down my spine. I was totally spooked!

I immediately asked the roofer to come into the house with me and help me catch the cat, and to accompany me if there might be a young male intruder actually in the house. We completely and thoroughly searched and searched the house, but did not discover anything or anyone. For obvious reasons, I did not want the roofer to think I was losing my mind, or hallucinating. I did agree to his recommendation to contact the local police regarding the unknown male figure at the window that was tapping to get his attention. I told him that I would definitely give the owner the information, and let her take it from there.

Towards the end of that day my daughter came to visit me. Using her new camera that had been given to her by her father as a birthday present, my daughter decided to take a few pictures of me. She wanted to send them to her grandparents back in Tacoma. She took a total of about 10 pictures of me in the living room, and in the outside in our nicely landscaped backyard.

My daughter had the pictures developed within the week and asked me to look at them before sending them off. I was surprised to notice that all the pictures she had taken of me had large white spots in them, which I knew were orbs. Some of these orbs were to the side of me, some in front of my chest and two were half hidden behind me—actually peeking out from behind my left side. We decided not to send these "damaged" pictures and instead took a series of others to replace them.

I informed my daughter about the new incidents regarding the mysterious cat, and she told me that she had a friend whose mother was a believer in ghosts and the paranormal. She asked me if she could tell her friend's mother about what might  be the cause of the strange cat. I said, "Sure why not?"

The mother of my daughter's friend contacted me by phone that day and introduced herself. She stated that in her manner of "feeling things," she felt that there were many cats in the house. More than she could count. And there was a young man that enjoyed looking out of the house's windows. He used to live in the house many years ago. I asked her, "Well, why now? Why are these things taking place now?" She responded that her impressions were that the young man used to torture and kill cats that he would trap in the backyard. I had had enough of this and politely ended the call.

When Pamela returned the following week, she informed me that she had decided to sell the house and move to Florida. I was overjoyed with the news. I had already planned to tell her that I was going to end my employment with her for personal reasons. Now, this good news spared me the trouble of having to follow through with my own bit of bad news.

I don't know why these ghostly things waited for me to come along so they could present themselves. Logistically, it all just doesn't make sense. The whole realm of spirits never made any sense to me. I've never held much trust in such things as mediums, fortune-tellers, and "woo-woos." But my experience at the Dover house has sure given me a new focus on this. Today, I'm a little more open to the possibilities that there is life-after-death and it may not only be for human beings but animals too!"

GUEST LODGINGS

ALBUQUERQUE, NM

THE PAINTED LADY BED & BREW, JESSE HERRON'S STORY

I'm a native born New Mexican. I never considered opening a B&B until after the success of my trolley tour company here in Albuquerque. I found myself wondering what more I could do that would fit in with the hospitality and tourism services. The idea gained hold when I found this property because it came with a lot of great history and needed to be preserved. It was a neighborhood eyesore and there were stories that no one knew about.

I was living on the Westside of ABQ for about eight years and felt really detached from the cultural corridor of the city, it was about a forty-minute drive and wanted to be closer to the Old Town area. I drove by this property and with the help of a realtor friend purchased it Feb 2, 2014. We found out that the building had once been a former brothel and saloon, stories of Billy the Kid and Pat Garratt staying here and my interest in learning about these definitely influenced me to purchase this property, no matter what.

I was not given any information from the sellers regarding any paranormal activity but one day while standing out front, a man approached me and asked if I was thinking about buying this property. I said yes. He said "Do you know the history?" When I told him I knew a little bit, he

Jesse Herron,
Bed & Brew Owner.

immediately said "You don't know s#@t!" Turns out he was the next door neighbor and he and his family had lived there for many years. He also stated that his family had built the building back in the 1800's. So, I grabbed my phone and switched on the voice recorder and started recording.

While he was describing all the things he remembered most about the property, he stopped and pointed to one of the rooms, which now serves as my office and apartment, and said that the people before me would never go near that room. I can honestly tell you that now that I've lived here for eight years, that room is one of the most haunted and active so far.

When I purchased the property, it was set up as a triplex with three individual apartments, the saloon on the far west end, large middle apartment in the center and the owners apartment at the opposite end. We converted the large middle apartment into two single apartments, one is a one bedroom and the other has two bedrooms. We took out the old shag carpeting which had preserved the original hardwood floors, removed the drop ceiling to expose the beautiful eleven and half foot-high bead board ceilings.

These apartments were popular and used through the 1980's without many improvements. Today, we have added private baths, full kitchens and amenities, i.e., flat screen Apple TV, heating/AC while keeping the best of the historic look and feel of each living space.

During the renovations, we removed and replaced all water damaged wood and support beams with new materials. While the floors were removed mainly from the former brothel room, we could see the dirt below the building and discovered a treasure trove of items from around the 1800's. We uncovered several ladies razor blades, the sole of a woman's shoe, a linoleum piece of flooring, pill bottles, a tattered piece of cloth from a dress and wall paper scraps. We've got many of these items now preserved behind wall display cases and placed throughout the guest rooms.

The first time I learned about the properties paranormal history was from the neighbor back in 2013 but the very first night I slept here in

February 2014, we began experiencing activity. Lights clicked on and off, things moving within the room, and the experience of a small statured person crawling into the bed with me. I thought it was kind of cool and something I had never experienced before.

Even my dog named, Bill Murray, had seemed to react to unseen things happening. When I felt activity, I would look at Murray and he at me as though he also sensed something.

I remember one time, I let him outside to go to the bathroom. I had his food dish placed outside my bedroom, and it makes a certain noise as he's eating. He's licking a plastic bowl that sits inside a metal bowl and when the plastic bowl hits up against the metal bowl, it makes a distinct noise. As soon as he came back in, just before I closed the door behind him, I heard that distinct bowl make that noise. I looked over at Murray, he stopped and growled. I walked over to the bowl and immediately sensed an energy and thought it might be a ghost dog. That was kind of cool but Murray would always seem to be watching and sensing things around us.

I also remember one night while watching a movie in the living room, I heard Murray yelp from my bedroom. It was not a normal yelp but one caused from feeling pain. Like when you accidently close a door on the dog's tail or step on his paw kind of yelp. He yelped two or three more times that evening.

The next night, I was watching TV again and he came over to me in the living room and sat right next to me. I remember reaching over to stroke his head and felt this dry crusty fur on him. I got my flashlight to inspect it and found dry blood on his fur. It was in an area on his back that he could not touch himself and appeared to be straight claw mark scab. These are some of the most viv-

Painted Lady Portal.

id experiences I recall that happened to Murray who has since passed away.

In February 2020, before the pandemic. I was sleeping in my bedroom. I had repurposed one of the old brothel doors into a headboard for my bed. I remember waking up to a

Jesse's Headboard.

load noise, not sure what it was but it woke me up from a dead sleep. I heard this whooshing noise coming out of the headboard, above me, right behind my head.

As soon as my eyes adjusted to the darkness of the room, there were these one-dimensional shapes with jagged angles, not squares or triangles but approximately one by one inches in size, a couple of hundred of these all swirling in a counterclockwise direction. The swooshing noise and unusual display continued for about several minutes all the while as I lay in bed.

It wasn't scary or threatening and as soon as it stopped, I fell back to sleep. That happened just that one time, and could have been a spirit portal opening from the brothel door headboard, right over my head. It was some kind of a vortex and truly amazing. It never happened again or since that one time. The energy around the property seemed to calm down and remained absent for months thereafter.

In August 2020, the paranormal TV show Ghost Adventures came out and spent a few days investigating the property. I remember thinking I know the place is haunted, but nothing paranormal has been happening and I wasn't sure if they would capture anything. I was interviewed, as was my neighbor Samantha Madrid, also a member of the property seller's family. Samantha introduced herself as a psychic/medium who has been successfully confronting and cleansing negative spirits from properties for many years. Samantha had cleansed my property very early on and from one particular negative spirit.

Original property doors creatively preserved.

From the very first night the Ghost Adventure crew arrived, things started to happen and the energy intensified with that same negative spirit I thought had been cleansed. What was most interesting was that I had not spoken or seen Samantha in several years since her first cleansing of the property but as soon as she arrived to be interviewed by Ghost Adventures, the first thing she said was that the evil energy she removed was back in the house. The second shocking thing she said was that there was a short young girl who likes to visit me in my bedroom, possibly a "Lolita" from the former brothel.

I couldn't believe what she just said because we had not spoken in years. I don't know if that aggressive, negative energy never left or if it actually came back because of some provoking by the Ghost Adventure production crew. I'm not sure what happened but as soon as the crew wrapped production and left, I spent the next month dealing with that awful energy all over again.

It also didn't help that this period of time also began the pandemic lock downs, isolation, over all darkness of deaths and the quarantine. I was feeling really, really down and depressed and was thankful for Samantha for offering another cleansing of the property and this time, it included me personally. I believed at that time that all these entities were removed.

I remember her asking me if I wanted her to get rid of all the spirits or just the bad ones. I told her just the bad one because I felt the good spirits were comforting. I didn't want to kick out any of the good spirits, and as long as they weren't harming me or my guest, they were welcome to stay. She offered a cleansing ritual of protection spells and that was it.

The next big thing that happened was in March 2021. Since I've been here for eight years now, I know can sense when there is something in the room or nearby. I feel this energy that is more than just the hair standing up on the back of your neck or get the chills. The male spirits that have presented themselves to me, have been very aggressive and oppressive. This is something like getting punched in the face energy, very strong and terrifying. The female spirits I've encounter here are more calming and protective in their nature.

One night while lying in bed on my back, I felt a male pressure pressing down on my legs as though being sat on or held down. I rolled over to my right side, away from this male energy and noticed a young girl standing directly next to my bed by the night stand. She seemed to be about 12-18 years of age. I looked right at her. I could see that she was Hispanic, she had eye makeup and a tight hair bun pulled up on top of her head. She stood facing the wall, not looking at me. I remember as soon as I saw her, I felt comfort and safe from the stronger, aggressive male energy coming from behind me. Eventually she disappeared and all was calm.

The next morning, I was so excited to report to my family that I had actually seen my first ghost. I'd never seen one ever in my life. She was short, barley taller than my nightstand, maybe 4 feet. I don't know if she was a prostitute that worked here or what her connection was to this property but I believe she was the "lolita" that Samantha had described months ago.

I've felt this spirit crawl into my bed several times since I've lived here. I feel she's looking out for me. I recognize her energy instantly. I sometimes feel her presence floating over me, when my heads on my pillow and I look up, I can almost sense her looking at me and it's a soothing and comforting energy.

I was told by Antonio, the author of this book, that it might be a nice gesture to make an offering to this spirit in the form of a few cosmetic items. I will give this some serious thought.

Next big episode, was January 2022. Nothing had happened since March 2021. It was about 4-5 am in the morning and a decorative lamp made of salt crystal turn on by itself. The click of it turning on woke

Jesse's interview session with Antonio.

me up. I looked at it and immediately thought ghost and asked my Alexa to turn off the light and it did.

I sensed a masculine energy, maybe three or four actually, walking down the hall toward my bedroom. I opened my eyes, the room was pitch black and I could see the outline of an older male figure. He was wearing a cowboy hat, carrying what seemed to be a paper doll and hobbling toward me.

He stopped at the foot of my bed and began tapping the mattress between my legs, very aggressive with the paper doll. I was terrified and didn't want to look. I held my pillow over my head, and felt my heart beating faster than I've ever felt before. It's the most terrified I've ever been. It felt like this masculine energy was draining me, somehow. I remember wishing that this would just go away and leave.

Eventually the energy left but quickly returned to hover over me with an even stronger intensity and sense of aggression. It was at this moment, that my space heater automatically turned on and the noise and dim light from it gave me some courage to turn towards the spirits and yell for them to, "Get Out." I grabbed a small mist bottle of juniper and sage scent, aimed and sprayed them directly. I also held a soft leather sachet of minerals including black obsidian, amethyst and quartz, that Samantha had given me for protection.

I finally fell asleep but now, every night since, I dread going to sleep because of the concern that these aggressive spirits remain and might manifest at any time. This episode was definitely not a pleasant or enjoyable experience.

I've thought about this quiet a bit and it felt these spirits wanted to suck the life force out of my lungs. It felt like I was being assaulted, violated and fearful similar to what I imagine it would be like when your car or home gets broken into.

I had never had any paranormal experiences and my family was not very religious when I was growing up. I basically got my knowledge from watching Ghost Adventures and those types of shows and going on ghost tours in various cities and just being a fan of horror films at an early age.

I was always a believer in ghost and had a few weird experiences when I was in my early twenties but nothing like living here and actually seeing the little girl ghost, its definitely changed me. I know they exist, I can tell you they exist but everyone has to have their own experience.

So, in the years that I've lived here, I've had several psychic healers cleanse the buildings and property. What amazed me was they each came at different times and not together. Neither one knew about the others cleansing but each of them described to me exactly what the other healers had attempted or done to remove the negative spirits.

The last psychic who arrived to investigate and cleanse the property, began by telling me that the property had already been cleansed in the past. I told her there had been several in recent years. She looked me directly in my eyes and stated that there remains one dominant evil spirit, who does not want to leave and is furious that I haven't move out. She said that the longer I let this thing remain, the more power it will become.

She said that when I was not around, this entity would torment my dog Murray and that was causing Murray to age rapidly. At that moment, I asked her what can we do. She told me that she would return in a few days with what she referred to as a demon trap. It involved burning a variety of spiritual items, in a small baking loaf pan using Epson salt and the herb cats claw to trap and remove

Demon Trap.

an entity.

The pan contents are lit on fire and this seeks out and draws the entity into the flame. I really don't know what else was in the pan, but the space smelled amazing afterwards.

 After all the cleansing attempts that have occurred, most of the evil spirits seem to have been silenced leaving only the non-aggressive ones. This property feels like an airport hub for spirits, like a portal for spiritual activity. It's always something. It's like running this Bed & Brew, you can't control who pays and stays here or what they bring with them.

Most guest are awesome, and treat the history and paranormal claims with respect. Others, not so much and just want to conjure up whatever paranormal activity they can, without considering the consequences this leaves for me to deal with after they leave.

In room #3, the Lotty Suite, there is a large dry blood stain on the wooden floor. During the renovations, the flooring repair crew made numerous attempts to sand away the stain. They told me they tried everything they had to remove it but ultimately stopped because I told them it was pretty cool thing to have and share with visitors.

I told them to leave the stains as they were exposed and just covered it with a large area rug. I've learned also that in the early 1900's this room was known as the swastika saloon and had been reported in the local newspapers of the time, for its reputation of frequent knife stabbings and gun fights. I image there's blood stains all over this place but this was the largest one we've found so far.

The truly odd thing about having Ghost Adventures here for three days of investigating was that after I was interviewed, I had no further communication with anyone from the program. They packed up on the third morning and left without a word about what they found or experienced. It wasn't until three months later, when the show actually first aired that I heard the host proclaimed that the Painted Lady Bed & Brew was enveloped in pure evil and that I, the owner, needed to exit this place for good. I was blown away but disappointed that I had to learn about their negative experience on tv, along with the rest of their viewers.

I am not religious but am now a true believer in the paranormal, ghosts and potentially demons, things that have not felt human that intent on attaching to me or negatively draw energy from my life force. I am much more sensitive to energy changes and can sense when spirits are present. I welcome positive encounters in the future but reject experiences like those where the male entities threatened me.

Blood stained floor.

I welcome guest who come to experience a paranormal encounter without using Quijia boards, pendulums, or rituals using candles or incense to summon or agitate ghosts. I've seen the aftermath of these actions by former guest and it always kicks up lingering activity. I often tell these guest that this might be cool for you because you don't have to live here but I always do with what's left. Honestly, I find this behavior pretty inconsiderate and rude when someone leaves me with what they've conjured up. I guarantee you they wouldn't appreciate me doing this in their home after I visit!

SAMANTHA MADRID'S STORY

I'm 34, I have been around metaphysics since I was a child. I come from a line of healers and people that praise the earth. My family came to this area from the Yucatan jungles of Mexico and moved here before any Country borders ever existed.

As a child, I got in trouble a lot over metaphysics, I didn't understand what was going on. I would get pinched and I would say things and things would happen. I didn't understand it until my great grandma told me you have a vision that no one else has and a lot of people will feel weird by the things you say and know. You need to see if they want that, before you say anything. I didn't know what she meant until I got older and involved with the healing aspects of life. I understood that I shouldn't solicitate but let people find me.

Samantha Madrid.

At 12 years-old, I learned to read the tarot cards and would do readings for my aunt, telling her about experiences I didn't know, and about her man and relationships. There were a lot of spiritual things and behaviors that I now know as an adult, what they meant and what purpose they served. At 14 years of age, my great grandmother passed away and I experienced her soon after letting me know that I had everything I needed to understand death and the afterlife.

Jesse purchased the property next door from my cousin Michael. We were shocked to learn that someone had purchased the property because it had been vacant for many years. It used to be rented out as a triplex but tenants wouldn't stay very long and often moved out.

Jesse and his girlfriend moved in after he purchased the property, began renovations and built a privacy fence around the property. My uncle was outside watching them, and was making comments to us saying, "Let's see how long they'll last?" "Good luck!"

One day, my uncle told Jesse that he should meet me, because I was very open to the spirit world and would be willing to help him if he need help. Jesse didn't seem interested and shook the offer off, mainly because he didn't seem to believe in paranormal stuff. And then soon after, Jesse called me and said that things were happening around the house and he didn't know how to ask for my help because he didn't know what was going on.

He told me, "Your uncle gave me your number and told me to contact you anytime if spirit activity or concerns regarding strange things happening in the house occurred."

We set a date to meet on the property. I told him that I was also going to invite several spiritually sensitive healers to join us because I already know your property and I'm not going to influence their investigation.

I'm going to stay quiet, and let these psychics tell you what they are sensing and seeing. I'm not going to give them any details or information about the property. They will give first hand impressions and report what they find to us.

There were four physics who joined us, none of them had ever met Jesse or had seen the property before. As I was escorting them on to the property, I was overwhelmed with fear. I was thinking to myself, "What has happened here?" I moved away and came back but instantly sensed something seriously wrong. I also notice the Jesse's appearance was not how I remembered him. He didn't look well. I stayed quiet and just observed the others.

We walked through all the rooms of the property, and each psychic began telling us what they saw and learned in each space. They were making references to the history of the property, people who had lived and worked there, all in details that no one could possibly know.

Jesse was totally surprised to hear them describe recent incidents that had occurred between him and his girlfriend. For instance, one where his girlfriend felt someone pulled her wet hair while she was showering. An intimate setting that no one outside of Jesse and his girlfriend knew.

While we were in Jesse's apartment space, I notice off to the corner of my eye, two red glowing eyes. As soon as I turned to look, they disappeared and I received a warning saying "Ha, you can try, but I'm not going anywhere." I stayed quiet.

I then also told Jesse, that he needed to get his dog away from this space. As I was expressing this, one of the other physics jumped in and also said that something was trying to get to him through his dog.

We both recommended that a spiritual cleansing be conducted on the property and I chose to let someone else perform this instead of me. My family and I had been too personally close to this property and I thought an outsider would be better to help cleanse everything. A cleaning was done and the entire atmosphere improved and most of the disturbing activity stopped.

Four years had passed and I had not seen Jesse since that cleansing. He asked me if I would be a part of a national paranormal investigation program filming at the property. I hesitated accepting because my experience with these "shows" has not been positive and usually involves provoking spirits. Jesse told me that he would appreciate the support so I agreed.

The moment I approached Jesse at the property, he looked physically drained and exhausted. I told him, "That spirit that was cleansed four years ago, was still in your house!" "It watches you and laughs," I said. I told him that, even though I can't see anything from my property into yours, I know that you sit out front here in this rocking chair. This spirit watches you sitting here with your laptop too. Jesse's eyes opened wide and he told me we need to talk. I said, "I know we do."

I approached the program producers and hosts telling them that this spirit is mocking them and thinks you're all a joke. They offered to help Jesse after they finished filming but did absolutely nothing, they just left him hanging. They didn't send him a priest, nothing. A few days after the film crew departed, Jesse was feeling even worse.

I told Jesse that we needed to do another cleansing and I scheduled it with several other psychics to join us. As soon as we cleansed the property, Jesse's health appeared to improve, his natural color came back to his face and he seemed healthier. He was out and about, smiling and much more active. I hadn't seen him this way in years.

To this day, Jesse told me "I only want you to remove what's bad but I want to keep the good spirits." Because there was a lot of blood shed on that property, through violence, it is very difficult to not be able to cleanse everything else, to bring in that peace. I was only able to do what he was letting me do.

When I was 7 years old, and there was no fencing surrounding that property, I had an older cousin, Christine, move into one of the former rental units. She was very independent and hippy type of personality. She burned incense and candles and I liked it. She lived in the same apartment space that Jesse now lives and I sensed an unseen presence even as a child. I didn't ever feel welcomed because of the presence and would never visit Christine's apartment if she was not home.

Two weeks after moving in, Christine suddenly moved out in the middle of the night. She told the family that the entire house would shake, the cabinet doors would open and items would move without her moving them herself. When I heard about her moving out, I had a strong sense that she may have messed with the Ouija board in an attempt to figure out what was going on but instead opened up something she should not have.

These experiences happened to me as a child, BEFORE, Jesse purchased the property: I also remember a little boy spirit I would see and run after as he ran away from me. I felt as if he was playing a game of hide and seek, but I could never figure out how he managed to totally disappear around the corner of the building or wall. I remember he wore little short pants and didn't wear shoes.

I remember one day, deciding to take my scooter over to offer it to this boy to play and when I noticed him looking at me and my scooter, I called him over to come play. He just smiled and ran away.

I also specifically recall seeing another figure of a short woman with her hair up in a bun, very motherly and always seemed to be concerned with what I was doing at the property. I didn't understand that they were actually spirits as a child. This woman told me that I should not be coming over to the property and that I needed to go to my own house. She never came outside but spoke to me from inside the apartment next door to Jesse's apartment.

I was seven and she looked older to me. She was young and close enough to my height as a child. Now, that I'm in my thirties, she could have been between 18-20. I feel this spirits energy is still very present and familiar with that property. This Lolita figure is who both Jesse and I have seen.

The last thing I want to share is that even now, when I'm outside walking past the nearby alley, I feel the need to run past the property. Back when I was a child, there was no privacy fence and you could see the building from the street. I always felt this vibe not to look in the direction of the building.

This one night, I was walking home from my friend Maria's home, and I heard footsteps behind me. It was dusk, but light enough to see but not details. I saw a tall man, dressed nice, like he was going to church. As I'm walking near the now Bed & Brew property, this man suddenly appeared much closer to me but without making any quick footstep sounds.

I sped up and got close to the property but when I turned to look back, instead of the tall man, there stood a huge black cat in the street, glaring directly at me. I watched that cat bolt over towards the building and disappear. No explanation for any of this but completely unforgettable!

When you live in a haunted location, a part of you gets so comfortable with that setting, change scares you. Jesse wants the property to be spiritually unique but he doesn't want the bad stuff to be there. There is no in between, you clean it, you heal it and you fix it or you leave it haunted."

BISBEE, AZ

The town of Bisbee is located approximately 100 miles southeast of Tucson, directly in the heart of the Mule Mountains at 5,300 feet above sea level. The quaint town was founded in 1880, and thanks to its rich copper deposits, quickly developed to become the most populated settlement in the state.

The town's mineral wealth did not go unnoticed by the Phelps Dodge mining company, who built a railroad into the town in 1880 and soon began to mine the rich ore. The many years of prosperity ended in the early 1970s when Phelps Dodge decided to cease operations. This in turn forced a good number of the town's residents to leave Bisbee and relocate elsewhere.

Today, Bisbee is a haven for artists who have settled in the historic buildings and have restored them to their past glory. Bisbee has become a city of diversified yearly events featuring music, crafts, and the arts.

HISTORY OF THE COPPER QUEEN HOTEL

The Copper Queen Mining Company constructed the Copper Queen or "The Queen" Hotel in the early 20th century. With 45 guest rooms, two lobbies, Copper Queen Saloon, patio, swimming pool, and dining room, "The Queen" is Bisbee's major historic landmark. The hotel is a well-preserved Victorian style hotel that is decorated in the manner of the pioneer West. Given the hotel's history of hosting such notables as "Black Jack" Pershing and the young Teddy Roosevelt, it is no wonder that a ghost or two (or three) would find such an inviting hotel perfect for an extended stay.

CRAIG H. ROTHEN'S STORY

The following accounts by the hotel's general manager and the front desk clerk will provide further evidence for the existence of "other types" of guests at the Copper Queen Hotel.

—Antonio

I have been the general manager at the hotel for one year. Prior to working at the Queen, I was living in the Phoenix area and working as a hotel and restaurant consultant for a corporation in Northern California. Not long after beginning my position at the hotel, I began to hear individual stories from several employees regarding the Queen being haunted.

At the time, I regarded all of these stories as nothing more than simply interesting and consequently funny. I myself have never had any experience with such things as ghosts or hauntings, so I found these accounts truly strange. After about six months into my job, I soon changed my mind when I received a call from two hotel guests who were staying in room 309.

The guests were complaining about their room being unusually very cold. I assured them that I would move them into a different room. Once moved, they were pleased with the new room. Later, at approximately 9 a.m., I decided to enter their now vacant room #309, to investigate the cause of the cold temperature. Room #309 operates on its own thermostat, and I thought that perhaps the

Craig Rothen,
General Manager.

I heard someone call my name.

temperature gauge might be broken.

As I entered the room, I immediately felt a chilling cold envelop my whole body. I walked around the room looking for any open windows, or any indication of its source. Every window was shut. The air vents were closed as they were supposed to have been. Finding myself now standing in the middle of the room, I was at a loss for where this freezing cold air was coming from.

Suddenly, the window directly in front of where I was standing opened wide! I was startled, but not scared. The hotel's windows are not spring loaded so I was most interested in finding out how exactly this window just opened as it did. I walked right up to the open window and did not see any unusual wires or loose springs. I attempted to close the window, and placed both hands on the top window frame and began to apply an even downward pressure. As I began to push down on the frame, an equal amount of pressure from an unseen force began pushing up! I actually felt the power of an invisible force resisting my effort to close that window!

Just then, I noticed something, a movement right next to me on my left. As I turned I saw the foggy white image of a presence—a figure! I immediately let go of the window and instinctively moved my hand right inside this hazy cloud. It felt icy cold to the touch. I withdrew my hand quickly! I knew that whatever this was, was completely unexplainable. I got an eerie feeling, and I knew that I was not dealing with something normal. Somehow I found the courage to say out loud, "I am going to close the window—now!" Once more I placed my hands on the window frame and pushed down. This time it closed easily. Surprised by this, I wasted no time in leaving the room.

About a month after that incident, late one afternoon, our office had run out of computer paper. I went up to the 4th floor, and entered the storage closet to retrieve some paper. As I was leaving the storage closet, I heard someone call my name, "Craig, Craig." Thinking it was a co-worker calling my name I answered, "Yes?" But there was no response, I looked around and immediately realized I was totally and absolutely alone.

I quickly walked down to the third floor where a couple of workers were remodeling a room to ask if they had called for me. The men answered, "No, we've been busy down here making the repairs. We haven't even taken a break yet." Then they added jokingly, "Mr. Rothen, it must have been the ghost." Not wanting to sound too alarmed by this statement, I answered, "Yes, it must have been the ghost, thank you," and I walked away.

Within the first year that I've been employed at the hotel, I have had employees come to me with their own stories of ghost encounters within the hotel. One of the housekeepers remarked to me that as she was working during the day shift on the third floor, she saw a little boy, wrapped in a towel appear to her, only to disappear a few seconds later.

Another housekeeper reported to me that again on the third floor, that some doors would open and close on their own. The curious thing to me is that the hotel has kept several logbooks of reported ghostly activities over the years. These written reports give detailed descriptions of the ghostly events including specific dates, times. These log books date back over six years. I'll share with you just two short written accounts of what has been reported.

A particular night auditor quit the hotel saying "I heard someone call my name but was working alone at the time," shortly after he wrote the following:

June 8, 1995

"I know the ghosts are stirred up again. The phone rang and a gentleman's voice asked for "Howard." I asked Hector, our maintenance man, if he knew who Howard was. Hector had a stunned look on his face. I didn't know this but Howard was a popular, long-time, former front

Howard, seen wearing hat, was a hotel front desk clerk in 1910.

desk clerk but in 1910. When I placed the phone up to my ear to reply, the line was dead. Rose, a co-worker, was standing by me and said, "It's just Howard checking up on the hotel. Here we go again."

Another employee entry the same night listed, "Guest checked out from the third floor. He was awakened by the presence of a ghost. And another guest checked out this morning from the third floor. He said he was awakened at 2 a.m. by a beautiful lady, dressed in black, who disappeared."

LAURIE DOLAND'S STORY

I've worked for the Copper Queen as front desk clerk now for almost a year. My first ghost experience happened just three months ago in June at about 2 a.m. I decided to get a drink of water and walked into the dining room, on my way to the kitchen. As I entered the dining room I saw a strange woman standing against one of the columns. I clearly saw that she had reddish brown hair, which she wore up in a bun, brown eyes, and a healthy pink complexion. She also wore a high collar blouse and I'm guessing was in her mid-twenties.

Immediately I knew this woman was a ghost! I knew this since I could only see her body from the waist up! Spotting her, I stood there, startled. I had come upon her so suddenly that I felt shock, but eventually, my shock turned to an intense fear. We both stood in place staring at each other for only a few seconds, until by chance, the owner of the hotel also

walked into the dining room.

The ghost woman must not have wanted to stay around because she quickly disappeared! I described what I had just witnessed to the owner, but she refused to believe me. Since that time, I have not seen the ghost woman again. I have no idea why she chose to appear to me as she did. However, from time to time, as I'm alone in the dining room, I have heard both the

Laurie Doland, front desk clerk. footsteps, and the movement of a long, crisp skirt—as it moved across the dining room floor.

I saw a strange woman standing against one of these columns.

Sometimes at night, I'll be visited by yet another spirit. I'll be alone at the front office, working at the hotel's computer, when suddenly I'll feel the presence of someone walk into the office. I always can tell when this spirit enters the office because the hairs on my arms stand on end, and an obvious thick atmosphere will fill the room. I'll feel a chilling sensation come over me and soon I'm covered from head to toe in goose bumps.

This has happened to me about five times now. Fellow male employees have told me about seeing a woman dressed in a black dress walking up and down the staircase in our lobby. The stairs are located directly to the front of the main desk. Interestingly enough, this woman in black chooses to only make appearances to male employees and guests. The latest incident with her took place in July, at approximately 3 a.m. The employee saw the ghost walk down the stairs and enter the dining room. As she walked up to the dining room doors she disappeared right through

The ghost walked down these stairs.

them! The employee described the ghost wearing a dress from an early 1900's era style of clothes.

A female employee also reported to me that late one evening as she walked through the dining room, she felt someone physically tap her on her shoulder. When she turned around, there was no one. That was the last time she has ever entered the dining room alone, day or night!

The sound of a man's heavy shoes walking down the hallways is very common and one that both guests and employees continually hear in the hotel. I myself have heard these sounds on several occasions. Some nights, while standing in the hotel lobby, I have heard the sounds of unseen people engaged in an uproar of conversation from different nearby areas. I can't tell what they are all saying, but they sure do make a ruckus!

What has also become commonplace is many employees hear their names called out, and as they turn around to answer the person they think is calling them, of course there is no one there. This happens so frequently that we all now take it in stride. Our thought is that the ghosts are keeping their watchful eyes on us.

Another frequent and unique ghost that employees have witnessed in the hotel is a boy that runs up and down the halls of the third floor. We also recently had two guests inform the front desk of a woman ghost that they saw dressed in a stripper's costume. The guests reported that this strangely dressed woman walked down the hall and opened the doors to the third-floor veranda. As the guests followed her, she apparently enjoyed the audience, because she started to do a striptease. The dancing ghost did not last for long. In just a few seconds, she had also vanished before their disbelieving eyes!

Guests in room #312 have reported to us strange bell sounds that wake

The sounds of a man's heavy shoes walking down the hallway is very common.

them from their sleep. Once, two women that were staying in room #312 reported that a man's hat "appeared" to them, it floated across the room, and then heard the sound of a man's heavy shoes walking down the hallway. The employee saw the ghost walk down the stairs and simply disappear. In Room #212, guests have reported "strong winds" rattled the doors and windows and kept them up all night.

Once these winds rattled a window to the point that it shattered, now that's a lot of force! I am definitely convinced that the hotel has ghosts, and I'm not the only one who will admit to this. Many employees, both past and present, will say the same. The employees are not shy about describing what they have heard and seen.

Thankfully I haven't heard of any ghosts within the hotel hurting anyone. I think that when these people were alive many years ago they truly enjoyed the Copper Queen, and they still find it difficult to part from it. As far as I can tell, even death has not changed their strong attachment to the hotel.

BISBEE, AZ

BISBEE INN

In 1916, owner Mrs. S. P. Bedford constructed a 24-room hotel building that today is named The Bisbee Inn. The hotel was furnished by Mrs. Bedford and then leased to Mrs. Kate LaMore who renamed it the Hotel LaMore. Rooms at the hotel were $2 per day or $8 per week. At that time, the hotel was advertised as being "the most modern in Bisbee."

Between 1922 and 1923, Mrs. LaMore's hotel lease reverted back to Mrs. Bedford. Mrs. Bedford operated the hotel under the same name (Hotel La More) until she sold it to Grace V. Waters. Various individuals have since owned the hotel.

In 1982 Joy and John Timbers bought the property and partially restored it. Under their ownership, they ran the hotel as The Bisbee Inn Bed and Breakfast. In 1996 the inn was sold to Elissa and Al Strati, who completed the total restoration of the property.

The current inn is a wonderful and romantic bed-and-breakfast. Comprised of 20 guest rooms, eight with private baths, the hotel today is a certified historic property. The original oak and period furnishings, together with the walls decorated with photos and maps of years gone by, reflect the present inn's early days of Victorian elegance.

JULIE M. CROTEAU'S STORY

I interviewed Julie on the front porch of the Inn on a very warm summer afternoon. My question was direct: "Have you ever been told by guests that there are any ghosts in the Inn?" Julie responded, "Sure, of course, and I'll also tell them of my own personal experiences that I've had with ghosts in the building, and I've had my share—believe me!"

—Antonio

I've been working at the Inn as a maid, laundry person, and front desk clerk for about one year. My first experience with the ghost of the Inn took place in January 1996. It was around 5 p.m. and I was in the back lounge where the television room is located. Between the lounge room where I was seated and the dining room were French doors that were locked.

I noticed something moving, and when I turned to look in that direction, I saw a tall man standing in place. I remember he was wearing a vest and his jeans were tucked into his high boots. I got the feeling that this was a bizarre guy just by the manner of his dress. Thinking it was a homeless person who had come in off the street looking for a handout, I said, "I'll be right there." I walked down the hallway around to the opposite side of the Inn, through the lobby, and then into the dining room. When I entered the dining room, he was gone. I could not have missed anyone passing me in the hall. There was only one way in and one way out. I immediately knew something strange was going

Julie M. Croteau.

on.

When I later mentioned my experience to other employees, they surprised me with their responses: "Oh, yeah, that's the ghost of the miner guy." "What?!" I said, "You mean you know who I'm talking about?" "Oh, sure, his ghost appears to all of us every now and then. You just had your first visit."

So apparently, I was not the only person who had experienced this ghost. After that, I didn't want to think too much of it, but I've always kept the experience in the back of my mind. I guess the ghost liked me because of what took place next.

A few nights later I was in my own home, seated on the floor watching television. Suddenly, materializing between the television and the heater, I saw the image of the ghost I had seen within the Inn, only this time, he was the size of a large doll! Standing as he was, he was only about three feet tall! I sat there in awe, staring eye to eye with this thing.

Again, he was wearing the same outfit as before. He didn't say anything, but slowly began to disappear. So, I thought, he's now followed me home!

But I want to tell you about another ghost that employees have also seen. This ghost is of a Chinese man. I don't know much more about him; the employee who described the man mentioned the experience to me doesn't wish to bring up the subject any more than is necessary. Apparently, he made a negative impact on her.

Sometimes, I'll walk down a hall of the Inn, and spot the movement of a shadow at the end of the hall. By now, I'm apparently getting very familiar with these shadows. I know that the eyes can play tricks on a person, but there have been so many of these incidents that I'm convinced there has got to be more to these experiences than just blurred vision.

All the employees, including myself, have heard doors slamming shut or the banging of metal objects from time to time in the Inn when it is totally empty of any living being. There are cold spots in certain areas of the Inn and one in particular and very obvious on the stairs. I don't know why this happens, or if there are any rational explanations for these things. I know I've heard these noises and have seen the ghostly shadows. I know that others not familiar with such things might consider me to be odd, but I know that what I've seen is of the paranormal—I've seen these things!

I can also tell when something unusual will take place because of a particular flowery scent of lilac perfume that will permeate the air. It's a pleasant, lingering perfume I've noticed in the air of certain rooms of the Inn. I'll be dusting or simply just passing a room, and suddenly the scent will overwhelm me. The scent will come and then leave after a few minutes. The two rooms of the Inn where I've experienced the scents are rooms #8 and #12. I have mentioned this to my co-workers, and they have all also confirmed this scent, but added, "It's just the ghosts, so what's the big deal?"

CIMARRON, NM

THE SAINT JAMES HOTEL

The Saint James Hotel Cimarron and its vintage hotel are indelibly marked by the turbulent days of westward expansion in northeast New Mexico. The St. James is linked to a veritable Who's Who of early land grant settlers, ranchers, and desperados (mug shots available on request).

The cast of characters included such notable settlers as Lucien Maxwell and Carlos Beaubien, Buffalo Bill Cody and his cohort Annie Oakley, Kit Carson, Frank and Jesse James, Wyatt Earp, Billy the Kid, and Blackjack Ketchum. The notorious gunman, Clay Allison, allegedly danced naked on the bar, once part of the present dining room, which still has bullet holes in its pressed tin ceiling. It was Henri Lamber, personal chef to President Abraham Lincoln, who in 1872 established the saloon; by 1880 it had evolved into the St.

James Hotel.

For those inclined to the paranormal, the Hotel has a long history, even right up to the present, of reported ghosts and supernatural happenings. But in spite of an occasional friendly visitation, the list grows longer every day of happy, relaxed, and rested folks who will testify to the charm and hospitality of this way station in the Rockies."

—Reprinted from the Hotel's brochure

ED SITZBERGER'S STORY

My interview with Ed Sitzberger, hotel owner, was conducted in the hotel's dining room. We sat by one window overlooking the street directly in front of the hotel. As more questions than answers followed, occasionally Ed would point to an area of the dining room and say, "This took place here, or that's where the bullet hole is, or the flatware was moved all around the tops of those tables over there."

A few employees also joined in to offer their own personal experiences of having had an encounter with the ghosts of the hotel. I've included their stories as well. Ed and his staff were very open to discussing what has been a major draw to the property and when the interview was over, directed me with a personal tour of the whole hotel. I must say I was impressed by what I saw.

The hotel is impeccably decorated with an authentic old west flare. Due to the early winter season, there was not a hotel guest to be seen, however this offered me the solitude and contemplative atmosphere I had hoped for. As I walked the second story halls, each of my footsteps echoed against the red velvet wallpapered walls. My imagination could only grasp at the historical individuals who passed this way.

It would benefit you to visit this hotel and surrounding hills. The peace and history will no doubt fill you with awe. Oh, and don't forget to visit the town's cemetery!

— Antonio

"I was born and raised in Cimarron. I attended both grammar and high school in Cimarron. After graduating from high school, I attended college at Highlands University in Las Vegas, New Mexico. I attended two and a half quarters of schooling there. I joined the Air Force right after. After leaving the Air Force, I attended the University of Colorado for four years and received a degree in Mechanical Engineering. Soon after, I moved to California and spent 16 years there. I left California and returned to Colorado, then moved to Los Alamos and worked for ten years at the laboratory.

The original owner who built the hotel was named Henry Lambert. In 1985, I purchased the hotel. I was very familiar with the property because I was born and raised in a house across the alley from the hotel. I was also familiar with the hotel owner's daughter, Toni Hagler. Toni and I were of the same age and were childhood friends, always playing together either at my house or at the hotel. Interestingly, as a child and growing up in the town, I never heard any reference to the hotel being haunted. Never a word about ghosts or anything close to it being haunted.

The first time anyone mentioned to me about the hotel having ghosts was when the woman who sold it to me mentioned it. In fact, she outright told me, "The hotel is haunted." Being an engineer, our profession is science-based so when I heard her words I thought to myself, Yeah, sure—whatever. Given this, we still proceeded with the sale and in July of 1985 we purchased the hotel and didn't get possession of the property until October 3rd. The previous owner operated the small bar and the restaurant. The actual hotel had been closed for over twenty-five years. The previous owner stated that she had the hotel closed due to the ghosts. Interestingly, at the opening archway that lead into the bar, she hung a silk stocking with several items or talismans to ward off the ghosts. I personally never had any cause to believe in ghosts so all her talk about them simply made no difference to me. As I said, having an engineer's degree gave me a reality-based view; I was not a believer in ghosts at all.

My first encounter with the spiritual world took place on Christmas evening of that year. Having taken possession of the property, although the hotel portion of the building was not yet running for business, we left both the restaurant and bar opened. What transpired that evening really made me rethink the notion that spirits might in fact be dwelling within the hotel.

That early evening, after having closed the building for the Christmas holiday, we prepared a family dinner in the restaurant. Strangely, throughout the dinner, we kept hearing the opening and closing of doors to some of the hotel rooms. These sounds were very loud as if someone was angry and slamming the doors shut. I'd excuse myself from the dinner table in order to investigate. Obvious as these sounds were, after walking the hallways, I never did discover anything out of the ordinary. After finishing up with our dinner, we gathered the dishes, washed them, then stacked them on the shelves.

My brother, who lived across the street from the hotel, suggested we go to his house for after dinner drinks. I made sure to lock up the doors and we proceeded to his home. At his house, someone asked if my brother had a specific cream liquor. My brother was out of that particular liquor, but I chimed in stating, "I now own a hotel with a full bar. I'll go get a bottle from the bar."

As I unlocked the door and entered the hotel, I heard the phone in the kitchen double ringing. It made to short rings, paused then two more short rings. This was a code ring, which a phone repairman had instructed us how to use within the hotel itself. The purpose of this was to alert fellow employees to pick up the phone; something like a house intercom system.

I picked up the receiver and said, "Hello," but there was no answer. I thought this was weird. Not thinking further of this unusual incident, I walked over to the bar and picked up a bottle of the liquor, walked outside, and locked the door. After informing everyone at the house about the strange phone call, we all decided to phone the police thinking it might have been a burglar and that he still might be in the hotel.

Two policemen arrived and as they were walking within the interior of the property, the rest of us circled the outside. Not wanting to miss a single hiding spot, we looked everywhere. We never discovered a burglar or anything out of place. Immediately, the thought had crossed my mind that I better start paying attention to future incidents of this kind.

In the days following this, both my wife and I decided to move into the hotel's second floor while renovations to the first floor were being done. During this time, I can remember quite a lot of strange occurrences my wife and I experienced, as did our employees, and guests. Again, I was not a believer in the existence of spirits, but my beliefs were definitely headed for a change.

I can clearly recall one late afternoon when I entered the restaurant area about three months following our Christmas dinner. The dining room was the first room built in the hotel. It originally served as a saloon and gambling hall. The reason for this was to create an income producing venture from which the hotel could then be built. As I walked into the dining room, I spotted a man sitting at a table right in the middle of the room. I got a good look at the man who was of a short stature and his chest was leaning against the table. I also remember he had a receding hairline, but the hair he did have was long and blonde. His face was pocked marked and clean-shaven and he looked to be about the age of 60 or so. I took a few steps closer and he disappeared!

Surprisingly, especially to me, I was not scared at all by the apparition of the ghost man. Over the past years we've had several sensitive persons, or mediums, investigate the property. These folks have always mentioned that the hotel is very much inhabited by spirits. This, together with all the personal experiences that our employees have encountered and brought to my attention, has left me with a straightforward understanding that these things do in fact exist.

One medium stated that when the spirit of one of our better-known ghosts "T.J. Wright" was contacted, the spirit stated that he had no problem with me or with the renovations I was doing to the property. T.J. Wright's personal story is that he won ownership of the hotel in this game of poker. He was betting for the hotel against a herd of cattle that he owned. After winning the property, he went to the owner to collect the property's deed. A scuffle ensued and T. J. was shot and killed in the poker room on the second floor. T.J. won the deed fair and square, but the loser wasn't so eager to turn the hotel over to him and chose instead to do away with him. Room #118 was T.J. Wright's room.

After my wife and I purchased the hotel, we never did anything to his room, just locked it up and it's been in this condition ever since. Strangely, there have been occasions when, without reason, the transit window above door to room #118 would open on its own. When the window is closed, the locking mechanism locks it securely. That locking system is within the room itself, so why or how this happens remains a mystery. To this day, the room is not rented out. We believe that T.J. needs to have this personal room to himself. So, it's always locked.

A strange thing took place one day while I took a walk outside of the hotel. I was imagining remodeling by extending the rear wall of the hotel, so I was standing in the area of the yard next to a clothesline. Standing by the metal pole of the clothesline, I noticed a flat stone that was being used as a step stone. I took a hold of one side of this stone and turned it over. To my surprise it was a tombstone! On its face was carved the name Rev. Toby. I later discovered that this reverend was killed in nearby Cimarron Canyon. He was a member of the Santa Fe ring and was on the opposing side. He was killed and more than that I have no information. Given the unusual history of the stone, I decided to place his tombstone in our hotel lobby for the benefit of tourist.

One incident took place when I was standing at the front desk of the hotel. A couple came walking in through our front door followed by a third man walking a few steps behind. The couple opened the door, and a second after, the man that was following behind grasped the knob to open the door, but was unable to open it because it was now locked! Apparently, a spirit wanted to make its presence known because the only way the lock on the door could be bolted shut would have to be by physically grasping the sliding bolt and engaging the lock. It would be quite impossible to "accidentally" lock on its own, without human, or in this case, "spiritual" assistance! This specific incident has taken place on more than one occasion, as our employees will attest.

A few years ago, we had in our front lobby, a large cage with several parrots. My ex-wife loved raising and keeping these birds as a hobby. Well, the spirits enjoyed molesting and teasing these birds. The poor things would become so agitated they would fall ill. My wife would re-move them from the lobby and take them to our home in an attempt to nurse them back to health.

After a couple of weeks, she would return them to the lobby and soon after they would become stressed just as before. It got so bad my wife would openly speak out to the spirit saying, "Okay T.J., I want you to stop bothering my birds or else you're going to have to leave this hotel!" I'm not too aware of the full details from then on, but the birds didn't seem to have any further trouble.

In years past, before the room was converted into the hotel's dining room, it was a saloon and gambling hall. Twenty-six people were killed or shot to death in this very room in the late 1800's. Because of its ill reputation, the man who took over ownership of the hotel in 1931, Will Hagler, decided to make a change to the notorious gambling hall. At the time of the purchase, the hotel was named the St. James, but Mr. Hagler chose to rename the property The Hotel Don Diego. In addition to this change, he commissioned a portrait of Franciscan Padre, Junipero Si-erra, a man of peace to counter balance the existing portrait of Spanish conqueror Don Diego de Vargas, a man of war. Mr. Hagler decided to permanently removed the bar and no longer sell liquor.

Over in the dining room, we set each table with napkins, glasses, and flatware at 5 p.m. The waitress in charge of dressing the tables had a large tray on wheels that was neatly organized with all the necessary items for each table. This included the flatware. Well, one early evening she rolled out the tray into the dining room and began to set each indi-vidual table. After she finished doing this, she returned to the rear of the kitchen, taking the now empty tray along with her.

As she described the incident to me, she heard a loud banging noise of metal on metal. She made her way quickly back to the dining room and was shocked to discover that all the tables she had taken the time to patiently dress, were now missing all the flatware. Most interesting, was finding all the spoons, forks, and knives all piled high on one table! This dramatic change all took place in a matter of seconds and left her quite upset.

Another incident, a well-known one in fact, took place in the kitchen. At the time one of our cooks was busy cooking when he suddenly experienced an unexplainable incident. He stated that he caught movement behind him, and as he watched, he witnessed a single drinking glass move on its own. The glass was resting on a shelf with other glasses, when it suddenly moved up off the shelf, hovered in midair, then returned to the shelf! It was as if an unseen hand was teasing or playing a strange game of "Look what I can do to you and you can't even see me!"

One time a busload of paranormal investigators came to the hotel to conduct a series of experiments. They set up their equipment and placed a grouping of helium balloons in the lobby. The teacher would ask a question to the spirits and one of the balloons would drop as if an unseen hand was pulling on the string. This would indicate a yes answer to the question, if the balloon remained in the air, it would indicate no. This happened a few times and was so fascinating to witness at the time.

In 1986, a couple of friends of mine, stayed in Room #17 during the entire month of February. Many years ago, this room belonged to Mary Lambert, the co-owner of the hotel. One morning they reported that during the middle of the night an intense heat awakened them. One of them got up and opened the window, and heard a very loud bang come directly from the window. He got up and closed it. This took place twice. After the second time, they decided to just leave the window closed. Oddly enough, the room returned to a cooler state and they were able to finally get some sleep.

There have been times when entering Mary's room and guests will catch the scent of a woman's old fashion lavender or rose perfume. I personally have experienced this. One time, we had a friend stay in Mary's room and told us that her perfume bottle suddenly disappeared from the fireplace mantle while she was in the hotel. Three weeks later our maid discovered the missing perfume bottle in the room on the mantle. There had been two men staying in this room for several days before this discovery so could not have been theirs.

One day a couple staying at the hotel approached me with a concern. They stated to me that when the woman left her husband in the room to

nap, upon her return, he told her that he had actually heard "a voice." The husband was a psychiatrist and told me, "I'm a psychiatrist, a doctor, and I know I'm not crazy. I wasn't imagining things. I heard a woman speak, she identified herself as Mary, and stated, 'I didn't die at the age that people think I did. I was your daughter's age when I died. I was thirty-five years old!"

Today I would definitely welcome experiencing an apparition or ghost fully manifesting itself to me. I believe in God and people who died in a not so peaceful state of mind tend to linger around. This is what I believe is going on here at the hotel. The spirits of these folks, for whatever reason, feel the need to hang around and want us, the living, to know they are still here!"

SANDY SITZBERGER'S STORY

"I've been working at the hotel since October 16, 2007. I'm Ed Sitzberger's wife and I'm the hotel's co-owner and bookkeeper. There are times when I'll have to stay at the hotel late into the night. These are the times when I'll experience ghosts. Oh, I've heard the stories of ghosts associated with the hotel, but never really paid them much importance. But after moving into the hotel, my first-hand encounters really changed my thoughts about all this.

I heard stories from our staff of all the things taking place, such as in the dining room with straws being moved off the table and thrown about the floor. Or in the rooms with pillows placed on the beds, which were then tossed onto the floor. Things such as these incidents were commonplace. As for my own personal experiences, well I do have a few. All these experiences have taken place with me on the second floor.

I've heard the ghostly sound of footsteps walking down the hallway, heavy footsteps very, very regularly. The footsteps are loud and distinctly from a man's boots. After hearing them, I'll jump off my chair and take a peek around my office door but see nothing. Like I said, this is a regular occurrence and takes place about eight or ten times a week! There is no set time of day, but generally they do tend to take place for me, during the late evenings. In addition to these footsteps, I've also heard the sad sound of a young woman crying. This sound in particular has left me with "goose-bumps" and often leaves me sad. Other sounds I have heard are doors knocking, opening and closing on their own.

Once these sounds took place for two solid days. After that, I've never heard the doors knocking since. Lights that have hanging chains that need to be pulled in order to be turned off or on are switched without anyone being present. This also happens often. There is no rhyme or reason; they just take place night or day, and year-round.

Sometimes, while I'm busy at work, I'll feel the presence of someone standing next to me or of as if someone has just walked in through the doorway. I'll stop and turn to see who it is, but no one would be there. At other times, I'll visually see the shadow of a person quickly move away. I can't explain these things. They just happen. Sometimes, I'll be walking the halls when I'll suddenly feel the presence of a someone following me. That's when my fear takes over and I'll run down to get away!

An unusually painful incident took place one day while I was in our house located right behind the hotel. I felt a hand actually give my rear end a forceful "slap!" No one was in the room with me, so I knew this was from a ghost.

I know that if any of the ghosts were to actually appear to me, I'd run like the dickens! I do believe in ghosts and it would be interesting, but I'd be very scared. I don't believe the ghosts we have here at the hotel ever intend to harm anyone; they appear to be friendly, and maybe are just interested in what the living are up to.

Before I forget, I want you to have this photograph and take it with you. It's one that a past hotel guest took and gave to me. This guest mailed it to me with a note describing what they believe is the image of a ghost

they caught on film. Here, take a look!

You can easily see there definitely is a foggy image, a spiritual being that was caught in the hotel's bar. I've kept the picture here on my bookshelf. As I look at it, it makes my skin crawl. Go ahead Antonio; take it with you. I don't want or need it in here anymore!"

MICHAELA WOLFE'S STORY

"I was born in Cologne, Germany and grew up in Bavaria. I came to the U.S. a little over ten years ago, I lived ten years in Chicago and now I've been here in Cimarron for about six months. In April of this year, my husband and I arrived in Cimarron and due to unfortunate personal issues, he has since moved away while I've chosen to remain. Prior to moving to Cimarron, I had never heard of the town or of this hotel's ghostly history. It was at the time I was filling out my job application with the hotel that someone mentioned, "You do know that the hotel is haunted—right?" I didn't believe in ghosts and, especially since the hotel attracts many tourists, I thought that the hotel staff might have made up the rumor to attract even more guests. Well, after I was hired as front desk clerk I was doing well for the first two weeks I began having my own experiences.

In Europe, I was raised hearing the stories of haunted houses and the paranormal. Not wanting to encourage such beliefs, our parents urged us not to believe in spirits or ghost, but at the same time also cautioned us not to go anywhere near supposedly haunted properties.

The hotel rooms here have no televisions or radios. The only modern electrical devices you'll find in the rooms are electric alarm clocks. The owners feel this is in keeping the hotel's original and authentic "Old West" atmosphere.

My first experience with the ghosts took place two weeks after beginning work at the hotel. I remember it was on a Sunday around noon. I was on the second floor conducting an inspection of room #17 after a guest had checked out. Room #17 is also known as the Mary Lambert room. As I entered the room, I noticed the clean towels the maid was to have replaced on the towel rack in the bathroom were instead scattered about the bathroom. Some towels were on the toilet seat, some in the bathtub, and one was half suspended on the towel rack.

I took it upon myself to gather the towels, fold them, and replace them onto the towel rack where they should have been. While I was doing this, I heard the sound of footsteps outside the room. I thought it might be a guest returning, so I stopped what I was doing and walked out to see who it might be. The hallway was clear of another living soul. I reentered room #17 and within a few seconds heard the sound of someone walking about the hallway once more. At this moment, I realized that the house-keeping staff were all out on lunch break and I was all alone. This time I began to feel uneasy and even a bit scared.

Once more I cautiously walked into the hallway and spotted no one. I decided to take a walk to inspect the rest of the second floor in order to ease my mind. I encountered no one. The strange thing about the footsteps was that they made the sound of a large man wearing heavy boots walking on hardwood floors. This is doubly strange because the hallways are all carpeted! So, you might have guessed by now, and would be absolutely correct, that I was nervous and very freaked out.

After reentering Mary's room, I quickly looked all about making sure nothing was out of place. As I was about to exit the room, the door suddenly moved on its own, slammed shut, while I was still in the room! A strong wind was not the cause since all the windows were shut. I took hold of the doorknob, quickly opened the door and ran out of that room! In my panic, I left my cell phone in the room.

I approached the front desk and briefly explained what had happened. I also asked one of the gals if she could accompany me to Mary's room to retrieve my phone. We reached the room I opened the door, found my phone, closed the door, and quickly returned to the first floor without any incident.

Just a few weeks ago we had guests, a couple who were in the process of settling into their room when the woman reported all the towels in the bathroom lifted themselves off the rack and were "thrown" about the room! The woman was in no state of mind to deal with ghosts, so they quickly repacked their luggage and checked out! Some guests have reported knocking sounds being made on the window of the room from outside, even though there is no place for anyone to stand outside on the second floor! Other guests have reported knocking sounds coming from a corner of this room when they were alone in the room. I have also heard these sounds. Some guests have reported the sudden, strong aroma of a woman's rose scented perfume in Mary Lambert's room. I have experienced this very thing, too.

Once I was called to enter Mary's room by a housekeeping staff. She reported that the bed in Mary's room had been moved close to the window after the maid had cleaned and prepared the room for another guest. No one had entered the room but the maid. When I entered the room with the maid, we found the bed had been moved just as the maid had found it, over by the window. We both took hold of the bed frame in order to move it back in place. And with much pulling and tugging, we were unable to move it one inch! It was as if an unseen person was lying on the mattress and because of their weight, did not allow us to move it back into place! The maid and I decided not to aggravate the ghost any further, so we left the bed where it was and decided to wait then attempt to move it again in a few hours. Later that afternoon, we returned and without much effort, we moved and placed the bed where it originally had been.

Other incidents that I've personally experienced in this room have been witnessing articles being moved about by unseen hands. One day as I was in Mary's room, and noticed a tissue box moving along the inside of the window ledge. I walked past the bed, reached for the box, and placed it on the table by the fireplace. As I turned around, I noticed the pillows that were one second ago arranged carefully on the bed, were now on the floor! I didn't hear a thing; they were just moved in the blink of an eye! I was somewhat in shock, but wanting to get out of there as soon as possible, I said out loud, "Okay, Mary I'm going to pick up the pillows and put them back on the bed where they belong, then I'm going to leave." We also get reports of the door leading into Mary Lambert's room opening and closing on its own. Some guests have even taken small movie cameras and filmed this occurrence.

One evening, as I was on duty, I walked up to the second floor to do a visual security check. I noticed one of the chandeliers suspended in the hallway was turned off. I walked up to the chandelier and pulled on the chain. Later that evening as I walked up to the second floor, the chandelier was again turned off. Apparently, the ghosts enjoy playing with the lights. People have taken pictures of the hallway and have "captured" several "spirit orbs." Some of the orbs are very large.

I must add that the sounds of heavy, booted footsteps are a frequent occurrence in the hotel. I can bet money that if someone is alone on the second floor, they will hear these footsteps. No matter which end of the hotel you're standing in the sounds of these ghostly footsteps will be at the end of the hallway making their way towards where you are. They are not in any hurry, but simply a slow, determined, and strolling walk.

A few months ago, we had a group of ghost hunters from Michigan here conducting a fact-finding session at the hotel one evening. I accompanied the small group into room #5, the Jessie James room, located on the first floor. I was standing in the bathroom with one of the team members while the others were in the main room. Suddenly the other woman and I felt a very cold breeze envelop the bathroom. This breeze was so cold that as we exhaled, our breaths actually became a misty fog. As soon as I finished stating, "Did you feel that cold change in temperature?" one of the other team members yelled out a loud scream and ran out the door!

We asked what had happened and she stated that she felt the coldness, only in her case it became so intense that she panicked and caused her to want to escape, so she ran out into the hallway for safety. This woman didn't want to continue the investigation any further. She stayed away from the team for the remainder of their investigation.

As the others made their way up the stairs to the second floor, they approached Annie Oaklie's room when suddenly we all began to hear a whimpering, soft crying coming from inside the room. I opened the room and discovered another absolutely empty room. The interesting thing I need to mention is that the sounds of a conversation taking place on the second floor between a man, woman, two men or even between two women is not unusual. Both staff and guests report this all the time. These sounds are so distinct that it's difficult not to believe that there aren't others in the hotel, be they living or not, with you. I am often amazed at the amount of guest looking to experience a ghost. The most often request from guests during the checking in process is, "Can we have one of the haunted rooms?" If it's available we check them into room #17, the Mary Lambert room.

Just two months ago, one late evening as I was using the copy machine on the second floor, I heard footsteps in the hall. I walked to the door and looking down the hall, I noticed a man wearing a large, black cowboy hat walking about the hallway. The hallway was dimly lit and he was at the very end of the hall, so it was a bit difficult to see any of this person's detail in full. I immediately thought it was a similar looking man I had checked into the hotel earlier that same day. The man stopped, looked in my direction, took hold of the front brim of his black hat and tipped it in a friendly greeting.

I didn't think much more of this, but after I finished my copying I walked down to the lobby and encountered the guest who I thought was the cowboy I had seen on the second floor. The guest was wearing a hat, only this hat was white and he told me he had not been on the second floor. This chance encounter really was unique because the ghost in the black hat acknowledged my presence, something that rarely ever happens, at least to me. As I said before, a lot of unusual sounds and sights take place on the second floor.

I remember one interesting thing that happened in the prep area of the dining room. In the dining room is a large wall that separates the dining area from the kitchen. Behind this wall are serving dishes, napkins, coffee machine, straws, etc. At the time of this latest incident, I was working the front desk late one night and was positive that there was nothing out of place behind this wall because I passed it several times that evening. Well, having to pass by this area again, I was surprised to see that the straws, which had been neatly stored in their place on a shelf all evening, were now strewed about the floor! This gave the appearance of a mischievous spirit who had decided to send a message of who knows what. I would love to be able to communicate more directly with some of these ghosts, just to find out why they move things or cause certain behaviors to be observed by us living.

Just last Sunday as I was in the hallway walking towards room #24. I suddenly felt someone's hand on my shoulder, followed by a tug on my shirt. Before I realized what just happened, I felt a hand on my arm, pull at my arm! I froze in place and while attempting to make sense of this, I felt an even stronger tug on my shoulder! I instinctively yelled out, "Knock it off!" This particular episode of being touched, pulled on by a spirit went way over the line and actually left me feeling very angry.

You know, for the most part, I really do enjoy working at the hotel. My concerns these days is in knowing that being touched or grabbed by a ghost, are now very real possibilities but for what reasons and to what level of frightening intensity, I'll never know. The hotel is a very nice one, but I would never sleep here overnight. I don't want to be surprised, touched or grabbed by one ever again. As I stated in the beginning of this interview, I never believed in ghosts, but after working at the hotel, I certainly do now."

GALLUP, NM

Gallup was founded in 1891 as a railhead for the Atlantic and Pacific Railroad. The city was named after David Gallup, a paymaster for the Atlantic and Pacific Railroad. It is the most populous city between Albuquerque, New Mexico and Flagstaff, Arizona. Gallup is sometimes called the "Indian Capital of the World," for its location in the heart of Native American lands and the presence of Navajo, Zuni, Hopi and other native nations. One-third of the city's population has Native American roots. Route 66 runs through Gallup, and the town's name is mentioned in the lyrics to the song, Route 66.

In 2003, the U.S. and New Mexico Departments of Transportation re-named U.S. Highway 666, the city's other major highway to Route 491 since the number "666" is associated with Satan and devil worship thus, it was offensive to many people. Local Navajos, some who are superstitious, felt the name change would lift the route from being "cursed". Gallup is a forerunner of racial diversity and civil rights issues. The city long opposed racial discrimination of its black residents; the majority of them lived in the city's west side in the 1940s before the U.S. Civil rights movement took place. During World War II, the city fought successfully to prevent 800 Japanese American residents from being placed in wartime internment. A sizable Palestinian community of about 600 persons can be found; they first arrived from Palestine in the 1970s and are found in the Southwestern arts and jewelry industries.

Gallup has more millionaires per capita than any other town in the United States. There is controversy surrounding this, as it is widely believed that most of the so-called Indian Jewelry Shops and Southwestern arts and jewelry industries business are exploiting the local Native American people. Most companies that deal with jewelry from Native American's often buy the jewelry for as little as 10% of the worth but turn around and then sell the items for hundreds of dollars with the artist receiving much, much less for his/her work.

HISTORY OF THE EL RANCHO HOTEL

"Charm of Yesterday, Convenience of Tomorrow." Thus, is the historic El Rancho Hotel's slogan. It's also known as the "Home of the Movie

Stars." Of note is the impressive guest lists of Hollywood's notable stars from years gone by that have lodged at the hotel. This list includes the likes of Ronald Reagan, Allan Ladd, Jane Wyman, Betty Hutton, Jackie Cooper, Katherine

Hepburn, Kirk Douglas, Paulette Goddard, William Bendix, Humphrey Bogart and Jack Benny. Today autographed photos of these and other stars adorn the fabulous two-story open lobby, along with mounted trophy animal heads and Navajo rugs.

Historically, the hotel, built by the brother of the movie magnate, D.W. Griffith, opened its doors on December 17, 1937. The Gallup area was well known to Hollywood filmmakers at the time due to all the westerns that were being filmed in the area. Conveniently located directly on historic Highway 66, the hotel is presently owned by and operated by Armand Ortega. Decorated throughout in the Spanish/ Indian tradition, it's quite a showcase for the eyes. Needless to say, for visitors it remains quite an interesting and unforgettable destination!

MARK CANNING'S STORY

I interviewed Mark while he was standing across from me with the hotel's registration counter between us. The hotel's lobby was silent, having a lull in check-ins during the late evening hour of midnight. The lights were low; the atmosphere was peaceful and the only break in this state of calm was the occasional ringing phone or nearby passing train. Mark is an easygoing type of person, very welcoming and no hint of agitation. Mark's responses to my questions were free flowing and he wasn't in the least scared or hesitant to inform me of his personal experiences with the paranormal at the hotel.

At the end of our interview he even accompanied me to the parking lot and to my car stating, "Maybe the next time you return to Gallup, if you have the time we can take a hike up to those mesas over there. There are a lot of interesting and historical things. I'm sure you'll be impressed by what you see." I told Mike I'd consider taking him up on his invitation but for now, I'll focus on documenting his ghost experiences. As you'll soon read, there is much to record and much Mark has seen throughout his fifteen years of employment at the historic El Rancho Hotel.

— Antonio

Mark Canning, Night Auditor.

"I'm from Montgomery, New York which is near West Point. As of today, I've been working at the hotel for about fifteen years. About eighteen years ago, I decided that I wanted to make a change in my life, so I moved to the Gallup area. One thing led to another and I got a job at the hotel. I worked various jobs at the hotel beginning as a desk clerk.

Today I'm the night auditor. When I began my employment, at first there was no mention of a ghost or ghosts inhabiting the hotel, but that soon change when I had my own unusual experience. I live upstairs in an area of the hotel that is reserved for an employee's living quarters such as myself. I had an apartment that is located in a connecting building, a building that originally housed chauffeurs, maids and other employees. My apartment was #228, that's over fourteen years ago. Having recently painted and fixed a few things in it, at the time I had only been living in the apartment for a few months. I had taken the time and care to make sure that everything in the apartment was in place and functioning properly.

My first night in the apartment proved to be a very disturbing one for me. I was abruptly awakened one night by the very loud sounds of items being moved in the room where I was sleeping. These sounds were coming from everywhere, so I couldn't pin point exactly what was going on, or what was being moved. But the noises were loud enough to wake me from a deep sleep.

Suddenly, the dishes, pots and pans that I had carefully placed in the kitchen began to rattle. I got up and look around the apartment but saw nothing. I was 'creeped out!' I went back to my bed and as I started to doze off, once more the noises started up. I also distinctly heard what sounded like a large four-footed animal walking above my ceiling!

The footsteps were very heavy and obvious. It was as if something or someone wanted to make themselves known to me by first, waking me up, then 'they' rushed into the kitchen to rattle the pots and pans. This took place the first night of my stay. Then nothing happened for approximately a span of about six months. Because I'd not had another such experience like the one on my first night, I thought it was now all over, but this was not to be the case.

As I said, about six months later during one night, as I was sound asleep, the loud noises in my apartment started up once again! I jumped out of bed several times, and looked all over the apartment and as before saw nothing out of place. The following morning, Manuel, the bar manager at the hotel whose apartment was several doors down the hall from mine, remarked to me that he had had some really bazaar 'going-ons' the night before; the same evening as me. He said that similar to my experience, he was awakened in the middle of the night by loud noises around his bed. Then the noises moved into the kitchen, he also rose out of bed to investigate and found nothing out of place.

We decided to check for the possibility that mice were in our apartments, so we looked for the tell-tail-signs of mouse droppings and any evidence of rodent damage, but discovered nothing to indicate such. I was somewhat glad that we didn't find mice; and was not looking forward to encountering any mice or having to eradicate them. I remember back to a time when I lived in New York, I accidentally discovered that my house had mice. One morning as I was going about my usual breakfast routine, I placed two slices of bread in my toaster and within a few minutes discovered that along with the bread, I had toasted a mouse that had entered the toaster the night before!

My wife, who is Navajo, has had her own experiences in the apartment. She tells me she has had numerous occasions when she has heard a male voice speaking to her in the room. This male voice surfaces every now and then. Even to this day, not much time transpires when the voice will make its presence known. She tells me that it is definitely a masculine voice. Interestingly, there was a time when she could make out a few sentences. The voice stated to her, 'Relax, I'm not going to bother you, I just want to rest a bit.' I tend to believe that this spirit might be a relative of mine. I believe this because of my furniture.

All the furniture in the apartment I brought to Gallup from New York.

I think that the spirit in the apartment is somehow 'attached' to the furniture. I got to admit that the furniture is very 'spooky' looking. Even though it's in good shape, it's dated from the late 1940's. We don't feel threatened or in any harm by this male spirit; I think he just wants us to know he's still watching over his furniture. People get attached to material things, so this is just one of numerous possibilities that I can think of.

Another strange incident took place on the hotel's third floor. It is not unusual for our housekeeping staff to describe that they have been touched on their backs by an invisible hand. I remember one night about five years ago as I was seated at the front desk, a female guest staying in room #305 came up to me and reported something strange had just taken place. In the room above the bed is a framed poster by a Navajo artist named R.C. Gorman. Prior to this woman's experience, the artist had died two weeks before. Well, this guest came up to me and stated that the glass framed print had come away from the wall but floated, suspended by unseen hands, through the air and down to where she was! Instinctually she swung at it, made a direct hit, and broke the glass! She kept repeating that it floated off the wall and hung near her in mid-air!

She asked to be moved to another room and was without further questions or discussion. Today the print has been re-framed, with new glass and re-hung on the same wall.

Manuel, informed me some years ago, that one of the bartenders reported witnessing the ghost of a woman floating down the stairs in our lobby. The woman's most notable feature is her long white hair. As the ghost made her way down the stairs, reaching the halfway point, she stopped, turned to look in his direction and apparently making sure he had a good look at her face. Once this visual connection was made, she broke out in a loud crazy laugh!

The bartender wasted no time in leaving the hotel at that very moment for good! He quit and never returned. The man still lives in Gallup, but refuses to enter the hotel. He won't even look at the hotel when he drives by in his car. I have heard similar stories about this apparition, and the stories all mention the ghost's long, white hair. Guests also mention that they see the long, white haired, spirit woman seated in our dining room. When they attempt to approach her, or even stare just a little too long she will dissolve into thin air before their eyes!

I am at this counter every night and I must admit that I've heard unusual noises in the lobby, and I've even seen what appear to be shadows of people walking about, but I think this might be due to all the ornate glass and mirrors decorating the lobby. At least, I want to convince myself that this is the case.

The freaky thing that not only have I seen, but lots of others have witnessed also, is the apparition of a ghostly light that moves up and down the rail road tracks. The train tracks that run through town are located directly across the street from the hotel and the trains pass several times day and night. Oddly, this ghostly light is seen moving along the tracks, it reminds me of a safety light that's fixed on the front of a bicycle, and you never hear a sound—it's completely silent. It jumps, speeds up, stops and then floats up in the air without any visible means of suspension, it's a very freaky thing to see!

People in town speak of the lights belonging to the spirits of those folks who have died on the tracks. I read of several incidents involving individuals who have been killed by the passing train. In fact, just recently there was an article in our newspaper reporting another such death. I've seen these lights quite a few times, and always in the early mornings. I've looked at my watch and have noticed that the lights appear between three and four in the morning— always within this hour.

As the front desk night auditor for the hotel, from time to time I've had guests come up to me asking, 'Is this hotel haunted?' I try not to engage them in this topic only because I can't tell if they sincerely are interested, or if they were looking for an excuse to seek lodging elsewhere. I try to give indirect responses to this question, but I personally don't have a problem with ghosts. I was raised in an area of New York where the writer Washington Irving wrote his story, 'The Headless Horseman'. The whole area where I grew up is spooky looking, especially during the fall and winter months when the trees are bare and the moon shines. So, having grown up in old farmhouses with huge foreboding barns, I don't have a problem at all with ghosts.

Aside from these reports, the only other incidents that have taken place during my time at the front desk are when local Navajos come into the lobby seeking refuge from 'skin walkers.' Navajo's believe that skin walkers are supernatural beings part human and part animal—usually coyote. They believe that skin walkers do harm, cause illness and even kill. This is a very common belief among the Navajos. Well, I've

had several incidents when I'd be working the front desk late at night, the front doors would open and in would walk a Navajo, visibly upset and seeking protection from what he stated was a skin walker following him. After a few minutes of conversation, the man would reluctantly leave the hotel. 'Navajo skin walkers, or 'Yeenaaldlooshii,' literally translated means 'with it, he goes on all fours' in the Navajo language.

A Yeenaaldlooshii is one of several varieties of Navajo witch, specifically an 'ánt'!!hnii or practitioner of the Witchery

Way, as opposed to a user of cursed-objects ('adag'sh) or a practitioner of Frenzy Way ('azh! tee). Technically, the term refers to an 'ánt'!!hnii who is using his (rarely her) powers to travel in animal form. In some versions, men or women who have attained the highest level of priesthood then commit the act of killing an immediate member of their family, and then have thus gained the evil powers that are associated with skin walkers.'

One incident worth mentioning that my friend Mike and I experienced about five years ago, took place one Easter night outside of the hotel. Mike and I were both employed at the hotel and on our day off decided to go for a hike. For the sake of the story I need to mention that Mike is part Apache. We decided to enter an area of the surrounding cliffs, which historically, the local Navajos are hesitant to enter due to their idea that it's filled with spirits, and is also a known area where evil medicine is practiced. We chose to hike the White Cliffs area because it is so attractively beautiful. We weren't at all thinking of ghosts.

Mike and I hiked up to a mesa, which is called Jesus Rock due to its highest formation appearing like the crown of thorns. The night was windy and as we hiked the area we discovered evidence of the ancient Anasazi people and a few kivas, or ceremonial subterranean sites. Today, they are all now in ruin but none the less still remain as evidence of human inhabitation in the area going back several thousand years.

Reaching the top of the mesa, we encountered an area that was totally flat and surrounded by very large boulders. Mike wanted to make our camp there in the middle of this spot, but something told me to move on. So, we agreed to walk away and eventually settled in another area where we pitched our tent for the night.

During the night Mike kept stating to me that he was hearing footsteps walking about the outside of the tent. I didn't hear anything, and mentioned to Mike that what he was hearing were squirrels.

Later that night, I had an unusual dream. I dreamt I was beating on a drum. Interestingly, the rhythm I was beating on the drum, without having a personal knowledge of Navajo music, was a very proper and correct one. Suddenly, I woke up and noticed at the same exact time I awoke, that Mike also woke and stood up from his sleep!

Without speaking a word, we jointly heard the sound of distinct, human voices chanting. The chanting appeared to be echoing from the top of the nearby mountain. Just then Mike began to once more hear the sound footsteps walking about the outside of the tent. We spent the remainder of the night in conversation until our lack of sleep got the better of us. Because I've never been directly bothered by ghosts, I'd like to think that if one were to appear to me, I'd take it in stride and perhaps react with a calm attitude, but I'm not so sure. I'm a pretty spiritual person. I pray a lot and have actually lived in a community of Hare Krishna worshipers. I feel I'm protected from spiritually negative forces. I studied the ancient texts and found it to be a very positive experience. But when it comes to ghosts, well, who can say until there is an actual sighting or encounter?"

SAM P. ANSON'S STORY

A mutual friend of ours who lives in Albuquerque referred me to speak with Sam P. Anson. I had never met Sam, but after just a few minutes of conversation, found him to be very interesting and also discovered that although he is Caucasian; he is fluent in the Navajo language. His story is a remarkable one in the sense that, unlike most, his ghost experience took place during the day. I can't write much more about Sam, because he is hesitant to have others possibly identify him. "You can't begin to imagine how the local Navajos would avoid me, once they discover that I actually had an encounter with a ghost! That would be very bad for business," he said.

In my experience, I've only had a few such stories when a ghost has made actual contact with the living in broad daylight. It's not a common occurrence, but why should it not happen during the day? After my interview with Sam was over, I drove over to the site where he had his encounter and actually spoke to a couple other individuals in the immediate area who were very well aware of the spiritual haunting. They stated to me, "I'm not surprised by what goes on here. Several people are killed on those train tracks every year. Drunks lay on the tracks and the train runs them over.

I'm not surprised by any of it at all." And another shared, "Ghosts here in Gallup, sure I've heard some of the stories-some are true, some are not, but I know the spooks hang around town."

—Antonio

"I've lived in Gallup for all my life 55 years and I attended the public schools from grammar to high school. Because of this, I'm familiar with the town and outlying country very well. One weekend I decided with some friends to do a little inexperienced rock climbing in the area known as Mentmore Canyon. I say inexperienced because I wasn't using any ropes, just my sneakers and bare hands! It didn't take long for me to take a tumble. I fell about forty feet—landing on both feet!

Regrettably, I broke both ankles and had to be carried out of the canyon. It was the worst pain I'd ever experienced in my life! To this day I still tend to limp a little when I walk. Being of Anglo heritage, my family and I were not much into discussing apparitions, ghosts and hauntings-we couldn't care less about them. We just didn't believe in these things, and preferred to leave what we regarded as fake but fun stories to the Navajos. I have to say this at the start of my story, in order to give you an idea as to how difficult it was for me to finally have to admit to actually having had my own real ghost encounter.

Since my family had a jewelry store in town, both my parents were always busy interacting with Navajo jewelers coming into our store with silver and turquoise bracelets, rings and necklaces to sell. After my parents passed away, I was left with the family business, and today it remains my livelihood. I still live upstairs on Coal Street with the jewelry business located on the first floor at street level.

It's no secret that alcoholism is a problem with a lot of the Navajos in Gallup. It's a problem that affects everyone, even whites, but is most obvious when you personally witness so many Indian drunks passed out along the streets and alleys. It's really sad to see such a waste of humanity. I know the tribe has attempted to tackle the problem of alcoholism among its members, but it must be a very strong addiction, or disease to conquer because you can still see the evidence of its terrible effects all

around town.

I first became aware of the stories of ghosts and witchcraft in and around Gallup when as a child; I'd gather together with the other children after school and tell stories. The stories most commonly shared were the ones that were told by the Navajo kids regarding 'skin walkers.' Skin walkers are witches who have turned themselves into animal forms then go about causing harm to others. They were very much feared by the Navajos then and even to this very day. Aside from the skin walkers, I was made aware of a few haunted places in town and in the surrounding hills and mountains.

When I got home, I'd attempt to explain all these stories I had heard to my parents, but my father in particular refused to hear them and forbid me to even mention anything that included the subject of ghosts in his home. I later discovered the reason for his strong aversion when my uncle informed me that when he and my father were children, they experienced a terrible ghost in their home. My uncle never went into detail regarding what that experience was like; he just made me promise not to bring the subject up ever again—and I never did.

Well, thirteen years ago this winter, when I turned forty-two, I had my own encounter with a ghost. My experience took place on a Saturday morning within an alleyway, just one half block south of Coal Street. The time was approximately ten in the morning. I was walking south on Second Street from Coal Street and was about to pass the alley that runs through the middle of most of the blocks going north and south. As I began to pass the alley, I happened to hear a man's voice say, 'Hey brother, can you help me?' I looked over to the direction of the voice and spotted a young Navajo man wearing jeans and a dark shirt.

The guy was about thirty yards away from me and was leaning with his back against a building. I stopped walking, turned and faced the man.

Immediately I thought he was going to ask for money, but instead said, 'I've been hurt and I need to see a doctor.'

Because of his need for medical attention, I cautiously decided to walk over to him to investigate. Normally, I would have just kept walking, but that day for me was somehow strangely a different one. As I got to within ten or so yards from him, he lifted his head and I got a good look at his face as he turned in my direction. His facial features indicated that he was a full blood Navajo, I was so surprised to see his face completely drained of any color, and was a very, very pale light white or yellow/grey!

He kept saying over and over, 'I need to see a doctor. Take me to a doctor.'

After seeing how unnatural this guy's skin looked, I was even more hesitant to approach him. I had never seen anyone who looked in this state of shock or poor health. Something within me, my instinct said, this is pure death, plain and simple. This guy is dead!

As he continued pleading for help, I walked up to him and asked, 'What the hell happened to you?' He responded, 'I was hit by the train. I need to see a doctor.' I was confused by his answer because if a train had hit him, he would be dead at the tracks, not standing in an alley. I didn't smell any alcohol on him, but as I was about to ask him another question he began to slide to the ground. I caught him and he spoke, raising and pointing his finger, 'Can you take me over to the Catholic Indian Center – they'll help me.'

The Catholic Indian Center was located just across the street, so I told him I would help him to cross the street. I placed my right arm around his waist and immediately felt a coldness that I can't explain. He felt so cold that I knew this guy's situation was a serious one.

He appeared not only sick, but also dead to the touch! We struggled across the street and walked around to the front of the building. I helped sit him down upon the stairs at the entrance to the center. The whole right side of my body, at the area during our short walk where I had supported his body, was ice cold! I thought the poor guy was ready to die any minute.

I walked up to the door of the center and began to knock loudly and with force. No answer. I couldn't wait so I told him I was going to walk next door and see if I could find someone. 'I'll be right back,' I said. I left him seated bathed in the morning sunlight on the stairs and ran over to Coal Street and found a shopkeeper about to open his store for the day standing outside his building. I explained to the shop owner, whom I knew, that I needed to get the guy some medical attention.

The shopkeeper seemed very calm and advised me not to be so concerned. 'The guy must be drunk. Just another drunk Indian that's all,' he said. I told him that this guy was not drunk but has something more serious. The shopkeeper turned the key to lock the door, took out his cell phone, and we both walked back to the Catholic Indian Center. This was only a short distance of about a half block.

When we arrived at the stairs, the guy was nowhere to be seen. I looked all around the building and glanced at the empty parking lot, I just stood there on the stairs, very confused. I thanked the storekeeper and decided not to give the incident more thought. But I remained perplexed and bothered by everything that had transpired.

I decided to walk back to the alley, and was so shocked to see the same man standing against the same wall! This time I had no hesitance to approach him and ask for an explanation. As I stood at the sidewalk facing in his direction, again about thirty yards away, I yelled at him, 'What are you doing here? I thought you wanted to see a doctor? I went through a lot of trouble for you.' As I walked up to him, he turned to face me and said, "It's too late, but everything is okay now."

I stopped and as I kept my eyes on this guy, he slowly began to disappear, in broad daylight; he faded away and just absolutely vanished! All I remember saying out loud was, 'Oh, God. Oh, God. Oh, God!' At this point I was shaking with fear. I walked out of the alley and back to my home very much dazed and confused. I didn't dare speak of what had happened to anyone. I was both sacred and dumbfounded.

The only people I've ever told this story to are Jon, a fellow neighbor of mine who moved to the state of Delaware a few months ago and the other is a Navajo woman, Josephine who has been a friend of the family for many years. She lives in a very traditional manner on the reservation, does not speak of ghosts at all. But after hearing my story she did arrange for a medicine woman to conduct a 'cleaning ceremony' on me. Because of its sanctity, I'm not allowed to describe the ceremony, but it did help me deal with the after effects of the experience I went through with this ghost.

At this point, I'll never forget what it was like to actually touch a ghost; it was cold and absolutely the most unforgettable thing I know I'll ever go through. You can't imagine how awful it was to unknowingly hold on to a ghost as I did, holding a person that is lacking any body warmth or feeling of life. The only thing that comes close to this is if you were to visit a mortuary and lift a body out of its coffin. I guarantee it will change your life forever.

Today whenever I drive past the alley, I try not to look at the exact place where I spotted that man. Even though I try not to look, curiosity always makes me sneak a quick glance. I haven't ever seen this guy again but always hope he has found peace."

GREEN BAY, WI

CARL BEMIS' STORY

My first and only experience with a ghost thus far took place just a year ago in Green Bay, Wisconsin. I am hesitant to tell you that this experience will be my last because in my soul I know, and am confident that, it will not. This personal thought is strong and directs me to seek out reading material and resources regarding the subject of life after death. At the time, I was and still am, employed as a realtor for Century 21. I am also a writer for a popular local, monthly reality magazine.

One particular spring I was doing research for a segment of the magazine featuring several Bed and Breakfasts for an April deadline. Prior to beginning my assignment, it was not my intention on any level to focus on the paranormal or haunted nature of these inns, but a horrifying experience sure change my perspective on the subject for good.

My assignment happened to take me to Green Bay and to a nationally registered three storied Victorian house that the owners were running as a Bed and Breakfast. My visit was pre-arranged one month in advanced together with my booking of room 202 for the night.

I arrived at 6 pm and before entering the front door, I made a mental note of the property's beautiful architecture and began taking numerous photos particularly of the attractive, eye-catch top most turret with its beautiful stained glass windows. Stunning!

I asked the owners if the turret was also a room that was rented out for guests, the husband quickly responded, "Oh yes, it is but, only for the most adventurist guest." I ask him to explain and without missing a beat he spoke with a serious face, "That's Mrs. Cassoway's room, she's our resident ghost and she enjoys making her appearance to male guests."

I smiled and asked if I might have that room instead of room 202? "Not a problem," he answered, "Guests tend not to book that room anyway due to all the stairs needed to climb up to it. Just remember what I'm about to tell you, Mrs. Cassoway might attempt to seduce you but not to worry, she's harmless."

I was taken aback by his last comment and thinking our conversation was headed in a direction I had not planned on, I just took the key when it was offered, lifted my small suitcase by the handle and made my way to the seemingly endless staircase leading up to the turret room. I didn't even mention to the owners that I was a non-believer, and not interested in Ms. Cassoway's sexual advances since I've been gay all my life.

Upon entering the room, I was visually struck at its simplicity, predominant lavender colored walls and matching bed spread, but what stood out most were the beautiful leaded glass windows that encircled the room. I then decided to take a quick shower before heading out for a light dinner in town.

After I arrived back at the bed and breakfast I watched a few minutes of television before getting under the covers at about 10:30. The last thing I remember before falling asleep was watching the light from the crescent moon as it shone through the colored glass window panes, displaying a rainbow of light on to the wooden plank floor. A visit from a ghost was the furthest thing on my mind, but a visit was indeed what was soon to come.

At 3:20 am the digital arm clock on my nightstand displayed the time as I was awakened from sleep by the sound of the bathroom door slowly opening on its own, it made a squeaking sound. From the position of the bed against the opposite wall, I had a direct view of the bathroom door. There was no way to mistake that sound as something else. I watched the door open while making the squeaking noise, right in front of me!

Almost immediately after the door opened, came the distinct sound of footsteps slowly approaching the opposite side of my bed. Once they reached the bed I caught an over powering aroma of fresh flowers, not any one type of flower in particular but flowers none the less. I must admit that this shook me up the most, the aroma was definitely emanating from whatever was now in the room with me.

I was unsure whether to jump out of the bed or just stay put, but my intense fear made me stay put. Thinking back to that moment it was sheer terror that directed my every thought and paralyzed movement. What followed was a silence of unimagined stillness, an uncomfortable emptiness.

Soon I experienced what I can only describe as something not of this world. At first, I began to slowly feel a slight movement in the bed, centered to the right of my feet. I turned to look at this spot and got the fright of my life!

The comforter began to move, slowly at first then it rose about six inches off the mattress. This was followed by the pressure on the mattress of 'someone's' body weight attempting to get in the bed with me! Then I felt a leg, then of a full body lying next to me, the whole bed was enveloped with the strong familiar scent of a woman's perfume, but this was not the worst of it.

As I lay flat on my back in bed and frozen in fear, I actually felt a woman's soft face start to press against mine, but what I find most difficult to erase from my mind is of her heavy breathing in my ear! First the slow inhaling followed by her labored exhaling, while all the time having to smell that God-awful floral scented perfume. In between each breath she would actually also sing a short, faint melody, then take a breath and sing once more. This went on for about 30 seconds until I had had enough.

Something within my soul snapped and gave me the strength to take in a deep breath of courage and yell out, "Mrs. Cassowary I'm not interested in you. I'm a gay man, get away from me, go away now!"

As soon as I said this, I felt the ghost leave my side, the energy in the room felt lighter and the overpowering floral scent cleared out. As I said, it was immediate, her ghost was gone in the span of a second or two!

What this experience has taught me is to not discount the existence of spirits. I know they are real and I respect them for what they are, former human beings, now souls that have the capability to somehow interact with the living. Why shouldn't they? They were once living human beings now present in a different form. But honestly this experience that night doesn't ever leave my memory, it's just something that I'll never forget and causes me to frequently question what I believe to be reality.

GROVELAND, CA

Groveland has a rich history as one of the towns that grew up around gold diggings during the California Gold Rush. Although gold brought the area its first rush of people, water also played a major role in the town's fortunes. Today, Groveland serves tourist from all over the world as well as its more than 7,000 area residents.

Originally, Groveland and Big Oak Flat were named Savage's Diggings after James Savage, who discovered gold there in 1848. He left in 1849 when the Gold Rush started. By 1850, the camp was named Garrotte for it swift and harsh frontier justice. The Golden Rock ditch from the South Fork of the Tuolumne River near Hardin Flat was completed in 1859, assuring though water for hydraulic mining and by 1860, Garrotte was a boon town.

The Big Flat Flume, a link in the ditch, fell with a spectacular crash in 1868. By the 1870's most of the "easy pickings" were gone. Garrotte became a quiet town catering to cattle ranches and a few tourists taking the Big Oak Flat Road to Yosemite. The Big Oak Flat Road to Yosemite was unpaved, narrow and winding. Traffic was one way, and the road was closed during winter months.

In 1875, Ben Savory, owner of what is now the Groveland Hotel, convinced his fellow citizens to rename the town Groveland. In the late 1800's Groveland had a second boon with deep shaft mine and milling operations. The mining boon was over by 1914, but San Francisco had received congressional approval to build the Hetch Hetchy Water Project. Groveland was selected as the mountain division construction headquarters, but Groveland received none of the water, so when the project ended, Groveland returned to the sleepy town it was before. During World War II, the town was dark and quiet. Everyone was fighting overseas or working in the shipyards.

When the war ended, America started building homes. Groveland had another boon, although it was short-lived. Twenty-two small lumber mills were opened, but the lack of water kept the area from growing. Private wells and springs ran dry every summer.

Today, Groveland is a natural stopping spot on Highway 120 on the way to Yosemite National Park, and it is a vacation destination in its own right, from which many take day trips to Yosemite.

GROVELAND HOTEL

The Hotel is the largest adobe building in Groveland, and is one of the oldest buildings in the county. Now listed on the National Register of Historic Places, in years past the structure was first used as a trading

post, owned and operated by Joshua D. Crippen and Company. The property was later owned and operated as the "Garrote Hotel" by Matthew Foot, a prospector who arrived during the Gold Rush. In 1857 it became known as The Groveland Hotel.

By 1900, Groveland's economy was driven by the mining industry. The miners' affairs were centered at the Groveland Hotel and Bar, a neighboring dance hall, and the nearby saloon. Although by then, there were at least two other hotels in town, The Groveland Hotel was still the largest and most impressive.

By 1914, mining had lapsed into an irreversible decline and the second personality of the Hotel was "born." The Hotel was purchased by Timothy H. Carlon, a successful cattle rancher with extensive holdings both inside and outside the county. Timothy Carlon was described as Tuolumne County's first "millionaire cattleman."

Walter A. "Peach" Pechart leased the historic hotel from Timothy Carlon and quickly set to work putting in games, hiring bartenders and converting some of the rooms at the back of the hotel into a small "bull pen." Although the Groveland Hotel's bull pen was best remembered for its girls, it was only one of many "sporting houses" in full-steam operation during this period.

Present owners, Peggy and Grover Mosley took over in 1990 and in 1992, completed a million-dollar restoration.

The hotel today has 17 uniquely decorated rooms, an elegant Victorian dining room and a cozy "saloon." The Grover's' have worked hard to preserve the hotel's historical integrity.

PEGGY A. MOSLEY'S STORY

Originally I'm from Memphis, Tennessee, and my 'claim to fame' is that I was actually a neighbor, classmate of singer and idol, Elvis Presley.

I got to California by way of my military service and being stationed at the Norton Air Base, in San Bernardino. I spent 13 years in the U.S. Air Force, then at my discharge, eventually made my way to northern California, where in May of 1990, my husband and I purchased the hotel and property.

When we came upon the hotel, it was in complete disrepair; the windows boarded up, in need of much care, and money. We really had no idea that under all the dirt,

Peggy A. Mosley.

rot, and neglect, there was a hidden priceless treasure.

We purchased the property with the goal of restoring, and operating it as a historic inn. As the remodeling progressed, we began to uncover little glimpses of its history. The property also included an original gold mine, located across the creek, in back of the property.

Once we acquired the property, local folks 'opened up' and began mentioning their experiences regarding the building. An older gentleman in particular named, Ernie Beck, who 8 years ago died at the age of 103, gave us the history of the property as he knew it, including stories of the ghost. I'll never forget Ernie's words, "Oh, you're going to be sorry."

Within a short time after moving in, we began to experience really strange things. The remodeling got underway when a group of 19 of our friends came to town specifically to help us with the restoration. During that time, all of us experienced doors in empty rooms being opened and shut, buckets of paint would be turned over spilling paint on the floor, and numerous other unexplainable examples that indicated to us, we were not alone.

Most importantly, we were also told by locals that a gold miner named, 'Lyle' had lived on the property. Lyle worked the mine on the property, and was known to be a very private man. One day, in 1927, someone notice after three days, that Lyle was missing. Soon he was discovered in his hotel room, dead. Since then the stories that are circulated, are that

Lyle's spirit wanders the hotel. All my employees, past and present, have stories of personal encounters with Lyle's ghost. Lyle's spirit tends to become most active in the winter months. I wish I had a photo of him, so that we could identify his face, with his spirit. l think it would be great to be able to see what he actually looked like.

The first significant paranormal thing that my husband and I experienced within the building, took place during the winter of 1990. My husband was in one room watching television, while I was across the hall in another room, attending to paperwork. My husband came into my room and asked, "Do you hear that? It sounds like a shower in one of the rooms is on." I responded jokingly, "Oh, it's probably Lyle taking a shower." My husband decided to investigate and walked upstairs to the room where the sound was coming from. I watched as he walked down the hall, about half way towards the room, when suddenly the sound of the shower abruptly stopped. He came flying back, and said, "Did you hear that, the shower stopped!" I said, "Well, I guess Lyle finished his shower." My husband didn't think my response was very funny. He refused to believe in the existence of ghosts, but I could tell he was quickly becoming a believer.

Another weird experienced took place one late evening at about 11:30.

Humes high school, Memphis, TN. Peggy Simmons (Peggy A. Mosley) Front Row, left to right, seated left of books. Elvis Presley, back row, standing at extreme right.

The hotel was up and running by then, and we had a group of 18 travel writers, employed by Delta Airlines, who were attending a meeting on the first floor of the hotel's dining room. Part way through my brief introduction, I was asked to describe a few interesting facts regarding the hotel, I shared a short overview of our resident ghost and things began happening. As soon as I mentioned Lyle's name, the lights in the room became dim, then bright, then dim, numerous times. A definite invisible presence, and coldness was felt by everyone. I noticed that a few guests were becoming uncomfortable and even gave out audible gasps of surprise as

A wooden chair that was placed against the wall, was now against the bed touching her mattress!

the lights flickered on their own. I ended my introduction with a quick, but courteous thank you, and exited the room.

After the meeting ended, I was approached by a female guest staying alone in Lyle's room, and reported being awakened in the middle of the night by a disturbing noise in her room. She opened her eyes to find a wooden chair that had been placed against the wall, opposite the bed, was now leaning against her bed's mattress! She asked if this might be something that Lyle has done before to other guest staying in his room. I told her, this was the first I had ever heard about but wouldn't be surprised if it was Lyle's doing.

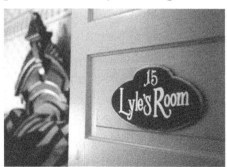

Another female guest who had also spent a night in Lyle's room stated that she was also awakened one night to find a tall, slender man, with a beard, wearing a straw hat, standing next to the sink! When she spoke to him, he faded away. She couldn't believe she actually witnessed Lyle's ghost but said she always keep this encounter as a highlight of her stay.

Apparently, Lyle also does not tolerate women's cosmetics in "his" room. He will routinely move them around the room to show his displeasure. We had a group of four couples, all attending a golf tournament, that were guests at the hotel. One of the women staying in Lyle's room, approached me one morning and asked, "Would you rather I not place my cosmetics on the dresser?" I was caught off guard by her question and answered, "No, not at all." I asked her to explain, and she told me that twice after leaving her make up on the dresser, she'd return to the room to find it all in the sink! I assured her that I would check with the housekeeping staff. As a result of my questioning, none of the staff mentioned moving the woman's cosmetics, or moving them into the sink.

At another time, a woman check into the Lyle room, and not more than twenty minutes later, she returned to the front desk stating." The strangest thing just took place in my room. As soon as I placed my box of make-up on the dresser, it 'hopped' onto the floor! It didn't fall, it hopped off!" This woman didn't know anything about Lyle, so I thought she'd enjoy hearing about him. I began to describe our resident ghost to her, and she was delightfully entertained by the story. She also told me that she would "have a talk" with Lyle to politely ask him for permission to stay in his room.

She told me that twice after leaving her make up on the dresser, she'd return to the room and found all of it in the sink!

Another time a chef, an employed with the hotel, was in the kitchen baking bread. He placed the dough into the oven and was apparently distracted by other tasks, because he totally forgot about checking on the bread in the oven. He stated, that without warning, and at the appropriate time, he was startled to see the oven door swing wide open, exposing the perfectly baked bread! It appeared as if Lyle was also volunteering his kitchen skills, making sure our chef didn't burn the bread.

If you were to ask me, if believe in ghosts, I would answer with a definite, yes! In the twelve years that we've been operating the hotel, we've only had two people who were bothered enough by Lyle, to actually want to check out. That's a good record, I think. Believe it or not, Lyle's room is our most popular and requested room. The public loves him. And as I said before, we all love him. Although our resident cat, "Miss Fat Cat," acts strangely sometimes, as if some invisible person has been teasing her, our staff loves Lyle, and he's never touched, or done anything mean to anyone.

JAMESTOWN, CA

Col. James H. Carson wrote: "On the long flat we found a vast canvas city under the name of Jamestown, which similar to a bed of mushrooms, had sprung up in a night. A hundred flags were flying from restaurants, taverns, rum mills and gaming houses...the whole presented a similar to that of San Francisco during the winter." Col. James Carson suffered financial losses and left in the summer of 1849.

The town slumbered after the gold seekers left for new diggings but was revived in 1896 when a group of Bostonians purchased the Wiskey, Hill Consolidated Gold and Silver Mining Co. and opened it as the Harvard Mine Sierra Railway arrived in 1987, bringing world commerce to the county.

Everything about Jamestown seemed to slide during the 1920's after the gold mines closed, but the image started turning around during the 1970's, when students and business owners began clearing the town and raising funds

JAMESTOWN
~ GATEWAY TO THE SOUTHERN MINES ~

FOUNDED IN 1848, ONE MILE FROM THE FIRST GOLD FIND IN TUOLUMNE COUNTY, AT WOODS CROSSING.

ARRIVING IN 1849, COL. GEORGE F. JAMES, A MERCHANT POPULAR FOR SUPPLYING FREE CHAMPAGNE TO PATRONS, WAS ELECTED ACALDE. AND THE TOWN WAS DUBBED "JAMESTOWN."

POOR MINING INVESTMENTS INDEBTED HIM AND HE QUIETLY LEFT TOWN. ANGRY MINERS CHANGED THE NAME OF THE TOWN TO "AMERICAN CAMP." EVENTUALLY, "JAMESTOWN" WAS RESTORED.

JAMESTOWN'S POPULATION WAS APPROXIMATELY 4,000, BEFORE THE DEVASTATING FIRE OF OCTOBER, 1885.

DEDICATED - MAY 26, 1991 (5996)
MATUCA CHAPTER 1849
E. CLAMPUS VITUS
CREDO QUIA ABSURDUM

to build a gazebo and park on Main St. The park has since become a focal point for community events.

At the same time, the rest of the historic downtown began to be revived. Buildings were renovated in keeping with their original purposes, and many of the Victorian homes were turned into shops that feature artwork, gifts, collectables and antiques.

THE NATIONAL HOTEL AND SALOON

The authentically restored Historic National Hotel in Jamestown (one of the 10 oldest continuously operated hotels, established in 1859), is filled with historical reminders of California's gold-rush past. Located in the center of Jamestown, the National Hotel has played host to travelers for over 140 years. Guests return again and again to enjoy the National Hotel's quaint accommodations, outstanding cuisine, and warm and friendly service.

Each of the hotel's nine restored rooms is furnished with wonderful brass beds, regal comforters, lace curtains, and the feeling that lingers from the days when the hotel was in its first glory. Among the newer amenities are modern plumbing with oak pull chain toilets. All rooms have private bathrooms. Each room is charmingly authentic, individually appointed and includes most of the original furnishings.

The Gold Rush Saloon is furnished with its original 19th Century redwood bar over which thousands of dollars in gold dust was spent. It's not difficult to ponder what it may have felt like to be a gold miner in the 1850s drinking at the bar.

STEPHEN WILLEY'S STORY

I'm the owner and general manager of the National Saloon since it was opened in 1974. I'm originally from the Monterey Bay area of California. Born in Salinas, and brought up in Watsonville.

The hotel is one of the 10 oldest, continuously operated hotels in the state, and it dates back to 1859. As historical records show, the other, older original hotels in the area that were built of wood, caught fire and burned to the ground. In the 1850's, the newer ones were built of stone. Within the present hotel, we currently operate an upscale restaurant and full bar.

Stephen Willey.

I was never told, or informed, of any ghost activity on the property when I purchased it. But, immediately after moving in, things started to happen, that I can only describe as 'unexplained'.

Reports from visitors were noted by employees, that described accounts of a woman's spirit wandering the property. Because of these reports, we decided to give the woman's ghost the name "Flo." I've not found any historical records describing this ghost, and she's never cause any harm, so I can confidently say she's a contented ghost. She also appears to be happy, enjoying her role as a prankster. She's never been malicious, angry, or scary to those who encountered her. Given this, we all continue to welcome her surprising visits.

I, myself have encountered her only once, at my home that's attached to, and located directly behind, the hotel. I recall the visit, when I was standing on my porch on a hot summer, breeze free day. Suspended from the porch, were several wind chimes. Suddenly, the largest of the chimes began to vigorously ring. I thought it was odd for only the heaviest and biggest of the chimes to start moving. Quite curious, I walked over to the grouping of suspended chimes, and expected to see one of my cats taking "paw-swings" at them. There was no cat in sight. As I got

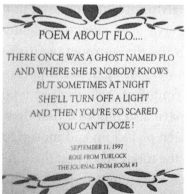

POEM ABOUT FLO....

THERE ONCE WAS A GHOST NAMED FLO
AND WHERE SHE IS NOBODY KNOWS
BUT SOMETIMES AT NIGHT
SHE'LL TURN OFF A LIGHT
AND THEN YOU'RE SO SCARED
YOU CAN'T DOZE!

SEPTEMBER 11, 1997
ROSE FROM TURLOCK
THE JOURNAL FROM ROOM #3

Poem written Sept. 11, 1997 by Rose, a guest who spent a night in room #3.

directly in front of the tinkling large chime, it immediately stopped ringing. I studied the situation, and found absolutely no cause for this. There was no wind causing the chime to move as vigorously as it had done. I gave up trying to figure out a reason, and turned around and began to walk into the house. As soon as I took a couple steps, surprisingly, the chimes started up once more, ringing and moving as if shaken by invisible hands. With a strong sense of resolution in my voice, I loudly spoke, "Flo, stop it!" Immediately, without any further delay, the chimes came to a full, and sudden stop.

Our employees and guests have had many, many encounters with Flo. Most of these encounters happen in the hotel. Housekeepers have reported to me that as they set a stack of clean towels on one side of a bed, and momentarily turn their back, the towels would be moved to the opposite side of the bed! Other times, when the housekeeper would

Guests report a young woman, about mid-30's, strikingly pretty, a very self-assured type lady.

pull a shade up, or down, then go into the next room, at their return, they'd find the shade in an opposite position. Housekeepers always expect for Flo to move things around. These little "things" happen continually, and are expected.

Our hotel records report that guests have seen a young woman, in her mid-30's, who is strikingly pretty, and dressed in a long Victorian style gown, that confidently walks through the dining room, as if she knows where she's headed. She appears to be a very confident, self-assured type spirit. Guest have also reported that their luggage has been picked up and moved to other areas of the room. Also, that the window shades have been pulled down in the middle of the night.

I've noticed that Flo doesn't make footstep sounds, and the scent of perfume occasionally found with female ghosts, has never been associated with Flo.

Guest also write personal short reports about Flo's activities in the hotel room guest ledgers. Each room has its own ledger, and those books are filled with detailed accounts about Flo.

Flo doesn't seem to favor one room over another, she 'hits' them all. But we do have returning guests, who specifically book rooms #3 and #7, because these guests state that those rooms have the most activity. But who knows.

We have had very few guests, but not a significant amount, who out of fear, have cancelled a stay at the hotel when they've heard about Flo. Most guests have a good time knowing that a classy spirit like Flo, is watching, and making sure they're being treated in the correct, and proper manner she was accustomed to.

I'd love to actually have her appear to me. But, just so long as she gives me a little warning first. I have no absolute thoughts about Flo, I just enjoy having her around.

JEROME, AZ

HISTORY OF THE GRAND HOTEL

The Jerome Grand Hotel, a National Historic Landmark, was built in 1926. Formerly the United Verde Hospital, it opened in January 1927 and was one of the most modern hospitals in the Western States. It served the Town of Jerome and the surrounding communities until closing in 1950. The Hospital was kept in standby condition—fully furnished, equipped,

and ready to reopen, if needed until the 1970s. It was purchased in 1994 from the Phelps Dodge Mining Company to be historically renovated and reopened as Van Alan's Jerome Grand Hotel in 1996.

Despite more than three years of renovation, the building has maintained over 95 percent of its original integrity.

The Otis elevator is once again providing service to all five levels, and heat for the hotel is provided by the original Kewanee boiler system installed in 1926.

As one of the highest public buildings in the Verde Valley, (elevation 5,260 feet), Panoramic views of the San Francisco Peaks, the Red Rocks of Sedona, and the entire Verde Valley are breathtaking. The hotel is located within walking distance of downtown Jerome. Along with the hotel and gift shop, the historically renovated 1920's style lounge and restaurant are now open, making the Jerome Grand Hotel the only full-service hotel in Jerome in more than 40 years.

THE DEATH OF CLAUDE M. HARVEY

On April 4, 1935, The Prescott Evening Courier reported that Claude M. Harvey, an employee of the United Verde Hospital and a well-known resident of Jerome, was instantly killed in the basement of the hospital. The man's unavoidable death was caused when his head was pinned under the elevator. Further, there were no eyewitnesses to the tragedy.

Born in Scotland on February 20, 1872, Mr. Harvey had been employed as the hospital's fireman engineer from 1932 until his death. Mr. Harvey was known to the community of Jerome simply as "Scotty" or "Dad."

John Zivkovich, a hospital employee, discovered the body. Dr. M. S. Meade examined the body, and Mr. T. C. Henson, electrical engineer, removed Mr. Harvey's body from the accident scene and testified that the elevator was in perfect working order.

Given all the testimonies following the death, presented to the coroner's jury, there were many individuals, then as now, who believe that Scotty Harvey was murdered. Various theories of the possible crime exist among present employees of the hotel and towns folk. These circulated stories lead the listener to wonder if Scotty's ghost is not yet resting in peace. Could the shadowy figure of a short man, seen darting about the hallways and boiler room of the present hotel, be the ghost of Scotty? Could the presence that is sensed of a man on the second and third floors of the hotel be that same spirit?

ELIN HEARD'S STORY

I'm originally from Wales and I am the bar manager of the Grand View Lounge. Prior to working
at the hotel, I was told about scary things that had
taken place in the building. My only experience
with a ghost took place right here in the bar of the
Grand View Lounge. As I was entering the lounge
one day, I saw a fellow worker, Lisa, standing behind the bar. Strangely, standing directly behind

Elin Heard.

Lisa was a woman whom I did not recognize. The mystery woman was
not very old, she seemed to be in her late 20s. She had long dark hair,
pulled back, and was wearing a white Elin Heard blouse with a high collar. Over the blouse, she wore a dark jacket. My impression was that this
woman was wearing clothing of a by-gone era.

I soon could tell that this woman did not want me looking at her, because as I stared at her, she quickly turned around and went through the
doorway into the rear storage room of the bar. There is no exit door in
the storage room—just one door in and one door out.

I asked Lisa, "What the heck is that woman doing here in the bar?"

She quickly turned around and went through the doorway into the rear storage room!

Lisa was perplexed at my question,
and responded, "What woman? There's
no one here." I told her that I had seen
this woman standing right behind her
and that she had just walked away into
the storage room. Lisa was speechless
because she did not see any woman. I
decided to investigate the storage room.
When I did, I found no one in sight. I
knew immediately that the mysterious
woman I had just seen was a ghost. I
have lived in a lot of places where ghosts
were regularly seen. I am accustomed to
such things and do not get very excited.
I accept them for what they are, and I

243

leave it at that. I have not heard of other staff or guests seeing this spirit in the lounge. Some people might not want to acknowledge or talk about ghost encounters. You just never know.

However, one story in particular that I remember is about a female guest. One evening, a guest removed her gold necklace and earrings and placed them on the nightstand by her bed. When she woke the next morning, she reached for her jewelry and discovered that her necklace and earrings had somehow fused together into a clump of melted gold! Everyone was shocked and couldn't believe what they were looking at. I have also heard talk of a ghostly little boy, about the age of six or seven, who appears on the third floor. He is seen with a playful grin on his face, and then he disappears.

JENNIFER A. EDENS'S STORY

I've been working at the hotel as the front desk clerk and gift shop cashier for over six months. Prior to working here, I definitely was told about the building being haunted. Growing up in the not-so-distant town of Sedona, local people are well aware of the hotel's ghostly reputation.

I consider myself to be a logical woman, and I have tried to make sense of what I have experienced here. I also know that what I have seen at the hotel is not normal and can't be explained in logical terms.

My experiences happened just a few weeks after I started my job. One evening I was alone, working the 4 p.m. to midnight shift. I was seated at the phone switchboard when I heard noises coming from the

Jennifer A. Edens.

gift shop area. I got up from my chair to investigate. I saw that several items, which I had securely placed on the gift shop shelves earlier, were now on the floor. Some unseen force had actually tossed small dolls and other bric-a-brac off the shelves! Other items that I had personally placed on the shelves went flying before my eyes! I was shocked. Then everything stopped just as quick as it started and I have not had anything like this happen since.

Another time, I arranged the chairs in the sitting area directly in front of my desk, and turned my back. Moments later, they had been returned to their original position by an unseen hand. I know this might seem nutty, but I was the only person in the room, and this really does happen.

At night as I am seated behind the desk reading a book, I sometimes get the feeling that someone is watching me. I can "feel"

Sometimes I get the feeling that someone is watching me.

the glaring eyes of a man staring at me from the stairs just a few feet away.

Once, when this feeling became too overpowering, I quickly turned my head and looked toward the stairs. As I did this, I got a glimpse of the shadowy figure of a man! He stood still and then walked up the stairs and out of my sight. That really shook me up. I was quite alert throughout the rest of the night.

You might have heard about the employee, Mr. Harvey, who once worked at the building and who committed suicide? Some say he was murdered. Well, they found his body at the bottom of the elevator shaft, which is just a few feet away from my working area. That sure gives me a lot of cold comfort knowing a dead man's body was found over there!

Once, as I walked down to the basement, I entered the boiler room and saw the shadowy figure of a man walking about the room. I didn't think much about this at the time, because I thought it was the manager of the hotel. I soon found out that the same day I was downstairs, the manager was out of town. The thought of encountering that ghost down there alone just sent shivers down my back. Eventually, the word got around about my boiler-room experience, and other staff members came forward to tell me about seeing the same shadowy figure in other areas of the hotel. I know that there has got to be a reason for this ghost appearing to all of us. Could it be the spirit of the man that died here?

245

Who can say?

I had another strange thing happen. My switchboard has received calls from rooms that are empty. This switchboard is an old one, but works perfectly fine. I have never had any problem with the system. I began to get these unusual calls from rooms that had not be occupied by a guest.

Once, when I checked out an elderly couple, from my window, I saw them get into their car and drive off. No sooner had they done this, the switchboard began to ring; the call was coming from the room they had just left. I carefully picked up my receiver and said, "Yes, can I help you?" All I heard was static at the other end. I felt as if someone was playing with me. The thought did cross my mind that perhaps it might be the maid playing a trick on me, but I know the maid and she has been so shaken up by these experiences that she would not play around with me like that.

I hope I don't ever see any more shadows or hear any more noises and ringing phones. I work the evening hours, and I don't need these distractions or to be shaken when I am all by myself.

LAINA R. GALLOWAY'S STORY

I have been working as head housekeeper of the hotel for seven months. I was born in Jerome and moved away for several years before returning. Growing up, I always heard local stories about the hotel being haunted, and one day I personally experienced strange events at the building for myself. As a child, I lived with my family in a home just above the hill from the building that used to be a hospital before the present owners turned it into The Grand Hotel.

Well, one day my sister and I walked down the hill towards the building. Suddenly, we both clearly heard a woman's screams coming from within the abandoned building. The numerous stories that people used to tell were about screams and other noises coming from the old hospital. Now we were hearing them for our-selves. Of course, there could have been someone in the building playing a trick on us, but it all seemed so spontaneous and real at the time. Not wanting to in-vestigate any further, we ran home.

A few days after I began my job at the hotel, I began to hear strange sounds coming from other rooms I knew to be empty, the sound of people conversing

Laina R. Galloway.

with each other. Even now I get scared and uneasy when I think about all this. My sister, who also works in housekeeping, has also heard the voices in other rooms. Most often we hear them on the third floor, in rooms #31, #33, #39a, and #39b. Those days, I get scared working alone in those rooms.

In one room, I saw the strangest thing: a shadow of a man walked right past me! As soon as I entered the room, I began to see a hundred little lights floating around. It was as if they were moving as a group in mid-air, much like a school of fish might behave. The lights really appeared to be like someone had thrown handfuls of sparkles into the air. After a few seconds, they slowly disappeared.

Another time, while in a room, I heard the sound of an old, large cart being wheeled across the hall. I could tell it was an old cart because of the squeaking sounds its metal wheels made. At the time, I was using the hotel's only cart, and it was in the room with me. Curiosity got the better of me, so I walked into the hallway to investigate. The hallway was emp-ty. Could that sound be the noise of a hospital cart, used years ago when the building was a hospital? Or could it have been a hospital cot being pushed by the ghost of a nurse?

Again, alone in a room, I'll hear my name being called out. I'll turn and face the direction of the voice, and there will be no one. My sister has had this happen to her, but "they" actually scream out her name in her ear. Of course, this upset her, but what could she do?

I'll also have doors slam shut while I'm in a room. There is no wind

I refuse to go into that room without someone else being with me.

to cause such a thing to happen, so what would cause closet and room doors to close with such force? Whenever a door slams on me, I instantly say, "Stop it and leave me alone! Can't you see I have to work?" Things will subside for a few days, only to start up again. I would like for the spirits to leave me alone. I have no idea why they enjoy bothering me this way. They seem to be at their most annoying during the day, because everything that I have told you has happened to me only in daylight hours.

One day, as I was vacuuming the third-floor hallway, a shadowy figure came right up to me and brushed against my left side. The shadow was moving quickly, and I had the impression it was that of a man. It also seemed to be threatened and angry, because of the manner in which it pushed me. I was so scared that I dropped what I was doing and ran away from that part of the hotel. Because I needed to finish cleaning, I located a co-worker and asked her to accompany me until I finished. She did and from then on I refused to go into that area without someone else being with me.

A friend of mine who used to work at the hotel once told me that she had seen the ghost of an old lady. That ghost appeared twice to my friend. There is also a male employee who works the front desk, tell me that on several occasions he has seen the ghost of an old woman. He told me that the ghost appears on the stairwell by the elevator, dressed in a white dress.

I also recall another employee, who actually only worked for the hotel for a day. She was hired as a maid, and while she was cleaning a room, she was actually attacked by a ghost! She told me that the ghost grabbed hold of her body and would not let her go! She struggled and struggled, but it held on. The supervisor soon called an ambulance that took her to the hospital.

After that experience, she never returned to work. I do not want to see ghosts anymore! I try to be firm with the ghosts when they start to play tricks on me. Today, before I start my shift, I make it a point to tell these spirits to understand that I have to work for a living, that I don't want to be scared and to please leave me alone. I really don't like to be alone in empty rooms, but what can I do? It's my job. I don't have much choice, do I?

LAS VEGAS, NM

THE PLAZA HOTEL

Located on the historic Old Town Plaza in Las Vegas, New Mexico, the Plaza Hotel was built in 1882. Benigno Romero formed the Las Vegas Hotel and Improvement Company in 1880, which was to provide Las Vegas with the finest hotel in the territory. Since the beginning, the  hotel was home to early silent film stars and producer Romaine Fielding. Just over a century after it was built, Plaza Partnership, Ltd. acquired the hotel and rehabilitated the property. This positive action spurred the city to reinvest in the Old Town area resulting in civic pride with the Plaza Hotel being the main focus of attention.

SANTIAGO VIGIL'S STORY

"As of today, I've been employed at the hotel as Front Desk Assistant Manager for close to five years. I was born in Albuquerque but at the age of nine, my family moved to Las Vegas where I've lived ever since. Prior to working at the hotel, I'd not heard of any ghosts inhabiting the property, but at my first day of my employment, the person who was training me informed me that the hotel had a resident ghost. In fact, to this day the front desk has a short print out that is given to any guest that wishes more information about our ghost. The information in the handout describes the previous owner of the hotel, Mr. Byron T. Mills, and his supposed spirit that haunts the property.

Personally, at the time I began my employment, I was a disbeliever. My family did not believe in such things as ghosts and spirits, but that mindset didn't take long to change after working at the hotel. Working different shifts, including late in the evening, I heard unusual sounds that were emanating from different areas of the hotel, including right here in the lobby. I was convinced that the sounds I was hearing were all in my imagination, however one particular night, six months into my employment, my perspective began to change.

I remember my first experience at the hotel when an elderly guest requested I come to his room #217. He was experiencing a problem with his television. The guest explained that the television set in his room had switched on without him physically touch it. And now, try as he might, he was unable to turn it off. When I arrived at his room, I reached for the remote, pressed the off button and nothing happened. Next, I pressed the off button on the set itself. Again, nothing happened. Not having any success, I decided to unplug the cord from the wall. The television set had been placed within a very large armoire and this large piece of furniture was very heavy to lift. Nonetheless, I attempted to move it, but quickly discovered I'd need two men to do this job.

After a few failed attempts, I did manage to move the armoire a few inches from the wall, thereby allowing me to squeeze my hand and arm between it and the wall; I reached for the plug and disconnected it. I pulled on the plug and the television turned off. Then after making sure the set had gone out, I plugged the cord back into the electrical socket again. But what happened next really surprised me. As I placed my hands on the armoire and began to push, expecting a struggle, surprisingly it very easily moved back into place, without any effort at all! It was as if there were an "extra pair of hands" doing the pushing for me. Even the guest who was there witnessing this commented in amazement and disbelief.

My second ghost-like experience at the hotel took place during the time of my Grandmother's funeral. My Uncle arrived in town for the funeral and had booked room 315 at the hotel. I got the impression that he did not wish to spend the night alone, so wanting to be of some comfort to him, I decided to share his room.

Throughout the night I kept having the very strong, uncomfortable sensation that someone was constantly watching me. I woke up during the night from a sound sleep and sat up in bed. I focused my eyes into the darkness and noticed the dark shadow of someone standing in the room with us. I immediately reached for the light and turned it on! My Uncle woke up and, after explaining to him what I had seen, he reassured me that as long as we were both there, nothing would hurt us. A few minutes later, fatigue got the better of me and I fell fast asleep.

Guests do report that the lights in their rooms turn on and off, glow brightly, then suddenly dim, especially in room #310. Room #310 is recognized as having repeatedly odd occurrences such as personal items being moved around when your back is turned. Within their room, as a guest moves from one room to another, returning just a few seconds later, discover a personal item has been mysteriously moved from one room to another. We receive reports of this weird activity to the front desk all the time.

From time to time, the hotel has had groups or teams of ghost hunters that have conducted investigations and apparently have "caught" evidence of spirit activity. Guests in general have taken their digital cameras and captured what they believe to be spirit orbs or balls of spirit energy. They've shared these photos with the hotel staff. We've kept a copy of one of these photos that was taken by a prior guest outside their room. Now, room #311 is also another room in the hotel that is purported to have some type of spiritual energy. Just outside room #311, in the sitting area, is where guests have reported actually seeing the ghost of a man seated in a chair with his arms outstretched as if reaching across the table for something.

As for my own attitude on any of the ghosts at the hotel, I hope I don't ever have one actually appear to me. I don't think my reaction would be a positive one."

JANET MARTINEZ'S STORY

"My positions at the hotel are as Reservations and Guest Services Manager and I have been employed at the hotel for over sixteen years. I was born in the northern town of Raton, NM and moved to Las Vegas, NM in 1986. Before starting my employment at the Plaza Hotel, I never heard of any talk of ghosts inhabiting the hotel, but now when in the course of a conversation, I mention my place of employment, the most common question asked of me is, "Oh, is the hotel really haunted?"

My first experience took place shortly after beginning my employment, in the fall of 1992. I began to hear reports from guests reporting disembodied voices, unusual noises and even the ghostly shadows of figures walking about in their rooms. These incidents most always took place on the third floor in rooms #310 and #316.

Although the incidents are most active on the third floor, that is by no means the only portion of the hotel where things are experienced. The entire hotel has a history of unusual ghostly activity. The most frequently reported accounts are of a man's spirit that moves personal belongings from one room to another. And women are in particular the focus of this spirit's activity.

I recall one woman who reported to me that as she was alone in her room sitting on her bed, she caught the scent of cigar smoke. As she was wondering where this aroma was coming from, she also felt the presence of a man standing directly next to her. Soon after, she felt the bed's mattress slowly depress right beside her as if an unseen person had decided to sit right next to her!

Other reports are of television sets turning on and off on their own and the distinct sounds of footsteps either walking up the stairs or descending down to the lobby area. The aroma of either strong cigar smoke or of a man's cologne usually accompanies these sounds. Given these reports, the hotel staff is convinced that the spirit of the man must be one of the previous owners of the hotel of years past—Byron T. Mills!

The most impressive report I personally experienced was early one fall morning. I had just entered the hotel to begin my shift. I was standing behind the front counter when I heard loud footsteps descending the stairs. I looked up and spotted a female guest dressed in slippers and a nightgown, who came dashing down the stairs to the lobby. As soon as she spotted me she began yelling hysterically, "Oh my God, there is a ghost in my room!"

At that moment Cathy, our hotel's head of housekeeping, was in the lobby and also heard the guest's outburst. I asked Cathy if she wouldn't mind accompanying the guest back to her room, number #310. Cathy returned to the room, without the guest. The woman was so shaken by what she had experienced in her room that she stated, "I'll never go back into that room again. I'll contact you later this evening!" Saying that, she walked out the front door still only dressed in her nightgown and slippers. After Cathy returned from investigating the woman's room, she reported to me, "Janet, I didn't see anything out of place. The room looks absolutely fine."

Later that night, this guest returned and I asked her for an explanation. She said that as she was sitting on the side of the bed, she suddenly felt someone sit right beside her! The presence sat on the mattress between her and the nightstand. Since the phone was on the nightstand, and the spirit figure in between, she would not call for help and said her only option was to run for the door and down the stairwell towards the front desk, which is when I spotted her.

One other time we had a guest who was both an antique collector and a police officer from Arizona. He was fascinated with the old furniture we have in the rooms, halls and lobby of the hotel. I noticed he had a camera and was busy taking photographs of some of these antique pieces of furniture. I spoke to him for a short while and after returning to Arizona, just a few weeks later he called and spoke to me regarding a weird thing that unexpectedly appeared in one of the photos. He also told me he would send me a copy of it.

After his photo arrived in the mail, I opened the envelope and was so surprised by the image captured on our third floor of a ghostly apparition seated at a chair reaching over the table! The picture was quickly passed around the hotel staff and now is displayed directly behind our front desk.

One other time we had a family with young children who had taken a few photographs of their kids at different areas of the hotel. Again, they were in room #302. Well, after their photos were developed, in several of them is clearly seen the images of large, balls of light or spirit orbs. The mother emailed these photos to me because she was curious to know if anyone else had had her similar experience.

Recently, in room #302, we've been having a strange occurrence. In all our rooms, guests have the option to secure their rooms by engaging a deadbolt. Obviously, the deadbolts are located within each guest's rooms and can only be locked from within the room. Well, we have been having reports of the deadbolt, particularly in room #302, being engaged when no one is in the room. Our maintenance crew has inspected the lock and has found nothing that would cause such a strange malfunction to occur. I do recall this same situation with the lock-taking place when I first began working at the hotel. It seems that "whatever" is responsible for this, is now back to their old tricks.

You know, I never really believed in ghosts until I began working at the hotel. One personal incident I recall having had in the hotel happened one fall evening shortly after I began my employment. The hotel was for the most part empty of guests and I was standing behind the front desk charting on a hotel log.

Suddenly, I heard a noise emanating from the room named The Conservatory. I looked up from my writing and noticed that the two large doors began to slowly and simultaneously fully open, as if unseen hands were pushing them outward! Stranger still, just a few seconds later, they both began to move in reverse with both doors returning to their original closed position! All I could manage to say to myself at that moment was, "Oh God!" Even though the experience I witnessed was an unusual one, I immediately knew I had also just witnessed something of a spiritual nature. I have to say that I didn't feel threatened at any time during the course of this event—not in the least. But I knew this was not something that would naturally be considered commonplace.

Most of our housekeeping staff swears that they've all witnessed things in the hotel. Things that give them cause to believe that ghosts in the hotel are an ongoing reality. Several past employees are very convinced of this.

My personal belief is that Byron T. Mills, still to this day is concerned about the welfare of his hotel. Because of this, his spirit is felt and even seen now and then. I don't think he is evil, dangerous, or mean just concerned and wants to "keep on top of things." I know that he particularly enjoys visiting the hotel bar because a previous bar manager named, Gerdie experienced a man's ghostly hand that had stroked her behind! No one else was in the bar with her. This incident took place one early morning as she was stocking the bar. Suddenly, as she described the incident, she felt the ghostly heavy hand, which she had no doubt was that of a man, gently, but firmly stroke her rear end.

Ernestine, our restaurant waitress reported to me one morning about seeing a ghost. As she was facing me from across the front desk, we were conversing about exchanging bills for coins. From where Ernestine was standing, she had a clear view of the bar, which at that early morning was empty and locked. Suddenly, here facial expression changed to one of fear. I asked her, "What's wrong, are you okay?"

She responded, "Janet, I'm seeing the ghost of a young boy who's standing in the bar!" "What are you talking about?" I said. "There in the bar is the foggy image of a little boy dressed in old fashion clothes with his arms outstretched as if he's holding something." At that moment, I turned to look, but I didn't see any ghost.

Even though I personally have never seen a ghost just the actions of ghosts, like doors opening and closing, I think I'd have a good time if one were to appear to me. I bet I'd be in shock, but knowing this, I'd still like to see one. Who wouldn't?"

MANITOU SPRINGS, CO

At an altitude of 6,500 feet, and with a population of 5,000, Manitou Springs has been the most typical example of a tourist town since the 1870s. "Manitou" is the Native American word for "Great Spirit," and both locals and visitors alike describe this beautiful mountain community as "magical." Interestingly, the town's name is an actual reference to an Indian spirit in Longfellow's poem "Hiawatha."

Not unlike other towns and cities established within the mountainous areas of the state, Manitou Springs has its own share of hot springs. A little-known fact is that nearby Colorado Springs was named for the abundant mineral springs located in Manitou Springs. There are nine named mineral springs that meander throughout the community. These springs are continuously fed by the snowmelt that gathers atop Pikes Peak. The Utes, being the first humans to inhabit the area, knew well the source and healing properties of these mineral springs. Today, these ancient springs are available to the general public, free of cost!

The town is situated between two major tourist destinations, the Garden of the Gods and Pikes Peak, Colorado's most famous mountain that reaches an altitude of 14,110 feet at its summit. Historically, before the coming of the white man, Native Americans such as the Ute and Cheyenne considered the area within the present-day town site to be sacred. Today, Manitou Springs supports a well-known enclave of talented artists and can also boast to being the home of many excellent restaurants and quality accommodations. It is said that there are even a few practicing witches' covens somewhere in town.

The arts thrive in Manitou Springs as there are many galleries and shops that showcase the town's excellent artists. Locally made arts and crafts are available at Common Wheel Artist's Co-op and the Business of Art Center. The town is so uniquely blessed with history, natural wonders, and the arts that it was named a National Historic District.

Additionally, among the scenery that awes visitors, nestled among the pines and mountainsides are many historic, and uniquely beautiful, classic Victorian bed-and-breakfasts.

RED CRAGS INN

Few homes in the United States have the stature to be known by their name, not address. Red Crags is a magnificent four-story Victorian mansion that has been known to all in the Pikes Peak area for more than 120 years.

The main house is over 8,000 square feet and dominates the 1.5-acre estate. Prominently situated on a bluff, the unique combination of views includes Pikes Peak, Manitou Valley, Gardens of the Gods and the city of Colorado Springs. Once inside, high ceilings, hardwood floors and beautiful antiques predominate.

The name, Red Crags, first appears on the abstract on March 15, 1870. It was on one of the villas that Dr. William Bell, and his associates, who built the property, were trying to sell to outsiders. Countess de Noailes, from a prominent French family, purchased the villa, named Red Crags, in 1870. The Countess must have lost interest in the property, because Dr. Bell bought the property back on August 11, 1880.

Dr. Bell, in association with Dr. Donaldson, intended to use the building as a hospital, according to some early accounts, but there is not much evidence that this venture was successful. Two rooms in the building were apparently built as sun porches for the treatment of tuberculosis in the early 1900s.

Throughout the preceding years the building has changed owner-ship many times. On March 9, 1908, the property was sold to Eloise G. Smith, and then to W.D. Swain on November 29, 1912. He died in 1924 and the property was deeded to his wife, Laurie Persis Swain.

In the summers of 1924 and 1925, as portion of the house was occupied by artist Birger Sandzen. He was associated with Bethany College in Lindsborg, Kansas. He taught art in the art school in Colorado Springs—out of which grew the Fine Arts Center.

His daughter reported that he used the southeast room on the second floor as his studio. She also remembers listening to people's loud comments on El Paso Blvd. pointing to the house and saying, "Look at the haunted house."

On August 3, 1934, the property was sold to Mr. C. Louis Smith, for taxes owed by Eloise G. Smith Haas. On March 10, 1938, Aldrin E. Smith took possession. The property has had a total of 16 owners since that time. Today, the present happy owners are brothers, Kevin and Brett Maddox.

DEBORAH HENDRIX'S STORY

Deborah and I spent a couple of hours for her interview. She gave me a personal tour of both properties, opening doors, walking into rooms, and sharing personal notebook notations that had been written by guests and owners in the past.

Without question, the property is impressive and historically rich. Situated on a hill, overlooking the valley below, it is clear that the original owner and builder was well aware of getting the most from the natural setting and location of the land.

My personal experience of the property was an eye-opening one, one that I'd definitely recommend to any future guest who might consider staying at a historic bed-and-breakfast. As far as I am aware, the unexplained activities continue to take place, just as they have done for many years.

— Antonio

"I've not lived in Colorado for very long. I was born and raised in Charleston, South Carolina, and arrived in Manitou Springs in March of 2005. I presently have the title of Assistant Inn Keeper at Red Crags, but I am also the Inn Keeper of our sister Inn, Onaledge. Onaledge is just a short walk from The Red Crags Inn. Given the short time that I've lived on the property, I've already had a fair amount of ghostly activity that has presented itself to me. During these experiences, the inn has always been empty of guests.

The builder of the house, Dr. Bell, was from England, and given the town's reputation as being a health-conscious area of rejuvenation, his vision was to have the house function as both a health wellness spa and sanatorium for tuberculosis patients. The solarium of the house has since been enclosed, but during the early years, it was a large open area for tuberculosis patients to use. Because Manitou Springs actually does have artesian springs dotting the area, people throughout its history have believed that these springs do in fact have the ability to heal physical illnesses.

Another known fact is that Dr. Bell's partner, Dr. Donaldson, was a Rough Rider with President Teddy Roosevelt. We have a large, framed picture that is prominently featured in the living room of this very house. The picture displays President Teddy Roosevelt astride his horse, in our front yard. He actually spent several nights in this house.

President Teddy Roosevelt on horseback on the property.

To this day, on each wall, there still exists, as in years past, in each room of the house a little black button for the patients to buzz and alert the nurses. The nurses' station and original switchboard were once located where our gift shop is today. In fact, that very switchboard remains in our gift shop.

My first paranormal incident took place one evening within my first month of arriving. I was at the Red Crags Inn, within my personal residence, located in the basement, or as we refer to it, "The Garden Level." The time was somewhere around 9:30 p.m. Except for my dog Lobo, who was with me, I was all alone in the entire house.

I distinctly remember that I had closed and locked all the doors to the house. I was in my room, reading, and watching television. Suddenly, I heard one of the upstairs' doors slam shut with such a loud bang that it scared me to death! I'm not easily frightened, but this bang was so loud and so sudden that I refused to leave my room and investigate. I looked over at Lobo's reaction and could he also was on high alert as his ears shot right up! The sound was extremely loud and frightening to us both. I've been told that animals are keenly aware of ghost energies, that ani-

259

Deborah Hendrix and Lobo.

mals have an instinctual ability to sense, and to see, figures and ghostly things that humans are unable to. Well, Lobo definitely was aware of something in the house and immediately stood up on all fours, started barking, running back and forth, all around the room.

As I watched Lobo's reaction, I became even more uncomfortable. It was very, very unnerving. I was terrified and who might be inside, and refused to leave the safety of my room. That's how it was for me the entire night. The next day, as I went about the house searching for the cause of the disturbance, I found absolutely nothing. I decided not to dwell on it, and did my best to forget the whole incident.

Not long after, Lobo and I were at nearby Onaledge Inn assisting Brett, the co-owner of the property. Lobo and I happened to be downstairs in the carriage house, that today has been converted into one of the inn's narrow guest room.

Well, once again, without any visible reason, Lobo began to bark and run circles around the bed as if he was chasing something. Then he cornered whatever it was against the rock wall behind the bed. Lobo just kept barking and barking at a spot on the wall, about six feet above the floor. Because of his intense reaction, I knew that "something" was in the small room with us. Although I didn't see anything, the feeling I sensed that we were not alone. As I eventually found out, there have been many unexplained occurrences posted over the years, about this very room, in our guest comments journal.

A few weeks later, while I was alone at Onaledge, I clearly heard a robust laughter coming from upstairs. This laughter

A spirit orb captured within the house.

was the type of laughter that two overjoyed people would share—the laughter of a very content and overjoyed adult and child. I sounded like laughter between a parent and a child. Knowing that I was alone in the house, I knew immediately that there these sounds from ghosts in the house, clearly having fun. I didn't feel threatened at all. I actually found comfort hearing them and was not afraid. It was nice to know that these two spirits were having such a pleasant time.

The house has a history of spirits laughing and who tend to carry on regularly at the house. Interestingly, this always takes place when I'm downstairs. I'll hear the laughter start up, then it just goes on and on for several minutes. When my curiosity gets the better of me, I'll walk upstairs to investigate, and of course I'll see no one. I do speak out loud to the spirits and ask, "Who's here?" But, to this day, I've never gotten a response.

Since the short time I've been here, I've not had any recent guest come to me saying that they have seen or heard any ghosts. But, past guests definitely have. I've even had some who have taken photos of ghosts at the Red Crags Inn!

The most remarkable photo proof came from former guest, who identified herself as Kathy Squire. The first thing she asked me after identifying herself, was "Is the house still haunted?" Surprised by her question, I asked her to elaborate. She stated that the last time she and her husband had stayed at the inn, she had taken a picture of the inside of their room, the Pikes Peak Room. Kathy further stated that she would be happy to send this picture to me, and once having had the chance to look it over, she would like for me to call her, and to give her my opinion and feedback, as to the unusual "object" that turned up in the photograph. The picture arrived in a brown envelope and when I opened it, I immediately had chills from head to toe. In the photo, in the upper right corner of the room, is a clear image of a woman's head that appears to be "floating" between the wall and the bed!

Note: There is NO space between the bed and the wall!

I got a magnifying glass, and held the photo over a light to see if it was somehow faked. I was unable to see anything that lead me to believe this

Clear image of a woman's head "floating" between the wall and the bed!

was an altered photo. It was genuine and clearly not altered in anyway. As I examined the head closer with a magnifying glass, I discovered that the woman's teeth are grossly misshaped, and deformed.

I called Kathy and told her that I had received the picture and couldn't believe what she captured in the photo. I also told her that the misshaped teeth were what struck me the most. She agreed with me. Well, not long after I spoke to her, I answered another phone call from a former guest who wished to make a reservation and again asked, "Is the house still haunted?" When I asked her to explain further, she stated she had rented the Cara Bell Room at the Red Crags Inn.

During her stay, she had entered the room's small closet, when suddenly someone invisible, a spirit, had pushed her into the closet, shut the door behind her, then immediately heard someone laughing on

Suddenly someone invisible, a spirit, had pushed her into the closet!

the other side of the closet door! I was at a loss for words and replied that I was unaware of any ghosts in the house, but if she was interested in renting the Cara Bell room again, she would be most welcome. She ended the conversation by stating, "I'll get back with you." But never did.

I've only been here a short time, but would welcome any of the ghosts to appear to me. I have a strong faith in God, and I'm confident I would be protected from any ghosts, even if it was of a negative or evil nature. However, I don't believe any of our ghosts are evil at all. They seem to be happy and joyful."

MURPHY, CA

MURPHY'S HOTEL AND LODGE

Murphy's Hotel is a registered landmark and was originally owned by John Perry and James Sperry. These men opened the hotel in August of 1856 under the name Perry and Sperry Hotel. Among the hotel's notable list of guests were Horatio Alger Jr., Mark Twain, Thomas J. Lipton, John Jacob Astor, J.P. Morgan, and former President Ulysses S. Grant.

A great fire destroyed the town and hotel in 1859, but in March of 1860, the hotel was rebuilt and soon sold to, Henry Atwood, who then sold it the following year to Harvey Blood, who sold it to C. P. Mitchler, who renamed it the Mitchler Hotel. Mitchler died and the hotel was sold by his brother's widow to Mr. and Mrs. McKimens in 1945, they renamed it Murphy's Hotel.

In 1963 the hotel was purchased by 35 investors who added the second story as was in the hotel's original design.

Today, walking within this unique hotel is like taking a step back in time. The guest rooms are furnished with period antiques, and have shared baths in keeping with the ambiance of 1856.

HEATHER BOWERS' STORY

Heather Bower.

I've began working at the hotel while attending high school. I started out as a bus girl in the dining room, today I work the front desk. I'm very familiar with the hotel's ghost stories associated with its history. It's rumored that the second floor of the hotel is haunted by a male and female ghost. It's a wonderful place to work at, and the staff generally doesn't make it a point to mention our ghosts to new guests, especially when they are accompanied by small children.

My first indication of a ghost haunting the hotel was when a hotel front desk manager informed me and was sitting right where I am now. Her story still sends shivers down my spine. She told me that there was nothing unusual about that particular evening. She was on the phone taking a reservation when suddenly the antique chandelier directly above her began to sway in a slow, circular motion. Within a few seconds, it quickly, and violently moved with such force, that it broke free of the ceiling-electrical wires, bolts and all! It dropped down and crashed right next to her, missing her by just five inches!

Another employee, the hotel's banquet manager, also told me about the time she was in the banquet room, when an unusually weird thing took place. She described finishing with straightening up the room, she pulled and closed all the heavy drapes covering the windows. After doing this, she stepped out of the room for just a few minutes, but when she returned, was shocked to find every one of the drawn drapes had not only been removed from the rods, but "torn" and scattered about the floor! She was so scared by this, that she refuses to discuss the event any longer. She has often told me that this experience has made her frightened, and to this day, she doesn't feel safe going into that room alone.

Just a couple of weeks ago, the street directly in front of the hotel was closed for repairs. The hotel had very few guests at the time. One afternoon, the housekeepers were all gathered on the ground floor attending a staff meeting. I was seated behind the desk. Not one person was on the second floor. As everyone was gathered together downstairs, we began to hear voices coming from the empty second floor. The voices were loud and obvious, and I had no trouble recognizing them as being the sound of a man and woman engaged in loud conversation. It sounded as if they were just at the top of the stairs. Keep in mind that the second floor is also the same spot where the dining room is located. The same dining room where the drapery was torn off the rods. No one was on the second floor at the time. The entire staff kept quiet, nervously listening to the voices. Soon the voices slowly faded away and everyone in the room stared at each other in amazement. Most all staff members by then had grown somewhat accustom to these activities and the meeting continued, business as usual.

Other common sounds that employees continue to hear are the ghostly footsteps that walk about the second floor. As I said, this is a common experience that does not ever seem to go away. I've noticed that the footsteps are more commonly heard in the early morning hours. I begin work at the hotel at 6 am, and I've noticed that the ghosts start their walking at about the same time.

One historical incident that is well documented, and actually took place at the property, is the time a man was shot directly outside the hotel entrance. His name was William Holt. Historically, Mr. Holt was one member of an old-time gang of bandits in the Murphy area, and was fatally killed as he was entering through the hotel's entrance. His signature, written in his own hand, can be viewed in the hotel's registry. I don't have any way to prove if his ghost is the one that inhabits the hotel, but it makes sense to me.

A friend of mine, Angela, who used to work at the front desk, told me about a few incidents she experienced at the hotel. Several times, while alone, and standing in the lobby, she would sense the invisible pres-

It began to sway in a circular slow motion.

265

The maid was nervous and unsure if she should enter the room.

ence of someone with her. She told me that this presence was that of a man. She could easily see that no one else was in the room, followed by the sudden scent of burning tobacco smoke. After a few minutes, this scent would disappear, and a new scent of Lilac perfume would take over. She had no explanation for this, but always felt that the hotel was without question, haunted.

One day, a maid approached Angela, asking if she would accompany her to room, #9 on the second floor. The maid was nervous and apprehensive about entering a guest's empty, unlocked room by herself. The door was apparently left open by the guests, and because of strict security issues, she wanted another staff member to serve as a witness, and accompany her when she entered the unlocked room. Both Angela and the other housekeeper walked upstairs and knocked on the door loudly announcing, "Housekeeping, anyone in the room?" When there came no answer, they walked inside. Looking around the room, and not seeing anyone, they decided to leave. When Angela grasped the knob, attempting to close the door, someone within the obviously 'empty' room began to hold open the door! Apparently, the ghost wanted it to stay opened. A tug of war ensued, and after a few seconds, Angela using a lot of force, shut the door and locked it.

The second floor of the hotel, to this day, still gives me a creepy feeling which is difficult to shake. I know that the ghosts of the hotel have never hurt anyone, but it's not easy for me to remember this when I encounter unexplainable things. Don't get me wrong, I actually do enjoy 'ghostly' things, reading books and talking to people about the paranormal. I just don't understand why would I fear actually seeing one of the ghost? I guess it would freak me out at first, but crazy as it might sound, I would welcome such an appearance, I think!

PONCHA SPRINGS, CO

Situated at the junction of state highways 285 and 50, this small town with a population of 474 is situated at the northern most point of the Sangre de Cristo mountain range, within the Upper Arkansas Valley. Poncha Springs is surrounded by Colorado's most concentrated series of 14,000- foot mountain caps, which include one of the state's tallest, Mt. Antero, at 14,269 feet. Poncha Springs lies at the south end of the Rocky Mountain range, thus giving skiers a prime location for easy access to Monarch Pass. The town was founded in 1880 and was named by frontiers-man, Kit Carson, after a local natural hot spring. The water from this spring is today piped into the neighboring town of Salida, to provide the hot water for the Salida Hot Springs Aquatic Center.

THE JACKSON HOTEL – ALLAN FORSTER'S STORY

I interviewed Allan at his home in Salida. He had a difficult time staying on schedule with our appointment, due to the fact that a heavy snowstorm over the mountains had caused Monarch Pass on highway 50, which travels through the Swatch Mountain Range from Gunnison, to close for a day. Allan was in the town of Gunnison, so our interview was delayed for more than a day.

When we finally did meet, as he began the first few sentences of his story, I could tell that his story was well worth the delay. Allan never gave me the impression that he was seeking attention in being in this book, rather, he was genuine in his mannerisms and recollections, and when addressing his experiences regarding ghosts, he became visually nervous and apprehensive.

Today, the hotel in Allan's story is much the same as it was in 1982 when he worked there. The area surrounding the property is in need of some landscaping, but its appeal, being a historic property, easily draws visitors to walk up and peer through its windows, hoping to catch a glimpse of Colorado's Victorian bygone era. Whether there are still spirits in the building is difficult to say, but as of the recording of this interview, the property was for sale. If you happen to be the purchaser, I'd appreciate it if you'd let me know.

— *Antonio*

"I moved to Poncha Springs in 1982. Before then, I lived in Colorado Springs, where I was born and raised. I was 17 when I was hired to work at The Jackson Hotel. My job was to cook lunches and I'd also work around the hotel doing a bit of plumbing, yard work and anything else that might be needed. I enjoyed it for the short period of time I was employed. I didn't much care to be frightened though, that's the main reason that I left. It was the constant knowledge of being watched and having the ghost "pop-up" without notice that made me nervous. I started my work in January of 1982 and only lasted a little over a four-month period.

One early morning, on my third day of employment, I was left alone at the hotel. I was told that the mid-winter season tended to be a very slow time of year for guests, given the extreme cold weather and dangerous snow covered highways. But that particular day was sunny, fine for raking up leaves and other yard work. There was a thin, wet, slushy layer of snow covering everything, but not enough to make my job too difficult.

As I was outside in the backyard of the hotel that morning cleaning up overgrown vines and brush, a movement in the upper second floor window caught my attention. I looked up at the second story window and spotted a man with a top hat looking back at me. Automatically thinking he was a potential guest looking to rent a room, I nodded back and waved my hand in a greeting gesture, then yelled out, "Hello, I'll be with you in just a minute." Strangely, the man did not acknowledge my greeting and just stood in place. I thought that was odd of him. As I stared a little longer, I noticed his unique manner of dress.

Of course, wearing a vintage looking top hat was strange in itself, he also sported a full, long beard that came down almost to his belly, and his clothes were dark, almost black. I put aside the rake, and hurried to the back door and made my way to the front entryway. I called up to him from the bottom of the stairs, "Excuse the way I look, but I've been getting the yard ready for our guests." No response came.

I walked up to the second floor and checked each room. No one was in the hotel. That's when I started to get a little spooked. I quickly walked back down the stairs and checked every area of the first floor but spotted nothing out of the ordinary. I walked over to the front door, and then to the large windows that face the street. I looked out the windows and noticed that there was not one car parked on the street. I kept thinking to myself, where did this guy go? I started to get a little bit more nervous. My nervousness was turning into fear. When I looked to the floor and then the stairs, I could only see the wet footprints that I knew were my own. There was not any evidence of another person's wet footprints in the entryway, just my own. Had there been, then that might have proved that a man had come in from the outside.

I decided to keep this experience to myself, but I knew I saw someone up in that window of the hotel. I was convinced of that. I did not even want to think that my imagination was playing tricks on me, because he was real, and if he was no longer in the hotel, then he had to be a ghost—plain and simple!

After locking the front door, I returned to the back yard to finish up with the job. But I was so unnerved by what I had experienced, that I did not even dare look up at that second story window again. I guess you can imagine how I must have passed the time in the backyard, just thinking all the while about the possibility of a ghost keeping a close watch at me. I'm not embarrassed to say that I was shaking a little.

The second time I experienced something supernatural at the hotel I was alone again. This time, it took place the following day after my first experience. I decided to bring a small radio with me, to keep me company and to help pass the time. I turned the music up a little loud, but not very loud. I also made sure to lock all the doors. I didn't want another episode to take place like the day before, with the possibility of a "living" person walking into the hotel unnoticed.

At the time of this second incident, I was in the men's bathroom sitting on the commode. Yeah, I was on the commode. I suddenly heard the sound of footsteps walking about the floors, and I thought it must be the owners. I kept quiet and then I heard a door slam. That's when I said, "I'm in the bathroom, I'll be right out in just a minute." I didn't hear an answer, so I repeated, "I'm in the bathroom!"

Just then, I heard the footsteps begin to walk towards the bathroom. Right as I heard them walk up to the bathroom, I spotted a shadow pass under the door. There is a small gap between the floor and the bathroom door, and I saw the dark shadow of someone pass in front of the door. I got freaked! I kept quiet, and stayed sitting on the commode for several minutes, until I decided that enough was enough. I got up and took hold of the door's knob and got out of there! I rushed right to the front door, unlocked it and was thankful to be outside. Once out in the open, the fresh, cold, afternoon mountain air helped me think clearly. I decided that if there were going to be ghosts in the hotel with me, I'd just have to make the best of it. But let me tell you, it took a lot of courage on my part to finally be able to admit that.

Another example of strange experiences were the cold spots. For whatever reason, the areas of the hotel where I'd experience these bone-chilling cold spots were in the dining room, the area in the middle of the stairs leading up to the second floor, and throughout the second floor.

Also, another day when I was coming down the stairs, I felt the quick rush of cold air come from behind me. It felt as if the cold invisible mass passed right through me! A few seconds after that, I spotted a strange little white ball of light flying right by my right side, it went down the stairs and disappeared into the wall! It was a very small flying ball of light. At first I thought it might be a moth, but this ball went at a great speed. A moth would not be able to fly that fast. I'd also experience lights like that one rushing by me a few more times in the hotel.

Sometime, after I had left the hotel for good I was informed by a friend that the lights are called spirit orbs, ghost orbs, or energy balls. I didn't know it at the time. I just thought they were reflections that were coming in through the windows from the outside. I just didn't think that they might be associated with the ghosts in the hotel. I thought they were reflected lights. But how they appeared inside the rooms and on the stairs, didn't ever make sense to me. Day or night I'd see these shooting balls of light.

Once, when I was in the kitchen, I began to hear the familiar footsteps of someone walking directly above me, on the second floor. I felt a little more at ease because one of the owners was in the backyard at the time. So, at least I was not totally alone as I had been all the times before. As I stopped what I was doing, I heard them moving about the upstairs room then suddenly stopped. I waited about a minute then I resumed my work. What happened next really freaked me out.

I was in the kitchen wiping down the refrigerator when suddenly I heard the sound of a door's knob being turned. I looked around the kitchen, followed the sound to its source and spotted the cabinet door knob start to turn by itself, about 10 feet from where I was standing!

That was the last thing that I ever experienced at the hotel, because I quit working there that very day! I have not had any supernatural things like that happen to me since. I didn't even believe in ghosts. I thought the subject of ghosts was all made up from people's imaginations. Never did I ever think that I would actually experience them, and I certainly never thought I would be talking to you and have my experience put in a book about ghosts. It's strange how things turn out, huh?"

SANTA FE, NM

ANTONIO & HANK'S ADOBE GUESTHOUSE B&B – JOSEPH NIGHTWALKER'S STORY

I conducted Joseph's interview one day during a two-hour drive from Santa Fe to Taos. With the tape recorder placed between us on the seat, he freely described he and his wife, Ruby's experience at a bed and breakfast in Santa Fe. Take from his story what you will but remember that sometimes all our attachment to what used to be our home, can prove to be so strong that even after death we find it difficult to move on.

— Antonio

"My experience with a ghost took place in Santa Fe several years ago. My wife, Ruby, and I wanted to get away for a couple of days, and wanted to stay in an upscale hotel. Because of our last-minute plans, we found out that all the hotels were booked up. Our second choice was to look into staying at a bed and breakfast. Santa Fe, among other things, is a city known for its excellent variety of accommodations. An employee at a chain hotel in the Plaza area recommended that we contact 'The Adobe Guest House' on the south side of town. Ruby called, spoke to the owner, Antonio, and booked the room.

The bed and breakfast was very nice. The large, authentic adobe home had four guest rooms; our room was located down a long hallway near the front of the house. During our check-in, Antonio handed us a sheet of paper that described the history of the house. Then he showed us to our room. As Ruby unpacked the suitcase, I started a fire in the corner kiva fireplace. We got comfortable and I started to read the sheet of paper that was given to Ruby.

A family named Martinez built the house in the early 1920s, and it was the first adobe house built in that part of Santa Fe. I read that the house was bought from the Martinez family by the first female archeologist of New Mexico, Dr. Burtha Dutton. The two B&B owners, An-

tonio and Hank, bought it from Dr. Dutton. I remember these details because, being an artist myself, I knew about Dr. Dutton and the stories about her association with the well-known artist, Georgia O'Keeffe. These two names certainly were not easy for me to forget. I put the sheet of paper back on the nightstand, and my wife and I took a short nap.

About 45 minutes later, Ruby and I woke up and drove into town for our dinner reservation. After dinner, it started to snow, slow at first, then harder and harder.

We walked around the Santa Fe plaza, window-shopping, but when we

A&H Adobe Guesthouse Courtyard.

saw how heavy the snow was falling, we decided to call it a night and drive back to the B&B. When we got back to the room, I looked out the window and saw about a foot of snow covering the ground. I also noticed that there were four other cars parked in the parking spaces. There was a full house at the B&B. Ruby and I got into bed, and quickly fell asleep at about 10 p.m.

I was awakened suddenly from my sleep when I heard the sound of breaking glass coming from down the hallway. I looked at my watch and saw that it was 3 a.m. I turned to see if the sound had also awakened Ruby. She was sound asleep. When I didn't hear any more noise, I thought that I had imagined it. I closed my eyes to go back to sleep, but soon I heard the sound of footsteps walking down the hallway towards our room. As the footsteps got closer, I heard them stop on the other side of our door. I kept quiet. Then I hear the doorknob slowly turn. By this time, I was wide-awake, and fully aware of what was going on. I kept my eyes focused on the doorknob, but because of the darkness, I only heard the knob turning, but couldn't see it actually turn.

Then the strangest thing happened. I saw a short white misty figure come right through the door! It didn't have any particular shape; it was just like drifting smoke. I decided to wake Ruby, so I hit her side with my right elbow. As she woke up, I whispered to her to look in the direction of the door. The smoke then started to change into the outline of a small woman! Ruby saw the same thing and said, "Joseph, it's a ghost, Joseph!"

Then she pulled the covers over her head and didn't move a muscle. Somehow I found my courage, because I yelled out to the figure, "Get away, get out of here!" The ghost took two steps towards our bed. I grabbed my pillow, threw it at the ghost, then reached over to the lamp on the nightstand and turned on the light. As soon as I turned on the light, the ghost and smoke vanished!

Ruby and I slept with the light on the rest of that night. In the morning at the breakfast table, I asked Antonio and Hank, if the house was haunted. They looked at each other, then Hank answered, "Not that we're aware of. No one has ever mentioned anything about ghosts in the house. Why do you ask?" As Ruby and I told them about our experience the night before, the other guests seated at the table began to tell their own similar experiences of hearing breaking glass sounds.

Although the others didn't mention seeing any ghosts, they all said they heard the sound of breaking glass, and a few even mentioned hearing footsteps in the hallway. Ruby got nervous talking about the ghosts, and asked us to change the subject.

We finished breakfast and went back to our room. Some of the guests returned to their rooms, while others drove off to explore the sights of Santa Fe. After a few minutes passed, there was a knock on our door. I opened it and Antonio was standing there asking if he could talk to us. I invited him in. He started to tell us a little bit more about the house. He had a nervous smile on his face, and then apologized for not being totally honest with us at breakfast. As he put it, "I didn't want to upset the other guests who might be uncomfortable or concerned about ghosts and paranormal activities in the house." But now he wanted to set the record straight and admit that the guesthouse was haunted, and yes, there have been several other guests who have seen ghosts in the house, including himself.

He said the previous owner, archeologist Dr. Dutton, kept a collection of American Indian artifacts in one room of the house. During her many archeological digs throughout the southwest, she would return to this house with stone axes, pottery, and various other samples of pueblo culture. In fact, in one room of the house she kept several medium size cardboard boxes stacked one on top of another, with actual Indian skeletons! He added that our room was not the room where the skeletons were kept, so we could feel safe about that, but that our guest room used to be Dr. Dutton's bedroom. He also mentioned that Dr. Dutton was still very much alive, and living in a nearby convalescent home—which shocked Ruby and I. He said that, throughout the seven years of owning the property, both he and Hank had witnessed many ghosts in the house.

Antonio said there were many times when he would be in the kitchen and notice a shadow of a person walk from the hallway into the living room. He'd investigate only to discover there would be no one there. Other times he'd hear his name being called from an adjoining empty room. When he would walk to the room, he'd see the fleeing image of a shadow! Antonio's partner, Hank, also later spoke to us about similar instances he had experienced in the house. Antonio mentioned that guests to the B&B had the common experience of hearing ghostly footsteps and the breaking sound of glass. Ruby asked, "What have you done to rid the house of these ghosts?" Antonio said that he and his 75-year-old father had conducted a cleansing ritual throughout the entire house, and since that time, the appearances of ghosts had stopped. But now he was unsure of the reason why the spirits had decided to return.

We talked a little more about several things before he left to make up the vacant guest rooms. My wife and I felt a little better after this conversation. We left to do a little shopping in town, and when we returned to the house, we noticed the faint scent of burnt sweet grass incense. Antonio once again knocked on our door, this time to inform us that he and his father had once again blessed the whole house. That night was spent without any further visits from a ghost. The prayers and incense had chased whatever was still in the house.

Hank Estrada and Antonio Garcez, seated in foyer of their haunted Adobe Guesthouse B&B.

A few days after Ruby and I returned home to our Pueblo we got a phone call from Antonio. He mentioned that we should read the local newspaper, because on the front page was an article about the recent death of Dr. Burtha Dutton.

Apparently, Dr. Dutton had died at a local convalescent home, less than a mile from her old home, now the B&B. Antonio said we should take particular notice of the date of her death. She died the same night that the short smoky-white figure visited our guest room! Was the ghostly woman who visited us that night indeed the ghost of Dr. Burtha Dutton? This sure could explain the experience. I just don't know how this could be proven, but we were in her beloved former home, in her bedroom on the night that she expired. It just makes sense to us."

SILVERTON, CO

With a population of just 500, and resting at an altitude of 9,318 feet, the town of Silverton has been designated a National Historic District Landmark. Surprisingly, nestled between three major mountain passes— San Juan, Molas and Red Mountain—the town of Silverton was built within a bowl of an ancient volcanic caldera. Unlike most mining towns, Silverton has never had a devastating fire, so it has not changed its outward appearance since its founding as a mining supply center in the late 1800s. Silverton remains an ornate and magnificent Victorian town.

Silverton used to be full of activity, supplying individual gold seekers and other much smaller mining towns scattered throughout the magnificent San Juan Mountains. Today, Silverton generates much tourist activity, and its wonderfully appointed hotels, boutiques, and shops continue to preserve the atmosphere of this alpine town's past.

Charles Baker was the first non-native who came upon the area together with his gold-seeking buddies in the mid-1800s. The town was then known as Baker's Park. Soon after that the native Ute people grew decisively protective of their homeland, and drove Baker and his men off their prime hunting lands. A few years later, a more enforced and resolute group of Anglos took advantage of the Brunot Treaty, which removed the Utes from their area, and established the present town of Silverton.

A major draw to the town is The Durango & Silverton Narrow Gauge steam locomotive Railroad which offers daily tours to and from Durango and Silverton. The train's steam whistle is always an eagerly awaited signal that blares its echoing shriek throughout the town and valley. Today, Silverton remains interesting, friendly and because of its remoteness, a special place to visit.

THE WYMAN HOTEL & INN – LORAINE LEWIS' STORY

I interviewed both Loraine and Tom Lewis in the lobby of their hotel. When I first approached Loraine, she seemed a bit nervous, and although willing to talk to me, asked that Tom be present.

After speaking with Loraine, Tom asked me to accompany him up to the second floor. There, he confided to me that guests have reported to him that they've seen the ghost of a woman walking in one area of the hall. Not wanting to alarm his wife regarding any further ghostly episodes on the property, Tom asked me to not mention to Loraine our discussion, until after the book has been published.

— Antonio

"My husband, Tom, and I have been the owners of the hotel now for close to nine years. I'm originally from New York City. I've always dreamed about owning a bed-and-breakfast and living in a beautiful area. I was never approached about anything ghostly or strange associated with the hotel. Not until I had

The Wyman Hotel & Inn, 1371 Greene Street, Silverton, Colorado 81433.

already purchased it did I begin to hear about its paranormal activity.

This began about a month after my husband and I moved in. One woman who worked for me at the hotel informed me that Mrs. Wyman walks the halls of the building. I found that information strange, and never followed up with the conversation.

Soon after, little things would begin to disappear. I would place something ordinary, for example a book, on a table then return to find that it

had disappeared. The object would reappear sometime later, at the exact spot where I had left it. Papers, pillowcases, anything that I had simply touched, I'd turn my back, turn around, and it would be gone. Some of these items would reappear in about a week's time. I've recently been noticing a shadowy figure that walks about 10 feet from me. Guests have also had their own experiences, which I'll tell you about.

One major instance where a very strange thing took place was one morning a year ago, when I spoke to my husband Tom about how exhausted I was with all the work involved in running the hotel. I mentioned that we might consider selling the property. He said he'd think about it. Later that morning, Tom was in the laundry room and discovered a clock on the floor. The clock was always hanging on a wall, a distance away, and was now broken on the floor.

For some unknown reason, I immediately thought that the spirit of Mrs. Wyman, was upset that I spoke about wanting to sell the hotel. I can only guess that due to all the upgrades and remodeling that Tom and

I had completed, Mrs. Wyman may now be dissatisfied that we might be leaving. Maybe this broken clock was one way for her to get our attention to reconsider leaving.

Recently, we have had some strange things take place on the second floor in room #11, named the 'Molas' room. It's named after Molas Pass. One day I heard music coming from the second floor. I walked up the stairs and, using my key, I entered the locked and empty room. When I opened the door, I noticed the music coming from the radio speaker but the button was set in the 'off' po-

When I opened the door, I noticed the radio had been turned on!

sition. Somehow the music was playing without the radio actually being turned on.

Of particular interest to us was the fact that certain objects associated with the room, such as the keys, were beginning to disappear. Remember I said that things in the hotel tend to disappear then reappear for no known reason? Well, this pattern began to take place with objects associated with the Molas Room.

One day, as I was leaving for a day trip to Durango to purchase supplies for the hotel, another strange thing took place. With my arm's full of folders and paperwork, I walked to my car parked to the side of the building. I happened to glance on top of the folders I was carrying, and noticed that the keys to the Molas Room were on top of the folders. I hadn't picked them up, and didn't have them with the folders when I left the front door. Why would I? I returned to the hotel and asked Tom, "Did you just give me these?" He answered, "No." This was one of the strangest incidents I recall and in broad daylight!

Guests also began reporting unusual things taking place on the second floor, in room #5, named the Railroad Room. During the hotel's history, there was a ballroom once located on the second floor of the hotel. Over the years, the second floor was remodeled and the Railroad Room was created within the ballroom. One former guest who stayed overnight in the Railroad room reported to me that his bed began to move entirely on its own. Not violently, but with an obvious rocking motion. I remember this guest did seem a slightly upset and embarrassed, as he reported the incident to me.

A couple that spent the night in the same room had reported seeing the spirit of a woman walk from one side of the bed, to the other side. These guests did not seem to be upset or disturbed by the spirit's sighting. I got the impression that they were actually 'entertained' by her appearance."

His bed began to move on its own!

279

TOM LEWIS' STORY

Tom and Loraine.

"I've experienced objects moving on their own in the hotel, such as pots, pans and large cooking woks. These objects have to be stored in designated storage areas or in own holders. Some of these items hung above the stove turn up missing one day, then are discovered sitting on the dining room table! I know that Lorraine would not place a pot on our nice dining room table, especially knowing that sometimes the bottoms of these pots could be greasy, or might be wet from having been washed. Placing the pot on our table could also damage the table's finish. I would never place it there and I know Loraine would not either.

Also, random objects tend to disappear regularly for some unknown reason, they will reappear in the most unusual areas of the hotel. This all strikes me as being so bazaar. I don't understand the reason behind any of it. I know Loraine has shared her thoughts about possible reasons for this, but still, I'm not convinced.

We currently are both so busy with running the daily business that we tend to just go about our routine and allow what happens to happen. I'm certain that there remain other things that I've experienced that I've forgotten to tell you about, but the disappearing objects are the most obvious for me. I know that when you leave here today, the objects will start to disappear again; they'll just start up and continue to happen as they always do."

THE GRAND IMPERIAL HOTEL

The hotel was built in 1882, and surprisingly completed very quickly within one year later. Known originally as the Thomson Block, it was built by an Englishman, W.S. Thomson. The name used by the locals to describe the hotel was 'Grand Hotel', but it was later named The Imperial Hotel and finally, The Grand Imperial Hotel.

Historically the hotel has housed a variety of businesses such as a newspaper office and a clothing store. Interestingly, the hotel's second floor was used as a courthouse. Today, within the hotel is a saloon and restaurant. Its rooms with private baths are appointed with period decorations and the hotel is open all year.

The Grand Imperial Hotel,1219 Greene Street, Silverton, CO 81433.

DEBBY FOSTER 'S STORY

Debby was a delight to speak to. Her interview was conducted in the saloon, front desk and within each of the rooms that were reported to be haunted. She held nothing back when describing her experiences, and particularly, those of the hotel's guests.

She also obviously took pride in informing me that she personally has decorated each of the hotel's rooms. If you choose to stay in the hotel, do request one of the haunted rooms. The front desk personnel will be well aware of this request, which otherwise might seem strange in another establishment. However, at The Grand Imperial Hotel, this would not be an unusual request to fill at all.

— Antonio

"Originally I'm from Denver, and both my husband and his father have owned the hotel since 1990. It's well known that the hotel is haunted. Many people have told us so—even before we purchased it. In fact, it's the talk of the town. To my knowledge, the ghosts have never harmed anyone, and they're pretty harmonious.

My first personal experience with the ghosts took place in room #314. I'm the person in charge of decorating the rooms, wallpapering, etc. I know that the room has a questionable history in that, in 1893, Dr. Luigi rented this room and committed suicide. Apparently, he was distraught over the fact that the woman he was in love with, who lived on Blair Street,

Is this strange or what?!

had announced she was leaving him. So, in emotional agony, he decided that living was no longer an option for him, he ended his life in room #314.

People have reported seeing his spirit walking the halls of the hotel, and is frequently seen by guests in room #314. He's also been seen bending over a guest's bed and attempting to 'doctor' them. Those who have seen his spirit, unaware it's a ghost, claim that he appears so lifelike that we have even had guests approach us in the morning asking, "How much do we owe you for the doctor's visit last night?"

When we ask them to explain, they respond by saying that a doctor Luigi knocks on the door then introduces himself. After entering the room, he checks their health and then leaves. The doctor will not ask for any money, and soon leaves the room. This behavior might seem strange, but because the doctor is so professional in his approach, the guests are overwhelmed by his sincerity, and allow him to do what he wishes. He doesn't discriminate between men or women. He treats them all the same.

Once we had a female guest who reported seeing a spirit standing against the wall in the reception area. The woman stated that the ghost was standing by the door, with both arms extended upward, reaching up the wall with the palms of his hands. Is this strange or what? I've never heard of a ghost ever being seen in such a "descriptive" position. Clearly it made an impression and the guest never forgot it.

Room #301 is also another room where guests have reported seeing a male figure

Bent over his lifeless body is a woman wearing a Victorian period hat and a dress.

lying on the bed, who appears to be dead. Bent over his lifeless body is a ghostly woman wearing a Victorian period hat and a dress. Her dress comes right below the knee. This spirit will then move away and walk back and forth in the room.

I have also heard reports from guests who have smelled a man's cologne and a woman's perfume in various areas of the hotel. Lights turn themselves on and off in these rooms, as do the lights located directly outside of the rooms, in the hall. Another very common incident that guests have reported are the sounds of heavy ghostly footsteps walking the halls, day and night.

People commonly mention the ghosts in the hotel. They really do like them. Some will even approach the front desk and ask to book one of the known rooms with the ghosts. This has happened so many times that I mentioned to my husband, "We need to include this information in our brochure." He was hesitant at first, thinking it might scare potential guests away. But he's noticed the incredible number of calls we receive throughout the year, asking for the haunted rooms. He's decided that it might not be a bad idea.

Personally, I always have the feeling when I am alone in the hotel, that there is someone watching me. I think that if I were to see a spirit, it would sure scare me. I have witnessed the lights going on and off, and heard the sound of someone walking about, when no one else is in the room with me."

HOSPITAL FACILITIES

CASTLE ROCK, CO

The town of Castle Rock is located 20 minutes south of Denver. Castle Rock is named after a huge rock outcropping that naturally replicates a European fortress. The town's very visible landmark is difficult indeed not to be noticed. As a natural signpost, it has historically served as a landmark throughout the centuries for both Native Americans and early settlers.

Modern-day travelers gravitate toward Castle Rock's Factory Outlet Shops that are a financial draw to all bargain hunters. In addition, each summer the city host's a large, 100-mile bike tour event—the Elephant Rock Cycling Festival. The bike tour begins and ends in Castle Rock.

Another of the town's celebratory events is the Wine Fest. This wine and music outdoor gathering is held at The Meadows within Castle Rock's historic center. Over 29 wineries and food vendors of every description are represented. Gastronomical creations from local chefs are always a big hit with the public, in addition to the amazing ice sculptures.

KATHY PETRO'S STORY

I conducted this interview with Kathy at her home. I couldn't help but notice that Kathy's residence was decorated with many framed photographic memories of her late husband and family.

It wasn't until the actual interview began that I found out about her tragic personal history. There were a few moments when she looked like she was about to break down in tears, but to her credit, she "held it all together," in order to give me her side of a most unusual encounter with the spirit of a young man.

— Antonio

"I've lived in Castle Rock for 40 years. I lived in Los Angeles and moved to Castle Rock after my late husband, Josh, was killed in an on-the-job accident. This terrible and tragic circumstance was multiplied 10-fold when my husband's own sister was murdered in Los Angeles just a week after Josh's accidental death. It didn't take me long to decide that I needed a change of environment. I had gone through a very rough time. Friends and family were helpful, but when all is said and done, only the person directly going through such an awful period can feel the full impact of the emotional stress. I was a total mess, and needed to get away, very far away from Los Angeles. My younger sister, Loraine, lived in Castle Rock and asked me to come and live with her in the winter of 1966. Since then, for most of those years I've lived on the south end of town.

When I had an encounter with the ghost that I saw one evening, I was not drinking or under any narcotic influence. I know that what I saw was real and no one can make me think otherwise. I saw what I saw, and it was a real ghost!

I was driving home around 7:30 p.m. I had just finished a little shopping and had groceries in the back seat of my Volkswagen bug. The sun was still up in the sky and there was plenty of light. As I was coming to the end of a slight turn in the road, I spotted a young man about 17 years old, standing by the side of the road wearing a light-colored shirt, Levis and a dark baseball cap, holding a long handkerchief to his head.

Given the murder of my sister-in-law just a few years before, I had been overcome with not trusting anyone I did not know. The human quality of having hope and confidence in others was a very challenging for me to buy into and accept. While trying to cope with the trauma of my sister-in-law's murder I was often filled with negative thoughts, and even went through a period of panic attack episodes. Thankfully, I sought the help of counselors and this helped me very much.

So why did I do what I knew to be the opposite what I knew to be good for my own safety? I can't come up with any good answer or reason. All I can say is that I saw a young man who appeared to be in some trouble, he looked so wounded, and so very helpless. I decided to stop and ask if he was alright. It was a very stupid thing to do. But something powerful, and so spiritual, compelled me to stop. The area where we were had plenty of sunlight, and there were a few cars on the road, so I felt reassured there was plenty of visibility all around me.

I slowly pulled to the side of the road, I rolled the window only half way down and asked him if he was all right. He turned to look at me and said, "Oh, could you please take me to the hospital, I'm not feeling very good." I could sense that he was in no physical condition to harm me and by the way he was speaking. He kept repeating how much pain he was in, so I said, "Sure, hop on in."

As he entered my car I asked, "What's your name." He said, "Thomas Mitchell." I asked him what happened. He said, "I hit my head really hard somewhere and all I remember was crossing a street, then bam!" I responded, "Did you fall? Did something hit you? He said, "No I guess a car must have hit me, I'm not feeling very well." I answered, "Well, we're headed to the hospital right now so just hold on and stay calm, okay?" I realized later that I never did see any blood on his shirt or handkerchief. This in itself was strange, and he didn't say much more during our drive to the hospital.

It only took me a few short minutes to get to the hospital's emergency entrance, and as soon as I drove up, Thomas opened the door and told me, "Thank you." I asked him if he needed me to wait for him, but he quickly walked away from the car, right up to the emergency room sliding doors, and walked through. I decided to find a parking spot and follow him inside. I thought I could call his mother, or offer some further assistance.

As I entered the ER waiting room, I noticed that the area was empty. I walked up to the receptionist and asked, "Where is the young man who just walked in a few minutes ago?" The woman responded, "I don't know, he might have gone into the bathroom, but I haven't seen anyone come in these doors in hours."

I thought that was odd, but I did walk over to the men's bathroom and knock. When there was no answer, I opened the door slightly and asked, "Anyone in there? Thomas, are you in there?" No answer. I walked a few feet down the hallway and asked an older gentleman if he could search the bathroom for a friend of mine. He said he would, and after coming out of the bathroom, he told me there was no one in there. I then walked back to the receptionist and asked her once more if she had seen a young man with a baseball cap. She said she had not. I didn't know what to think and wondered where Thomas could have gone. I was torn with the decision to continue searching or to just leave but decided to leave. As I walked outside to my care, I looked everywhere for Thomas but didn't find him. I got back into my car and drove home.

A few days later, while at my job, I took a lunch break and overheard co-workers talking about a radio news flash regarding a young man's body found early in the morning by some highway construction workers in town. The local paper reported a story about a young man's beaten body that had lain in a shallow ditch for about two days before being discovered. The picture of the area where the body was discovered showed the ditch and a large metal building in the background. It was the exact place where I had stopped to pick up Thomas Mitchell! I was left with my mouth wide open from shock. I remember actually opening my mouth in disbelief.

I didn't tell anyone about my encounter but was so shaken up that I left work early and drove straight home. A few hours later, I phoned my sister Loraine and described everything to her. I was surprised to hear her reaction, "We both know how much stress you've been under lately. You must have imagined it all. You know how upset you've been with Josh and his sister's death. Of course, you imagined it all. You must have heard or read something about this boy's murder and your mind somehow created the whole meeting and drive to the hospital story around the unfortunate incident."

I chose not to pursue the subject any further with Loraine, so I agreed with her and kept my true thoughts to myself. But I knew better. I knew I had not imagined any of it—the boy, his clothes, the hospital—none of it was made up by my imagination. I never read anything about his death in the newspaper before. It really did happen and in my soul, and heart of heart, will forever believe this to be my true experience.

I never did find out the boy's actual name, the paper did not print further details due to him being a minor, and the pending police investigation. And I never again brought up the subject of the boy's death to my sister again. I'll always carry this experience with me until the day I die.

I do feel confident in knowing that I did try to help that poor spirit as much as I could at the time. The experience gave me more in return than what I could ever hope to give the spirit of Thomas Mitchell. Thomas has never visited me since, and I hope he has found his final place of peace. I feel grateful knowing I might have helped him on his journey. I do wonder if other drivers on that stretch of road have also had similar encounters, but guess I'll never really know."

LOS LUNAS, NM

LOS LUNAS HOSPITAL AND TRAINING SCHOOL – SHARON L. TREGEMBO'S STORY

"I've lived in New Mexico since 1971, but I'm originally from the state of Michigan. I've lived in Los Lunas for about twenty-five years. At the time of our move, my husband was stationed at the local Air Force base. Soon after I arrived at Los Lunas, I found a job with the local school district. Eventually I had a position working with an intervention program at the Los Lunas Training School targeting at risk children. I held the position of teacher for two years at the school with children enrolled from grades 1 to 6.

I began working at the Training School in 1998. Prior to my employment, the school's building had been empty since the mid-eighties. During my employment, the facility housed children referred to us who had a history of social problems, anger issues or simply labeled "at-risk kids."

During that time, the school was linked to a national program was done away with and all the residents were then released to private homes. The facility was called a "school," but it was more of a hospital than anything else. The children were profoundly handicapped and considered un-trainable.

Sadly, because the resident children were deemed severely even profoundly mentally disabled, their parents brought them to our facility as their only last recourse. Regrettably, some of the residents' parents chose to simply drop their children off at the school and then never, ever visit them again. Some children were referred to the facility as newborns, spending many years within these  walls; some for just as long a time until death took them. For many, their lengths of stay could be a few months to a few years or, in some cases, until their deaths.

The state of New Mexico owned the land upon which the building stood and rented the land to the Training School for only one dollar a year. Again, it was a program affiliated with the Los Lunas schools. Because of all the empty, but useable buildings at this location, the state officials ordered the buildings to be rented for the purpose of generating revenue.

Within the facility were two classrooms; the remaining rooms were offices for diagnosticians where children were tested in order to place them within their appropriate levels of training. At its highest count, we had a student population of 25. The goal of the program was to ultimately mainstream or enroll the students into the general overall population of public school students. Entering foster care homes was common for them and once adopted, most of the children were forgotten by the state. Social workers were not required to make followed-up visits, so who knows how their lives ultimately ended.

Prior to working at the school, I didn't know of or hear talk about the facility having ghosts. It was only after having worked at the facility and experiencing unusual things that got me thinking that there was something on a paranormal level at the facility. Employees would definitely speak of having such experiences among themselves.

A common experience noted was to smell the aroma of food being cooked. In my particular classroom, myself and others would catch the aroma of fried eggs, bacon, cookies, etc. Oddly, there was no kitchen anywhere near the classroom. The children would sometimes also comment, "The ghosts are cooking again!" I happened to mention this to a bi-lingual teacher and he stated he had the same experience two years ago in his classroom within the building.

I also had an assistance teacher who was adamant about not being left alone in the building. She stated to me, "I know the ghosts will get me, don't leave me alone." Because of her fear, she would never be left alone in a room. Commonly experiences included personal items moved or relocated from one spot to another, music boxes would play, office radios turn on and off, and of course doors opening and closing all on their own. Employees who stayed after hours would always report hearing the sounds of children crying. Hearing crying, weeping sounds coming from empty rooms was common.

One of my very first experiences seeing a ghost in the facility took me totally by surprise. A meeting had been scheduled between myself and another teacher named Sharon. As I was walking past Sharon's classroom, on my way to my own classroom to retrieve a folder, I spotted a young girl about four or five years of age, standing behind Sharon's chair. This perplexed me because I didn't recognize the little girl as one of our students and secondly, why isn't she outside with all the other students? I paused in my tracks, look directly at her and remember her brown-hair. She didn't move or make a sound. She wore a long patchwork patterned dress over a brown pinafore, she stood on her tip toes and held on to the back of the chair. All along she was watching Sharon intently, observing her actions.

After a few seconds, I walked over to my classroom, then something "clicked" in me. I turned around and walked into the classroom to speak to Sharon to ask her who the little girl was. As soon as I entered her classroom, the little girl was nowhere to be seen. She had disappeared! Sharon took notice of me standing there, and asked, "Wow, it looks like you've seen a ghost!" After briefly describing to Sharon what I had seen, she freaked out!

Hearing about my experience with the little ghost girl others in the building began feeling more comfortable reporting their own experiences of hearing voices, whispering, talking, and some even reported hearing screaming! Employees stated that these sounds reflected the early history of the school when allegedly the staff traumatize the children, giving them forced cold baths and other disturbing treatments. I don't believe all former staff members acted this way because I knew some and they never appeared to me to have the disposition to do such terrible things. There have always been stories of mistreatment of children by former staff and throughout the schools' history.

At its height of enrollment, during the 1950's and 60's, there really was no place to rehabilitate such profoundly handicapped children. As I've said before, after being dropped off, many parents never returned. At the rear of the property to the north, there is a large area of land that was set aside for a graveyard for these abandoned children who died while on the property.

I'm aware that the facility had one terrible year, several years before I worked here. For some reason, that particular year recorded a high number of child deaths at the facility. If you read the tombstones in the graveyard, you'll see what I mean. Just notice the year of their deaths, many died in the same year. Some of the children's deaths took place when they were only a few days old. I recall one of our oldest clients died when he was in his eightieth year of life. Some of the graves have caved-in over the years, due to the weight of the soil above, crushing the coffins below. I've notice that these graves have had new fill dirt added to keep them level with the top ground level. It's so very sad, and unfortunate.

I haven't returned to the property for over eight years. As we're now walking about the grounds, making our way between the buildings, you'll notice the broken windows, damaged walls, and unkempt grounds. To prevent further vandalism, the state has erected the chain-linked fencing that today sur-

Los Lunas Hospital and Training School Cemetery
Lives remembered with gratitude and love
Souls honored with dignity and respect
Spirits resting in gentle peace

rounds each building. It's so depressing to see how the whole property is now in such a neglected state. I remember when there used to be flower-beds here and over there, but now it's just spooky, kind of scary. It didn't look like this when I worked here. It was in these very buildings that the staff used to hear the ghostly screams. Because today the buildings are in such bad shape, they give the appearance they are all haunted. Since you now know the history of this property, I tell you I wouldn't want to ever be here alone at night. It's bad enough being here with you touring the place!"

MIAMI, FL

BAPTIST SLEEP CENTER AT MIAMI LAKES SLEEP TECHNOLOGIST / RESPIRATORY THERAPY – CHET BENSON'S STORY

"I've been employed at this facility going on five years this Christmas. Originally, I'm from Montana, and after falling in love with a man from Sarasota, Florida, this is where we both ended up settling down and making a life for ourselves. My first partner of thirteen years, Daniel, was murdered during a hate crime in broad daylight at a supermarket parking lot in Missoula, Montana. His murder was extremely difficult to understand and ultimately accept. Adding to this horrific crime, Daniel was deaf since birth. We met while attending a deaf conference in Se-attle. Like Daniel, my older brother was also born deaf, and because of this, my whole family and I are well versed in American Sign Language, or ASL. I knew I had to move away from Montana if I was going to ever attempt to find the necessary courage to move forward with my life.

I graduated with an AMA bachelor's degree in respiratory care seven years ago and am currently licensed to practice respiratory care in Flori-da. I am registered as a respiratory therapist with the National Board for Respiratory Care. Additionally, I am certified and currently registered with the Board of Registered Polysomnographic Technologists.

My current job involves my performing a variety of tests and studies related to the diagnosis and treatment of sleep-related breathing dis-orders. The facility has recently hired a new director to head the new sleep study research program. This particular program performs and evaluates the technical aspects of overnight sleep patterns and nocturnal pulse oximetry. Some of my responsibilities are to set up and apply polysomnographic monitoring devices, ensure patient safety with accurate test results, and provide summary analysis and reports of all studies for physician review.

Because of my skill in sign language, I'm at times called upon to assist deaf and hearing-impaired patients communicate with staff in other areas of the hospital. This being the case, one early morning at around 3:00, we had a middle-aged African American deaf woman brought into the hospital by ambulance who was being prepped for emergency surgery for having taken a terrible fall that resulted in internal bleeding. She was found semiconscious in her backyard by a neighbor hours after her fall. Her prognosis was not very positive. When I arrived at her side, I could see she was in severe pain, in shock and terrified. She definitely needed someone who could sign to offer reassurance and to walk her through the emergency room process she was about to experience. I introduced myself in sign language, and the tension in her face turned to relief.

I could immediately tell that her whole composure was beginning to change from that of dread to a more tranquil demeanor. Within a few minutes, she was sedated and taken into surgery. Before closing her eyes, I assured her in sign language that all would be well, and I promised her I would be at her side in the recovery room. I held her hand until she fell into controlled unconsciousness.

Sadly, the poor woman never made it out of surgery and died in the operating room. Her death affected me deeply. Having a deaf partner and now this deaf patient die hit an extremely sensitive nerve with me, and I fell emotionally apart.

Looking to recover and compose myself from this tragic moment, I walked over and entered the brightly lit break room just a few doors from surgery. I was exhausted. I reached for the light switch and turned off most of the overhead lights, leaving only one light on. I planned to sit quietly in the darkened room before going back to my station.

As I was seated in our small break room, I bent over the table, rested my head on my arms, and fell asleep. Suddenly, the loud voice of a co-worker shouting at me in the break room doorway woke me up. "Chet, Chet, quick, look!" He was pointing as I sprang up off my chair, I looked to where he was pointing, and was shocked to see the deaf patient who had just expired. My coworker said, "Do you see her, Chet? Tell me you see her too!" I sure did, she was standing before me, clear as life!

I was dumbfounded by the woman's apparition. I could see that a thin, blue, glowing light surrounded her, and the expression on her face was of peace and calm. Nothing about her displayed any sense of pain or fear.

Then in one smooth movement, she raised her right hand, touched her fingertips to her lips, and dropping her hand back toward me, giving me the 'Thank you' sign. I was so completely unprepared for all this and couldn't think of the proper 'You're welcome' sign to acknowledge her. Apparently not bothered by my oversight, she smiled, turned away, and disappeared right through the wall behind her. My co-worker and I knew that what we had just witnessed was a beautiful and unforgettable gift of a life-time.

I felt so very lucky to have another person actually experience this with me. I am confident that each of us are provided with opportunities to share positive life energies while alive but now also believe, in continuing this very real capability, when we transition into an afterlife."

SAN FRANCISCO, CA

ADULT ACUTE CARE PHYSICAL THERAPIST AT UCSF MEDICAL CENTER – GARTH A. MASSINGILL'S STORY

I was born in Rockford, Illinois, and graduated with a degree in physical therapy from North Park University in Chicago. I moved to San Francisco in 1996, where I was immediately hired at UCSF Medical Center at Parnassus as an adult acute care physical therapist. I've been employed here ever since. I'm responsible for administration of physical therapy treatment and patient programs, coordinating discharge plans, and so on. Lots of paperwork is involved as well. Overall, I view my work as a team effort between myself and other hospital staff members. Surprisingly, my ghost encounter took place just two months ago.

I started my day going through my regular routine at the hospital's physical therapy and rehabilitation clinic. I had a 10:00 a.m. appointment with Carl, a forty-two-year-old man who was in therapy for an ischemic stroke. This stroke affected the movement on the right side of his body, and from the point when I first met Carl, he had been a patient of the clinic for three months. He was required to continue lengthy ongoing therapy and to be evaluated every six weeks.

The clinic had several patients undergoing similar therapies with high degrees of achievement and success. Carl's brother always accompanied him to therapy sessions by pushing Carl's wheelchair, and was helpful in providing feedback as it pertained to Carl's rehabilitation progress. Our staff grow emotionally attached to patients like Carl, especially those enrolled in our long-term program. This was particularly the case with my interactions with Carl and the establishment of a bond of sincere caring between us.

Although I am a 100 percent heterosexual man, Carl disclosed early on to me that he was gay. He held no reservation in telling me this, and I respected him for his honesty and trust. This personal information allowed our future conversations from that point on to be free from any misunderstandings or assumptions. We became buddies.

When Carl failed to appear at the appointed time, I phoned his home and spoke to his father. Sadly, I was informed that Carl had taken his life the week before by overdosing on the prescription sleep aid Ambien. Carl's father apologized profusely for the family's lack of communication with our office and had only this tragic family nightmare as an excuse. I offered my condolences, and after ending the call, I remained silently seated at my desk in absolute shock from hearing this terribly sad news.

From what I learned, Carl had committed suicide after fighting an ongoing state of depression as a result of the over-all debilitating consequences from his stroke. Prior to his stroke, Carl had been an avid Bay-area cyclo-cross bicyclist, and given his intense love of the sport and now his limiting conditions, I can only imagine the depression he must have struggled with. Apparently, the hurdles of having to adjust to his new wheelchair-bound reality were far too much to bear for this active, vibrant athlete.

It was just four days after Carl's funeral, a Monday, and I was working late that evening. I took my dinner at the hospital's cafeteria, and due to a hard down pouring rain outside, I stayed inside the building for close to an hour. That particular week, I was having transmission work done on my car; it had been in the service department at the dealership for two full days. I was depending on public transportation to get me to and from work, and I didn't want to sit outside on a wet bus bench waiting, but had I no other choice. I remember taking a large plastic trash can liner from the cafeteria kitchen and positioning it above my head as a makeshift umbrella. I made a dash out the cafeteria's side doors and found myself on the long walk to the nearest bus stop at the opposite end of the hospital complex.

Not surprising, I was the only person outside on the otherwise heavily traveled sidewalk. As the rain was coming down all around me, I spotted a tall man about fifteen yards ahead, walking with the help of the illuminated walkway lights, looking straight at me and coming toward me. Then he abruptly stopped in place while I kept my pace and reached him. It was Carl!

Still holding the trash can liner above my head, we stood in place with no more than ten feet between us, facing each other. I said, "Carl, what's going on? What are you doing here? Your father told me ..."

Then it hit me like a lightning bolt. The person I was speaking to, Carl, was actually standing before me and out of his familiar wheelchair. I stared at him as the rain was coming down on both of us, but surprisingly, he showed no sign of being wet. In fact, his clothes and hair were neatly in place and bone dry.

While our eyes locked, Carl smiled raised his palm toward me in a 'hello' gesture and suddenly I understood to mean, "It's all right, I'm fine." Without saying another word, I stood frozen in place watched Carl turn around, take about five steps away from me, then just disappear. I was stunned but got the courage to speak, and said, "Take care of yourself, my friend." I knew and was totally convinced that I had seen Carl's ghost. I wasn't afraid or apprehensive at all. I was, on the contrary, filled with an all-consuming sense of peace, comfort and elation. Because this spirit was not threatening or unpleasant, I felt remarkably relaxed. I knew I had just experienced something extraordinary and wonderful.

I chose not to mention this experience to anyone, but when I feel the time is right, I'll share this with Carl's brother. He's the second person I'll describe my encounter to. This happened only two months ago, so I need a little more time to think things through. It was really a remarkable encounter that will change my life in ways I have yet to discover.

HISTORIC & TOURIST DESTINATIONS

AZTEC, NM

AZTEC RUINS NATIONAL PARK

Early settlers mistakenly thought that people from the Aztec Empire in Mexico created these striking buildings. They named the site "Aztec," a misnomer that persisted even after it became clear that the builders were the ancestors of many Southwestern Tribes. The people who built at Aztec and other places throughout the Southwest were called "Anasazi" for many years. Archeologists had adopted a word from the Navajo language that they understood to mean "old people," and then popularized its use. Most Pueblo people today prefer that we use the term "ancestral Pueblo" when referring to their ancestors.

Aztec Ruins, built and used over a 200-year period, is the largest ancestral Pueblo community in the Animas River Valley. Concentrated on and below a terrace overlooking the Animas River, the people at Aztec built several multi-story buildings called great houses and many smaller structures. Associated with each great house was a great kiva—a large circular chamber used for ceremonies. Nearby are three unusual tri-walled structures—above ground kivas encircled by three concentric walls. In addition, they modified the landscape with dozens of linear swales called roads, earthen berms and platforms.

An interesting 700-yard trail leads visitors through the West Ruin, an excavated great house that had at least 400 interconnected rooms

built around an open plaza. Its massive sandstone walls tower over 30 feet. Many rooms contain the original pine, spruce, and aspen beams hauled from distant mountains.

Archeologists excavated and reconstructed the Great Kiva in the West Ruin plaza and it now evokes a sense of the original sacred space.

The construction at Aztec shows a strong influence from Chaco Canyon, the site of a major ancestral Pueblo community to the south. Aztec may have been an outlying community of Chaco, a sort of ancillary place connected to the center to distribute food and goods to the surrounding population. Or it may have been a center in its own right as Chaco's influence waned after 1100.

Excavation of the West Ruin in the early 1900's uncovered thousands of well-preserved artifacts that provided a glimpse into the lives of the ancestral Pueblo people. A remarkable variety of food remains as well as stone and wood tools, cotton and feather clothing, fiber sandals and mats, pottery, and jewelry made of turquoise, obsidian, and shells each revealing much about their use of local resources and trade with others.

About 1300 A.D. the ancestral Pueblo people left the region, migrating southeast to join existing communities along the Rio Grande, south to the Zuni area, or west to join the Hopi villages in Arizona.

Aztec Ruins National Monument connects people of the past with people and traditions of today. Many Southwestern American Indians today

maintain deep spiritual ties with this ancestral site through oral tradition, prayer, and ceremony. The site offers visitors opportunities to learn about these remarkable people and their descendants and to forge connections with the monument's timeless landscape and stories.

FLORENCE BEDEAU'S STORY

"I've lived on East 20th Street in Farmington, New Mexico for most of my life. Both my parents were Cajuns from Baton Rouge, Louisiana. I'm telling you this so you'll understand that in my family, we are very much aware of ghosts and voodoo and witchcraft. When I was born, two of my aunts took me to a voodoo man for his blessing after which he presented my parents with a "protection bag," which I was to carry with me throughout my life. I still have this mojo bag. I've never opened it, but as I use my fingers to feel its contents through the red cloth, I'm able to sort of make out several of its contents. I know there is a small bone and something that I think is a rock. There is also a small glass bottle that contains who knows what. The rest of the contents remain a mystery to me.

The voodoo man's name or what he preferred to be called was Grandpa Asakra. He died, or better yet, was murdered by his third wife. She was also murdered a week after his death. Her murder was never solved. My two older sisters also have their own mojo bags that were given to them by Grandpa Asakra. Like I said earlier, I'm telling you this because as you'll find out later in my story, his power remained very strong all these many years after his death.

My story begins one summer day after my sister Lucy and I returned home from a two-month's stay visiting with our grandparents in Louisiana. At the time, I was seventeen years old and my sister Lucy was nineteen.

Our cousin Roberta decided to accompany us on the bus ride home. She had never been outside of Louisiana so was very eager for the trip. Her parents only allowed her to stay with us for one month, and since my parents were Roberta's Godparents, our family's relationship was very close. Lucy and I were so happy to have Roberta with us especially since our father had died earlier that year. It was a comfort to have Roberta with us. When we arrived home, we wanted to show her all that Farmington had to offer including the Aztec Ruins. We even talked about the ruins while in route home on the bus. Just a few days after arriving, we got into Lucy's car and drove to the park.

When we arrived at the park, we took a few minutes to look over the visitor center's books and souvenirs, but were obviously more interested in seeing the ruins. Walking on the trail that led to the actual site, Lucy suddenly got a painful fit of cramps. We stopped and sat with her on a bench until they subsided. Lucy asked us to go ahead of her, "I'll be alright. Go ahead, I'll catch up with you in a little while." So, off Roberta and I went.

When we walked up to one of the many rooms that make up the site, Roberta asked, "Do you think these people were cannibals?" Taken aback by such a question, I asked her why she would say such a thing. She responded, "Well, I heard some stories that Indians would steal and rape the women who were traveling to the west in covered wagons." I found it difficult to believe that my own cousin, was actually thinking in such a bigoted manner. All I remember saying was, "No, Native Indians didn't do such things. These kind of ideas, are falsely based on Hollywood story lines and movies. They're all just a bunch of lies."

The remainder of our visit was spent walking about the ruins from room to room. Suddenly it hit me; my sister Lucy hadn't joined us? I left Roberta and quickly returned to where we had left Lucy a few minutes earlier. When I arrived at her side, I could see that she was suffering badly. I stayed with my sister for about ten minutes and then decided it would be better for all of us to return home to have our mother look after her.

I returned to where I had left Roberta in the ruins and eventually found her sitting on the ground, leaning against one of the walls inside a room. I called her name but she either didn't hear me or chose to ignore me. When I stood over her and spoke, she looked up to me with the strangest in her eyes. "Roberta are you alright? You look terrible." I said. She tried to stand up, but as she tried she fell to the ground. With my help, I picked her up and I eventually managed to stand her upright.

She said, "Oh, I don't feel too good Flo. My entire body hurts." I didn't know what to do, so I said, "I'll get some help. You stay right here."

As I turned to leave, and without any indication that she had been in any trouble, Roberta answered, "Oh, I'm much better. Look I can even pick up this rock and throw it. Look!" She bent down, picked up a rock, and threw it at the opposite wall. I didn't know what to think. What the heck was going on here? Convinced that she was fine for the moment, although not totally convinced, I agreed with her, but decided for the three of us to leave and return some other day.

When we arrived at home, mother took Lucy into her bedroom and left both Roberta and me in the kitchen to begin preparing dinner for that night. Although Roberta seemed normal again, as I said, I was not totally convinced.

After dinner, we gathered in the living room and watched television. Lucy looked much better but said she was going to excuse herself and head off to bed early. Roberta said, "I'm tired too. I'm going to take a shower before going to bed." After saying this, she lifted herself off the couch then walked to the bathroom.

I said, "I'll take one after you're done." Within a few minutes we heard Roberta turn on the water and begin to shower. I took advantage of this personal time with my mother and told her all about the day's episode with Roberta.

Mother was surprised by what I told her, then said, "Well, she looks normal now. I don't think there's anything to worry about." As mother rose off her chair to reach for a cookie on the coffee table, she let out a scream. "Look at that!" she said, "What are those things!" Pointing to the area of the couch where Roberta was sitting, I got up off my chair, walked over to the couch and saw about a hundred sow bugs! Mother ran to the kitchen and returned with a small broom and an empty mop bucket. Carefully we swept the bugs into the bucket, being very careful not to miss a single one!

"Why and how did these things get into the house? I don't know how this has happened!" Mother kept saying over and over. I, on the other hand, was totally grossed out. I took the bucket of bugs to the street and dumped them out on the curb. Then I left the empty bucket and broom out front on the porch.

About a half hour after we heard Roberta finish her shower and enter her bedroom, I gathered my clean clothes together and walked into the bathroom. As I reached for the water knobs to turn on the shower, I put my hand over my mouth and ran for my mother. As she entered the bathroom I pointed to the bathtub and said, "Mother look, there!" The tub's drain was full of sow bugs! My mother gasped and due to her spiritual knowledge and experiences immediately said, "This is not something normal. Something is wrong with that girl and it's not anything good!"

Then, being careful not to touch any of the bugs, I grabbed a pair of scissors, carefully removed the drain cover from the tub and turned on the hot water sending every one of those gross bugs down into the plumbing! At this point, I didn't have much of a choice, so I continued with my shower and before going to bed, mother not to worry too much about what we had seen and not to mention any of this to Roberta. Mother promised me that she would take care of the situation the very next day.

Somehow, given all the bizarre stuff that I had seen that night, I did manage to fall asleep. But I kept thinking over and over in my head about the day's events. However weird as it might appear, I was most concerned for the safety of my sister and mother. I was not sure why, but there was an overriding fear that I had for them and not for me.

The next morning during breakfast, mother mentioned to me she needed help moving a box in our garage. By the tone of her voice, I knew this had nothing at all to do with moving a box. I walked outside and behind the garage wall she quickly described a phone conversation she had early that morning with Roberta's mother. After mother described all the strange behaviors Roberta had been experiencing, including our experiences with the sow bugs, her mother informed my mother that Roberta was definitely having some type of paranormal issue and she knew why.

Prior to Roberta taking the trip to New Mexico, she and another girl in her neighborhood had gotten into some trouble. The other girl's father was a known voodoo practitioner and after some words were exchanged, Roberta and the girl actually got into a fistfight. Roberta left the other girl with a badly scrapped arm and leg after pushing the girl down onto the concrete drive way. The fight was over a popular song, nothing of any serious value, just over a stupid song!

The other girl's parents got involved by threatening Roberta and her parents. The father swore that Roberta would pay for this. Roberta's family understood what they meant by this. Actually, the father of the girl clearly said that he would send the devil to Roberta's house! This altercation took place just a few weeks prior to our visit to our grandparent's home. Obviously, this was an embarrassing situation, at that time we were not told any of the details about the fight or the threats. But what was now clear to Roberta's mother as she spoke to my mother was that, given Roberta's strange behavior at the ruins and our experience with the sow bugs, the girl's father was making good on his magical threats.

Just before mother was finishing her story, we stopped when we heard what sounded like a disturbing laughter coming directly from above where we were standing! Mother got quiet and gazing up within the branches of the tree said, "No, no you don't. This is not something you are going to win. Leave now and forever or you'll have me to deal with!" I was shaking with fear. Mother said to me, "Flo, I'm going to handle this the way my parents would. This is a terrible thing that Roberta brought with her, a spiritual force that is evil. But don't worry, this spirit is not going to last another minute in my house!"

Later that morning, mother asked me to inform my sister Lucy about what had happened, but not to mention any of it to Roberta. Further, we were to take Roberta for a ride, just to remove ourselves from the house for a few hours so mother could "take care of things" at the house. Mother said that she was going to do battle with this spirit and totally cleanse all of Roberta's clothes and bed with incense and prayers that her parents used to recite back in Louisiana. I mentioned to mother that I would be driving the car, so I'd make sure that we would return in about three hours.

About an hour into ride in the car, Roberta, who was seated in the rear seat, began to act a strangely. At one point, she was laughing at a joke I had told her, in fact, we all were laughing. Then, in just a split second, she became very, very quiet and began to strike out punching with her closed fists at the back of the seat that Lucy was sitting in! With all the force she had, Roberta was striking and yelling out obscenities saying,

"You'll suffer like we all suffered. You're dead, you'll suffer—SUFFER!"

I immediately knew Roberta was being possessed by something evil. I remember that as I was driving over the Animas River on W. Murray Drive. As soon as we crossed the river, I pulled over to the side of the road and stopped the car. Roberta began to loudly cry. I got out of the car and opened the rear door then got into the back seat and hugged my cousin. Since Lucy had already been made aware of what was going on back at the house, I decided to tell Roberta what my mother was doing back home. I felt it would be a good thing for her to know what we were doing for her benefit. Roberta became calm and said, "Oh, God, I hope your mother takes care of it. I'm so scared. I woke up this morning and found my mouth and pillow covered in little bugs. I didn't want to tell any of you. I'm so sacred!"

After two more hours passed, we drove back home. Mother was seated at the kitchen table smoking a cigarette. As we entered through the living room door, the whole house smelled of church incense and the atmosphere was so different, different in a good way. The moment we walked into the kitchen, Roberta ran to mother and hugged her tightly. She sobbed and sobbed, thanking mother for her help.

Well, after that experience and house cleansing, nothing ever again took place in the house with bugs or ghostly laughter. Mother had certainly taken care of things. Roberta returned to Louisiana and informed her own parents of what had taken place. Everything turned out fine. I could tell you more details, but I promised mother I never would. What I just told you, you'll know why I am now such a believer in ghosts, witchcraft, and voodoo. Even here in little old Farmington, New Mexico witchcraft traveled from Louisiana and made its active presence known. So, what does the future hold for our family? I can only hope for more positive, healthy good things from now on."

BLACK CANYON OF THE GUNNISON NATIONAL FORREST, CO

While the people of the Ute bands knew of the Black Canyon of the Gunnison, for hundreds of years to many explorers it was an obscure geographic feature. The Spanish were the first Europeans to canvas western

Colorado with two expeditions, one led by Juan Rivera in 1765, and the other by Fathers Dominguez and Escalante in 1776. Both were looking for passage to the California coast, and both passed by the canyon.

Fur trappers of the early 1800s undoubtedly knew of the canyon in their search for beaver pelts. They left no written record of the canyon, though, probably because they couldn't, in fact, read or write.

By the middle of the century, exploration of the American West had captured the nation's attention. In turn, expeditions came to the Black Canyon searching for railroad passageways, mineral wealth, or in a quest for water. Eventually, explorers came to see the canyon, not for commercial wealth, but for the renewal and recreation that it offered.

Today, you can walk in the footsteps of some of these hardy and inquisitive forbearers'. The canyon still offers a rugged and demanding experience, even as it did more than a hundred years ago.

RITA MANSON'S STORY

Rita and her best friend, Jeanette, were seated in Rita's living room as I conducted the interview. Rita shared photos and personal stories unrelated to ghosts, regarding her husband and their life together. Jeanette was very interested in the subject of ghosts, and would occasionally interject with her own personal opinions. It was obvious to me that these elderly ladies were the best of friends, and at one time during my visit, Jeanette informed me that she had even once dated Rita's husband, Bruce, when they both had attended high school, many years ago.

That being said, Jeanette remained quiet once Rita began her personal story. Rita's story offers insight into the spiritual mysteries that many Native Americans know exist, to this day, within the wild and rarely traveled areas of North America. Rita and her husband were witnesses to such an example of this, and as you'll read, were never the same after their experience.

*— **Antonio***

"Both my husband, Bruce, and I were born and raised in Montrose,

Colorado. Bruce died six years ago at the age of 75. The story I'll be telling you took place when we went camping one week in the park. We were both in our early fifties, still very active and physically fit.

The national park is a bird watchers' wonderland. Both Bruce and I were avid birders and even helped the park with counting migratory and non-migratory birds that nested, and yearly visited the park. My favorites were the raptors, such as hawks and eagles. Bruce enjoyed the park's resident birds such as the American dippers, ravens, and jays.

Shortly after hiking into the backwoods for several hours, and after having finished setting up our camp for the week to come, we decided to take a short walk into the woods. If you know the park, our camp was located off the North Rim Road, not far from Grizzly Gulch. Isolated, and yet very nicely situated for our data gathering requirements.

Bruce and I went for a short hike and eventually came upon a meadow. It was midday. When we entered the meadow, I began having a strange feeling come over me. I knew something was about to happen. It was a sunny day, and I had no health problems, but I began to feel weak and an oppressive heaviness began to affect my normal breathing. I was gasping for air. Bruce took hold of me and lay me down on the grass. I began taking shallow breaths as he shook me and spoke, "Rita, talk to me, talk to me!" At one point, I came to and began to sob like a little girl. I don't know what it was that had affected me so severely, but whatever it was came and quickly left my body. I composed myself and told Bruce, "That was the strangest thing I have ever experienced. I've never felt so sad and depressed."

There was no reason I could think of, no allergic reaction, or anything that would have caused me to have such an unusual breathing and crying attack to that degree. We held on to each other for a few minutes until I felt well enough to continue. But I did notice that once we walked out of that meadow, I felt as if a large boulder had been lifted off my chest. Somehow, I felt that there was something on the level of the mystical, or spiritual, that dwelt in that area, and that I should never go back into it. Just minutes afterward, I totally recovered and was breathing just fine again. As we continued on our hike, and for the remainder of that day,

I remained confused and concerned about what may have caused this experience and such an intense reaction.

Later, after we had finished our campfire dinner, I decided to write in my journal. I entered our tent and lay on top of my sleeping bag, and began to jot down my thoughts. Bruce stayed outside. The night was a bit windy, with large, dark clouds that at times past in front of the crescent moon. After about an hour, we went for a short walk to a mound of boulders, climbed the largest of these, and drank a cup of wine from a bottle I had brought along. We spread out a blanket over the ground, gazed up at the night sky, while Bruce pointed out several constellations of stars that stood out in the darkness.

I was not in the least thinking about ghosts, or anything supernatural. But from the corner of my eye, I noticed the movement of someone's outline, or shadow, walking about the trees—just about twenty feet from where we sat. I turned my head and spotted a short man about four feet tall looking in my direction. He was clearly standing there, just staring at me. His left arm was bent at the elbow, with his left hand on his waist. His right hand was holding something small, resembling a bag.

I softly directed Bruce to look in the direction I was staring and asked, "Do you see that man over there, by the trees, look, over by that tree with the broken branch that's touching the ground?" He said no, there was no one there he could see. Thinking my imagination was playing tricks on me, I said, "Bruce, I think this wine is stronger than I imagined. I've had enough for tonight. I'm starting to see things. Here, you can finish the rest of mine, I'm going to turn in early." Bruce remained while I walked back to the tent and went to bed.

After just a few minutes, I heard what I thought was Bruce walking the short distance north of our camp. I called to him, but he did not answer. I got up, stepped out of the tent and heard footsteps coming from nearby pine trees. I grabbed my flashlight and walked over to the trees. Again, I called to Bruce and this time I heard his voice answer, but it came from the opposite side of our camp.

"Bruce," I called, "I'm over here. Do you see me?" I waved the flashlight attempting to get his attention. I was unable to see him, but I could tell by the distant sound of his voice that he was quite a bit further away from where I was.

At that moment, I heard a noise coming from behind me. I looked up toward the top of the trees and that's when I saw that figure of the small man I had spotted earlier. I noticed what I could only describe as a very weak amber colored light, and within this light was the short man, standing on one of the limbs, appearing to hover, somehow suspended in midair! I was terrified! As I turned to run, I tripped and fell to the ground. But as I fell to the ground, I hit the trunk of a tree and received a nasty gash across the top of my left eye and upper lip. I turned over on my back and placed my hand to my head. As I lay there for a few seconds, I felt the blood running down my neck and shoulder. I looked up and in the darkness, I saw a strange hand reach down to take hold of my right arm. The strength this person had was obvious when, with just one pull, I was on my feet.

I looked at my arm and saw the hand and arm of the ghostly being still holding on to me. A wave of fear surged over me, as I took a couple of steps back and gazed directly at the face of the spirit. All I remember was its unnaturally large eyes, and the smile that was filled with two rows of cream-colored teeth, outlined in dark shadowy lines!

Terrified of the apparition, I screamed, and it immediately disappeared! I quickly turned around, and ran in the darkness toward my tent. I had not run more than a few feet when once again, I tripped over something, and fell to the ground. I lay on my side stunned. I somehow managed to turn over on all fours, and began to crawl my way back towards camp. Screaming Bruce's name, he finally located me lifted me up. I was a complete mess, covered in wet earth mixed with blood. It took me a few seconds to calm down, but when I did, I described to Bruce exactly what I had just experienced.

Confused and unsure of what to believe, Bruce walked me to our tent and helped dress my wounds. Because it was so dark and the weather unstable, we decided to spend the night in camp, and leave for town in the morning. We spent the night huddled together, listening and watching for something but didn't really know what.

I kept explaining to Bruce that what I had seen was not in my imagination, but something real, and definitely not anything close to a living and breathing human at all! Eventually, I fell asleep and in the morning, I looked in the mirror and saw how swollen my face was. After seeing a doctor in Montrose, I was given sedatives and had my two small cuts stitched up.

The drive home was interesting in that, Bruce confided in me that he had stayed up most of the night, worried about me and oddly enough, confided to me that he had kept hearing the strange sound of what he thought sounded like a cross between a singing bird and a person's laughter. It surprised and really frightened him. Bruce was not a man to frighten easily, but this unearthly sound really did frighten him.

In the few months following my ghostly incident in the park, I've mentioned what I experienced to a few people, but everyone, without exception, stated that they felt compassion for what we went through but could not believe that it was anything that had to do with a ghost. I once attended a forestry workshop and met a Ute man. I mentioned my ghostly experience to him and he answered, "Sounds like something the Crow Indians of Montana would be experts in. They have a mythology within their tribe about the little people that inhabit the outlying hills surrounding their reservation. Their stories about the small spirits that live in those hills go back generations, and they tell about the discovery of a few, small, fully developed skeletons of human-like beings that have been found in shallow rock caves. I'd keep away from that area of the park. Something in your spiritual makeup is attractive to them. It's a "medicine" that they might want to tap into. You might want to talk to a person of the Crow tribe, but I don't think they would offer you much information because they do not talk openly about their traditions to outsiders. It's rare for them to even hint at this subject at all."

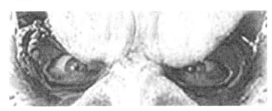

Since that time, I have not ventured onto the north side of the canyon. I tend to stay within other areas of the park, but even then, not without a bit of trepidation. I know what I saw was real and not spiritually positive. I'll keep the pleasant thoughts and memories I have regarding the good times I spent in the canyon with my husband. The others, I hope, one day will completely fade away with time."

CAÑON CITY, CO

MUSEUM OF COLORADO PRISONS

The museum is unique in the fact that it is the only prison museum located adjacent to an actively, operating prison. Behind the walls on the west side of the museum is Old Max, now called Colorado Territorial Correctional Facility; it was originally built in 1868 as the Territorial Prison. On June 13, 1871, it received John Shepler as its first inmate. In 1876, when Colorado became a state, the Federal Government deeded the Territorial Prison to Colorado, and it became a State Facility. Today, there are approximately

700 medium security male prisoners housed at CTCF. There are nine State Facilities and four Federal Facilities located in Fremont County, and these are the largest employers in the area.

PAT KANT'S STORY

I interviewed both Pat and Melissa for their stories in Pat's office. Both women were very helpful in taking me around the inside of the property and pointing out various items of interest. Pat provided me with additional hearsay information, prison terminology, and factual details.

The prison today appears strikingly austere and somewhat odd. The stairs that lead to the main entrance is flanked on the left with a large gas chamber. Peeking inside the green tinted window is the

actual chair of execution—leather straps and all. Not bad as an introduction, for what awaits within the main building itself.

— Antonio

"I've been the Executive Director of the museum for 12 years. Prior to this position I owned a small business in Cañon City. Because of some financial problems that the museum was going through, I was chosen to straighten things out for the foundation. Having owned a business for some time, I had the knowledge and ability to make organizational decisions that ultimately did turn things around. We had a large debt on the building, and in a short time that financial debt was paid off.

My position at the museum has given me the opportunity to interact with the public. At the end of their tour through the museum, it is not unusual for visitors to report to me, or to my staff, how eerie the experience has left them feeling, or that they even sense the presence of ghosts in the building.

Personally, I recall numerous times when, after I first began working at the museum, employees would describe unusual things taking place. They reported decorations and ribbon barriers being removed from the entrance to the prison cells, without anyone else being in the building.

As part of the museum experience, prison cell doors are left open for the public to view the inside of a cell without having to actually walk inside. These cells have ribbons strung across the openings, to prevent vis-

Pat Kant.

itors from entering them. Staff would make sure that these ribbons were securely tied at each end. Before closing the museum's doors for the night, a visual security check would be conducted by the employees on duty. The next morning, employees readying the museum for a new day of visitors, would conduct a final walk through and discover that every one of the ribbons had been physically untied and were lying on the floor. Soon the talk among the staff was that this activity was enough proof that the ghosts of the prison were 'at it' once more.

A past warden, Wayne K. Patterson, who died just two years ago, was one of our board members. During his tenure, he happened to be the appointed warden when women were being housed in this building. The warden mention to me that at the time of his tenure, there was a particular woman prisoner who was kept in cell number 17. The prisoner was extremely angry about being incarcerated. She made it clear that she did not want to be here at all. Apparently, she would regularly make comments stating, "When I die, I'm

Cell #17.

going to return to this prison as a ghost, and I'm going to haunt the hell out of it. I'm going to haunt all of you!" Her criminal history states that she lived in Denver and was employed as a nurse. She was incarcerated at the prison because she murdered her boyfriend. Her boyfriend coincidentally happened to be a police officer.

Well, after her death, other prisoners began complaining to the warden about all the strange noises that would be coming from her now empty cell #17. They complained about hearing what they say sounded like large furniture being dragged about, and silverware, or metal objects, being thrown against the walls of the cell, and dropping on the concrete floor.

Warden Patterson told me about another incident in the 1960s when two prisoners were downstairs in the kitchen and a fight broke out between them. One prisoner took a knife and stabbed, killing the other. The attacker must have hit an artery, because a great amount of blood was spilt all over the kitchen floor. The floor was mopped and cleaned, but the blood strangely kept reappearing. Even though prisoners and employees witnessed the blood being cleaned right after the attack, in just a day or so, fresh blood would reappear upon the floor as if it had never been cleaned. I have not witnessed this, but I know people who swear that this did indeed happen. Gratefully, I've not had the blood re-

Colorado's last legal hanging. This noose was used to hang Colorado's last condemned man, Walter "Shorty" Jones. Jones was hanged on the night of December 1st, 1933. Both Jones and Monrad J. Nelson were arrested in Salida, for the murder of Hartford Johnson. They were transferred to the prison where they were tried and convicted. Nelson received a life sentence.

appear since I've been here.

Interestingly, during the summer months, Cañon City sponsors a 15- block ghost tour. To add a little extra enjoyment to the tour, the tour guide will assume the role of either a female or male local historical character while reciting stories. The tour begins at the prison proceeding into town. Local, historical information is shared with the public regarding the buildings and the town's forefathers. They also tell the history of the K.K.K. who once made its home in Cañon City, and describe the stories of some inmates who made prison escapes. They also recount the stories of prisoners that were hung on main street, and the strange story of a local doctor who, because no one wanted to claim it, displayed for years in his office the actual unclaimed, embalmed body of an executed inmate!

There are plans afoot to eventually expand the museum by including the two buildings that are situated in front of the museum. The museum frequently adds to its prison collections, thus, the more we collect, the more space is needed to house them.

As for my own experiences with ghosts at the museum, there have been times when I've been alone at the museum and I have clearly heard women's voices. These voices sound like they are coming directly from down the halls and from within the cells. During those times, I've gotten up off my seat and walked down the corridor to investigate. I've never found anyone else but myself in the building. Now, given everything that others have reported to me, and all that I've personally experienced at the prison, I still don't believe that the ghosts will appear to me. I know that others have seen them, and that they're in the building, but I don't think they'll appear to me. Anyway, I hope they don't."

MELISSA DARWIN'S STORY

Melissa Darwin.

"I don't believe that people should mess with the spirits that I know definitely dwell in the prison museum. I've read the stories that describe what people have actually experienced here, and I don't want to mess with any of them. I believe that this building belongs to "them" and I'm just an intruder on their property. I have heard sounds in the museum, but do you think I'll take a walk inside to investigate— no way!

C- House.

I find interesting the old house that is located at the corner of the prison property. The tall, old, stone house that you pass when arriving up to the prison itself. That house was named "C" house.

Years ago, the assistant to warden Roy Best, lived there. Warden Roy Best was indicted for his mistreatment of prisoners and also for financial impropriety.

During the court procedures, trial and negative media coverage, the warden's assistant assumed that he was going to be likewise implicated as was the warden, so he committed suicide and was found dead in that house. There must be paranormal activities in that house. Because of the tragic things that have taken place there, there must be.

By the way, did you happen to see, right at this museum's entrance the gas chamber? That chamber was actually in use until just a few years ago. It's an unusual artifact

With Cigar in hand Warden Roy Best stands outside the gas chamber door.

315

George Witherall sentenced from Douglas County for killing a sheep-herder. He escaped in 1874. His escape likely caused warden Anson Rudd his job, though the warden was likely not to blame. The tools used in the escape were apparently hidden during the time of the previous warden's time in office. Witherall was caught and returned to prison, though in for murder, his sentence was commuted by the governor and released. Witherall was traveling from Pueblo to Cañon City with a man and wagon, Witherall killed and robbed the man and took the man's wagon to Denver. He was then caught and returned to a city jail. That evening a small group of men took him from the jail at First and Greenwood streets, and hung him from a telephone pole at First and Main Street. Notice that in his haste to dress, he placed his own shoes on the wrong feet!

that strongly attracts our visitor's curiosity. Kind of spooky, wouldn't you say?

Today, the actual state prison is still in operation, housing over 800 inmates. It's located right beside this museum. Just take a look, you can see over in that direction, behind that high stone wall that separates the museum property, that wall, behind it is the working prison. At this very moment, you'll spot at the top of that guard tower an armed man. Don't think for one second he won't shoot to kill if anyone tries to escape!"

THE ROYAL GORGE PARK

Fremont County is very fortunate to have within its boundaries one of the most visited and scenically beautiful historical landmarks—the Royal Gorge Bridge and Park. Spanning the gorge is a very popular and frequently photographed landmark—the world's highest suspension bridge. The bridge, built in 1929, spans the gorge, a chasm 1,053 feet deep! Given its height and the unimaginable human labor involved during the construction of this awe-inspiring bridge, not one single loss of life occurred.

Directly below the bridge flows the historic Arkansas River. Its origin is in Colorado's Rocky Mountains. If you were to ride upon the surface of the river, beginning at its origin, then pass through the gorge on its

315-mile journey within the state, you would experience some of the most spectacular landscape ever to be seen. Not to mention the Class-V whitewater rapids.

Another great adventure is to get on board the Denver & Rio Grande railroad and take the 24-mile ride named the Royal Gorge Route. This trip has been named one of the most scenic train rides to be experienced in the world!

Note: The long drive to the gorge could be worthwhile, unless you have a family and funds are tight. The Cañon City government would be wise to reconsider its enactment of its excessively high entrance public lic fees to the park. Further, the 'tourist trap,' theme park atmosphere, created by the present, private concessionaire, who the Cañon City government contracted, adds little to the natural beauty and setting of the gorge. All that being said, the gorge remains an extraordinary wonder to behold.

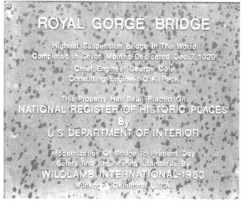

KRISTINE SARGENT'S STORY

I met Kristine at a Cañon City Mexican restaurant where the interview took place. Over a plate of tacos, I asked about her experiences at the park and she responded by giving me an unusually personal description of meeting up with a ghost in broad daylight!

Kristine, as she explained, like most never had much of an interest in the subject of ghosts, but after her experience, she has become quite knowledgeable. She has attended meetings of paranormal investigators, and even was an attendee at a séance or two.

Today, Kristine lives in Cañon City with her life-partner, Chelsea, and works for the city's department of labor."

— Antonio

"I presently live in Cañon City, and worked for the Royal Gorge park in the summers of 1994 and 1995. My job at the park was to operate the Incline Railway car that would take visitors down the natural gulch in the gorge to a total depth of 1,550 feet. It's a 100% grade drop, at a 45-degree angle, so it's quite a ride down to the Arkansas River. It is considered to be the world's steepest incline railway.

I really did enjoy my work and especially liked conversing with the tourists who would visit from all over the world. I enjoyed answering questions and especially hearing their loud cries of excitement, as they'd start the descent into the gorge. It's a very scary ride for someone who has never experienced anything like it. I recommend that everyone should take the trip, at least once in life. It's great!

When I spent the first summer at the gorge, I recall the day when I was having lunch with a co-worker named Roger. Roger and I were discussing different things associated with the building of the bridge that spans the gorge, and for some reason we got to conversing about suicides that have occurred at the park. Surprisingly, there have not been many that he was aware of, but for obvious reasons, if there were any, the park administrators would most likely want to keep these statistics quiet.

Anyway, as we were talking, another employee interrupted and said, "How about the spirits in the park, have you heard the stories about the spirits?" I answered, "No, I haven't." Roger added, "Oh, yeah I've been told there are spirits of several people that wander about the area. One popular story is about a guy that hangs out at the bridge, and there's another one about a guy that's been seen at the bottom of the gorge. I've never seen anything like that, but maybe ghosts aren't attracted to me." Our talk got me a bit curious about the subject of ghosts at the park, but that was all the information I was told, until a few nights later when I spent the night with my girlfriend Chelsea.

Chelsea was renting a cabin in a nearby campground, and from time to time we used to spend a few nights together. We met at the park, and our friendship soon developed into a romantic relationship. It was also convenient for me to stay over with her, because it saved me from making the long return drive alone at night to Cañon City.

Chelsea herself had worked for the park twice before, so she was familiar with several of the employees. One afternoon, I asked her if she had heard talk among the staff about anything regarding ghosts in the park. "Oh, yeah, there are a few that I know of. Why do you ask?" she said. "Oh, just curious, that's all," I responded.

Then Chelsea began to tell me about a black dog that employees believe is an animal spirit, that has appeared for years at the park and that won't allow anyone to approach him. She said, "He always makes his appearance at night. Sometimes he'll just follow a person for miles during a hike, then "poof" he's gone! But, like I said, he's been spotted around here for many years. I don't know if that could be considered a ghost, but he sure does act like one." Another story that Chelsea shared with me was about the white figure of a woman who is seen walking, or better yet, "floating" against the gorge walls. Chelsea said, "She'll appear for just a few minutes some nights. She moves a short distance and seems to be in the act of walking, but she seems to float against the granite walls of the canyon! Of course this is impossible for any living person to do, but being a ghost, she has no problem in maneuvering this way. She does not appear very often, but she is seen from time to time as a small figure at the west wall of the gorge."

I asked Chelsea, "Have you ever seen her?" She responded, "I myself saw what I thought appeared to be her ghost one night. I was walking alone on one of the trails at the opposite side of the gorge. This was before anyone informed me of her, so I didn't really know what that white, little moving object was at the opposite wall, way over to the other side of the gorge. She looked like a small flame from a lit match, just slowly bouncing around the walls. But that's all I've seen of her since I began working at the park. I've often heard footsteps along some of the trails that I have been hiking on. I was sure someone was behind me, following me, but when I'd turn around and there would be no one. Now that's kind of weird and creepy. But other than that, that's about all I've seen, and heard, as far as ghosts are concerned."

I didn't mention to Chelsea anything more about ghosts, or to anyone else for a long time. But one day my curiosity did begin to change. I had what I believed was a ghost experience that took place, not at night, but late in the day.

I was assisting Buddy, one of the park staff, helping him move some boxes from one office to another. I needed to use the bathroom and told Buddy I'd be right back. On my way, I walked past one small building. As I turned the corner, I spotted an older man several yards away, alone and leaning against one of the buildings. Strangely, I didn't think of asking him if he needed anything, but I should have, because the park was closed for the day. It's strange, but something at that moment just compelled me to keep on walking and avoid this guy.

He was not threatening in his appearance, but he did have an overall appearance of 'darkness.' Again, it's difficult to explain, but he gave me the impression that I was looking at a 'shadow.' Again, I would not usually react so flippantly as to simply disregard a guest even one with such a weird looking appearance, but something came over me that I believe was protecting me by having me keep a distance. It's weird, but even I can't understand it myself. Avoiding this guy, I walked past him entered the bathroom, and went into a stall. I began to think a bit further about him and my reaction.

Then it came to me, I must have been subconsciously afraid to confront him, so I chose to avoid a possibly negative situation. As I was thinking about this, suddenly I heard the sound of footsteps walking around the outside of the bathroom. Without hearing the door open, I heard the faucet being turned on. I said, "Is anyone there? I'll be out in just a second." No one answered me. Again, I said, "Is anyone there?" Nothing.

Not wanting to stay another second in the bathroom, I decided to get out quickly! But right after I exited the stall, the bathroom stall door opened wide, and then slammed shut with a huge bang! I stood as solid as stone with fear! The faucets were still running and I shot out of there like a bullet!

As soon as I arrived back at the office, I told my co-worker what had happened and surprisingly he just stood looking at me. I was not crying, but was close to it. I yelled at him, "What the hell's wrong with you? I'm serious, I just saw a ghost!" He came over to me and gave me a hug, "I know, I know, other's here have also seen him too. Don't let him scare you, he'll always keeps his distance. He never hurts anyone."

I was so surprised by his response that I said, "You mean, you've known about this ghost, and not one of you guys ever bothered to tell me about him?" He said, "Yeah, well the dude hasn't appeared for a long time. The last I heard, he was spotted by a hiker on one of the trails last year." Then Buddy asked, "Was he wearing a uniform?" I answered, "No, I don't think so, he was just a dark shadow." "Well," he said, "He usually always is seen wearing a military type of uniform, something from the Civil War era, or because of where we are, a uniform from the U.S. Cavalry. He also staggers or walks with a limp. Probably from having been shot in the ass by an Indian, who knows."

I didn't appreciate Buddy's devil-may-care attitude. I was in no mood for jokes, and I was still shaking. Fortunately for me, Buddy said he would finish moving the boxes and told me I could clock out for the day. I left in a rush, got into my car, and drove to the cabin, where Chelsea was making dinner. I told her about what I had experienced and she said, "Oh, that's right—the soldier! I haven't heard about him for a while. You mean you actually saw him!" I said, "Yes, yes, yes I did, but everyone seems to think it's no big deal!"

Chelsea answered, "Did you really see him? I mean, Kris, did you really see the ghost of the soldier?" I answered, "Hell, yes I did!" Well, I spent most of the night describing to Chelsea in great detail all that I had experienced, and soon I felt at ease enough to finally put it past me.

I never again spoke about it to the other co-workers, even though some asked me, I just gave them little details, but nothing more. I knew I saw a ghost that day—a real ghost! Since that time, I've read all the magazines and books I could get my hands on that describe ghost sightings, encounters and hauntings. There must be others at the park who have seen one or two of the ghosts, there must!"

CHACO CANYON, NM

CHACO CANYON NATIONAL PARK

The cultural flowering of the Chacoan people began in the mid-800's and lasted more than 300 years. We can see it clearly in the grand scale of the architecture. Using masonry techniques unique for their time, they constructed massive stone buildings (Great Houses) of multiple stories containing hundreds of rooms much larger than any they had previously built. The buildings were planned from the start, in contrast to the usual practiced of adding rooms to existing structures as needed. Constructions on some of these buildings spanned decades and even centuries. Although each is unique, all great houses share architectural features that make them recognizable as Chacoan.

In the 1100's and 1200's, change came to Chaco as new construction slowed and Chaco's role as a regional center shifted. Chaco's influence continued at Aztec, Mesa Verde, the Chuska Mountains and other centers to the north, south, and west. In time, the people shifted away from Chacoan ways, migrated to new areas, reorganized their world and eventually interacted with foreign cultures. Their descendants are the modern Southwest Indians. Many Southwest Indian people look upon Chaco as an important stop along their clans' sacred migration paths, a spiritual place to be honored and respected.

REX HENDERSON'S STORY

My interview with Rex took place at his parent's home in the northeastern area of Albuquerque. We sat in his living room surrounded by examples of southwestern art and family photos taken several years before. Said Henderson, "My father enjoyed photog-

raphy, that's why in most every room of the house you'll find has at least two or more examples of his work. On the wall and on the table, you'll find dad's passion. He loved taking pictures of nature and Indian ruins."

During our interview, from time to time Rex would need to excuse himself after becoming overwhelmed when reminiscing about his and his father's relationship. "I really loved my father. I miss him deeply," he'd tell me. Although I had heard of strange occurrences that others had experienced at Chaco, this would be the first I'd record. I hope you enjoy this particular story. Not simply for its narrative, but for its view into a historical past unique to New Mexico.

— Antonio

"Let's see, I guess to date, it's been about eight or nine years since my encounter with a spirit. Coincidently, I had recently been divorced from my wife. As bad-luck would have it, soon after our divorce was finalized my father died. My ex-wife Sherry and my dad got along very well, and when she heard about his death, she took it pretty hard. Sherry was not a terrible person at all, in fact she was the best person to have ever had come into my life. But as in most things, change comes and sometimes we just have to admit to ourselves that it's time to accept and move on.

During our twenty years of marriage, Sherry and my mother were the primary caretakers of my father. He was a very active man before being diagnosed with Alzheimer's, but in the end, it actually wasn't the Alzheimer's disease that killed him. One afternoon, without anyone noticing, my father walked out the side gate in the backyard; and in broad daylight quietly slipped away. He was aimlessly wandering the streets several blocks away before my mother noticed that he was missing from the back yard.

The police report noted that a witness spotted him standing between two parked cars. She stated that my father darted out into the street and an oncoming car hit and killed him. The hospital report stated that due to massive head injuries, he died instantly. It was a very distressing time for my family and I. Together we somehow we managed to push through all the sadness and depression.

My father's body was cremated and I held on to his ashes for over a year before my mother, Sherry, and I decided we needed to either bury or disperse the ashes in a proper place. I proposed to my mother that I spread his ashes in the Sangre de Cristo Mountains that surround Santa Fe. My mother made it very clear that she was not in favor of this idea. Sherry spoke and said, 'Rex, your father enjoyed reading about southwest anthropology. Do you think he would approve if we were to spread his ashes somewhere over in Chaco Canyon or maybe even the Grand Canyon?'

I thought about this and because Albuquerque was not that far from Chaco Canyon, it became my first choice. Arizona's Grand Canyon was close to a day's drive away—much too far a drive. Chaco was closer and for personal reasons I wanted to keep him in New Mexico. We all decided on Chaco Canyon and even though we knew it had to be against the law to spread cremated remains in a national park, we decided to do this anyway.

On the day of our trip, with dad's boxed ashes lying on top of our jackets in the back seat, Sherry and I drove the four or so hours out to the park. My mother was unable to accompany us but sent us off with her blessings. This visit to Chaco Canyon would be a first for Sherry and I. We arrived at 3pm and upon entering the park noticed not many other visitors or cars in the visitors parking lot.

We parked the car and placed the box containing my father's ashes in my backpack. We hiked about a mile to an area of the park that seemed pretty isolated and noticed a sign nearby with the name 'Pueblo Bonito'. I never would have imagined how huge and spectacular the ruins would be but they were incredible! It was so overwhelmingly large. Admittedly on a spiritual level the area seemed magical. We were totally amazed by the impressive ruins, overall beauty and solitude.

We walked around for a few minutes until Sherry found the perfect spot at the base of a very tall, stonewall for spreading the ashes. Directly above this wall was a window outlined in stone and at its top, an ancient wooden lintel constructed many hundreds of years ago. It was obvious to us that we were totally alone. We stopped talking and immediately noticed how absolutely still and silent the entire area was. Everything was quiet, not footsteps, voices or conversations from other visitors, just total silence. Not wanting to risk being discovered, we quickly spread my father's ashes along the base of the wall.

As I returned the empty box to my backpack, we offered personal prayers also in silence. But within a few seconds, we noticed a forceful wind start to kick up. And not just wisps of wind, no this wind was strong and completely out from nowhere. It was strong enough to blow my father's ashes up and over us! Most of the ashes had been carried up off the ground as Sherry and I ran to the opposite side of the area just to avoid being covered in the swirling cloud of ashes! For sure this was unusual and so surprising.

For as long as I've lived in the southwest, I've never encountered wind coming up so quickly, suddenly and with such force. Together with the ashes, bits of debris were also being blown around. A fear came over us and Sherry yelled at me, 'Let's get out of here—now!' We climbed up and over the rocks and made our way out to an open area away from the ruins.

As soon as we walked into the area at the outside of the ruin, the air was as still as it could be. No breeze or wind of any kind, just the silent stillness we first encountered when we first arrived. We had no doubt that what we had just witnessed was something unusual, maybe even paranormal. This windy occurrence was not a random thing; it definitely had something to do with our scattering my father's ashes. In both our hearts, we knew it had to be.

We thought about the possibility that the sudden burst of wind was a sign of my father's presence. We hoped that my father would have been pleased to be honored in such a manner. No, this was not what I'd call a positive experience. Sherry and I were left wondering if the spirits of the ancients were angry with us. We would soon find out.

That evening as we drove out of the park, it was just too late to continue on to Albuquerque so we chose to stay at a motel off I-40 in Thoreau, several miles south of Chaco. Here's when things got even stranger.

We had a disturbing experience that made us think that perhaps the spreading of my father's cremated ashes was not welcomed by the spirits and ancestors of Chaco. In the middle of the night, I was the first one awakened by the loud sound of a glass breaking in our room. I still don't know what it was, but it sounded like the glass window of our room had broken. I opened my eyes and looked all about the room, nothing was disturbed. Sherry awoke and asked me what was going on? I told her that I had heard a sound. She kept still.

She kept quiet because as soon as I answered her, we both caught the scent of something musty and moldy. It was an awful odor, something that gripped the back of my throat and even made my gag reflex react. Sherry immediately sat up in bed and asked, "What is that smell?" The smell became overwhelming to her, and as we were sniffing the air, I notice that the odor getting even stronger. I said, "It smells like rotted, musky tanned leather."

As soon as I said this, we were terrified to see a large, dark shadow, more of a mass of darkness; begin to come out from the wall in front of us. I'm not ashamed to say this made us jump back against the head-board! Right after seeing this, an arm and hand materialized! The arm reached out from the darkness towards our bed: the arm was not attached to a body it was just an extended arm with an open hand!

Surprisingly, it made a swaying motion, something like a hula dancer would make. We both saw it and there was no doubt that this thing was a ghost! I immediately grabbed and pulled away the pillow Sherry was clutching and threw it at the ghostly arm—making a direct hit!

I got out of the bed, reached for the light switch and turned it on. The only evidence of having been visited by the ghost was the pillow on the floor that's all. The odor had disappeared and cleared out. We were shaking and Sherry very much wanted to get back in our truck and drive home that night. She said, 'I don't want to go through anymore ghostly stuff like that again.' I left the light on and answered, 'Sherry let's just try and go to sleep, I don't think we'll have any more visits.' Before I could finish talking, Sherry said, 'Nope, I'm not going to stay here another second. If you want to come with me, I'll drive us home, but I'm leaving with or without you—I'm out of here!'

In less than ten minutes, we packed our few clothes in a plastic bag, got into the truck and headed home. During our drive home, we discussed the situation and both agreed, a ghost visited us, if only by an arm, it was a spirit nonetheless. The action of the wind at Chaco earlier that day, followed by the hotel experience later that night, was evidence enough for me that having innocently disposed of my father's ashes in such a sacred site, was not appreciated by 'someone.'

Today, I worry that the spirits at Chaco may have held my father's spirit accountable for my actions because he had nothing to do with what Sherry and I did. I regret it, but what was done was done. You can't go back and change it. Frankly, as beautiful a place as it is, I never want to set foot in that park ever again!"

COLUMBIA, CA

COLUMBIA STATE PARK

Columbia is a rich gold town which has become a living history museum. Columbia State Historic Park started life in 1859 as a commercial hub for the areas miners. Today, Columbia State Historic park is an educational sightseeing attraction for people from all over the world. It is also a vital, living community for those who live in and around it.

The original buildings with their iron doors from the 1840's have been restored to house businesses in keeping with the historic theme of the park. Approximately 96% of the buildings are original. In 1860 a fire destroyed several of the buildings; they were replaced within the year.

The town was accepted as a state park in 1945 at the urging of area residents who wanted to preserve the Mother Lode's most intact Gold Rush town.

The history of Columbia is rich

in gold. According to most reports, the first miners arrived there in 1850. Dr. Thaddeus Hildreth, his brother George and a handful of other miners found gold while camped near today's main parking lot. Another version said a group of Mexicans panned for gold at the same spot in relative secrecy for four or five months prior to the Hildreth party happening upon them. Within a month, about 6,000 miners lived in a tent and shanty town called Hildreth's Diggings. The name was changed to American Camp, then to Columbia all in 1850. By the end of 1852, the new town had more than 150 stores, saloons, and other businesses, a Sunday school, Masonic lodge and a branch of the Sons of Temperance.

In addition to being a state park, Columbia has been the setting for many movies, television shows and commercial productions.

PARK RANGER LOGAN TEJON'S STORY

My story took place over 16 years ago. I was employed with the California State Park Service. I'm a Native American from the Tule River Indian Reservation just west of the town of Porterville. My mother who worked for the tribal office, informed me of a job announcement that the tribal office had received through the mail. The job was for a park ranger at the historic village of Columbia. I fit all the required criteria for the position and after submitting my application, I was hired a few months later.

After I found a small house to rent in the nearby town, I started my new job at the park. My position was Historic Interpreter. Like everyone else who was employed at Columbia State Park, our positions did not just limit us to function within our professional title. We were required to understand other obligations at the park, this usually meant that we 'crossed over' to assume the duties of other jobs whenever necessary. For example, I might be asked to lead a tour during the day, then do security watch the following night, etc. On a few occasions, I would substitute in other areas of the park when an employee called in sick, or missed a day or two.

My ghost experience at the park took place one early evening as I was taking a group of tourist on an interpretive walk. I had no idea that within a span of a few hours, my entire outlook on the paranormal would change as much as it did on that tour.

Towards the end of the tour, one member of the group who was about thirty years of age asked, "Excuse me but do you know if the park is haunted?" I answered, in as much of a professional manner as I could, "Well, that's a common question. Due to the antique look of the buildings, and the town's exceptional rich history, I can see how some people might associate it with ghosts." I also informed the woman that I personally had never had any type of encounter with a ghost at the park. However, by her negative facial reaction, I could tell she was not convinced in the least by my answers.

When I informed the group that the tour would be ending in just a few minutes, the same woman and her boyfriend both came forward and asked me if I could spare a few minutes alone with them, so they could describe a ghost experience they recently had at that park. I told them that would not be a problem. And at the end of the tour, we sat at a bench under a tree where they proceeded to tell me their story:

Last night at about 9pm my boyfriend and I were walking through the park when we both spotted the ghost of a small man standing next to one of the doorways. He was dressed in dark clothing, and as we walked past him, he simply stared at us, not giving us a wave of his hand, or any courteous gesture."

Surprised by her story, I asked her, what made her think this man was a ghost? She said, "As we walked past him, we noticed that his face was very pale and had distinct dark outlines. This left us with a creepy, scary feeling." The boyfriend continued by saying that he said, "Let's stop across the street and watch what he does." She said, "We acted as if we were tired from walking, and sat down on one of the public benches. We were only about fifty feet away from the man, so even though it was dark, we easily had a clear view of him. The boyfriend then said, "The man might be a tourist acting out a fantasy of playing a ghost and scaring people, or he might even be employed with the park service.

The woman continued the story by telling me they both watched the man for about five minutes until she had had enough, and told her boyfriend the ghost was scaring her. The ghost man was still as could be, staring straight ahead, and this was freaking her out. She said, "My boy-friend saw how this was affecting me and approached the man, "Hey, what's up?" At that, the ghost man slowly turned away from us, and seemed to float towards the doorway of the building directly behind where he had been standing. As he reached the door he disappeared in the darkness!

We were immediately shocked and amazed. My initial fear left me and I convinced my boyfriend that we should walk over to the door and in-vestigate. We cautiously walked over to the building, and looked through the door's window. It was dark, but for the dim light from a small ad-jacent room. We turned the door knob, but it was locked. As I said, we followed this man immediately after he disappeared. He did not have enough time to place a key into the keyhole, open the door, or enter with-out us watching him. And for God sakes, he floated above the ground!"

I attempted to explain to the couple that as far as I was aware, the park service did not employ actors to play the role of ghosts, especially after closing hours. They were not convinced, and urged me to discuss their experience with a park superintendent. I assured the woman that I would try and find out who was behind this. They were so concerned with what they saw, that she gave me her home phone number and ad-dress so I could update them as to the outcome of my investigation.

The next day, I asked several employees and no one knew anything about any employees or actors dressing up, and portraying ghosts. I filed a report with the supervisor, and left it up to her to do the remainder of the follow up investigation.

Some months after this incident, a film crew had scheduled to shoot some footage in Columbia. The old west setting of Columbia attracts sev-eral film crews throughout the year to the park. Not only does Hollywood love the historic shooting location of Columbia, but film companies from other parts of the world also appreciate access to its variety of unique at-tractive locations. Columbia's old buildings offer a historic and authen-tic aura of the old west, because we get production crews into the park throughout the year. This particular time, the film company that came into the park had traveled from London.

The crew arrived without incident, and began setting up their trailers and positioning their lights. I was employed to provide security for the set, and was also hired by the production crew to tour their staff around the park, nearby towns, local restaurants, and other points of interest.

One staff crew member searching for the best locations to film, was in charge of operating a mobile camera unit. I accompanied him as he set up his camera and actors at different lo-

He simply stared at us.

cations throughout the park. His shots were taken in buildings, under porches, on top of buildings, and generally throughout the park. At the end of the day he and I met to discuss the shooting schedule, for the following day. The reason for the schedule was to shoot around, and not to disrupt the flow of, visiting tourists.

I remained with him as he entered a movie trailer filled with the company's editing equipment. After he took a quick review of what he had filmed that day. He seemed strangely baffled by what he had seen on the film. He rewound the video and appeared just as perplexed. He asked me to take a look at the video screen. We both spotted a strange person who appeared in one of the shots, that was not part of the acting crew. He asked me if I knew who this individual was, or if he was employed with the park service. He re-ran the video for me, and sure enough there appeared a small man dressed in a dark hat and clothing, standing by one of the old buildings. The video caught this strange man as he stood by the building, turned and walked towards a very old large tree. He turned to his left, then "disappeared" by a doorway. He didn't just walk into the doorway to enter the building, he "disappeared" under the doorway. I had no idea who this person was, but I immediately recalled the story the couple on my tour had described to me about the ghost they had seen, just two months before.

I got chills, and asked the camera man if this man had appeared in other shots. He said this was the only one, then said, "Logan, if I didn't film this myself, I would have thought this guy was staged, but I think we've captured a ghost on film." I was shocked. I could only respond with a nervous, "Wow!"

Once word got around about the ghost caught on video, several other park staff eagerly asked to view it. One female employee related to me in confidence, that she had never seen the ghostly man, but she had her own experience with voices in that same building! She said she had not told anyone about her story, because she hoped she'd ultimately and eventually forget the memory of it. But after viewing the film, she decided to described to me exactly what happened to her one afternoon:

"At about 6:30 one evening, I entered the store to check on a light I noticed had been left on. When I walked to the rear of the store, I immediately felt the presence of someone in the room with me. This was strange because I knew I was alone, and I didn't hear footsteps, or the door open behind me. There was still enough sunlight entering from the windows, so I was not at all in a darkened room. As you know Logan, the room is also not very large, so I could obviously tell if I were alone or not. The powerful sense of someone standing right next to me was very strong. I turned around and faced the front windows. I asked, "Anyone here?" Suddenly I clearly heard a male voice state, "Women don't belong here, women don't belong here!" I froze in place and said, "Who is there, whose there?" I kept still. Without warning, I felt the pressure of a 'cold hand' placed on the area between my shoulder blades! That was enough. I shot out of that room like a bullet! I've not told anyone about this experience before. But since that day, every time I pass that store, I turn away not wanting to see what might be glaring back at me from the inside the window."

As for myself, I've still not had any direct sighting, or contact with anything paranormal here in the park. And aside from these incidents I've shared, I've not heard of any guest reporting other ghostly activities at Columbia. I wouldn't be surprised to know that other visitors have witnessed something strange at the park. Given the large influx of tourists who visit Columbia each year, I sure someone must have captured an image or two of a ghost, they just never noticed or knew to look for one in their photos. As I said earlier, I haven't worked at Columbia in over 16 years but a lot of visitors have toured and taken thousands of photographs here in those 16 years. I would think that this ghostly figure must have been captured in some of those photos during all these years, we'll just never really know."

DENVER, CO

BUFFALO BILL MUSEUM

Located just 30 minutes west of Denver the museum was opened in 1921 by Buffalo Bill's only foster son Johnny Baker. Johnny wished for the museum to record the life and times of and particularly the legend of, William F. Cody. Firearms, artifacts, and Native American memorabilia of the spectacular Wild West Shows are all on display.

Named after William F. Cody's more recognized nickname of "Buffalo Bill," the museum offers visitors an unusual collection of western memorabilia. Housing such priceless artifacts as Sitting Bull's bow and arrows, Buffalo Bill's elaborate show outfits, and an original Frederick Remington, "Portrait of a Ranch hand," the museum contains many other items from this man's well-known career as a western showman.

In 1886, he was contracted by the Kansas Pacific Railroad to hunt buffalo for the purpose of providing meat to the crews that were laying railroad tracks. He also proved skillful in hunting buffalo, thus acquiring his nickname.

In 1913, he tried to preserve the few remaining buffalo by starting a protected herd. The City and County of Denver took notice and itself took decisive action by starting its own protective herd just five miles west of the museum's present location.

William F. Cody, aka Buffalo Bill.

333

Born in Oakley, Kansas, and laid to rest in Lookout Mountain within the Colorado town outskirts of Golden, the museum pays a lasting tribute to this legendary man, who died in 1917 at his sister's house in Denver. Among what has already been stated, the museum grounds are also the chosen resting spots for the graves of both William F. "Buffalo Bill" Cody, and his son, Johnny Baker.

KIMARY A. MARCHAESE'S STORY

I interviewed Kimary outside the museum walls where we sat on a picnic table, encircled by the magnificent, panoramic vistas that surround the museum's perch top location.

Kimary was very knowledgeable of the museum, sharing her own personal religious beliefs and describing to me how they have provided her with, as she stated, "the strength to withstand any demonic or evil influence."

After our interview was completed, I was given a short but adequate tour of the museum itself. The museum contains a better-than-average collection of artifacts and related memorabilia, much of it significant to the history of not only the west, but also the nation. I would highly recommend that if the opportunity ever comes your way, that you definitely make it a point to visit this museum. The museum staff, and a ghost, or two, or three, would appreciate your visit.

— Antonio

Kimberly Marchaese.

"My position at the museum is Exhibit Coordinator and Artist. I was born in California and raised in Hawaii, and arrived in Colorado in 1978 to attend college. During the period that I was attending school, I obtained a job at the museum, and have since been employed at the museum for a total of 14 years. Admittedly, I was not familiar with the stories of ghosts which, I discovered later, exist in the museum but that soon changed. During my first month of work at the museum, I had a conversation with the museum's curator, Jan. Jan expressed to me her concern regarding how uncomfortable she felt while working alone in the building. As we talked a little more, Jan informed me that these uncom-

fortable feelings originated from the strange events she had experienced within the building. Small items would move about on-their-own, and sometimes she would even hear the "clinking" of metal boot spurs, as if a cowboy would be walking the halls. Finally, she added that she was always aware of feeling the presence of Buffalo Bill's spirit, who she believed continues watching her every move.

Another employee named Keith Allen also worked at the property.

William Frederick Cody "Buffalo Bill"—February 26, 1846 – January 10, 1917.

Keith was a city employee of Denver's Parks and Recreation. Sadly, six years ago Keith was killed in a car accident. Keith was one man who took a keen interest in the paranormal experiences that visitors at the museum would regularly report having had. On several occasions Keith described to me the things he would see on the property.

Keith not only worked but also lived on the property. He also had the advantage of spending a fair amount of time discussing the topic of ghosts with the public. Keith lived within the building named 'Pahauska.' Today, the structure is used as the museum's gift and snack shop. Pahauska, in the native Lakota language, is a word that translates to 'long hair.' Long Hair was the name given to Buffalo Bill by the Lakota. Keith was a museum interpreter of Buffalo Bill's life, and would dress the part of Buffalo Bill,

in full costume.

Many of these experiences reported to Keith would take place at Buffalo Bill's actual graveside. That grave is located just a short walk to the south of the museum. The most frequent spiritual episodes reported to him were the sounds of a man's booted footsteps and his "clinking" metal spurs, about the graveside. The distinct sounds of spurs are also reported by other employees and visitors within the museum. Keith reported to me that the visitors stressed to him that they were absolutely telling him the truth and that they were not making up stories. Keith stated to me that the sincere and serious tone in their voices was very convincing.

One evening, Keith had his own funny encounter, as he was returning to the museum from an event in town. For the fundraiser, he was required to dress in an interpretation of Buffalo Bill's full costume. As he got out of his car, and walked toward the Pahauska building where he lived, he heard the sound of voices coming from the direction of Buffalo Bill's grave. Keith decided to walk up to the site to see what was going on. Arriving at the graveside, he told me that he heard the loud terrifying screams and shouts of teens as they scrambled into the woods.

Keith had unknowingly surprised these naive and susceptible teenagers, who by coincidence had been conducting a séance in their attempt to contact the spirit of Buffalo Bill! When these teenagers spotted Keith approaching in full costume, they apparently believed that Keith was Buffalo Bill's spirit and scampered willy-nilly into the woods!

An unusual and unique tradition that the public has been engaged in for many years is to leave coins on Bill's grave. The museum staff has researched and investigated this unusual habit, and found that years ago someone began to toss buffalo nickels upon the grave's stone. Today, since the buffalo nickel is no longer being made, regular nickel and other coins are tossed. This tradition is a curiously odd one, and seems to be thoroughly enjoyed by the public. The museum benefits from this by regularly gathering up the coins that are then added together with the money raised for the general museum Education Fund.

If you happen to look at the reverse of an original buffalo nickel, you'll spot the side view portrait of a Native American. A very good friend of Buffalo Bill's was a Native American

man called Iron Tail. Iron Tail was employed and performed within Bill's Wild West Show. It is assumed that Iron Tail's likeness was the model that was most likely used for the nickel's portrait.

Another item frequently tossed onto the grave are bobby pins. The tradition of doing this dictates that single women who toss bobby pins on Bill's grave will soon find a husband. I personally know of a group of six women who visited the museum. They walked to the graveside and all but one woman tossed a bobby pin. Within the year, all were engaged to be married—all but the one!

A local newspaper got wind of this and ran with the story. The paper soon sponsored an event at the museum that coincided with the anniversary of Buffalo Bill's death. The women were invited to return to the graveside with a hand-full of bobby pins. The women complied, at which time bobby pins were distributed to the gathered crowed and the pins were tossed on the grave. I personally got into the action that day, and also tossed a bobby pin. I don't know if it will do any good, so you'll have to check back with me in about a year's time to see if it actually worked.

Strangely, most of the ghostly events the public experiences tend to take place at closing time. Of course, as I've said before, some of our employees who work alone within the museum do report unusual activity. I also work alone many times at the museum. Personally, I'm not afraid of spirits, because my personal religious beliefs tell me not to be. I do, however, believe that such things do exist, but truthfully, I'm not afraid. I know that nothing evil or negative is in the building, so that gives me comfort."

ALBERT HALBERSTAM'S STORY

"I was born, raised, and still live in Denver. Close to three years ago, my wife, Wendy, and I decided to take our nine-year-old daughter on a weekend outing to the Buffalo Bill museum. We were not ready, or even expecting, to have a ghost manifest to us, but that's exactly what happened. Our encounter happened in the museum basement, where the large stuffed buffalo is displayed.

As Wendy and I were taking our time strolling through the numerous displays and reading the informational descriptions, our daughter, Christine, let go of my hand and made a beeline directly towards the stuffed buffalo. The stuffed buffalo is roughly about five feet tall from hoof to shoulder, and is surrounded by a wood fence. Because of its realism, I could understand how it might be very attractive to both children and adults. As was the case, my daughter ran right up to it.

Keeping a close eye on our daughter, I watched her fascination with the display as she took her time scrutinizing each inch of the animal. Wendy was at the time marveling at a glass case where a number of Native American artifacts were displayed. I decided to walk into another small room nearby where I heard what I thought was the recorded voice of a man describing something. His voice had the effect of being very sure of himself, and direct and somewhat commanding.

Upon entering the room, I found it empty. I glanced around the displays, hoping to find a button that would enable me to press it and listen to the pre-recorded tape but there were no such buttons.

I thought this was strange, because I had heard the voice of a man talking in that very room. Stranger still, while this thought was going through my mind, I began to feel a sudden weakness come over me, almost as if I were about to faint. Then the lights started to flicker off and on. An unusual cold came over me, enveloping my shoulders, I walked out of that room and approached my wife who was looking at a display of rifles. I said to Wendy, "I don't know what's going on, but I suddenly don't feel very well. I'm going to step outside for some fresh air."

I walked over to the buffalo display to ask Christine if she wanted to join me outside, I spotted her standing and staring at the bottom of a ramp that led up to the first floor. I asked her what she was looking at and she answered, "The tall man with the hat." I looked down the ramp, and did not see anyone, so I asked her, "Where is he? I don't see anyone." She answered, "Daddy, he's waving to us, over there, see?"

I got the weirdest feeling that is difficult to explain. I imagine it must have been fear because I took hold of my daughter's hand and walked over to Wendy. I said, "Honey, I think we need to go outside, I'll tell you what's going on after we're outdoors." Wendy looked at me with apprehension, but didn't argue. As we exited the museum, I explained to Wendy what I had experienced in the room, and about the man in the hat Christine had seen. Not wanting to alarm Christine, we spoke in soft tones and asked her to tell us all about the man she had seen waving to her.

Christine responded in her innocent voice, "He told me that buffalos are dangerous, and I should never go out to the corral alone. I told him we don't have a corral, and he walked away. That's all he said."

We didn't press Christine with any further questioning and decided to head home and not mention the man with the hat to Christine again. Before we headed to the car, I told Wendy that I was going to use the bathroom.

Instead of going to the bathroom, I walked over to the front desk of the museum's entrance and spoke to a woman. I asked her if there was a costumed man wearing a hat walking about the place. She answered that there was no one fitting that description, or any man dressed in a costume in the museum. "Are you sure," I asked. "Yes, yes," she answered. Then hesitating a bit, while looking at me straight in the eyes she said, "Why, did you see our ghost?" "Nah," I said, I was just wondering, then I walked away. I couldn't believe she asked me if I had seen their ghost but have thought about this ever since. I may not have seen a ghost but certainly felt things I never have while inside the museum.

Well, that's all I can tell you about

what I experienced, and what my daughter saw at the museum. It's not that frightening, but it's still somewhat creepy and scary don't you think?"

DOLORES, CO

MESA VERDE NATIONAL PARK

Situated just west of Canyon of the Ancients National Monument and northeast of the Ute Mountain Tribal Park, Dolores is considered the gateway to Mesa Verde National Park. To the southeast of town are the world-famous cliff dwellings at Mesa Verde National Park. Colorado's second largest body of water the McPhee Reservoir, is located just northwest of town.

It is not uncommon to experience such large animals as deer or elk as they graze in the nearby hills, or even cross the highways. Such big game attracts seasonal hunters, as well as photographers who, thankfully, prefer to take aim and shoot with a camera.

During the height of Dolores's history, the town was a major railroad stop-over along the Rio Grande Southern route that lay between Durango and Ridgway. Given its railroad history, the town displays an exact replica of the original train depot on Railroad Avenue. It is housed within the Rio Grande Southern Railroad Museum and Dolores Visitors' Center. In addition, a curious visit that a tourist might also enjoy while passing though Dolores would be to its well-known Galloping Goose Museum.

The Anasazi Heritage Center is an archaeological museum that displays and preserves artifacts and records from excavations on public

lands in the Four Corners area, one of the richest archaeological regions in the United States. The museum is also the headquarters for Canyons of the Ancients National Monument. Their goal is to increase public awareness of archaeology and

cultural resources in the Four Corners area of the southwest.

Anasazi is the Navajo name for
a farming people who lived in the
Four Corners between AD 1 and
AD 1300. The population size varied over time, but at its peak many
thousands of Anasazi families occupied the southwest corner of Colorado. Their modern descendants, the Pueblo Indians of New Mexico and
Arizona, prefer the term Ancestral Pueblo rather than "Anasazi." The
Spanish word, 'Pueblo', refers to the traditional apartment-house style
of village architecture that survives today.

The museum features permanent displays on the Ancestral Pueblo
people, and on techniques that allow modern archaeologist to reveal the
past. Many exhibits are hands-on and interactive. Visitors can weave on
a loom, grind corn meal on a metate, examine tiny traces of the past
through microscopes, and handle real artifacts. Changing special exhibits and events feature topics of regional history and Native American
cultures.

The museum's pueblo-style building was created during the McPhee
Dam and Reservoir project, which included the Dolores Archaeological Program, the largest single archaeological project in the history of
the United States. Between 1978 and 1984 researchers mapped about
1,600 archaeological sites, including hunting camps, shrines, granaries,
households and villages, along the Dolores River in the reservoir area,
and excavated about 120 sites to salvage their information value. The
artifacts were removed from the area scheduled to be flooded by the
McPhee Reservoir project. Many of these artifacts are displayed in the
museum; the rest are available for study and research.

The museum is 7,000 feet above sea level at the foot of the San Juan
Mountains in Southwest Colorado. It overlooks McPhee Reservoir and
the Montezuma Valley, and is about 17 miles by road from Mesa Verde
National Park. On the museum grounds are two 12th century settlements,
the Dominguez and Escalante Pueblos, named after Spanish friars who

explored this area in 1776 and became the first to record archaeological sites in Colorado. The pueblos were excavated and stabilized 200 years later.

MICHAEL DEVLIN'S STORY

My interview with Michael took place at this home in Cortez. I had heard about his spiritual experience from another interviewee in Denver the week before. I made it a point to contact Michael and travel specifically to Cortez to schedule an interview with him. Michael's home is intricately decorated with a Native American theme in mind. On one wall are framed lithographs, on another a bob cat pelt, and earthen jars filled with feathers of various birds. The living room gave me the appearance of it being a mini museum.

Michael pointed out a specific old, small earthen jar that was topped with a clay lid. Michael stated, "This small pot contains a few human bones. I located it in southern New Mexico at a dig about 10 years ago. The site was a burial." When I pressed him further regarding his purpose for removing it from the burial site, Michael answered, "I know I should have left it where it was, but there were so many pots like this one at the site, I didn't think taking one would matter much. Anyway, I plan to return it at some time."

This manner of disconcerted thinking is, in my view, very disrespectful and adverse to a positive focus regarding Native Americans. After my interview with Michael, I did not mince words when describing my disagreeable thoughts on his keeping such human remains in his house. Michael agreed to return the pot to its rightful resting place. In fact, three months after our interview, I received a letter that included two pictures showing Michael placing the pot in the pit where he had originally removed it.

Since our initial meeting, I have kept in contact with Michael, and I am assured to know that he has remained true to his word in respecting the remains of the dead he has, and will, at times come into contact with.

— Antonio

"I've worked at the Anasazi Center just outside of the town of Dolores for several years, and never in my life would I have believed that what I experienced within the park could have happened to such a disbeliever of spiritual things as myself. Today, I'm still able to clearly recall the memory, and the impact the experience had on me. I know that I have been changed spiritually. I now have a better understanding and respect for those individuals who report their own experiences with ghosts.

When I first studied at the center, I was under the tutelage of a professor of archeology from Denver. Beginning with my first graduate study semester, I was one of two students that was chosen for the archeological 'dig' the other student's name was Bob. Both Bob and I were working on completing our Masters degrees in archeology that summer. After successfully completing our respective research papers, we would graduate in the Fall of that year. We were both excited to begin the archeological 'dig'.

During the first week of our research, Bob and I began mapping out a 40 by 30-foot area of land. This area was marked out using stakes and tape. Then we transferred this information onto a grid in our notebook. Within the first week this mapped out area began to take shape as we cleared its top surface layer of weeds, stones and debris. All the soil that we had removed from the site was passed through a mesh screen to separate any artifacts that might have been overlooked. The work was tediously slow but very necessary.

Within the first week we advanced a little more than halfway through the process, and by the following week we had already discovered a tray full of pottery shards and one deer bone awl. Awls were used by the ancients as a leather hole making tool. In additionally, we also found several examples of shell and stone beads. Without much digging, all these artifacts were recovered from the surface, which was quite fortunate for us. We knew that given these initial discoveries, the area had to be a rich source of more significant artifacts and other examples of ancient human evidence.

One day, during the first month of my work, I received some bad news. My brother, while working for an oil company in Germany, had been terribly injured. Thankfully he was alive, but he had lost the sight in his left eye. He would also need numerous plastic surgery operations on his face in the future. This terrible news affected me to my core. I cried for most of the day, feeling helpless and very sad. The news was a burden that I carried throughout the day and into the night. I needed to clear my mind so around eight that evening, I decided to drive the six miles to the site, and find a large rock where I could sit and contemplate my brother's future, that now included his being partially blind. Gazing upon the heavens I was comforted sitting there in the open desert, viewing the stars that were so bright. The night was clear and the moon was full. This time to reflect was just what I needed.

As I was about to rise up off the rock, in the near distance I spotted what I thought might me a coyote moving about 40 feet away from me. I sat back down and waited, hoping to see where it was headed, but I soon noticed that what I thought was a coyote was instead a man! I waited to see what this guy would do next.

He moved about the ground in a sweeping motion. That's the only way I can describe his movements as swaying from side-to-side. In my mind, I struggled to know just who this person was and what to make of his strange movements. There was nothing for me to do but watch.

Strangely, I was not in the least bit scared as he turned to face me. I looked him straight in his eyes and spoke, "Yeah, I'm over here. What's going on?" He did not respond but within a split second, he was standing right in front of me! I was totally shocked by this and tried to scream, but I couldn't, I was frozen stiff! I looked him straight in the eye and was transfixed with terror.

He glared at me and I noticed that his skin was so pale, and appeared as though he had never been exposed to sunlight. His eyes were a clouded light gray color, without showing any life in them at all. I immediately knew that the person standing in front of me was a ghost, and I was scared! I was so filled with fear I began breathing rapidly and with difficulty. The next thing I remember was waking up with my face flat on the ground, clearly I must have passed out!

The night was still dark and I had no idea how long I must have been laying on the ground because I did not wear a watch. I struggled to slowly get up and once I did, I walked to the truck and drove back to the center. As soon as I entered my sleeping quarters, I laid on the bed, and fell into a deep sleep. I was out cold!

When I awoke in the morning, I felt as if I still needed more sleep, so I fell back to sleep. I didn't wake up until 11 that morning. I have no idea why I was so tired. I just know that my body felt totally drained of energy from the night before. I was fully aware of my surroundings and did not feel as if I had been drugged, and why would I have been? I felt a strong desire to get up and out into the fresh air.

Once I stepped outside, with the warm sunlight washing over me, I felt much better. I can only describe this feeling as the feeling I got when I spent a week in a hospital when I was a young boy. I had had my tonsils removed, and an infection developed, so I was kept in the hospital for a week. When I was released, my father carried me in his arms to the car. As my father walked into the sunlight, such a refreshing feeling of peace came over me, one I'll never forget. That exact same feeling came over me as I was standing in the sunlight that morning. It was a wonderful feeling of safety and peace.

I don't know why that dark and menacing spirit approached me that night in the desert, and what I could have done to prevent the fear that gripped me, from taking over me like it did. I wasn't drinking, nor was I under any medication that could have caused such an intense experience. It was nothing my imagination created. I was not even thinking of anything paranormal at that time. I do believe that what confronted me was a ghost and its reason for doing so remains a mystery. I like to think that because of this encounter I am now more sensitive, informed and aware of the possibilities and potential for further encounters resulting in my line of research work.

EAGLES NEST, NM

VIETNAM VETERANS MEMORIAL – FRAN MULLEN'S STORY

"My story took place just last year when a girlfriend of mine, Sarah Tobias and I were visiting the memorial. My older brother, Sgt. First Class Samuel Higgins was in Viet Nam and I was told he was killed as he slept in his tent. Apparently, Sam had the misfortune of being the first person, among nine others, who the Viet Cong had killed before they attacked the remainder of his particular battalion. Because of my brother's death, I thought it might be a form of healing for me to visit the memorial and offer a few prayers in his honor. Since I live in Taos and the memorial is just under an hour drive to Eagles Nest, this would not be a very long drive or out of my daily routine. But, since I don't drive, I had to depend on my friend Sarah, who does drive, to take me to the memorial.

We arrived in Eagles Nest at around ten or so in the morning and decided first to have breakfast. I remember that the day was warm and without any wind. After leaving the restaurant, we located the memorial without any problems.

I brought with me a ring my brother had given me before he left for his tour of duty in Viet Nam. A girlfriend who had broken up with him months before he had enlisted gave the ring to him. I had always mentioned to Samuel how much I liked the ring's blue stone. I knew that the stone was nothing more than just cheap glass, but I liked it anyway. Samuel kept the ring for the few months after he and his girlfriend called it quits. So, when the day came for him to leave, he handed me the ring and with a big hug he left for California's southern marine base in 29 Palms.

I had decided to bring the ring with me and to leave it somewhere at the memorial, perhaps on the memorial's place of honor. I don't know where exactly, but I had heard that there were areas on the grounds where visitors could or would place such mementoes as mine in honored areas of the memorial.

At the time of my brother's funeral, the Marines presented my parents with a few of his belongings. Among these were his hat, or Garrison cover, irreverently called a "Pisscutter," and a globe and anchor pin insignia that was still pinned on to his Garrison cover. During the funeral, I was an emotional mess, my parents gave me my brother's hat to keep. I still have it even after so many years; I keep it next to my son's picture. My only son, Robert died at the age of six after being diagnosed with leukemia in 1974. I keep both Robert's picture and Samuel's hat and ring on top of a table in my bedroom.

At this point in my story, I need to inform you about the reason, what prompted me to visit the memorial after having lived in Taos for so many years, in relative proximity to Eagle Nest, but never having the need to actually make the short trip. It all revolves around a reoccurring dream of my brother that I kept having a week before my visit.

One night, as I was in a deep sleep, I was having another one of these dreams, but this night was different. I was abruptly awakened by the sound of my brother's voice calling my name. As I lay in bed, with my eyes now wide opened, I heard footsteps coming from down the hall. The sound of these footsteps at first caused me to panic thinking I had a prowler in the house! But soon as the footsteps came closer to my opened bedroom door I could see there was no need to be afraid because standing right at the door was the faded, but visually distinct image of Samuel! Just a couple of feet away from my bed, my brother stood just as I remember him. I found it difficult to speak, but I did call out to him, "Samuel, Samuel, where have you been?" I didn't know what else to say at that very moment. The words just came out of me without any rational thought.

Strangely, as I watched him, I had no doubt I was looking at my brother, but unlike a living person, he was emanating a strange yet comforting light. The light seemed to come from behind and through his image. It was a light blue colored light, something that I can only describe as being like a dim colored light, but not bright at all. The more I think about it, it was a pale blue light.

My brother stood in place and I watched as he gave me such a reassuring smile that it left me feeling very peaceful. I was in total bliss! I automatically reached my right arm over to the lamp on my end table and switched it on. I'll forever regret doing this because as soon as I switched the light on, his image disappeared!

Sitting up in bed, I looked all around the room, but he was gone! I slowly laid back down with my head facing the door, crying and softly calling out his name. I remember turning out the light and due to my exhaustion, I fell back to sleep. As I said, I'll always regret switching on the light; I'm such a stupid woman, I could kick myself!

Since that night I couldn't get my brother's image out of my mind. I needed to somehow be at peace and put an end to my torment. Somehow I got the idea to visit the memorial in Eagle Nest. And that's how Sarah and I came to find us at the memorial that day.

After breakfast, Sarah and I drove up the short hill to the memorial, parked the car, and walked to the entrance. An actual large and impressive helicopter was placed at the level of the parking lot and we got a good look inside the control panel before walking down the stairs to the chapel. But before reaching the chapel's door, we came upon a short little marble monument with a collection of personal items that visiting relatives and friends had deposited upon its flattened top. When I spotted this, I knew that this was where I would lay the ring my brother had given me so many years before.

After I was done visiting the chapel, I decided that I would return to the marble monument and place his ring among the other mementos. Sarah and I walked away from the monument then toward the few steps to the chapel; we then walked inside and took a seat at one of the rear pews. It was one of the most strangely quiet and sorrowful moments I'll ever experience in my life. Sitting within the chapel and having to hear the tearful weeping of a few of the fellow visitors became too much for me to bear. I whispered to Sarah that I needed to get out of there. So, we rose from our seats and walked out the entrance.

Once outside I mentioned to Sarah, "You know, even though I will always miss having my brother with me, having to hear those poor people weeping with grief for their loved ones has made me realize more than I ever could before that my brother is in a good place. Sarah, you remember that I mentioned to you about how Samuel appeared to me a just a few weeks ago in my bedroom? Well now I can see his death in a way I never could before. Somehow I knew that Samuel was always with me, and that he will always be with me until the day that I die. I am no longer missing him like I used to do. I know he is with me—and I know he's with me right now!"

After saying this to Sarah, we walked through the museum and then took our time to walk up the stairs to the parking lot. But before doing this, I reached into my jacket and brought out Samuel's ring. I kissed it and set it upon the stone monument, speaking out loud the words, "I love you."

But you know, right after I spoke these words, I heard my brother's voice as clear as can be speak in my ear, "I love you too, Frannie." That was all I needed to hear; I took hold of Sarah and began to cry on her shoulder.

Poor Sarah didn't know what to do as I cried and struggled to get my words out, "Sarah, Samuel just told me he loved me!" Sarah responded, "Yes, he does Fran, he loves his sister, he sure does."

During our return drive home, I was so moved by the experience. I know I must have been driving Sarah crazy with my non- stop talking, but I was so happy and content that I just needed to get my thoughts out!

Well, there you have my story. It's not a scary story but nonetheless I hope people will take away something positive from my experience. I do believe that spirits are not always harmful, especially when they are loved ones that have passed. My brother visited me and told me that he loves me still, and that is so comforting to know and to understand. It's a wonderful thing to carry through this life, don't you agree?"

FORT UNION, NM

FORT UNION NATIONAL PARK 1851-1861

When New Mexico became United States territory after the U.S.- Mexican War, the army established garrisons in towns scattered along the Rio Grande to protect the area's inhabitants and travel routes. This arrangement proved unsatisfactory for a number of reason and in April 1851, Lt. Col. Edwin V. Sumner commanding Military Department No. 9 (which included New Mexico Territory), was ordered "to revise the whole system of defense" for the entire territory. Among his first acts was to break up the scattered garrisons and relocate them in posts closer to the Indians. He also moved his headquarters and supply depot from Santa Fe, "that stink of vice and extravagance," to a site near the Mountain and Cimarron branches of the Santa Fe Trail, where he established Fort Union.

In 1851, in order to get the troops out of the towns where rent was expensive and closer to where the Indians were, Colonel Edwin Sumner moved most of his Santa Fe Command to the "Ponds on the Prairie, Los Posos" about six miles north of where the Mountain and Cimarron Branches of the Santa Fe Trail intersected. The essentials for a Lt. Col. Edwin V. Summer military post were there; water, wood, grazing for their stock, and most of all it was healthy.

With the post being established in mid-summer, work was begun at once on the quarters. Logs were cut and put up without even taking the bark off. Yet quarters were not completed for occupancy until November. One officer's wife enjoyed her new home, but the dust that came with the wind bothered her. She enjoyed the climate, her companion wives, and the "excitement" of living on a frontier. Her husband had a different opinion as he expressed, "...for if ever there was a country which our creator had deserted, forsaken and left to its own means of salvation, that country must be New Mexico."

The post later consisted of a garrison, a quartermaster supply depot, and an arsenal. Troops chased after Apache and Ute Indians as materials and goods came into the depot over the Santa Fe Trail only to be freighted out to other posts all over the southwest. At the time, Fort Union served as department headquarters.

With the onset of the Civil War and the threat of invasion by Confederate Texans, an earthwork was built across the valley because the position beneath the bluffs was indefensible. While most of the post occupied the new fort, a hospital and the arsenal remained on the first fort site. At war's end, a third fort was constructed near the second fort and the garrison and quartermaster occupied the new structures. Captain William Shoemaker, in charge of the arsenal since the beginning, built his arsenal anew on top of the old and lived in "splendid isolation" from the main post. With Shoemaker's death in 1886 and the abandonment of the arsenal in 1882, the site became a place for picnics and company pictures. The few remains and scattered foundation stones today recall past glories, joys, and sorrows. They are a reminder of the days when New Mexico was "forsaken."

WINSTON A. MYER'S STORY

"I'm originally from Illinois and moved to New Mexico in 1977. Arriving in New Mexico, I lived in the northern town of Las Vegas with my wife, Belinda and baby girl, Teresa. My wife worked as an office administrative for Highlands University while I worked as an asphalt mixer for the state highway department. After graduating from high school, our daughter Teresa married a man from Colorado and has since lived in Longmont. After I retired from the state, Belinda and I purchased a home and a few acres in Sapello, just north of Las Vegas and southwest of Ft. Union. We've been living here ever since.

Regarding any stories of ghosts, well yes, I can tell you a story that I've carried with me for several years. I'm not the only one who witnessed the ghost. My good friends Guero and our neighbor Alex, both of whom have since died, also experienced first-hand the ghost of a soldier who we believed was from Fort Union.

One spring morning I, together with my neighbor Alex Resendez, decided to visit a mutual friend of ours, Guero, in Mora. As we were driving from La Cueva on road 518 to Mora, I noticed a young man standing about a half mile up in the middle of the road. Anyone who has driven this short stretch of road knows that there isn't much out there but the road. This young guy stood in place and oddly, as I slowly approached him with my car, he stood his ground and didn't move a muscle. I immediately applied my brakes and slowed my car so as not to hit him. You have to understand, before I go any further that it was morning, the sun was out and the day was clear.

When I came within a few yards from him, I noticed that he was dressed in a dirty white shirt and wore an even dirtier pair of bluish colored trousers that were kept up by dark colored suspenders. I noticed that he was also barefoot and in his left hand he held a white cloth bag with its bottom covered in dirt. When I reached this young man, I rolled down my window and waited for him to say something. When he kept silent, I spoke, "What's going on?"

He looked directly at me and said, "Sir, I'm not ready." I answered, "What do you mean?" He responded, "Sir, I'm not ready."

Alex who was seated next to me said, "Keep driving Willy, this guy's nuts." Before I spoke another word to this stranger, he surprised us when he bolted from the road and ran, disappearing among the trees that grew along the side of the road! Alex said, "Willy, did you see that, he ran like a deer—that's crazy! Nobody runs like that. This guy's a ghost or something else!" Not sure of what had just happened in front of my eyes, I stepped on the gas and got us out of there—fast!

Alex couldn't stop talking about the guy. I could tell he was very anxious and even scared. I was shaken by the stranger, but was focused on my driving, so I let Alex talk. Then I interrupted by saying, "Alex, what the hell do you think that was? I mean really, what do you think that was—a ghost?"

Alex, immediately said, "Willy, when you think about it, how he was dressed and how he was so polite when he addressed you, yeah I think he was a ghost. I also think that he was from a long time ago. I think he was a ghost soldier from the fort!"

I remained silent for a few seconds then said, "Oh, God Alex. I never thought I'd see a ghost, but I think we just did!"

When we arrived at Guero's house, we told him in detail all we could remember about the ghost. He listened and with a serious and astonished look on his face, he didn't say a word until we finished. "I know exactly where you guys saw that dude. He's the same guy I saw standing at the road years ago. He did the same thing to me; stood in the middle of the road and waited for me to stop the car. When I asked him what he was doing, he told me, 'Sir, I need to say that I'm not ready.' Immediately after saying this, he turned towards the trees and took off running. But before leaving the asphalt and meeting the ground, he disappeared! Just like that he was gone. But you know, the strangest thing about this ghost was that, as his words were spoken, his mouth didn't move at all. I heard his words alright, but this face was motionless."

Alex asked Guero, "Did you ever find out who this guy is?" Guero answered, "No, but I think he was from Fort Union." I actually visited the Fort a couple of days after this experience and I asked a woman who was the supervisor at the time if she might help me find out who this ghost was. She looked at me like I was insane and said, "I'm sorry, but I have no idea what you want me to do for you. We don't keep a roster of 'ghosts' at the Fort." Because of her sarcastic response, I never mentioned the experience again. That negative experience made me think that I might have simply imagined the ghost, so I haven't spoken of it. Except for one time, I did talk to someone about it when I was in a museum in Washington, DC.

I was visiting an exhibit about the Civil War. As I stood in front of a glass cabinet that displayed a cap and uniform, I was totally mesmerized by the uniform. I was noticing that some of the clothing on the mannequin resembled almost exactly the clothes that the ghost was wearing. I was kind of scared because standing in front of the cabinet brought the whole ghost experience back to me. An employee who was walking by asked me how I was enjoying the exhibit and without thinking, I described to him my story. He looked at me with an odd stare and said, "Well, there are a lot of things in our world that we still don't have an answer for. My guess is that you might have seen the spirit of a soldier who may have deserted his post. Because of the disheveled manner he was dressed, he just might be the ghost of a deserter."

Returning to New Mexico after my short vacation, I was left with a reoccurring thought. What if the ghost I came into contact with on Road 518 was indeed a Fort Union deserter? If this be the case, then what was he doing standing there in broad daylight? And why did he run away from me? After all, at the time, I was not totally aware that he was a ghost; I was fully able to hear his words and to respond. I was totally willing to hear him out. It was only after he unnaturally dashed away and disappeared that I immediately knew this guy was not of the living.

So, that's my story. I don't have much more to tell you. There must be more people who have witnessed the ghost, people who can relate to my experience, but since my two friends, Guero and Alex have since passed away, I only hope their deaths bring them peace. I would hate to think that they or anyone else's spirits wonder lonely back roads. That would be terrible.

Do I believe that there are ghosts, I sure do! I know ghosts exist because of what I just described I witnessed in broad daylight several years ago. It's a strange thing, huh? But it's the real thing. If anyone doesn't believe, then they'll just have to take my word until they themselves get the opportunity—right?"

HOLBROOK, AZ

Holbrook is on the banks of the Little Colorado River in northeastern Arizona's Navajo County, which is high plateau country. In 1881 railroad tracks were laid in northeastern Arizona, passing through an area known as Horsehead Crossing. The following year, a railroad station was built at Horsehead Crossing and the community's name was changed to Holbrook in honor of Henry Randolph Holbrook, first chief engineer of the Atlantic and Pacific Railroad.

The town of Holbrook, at an elevation of 5,080 feet, became the county seat of Navajo County in 1895 and was incorporated in 1917. Holbrook is an important trade center for northeastern Arizona, ideally located on historic Route 66 and Interstate 40 and at the junction of four major highways. Positioned between the Apache Sitgreaves National Forest to the south and the Navajo and Hopi Indian Reservations to the north, Holbrook's local economy relies heavily on tourism.

HISTORY OF THE NAVAJO COUNTY COURTHOUSE

This historic courthouse is located at the northeast corner of Arizona Street and Navajo Boulevard. Currently within its walls are located the Chamber of Commerce offices and the Historical Society Museum. In 1976 a new governmental center was established south of the city. All county offices were then moved from the courthouse to this new location. In 1981

Holbrook Courthouse. the County Board of Supervisors requested that the Navajo County Historical Society open a museum in the old building. Local residents graciously donated furniture, keepsakes, and other wonderful items along with written family histories to include in the displays, which are currently on view in the museum.

Invitations to the hanging of George Smiley, which occurred in Holbrook on January 8, 1900, were issued by F. J. Wattron, Sheriff of Navajo County.

Aside from the many notorious trials that were held in the courtroom, only one hanging took place, in the courtyard on January 8, 1900, at 2 p.m. The name of the executed was George Smiley, who was hung for the murder of T.J. Mc Sweeney.

The first invitation, was sent out by the Associated Press, brought a letter of condemnation from then President William McKinley to Governor Nathan Oakes Murphy, of the Territory of Arizona. Governor Murphy severely rebuked Sheriff Wattron, and issued a stay of execution, whereupon the Sheriff Wattron sent out the second sarcastic invitation.

MARITA R. KEAMS'S STORY

I interviewed Marita at the courthouse, where she is currently employed as receptionist and information clerk for the Museum and Chamber of Commerce. Marita is a Navajo woman who has had numerous encounters with ghosts at the courthouse. She believes that perhaps one of the spirits that follows her around the property is the ghost of the executed man 'Smiley.' "I know he's around here all the time, I can feel him looking at me."

What follows is a detailed account of something that cannot be contained behind glass cases or roped off within museum rooms. When the lights are turned off at the Navajo County Courthouse and all daily business has ended, another type of activity begins to stir, an activity of curiously weird noises, voices, and more.

Marita can tell you what she has experienced, but of course the true challenge is to experience these eerie events for yourself. The museum's hours are 8 a.m. to 5 p.m.

—Antonio

I've been working at the courthouse for three years, and before that I was working at the Petrified Forest National Park gift shop. I have had numerous experiences with the ghosts in the building, and I also know of others who have experienced similar things firsthand.

My encounters gave me the impression that I was not welcomed in the building. I guess I was being tested. Being a Navajo, we are taught that if you keep any possessions of the deceased—a shirt, furniture, or whatever—the spirit of the dead person will attach itself to the item, and you might have some trouble on your hands.

In the museum, there are lots of items of the past that are displayed in the showcases such as old Native American grinding stones, arrows, clothing, as well as lots of non-Indian items. The museum director has informed me that some of these items that have been securely locked behind glass cases have been mysteriously found outside of these cases, and placed in other locations by "someone." Our museum's kitchen display seems to attract most of this type of activity. Utensils and other items are rearranged to fit an unseen person's own whim for order. A museum employee named Jane refuses to open any of the display cases unless someone is with her. She keeps her own experiences to herself. Interestingly enough, our own museum director is hesitant to be alone in the building as well.

All our employees have experienced our names being called out from the second floor. In my case, I heard a friendly female voice, but others have heard both male and female voices calling them when they are alone in the courthouse. Another employee who was the city's former tourism director had quite an eerie experience of his own.

His experience happened while he and his family were driving past the courthouse one late night. As they drove by the museum, he noticed that the lights had been left on the second floor, when they should have been turned off. He drove his car to the rear of the building and informed his wife and teenage son that he would return after finding out who was in the courthouse at this late hour. He opened the back door and just as he was about to enter, his wife called out to him from the car saying that there was a woman on the second-floor landing, looking out the window at them. He returned to the car, and sure enough, there was a woman whom he did not recognize staring back at them. He, his wife, and son entered the building and

Mariat Keams.

searched for the woman. Although they did a thorough search, they never found her but quickly shut off the lights and left the building.

Just a few months after I began working here, a group of kids took a Ouija board up to the third floor on a Halloween night, and apparently made contact with a ghost of the building. The ghost identified himself as "George." George just happened to be the man that was hanged right outside the courthouse in 1900.

I was alone one evening in the courthouse when suddenly; I heard a loud, banging metal sound coming from the second floor. As loud as it was, I was not about to go upstairs by myself and investigate. I just remained where I was, listening to the sound a few more times. The next day, I asked a coworker about the sound, and he said, "Oh, that happens now and then." I decided not to inquire any further.

A few months after this experience, I was once more in the building locking up for the day. It was dark, and I was on the second floor standing next to a window. Suddenly, I heard the sound of someone walking down the staircase from the third floor, approaching the second floor where I was. The doors were locked, and I wasn't sure who this could be. The thought crossed my mind that I could be in danger. As I kept quiet and listened for the footsteps, I noticed they stopped.

Trying to be as quiet as possible, I listened for any sound at all. There was no further noise coming from the stairs. I had heard others often speaking about the courthouse being haunted but I convinced myself that my mind was just playing tricks on me.

Suddenly, the footsteps started up once more! I cautiously made my

"Suddenly, I began to hear the sound of someone walking down the staircase."

way to the opened door, peered out onto the staircase and landing. I saw no one. I realized then that I must have been experiencing something ghostly. I sure didn't want to stay in the building any longer. I pretty much ran down the stairs, grabbed my purse and keys, and bolted out the front door! This sense of a presence of someone is strongest in a room where an old chuck wagon is displayed.

There is another thing I experience repeatedly during winter months: doors opening and closing on their own. Once I actually saw the door knob on the front door of the courthouse turn, then the door opened and closed, all on its own! We have double doors that are located directly behind the front desk, which lead out to the rear of the building. I once heard these doors swing open while I was alone in the building. I walked to the doors to investigate the noise, and found the doors closed and locked, just as I had left them.

Besides my own experiences, visitors to the courthouse have on numerous occasions approached the front desk to tell of experiencing cold chills or the feeling that someone is following them. Just like the visitors, I have also experienced these same sensations. I felt a sudden, unexplainable gust of very cold air pass right through me. I know this sounds strange, but I'm also not the only one that has experienced this. Visitors have told me that the room where this feeling is strongest is again, where that old chuck wagon is displayed. I was actually not surprised to have heard this because that is exactly the room where I have always felt the exact same thing.

Another disturbing thing that continues happening in the courthouse is when the faucets in the men's restroom somehow turn on by an invisible hand. I don't know why but I feel like something or someone is trying to get my attention by turning on the faucets. At the end of the day, I thoroughly check every corner of the courthouse, making sure that everything is as it is supposed to be.

There have been several instances when I'll return after checking the men's restroom and find the faucets turned on and water running. I don't know who could have done this, since I am the only person in the building. I have a suspicion that it is the ghost of "George."

I remember one day when I was seated at the front desk, and the greeting card rack began to turn and spin on its own, then abruptly stopped. I thought that there might be a small child behind it who was having fun spinning the rack. I rose from my chair, walked over to have a closer look; there was no one near it!

There was a time when for several nights after leaving the building, I would feel the presence of someone following me out to the parking lot and into my car. I felt the usual cold chills, and this presence would not leave me. I would frequently glance at my rearview mirror expecting to see something or someone in the back seat, that's just how strong this feeling was.

At other times, I'll feel an invisible hand of someone playing with my hair, and suspect that its George. I have also felt my body being touched so many times that I decided not to discuss this with anyone anymore. They might think I'm crazy. There are times when I'll be so annoyed with George's behavior that I'll yell out, "George, please stop doing this!" I won't experience any more activity for several days afterward, so I know he is paying attention to my anger.

Once we had a man come to us as a volunteer. This guy was ordered by the traffic court to do community work at the museum as a part of his sentence. Our employees' first impression of this volunteer was not a very positive one. This guy had heard some of the stories about our ghosts, and when he arrived for work, he began to make fun

"This feeling is strongest in a room where an old chuck wagon is displayed."

of George and openly stated that he was not afraid of ghosts. We didn't trust this worker and didn't want to leave him alone in the building unsupervised. In the museum, we have a donation box and a few small, valuable items in the gift shop that would not be very difficult to steal.

One day, I asked him to bring me some brochures from the rear of the building, where the old jail cells are located. We now use these original cells as storage areas for office supplies. Just a few seconds after he left, I heard him scream. He came running to me, saying that the bars and metal were making loud noises and the ghosts were trying to get him. I smiled and giggled to myself when he told me this because I knew that "our George" was also keeping an eye on this guy.

LA JUNTA, CO

La Junta, situated on the southeastern plains of Colorado, is a small town with a population of about 9,000. The town's name, when translated from the Spanish, means 'the junction.' The Comanche National Grassland lies to the southwest of town and the Koshare Indian Museum and Kiva is just northeast. This museum contains a collection of Native American artifacts and produces "Indian" dances to the public. The museum began as a Boy Scout troop's project in the 1930s. Today the dances are performed by non-Indian boy scouts. Continuing nine-miles northeast of the museum is Bent's Old Fort National Historic Site.

BENT'S OLD FORT NATIONAL HISTORIC SITE

This historic fort was established March 15, 1960, by Congress, its reconstruction was completed in 1976. The reconstruction was based on original drawings, historical accounts, and archeological evidence, and what remained of the original fort was studied by historians and archeologists. During the nation's bicentennial, the National Park Service took the daunting task of re-creating the large fort as close to its original condition as possible.

Originally erected in the 1833 by two brothers, Charles and William Bent, and their business partner Ceran St. Vrain. The fort was one of the significant centers of fur trade on the Santa Fe Trail, influencing economies around the world. The fort was the leading industry west of the Mississippi in the early 1830's. For 16 years, Bent, St. Vrain and Co. managed a prosperous trading empire.

The fort was located on the Arkansas River, the international boundary between two countries—Mexico on the south side of

At a distance it presents a handsome appearance, being castle-like with towers at its angles...the design...answering all purposes of protection, defense, and as a residence." —George R. Gibson, a soldier who visited the fort in 1846.

the river, and the United States on the north. Strategically located on an established road, it helped pave the way for the occupation of the west by the U.S. Army, and was an instrument of Manifest Destiny and the invasion of Mexico in 1846. William Bent was known to the Cheyennes as "Little White Man." His fairness and respect for the culture was the reason for the company's excellent reputation among the Plains Indians. The fort remained as the only permanent structure to be seen for hundreds of miles around.

In the decades after the 1803 Louisiana Purchase, even as the earliest explorers crossed the continent, America's economic frontier expanded westward. Trappers ventured deep into the Rockies for beaver. Plains Indians showed their willingness to trade buffalo robes, and the first wagons rolled between the Missouri River and Santa Fe, initiating regular commerce with Mexico. When traders Charles and William Bent and their partner Ceran St. Vrain sought to establish a base, they wanted to locate where they could take advantage of all these trades. So, in 1833 they built a fort (then called Fort William) on the north bank of the Arkansas River, the boundary between the United States and Mexico. It was close enough to the Rockies to draw trappers; near the hunting grounds of Cheyenne, Arapaho, Kiowa, and other tribes; and on the Santa Fe Trail, near a fort across the river.

While dining at the fort, the separation of social classes was evident. The laborers cooked in their quarters or ate from a community cooking pot. In the 1830s, beaver pelt (called "hairy bank notes") could be bartered for trade goods. As beaver numbers declined, buffalo hides became the basis of exchange. The fort was hardly the only sign of human life in the area—the high plains had long been home to thousands of Native Americans. But for travelers two months on the trail, it was a greatly anticipated haven, the sole place between Independence and Santa Fe where they could refresh themselves and their livestock, repair wagons, and replenish supplies.

The Bent's Mexican trade grew rapidly as their caravans plied the route from Independence and Westport to company stores in Santa Fe and Taos. There, goods such as cloth, hardware, glass, and tobacco were exchanged for silver, furs, horses, and mules. Thousands of beaver pelts passed through the fort in the early years, but as the market for beaver declined in the 1830s, the Indian trade became a mainstay of the business. The fort's traders swapped American and Navajo blankets, axes, firearms, etc., for buffalo hides and horses taken in raids—no questions asked. The Bent's positive reputation made their traders welcome in most villages and drew growing numbers of Indians to the fort. Before long, the company dominated the Indian trade on the southern plains.

The Bents, so effective as peacemakers, especially with the Southern Cheyenne, that in 1846 the fort (by then called Bent's Fort) was used as headquarters for the Upper Platte and Arkansas Indian Agency. That year, the quickened beat of military operations stepped up the pace of activity beyond that of the seasonal trade. America was going to war with Mexico, and the fort's strategic location on an established road made it the ideal staging point for the invasion of Mexico's northern province. Storerooms were filled with military supplies; soldiers were quartered at the fort; military livestock stripped the land.

"It is crowded with all kinds of persons: citizens, soldiers, traders to 'Santa Fe, Indians, Negroes, etc. The Indians were Arapaho, a fine-looking set of men, with mules to trade" —George R. Gibson, account from his 1846 journal.

Later, a growing stream of settlers and gold seekers disrupted the carefully nurtured Indian trade. In the face of polluted water holes, decimated cottonwood groves, and declining bison, the Cheyenne moved away. Escalating tensions between Indians and whites and a cholera epidemic was sweeping the area. Also, William Bent's first wife and three brothers had died. But the cholera epidemic finally killed the trade. After the death of Charles in 1847, St. Vrain tried unsuccessfully to sell the fort to the U.S. Army. It is thought that William Bent tried to burn the fort in 1849 before moving to his trading houses at Big Timbers, some 40 miles downriver, near present day Lamar, Colorado. He constructed Bent's New Fort there in 1853.

HAROLD ROONEY'S STORY

"I currently live in La Junta and have lived here all my life. My wife and I are both school teachers and have taken groups of students to the fort on several day trips. I'll be retiring from the school district in just a few years and I'm planning on writing my own book on the area's history. There are many sites of importance in this southeastern corner of the state, sites that have played a significant role in Colorado's history and, in my opinion, have not been covered in any major way. This, I believe, is very much needed. I plan to do this, do the research, and put it in final book form. My retirement will most likely provide me with the time to devote to this personal project.

I'll never forget one very, very notable ghost encounter that took place at the fort in late September. The morning was very cold and the experience took place during a school field trip. I had a few students with me who had been studying the history of Bent's Fort for the entire semester. Some of the students had previously visited the fort with their parents, but the majority had not. Although the fort is located in very close proximity to the town of La Junta, and is marketed extensively to tourists,

"The Billiard Room".

the actual residents of town, ironically, do not show much interest in this major historical site that lies right at their back door.

As I was saying, I was with a group of my students on a field trip, and they were excited to put to the test all they had studied months before of the fort's history. The day was not an unusual day given the time of year. It was cloudy, drizzly, and thinking back, perfect for sighting a ghost or two.

I turned the students loose, while I stood at the entrance and chatted with one of the interpreters that was dressed in period costume. We were scheduled to be at the fort for half a day, including a lunch break. Everything went well, and one student even brought along her drawing pencils and pads. The fort is an architecturally beautiful structure. Many people feel drawn to its massive adobe style of design.

After a few hours, we gathered for our lunch break during which the student with the most artistic talent shared with everyone her colorful drawings. One picture in particular stood out from the rest, in that she had drawn the interior of a room, located on the second floor. She named the room, the 'barrel room,' but in fact the room is named, 'The Billiard Room'. She so named the room because of an obviously placed wooden barrel, which stood in one corner. But she had drawn the image of a man, who was seated in a chair, which another student recognized as being the same man she had seen seated in a chair in another area of the compound. That room was located directly below The Billiard Room, in 'The Trappers' and Hunters' Quarters.'

What caused such a stir among the students was that while the student was drawing the man in Billiard Room, several other students claim to have seen the same man seated in the room below! They compared times and came to the conclusion that it would be impossible for the man to be in both rooms at the same time. Being young, their imaginations ran wild, and they immediately claimed to have seen a ghost in the fort.

I asked the students to calm down and rationally think about this situation. I asked the student who drew the man to describe her impression of him and to tell us all the information he related to her about the fort. I imagined he was another interpreter, and although I was not personally informed of his presence by the interpreter I was speaking to earlier, I assumed he had to be an employee.

The student stated that when she asked him if it would be all right to draw and reproduce his image together with the room, he turned to her and just nodded his head, indicating with this gesture his approval. Sensing that he must be 'in character,' she did not speak any further to him and continued with her sketching.

The other students who claimed to have also seen the same man in the room below stated that he was in their words, "weird." I asked, "How so?" They responded that as they had entered the dimly lit room, taking notice of him seated at a table, they courteously said "Hello" to him. He focused his stoic gaze on them and slowly nodded his head. The students found his response to be odd, but also thought he was in character acting a role for the visitors' benefit.

The oddest thing about both the artist's and the students' recollection of this man was that the he was very "authentic" in his appearance. He wore a red tunic, or long coat, and his pants were of a dark blue, heavy material. His shoes were light colored and rough in appearance. In fact, the man's overall appearance was 'rough.' He had a short beard, and under his stout and wide brimmed hat, his hair was short. But the most unusual and unmistakable trait was the color of his face and hands. They were pale, almost a gray/white color! The man never spoke a word to any of the students, giving them the impression that not only did he dress the part, but actually went so far as to apply professional looking makeup to his face and hands in the attempt to be truly authentic as possible.

As the teacher, and the more mature, rational thinker, I felt that my responsibility was to locate the interpreter I had spent the morning conversing with to inquire about who this other individual employee/character actor might be. I also wanted him to visit and personally meet with the students, which I'm sure they would have appreciated, then answer their questions about the fort.

I approached the interpreter, and mentioned the man in the red tunic, and he said, "We have no one else on the property interpreting today or that is dressed in a costume like you're describing. I'm the only person here in costume. The only other employees at the fort are in the corral area, and I guarantee those guys would never 'play dress up', not for any amount of money. I decided to walk over to the park's administration office, located at the entrance to the fort, and speak to the officer on duty about this situation. After introducing myself, and giving him the details I was aware of, he stated, "As far as I'm aware, no one else is providing the service of interpreter that your students claim to have seen."

Now, whether or not an actual ghost was seen by one, or 10, students at the fort that morning, is a matter of opinion, but I can say with full confidence that the students were absolutely, emotionally affected by what they saw. That man, they believed, was a ghost, and try as I might I did not sway them otherwise in the least. In all honesty, I had absolutely no evidence or explanation to offer them to the contrary. I don't know where to go with this. I do believe that there are things unknown to us regarding the hereafter. I'm not sure if someone can prove the existence of ghosts, but can anyone really disprove them?"

OLD SACRAMENTO, CA

Old Sacramento is a registered National Historic Landmark, within which can be found the State's greatest concentration of historic buildings. Adding to the historic charm, are no cement sidewalks, only board walks made of thick, wide pine planks. Built adjacent to the Sacramento River on the west, this original city site gave convenient access to boats unloading their merchandise to the eager citizens. The Gold Rush of 1849 transported the small town into a major area of new wealth and barter. Saloon locations were often used to exchange gold dust and nuggets for U.S. coins.

As the Gold Rush boon began to wane, the Old Sacramento area became a gathering place for migrant workers, and the original pioneer businesses were changed from bustling mercantile establishments to simple, unadorned warehouses. It fell into such a state of disinterest that during the mid 20th century, a wave of threateningly shoddy, and trashy bars and hotels succeeded to take hold. Sadly, the Old Sacramento area turned into one of the worst skid rows in the west.

Old Sacramento Main Street.

Fortunately, during the 1970's a positive trend towards redevelopment, turned Old Sacramento towards a dramatic and much needed new focus. A major reconstruction project was begun, and at its end, Old Sacramento took its place as a living link to California's historic past.

Today Old Sacramento offers many diversions and museums for its visitors. Four prominent museums of note are, The Discovery Museum History Center, The California State Railroad Museum, The Wells Fargo History Museum and the California Military Museum.

CALIFORNIA STATE RAILROAD MUSEUM – PATRICIA BAEZ'S STORY

In September of 1993, my husband Lorenzo and I decided to take a three-week trip from our home in San Diego, and travel up the California coast. At the time, I was also in need of a change of employment from my job as a surgery nurse at Scrips Medical Center in San Diego. Deciding to mix business with a pleasurable vacation, I took a folder full of resumes, which I dropped off at hospitals along the way.

We had been thinking of relocating to a new city months before, and decided that the furthest north in California we would consider to resettle would be Sacramento. After two weeks of traveling up the state, we eventually arrived in Sacramento and checked into a hotel. After breakfast, we toured the city, the State Capitol building, had lunch, and then did a little more touring. The next day we met with a realtor, and eventually found a house on the south side of town, which we bought and have lived in ever since.

To celebrate our home purchase, that very evening after we signed the real estate contract, we decided to visit Old Sacramento, where we enjoyed a wonderful dinner at a nice restaurant. The time was around 8pm. As we left the restaurant, Lorenzo suggested we take a stroll around the Old Town area. As we walked on the western boardwalk, we spotted the Rail yard, and the display of an actual steam locomotive. I remember how the old fashion light poles were lit, the romantic glow they gave off, and shadows they cast about the yard. It was a perfect evening.

As we walked arm and arm towards the locomotive, I mentioned to Lorenzo that aside from another couple seated some distance from us, we were the only others in the area. I asked Lorenzo if we could sit down on the bench, under the large metal shelter that protectively hung over the locomotive. We sat, talked for a few minutes, and noticed the other couple get up and leave.

Lorenzo got up and walked to the locomotive, while I remained seated on the bench smoking a cigarette. He busied himself investigating the wheels and smoke stack of the immense machinery. I was gazing at the beautiful buildings across the street, and allowed my imagination to place me in the era of the 1800's, when the town must have been quite a busy, and colorful place. The architecture of the buildings, the boardwalk and the darkness of the night, easily allowed me to grasp the feeling of that era, and what it might have looked like.

Lorenzo came over to me and said he was going to look for a public restroom, or else return to the restaurant where we had our dinner, and use their men's room. I didn't feel like getting up, so I told him that I would just wait for him there at the bench. I watched as he walked away. Remembering all the traveling that we had done up to this point, I felt a very peaceful feeling of contentment, and accomplishment settle over me.

All of a sudden, I noticed a small man in a dark suit walking on the boardwalk quite a distance away from me. I saw him pause twice to open his coat and check for something in his pocket. Because he was the only person in the area, and I was by myself, my eyes were focused, and did not leave him.

I also noticed that he had a strange manner of walking. He walked with a bounce to each step, and as I said, I kept my eyes on him because after all, he was a little strange looking.

He walked a few steps up to a display window of a closed shop, and when he turned around to face my direction, I spotted a bag he was holding. From my view point, I thought it was a bag, but it could have been something else. At any rate, I wasn't able to clearly make out what the heck it was. He made his way back onto the street, where he walked over near the railroad station, a few yards away from where I was seated.

I never felt afraid, or even concerned for my safety. I could see that the man was not very tall, in fact I was much taller than he, so I didn't believe he posed any real threat to me. But, my demeanor changed immediately when, I noticed the strangest thing about this man. As he came closer, I realized his footsteps were not making any sound! The street is composed of dirt with a top layer of gravel, so walking on this would naturally make a sound of some sort. But there was absolutely no sound to his steps!

As an uneasy feeling of fear started to well up inside me, I didn't dare take my eyes off the dark stranger. I suddenly began to feel very vulnerable sitting there alone on that bench. My instincts told me this little man was not real, and might even be a ghost. Slowly, he came, approaching my direction!

I attempted to stay very quiet, and to make myself as invisible as possible. I threw my lit cigarette to the ground, and with my right foot, slowly extin-

He walked over near the railroad station that was just a few yards away from where I was seated.

guished it. As he came even closer, he appeared very frail, and slightly bent over, because he produced a little shaking motion with each step. Again, I noticed that his footsteps did not made any sound. I was ready for anything to happen. Ready to immediately jump off the bench, and run for my life.

Fortunately, he turned away from me, and headed straight for the front door of the railroad station building. He stood at the door, and as I watched, he extended his hand to reach for the doorknob. I heard him jumbling and pulling the knob, then he walked inside. When I say, he walked inside I mean he walked inside without opening the door, he just 'past through' the door! I froze and couldn't believe what I just saw happen.

By coincidence, Lorenzo appeared at that moment, exactly at the same spot on the boardwalk where I first spotted the ghost. I yelled at him from where I sat, demanding he quickly come over to me.

When he got to my side, I hugged him and began to tell him what I had just witnessed. He of course did not believe me, and even jokingly made fun of my story. But because of how distressed I must have appeared, he stopped with the jokes. With his arm around me, we quickly walked away from the rail yard, all the while l repeated over and over, "I know what I saw, that was a ghost Lorenzo, a ghost!"

Just then, my story-telling abruptly stopped when we both heard the sound of invisible scrapping and scuffling footsteps, coming from the direction of where I had seen the ghost figure disappear. There were no other people anywhere but us. Lorenzo also heard the unexpected sounds, grabbed hold of my hand, and ordered me to just run. We flew across the street, jumped into our car, locked the doors and sped away faster than I ever thought possible.

I don't know of anyone else who has had a similar experience at the rail yard. I've lived in Sacramento several years, and have never heard of any other ghost sighting or encounter like this. I'm sure most people would be afraid to talk about this kind of experience and not be taken seriously. It was a truly terrifying experience and I won't go out there at night ever again. I have to be honest, describing everything that happened that night now for this interview, even though it happened over eight years ago, still scares me to death!"

OROVILLE, CA

Temple entrance.

OROVILLE CHINESE TEMPLE

Listed in the National Register of Historic Places and as a California Landmark, the Temple once served a community of 10,000 Chinese. In 1949, during California's Centennial, it officially opened its doors to visitors.

CISSY SANT'S STORY

I've worked at the temple for over six years, as its Caretaker/Tour guide. Prior to beginning my employment at the temple, I was unaware of any ghost-like activity on the property. No one ever came to me with any information about it being haunted. But all that slowly began to change the longer I worked there. I'd like to begin my interview with the spirits at this site, with a short history of this unique, and historic temple.

The first temple was built in 1863, and served the spiritual needs of the 10,000 Buddhist, Taoist and Confucians Chinese population of the area. The English translated name of the temple is "Temple of Many Gods." Notably, it is quite unusual to find three distinct religions being practiced together in the same complex. As such, it remains as the West's largest, authentically furnished Chinese temple of its kind and of its era.

In 1868 a two-story building was built directly behind this first temple. The Buddhist used the large second floor room, with the large circular doorway, as a prayer room. They named this prayer room "The Moon Temple." The Buddhist believe this circular doorway

Cissy Sant.

371

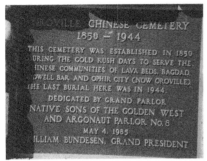

symbolized the circle of life, eternity and reincarnation.

Beneath the Moon Temple, on the first floor is located the Council Chambers. This room was used by the Chinese as a type of 'city hall.' Decisions effecting their community, and other important issues were regularly discussed here. Another interesting function of the room, was that it also served the Chinese community as a funerary preparation room.

Correspondingly located about two miles from the temple, on the southwest side of Oroville, is the original Chinese cemetery. It's located on Feather River Blvd., just past the Wal-Mart. It's easy to drive pass this important and historic part of California's past without noticing it. It's present unassuming condition definitely belies its historical significance.

After a body was buried in this cemetery, it was left in the ground for about 7 to 10 years. Following this time, a chosen person from the Chinese community would disinter the body, clean the bones, then bring them into the temple's Counsel Chambers where they would be religiously prepared to be returned to China. The Chinese believed that if a member of their race died in a foreign country, on foreign soil they would not go to heaven. Also, because of their traditional strong family bonds, the family back in China was morally responsible for the care, and to respectfully over see that the body and bones of the deceased were returned to the homeland.

In 1874 an adjoining room named "The Chan Room" was added to the temple. Initially the room was built for the sole use of the Chan family for their private ancestor prayer, and worship, but it also served as a community temple of Confusion teachings. The Chan family, aside from being Chinese, was one of the very few wealthy families in the area. Their wealth was based on mercantile.

Original Grave markers.

Initially, Mr. Chan arrived in the area to mine for gold, but soon discovered he could make more money, with less effort, by supplying the miners with retail goods.

Eventually, due primarily to the construction of the two newer temples, the original first temple became known as the Daoist Temple. Presently, within the original temple are three wood statues of Chinese Gods, Mulan (Woman Warrior), Huat'o (Doctor of Medicine— Renowned as the first person to do surgery, and who defined acupuncture pulse points and meridians), Tien Hau (Goddess of the Sea, Queen of Heaven—Protectress of Sailors, Prostitutes, and travelers in foreign lands.)

An odd historical point of Oroville's history are the many tunnels underneath the older part of town. Supposedly the Chinese dug interconnecting tunnels underneath the town, and as recently as a few years ago, the supporting pillar of a private residence, began to sink into the ground. I was told that there was a large pit, 40 feet deep under this house, with several side tunnels leading off which joined others. I've also read stories of sections of Montgomery street collapsing under the weight of trucks, due to these tunnels.

Now that you have a general idea of the temples' history, I'll now begin with my own encounters with what I believe are spirits that have made themselves known to me on the property.

One of the first experiences that made me think things were not 'right', happened during a period of days when I would walk into the main temple, and unusually cold chills would envelope me. These chills were unusual because the temperature outside was warm, and comfortable. I was not thinking of spirits, or anything close to ghosts at the time. Every time I entered the temple, a coldness would commence to envelope me. This continued for a number of days. Eventually I believe the spirits got used to having me around, or I got used to them, because the chills eventually stopped and I don't feel them anymore. On the other hand, I've had some visitors on my tour, tell me that they have experienced these same unexpected, and unexplained chills during the tour.

Each week I conduct several tours throughout the day, and there are instances when some of the guests will exhibit unusual behavior. I'll spot someone visible shake and shutter, and I'll ask them if they're okay. The response I'll get is that a cold breeze has just overtaken, or a sudden unknown coldness has come over them. I do believe that some people are more sensitive to unseen things than others. My response is to just shrug my shoulders, and continue on with the tour.

Admittedly, the temple might be a scary place for some, but I don't find it to be a scary place. It's definitely an unusual structure, given its aged and exposed brick walls, and having an alter as its focus. The exotic carved Chinese god figures, might also add a bit of strangeness to the overall atmosphere. But I don't find anything in the temple to be particularly scary by design.

Some months ago, I was visited by two ex-caretakers who asked me if the spirits have begun playing with me. I was caught off guard by this question, so I asked for a further explanation. I was told that when alone in the temples' office area, sometimes the sensation of small invisible fingers tickling and playing with their hair would commence. Actually, the feeling of invisible fingers stroking the middle of the neck would happen at different times of the day. I answered that I did indeed have that same experiences take place, but had chosen not to ever discuss it with anyone.

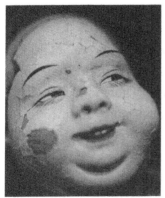

"A coldness would commence to envelope me."

I remember, very soon after I began working alone at the temple, feeling the sensations of being touched at the base of my neck. I rationalized these tickling sensations to be unnoticed spider webs, that I had unknowingly walked through. But there were instances when I would be alone, seated and reading a book, when suddenly the tickling sensations would begin. I would start waving, and batting my hands all around my head, attempting to remove whatever it was that was touching me. I knew that I was experiencing something unnatural, but I just did not want to admit it.

However, one particular day I recall being in an unusually bad mood. Again, I was seated in the office area, and the tickling started up once again. I was in no mood for play, so I spoke to the spirit in a very stern voice, "Go away, leave me alone!" The tickling immediately stopped, and ever since that confrontation, I've never had another tickling experience at the temple.

Another unusual thing that I've experienced in the temple is when our electric Open and Closed sign would turn on by itself. I know that a spirit is playing with me, because at the end of the day as I routinely lock-up, I've noticed when I turn the sign to its Closed position, it would turn back On. I've never actually seen it physically 'turn' but the sign always turns when I am facing away. I'm a very fastidious and detailed person, so for this to happen over and over again does bother me.

I've also seen people's shadows darting around the property. No matter where I'll be in the temple complex, some movement will catch my eye. I'll turn and see the shadows of people, or just dark images darting quickly about the area. These shadows most often appear in the courtyard area, just outside the Council Chambers.

Another fairly common experience for me are the 'voices' that I hear coming from the temple. I'll be alone, seated in the office which shares a common brick wall with the temple, and I'll hear low, whispering voices. I can't make out the words, if they are speaking English, or Chinese, but I know I am hearing the voices of two people in conversation.

My personal belief is that I'm open to ghostly experiences. I'm not afraid. I don't discount anything that I can't see as being unreal. I think that there are spirits here who are protecting their temple, and making sure that each visitor is respectful. As the temple caretaker, I'm required to actually live on the grounds, and I do feel protected by these spirits. Because I do see shadows, and hear the voices of spirits regularly, I've gotten to the point where I don't pay much attention to them any longer. This is their temple, and that's that. But, I've got to admit that sometimes the voices do still surprise me from time to time. It's interesting that most of my ghost experiences have taken place, or are most prevalent, in the winter. Would I welcome an actual visit from one of the spirits? I guess I'd like to see what one of these guys looks like face to face. I know I'd be a bit startled at first, but other than that, maybe I'd enjoy the encounter."

REDSTONE, CO

Located between the White River National Forest to the north, and Gunnison National Forest to the south, this quaint and small alpine community offers spectacular mountain views, fine dining, art galleries and a museum. Artists in town produce their handmade crafts to sell to the public from their home studios.

Historically, the Utes used this area as their summer hunting grounds. In 1872, prospectors over ran the area and, as is often the unfortunate and unfair case, the native people were forced out, eventually ending up in reservations in Colorado's neighboring state of Utah.

Redstone, a National Historic District, was known in years past as "the Ruby of the Rockies." The town was developed by a turn-of-the-century industrialist, John Cleveland Osgood, as a company town for the employees of his coal mining empire. Apparently his second wife, Alma Regina Shelgrem, prior to emigrating to the United States, was from Sweden, and rumored to have been a countess, persuaded Osgood to look beyond the all mighty dollar to seek a more humane, paternalistic approach to his employees. Due to her generosity and kindness, which she bestowed on the employees and their families, she became known throughout the area as "Lady Bountiful."

John Osgood abided by his kind wife's strong suggestions and took seriously the comfort of the employees; hence soon after he had constructed 84 cottages for the benefit of married workers' families. In addition, he constructed a 40-room inn for his bachelor employees. Both a rarity and luxury for the period, all these facilities featured indoor plumbing and electricity. Not ceasing his commitment to their comfort, he also built a modern bathhouse, and a clubhouse containing a library and theatre. His altruistic focus did not end there, and in addition he built a small but efficient school.

All this building activity motivated numerous other building projects to be started in town. Today, the visitor can view several of these historic buildings by simply taking a short walking tour through the center of town.

Lastly, the strong affection that Mr. Osgood felt towards his wife was evident when he announced the construction of "Cleveholm Manor," in her honor. This very lavishly appointed Tudor-style mansion home, containing 42 rooms and completed in 1902, is today known as "the Redstone Castle."

WALTER IGER'S STORY

Walter and I met at his home located a few miles north of Redstone, in the town of Carbondale. The interview went smoothly and before we got started, he gave me a tour of his drawings, looms and finished weavings. We discussed his art and his use of vibrant color combinations. It was during this discussion that he told me how he had learned the craft of weaving rugs.

During a two-year stay in Turkey, Walter met a man who worked within the U.S. State Department's American School. The man was teaching the craft of weaving rugs to a classroom of students. Although a teacher of English, and not a student at the school, Walter was initially so impressed with the art, that each day after his school responsibilities, Walter immersed himself totally in the art of weaving.

His experiences in Turkey also involved traveling to areas where native healers practiced their craft of divination, charms, spells and power over natural sources. Because of my own recent visit, and travels within North Africa, his stories fascinated me. We compared and exchanged experiences, and our time together was so enjoyable that the hours pasted without my realizing it. Although Walter's stories were interesting, none compared with the personal paranormal experience he had in Colorado.

-Antonio

"During the summer and fall of 2001, I lived in Redstone for just under a year. I found myself house sitting for a few months, for friends of mine who at the time were vacationing in Europe. This was the first time that I had visited Redstone, and I was excited to spend so many months in the Rockies. Strangely, I thought, I had been cautioned by my friends regarding the unusual goings-on in their home. They told me to expect this, and that they attributed the weirdness to the resident ghost. They had added that the things I might experience were not severe, nothing to the point which would make me run out the door with fright, just little things such as lights going on and off, and footsteps in the hallways, etc.

As the days pasted, I was looking forward to meeting the neighbors in the small community and also to working on the home's backyard garden, and doing general country crafts. I am an artist by trade, specializing in weavings and an occasional painting. I had brought along all my craft materials for my stay, and was prepared to produce many items for the following year's craft shows. I attend gift and craft shows as a vendor throughout the western states, and have had much success with my weavings. Staying at the house would be a perfect opportunity to work, giving me the uninterrupted time I needed for building up my stock of art projects.

Within the first weeks, I didn't notice any strange phenomenon take place, just an occasional creaking ceiling during the day and night. I knew this was most likely caused by the house settling and temperature changes. This took place at regular hours, so aside from these common noises, I thought nothing more about it. But on July 21, I did experience a very strange thing. I even went so far as to mark the day in my journal, so as not to ever forget the date.

After breakfast, I decided to take a break from my weaving and do a little sketching and drawing. I thought I'd go for a walk in the hills, overlooking the town, at the opposite side of the highway. Together with my pastels and papers, I packed a small snack and headed towards the old coke ovens, located at the south entrance to town. I climbed over and around the ovens, and hiked up the steep tree covered hills, and eventually located the perfect spot for my drawing. The view was fantastic, but not much more than an hour past before I felt as if someone was watching me.

I turned to my left and didn't see anyone. There were several large pine trees all around the small clearing where I was seated, so if

Redstone coke ovens.

anyone wished to spy on me, it would not be that difficult to do. I returned to my drawing and again the feeling of someone watching me caused me to stop my drawing and listen for foot-steps among the grass. Sure enough, I heard someone behind me, as I turned around, I was startled when I spotted a medium size man wearing a cowboy hat. He was about 20 feet away from me.

I said, "Hello, good morning. How long have you been standing there?" He looked at me and seemed to be staring right through me, then sternly responded, "Young feller, this is my land. What are you doing on my land?" I took notice of his piercing dark eyes and brown hair. He was also sporting a thick moustache and wearing a white shirt. I answered, "As far as I'm aware this is public forest property. If you have a problem with that I suggest you give a call to the BLM office, and have them take care of it. You can see that all I'm doing is sitting here. Why would you have a problem with this?" His position did not change. He simply kept looking at me. Then I broke the uncomfortable silence between us by asking, "Well, now what are you going to do?"

After I had finished my sentence, like a large beast he took two deep breaths, turned from me, and began to walk away. While he was taking his second step, he began to slowly, but absolutely, disappear in front of my eyes! I mean, as he walked, he vanished into thin air until he had totally and completely vanished! I wasted no time in standing right up, and was so frightened that I grabbed my backpack and ran down the hill, leaving my sketch pad and pastels right where they fell!

Because the morning was so sunny, I had no difficulty in retracing my footsteps as I zoomed down the hill towards town. I was very scared and had no doubt in my mind that I had actually heard, seen, and spoken

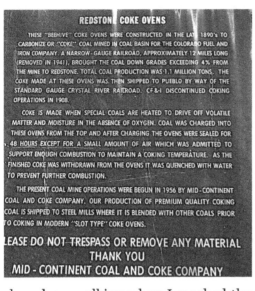

REDSTONE COKE OVENS

THESE "BEEHIVE" COKE OVENS WERE CONSTRUCTED IN THE LATE 1890's TO CARBONIZE OR "COKE" COAL MINED IN COAL BASIN FOR THE COLORADO FUEL AND IRON COMPANY. A NARROW-GAUGE RAILROAD, APPROXIMATELY 12 MILES LONG (REMOVED IN 1941), BROUGHT THE COAL DOWN GRADES EXCEEDING 4% FROM THE MINE TO REDSTONE. TOTAL COAL PRODUCTION WAS 1.1 MILLION TONS. THE COKE MADE AT THESE OVENS WAS THEN SHIPPED TO PUEBLO BY WAY OF THE STANDARD GAUGE CRYSTAL RIVER RAILROAD. CF&I DISCONTINUED COKING OPERATIONS IN 1908.

COKE IS MADE WHEN SPECIAL COALS ARE HEATED TO DRIVE OFF VOLATILE MATTER AND MOISTURE IN THE ABSENCE OF OXYGEN. COAL WAS CHARGED INTO THESE OVENS FROM THE TOP AND AFTER CHARGING THE OVENS WERE SEALED FOR 48 HOURS EXCEPT FOR A SMALL AMOUNT OF AIR WHICH WAS ADMITTED TO SUPPORT ENOUGH COMBUSTION TO MAINTAIN A COKING TEMPERATURE. AS THE FINISHED COKE WAS WITHDRAWN FROM THE OVENS IT WAS QUENCHED WITH WATER TO PREVENT FURTHER COMBUSTION.

THE PRESENT COAL MINE OPERATIONS WERE BEGUN IN 1956 BY MID-CONTINENT COAL AND COKE COMPANY. OUR PRODUCTION OF PREMIUM QUALITY COKING COAL IS SHIPPED TO STEEL MILLS WHERE IT IS BLENDED WITH OTHER COALS PRIOR TO COKING IN MODERN "SLOT TYPE" COKE OVENS.

PLEASE DO NOT TRESPASS OR REMOVE ANY MATERIAL
THANK YOU
MID-CONTINENT COAL AND COKE COMPANY

to a ghost! I was paralyzed with a great fear to the point that I felt like crying. At one point in my run, I stopped and turned to look back from where I had come from. I didn't see a ghost.

As I reached the Coke ovens, I scrambled over them and felt immediate relief when my feet touched the highway's asphalt. I can't remember when I had ever felt such fear. Not wanting to allow my fear to show, I slowed my walking when I reached the road into town. Arriving at the house, I walked inside and hoped that the ghost did not follow me home.

Eventually, as the days past, I did manage to speak to a couple of locals, in a roundabout way. I asked if anyone had ever seen, heard, or even had a personal experience with ghost-like things in the town, or anywhere in the valley. Everyone eventually referred me to the Cleveholm Manor. Apparently, the manor has had a few ghostly things that have taken place throughout the years, but nothing in town, or as was my personal experience, in the hills.

The ghost of the man that I had clearly seen that morning will never leave my memory. I'll always think back during that summer day and remember where I was, the moment I actually saw, spoke, and most importantly, had a ghost speak to me directly. I was scared, and I'll never want to experience another ghost again. Since that day, I have a new profound respect for ghosts."

SACRAMENTO, CA

SUTTER'S FORT STATE HISTORIC PARK

Sutter's Fort began its history in 1839 as a small settlement, founded by John Sutter, a German-born Swiss entrepreneur. This one time small,

lowly gathering of settlers would come to mark a supremely important position in California's history, and the great migration to the west.

John Sutter acquired the land grant for his settlement from the Mexican government and called it New Helvetia, meaning New Switzerland. However, the settlement generally became known, and was

soon accepted as Sutter's Fort. Self-sufficiency was paramount to the fort's survival. The Fort, primarily constructed with Native Americans doing the bulk of the labor, soon became widely known as a way station and trade center for pioneers.

Another aspect of the Fort's role in history was when it sent several rescue parties to deliver the doomed Donner Party that was trapped in the Sierra Nevada's during the severe winter of 1846-47.

Eight-year old Patty Reed carried this doll across the plains to California.

During the bitter snowbound months in the Sierra Nevada mountains, Patty had "Dolly" to confide in and to comfort her. She later donated the doll to Sutter's Fort, the original destination of the Donner Party.

Perhaps the most famous of its roles was in 1848, when John Sutter sent a work party to Coloma, to construct a lumber mill. During the building of the mill, construction foreman James Marshall spotted the glint of yellow gold among some stones. Efforts were made to keep the news of this discovery quiet, but to no avail. Soon word spread, and the rest of this worldwide rush of fortune seekers is the basis to California's history.

With much excitement and quick movement of Sutter's workers away from the Fort in search of wealth, to the town of Coloma, the Fort was soon left deserted. John Sutter was left without a work force, and by the 1880's, the fort's only original building, "The Central Building," remained. Today, the Fort was reconstructed in 1891, and it was based on an 1847 map.

Sutter's Fort and the California State Indian Museum are both located in an easily reached location in downtown Sacramento.

MICHAEL 'SPARKY' ANDERSON'S STORY

I'm originally from Michigan, and I've been at the Fort now for about 12 years. I manage the Fort's 'Trade Store' also known as the gift shop. I'm also the Master Blacksmith, and I present public demonstrations of blacksmithing techniques from the gold rush era.

It's commonly known among the staff, that the fort was built upon a Miwok Native American grave site. I remember before working at the fort, I was told many stories of the ghosts that dwell in the fort by several employees. Many of the ghost sightings center around a woman and man's ghost that are regularly seen at the Central Building. The Central Building, also known as the Administration Building, is the two-story

Michael Anderson.

adobe brick building, that incidentally, is the only original standing building within the Fort complex. When spotted, these ghosts are seen standing in this building's doorways.

I recall one Saturday night in 1989, when the employees, and docents were involved in a two-day event at the Fort. We all spent the night at the fort, and that was when I first heard of the ghosts of the man and woman, that inhabit the Central Building.

At the entrance to each of the Central buildings rooms, is a pre-recorded explanation of what that particular room was historically used for. This message assists with the self-guided tour, and is programmed by a motion detector, programmed to automatically play as a person's body passes in front of each doorway.

At the Central Building, on the second floor, there is one room that has a window named the Doctor's

"the ghosts can be seen standing in the Central building's doorways."

room. One of our docents told me that a woman's image is reportedly seen by visitors, as she gazes out of this particular window. The ghost is reportedly only seen in the evening hours dressed in early California style gold rush garb, about the mid-1850's.

One especially interesting account of a witness who spotted our ghosts, was told to me 4 years ago by a park visitor to the Fort. The sighting took place in the summer of 1998, that involved a group of Boy Scouts. The group of scouts were visiting the Fort from the San Francisco Bay area. This group was accompanied by another group of scouts that were visiting from Guadalajara, Mexico. They came to the Fort and set up quarters in the Fort's Central Building. After introducing myself, I engaged the Mexican Scout Master in conversation, at which time he began to tell me of a strange experience he had at the Fort.

He reported to me that the previous afternoon, he was sitting alone on a bench in the upper floor of the Central Building. Strangely, the pre-recorded message began to play on its own, as if someone had passed in front of the motion detector. Again, the Scout Master stated that he was the only person in the upper floor. Suddenly from the door opening on the west side of the room, entered two men dressed in period clothing. These men walked past the seated Scout Master, towards a wooden staircase. They proceeded to walk up the staircase, where they disappeared from his sight. The scout master said he immediately thought these men were associated with a costumed Fort reenactment of some kind, and enjoyed the show.

His curiosity being aroused, he decided to follow these actors up the

Inside view looking out of Central Building 2nd floor doorway.

stairs, to the third floor. He walked over to the stairs and noticed that there was no way to walk up the stairs, because a barrier of framed wood and wire had obviously been constructed by the park service, to prevent any unauthorized person from walking on the stairs. Immediately he felt unnerved because how could the two men have walked as easily 'through' this obvious barricade without any difficulty? The Scout Master said he immediately knew he had seen ghosts, and that the experience scared the devil out of him! He quickly walked outside the building, to gather his senses, and located a park employee. After describing the incident, he convinced the perplexed employee to follow him back inside the building, for the purpose of physically describing what he had just seen. The employee was at a loss for words, and had no reasonable explanation.

I have personally experienced the 'presence' of a spirit, the day I took over the Fort's Blacksmith Shop. Between the years 1988 and 1989, there was a fellow who used to work at the Blacksmith Shop by the name of "Slow Wolf." Slow Wolf was directly involved in setting up the shop's iron furnace and display, and was also the main interpreter of the blacksmithing art. He also belonged to a 'Mountain Man' organization, and the name "Slow Wolf" was the name he personally gave, and chose to identify with.

When Slow Wolf died, against the park rangers' directives, a group of his friends scattered his cremated remains, or ashes, all about the Fort's Blacksmith shop. I never met Slow Wolf, but I have been told a lot about his unique history at the fort.

At the time, I was still very new at the blacksmithing trade. I recall working one day at the same Blacksmith shop where Slow Wolf worked, when something very peculiar took place. As I was busy at the table working on a project, I suddenly got the sensation of someone standing next to me, looking over my shoulder. I turned my head to see who it was, and spotted no one. Immediately a prickly sensation came over me. I actually felt the physical presence of someone leaning over my shoulder to view my work! These creepy visits took place for a total of about six times during the first year that I worked in the shop.

I never mentioned these experiences to any of my co-workers. I just decided to keep this information to myself. There was no pattern to these visits, day or night I'd suddenly feel the presence of what I believe were Slow Wolf's visits. I didn't hear any footsteps, or actually see a person standing next to me. I would just 'feel' someone standing right beside me. I knew it must be Slow Wolf checking up on my blacksmithing work. I guess he was making sure I was operating the Blacksmith Shop in the correct manner he was used to doing.

Before I began working at the Fort, if someone were to ask me if I believed in the existence of spirits, or ghosts, my answer would have been, definitely no! But now I have to honestly say, I'm not so sure. My curiosity draws me to want to actually experience seeing a ghost appear to me. Others have, so I guess I'd welcome the possibility.

SAND CREEK MASSACRE NATIONAL HISTORIC SITE (NEAR EADS, CO)

"Each evening she would start telling us the story of Sand Creek ... she would always cry when she told the story, and I always wondered why she cried ... and then when I started growing older I began to realize what she had been through, seeing all her people getting killed..." — Nellie Bear Tusk, 2000

On November 29, 1864, Colonel John M. Chivington, a Methodist minister, ordained in 1844, led approximately 700 U.S. volunteer soldiers to a village of about 500 Cheyenne and Arapaho people camped along the banks of Big Sandy Creek in southeastern Colorado. Although the Cheyenne and Arapaho people believed they were under the protection of the U.S. Army, Chivington's troops breached the 1861 Treaty of Fort Wise by attacking and ultimately slaughtering over 150 people, mainly women, children, and the elderly. For protection of his people and as duly authorized and directed by the United States government, Cheyenne Chief Black Kettle had raised both the U.S. Flag and a white flag of truce, both of which were fully visible to the troops. Despite the display of these flags, Chivington's men marched ahead with their personal need to complete the utter destruction of these peaceful people. The Colorado troops then desecrated the dead and plundered the camp. Later, they were greeted as heroes in the city of Denver.

For the soldiers, losses were minimal, with about nine or 10 killed and three dozen wounded. After the attack, most of the surviving Cheyenne fled north towards the Smoky Hill, seeking refuge among relatives. After extending their expedition briefly southeast into the Arkansas Valley in pursuit of Littlie Raven's Arapaho, Chivington and the majority of his command arrived back at Fort Lyon around December 10–twelve days later they returned to Denver amid a hero's welcome. Dismembered corpses and body parts were paraded among the streets of Denver, with much glee and delight by the soldiers.

Chivington's decision not to pursue the Cheyenne north towards other large camps was greeted with disdain by some, including Major Scott Anthony. During the ensuing months, Sand Creek was investigated by a Military Commission, a Joint Committee on the Conduct of War, and a Special Joint Committee investigating the Condition of Indian Tribes. These committees condemned the action of Colonel Chivington and most of his officers and troops, labeling the event a massacre— their findings however drew the ire of many.

"I saw the bodies of those lying there cut all to pieces, worse mutilated than any I ever saw before; the women cut all to pieces ... With knives; scalped; their brains knocked out; children two or three months old; all ages lying there, from sucking infants up to warriors ... By whom were they mutilated? By the United States troops ..." — John S. Smith, Congressional Testimony of Mr. John S. Smith, 1865

"Fingers and ears were cut off the bodies for the jewelry they carried. The body of White Antelope, lying solitarily in the creek bed, was a prime target. Besides scalping him the soldiers cut off his nose, ears, and testicles-the last for a tobacco pouch ..." — Stan Hoig

"Jis to think of that dog Chivington and his dirty hounds, up thar at Sand Creek. His men shot down squaws, and blew the brains out of little innocent children. You call sich soldiers Christians, do ye? And Indians savages? What der yer 'spose our Heavenly Father, who made both them and us, thinks of these things? I tell you what, I don't like a hostile red skin any more than you do. And when they are hostile, I've fought 'em, hard as any man. But I never yet drew a bead on a squaw or papoose, and I despise the man who would." — Kit Carson

Colorado Territorial Governor Evans who ordered the bloody attack, and who's political career was subsequently ended because of this loathsome decision, wrote a rebuttal of sorts, his report was dated August 6, 1865; meanwhile Colonel Chivington, who had initially responded via deposition, addressed the people of Colorado with a synopsis of the investigation, this was published in June, 1865. Chivington, his counsel Major Jacob Downing, and others defended their attack at Sand Creek, claiming bias, political agendas and even officer jealousies had distorted and misrepresented the facts. Today, the Sand Creek Massacre remains as only one of many historical reminders of the numerous sorrowful events imposed upon Native Americans within their own land.

"I think that by locating these places and having an actual place to go and pay homage to the people who died there, for us it's going to bring closure to a lot of tribal pain that we are presently experiencing. — Dr. Richard Little Bear, 2000

In 1998 Senator Ben Campbell (CO-R) introduced a bill that resulted in legislation known as the Sand Creek Massacre National Historic Site Study Act. This legislation directed the National Park Service to identify the location and extent of the Sand Creek Massacre and define its suitability as a potential unit of the National Park Service. The Sand Creek Massacre Site Location Project used historical documentation, oral history, traditional tribal methods, aerial photography, archeology and geomorphology. Two documents, a "Site Location Study" and a "Special Resources Study and Environmental Assessment" were published as a summary of the project. On the basis of these findings, on November 7, 2000 President Clinton signed into law the Sand Creek Massacre National Historic Site Establishment Act. The Act recognizes the national significance of the Sand Creek Massacre and authorizes its establishment as a unit of the National Park Service.

Approximately 12,500 acres in Kiowa County, Colorado, are authorized for inclusion within the National Historic Site. The National Park Service is working in partnership with the State of Colorado, the Cheyenne and Arapaho Tribes of Oklahoma, the Northern Cheyenne Tribe, the Northern Arapaho Tribe, landowners, Kiowa County, and other partners in the process of establishing the National Historic Site. Currently 920 acres are in National Park Service ownership and the Cheyenne and Arapaho Tribes of Oklahoma own 1,465 acres. The Conservation Fund, a non-profit organization, is working to acquire additional parcels of land.

Over the years the area of the Sand Creek Massacre has continued to be visited and commemorated. An aging John Chivington smugly returned to the area in 1887, and in 1908 Veterans of the Colorado Regiments planned a reunion at the site. In August of 1950 the Colorado Historical Society assisted local residents and the Eads and Lamar Chambers of Commerce in placing a marker atop the bluff at the Dawson South Bend. Sand Creek Descendants remain active in tribal communities in Montana, Oklahoma, and Wyoming –– and Council Representatives continue to work alongside the National Park Service. Also, in 1978 the late Edward Red Hat, Keeper of the Cheyenne sacred covenant made "Cheyenne Earth" at the site.

Clearly, as defined in its enabling legislation, the Sand Creek Massacre National Historic Site shall remain a reminder of the tragic extremes sometimes reached during times of conflict; it symbolizes the struggles of Native American tribes to maintain their way of life on ancestral lands; and represents a significant element of frontier military and Native American history. Each of these mandates, historic sources and partnerships will help insure that the site is preserved in perpetuity for future generations of Sand Creek descendants and world citizens.

On October 6, 1998, the 105th Congress of the United States authorized the Sand Creek Massacre National Historic Site Study Act. This legislation (Public Law 105-243) was introduced by Senator Ben Nighthorse Campbell and mandated that the National Park Service identify the location and extent of the massacre area and determine its suitability and feasibility as a potential National Historic Site. The legislation also required cost estimates for potential acquisition, development, and operations and identified alternatives for administration of the area. Resulting from this legislation was a 366-page Site Location Study and a two volume Special Resource Study and Environmental Assessment. The Location Study identified the length and extent (the boundaries) of the Sand Creek Massacre. The Study used an interdisciplinary approach to its task –- oral history, archived sources, and other historical documentation, archeology and remote imagery, geomorphology, aerial photography, and traditional tribal methods were used. These efforts resulted in the partnering of the National Park Service, the Colorado Historical Society, property owners, volunteers, and the Cheyenne and Arapaho Tribes in Oklahoma, the Northern Cheyenne Tribe in Montana, and the Northern Arapaho Tribe in Wyoming.

During the Site Location Study, the Sand Creek Massacre Project Team was able to identify several areas along Sand Creek where, based upon the interdisciplinary methods, the Indian camp and much of the activity of November 29 and 30, 1864 likely took place. As a running engagement, the Sand Creek Massacre continued up Sand Creek and across its valley into the surrounding hills and prairie. As this research unfolded, a range of opinions developed regarding the exact location of the Sand Creek Massacre. Some debate continues regarding the specific locations of internal features. Potential areas initially considered included the Dawson South Bend and the northern edge of the Dawson Bend; the Bowen Middle and Bowen South Bends; the Rhoades/Bowen Bend; and the Dewitt/Ballentine Bend. These areas, with one exception, stretch across the open country of Township 17 South, Kiowa County into the southern edge of Cheyenne County. The final boundaries, agreed upon by all participants in the study, encompass about 7500 acres in Kiowa County — from the Bowen Middle Bend to south of the Dawson Bend. This area is now on the National Register of Historic Places.

Two years after the Site Study Act, the United States Congress concurred with the site boundaries and authorized the Sand Creek Massacre National Historic Site with Public Law 106-465, November 7, 2000. The

Act requires the National Park Service to acquire from willing sellers enough area to adequately protect, interpret, memorialize, and commemorate the site. The legislation also confirms the site's national significance, and provides an opportunity for tribes, the State of Colorado, and other entities to be involved in its support and development. Establishment will provide enhanced cultural understanding and define the conditions of descendant and tribal access for traditional, cultural, or historical observance.

Currently, through its partnership with The Conservation Fund and with Colorado State Historical Fund assistance, the National Park Service has acquired approximately 920 acres of the proposed 12,500-acre site. An additional 1,465 acres (the former Dawson Ranch) was recently purchased by Southwest Entertainment, Inc., which in turn intends to convey the property to the Cheyenne and Arapaho Tribes. It is anticipated this land may be legislated into tribal trust status, thence managed by the National Park Service. Most land within the authorized boundary remains under private ownership.

Within the massacre site boundaries are places of great historic importance — the location of the Cheyenne village and several Arapaho lodges; the point(s) from which the Colorado Regiments first spotted the encampment; the location of Indian pony herds; the area of flight, bordering Sand Creek, that the Indians took during and after the initial attack; the general path of battalion advancements, individual skirmishing and other collateral action; the military bivouac area for the nights of November 29 and 30; spots in the creek and along its banks where the Cheyenne dug sandpits/survival pits, and the points from which battery salvoes were launched into the camp and later into the sandpits. All of these areas are on land authorized for inclusion in the National Historic Site.

Over a century since the tragic event, the Cheyenne have finally begun to realize some sense of healing by honoring the memory of the Sand Creek Massacre victims through the on-going following efforts:

- Repatriation of human remains and artifacts held in museums taken during and after the massacre.

- Researching, gathering and archiving Cheyenne oral history of the Sand Creek massacre;
- Protecting and preserving the village site of the Sand Creek massacre through federal legislation the Sand Creek Massacre National Historic Site Act of November 7, 2000;
- Assisting the State of Colorado in reinterpreting the Civil War monument at the State Capitol to affirm that what occurred at Sand Creek on November 29, 1864 was a massacre of innocent men women and children a not a "Battle";
- Originating the First Annual Sand Creek Spiritual Healing Run of 1999 from the Sand Creek Massacre Site in Kiowa County to the steps of the state capitol in Denver.

OPHELIA CHANGING BEARS' (KIOWA/ARAPAHOE) STORY

Ophelia and I met prior to the beginning of a pow-wow one early evening. By coincidence, Ophelia's son David and I are both bead workers, making traditional crafts for personal use and to trade at pow-wows. It was during our conversation that David mentioned that his mother was knowledgeable in spiritual matters. After he introduced me to his mother she became very interested and willing to share her thoughts. A few months after our meeting, Ophelia has since "let go of her physical body and taken the spiritual road herself," but thankfully because of her willingness, I was able to record a bit of her personal remembrance for you.

— Antonio

"I was born in Anadarko, Oklahoma, in the year 1923. My mother was a member of the Kiowa nation and my father was from the Arapahoe people. Both of them had much to tell about their memories of the Sand Creek battle. I remember as a small girl, when we would visit Sand Creek, Father would always make offerings of tobacco to the souls that were killed at Sand Creek. I was told to never speak about, or to mention, the name Sand Creek without first bowing my head to honor our relatives. All of them were to be honored and prayed for.

I don't have too much to say about the stories; they are mine to carry with me until I also leave this life. What I will say is that I know that Sand Creek is a very sad place. Many terrible and sad memories still linger there. I haven't visited the area for over 60 years, but once when I did visit with my parents and two older brothers, we all knew and felt that that ground was holy. A hawk followed us everywhere we walked. It flew in the air and just kept up with us, just floating way up high where we could see it.

I hope people who visit will always remember to keep it holy and not to speak in a loud voice when they visit. The trees, the ground, and the wind all can hear what people say. Mother Earth knows what's in people's hearts. So, be reverent and make offerings. It's a sad but holy place."

RALPH COVINTON'S STORY

Ralph and I met for his interview at a Santa Fe city park. Ralph just happened to be in New Mexico for a gallery showing of his brother's artwork and my being a resident of Santa Fe at this time, found it convenient for me to meet with him in town. Seated at a bench one afternoon under the shade of cottonwood trees he described his spiritually rich encounter with one entity. Unexpected as the encounter was Ralph was, on this day, still visibly moved by what happened to him a few years earlier. I know this story will be one story you'll be thinking about for some time to come.

— Antonio

"Today, I live in the small town of Lamar, but I was raised in Eads, and born in Chivington in 1923. The town of Chivington is what most people who happen to visit might refer to as a ghost town. Not much is left of it, just a few houses and dirt, with lots of dead trees and open ranges, with a few cattle here and there. I left Chivington in the late 1960s. The only ones left from our family are just my brother and me, that's all, just the two of us.

As you know, the town of Chivington was named after the Arapahoe and Cheyenne Indian killer, Col. John M. Chivington! I don't hide my distaste for that terrible idiot! I had a couple of friends who were Native Americans, and I personally know how honorable those people are. My wife was a Kiowa from Oklahoma. I know about the way history can change things, for the worst, depending on who's writing it all down. Native American people are, by and large, the best thing this county ever had, and I hope your readers know this. I was around the age of 14 or 15 when I first began to have the experiences happen to me that I would call hauntings. I was visiting my grandparents at the time that also lived in Chivington, just a couple of miles away from where our family house was. My grandparents' house was a small, three-room house. No running water or electricity. When we wanted to take a bath, we had to heat the bath water on the wood-burning stove in the kitchen, and we would also share the bath water!

One spring evening after we had all gone to sleep, as I was lying in bed, I heard the sound of a dog barking in the distance. For some reason, this sound alarmed me. It was not unusual to hear this, the dogs in town would sometimes bark at foxes, coyotes and other dogs, but for some reason, this night was different. Apparently, no one else heard the dog because I could see in the darkness that everyone was fast asleep in his or her beds. I did finally go to sleep, but that night I had the worst nightmare I have ever experienced. I dreamt that a woman, an Indian woman who was covered in dirt, was standing next to my bed. I woke up on my back, in a sweat, and just lay in bed staring up at the dark ceiling. My brother, Glen, who was asleep next to me did not notice anything because he never woke up and was snoring away. But I felt that my dream was more than a dream because of it being so real. From that night on, I would have many nightmares of that Indian woman who would approach my bedside, but when I'd wake up, she would not be there. I knew I was dreaming, but the nightmares sure did seem very real to me as a child.

At around the age of 17, my dreams began to take on a new focus. The nightmares became more constant, and the nightly visitations by the Indian woman were becoming even more frightening to me. Until the time when she actually appeared to me!

One night, I was having a dream about running after our horses. It was a strange dream. I was barefoot and running as fast as the horses. As soon as I caught up to them, I suddenly woke up! I was on my left side, facing the wall. As I was lying there in bed, I began to suddenly hear the sound of footsteps coming up to my bed. A little bit scared, I didn't turn around. I just automatically froze, listening to the strange footsteps. Then I heard the steps come right up to my bed and then felt the hand of someone pulling at my hair! I acted like I was asleep—playing possum. Somehow, I eventually did fall back to sleep.

From that night on, my dreams of the Indian woman kept happening night after night and more constant. And as soon as she would reach my bed, I'd wake up. I'd look about the room and not see anyone. I knew that if I were to tell my mother or father about them, they'd think I was losing my mind, so I just kept them to myself. But one night things did change.

After having the usual dream of the Indian woman, I woke up and I remember that as I lay there in my bed, the smell of what I could only think might be wet wood was overpowering. It was a very strong aroma of something old and damp, resembling mold.

I lay there and thinking that a skunk or some type of smelly animal had "let go" in my bedroom, I sat up in bed and quickly visually scanned around the room. That's when I noticed that one area of the room was a lot darker than the rest. I fixed my gaze on this darkness and soon saw that it was beginning to move! This dark shadow area took the form of a person—the Indian woman in my dreams!

Her shadow moved slowly towards me and it began to grow larger and with more defined details. I lay silently in bed in shock! Despite the darkness I could see her fine facial features, and the pattern of her dress were becoming clearer. As she got to about five feet from my bed, something within me took over. Suddenly, instead of fear, I began to feel a deep concern and sadness for this woman. I could somehow sense that she was in pain, and sensed a deep pity come over me.

With a dry mouth, I spoke to her, "I don't know why you're here but I care about you and I'll try to help you." She slowly turned her head and opened her mouth, but I didn't hear any words come out. Then I again said, "I'll help you with whatever you need." She kept still and then I felt my face and body grow hot, as if a thick wool blanket had been wrapped around me! As I lifted my right hand to my face, I must have fainted because the last thing I remember is waking up in the morning. I knew I did not dream of the woman, she was real; the ghost was real because something inside me told me so. I was not dreaming I was sure of it!

The next night I decided that if I were to have another visit from this woman, I was going to make sure I did no faint. Somehow I was going to be braver and keep talking to her until she responded to me. I guess because of having had so many dreams of her in years past, she had become somehow familiar to me. Not as a friend, but as a sort of familiar being. I know this is a strange kind of relationship, but that's how I was thinking at the time.

Sure enough, about two nights later I heard a noise in my room and there she was. This time, as before, when she spoke to me her mouth moved but no sound came out. But after she closed her mouth, her words, or what I thought might be words, came after, as if in a delayed time. Something like if you were to clap your hands together, and just a few seconds later, the clapping sound is heard like an echo. This made no sense to me.

In a few minutes, she had disappeared. In the morning, I awoke with a sense that I could communicate with her if I kept it up, and persisted in allowing her to feel comfortable. I didn't know what else I could do, so the next night, before going to bed, I placed a small piece of a chocolate bar next to the table in my room where she would appear. I hoped she would appreciate that as my gift to her.

I didn't have to wait very long, because right after I placed the chocolate on the table and said, "Well, I hope you like chocolate," I felt the room grow cold, then the scent of wet earth filled the air. I looked around the room and didn't see anything unusual, but in the distance, I slowly begin to hear the sound of lots of commotion going on—the sound of yelling and gunfire! I looked outside from my window and didn't see anything.

The night was still and even the dogs weren't barking. I was wondering what this sound was, when I heard something moving in my room. I struck a match and didn't see anything, and the chocolate was still where

I had placed it. So, I decided to get into bed, but as I got under the covers, I felt a hard object between the wall and me. I reached out of the covers and discovered a stick!

I took a long slow breath because that night I was alone in the house. My brother Glen and mother had gone to Lamar to stay with my uncle for the week, and father was returning with the two of them in two days. My hands began to shake because I had not put that stick in my bed and knew it had to be the Indian woman who had left it there for me. I said, "Thank you" out loud. Then I placed the short, thick stick on the same table where I had left the chocolate bar. That night I did not get a visit from the Indian woman, and I have not had another dream about her since then.

I've kept the stick for many years and when I married my Kiowa wife, I told her the story about my dreams and how I had come to have the stick. She told me to wrap it in a blanket, sprinkle sage over it, and to place it upon a small bed of cottonwood and juniper branches. And most importantly, to keep it hidden from anyone's view.

We've always kept the stick wrapped up and hidden in a box, high up on a shelf in our garage. When my wife died in 1976, I brought the box into the house and kept it in my own bedroom. It's a small stick, about 23 inches long and about an inch around. I'll always keep it with me. I've told my brother Glen not to forget to bury me with it. I want to always have that stick, which was given to me by that Indian woman when I was a young man, even when I'm dead and leave this Earth. I hope that I will meet up with my wife, and that both of us can personally thank the spirit of the Indian woman for her gift."

SANTA ANA (TAMAYAME) PUEBLO, NM

The original location of Santa Ana Pueblo is unknown. Most of the pueblo's inhabitants were displaced by either voluntarily leaving or were killed during the Pueblo Revolt of 1680. Following the re-conquest of the New Mexico territory by the Spanish in 1692-1694, the pueblo originally known as Tamaya, or the Old Santa Ana Pueblo was founded in an area about eight miles northwest of Bernalillo. The present people of Santa

Ana pueblo tend to maintain two residencies; one area is a farming community along the Rio Grande while the other remains a traditional home located on the north bank of the Jemez River. Today most of the pueblo's population, about six-hundred-sixty-eight people, gather together at the Old Pueblo for their traditional ceremonies, social gatherings and festivals. This pueblo is rich in its ancient arts of pottery, woven articles and beaded jewelry.

SANTA ANA STAR CASINO

I chose to include this story due to my having been approached by several casino workers regarding their own encounters with spirits on the property. Granted, most individuals requested not to be identified in this book given their spiritual or tribal beliefs. However, for reasons known only to her, the following person in this story absolutely wanted her story told. Having traveled to many Indian owned casinos in and outside of New Mexico, I've discovered that for some strange reason, many without exception have some employee who has witnessed something paranormal or encountered spirit activity. Might this be due to the extreme desires of economic hope casino's offer given the slim possibility for a chance of wealth or that so many individuals have lost so much in the game of chance they offer? Could the fact that a burial gravesite exists just walking distance from the main entrance of this casino have anything to do with the following encounter?

I'll leave this possibility open for discussion. But if you're ever in the vicinity of this particular casino, enter, relax, and enjoy yourself. You just might return home with much more than pleasant memories or even winnings. You never know "what" might be standing nearby, watching your next move, waiting for an opportunity to be seen, recognized and honored!

—Antonio

KATIE MARQUEZ'S STORY

"I'm a tribal member of the Santa Ana Pueblo and I've worked at the tribe's casino for over nine years. I know there are some fellow pueblo people who would not want me to talk about the spiritual going-ons at the casino, but even though this is the overall feeling of the tribe, I know that employees talk openly among themselves about ghosts on this property. I've heard them and I also know that the tribal chairmen are aware of what employees have seen and spoken of. If my story helps others to recognize that what we're seeing is not in our imaginations, that there really are spirits in the building, well maybe they'll have a medicine man or woman bless the grounds again and put these restless souls at peace.

Speaking for myself, I'm scared of the spirits. I'm not going to lie; I'm really scared having to come into the building alone at night. I don't want to experience anything else like the experiences that I've had in the past. So, after people read my story, I hope enough pressure is put on the tribal council to do something about it. The spirits need to know that they are honored and they need to have prayers offered to them. I hope a ceremony is offered to them; the spirits need one and so do we.

It was just a few months after being hired, six years ago when I had my first experience with a spirit in the casino. Just before my experience, I was told by a fellow pueblo woman co-worker named Estelle about her own experiences with a spirit that she'd seen in the parking lot one early morning. Estelle told me that it happened when she was walking from her car to the sidewalk. She spotted a little girl about eight or nine years of age. The girl was quite a distance from where Estelle was standing. However, the strange thing about this girl was that she was running and jumping about the ground like a small deer. The little girl was making movements that a normal child could not ever do. That's what initially caught the woman's attention. The unusually strange, inhuman movements the girl was making.

Immediately the woman told me she knew this was of a spiritual nature, she quickly turned around, got in her car and drove around the casino to another entrance. As soon as she parked her car, Estelle sat inside and visually checked all around to see if there were plenty of people walking about. She left her car and dashed in through the casino doors!

She didn't dare mention to anyone about what she had seen, especially to co-workers. Estelle told me she was concerned people would think she might be losing her mind. 'It's difficult to explain to people about seeing a ghost. Some might say they believe; but most people don't. It wasn't until my second experience that I decided to open up to others,' she said.

She told me that it was about a year later when she was taking her work break in one of the bathrooms. Thinking she was alone in the bathroom, she was looking into one of the bathroom mirrors applying her lipstick. Suddenly she noticed the faint reflected image of a strange woman standing in front of the wall behind her. Surprised to see her, the employee turned around to face the woman, but she vanished!

She immediately dropped her lipstick, grabbed her purse and ran out the door! Estelle described the woman as about the age of thirty or thirty-five, five feet or so with long hair and definitely of native decent! This time because of how upset she felt, Estelle chose to speak to a co-worker, a Mexican woman, about the spirit. She felt confident to speak to her because for the four years they had known each other; they both had grown friendly and trusting towards each other. Soon after her second experience, Estelle left her job and didn't return to work for a full month!

Before returning to work, she requested a change of position, specifically a position where she might have plenty of interaction with the public. Estelle did not want to work alone any longer. The casino's human resources department chose to accommodate her request by giving her the job of pushing a coffee and soda cart throughout the casino floor offering drinks to the guests. Estelle felt satisfied and safe with this new position and stayed with the job for a few more years until she left the casino in 1991.

That same year I had my own experience with a ghost inside the casino's Events Center room. I, together with several other women staff were in charge of setting up the tables, chairs and decorations for events. The Events Center is a very large indoor area that host's concerts and conferences throughout the year and is equipped with a state-of-the-art lighting and sound system.

At the time of my ghost experience, I and two other employees, Elsa and Carolyn were in this large room setting up tables and chairs. I was the first to enter the room, and after turning on the lights, walked to the area where the chairs were stored. The other two women walked over to the opposite side of the room and began to remove the folding tables from storage. The only persons in the room were the three of us; absolutely no one else was in the room. Carolyn mentioned to Elsa and I that she needed a bathroom break. Elsa also decided to accompany her, so they both left me alone in the room for a few minutes. There were approximately forty tables to dress and decorate. I walked to each table placing folded tablecloths in the middle of each.

After doing this, I'd begin where I started and unfold them. I was very focused on the job that I was doing when suddenly I had the strangest feeling that I was being watched. I turned to look at the doors and they were closed. Then I looked up to the area of the stage and except for the microphone and podium, it was empty. I could see that I was totally alone in the room.

I was unable to shake off this feeling; it was unshakable, I knew someone was staring at me. I just knew it! I decided to stand quietly in place and listen for footsteps or perhaps a voice. All I heard was the slight humming sound of the air conditioner. But just as I was about to return to the job I was doing, I heard the sound of what appeared to be the dropping of dirt, or gravel on the floor.

The sound was not abrupt or very loud, so I was not startled just a bit unnerved. I looked in the direction of the stage and noticed nothing unusual, suddenly I heard the sound of a cardboard box being kicked very hard coming from what could only be the lighting room located up high and directly above me. The lighting room is located opposite the stage at the eastern end of the room. It's a small room that resembles a loft. In this room a person can operate the special lighting effects that are needed for stage productions. Because of its position, the interior is very visible to anyone standing at the floor level below.

I turned and looked up to face the lighting room and spotted the image of a person—a male, standing and starring directly at me! I stood in place wondering who this person could be. I waved at him with my left hand and I could see that he noticed me because he immediately moved from where he was standing just a few feet to his right. Again, I waved at him then said, 'Hey what are you doing, spying on me?' He stood in place gazing at me and literally disappeared as I blinked! I didn't know what just happened or if what I saw was real. I was frightened for sure and almost peed myself! I dropped the table linen's I was holding on the table and ran out of the event center!

I ran into the nearest bathroom looking for Elsa, gasping for air and calling out her name, but I was alone. I terrified to stay in the empty bathroom and ran down the hall to the buffet dining room. People were busy dropping their money in slot machines as I ran past them. Comforted by the noise and activity all around me, I stood in place, spotted Carolyn and ran up to her. I hugged her with all my might, but couldn't begin to tell her what I had just seen. Because of the serious look on my face, Carolyn stood still, and waited for me to speak. I couldn't keep this experience to myself and told her exactly what happened. She listened to my every word. Then said, 'I know you're telling me the truth because you're now the third person I know that has seen a ghost in this casino.'

She hugged and attempting to calm me down. She said, 'Katie, don't worry, he won't hurt you. He's probably lonely and is looking for a girlfriend!' Her silly joke made me smile, but I still had tears in my eyes as I broke into a little laugh.

I very hesitantly returned to the room with her and expecting to see Elsa, we entered the empty Events Center room. I didn't want to even accidentally peek at the lighting room. Clutching her arm, I asked Carolyn to take a look around the room for me. She said that there was absolutely no one living or dead that she could see in the room—it was empty.

Just when we were wondering where Elsa had gone, walking through the door came Elsa. She looked oddly. I asked her if she was all right, and she asked us not to laugh at her, but she was scared. She stated to us, "As I was extending the folded legs from one of the tables, I felt as if an unseen hand had touched my left arm. I turned around and didn't see anyone next to me, but I kept feeling the pressure of an invisible hand holding tight to my upper arm! I got so scared that I started to swat at my arm. When the 'thing' would not let go, I ran out of the room and into the safety of the slot machine room! I didn't notice when the invisible hand let go of me, but it finally did. I walked around for a few minutes until I felt ready to come back and look for both of you."

I told Elsa about my own experience and we both decided to call it quits for the day. Elsa and I reported the experience to our supervisor and we were surprised to hear that our experience with a spirit in the casino was not an isolated one. We were asked to finish up the day assisting in another department, but were strongly advised not to discuss our 'encounters' with any other employees. Carolyn and three other employees were left to finish up our job. I've spoken to my family about the spirit I saw at the casino as well as Elsa's experience. My mother told me that the spirits are members of our people who are keeping a watch over us. I shouldn't be afraid of them, just respectful.

My older sister Linda mentioned to me that there are graves on the casino grounds and in fact the graves are located just a short distance from the western edge of the casino's main doors; next to the main highway just behind the large wall with the sign that reads, 'Hyatt Regency Tamaya Resort.' The graves are directly behind that wall surrounded by a small wooden fence. I've also seen many photographs from around the property with round white circles of light called 'spirit orbs' in the photo. Lots of people have captured orbs by accident during public gatherings and other spaces inside the building. They'll appear flying about the room and even next to, and on, people. Just ask around, you'll see I'm telling you the truth.

The last thing I want to say is that people need to respect these graves and not climb over the fence and wander about. The ones who are buried in that area are ancestors; people like you and me. They lived and had families like everyone. It's best to show your respect by being silent when

passing the area on foot, or when driving by in your car. Offer a prayer, but never, ever disrespect this sacred resting place.

We pueblo people know that even though the remains of our ancestors are underground, the spirits of our brothers and sisters are always involved in our daily routines. So, please respect the area and keep away. I'm not concerned about what people may think about ghosts, I know I've had my own experiences and I'm personally afraid of them. I have confidence that our medicine people know about these graves, and that they gave the right offerings and prayers to our ancestors. I know that we, as pueblo people, need our ancestor's guidance and protection to help us all do good. But sometimes even though they may not intend to scare me, I always am. I really believe that perhaps our ancestor spirits need to be better honored with more prayer offerings, so they stop distracting us away from doing our jobs."

SANTA FE, NM

THE SANTA FE LABORATORY OF ANTHROPOLOGY HISTORY AND THE MUSEUM OF INDIAN ARTS AND CULTURE

As the 19th century came to a close, the American Southwest was undergoing enormous transition. Tourists from Europe and the East Coast of America flooded the area, drawn by word-of-mouth from early visitors and quick to take advantage of the railroad, which had just arrived in the West. Notably being the Southwest's major attraction— its vibrant Native American cultures. In response to unsystematic collecting by Eastern museums, anthropologist Edgar Lee Hewett

founded the Museum of New Mexico in 1909 with a mission to collect and preserve Southwest Native American material culture.

Several years later in 1927, John D. Rockefeller founded the renowned Laboratory of Anthropology with a mission to study the Southwest's indigenous cultures. In 1947, the two institutions merged, bringing together the most inclusive and systematically acquired collection of New Mexican and Southwestern anthropological artifacts in the country.

DOTY FUGATE'S STORY

I sat across the desk from where Doty was sitting when conducting this interview. Doty's office is located at Museum Hill, on the bottom floor of the Laboratory of Anthropology building. We were surrounded with long tables upon which were numerous archeological examples. Contained within cardboard boxes were carefully placed un-cataloged pottery shards and other artifacts. It was not difficult to feel an aura of ancient history that enveloped the large room as the afternoon sunbeams entered the narrow windows.

Speaking for myself, I was impressed by the array of ancient human evidence that lay just a few feet from where I sat. Not only were native people of the Southwest represented within arm's length of where I was seated, but in adjacent rooms were also artifacts from the Maya and other pre-Columbian high cultures of the Americas.

I found Doty to be quite informative of her experiences both within her chosen field of study and with the focused details of our discussion. "I'm familiar with the area of ghosts and the supernatural," she stated, "I've had my own experiences, so I'm not a disbeliever. I've also known of a few fellow archeologists who have had their encounters with spirits at dig sites; some good, some not so good." Doty Fugate has been employed at the laboratory for many years, and has regularly heard of the personal experiences from fellow staff, and additionally has had her own encounters inside this very building. Not included with this story for personal reasons, Doty informed me of a female child's spirit who is today making her presence known in the rooms and halls of the building. I hope

Doty's story will offer another evidential twist to whatever precon-
ceived ideas you might have regarding museum workers and their
vocation.

— Antonio

"In 1991, I began my employment as a day laborer at the Museum of
Indian Arts & Culture Laboratory of Anthropology. My duty at the time
was to organize and make sense of the anthropological lab, as it was in
desperate need of a thorough makeover. Prior to arriving in Santa Fe,
I was employed as Assistant Curator of Collections at Arizona's State
Museum.

Today my title is Assistant Curator of Archaeological Research Collections. Let be begin my story by giving you a little history of the lab and
building. Founded in 1928, the building's construction was completed
in 1930.

During that the time there existed a political conflict between the museum and the lab. Understand that the Anthropological Lab was independent of the museum.

The lab was owned and was supported by the Rockefeller family. At the
time, both archeologists, Jesse L. Nusbaum (1887-1975) and Alfred Vincent Kidder (1885-1963) were the administrators of the lab. That picture
of the two was taken in the year, 1907. The building when constructed
was actually built upon the original Santa Fe Trail, meaning it is situated
today astride the historic Santa Fe Trail.

"From 1915 to 1929, Kidder conducted site excavations at an abandoned pueblo in Pecos, near Santa Fe. He excavated levels of human
occupation at the pueblo going back more than 2000 years, and gathered a detailed record of cultural artifacts, including a large collection of
pottery fragments and human remains. From these items, he was able to
establish a continuous record of pottery styles from 2000 years ago to
the mid to late 1800s. Kidder then analyzed trends and changes in pottery styles in association with changes in the Pecos people's culture and
established a basic chronology for the Southwest.

With Samuel J. Guernsey, he established the validity of a chronological

Jesse L. Nusbaum and Alfred Vincent Kidder. In 1931, Nusbaum took leave from the NPS to develop the Laboratory of Anthropology, part of the Museum of New Mexico, in Santa Fe. He continued to serve as advisor to the Secretary of the Interior and Interior bureaus on archeological issues, and his title was modified to reflect this relationship, becoming 'consulting archeologist,' thus, modifying the title to the one still used today, Departmental Consulting Archeologist (DCA). By 1935, Nusbaum had returned to the NPS and held positions at Mesa Verde and the NPS office in Santa Fe, as well as serving as DCA, until the end of his long career in 1957. Following his retirement, he continued his involvement in archeology as an independent consultant until his death at age 88 in 1975.

approach to cultural periods. Kidder asserted that deductions about the development of human culture could be obtained through a systematic examination of stratigraphy and chronology in archaeological sites. This research laid the foundation and has become New Mexico's state repository, housing millions of artifacts. Generally, if it's dug up in the state, it eventually ends up housed here. For example, see those items sitting on that table over there? Well, those items were dug up at an excavation in 1974 at the Santa Fe Plaza, Palace of the Governors. As you can see, there is pottery, nails, and porcelain, from Santa Fe's Spanish era. Additionally, twine and cordage fashioned by native hands that has been collected is dated to be over 2,000 years. Pioneering archaeologists in other regions of the United States completed the transformation of professional methodology initiated by Kidder.

Like many other archeological parks in the Southwest, Bandelier National Monument was excavated before the National Park Service existed. Edgar L. Hewett was the most important early excavator and one of the few who made any record of his work. Beginning in the summer of 1897, he led a group that surveyed the Frijoles Canyon ruins. Hewett dug at Otowi in 1905, and in 1907 initiated work in Frijoles Canyon.

The lab building has both a basement and sub-basement. My office, where we are currently seated is the level of the first basement. I first knew something was unusually strange when soon after beginning my employment; I noticed that my trash can was not being emptied. When I asked the staff why, I was told that the maintenance personnel were afraid to enter my office during the night hours. Without hesitation, I was given the simple explanation, 'The basement and your office are haunted!' I did not recall ever being told in a direct conversation, or being informed prior to being hired, of any unusual activity regarding ghosts or spirits at the lab. However, one evening after hours, myself together with the museum's security staff met at a bar for a few beers. One of the security officers spoke in detail of witnessing spirit activity, and included similar accounts shared by fellow security staff. I made a mental note of the stories and eventually wrote them down. I've been recording all the stories I've heard about strange paranormal going-ons here ever since.

The main areas of the building where most of the occurrences of un-explained activity are frequently reported are within the library, base-ment, the boiler room and the small apartment. Once in 1991, we had a high-ranking administrator visit the lab and decide to stay at the apart-ment. The apartment that is located in the basement of the building is not that easy to get to. To reach the apartment you need to walk through the collections room, a small hallway, and through the boiler room.

Well, one night during this administrator's stay, he reported being awakened from a deep sleep by a very loud argument, or as he described to the security staff, the sound of an all-out, drag-out, violent, physical alter-cation taking place in the apartment!

He also let it be known that being con-

Alfred Vincent Kidder.

cerned for his safety, he had a loaded gun and would not hesitate to shoot first and ask questions later. The police were called and no evidence of an intruder or of a fight was ever discovered.

The unexplained movement of furniture has also been reported to occur on the first floor on the north side of the building; such as chairs and tables moving at various times of the day and night.

The building was meant to house a large and growing collection of American Indian arts and crafts such as pottery, baskets, weavings, etc. I was once informed of an incident regarding the Anthropology lab and the ghost of a little old, grey haired lady.

One evening, as a wine and cheese event was taking place at the lab, an older woman dressed head to toe in black, entered from the outside and walked among the guests. By her movement she apparently knew the lay of the building because she was observed meandering through the guests and eventually made her way to the room where our collections are housed.

Quietly, she was pursued close behind by a security staff member. As the staff member followed this strange woman into the secured room, he reported that she abruptly disappeared, was nowhere to be found and never seen again. There is a stairway, which leads to the basement where many historical artifacts are housed and catalogued. Let's now take a short walk over there.

This is the basement where at one time there were literally stacks of cardboard boxes filled with artifacts. These boxes were stacked on top of each other to the point that they actually reach the ceiling. In previous years, some of the boxes even held human remains that were gathered by way of excavating Indian sites, but that policy has since changed. We no longer do this.

Today, our policy is to house human remains off-site of this building. We used to have a collection of religious mural paintings that pertained to spiritual Native American sites, such as kivas.

Again, today these also have been removed and are housed elsewhere. It took a lot of hours and hard work to re-organize this large storage room. But as you can see, today it is well organized and everything is properly catalogued, as it should be.

Also in the past, that hand-cranked elevator located at one end of the room was
used to move heavy objects between the
upper and lower floor levels. It's a dinosaur, to be sure. Because of its iron cogs
and wheels, it reminds me of something
that would have been used in a torture
chamber many years ago. Admittedly,
when needed, it must have certainly gotten the job done.

I do want to make sure you see something else. The closet you see here is con-

sidered by our staff to be the 'center of unpleasantness.' It also gives me
the creeps! I know of individuals who refuse to come down here because
of this very closet. I was told by maintenance staff that, 'If I go down
there, that 'thing' in the closet will get me!' They didn't go into any details or explanation regarding the 'thing' but I could tell that they clearly
had one because of their reaction.

When you pay a visit to our research library, you'll note that it's located at the top floor just left of the main entrance. Let's now take a walk
over there. Security staff has told me of numerous instances when after
locking up the building and turning off the lights they would witness
'moving' lights, dancing within the building, and in particular within the
area of the library!

The security service staff for the building used to have a terrible time
with our motion sensors. The sensors would go off constantly. They
would have to quickly respond to these alarms and as you might guess,
they would discover nothing out of place and nothing to cause the alarms
to malfunction. I had three guards confide in me that at different times,
usually at the end of the day, they would hear a loud discussion between
women taking place at the basement of the building. The sound of these
women would travel as if the women were walking about the building
making their way up to where the museum guards were located on the

Original hand-cranked elevator.

first floor.

As soon as the voices of the women reached the doorway where the men stood, the voices abruptly stopped! One guard named Pete, described to me how, after hearing the voices; he quickly walked to the top of the stairs, where he had a clear view of the stairwell leading to the basement. As soon as he glanced down the stairs, he heard the voices move from the stairwell, reverse direction, then disappeared into another room! Of course, Pete and the other security staff would investigate the origin of the voices, but again, nothing would be discovered.

Another incident I'll describe, pertains to a lab staff member who happened to be a Native American man from the San Felipe Pueblo. He related to us that as he would begin the drive from his home to the lab, he would 'get spiritual messages' from his dead ancestors that would caution him not to go to work due to the lab being a 'bad place.' He didn't go into detailed description as to how he would receive the messages, but he was steadfast on this.

Speaking of American Indian spirits, another frequent report from our security staff involves the sighting of the ghost of an Indian. He materializes with such a frequency that we all refer to him as 'the big Indian.' He is always seen in a crouched dancing position. One guard was so startled to see him that he even drew his gun on the spirit! The guard encountered the spirit as the guard was walking down a hallway and turned the corner. Spotting the big Indian, and not knowing this was a spirit, the guard demanded he stop! When the spirit paid him no heed, the guard drew his gun and again demanded he stop in his tracks! The guard stated that the Indian who was very large in stature, turned to face the guard, gave him a very grumpy look, then preceded to disappear by walking right through the wall!

Another employee who happened to be a 24-hour live-in staff janitor, had his own apartment located in one wing of the basement. He reported seeing the ghost of an Indian man who at different times, would appear to him sitting at the foot of his bed.

One security guard stated that as he was responding to one of the motion alarms that was triggered, making his way through the basement, a 12' by 6' very heavy wood table actually moved on its own, blocking his access to the short hallway that leads to the boiler room! The table physically moved across the floor and came to a stop directly in front of him! The actual table is still stored down in the basement, exactly at the spot where it has stood for many years. Needless to say, he was quite alarmed and made the decision to get the heck out of there.

He scrambled his way up to the main floor when he noticed that the short wooden gate between the main room and the hallway was actually moving back and forth on its own. It appeared as if an invisible hand was pushing it! I have also had others directly report to me witnessing the unexplained movement of this small wooden gate as it swings back and forth on its own. Keep in mind, that throughout all this, the security guard was the only person in the building at the time!

It is well known among the staff that spirits frequent the boiler room. One reported incident states that the door to the boiler room once opened on its own, and as a work man was standing within the door jam, a very cold breeze passed through the now opened doorway and suddenly closed with a loud, 'slam!' The guy was fortunate to get out of the way in time, or else he would have had quite a bruise, maybe even possibly could have lost a finger or two!

I've been told by a few staff members that work at the Museum of American Indian Art and Culture, located directly next to the Anthropology Lab, of its haunted nature. You'd have to speak with staff from that museum for their stories. I bet you'd receive some very interesting responses.

As an anthropologist, fellow associates have shared instances of strange unexplained occurrences that have taken place

Short swinging wood doors.

Boiler room.

when at a digging site. One story in particular involved an archeologist who was asleep one night within a tent he had pitched at the site. He mentioned being suddenly awakened by the sound of crying children. He opened the tent's door to peer outside expecting to see someone, but didn't see a living soul.

Stories like these, experienced by fellow anthropologists are not as uncommon as you might think. I was once at a conference in the Pecos area located east of Santa Fe, which took place in the 1970's. There were some paleontologists who were also present. They described to me their experience when excavating within a cave. The cave was located next to the Zuni pueblo in the Malpais area. Their purpose was to excavate Pleistocene megafauna, or pre-historic animal remains. Suddenly, during their work they began to hear the sound of a woman singing; singing what they described to resemble antiquated Mexican songs.

Again, my own personal experience has given me much to believe that ghosts do exist. I don't doubt for one instance that there is an afterlife and that ghosts or spirits are very much a part of this life. I also believe that animals too have spirit, which carry on after they have died. I can recall my own experience I had as a young child, when my dog visited me sometime after its death.

As for the lab being haunted, no doubt this place gets very creepy. I don't find myself working here at night and neither would anyone else if they had any good sense!"

TELLURIDE, CO

The picturesque town of Telluride is located at an altitude of 8,745 feet, at the base of the inspiring San Juan Mountains. Lying within a glacial canyon, Telluride's emergence from a rough and tumble mining town to its present prominence as a home to celebrities, artists, and skiers is without doubt, quite an exceptionally story. Nestled in an area of natural beauty and Victorian charm, Telluride is host to numerous, festivals, celebrations, and definitely much visited by both U.S. skiers and internationally acclaimed sport professionals. A well-known, not-to-be-missed outdoor amphitheater celebration that takes place each June is the Telluride Bluegrass Festival.

Telluride is situated within an immense, towering box canyon, a location that is not soon forgotten. The first

Main Street Telluride.

non-Native Americans to move into the area were miners. They first set foot in the canyon in the 1870s. In 1963, Telluride was listed as a National Historic Landmark District. Much of the town falls within this listing, including residential neighborhoods, Main Street, the Lone Tree Cemetery, a warehouse area, and a very well known "red-light" district.

One interesting structure in town is the New Sheridan Hotel, which was built in the late 1800s, on the corner of Colorado Avenue and Oak Street. This building is just one example of a style of architecture common to Telluride's main district. The two-story hotel underwent a major change since its original building date in 1892, to 1899 when a third story was added. Amazing as it may seem today, beds in the hotel went for the princely sum of 50 cents but if you wanted sheets, an extra 25 cents was added, and only five people were allowed on one bed at a time!

Historic Red Light District as it looks today, minus the ladies.

Because of the rugged and steep terrain found in and about the area, the outdoor activities visitors may wish to partake in are numerous and some can be hair-raising. One waterfall named Bridal Veil Falls, at 425 feet, is listed as Colorado's largest, and is located just minutes away from town. For additional recommendations to all local points of interests, visit the Telluride Historical Museum, located right in Telluride's historic district.

MIRIAM SAGAN'S STORY

There are some people that I've interviewed who are hesitant to speak of their experiences. Ghosts frighten them, and they frankly want nothing to do with them. Miriam is one of those individuals. With this in mind, I will mention as little of our interview as possible. After reading her story and her experiences, you'll understand why.

— Antonio

"I first came to Telluride in 1995, arriving from Oklahoma City, and immediately fell in love with the town. No humidity, and the cleanest mountain air I'd ever experienced—this was what I was searching for. I was also recently recovering from my recent separation from a terrible marriage, so this new start was what I was very much looking forward to.

Within the month, I found employment at the New Sheridan Hotel where I worked for eight months in housekeeping services. I left after working for this short amount of time, when I needed to return to Oklahoma to finalize my divorce settlement and take care of other matters. I sold my house in Oklahoma and with that money I returned to Telluride, and bought a small home on the north side of town.

My first experience with a ghost in Telluride happened when I initially began my work at the hotel. At the time, myself and another maid were working on the second floor, cleaning rooms. I was in one room and

the other housekeeper was working in another room, down the hall. After cleaning the bathroom, I walked out to the hall to my supply cart, to get a few bars of soap. I immediately noticed an elderly man slowly walking out from one of the rooms I had just made up. He was short, thin and wore dark-colored clothes and a small hat.

What struck me immediately was that the door the man had just walked out of was closed and locked! I personally had just made up that room and locked the door when I moved on to the next room.

I stared at the man as he walked down the hall away from me, and watched in shock as he passed straight through a door and disappeared! This took place at about 10 a.m. The day was sunny, and the hallway was not at all dark. As soon as I saw this man 'fade' through the door, I screamed the other maid's name! She came running from out of a room, near the same area where the man had disappeared. I told her what I had seen and she told me that she also had her own ghost experiences. At the time, she wasn't comfortable reporting this to management, or even talking about it with anyone else. But she definitely had what she called a visit from a ghost.

She said that she had heard a man's voice in two separate unoccupied rooms twice before, but remained quiet about it. At the time of her experiences, she was only focusing on cleaning the rooms and nothing more. Then after a few seconds, she began to hear singing. The male voice began singing, "Rosemarie, why don't you dance with me, Rosemarie." She stopped what she was doing, look all about the room but did not see anyone. She even walked out into the hallway, and all was silent and still. Not another living soul in sight. This happened to her during the late morning on two other occasions. The ghost never appeared to her, and she never felt in danger, it just sang its playful song.

Another common experience she remembers is the sound of a man clearing his throat from an unoccupied guestroom she knows is vacant.

I felt comforted by her experiences, knowing my imagination was not on "overdrive," but I was not comfortable with, and definitely did not enjoy, having a firsthand experience of the ghost figure. I never wanted this, or any spirit to appear to me ever again. But this wasn't up to me because just a few months later, I had a second, then a third encounter.

I left a performance late one night at the Sheirdan Opera House, and decided to take a walk down Fir Street. I was only about a block away

I was only a block away when I approached a building with a long metal roof.

when I approached an old building with long metal roof. The building I later discovered is historic, and named the Stronghouse. The Stronghouse has a long porch that runs the length of the building. Under this porch I spotted a couple, who I assumed were arguing because at one point, from where I stood, I watched as the man took hold of the woman's shoulders and pushed her over the short porch railing! I yelled out, "Hey stop it!" I drop the coffee I had just purchased, and ran towards the couple. At that hour of the night, I was the only person on the street, so I knew I had to be careful.

Strangely, I never heard either of them make a sound, and she didn't even let out a scream when he pushed her over the railing. I kept my distance as I crossed the street and yelled again at them, "I'm calling the police!" I reached for my cell phone and as I glanced down to dial 9-1-1, I noticed that she got up, stumbled, and then once again, fell to the ground. The man threw himself upon her and again I yelled out for him to stop. As I screamed a few cuss words, I was fumbling to press the numbers on my phone. Everything was happening so quickly, and I was in such a hurry to get help that I had forgotten to turn my phone on.

I pressed the button on my phone to turn it on, and rushed over to where a car was parked on the street, physically keeping it between me and this couple. When I got as close as I could to where they were, they were gone! They had totally disappeared! I got goosebumps all over my body. I knew instantly that they were ghosts. They had made no noise, even though they were having quite a fight, they never made a sound. I cautiously walked

around all sides of the building and didn't see anyone on the ground, in a doorway or even inside. The building has no other structures where a person could hide, just a parking lot without any obstructions. It didn't take me long to realize that I had just seen not one, but two, ghosts!

The third time I witnessed ghosts in town took place on another evening. I was walking down San Juan Street, then turned to walk east until I arrived at Pine, then continued walking north. I was making my way to Pacific Avenue, and eventually to Colorado Avenue where most of the town's activity is. As I arrived on Pine Street I noticed a strangely dressed woman in a long black dress standing at the door of the Pick and Gad building. All she did was stare at me as I walked past her. I didn't want to stop because something within me, intuition I imagine, told me this woman seemed completely out of place, possibly someone with evil intentions, and I needed to move away from.

The woman was short in stature and her facial expression was stern and cold. The fact that she wore her hair pulled back and pinned up in a bun didn't help her matronly appearance. As I passed her, I saw her big, black eyes just staring at me. Her stare really creeped me out and I could tell this woman was up to no good. Without us speaking a word, I got that negative 'vibe' feeling from her. I'd never seen anyone like her in town before. I wondered, what was she doing at that hour of the night, standing under the porch like that, and without saying a word to me? She really did scare me, and given what I had just experienced weeks be-

fore, with the ghost couple fighting under that porch and in the street, just gave me the energy to run until I made it on to Colorado Avenue.

After I had gone a few feet, I glanced behind me and sure enough, she had disappeared! There were no cars where she could

Pick & Gad building.

have jumped behind, and hide. In less than a few seconds right after I passed, I turned back to look for her, but she was gone!

These have been the three ghost encounters that I've had in Telluride, but they have definitely left me feeling awful. I don't feel good about them. People whom I've told my story to stated that I should be happy knowing I was given the gift to see ghosts. Well, I certainly don't believe this is any kind of gift and don't ever want to see ghosts-like ever again! I'm afraid of ghosts and I don't believe they want to help me. They just want to scare me, and they've sure succeeded in doing that!

I spoke to a woman in town about a month after my experiences that describes herself as a spiritual-channeler. She told me that I am the type of person who "draws spirits" to me. I told her that I want nothing to do with them. She said, "It doesn't matter what you want, they will follow you and make themselves known to you any time, day or night."

Personally, I feel they all need to stay in the graveyards, away from the living. Now, because I've told you my stories, and you're going to put them in a book, I hope this doesn't aggravate them, I don't want to come looking for me just because I'm telling you about them. My nerves can't take it. I've had enough of them!"

TRINIDAD, CO

Trinidad, a Victorian and adobe city with a population of about 15,000 is nestled among hilly streets, and the confluence of the banks of the Purgatoire River and Raton Creek. The Mountain Branch of the Santa Fe Trail was no doubt the major factor in Trinidad's existence, as it lies at an elevation of 6,025 feet, and enjoys a four-season climate. Conveniently, Interstate 25 runs directly through Trinidad's historic center. Old Downtown Trinidad was also designated as Corazon de Trinidad National Historic District. Many of the truly splendid buildings within Trinidad's Corazon de Trinidad National Historic district were built with cattle money from the famous Prairie Land & Cattle Company.

Historically, Native Americans, Spanish Conquistadors, and French trappers all have left their legacy within the area. Prehistoric peoples also added richness to the area, adding their unique petroglyphs and artifacts. In addition, fossils that include the longest-known set of dinosaur tracks in the world can be found in the Trinidad area.

In 1876, the city was officially incorporated. The historic Santa Fe Trail, a noteworthy trade route, proved to be a superior trail of commerce between the three cultures, Indian, Hispanic and Anglo. Trinidad can boast both the famous and infamous as some of its past residents. These would include Billy the Kid, Bat Masterson, Casimiro Barela, Kit Carson, Doc Holiday, and Uncle Dick Wootton.

In 1862, coal was discovered in the nearby hills and immediately the call for a labor force to extract this valuable reserve went out throughout the U.S. and as far away as Europe. Europeans were ideally sought due to their history of being well trained and skilled in the mining trade. Thus, today in Trinidad it would not be uncommon to meet a citizen who can directly trace their ancestry to a diversity of European nationalities such as Greek, Irish, Italian, Lebanese, Polish, Slavic, and other northern Europeans.

Today, Trinidad's economy is still sustained by the important economic focal points of mining coal, farming, ranching, and natural gas production. Tourism is a welcome boon to the community as are Trinidad's top-notch community of artists.

LUDLOW MASSACRE

The Ludlow massacre of April 20, 1914, was one of the bloodiest assaults on organized labor in American history. As a result, 20 people were killed, including a dozen women and children. It took place in Ludlow, Colorado, (today a ghost town) northwest of Trinidad, and was the climax of an effort to suppress a strike by 12,000 coal miners.

Labor unrest in the United States in the years pre-

IN MEMORY OF

THE MEN, WOMEN AND CHILDREN.
WHO LOST THEIR LIVES
IN FREEDOM'S CAUSE
AT LUDLOW, COLORADO
APRIL 20. 1914.

ERECTED BY THE
UNITED MINE WORKERS OF AMERICA.

ceding World War I was particularly tense in the West. When a union activist was killed in the fall of 1913, workers at the Colorado Fuel and Iron Corporation's (CF&I) coal operations and other Colorado coalmines went on strike. The miners evacuated the coal mining camps on September 23 to protest low wages ($1.68 a day) and poor working conditions. Contrary to state law, miners were paid in scrip, which was redeemable only at the company store, where prices were high. Miners were cheated at the scales where the coal they dug was weighed. Many mines maintained two separate systems of weights: one for the miners' transactions, and another for the coal buyers.

In Colorado's mines, "dead work" was not paid. Dead work included timbering the mine for safety. The death rate of Colorado miners was approximately twice the national average. Miners frequently complained that company mules were treated far better than their human counterparts. Years after cave-ins and mine explosions, miners' anecdotes recount the first words of the coal operators when a mine collapsed: "Did the mules get out?"

Colorado miners had attempted to unionize periodically since the first strike in 1883. First it was with the Western Federation of Miners. Later (in 1927) they would join the Industrial Workers of the World. In 1913 they attempted to organize themselves into the United Mine Workers of America. The UMWA had demanded: "...recognition of the United Mine Workers of America as the bargaining agent for workers in coal mines throughout Colorado and northern New Mexico; an effective system of checkweighmen in all mines; compensation for digging coal at a ton-rate based on 2,000 pounds; semi-monthly payment of wages in lawful money; the abolition of scrip and the truck system; an end to discrimination against union members; and strict enforcement of state laws pertaining

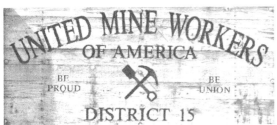

to operators' obligations in supplying miners with timbers, rails, and other materials in underground working places."

The strike provoked a

harsh response from the Rockefeller family, who controlled Colorado Fuel & Iron and effectively ruled the region. Since the companies owned the towns where the workers lived, they were able to evict strikers from their homes, leaving women and children, mostly from immigrant families, without shelter as the harsh Rocky Mountain winter approached.

Helped by UMWA groups across the country, the strikers were able to organize tent cities and carried on their strike. The union selected locations near the mouths of the canyons that led to the coal camps. Their purpose was monitoring traffic to the coal camps and discouraging replacement workers from breaking the strike.

The company hired the Baldwin-Felts Detective Agency to harass strikers and union organizers. Baldwin-Felts had a reputation for aggressive strike breaking. They supplied armed guards, gunmen, spies, and agents provocateurs to intimidate the miners. CF&I built an armored car mounted with a machine gun. The company guards called it the "Death Special." Because of occasional sniping on the tent colonies, miners dug protective pits beneath the tents where they and their families could seek shelter.

On October 17, Baldwin-Felts agents used the armored car to attack the Forbes tent colony. One miner was killed. A young girl was shot in the face, and a boy was hit in the legs by nine machine gun bullets. Confrontations between striking miners and "scab" replacement workers often got out of control, resulting in additional deaths.

Despite widespread violence, the workers refused to give in. On October 28, Colorado governor Elias M. Ammons called in the National Guard. The Rockefellers supplied the Guards' wages. The miners believed at first that the Guard was sent to protect them, but they soon discovered that they had come to destroy the strike. Even though the campaign of harassment increased and many of the organizers were beaten and arrested, the miners persevered through the winter.

It had been a difficult time for the strikers. Harassing rifle shots were randomly fired into the camps. Union organizers were kidnapped and intimidated. One tactic was to tell the union men that they were about to be executed and to force them to "dig their own graves" before beating

them and, finally, ordering them out of the territory.

After months of stalemate, Governor Ammons was growing concerned about the cost of keeping the National Guard in the field. He accepted an offer by the coal companies to put their men into National Guard uniforms.

Under the leadership of Lieutenant Karl Linderfelt, Company B of the Colorado National Guard stuffed barbed wire into the water wells of the tent colonies. They threatened miners and their families. Linderfelt told one immigrant miner that he was "Jesus Christ on horseback" and that he must be obeyed.

On March 10, 1914, the body of a strikebreaker was found on the railroad tracks near Forbes. The National Guard's General Chase ordered the Forbes tent colony destroyed in retaliation. Tension was growing, and the stage was set for all-out war.

The acting National Guard troops decided to evict the tent cities that sprang up around the mines, even though the camps had been established on private property leased by the union. Ludlow was the largest of the tent cities, located 18 miles north of Trinidad. On the morning of April 20, the day after Greek Easter celebrated by many Greek immigrants in the Ludlow camp, the troops opened fire with machine guns. They fired across the railroad tracks into the tents. Anyone who moved through the camp was targeted. The miners fired back, and the fighting raged on for hours.

In the afternoon, a passing freight train stopped on the tracks, allowing many of the miners and their families to escape to the east to an outcrop of hills called the "Black Hills." Louis Tikas, the camp's main union organizer went to the National Guardsmen to arrange a truce. Lieutenant Linderfelt assaulted him with the butt of his rifle, and the soldiers fired three shots into Tikas's back as he lay on the ground. As night approached, the militia descended on the tent camp and set fire to it. Two women and 11 children had been hiding in the pit beneath one tent and burned to death. When their charred bodies were found the next day, their deaths became a rallying cry for the UMWA, who called the incident the "Ludlow Massacre." In addition to the fire victims, 13 people were shot dead during that day.

GREGORY JOSEPH'S STORY

Gregory and I met at the Ludlow Massacre Site for the interview. He seemed very concerned throughout the interview, taking parting glances over my shoulder and turning around to possibly catch a ghost or see something unusual. Because I knew his discomfort was causing him obvious distress, I chose to make the interview a concise and brief one. Gregory's personal ghost experience was not a pleasant one for him. He has made great strides in coming to grips with actually having been visited by a ghost, but he still struggles with the knowledge that ghosts do in fact exist, and can cause distress.

— Antonio

"I've lived in Trinidad most of my life. My parents moved to Trinidad when I was seven weeks old. We moved from Pendleton, Oregon in 1952. During the years that I attended elementary and secondary public school, and during the time I was in high school, all my classmates heard about, and shared, the stories of ghosts in the area.

One evening I, and a group of friends, on a teenage whim decided to go on a ghost hunt into the local cemetery, but never did see anything close to a spirit. We just got drunk, using the excuse of a ghost hunt to get away from our parents' prying eyes. Not that they would have approved of our plan to enter a cemetery, but just to have a somewhat legitimate excuse to sneak away for a few hours. One night, close to 30 years ago, that all changed.

One year, my girlfriend's cousin Otto, who lived in Iowa, decided to visit her during Christmas school break. Otto and I got along well, and one day, I happened to mention to him about the Ludlow Massacre Site. Immediately he wanted to visit it. I myself hadn't visited the site for a number of years, but as it is when you have a visitor, and particular an out-of-state one, you feel obliged to share your town's interesting points of interests. I do remember that it was a cold winter day, and the wind was blowing a bit, however there was no snow on the ground. That evening we decided to drive the few miles north of town to visit the site.

As we were approaching the monument, we noticed there was an older gentleman standing by the chain link fence that surrounds the site. He was odd looking, dressed as he was, and appeared to be a homeless person. As I drove the car nearer, he began gesturing to us by waving his hands, inviting us on to the grounds. Given the very cold weather that must have deterred visitors, ours was the only car in the dirt parking lot.

After parking the car, we put on our jackets, got out and didn't even bother to lock it. It didn't take any longer than a few seconds to put on our jackets. Strangely, anticipating that the old guy would come right up to us, he was nowhere in sight. He was gone! One minute he was at the gate, then had just disappeared from the area. He just disappeared!

We looked at each other and wondered aloud, how strange this was. Even stranger was that we also noticed the non-stop barking of a dog in the distance. Although we never did see it, the dog's barking just kept up in the distance somewhere out of sight.

We walked around the grounds, and walked over to the open pit where the strikers and their families, in years past, had been burned to death. If you can imagine how eerie the area was at the time, with the cold wind blowing, the barking of the dog in the distance, and the older looking man who had disappeared at the gate, and now as we stood where so many people had been burned to death, you might be able to get a glimpse of how strangely eerie the whole atmosphere was.

We walked up to the tall stone monument that the miners' union had erected at the site, and read the inscription. Just a short time later we decided to leave the area and head back to town. Never catching any sight of, as we had named him, the "gate keeper" who had disappeared. In just a short time after we had driven out of the area, the weather tuned very snowy, and we were glad to have finally gotten home without any trouble. Later that night after having gone to bed, I had the strangest dream.

I dreamt that I was back at the massacre site. I was walking in a counter-clockwise circle around the open pit, and was being followed by the old guy who we had seen at the site when we drove up. In my dream, I kept walking and attempted to pick up my speed in order to get away from the man, but as much as I wanted to, my legs would not increase the pace. Slowly the man was gaining on me and I knew instinctively that he was not a positive force to tangle with. Within a second, the man had caught up with me. As soon as I felt his presence behind me, I suddenly awoke from my dream.

As I lay in bed, with my eyes wide open, staring at the ceiling, I caught the smell of something musty and old. As this disagreeable scent grew stronger, I began to feel uneasy and then the sudden, loud, startling sound of my closet door slamming shut caused me to jump, and made me sit up in bed!

I looked in the direction of the closet, I spotted the clear image of an older man fitting the description of the guy at the site, standing in my room! I gave out a loud yell, that more resembled a little girl's scream! He turned his head away from me then completely vanished!

I spent the rest of the night wide-awake on the couch in the living room, with the television on. Later, towards morning, I finally did fall asleep, but I could not forget everything I heard and saw.

Around 11a.m., I finally did relay the dream and ghost encounter with my girlfriend. She told me that perhaps the spirit visited me because he wanted us to be more respectful toward the people who had died at the site. Maybe he was some kind of spiritual caretaker of the site. She suggested that we needed to return to the Massacre site, and leave an offering to the ones who had suffered such a horrific death.

That very day, right after we finished discussing this, my girlfriend and I returned to the site after purchasing a bouquet of flowers at the local supermarket in town. I did not want to be there in the late afternoon, and chose to arrive at the site while the sun was still very much high in the sky. Not wanting to give my girlfriend any indication of the fear I was feeling, which I definitely had, I wanted to get to the site, spend as little time as I needed to there, and then get the heck out!

After parking the car, we walked to the edge of the pit, offered the flowers to the spirits, and left the bouquet. I asked the spirits to please not pay me any further nightly visits. Being a Catholic, I crossed myself and quickly walked away to the car with my girlfriend following behind. I felt better for making the offering, and I'm glad to report that I've not had any more dreams about, or visits from, the ghost man since then.

Since that time, there have been occasions where I've spoken to other locals in town who have visited the site, and without telling them about my own experience, have gotten some very interesting responses. There exist numerous areas surrounding Trinidad where people have heard and seen ghosts. Some of these places are located in, or not very far from, town. Some are homes, while others are located within the hills to the west of town, and within the Culebra Mountains. You'll never find me going to those places. Nope, I'm done with any form of ghostly investigating."

THREE RIVERS, NM

THREE RIVERS PETROGLYPHS NATIONAL RECREATIONS SITE – LAUREN GUTIERREZ'S STORY

Sometimes when we least expect to encounter a ghost, they might make their presence known in the daylight, symbolically in the form of an animal or even in a hotel room. Such was the case of Lauren and her husband Luis' experience. The spiritual world can be a consciously unfamiliar one for us. But that doesn't preclude us from connecting with it. Evidence to support this remains etched within native Indian culture and as is evident in the following story, literally etched in stone.

There are moments when we might encounter something so unusually weird that we are at a loss as to which way to turn. A recurring theme I've discovered among these familiar experiences is to focus on the positive and allow it to lead towards protection from the negative. Trust me, this works. As in the following story, Lauren discovered this to work well for her and her husband.

As a personal note, this area is the place from where my very own Apache great grandmother named 'Little Stars' or 'Little Crosses' described as being the originating homelands of she and my very own ancestors.

— Antonio

"Originally, I'm from Los Angeles and I've been living in Albuquerque for two years. In 1991, my husband Luis and I who are both originally from the Morongo reservation in California, were vacationing in New Mexico when we decided to take pictures and hike around the southeastern area of the state. The Morongo reservation is seated at the foot of the San Gorgonio and San Jacinto Mountains overlooking the Banning Pass. Luis' reservation extends more than 35,000 acres and was at one time one of nine small reservations set aside by President Grant by executive order in 1865. The Morongo reservation also has one of the oldest and most successful Indian gaming facilities in California.

We hadn't made the permanent move to New Mexico, so this trip was to tour the state and take in as much of the sites as our time permitted. We had just visited Carlsbad Caverns, which was spectacular. It was then we decided to take a drive up north from Las Cruces on Highway 70.

Our destination was Albuquerque and we decided to make the drive north and stop at Three Rivers for a few hours. The time of year for our trip was in the month of July, knowing that the weather was going to be quite hot, I brought along plenty of bottled water and sunscreen.

Arriving at the park, we loaded our backpacks with plenty of supplies for the hike and took off! The area was a wonderful place to view rock art up close. Luis took photos of most every bird, lizard and natural abstract design imaginable.

We both were very impressed by all the ancient art that was literally at our feet; surrounding us everywhere we looked!

I decided to walk over to a small ridge and investigate the area for more art. As I reached the ridge I was drawn to another ridge located a distance from where I was standing. I informed Luis to take his time photographing. Luis' lifelong goal was to be known as one of the world's best photographers. The year before our southwest trip he spent six months studying this art form in London England, living and learning at a renowned photography school. The Morongo reservation provided him with a few extra dollars for this endeavor.

But I was at the moment going to make the hike over to the distant ridge. Having to scramble and maneuver over the sharp volcanic formations with both hands and feet was a bit more than I was prepared for, but eventually I did reach the ridge. Admittedly, I was unprepared for the unusual surprise I was too soon encounter. Immediately as I looked around, I realized that I had stumbled upon unusual depictions of weird looking symbols, representing faces with wide screaming mouths and bodies having what looked to me to be 'claw-like' arms and legs. In all the times that I've come across ancient art on rocks walls, I'd never encountered such bizarre looking symbols. If I'd brought my own camera, I would have taken a few pictures of these but, I had counted on Luis with his own camera to be the photographer, and unfortunately he was quite some distance away.

I was captivated by these unusual depictions of who knows what, as I carefully walked among them. The area is known to have an abundance of rattlesnakes, so admittedly I was carefully making my way through the

rocks and brush. But wouldn't you know it; I soon heard the 'buzzing' sound of what could only be a rattlesnake! I froze in place and turned my head in the direction of the sound. Sure enough, just a few feet up ahead I spotted the snake, coiled and ready to defend itself.

Taking a few steps back, I missed a step and that's when I took my fall! With a thud, I fell right on my right thigh and rolled over on my back!

A little bloodied, I straightened up, and then sat down. The snake was a non-threatening distance away. My hat had also taken a fall off my head and landed in between two large rocks. I looked over to where Luis was and I could see the top of his head and his yellow shirt, but he was at least a half-mile from where I was. I decided to not make a scene and just do the best I could to make the return hike.

As I was seated on top of the sharp rocks, my eyes caught the sight of one large rock having a large collection of glyphs. Among these glyphs, was an unusual one that stood out from the others. All the glyphs depicted several large heads, but among these heads was one that was in the process of what appeared to be letting out a loud scream. This glyph in particular among the others, was most unusual because of the strange movement I notice taking place on its surface.

At first I didn't know what to make of it, but as I leaned in closer for a better look, I noticed that there were hundreds of bees actually crawling along the outline of the glyph! The bees were not randomly crawling all over the glyph and rock, no; they were actually following the outline of the artwork! It was so strange to witness how one bee was trailing the other like an insect 'conga line.' They were crawling, following the glyph's outline making it appear as if it were moving. I was so alarmed by this activity that I decided to get the heck out of there and fast!

I found my hat and made the strenuous return hike to the car. I was not in the most positive of attitude when Luis looked at me and asked, 'What happened to you?' I just remember almost yelling to him to help me into the front seat and then to give me a wet towel to wipe the now dried blood off my legs. However, one thing I do clearly recall saying was telling Luis that I had had enough of this place, and to get his things together because, 'We're getting out of here and heading back onto the highway!'

We arrived later that evening at Albuquerque, had dinner and then checked into a hotel for the night. Throughout the night I was visibly uncomfortable and Luis kept inquiring about my well-being. All I was able to tell him was that I felt a strangeness; a heaviness that just wouldn't go away. It was as if a heavy, hot fur coat had been placed over my body and even after I had taken a cold shower, it had no effect. I took a few aspirins and went to bed thinking this might blow over and I'd feel better in the morning.

During the night, I awoke and walked over to the large window on the tenth floor overlooking the city below. Gazing out the window into the darkness of the night, I suddenly noticed a white bird flying in the distance. My eyes were locked on this bird as it flew about the sky and then was surprised as it suddenly came fluttering over to where I was standing at the window. As soon as it came close enough for me to make out its form, I noticed what type of bird this was. It was an owl! I froze in place! As I stood at the window, the owl changed its direction and came flying directly right up to the window where I was! Fully aware of the negative implications that this symbol conveyed, when this owl came up to me I jumped back into the room and immediately woke Luis up.

We discussed the events of the day in addition to the owl, we thought it best to phone Luis's mother the following morning. She informed us that we needed to get home to the Morongo reservation as soon as possible, but before doing that, she instructed me to visit a local Catholic church and have the priest recite a blessing over me.

Oddly, I didn't feel in the least embarrassed to follow her instructions and after breakfast Luis and I found a church and priest. We met the priest after introducing ourselves to him at the church rectory office.

We were escorted into his office and there he heard our story. Without hesitation, he blessed both of us, making the sign of the cross on our foreheads. I wept a bit and thanked him. He said, 'There are many avenues which the negative force makes its presence known, but always remember that with all its power, there is one that is greater and even more powerful.'

A few years have passed since that day. Luis and I have moved from Los Angeles and now live in Albuquerque. Our lives are filled with peace and we absolutely would not change a thing. The move to New Mexico was the best thing we ever could have hoped for. And Luis is living his dream of being a professional photographer. An art gallery in the village of Corrales currently is doing well selling his work and I'm attending the University of New Mexico with a hope of graduating in three years.

Although the experience we encountered at Three Rivers Petroglyph National Recreation Site was a tormenting one, I did learn from it and came through the experience with a much more positive view of what is sacred, and the role I personally must play in making positive decisions in my life. That's what I took from that experience."

TOMBSTONE, AZ

Tombstone, in Cochise County, is probably the most famous and most glamorized mining town in America. Prospector Ed Schieffeling was told he would only find his tombstone in the "Apache-infested" San Pedro Valley and thus named his first silver claim Tombstone, and it became the name of the town.

On a mesa between the Dragoon and Huachuca Mountains at an elevation of 4,540 feet, Tombstone was incorporated in 1881.

While the area later became notorious for saloons, gambling houses, and the Earp-Clanton shootout, in the 1880s Tombstone was larger than Tucson and had become the most cultivated city in the West. Massive underground water in the mines and falling silver prices ended the boom in 1886. Having survived the Great Depression and removal of the County Seat to Bisbee, Tombstone in the 1930s became known as the "Town Too Tough to Die."

Tombstone's economy has changed drastically since its days as a mining town. The town's colorful history is the key factor in its steady growth. In 1962, Tombstone was designated a Registered Historical landmark by the Department of the Interior. A restoration zone was established and a commission organized for the preservation of its landmarks. Tourists flock to the town by the thousands, and their business is the mainstay of the economy.

Debbie K. Valdez, Teresa Rice, Tim and Macy Ferrick.

HISTORY OF BIG NOSE KATE'S SALOON

In the 1800's, "Big Nose Kate's Saloon" was once The Grand Hotel. Although the saloon itself was not in existence during Tombstone's rise to fame, it has on its own made quite a mark on Tombstone. The saloon is named after the woman who had quite a rambunctious relationship with John Henry "Doc" Holliday. Doc, a former dentist and a well-known gambler in town, never married Kate, although she remained his live-in girlfriend for many years.

This great hotel hosted such infamous personalities as Wyatt and Virgil Earp, Holliday, the Clantons, and the McLaurys.

The bar of the present saloon is located on the first floor, but originally, when it was The Grand Hotel, the bar was located downstairs in the basement. The present bar is the only Tombstone bar that is still in use to this very day.

LEGEND OF "THE SWAMPER

During the Grand Hotel's golden era, a man known as "The Swamper" who worked as a janitor also did odd jobs for the hotel in exchange for his room and board. He was a trusted and honest hotel aid. The Swamper had his own special bedroom, located in the dark basement of the hotel, which he used as his own private haven. He enjoyed the peace and solitude where, separated from the hustle and bustle of the hotel's many guests above, he could keep his secret of his silvery wealth to himself.

Throughout the years The Swamper had hoarded and concealed a small fortune of silver somewhere on the premises of The Grand Hotel. The basement where he lived was deep enough below the surface of the ground to afford entrance into one of the catacombing mine shafts that ran underground, beneath the hotel as well as beneath most of Tombstone. The Swamper spent many painstaking hours over a period of years tunneling an entrance into this silver mine shaft. Completing his task, he gained access to a thick vein of silver where he secretly extracted; ounce-by-ounce, glorious silver nuggets.

To this day it is unknown whether The Swamper spent his silver before his death or hoarded it in an unknown niche somewhere on the premises of the hotel. Employees of Big Nose Kate's Saloon however, swear that they have seen The Swamper's ghost wandering the halls and stairs. Photographers have caught the ghostly image of an unknown being on a photo as well as on the postcard of the saloon's interior.

Perhaps the Swamper in his afterlife, is protecting the silver still buried somewhere in this legendary building.

TIM L. FERRICK'S STORY

I interviewed the following employees of the present Big Nose Kate's Saloon on a very hot mid-day in July. I was thoroughly amazed by everyone's serene composure and easy-going manner as they described their stories.

At one point during the interviews, I was led down a narrow wooden staircase to the basement of the saloon where the owner, Mr. Steve Goldstein, pointed out the actual silver mine shaft from which many stories evolved, including the one of The Swamper. For safety's sake, the mineshaft can now be seen through bars of iron. Arranged around the shaft's opening is a collection of antique period furniture of the 1800s. This strange accumulation of dusty furniture, picks, shovels, mirrors, clothing, and oil lamps is made visible only by a few spooky colored light bulbs, which cast an eerie glow on what a miner's life might have looked like.

The stories of the ghosts of Tombstone's violent past will continually resurface. I present to you just a few of the testimonies from some living individuals who have been witness to weird happenings at Big Nose Kate's Saloon.

—Antonio

I am currently the manager of the saloon and have held this position for nine months. I'm originally from Southern California and have visited Arizona and Tombstone repeatedly throughout the last four years. During one of my visits to Tombstone, I visited my brother Mick, who at the time was the manager of the Saloon. He has since died and is buried at the local cemetery. Before my brother died, he mentioned to me that he had experienced "ghosts" at the saloon. About one month after his funeral, I made plans with my wife to return to Tombstone and meet with the owner of the saloon about taking over my brother's job.

We arrived at Tombstone in the late evening. The owner had closed the doors for the night, and we sat at a table at one corner of the saloon drinking sodas. We discussed a few personal issues, and for some reason, the conversation turned to the strange, ghostly things that employees have experienced at the saloon. Approximately, half an hour into our discussion, a sudden movement caught all our eyes. We all turned to look up in the direction of the ceiling of the saloon where a small balcony is located.

On the balcony were two mannequins, a man and a woman dressed in 1800s period clothing. We watched as the female mannequin, seated far behind the railing, moved to the railing of the balcony, leaned over, and fell to the floor! As we all sat in our chairs stunned by the noise of the mannequin making contact with the floor, I spotted the male mannequin facing us. I said to the others at the table, "Hey, take a look at the other mannequin." We all watched as the male mannequin's head quickly turned towards the direction where the female mannequin had been! Truly unnerved by this, we promptly got out of our chairs and called it a night.

The next morning, when I spoke to the manager, she stated that she had no explanation for what had happened. She considered it to be her first ghostly experience at the saloon.

My second experience at the saloon took place about one month after I had begun working there. It was about 7:30 a.m. when I started to hear doors opening and closing on their own. I walked to the now opened door—which I had closed and locked just minutes before from the inside—only to see it in an open position! Lights that I personally had turned off were now turned on. During these times, I was the only one in the building! Returning to my office chair, I suddenly began to hear noises coming from down in the basement where the mineshaft is located. These were the distinctive sounds of a man wearing heavy boots with spurs walking up or down the stairs. The sound was that of someone walking halfway up the stairs, then stopping in the middle.

A few times, after hearing the steps, I rushed to the stairs, hoping to catch a sight of the person making the noise. But as soon as I reached the stairs, the footsteps would abruptly stop! Sometime after these incidents, we decided to install surveillance cameras throughout the saloon. We spent several days installing the cameras in just the right locations, in key rooms of the saloon. The equipment functioned with motion detectors that would sense movement and automatically turn the cameras on to record whatever was present. These sensors were very sensitive to movement, and I was sure we would be able to record any burglar ghost on film. That night before we left the saloon, I personally turned on the motion detectors.

The next morning as I unlocked the back door and entered the building, my wife and I were shocked to see that all the cupboards, doors, refrigerator doors, and drawers were wide open! Nothing had been stolen from the premises. The alarm had not been activated, and I immediately phoned the alarm company to complain that their equipment had failed. The alarm company sent representatives over, they tested the system, and found that everything was functioning correctly.

Another experience my wife and I had one morning after I switched on the monitors that were attached to the cameras to scan each room. The camera that was placed in the dance floor of the saloon was picking up a noise. I called my wife over to the TV monitor, and as I turned up the volume, we both clearly heard the sound of booted footsteps walking across the floor! We immediately left the office and entered the dance room where we discovered nothing out of place. A few minutes later, we heard the same footsteps walking in the opposite direction. We knew that something ghostly was happening, but decided then and there to just live with it.

Throughout the years, we have had many patrons experience odd things. Just recently, I was called to witness a gentleman who was in the downstairs bar going through his own supernatural experience. I witnessed the jacket he was wearing being pressed flat against his body!

It was as if a large pane of glass was being pressed against him. His wife took a picture of her husband as he was going through the experience, and when she developed it, the large image of a butcher knife appeared floating next to his head! I must admit seeing this left me covered with goose bumps.

Other things that have taken place—strangely enough to just our female employees—have been trash can lids rising off the cans and dropping to the floor, rolling large circular patterns on the floor of the basement. This has happened several times to my own wife. My wife now refers to the ghost as "Felix." It's just a name she decided upon, to give the ghost a personality. The male employees have not experienced such things, only the women. We have since removed all the trashcans from the basement.

The current owner, Gloria Goldstein, and I heard Gloria's name being called out in a very loud, distinctive male voice. We both turned around as she responded, "Yes." There was no answer returned.

Other events patrons have experienced have been the sound of gambling dice being dropped to the floor, sudden cold winds, severe pressure changes in rooms, etc. A lot of these incidents take place randomly. Despite all this activity we have never thought much into contacting a priest to help clear out these spirits. We knew we had a ghost and that was it. I know that there is the presence of someone still here in the building. Perhaps a ghost is protecting the place. I'm not afraid, but I do let our employees feel comfortable enough to approach me with their concerns.

MARCY D. FERRICK'S STORY

My husband Tim and I began employment at the saloon at the same time. I was present in the saloon the evening that Tim has spoken about, when we had our first experience with the mannequins coming to life. I've got to say that what we experienced, that night with those mannequins, was enough to send us out of there fast!

My second experience with "Felix" happened when I was in the basement. As I entered the basement, suddenly the lid on the trash can popped off and began to roll on the floor. The lid made small circular movements, and then they got bigger and bigger. It just kept moving until I took hold of it and placed it back on the can. Then once more it popped off and repeated the same circular motions on the floor. Again, I took hold of the lid and placed it on the can. Well, this happened about five times until I had had enough. In a loud, irritated voice I said, "Stop it now!" Then it stopped. I think that "Felix" is trying to harass or tease the women. I don't get the feeling that he wants to hurt us, just wants to let us know that he is still around.

Just a couple of months ago, we had two patrons who were very drunk disturbing other patrons with their loud voices. I decided to ask them to leave. When I approached the table, I immediately felt the strong pressure of an invisible male hand on my shoulder. Before I had even said a word, the two drunks gazed with very wide eyes in the direction past my shoulder, and immediately put their beers on the table, got up, and made for the door! In that moment, I felt the pressure on my shoulder slowly lift up and disappear.

Another strange thing that happens is when I walk down the stairs to the basement. Sometimes I'll notice that the ceiling fan is turning. Thinking that it has been left on, I'll reach for the electrical switch and notice that it is in the "off" position! I'm at a loss to find an explanation for this. We have had the switches checked and have found nothing wrong with the electrical system. Given all that the other employees and I have experienced in the saloon, I am convinced that it is haunted!

I still hear the very distinct footsteps of a heavy-booted and spurred man, who walks up and down the stairs that lead to the basement. I think that the reason "Felix" is so active in the saloon is because he is trapped between the world of the living and of the dead.

The first experience I had with the mannequins shocked me and yes, I was scared, but all the other experiences since have just become a nuisance to me. I'm not scared to be in the building by myself, but you never know what "he" might decide to do next time.

THERESA RICE'S STORY

I'm originally from Tyler, Texas, and have been working at the saloon for seven months as a waitress. My first experience with the ghost of the saloon happened only two weeks after I started work. It was around high noon when I was standing on the south end of the bar. I was talking to a gentleman customer who was seated across the bar from me.

Suddenly, I felt the presence of someone behind me and just as quickly, felt two fingers give my rear end two hard pinches! I immediately turned around to confront the vulgar man who had rudely done this, but when I turned there was no one there! Other employees had told me that the saloon was haunted. After this experience, I was definitely convinced of this.

My second experience happened just about two months ago. Again, this took place at about noon. I was walking toward the bar, carrying a tray of drinks. Suddenly, I heard a loud male voice call out, "Theresa!" I turned and saw no one. This has happened more than once to me, and also in the presence of others. This initially left me with a confused feeling, but soon I realized that Felix was behind it. "Felix" is the name the employees have given to what we believe to be "The Swamper."

Anyway, I knew Felix was behind everything. I don't know why he chose to play these rude-natured pranks on me. Why is he trying to provoke me? I just wish he would just come out and speak to me. I don't think I would be frightened, but maybe I might be.

DEBBIE K. VALDEZ'S STORY

I'm originally from Whiteland, Indiana, and have been working as a bartender in the second bar that's located downstairs in the basement. I also have a country music band, "Black Velvet," that performs at the saloon. So, I'm both a bartender and entertainer. I've been employed at Big Nose Kate's now for seven months. My first experience happened five months after I had begun working at the saloon. It was in the early afternoon when I happened to look up to where the mannequins were located on the balcony. I spotted a very nicely dressed woman whom I had never seen before. She was dressed in the style of the 1800s—dark dress, holding a parasol, and her hair was done up in ringlets that were shoulder length. I could not keep my eyes off this beautiful woman. As much as I stared at her, she did not look in my direction, but appeared happy to just observe everyone else down below. At one point, I turned away from her for a sec-

Debbie K. Valdez, hesitant to be downstairs alone.

ond, felt ice cold air surround me and became frightened. I looked back again for her but she had disappeared, and I have not seen her since.

Another time, I was wearing my hair pulled back and held in place with a large white bow. Well, apparently, the ghost 'Felix' wanted to play with my bow because he kept pulling on it. I turned my head several times to see who was tugging at my hair and bow but there was not a living soul anywhere. After a few hours of this I got tired of his game and I said, "Now, you stop it!" After that the hair and bow tugging stopped.

The ghost also hides my pens. I will write a guest receipt and place the pen on the cash register as I hand the receipt to the customer. I won't even leave the register and as I reach for my pen—poof—it's gone! This has happened when more than one person is with me. We looked on the floor, behind the register, everywhere! Then in a few minutes, the pen reappears right where I had originally placed it! Now, is that weird or what?

I see lights go on and off in rooms when no one else is with me. I see this quite a lot. I have also seen a gentleman sitting at the basement bar, wearing a long-sleeved white shirt. He just suddenly appears, and then just as quickly will disappear. I get the feeling that the ghost does not intend me any harm, but I always experience very cold chills when I witness these things. The ghost is a playful spirit, and knowing this, I don't like to be left alone in the basement bar. If we have no patrons down below, I'll just walk upstairs to be with someone. I'm not scared, just a little nervous to be alone down there.

YUMA, AZ

Yuma is in the far southwest corner of Arizona, just below where the Colorado and Gila Rivers converge. Since prehistoric times, Yuma has been the best site for crossing the Colorado River. Yuma was named after the Yuman tribe, so called because of their habit of setting fires along the river (humo meaning smoke in Spanish). Fort Yuman was built during the gold rush to establish an Anglo presence in the area and to ensure a southern route into California.

First established in 1854 as Colorado City, the town became Arizona City and finally Yuma Incorporated under the name Arizona City in 1871, it was reincorporated as Yuma in 1873 and now serves as the Yuma County seat. At an elevation of 138 feet, Yuma remains a crossroad for air and land transportation, although steamboats no longer carry supplies to mining communities and forts "up river."

Agriculture plays a dominant role in Yuma County's economy. Tourism, composed mainly of cross-country travelers and winter visitors, creates estimated gross revenue of $368.8 million.

HISTORY OF THE YUMA COUNTY COURTHOUSE

Built during 1928 according to the design of San Diego architects Ralph Swearingen and G.A. Hanssen, the third Yuma County Courthouse is a good local example of the Second Renaissance Revival style. The building was erected at a cost of more than $100,000 to replace a similar facility on the same site destroyed by fire on August 18, 1927. As the seat of Yuma County since 1928, the Courthouse has acquired additional significance as a symbol of government and as a distinctive landmark within the community.

HISTORY OF ADOLPH TEICHMAN

Within the apparent safety of stone and concrete walls of the courthouse are employees who have their own, very different story of a ghost whom they identify as being that of a former bailiff, Adolph Teichman. Mr. Teichman worked and lived in a loft above the second floor of the courthouse. He died on Christmas morning, 1949, at 82 years of age.

In life, Mr. Teichman measured 5'7", was hunched over, and was known to walk with a peculiar shuffling gate. His demeanor was quiet and friendly. City clerks who worked—and still work—the evening hours have witnessed an elderly, hunched man who walks the hallways in a shuffling manner. Could this be the loyal employee of the courthouse who now refuses to leave his former home?

Mr. Teichman is buried in Yuma at the northeast corner of Desert Lawn Memorial Park, next to his brother. There is no headstone to mark the resting place for either brother. Perhaps, Mr. Teichman would now very much welcome a small token of appreciation from the citizens of Yuma, perhaps a small headstone? After all—death or no death—he still is very devoted to serving as caretaker of the courthouse. Just ask anyone who has worked during the late-night hours on the second and third floors. He's around all right, still keeping a watchful eye on "his" courthouse.

CECIL J. ROACH'S STORY

My interview with Cecil took place in the maintenance office, located in the basement of the courthouse. During the interview, Cecil nervously chuckled and wrung his hands as he related his experiences. He was quite aware of the skepticism people might have towards his story, and the perplexed attitude of those who have never experienced a ghost directly. Undaunted by this, he presented a straightforward and focused account of what he believes to be behind the unusual activity that begins in the courthouse when night falls.

— Antonio

As the maintenance foreman, I have been working at the courthouse for five years. Prior to working at the courthouse, I don't recall any stories of ghosts or hauntings ever told to me. However, once employed and

Cecil Roach.

well into my job, certain individuals did feel comfortable enough with my personality to open up and tell me about their own stories and experiences. Of course, I thought that behind these stories was another purpose. I thought people just wanted to have fun with me and have a good laugh.

Some of the secretaries have told me about their experiences of seeing the ghost of an old man dressed in a suit. Some of them have refused to work in the evening hours because of these ghost sightings. They say that the ghost resembles the photos of the dead caretaker, Adolph Teichman. Doors will open and slam on their own. I've also heard talk of file cards flying across the room while the secretaries are busy at their computers. They also hear footsteps and sometimes will even be touched on the shoulders. These scary things just don't only after hours and at night.

In the basement, during the day, workers have heard sounds of laughter coming from empty rooms. Assistants who work with me have told me about seeing the same old man who walks down the hall and then gradually disappears. One assistant came to me one early morning yelling, "Cecil, Cecil, there's a bum loose in the courthouse!" He explained that as he looked through one of the glass windows built into an office door, he saw an old man moving about the room. The assistant attempted to open the door and confront the old guy, but it was locked. He described the man as being about 80 years old and wearing an old, worn suit.

Another assistant told me about an old man who walked right past him, brushing against him in the hallway. When the worker turned to see where the old man was headed, he simply was no longer there and seemed to have just disappeared into thin air! There also was an instance when one of the office service bells had, we thought, been stolen. It was missing for more than a year, and then recently workers began to hear the sound of the ringing bell coming from the office. Maintenance workers informed me that they'd heard a ringing bell coming from that same office at 6 am. Of course, we looked and didn't see a bell, but just a few hours later, a secretary came to me holding the missing bell! She said that she had found it in the office and had no idea how it had reappeared after being missing for so long. What was strange to me was why that darn bell was ringing on its own in an empty office at 6 a.m.! It wasn't until I had my own first experience with the ghost that I began to slowly understand that I was working in a haunted building.

My shift always began at 3 a.m. I was given the responsibility of carrying the master key of the courthouse, and with that responsibility, I had to be sure to lock the doors behind me. Once in the courthouse I turned on the lights. I was always the only person in the building at that hour."

One night, 10 months into my job, I heard noises and footsteps of someone walking up and down the second-floor hallway and slamming doors. I was on the first floor, and I remember going right up the stairs to see who was making all the noise. I looked all around and called out, "Is anyone here?" There was no response and no one in sight. This happened off and on for a few nights, then the noises suddenly stopped altogether.

About a year later, at 4 a.m., I was alone again in the building buffing the hallway with a buffing machine, and over the soft humming sound of the machine, I heard the sound of someone whistling. I stopped the machine and listened to the fading whistle sound as it disappeared down the hall. I started up the machine to continue, and again the whistling began. I turned off the machine and walked up the hallway, opened each office door and looking inside to see if I could catch whoever was whistling. The place was empty. Because I didn't see anyone in the flesh, I somehow got the courage to return to finishing up my job. I returned to buffing the floor. The whistling started up again, only this time it was right behind me! Yeah, I was totally freaked out, maybe even a little concerned for my safety. I quickly gathered up my equipment and supplies and left the area.

After that odd experience, I have had others. Sometimes when I'm working, I like to have my radio playing in the hallway to keep me company. The music also helps to keep me active in the early hours. As soon as I would leave the hallway or room, it would shut off on its own! I thought perhaps there was an electrical problem with the outlet or even with the radio itself. As I returned to where I placed the radio, I noticed that the radio's electrical cord was lying on the floor, disconnected from the wall! Now, this might sound strange, and it might appear to be a problem with a certain wall outlet, but even stranger was that this happened on every floor and wall outlet I plugged the radio into. I assumed that my choice of music was not appreciated by the ghost nor was this the only thing that the ghost did not like.

My coffeemaker was also unplugged. Sometimes I brought my coffeemaker with me and plugged it into a wall where I was working. When I returned to see if the coffee was done brewing, I discovered that the cord had been pulled from the wall, just like my radio. One time I returned to find the extension cord I had connected to the coffeemaker was also disconnected and was wrapped around a trash can with one end inside the can! Now, can anyone explain that to me?

I soon started to notice these strange things happening more frequently in the month of December. Even stranger, the activity would intensify as the days got closer to Christmas. One year, at about 5 a.m., as I was getting out of the elevator on the second floor, a voice loudly called out my name, "Cecil, Cecil!" Of course, there was no one in the elevator with me, but I turned around anyway just to be sure. I saw no one. Now, that really gave me goose bumps and scared me, for sure.

As I began to walk past the door, it quickly and mysteriously opened wide on its own!

Just last year, two days before Christmas, I had an assistant helping me in the building. I was on the second floor where the courtrooms are located. Suddenly, I saw one of the doors to a courtroom open. Since the courtrooms are to be locked securely due to strict security procedures, I immediately investigated. I entered the courtroom, turned on the lights and looked around cautiously. I saw no one. I the locked the door behind me and walked down the hall. I came upon the door that lead up to the top floor where Adolph Teichman used to live. As I began to walk past the door, it quickly and mysteriously opened wide on its own! When this happened, I jumped out of its way so fast, I don't even remember how I reached the first floor!

Not long after, I was with another assistant when we had a joint experience so frightening that even to this day, I can't get it out of my mind. Again, it took place in the dark, early morning hours. We were seated in my office talking, when suddenly we heard noise coming from the hallway. The noise was of someone hitting and spinning the lid of a trashcan. Thinking that a security guard must had entered the building and caused the unusual noise, we waited for him to come to my office and pay us a visit. After a few seconds of waiting, I got up out of my chair and checked the hallways and doors. The doors were locked, and I clearly we were still the only two in the building.

We disregarded this latest incident and went right back to work. My assistant climbed the stairs to the third floor, and I remained on the first floor. Everything was going as usual until I heard a noise and then saw something coming down the stairs. You might think I'm crazy, but as I looked to the stairs, I saw a large black ball floating down the stairs, with a smaller black ball following behind! The larger ball was the size of a basketball. The smaller ball also followed the larger ball by about four feet. They were traveling quickly, as quickly as someone running down the stairs might move. As the balls reached the landing, they disappeared. I can't explain the thoughts and feelings that went through me. When I saw this, I was shocked and covered in goose bumps. It was a very frightening thing to witness, and one that I hope to never have again.

Throughout the years I have heard and seen lots of things in this building. There is definitely something here. I know there is. Because I still work in the courthouse, I would rather not see any more ghosts, or hear whistling and the ringing of bells, or any other unexplained sounds again! I mean it! I want the ghost to know that I just want to be left alone from now on."

YOSEMITE NATIONAL PARK, CA

YOSEMITE VALLEY

Often called "the incomparable Valley," Yosemite Valley may be the world's best known example of a glacier-carved canyon. The dramatic scale of its leaping waterfalls, rounded domes, massive monoliths, and towering cliffs, has inspired painters, poets, photographers, and millions of visitors.

The Park embraces a great tract of scenic wildlands set aside in 1890 to preserve a portion of the Sierra Nevada that stretches along California's eastern flank. Ranging from 2,000 feet above sea level to more than 13,000 feet, the park encompasses alpine wilderness, groves of giant sequoia trees, and the Yosemite Valley.

The Valley's sheer walls and flat floor evolved as alpine glaciers lumbered through the canyon of the Merced River. The ice carved through weaker sections of granite, plucking and scouring rock but leaving intact harder portions, such as El Capitan and Cathedral Rocks. Glaciers greatly enlarged the canyon that the Merced River had carved through successive uplifts of the Sierra. When the last glacier melted, its terminal moraine, left at its farthest advance into the valley, dammed up the melting water to form ancient Lake Yosemite in the newly carved U-shaped valley. Eventually sediment filled in the lake, forming today's flat valley floor.

Today Yosemite Valley is a mosaic of open meadows sprinkled with wildflowers and flowering shrubs, oak woodlands, and mixed-conifer forests of ponderosa pine, incense cedar, and Douglas fir. Wildlife—from monarch butterflies to mule deer and black bears—flourishes in these diverse communities. Waterfalls around the Valley's perimeter reach their maximum flow in May and June. Most prominent are the Yosemite, Bridalveil, Vernal, Nevada, and Ililouette falls, but some have little or no water from mid-August through the early fall. Meadows, riverbanks, and oak woodlands are sensitive and have been severely damaged by long-term human use.

A life-like statue of Chris Brown "Chief Lemee" Southern Miwok 1900-1956, welcomes visitors to the museum.

Native American people have lived in the Yosemite region for as long as 8,000 years. By the mid-nineteenth century, when native residents had their first contact with non-Native American people, they were primarily of Southern Miwok ancestry. However, trade with the Mono Paiutes from the east side of the Sierra for pinon pine nuts, obsidian, and other materials from the Mono Basin resulted in many unions between the two nations.

Chris Brown (Chief Lemee) dancing for park visitors in the Indian Village behind the Yosemite Museum, June 20, 1949.

Chris Brown (1900-1956) was a Miwok man born in Yosemite Valley. Known as "Chief Lemme," he performed Miwok dances for visitors to Yosemite from the 1920s until 1953. The dance regalia he is shown wear-

Actual photograph of Chief Lemee wearing a shoulder cape of great horned owl feathers, clamshell disc beads, and a bone whistle around his neck.

ing is a mixture of Southern and Northern Miwok style. He also made and used a Paiute or Plains-style drum which he decorated with designs of his own creation.

Demonstrations of Native American culture have long been popular with visitors to Yosemite. The Indian Village, located behind the museum, was built in the late 1920s, and is open year-round. Although daily demonstrations of Miwok dances are no longer presented, demonstrations of Miwok and Paiute culture take place there during the summer.

The native people of Yosemite developed a complex culture rich in tradition, religion, songs, and political affiliations. Making use of the varied local ecosystems, they used plant and animal resources to the best of their abilities. The pattern of oaks and grassland noted by early visitors to Yosemite Valley is probably a direct result of the intentional burning of underbrush practiced by native people.

MARIPOSA BATTALION ENTERS YOSEMITE VALLEY

Although the first sighting of Yosemite Valley by non-Native American people was probably by members of the Joseph Walker Party in 1833, the first actual known entry into the Valley was not until nearly 20 years later. After the discovery of gold in the Sierra Nevada foothills in 1849, thousands of miners came to the Sierra to seek their fortune. Their arrival resulted in deadly, racial conflicts with local native people who bravely fought to protect their homelands. Because of such interaction, the Mariposa Battalion was organized as an expedition under

Joseph Walker.

the authority of the State of California to inflict punishment to native americans, and ultimately bring an end to the "Mariposa Indian War." The Battalion marched into the Yosemite Valley on their search for Indians on March 27, 1851.

EARLY TOURISTS AND SETTLERS

Writers, artists, and photographers spread the fame of "the Incomparable Valley" throughout the world. A steadily increasing stream of strangers came on foot and horseback, and later by stage. Realizing he could make money off these people, James Hutchings became one of Yosemite's first entrepreneurs. Hotels and residences were constructed, livestock grazed in meadows where for centuries only deer browsed, orchards were planted, and as a result, Yosemite Valley's ecosystem suffered drastically. Native Americans could only watch with heavy hearted disappointment, as their sacred falls, meadows, trees, animals and mountains were being overrun with these invaders.

PROTECTION IS SOUGHT FOR YOSEMITE

Inspired by the scenic beauty of Yosemite and spurred on by the specter of private exploitation of Yosemite's natural wonders, conservationists appealed to Senator John Conness of California. On June 30, 1864, President Abraham Lincoln signed a bill granting Yosemite Valley, and the Mariposa Grove of Giant Sequoias to the State of California as an inalienable public trust. This was the first time in history that a federal government had set aside scenic lands simply to protect them, and to allow for their enjoyment by all people. This idea was the spark that allowed for Yellowstone becoming the first official national park a few years later, in 1872.

Later, John Muir's struggle against the devastation of the subalpine meadows surrounding Yosemite Valley, resulted in the creation of Yosemite National Park on October 1, 1890. Mili-

449

tary units with headquarters in Wawona, administered the park while the State of California continued to govern the area covered by the original 1864 grant. Dual control of Yosemite came to an end in 1906, when the State of California receded Yosemite Valley, and the Mariposa Grove to the federal government. Civilian park rangers took over from the military in 1914.

Two years later, on August 25, 1916, through the persistent efforts of Steven Mather and Horace Albright, Congress authorized the creation of the National Park Service. This department office was to administer all national parks in such manner and by such means, as to leave them unimpaired for the enjoyment of future generations.

Around the turn of the century, Hetch Hetchy Valley became the center of a bitter political struggle when the City of San Francisco wanted to dam the Tuolumne River inside Yosemite National Park, as a source of drinking water and hydroelectric power. In 1913, conservationists led by John Muir lost the battle when Congress passed the Raker Act, authorizing the construction of O'Shaughnessy Dam.

INCREASING VISITATION REQUIRES MANAGEMENT PLANS

The day of the horse-drawn stage drew to a close in 1907 with the construction of the Yosemite Valley Railroad from Merced to El Portal. While a few automobiles entered the park in 1900 and 1901, they were

not officially permitted until 1913. In order to reduce competitive expansion of facilities in the park, in 1925, two major concessionaires were consolidated into the Yosemite Park and Curry Company.

Impacts resulting from increasing visitation in Yosemite Valley became very apparent. People camped at random throughout its beautiful meadows, and the dramatically increasing automobile traffic haphazardly entering fragile areas, left the Valley eroded and drastically changed. As visitation, and need for year-round services increased, Yosemite Village was relocated from a location in the flood plain on the south side of the Merced River, to the present Yosemite Village site to the north.

Visitation exceeded one million in 1954 for the first time, and by 1976 over two million people visited Yosemite. In the mid-1990s, visitation topped four million. In the early 1970s, the National Park Service established one-way road traffic patterns, eliminated cars in the far east end of the Valley, offered free shuttle bus transportation in the Valley, converted the parking lot in front of the Valley Visitor Center to a pedestrian mall, and generally encouraged visitors to enjoy the park by walking or using public transportation.

Yosemite's General Management Plan, which was completed in 1980, articulated the needs for park wide visitor services, resources management, interpretation services, concessions management, and park operations.

SAVINA CORBALLI'S STORY

I've worked and lived at the park since 1994. What began as a temporary housekeeping or maid position, has turned out to be my full-time job. My girlfriend and I both began working at the park together after we completed two years of college. We were looking for summer jobs, and were told by a friend that Yosemite was always hiring summer, seasonal workers. We applied and were soon hired at Curry Village as maids. Although my girlfriend returned to finish college, I decided to stay on at the park. It's now been over seven years since that summer.

Although I haven't made very much money over the years, I have managed to save a few dollars. My meals and rent for a one bedroom cabin are both deducted from my salary, and I know I'll never get rich working here, but the location of working in such a beautiful environment like Yosemite, more than makes up for my lack in salary.

I've had several weird experiences at the park. Many of these experiences have not made me fear ghosts, but one in particular sure made me rethink this. This 'special' experience began in the spring of 1997, while I was hiking by myself in the back country of Tuolumne Meadows. I've hiked many of the back trails, before, and I especially enjoy the John Muir Trail. This has undoubtedly got to be among the most beautiful hiking trails in the world!

The meadows are beautiful in the springtime, and the spring of '97 was no different. I decided to hike alone, with only my backpack and adventuous spirit. It's not at all unusual for the employees at the park to do a solitary hike. Eventually most of the employees get the urge for exploring the park, and because of the availability of good trails, and time off of work, we definitely take advantage of opportunities to explore this beautiful park. However, staff accociates scheduals don't always match, so hiking alone is not uncommon.

One spring evening, I got all my gear ready for the 6-day long hike that I had planned. On day two of my hike, I reached my destination and set-up my base camp. This is where I would be spending 3 wonderful days alone, swimming in the streams, hiking and sleeping. What a life! I also brought two books with me, one that was written about the history of Yosemite Park, and one written about the Indians of the gold rush country. This second book was basically written about the sad history and ultimate extermination of the Indians. I wanted to get a perspective of what most Americans don't learn in public school. I know I certainly didn't get much of an education throughout my school years regarding the treatment of the native people of California. Like most visitors to Yosemite, I fell in love with the beauty of the area, and equally, was unaware of its terrible history regarding the white man's treatment towards the Indians. I decided to take this opportunity on my hike to read and educate myself. I also brought along a camera to take lots of pictures.

Coinciding with my hike, the park service was sponsoring a photography contest for non-professionals and I decided to enter. The first prize of $500.00 was something I wanted to take a chance on winning. I brought along about eight rolls of film. Everything was going well on my hike, until the the second day, things definately turned out differently.

It was a warm afternoon, and I was lying on my sleeping bag inside my tent. As I was reading my book I heard the footsteps of someone walking up to my camp. I looked out of the tent and did not see anyone. This really bothered me to so I got up, walked outside of my tent and looked all around. I saw nothing. I thought perhaps it might be a squirrel, a raccoon or bird. But the footsteps were very identifiable to me as a walking human would make, stepping one foot in front of the other. Even though the day was clear and bright, I saw no one around my camp.

After a short while of listening and watching for something, I disregarded this incident, and decided to take a short walk to the nearby stream. As I splashed myself with the cool, stream water, I began to think about my earlier experience with the footsteps. Subconsciously, the incident was still bothering me. I decided to walk back to my tent and get a snack.

As I rose and turned in the direction of my camp, about a quarter of a mile away, I noticed that someone was standing by the tent. I could tell it was a young guy wearing blue shorts, a blue cap, holding an orange backpack. I yelled out, "Can I help you?" The guy turned and looked in my direction. I held up my arm and made a waving gesture to communicate that I had my eyes on him. He said nothing, and made no movement, other than to face my direction, to indicate he knew I was yelling at him. I felt a bit alarmed and unsure about what he might be up to, or what I should to do next, so I yelled once more, "That's my tent, can I help you?" Keep in mind, I was alone in the woods, so I didn't want to necessarily get too close to this strange guy. I'm smart enough to know that there are lots of "kooks,' that would like to take advantage of a single woman in a situation like this.

When he failed to respond to my calls, I knew, and felt something was definitely not right. I decided that the best thing for me to do was to stay put. Then he slowly turned away, and walked towards the open foot trail directly above my camp. I kept my eyes on this weird guy, while at the same time, wasted no time, briskly making my way to my tent.

As soon as I got to my tent, I looked over everything inside and outside. It was clear to me that nothing was disturbed or missing. Though strangely, there was an area of water soaking the ground, directly below where this guy had been standing. Hoping to get a better glimpsed of him, I looked in the direction of the footpath. I spotted him, then notice something unusual in the way he was walking. He moved abruptly from side to side, kind of staggering with each step. I imagined this guy might be drunk, or under the influence of drugs. I sat down on the ground and observed as he continued to slowly walk away, until he slowly disappeared. And when I say disappeared, I mean DISAPPEARED! The path he was walking on was an open meadow without any trees, or large rocks to hide behind. It was midday, the sun was bright, high up in the sky and no shadows whatsoever. This guy was there one second, and in the next, he just suddenly disappeared!

I quickly stood up, thinking he must have taken a fall, and cautiously walked over to where he might have hit the ground. There was no evidence of the guy anywhere. No cap, no backpack, nothing! The meadow grasses and flowers were only about a foot or so high, so he couldn't have been hiding among the plants. I knew right then that the only explanation was that I had been visited by a ghost! And it had appeared to me in broad daylight no less! Admittedly, this shook me up. And as I returned to my tent, I decided to cut my stay short, pack up my things, and return back home.

As I gathered up my belongings, I noticed drops of blood on the paper bags I had next to my camp stove, and at the side of my tent! These were fresh drops, and there was only one way they could have gotten there—the ghost! In just a few minutes, I high-tailed it out of there. Because of all the adrenaline that was now coursing through my body, I got on the trail, and walked at an accelerated speed, almost running.

I soon met up with two women hikers from Germany who were also headed back down to the valley floor. Although I'm sure they must have noticed the tormented look on my face, they said nothing. I attempted to act as normal as possible. I told them where I had camped the previous night, and they said they had seen my tent pitched in the meadow. They were pleasant, and soon invited me to join them as they walked back down the mountain. Not wanting to alarm them, I didn't dare tell them about the ghost I had seen.

The three of us made camp that night, without any strange incidents, then we all got up early the next morning, had our breakfast, and were soon back on the trail. After reaching Yosemite Valley at around 1pm, we went our separate ways. I was so grateful to be among familiar surroundings, and both mentally and physically exhausted.

As I crossed the last stone bridge that led to my residence, I noticed a gathering of people to the side of the bridge who were all wearing blue caps and shorts. They were holding candles and praying. An uneasiness came over me. I recognized the outfits as the same one the ghost had been wearing. I asked one gentleman what the gathering was for. He said that a friend from their group named "Russell," had died two days ago while swimming in the river. The gathering was to offer prayers for Russell before their return trip home.

With emotion in my voice, I asked him, where Russell had died, and how old he was. He told me Russell was 17 years old, and had gone with a group of four on an overnight hiking adventure to Tuolumne Meadows. Apparently while swimming in one of the deeper streams, he had misjudged a rocks' slipperiness, slipped, and fatally struck his head on a rock. As he finished explaining, I felt shivers and goosebumps all over my body!

I didn't ask any more questions. I walked a few feet away from the gathering, and I began to silently sob. I couldn't bring myself to tell him that I had seen the ghost of his friend. I was shaking all over. I watched as the group got into their cars and drove off.

I was an emotional basket case. I felt numb and unable to do much more other than think over and over, what I had experienced. Thinking took over the remainder of that day, and the next. My thoughts were of life, death and unanswered questions I had of the afterlife. I knew I had seen Russell's ghost. The puddle of water, blood drops, the cap and shorts, and the manner in which he disappeared on the trail, was all the evidence, and proof I would ever

He had misjudged a rocks' slipperiness, slipped and, fatally struck his head on a rock.

need. I had seen a ghost!

My experience with Russell's ghost took place only four years ago. Since then I've told only a few trusted people. I've discovered that whenever I would tell my story to someone, it would motivate them to share a story of a ghost experience at the park of their own. Although my personal experience is a hard one to top, fellow Yosemite park employees have some stories that are also real chillers.

These days, I won't go hiking alone into the woods again without a partner. I'm not necessarily afraid of encountering bears or snakes. It's the 'other' type of encounters that I don't ever want to have again. I think you can understand why.

KIMBERLY H. CUNNINGHAM-SUMMERFIELD'S STORY

My foster parents are from the Toulomne Rancheria. My birth family is from Yukia California. I am by birth, Tsa'lagi or 'Cherokee,' but I was raised by my foster parents, in the culture and ways of the Yosemite Miwok. I began working at the park at the age of 15, as an Indian Cultural Demonstrator. Today my title is Park Ranger/Interpreter, and I'm also a member of the Park's Indian cultural staff.

The Indian museum is housed in a park building that was dedicated in 1926, and is constructed of local stone granite. At one corner of the building is an Indian burial whose location is kept secret from the public. We don't give out information as to the location of the burial, we respectfully kept that information to ourselves.

I know of many spiritual experiences at the park, Yosemite is fill with spirits. And as native people, we believe in the existence of both human and animal spirits. They dwell within the valley mountains, streams and waterfalls. They can be seen, and heard moving about, and

Kimberly H. Cunningham-Summerfield. at times even singing. We believe this. Personally, I'm always experiencing spirits at the park. Right here in the museum, are many spirits who regularly make themselves known.

Just last week, my two co-workers and I were in the process of closing the museum for the day. We turned off the lights, and turned on the alarm system. Finally, standing at the entrance, before locking the doors, we took one last glance at the interior and left. The next morning, I came to work at 7:30, and as soon as I stepped inside the museum, I "felt" that things weren't right. It was a feeling that just came to me, something was out of balance. People say that when a spirit is present, the

Right here in the museum, are many spirits who regularly pay their visits.

room will get cold. Maybe that does happen, but I've only experienced the room changing to a very warm temperature, when something of a spiritual nature is about to take place.

Suddenly, the display lights, located in the middle of the museum, specifically spot-lighting the collection of ceremonial regalia, began to flicker. They'd dim, then slowly get bright, and flicker. It appeared as if someone were playing, or sending out a 'light code'. I explained to my

co-worker, "I don't know what's going on, but I'm not going in there!" No one has ever fully explained to me why the lights that focus only on the ceremonial displays, behave the way they sometimes do.

All I can say about this is that I know there are spirits in the museum. I've seen them as they walk by, and approach the area where I am standing. Shadows of people will move about the museum. I've gotten so used to seeing them, that I even talk to them. I know that they're always around.

It appeared as if someone were playing, or sending out a 'light code'.

Artifacts that are kept under glass, in display cases, occasionally get moved around.

457

Not only did he hear the spirit voices, but he actually saw them!

I imagine that the creators of these beautiful baskets and such, are still emotionally attached to them. It's understandable because of the love, and care, the creative energy those people put into each of their creations.

We have one park ranger who we confided to about the spirits in the museum. He made no qualms about his disbelief in the supernatural. But one evening, as he was closing the museum for the day, something abruptly changed his mind. He said that as he was doing a walk-through of the museum, not only did he hear voices, but he actually saw the spirits! Since that evening, he's not been the same.

Again, I believe that the artifacts we have in the museum, were very personal to the people who skillfully, and lovingly made them. I've never gotten the feeling that the spirits are angry, they just are checking up on things. The museum does not display anything that is disrespectful to Indian people. The park staff places much importance about not displaying burial jewelry, or offerings.

I need to tell you about the mannequins in the museum. The diorama displays are actually molded from actual Indians faces, cast from living people's faces. There are moments when I'll hear loud shrieks being yelled out by visitors who swear that they've seen the mannequin's heads turn to look at them! I've had visitors become so scared by the mannequins, that they will quickly leave the museum without speaking a word. But I know what took place. Visitors have reported to me that they've seen the eyes, or mouth move on these mannequins.

My Aunts always cautioned me as a child, never to look, or stare at a spirit straight on, because that can cause the spirit harm. I was told that if spirits chose to appear to us, it's because they have a lesson, or news to give. I was also taught never to be mean, disrespectful, or talk rude about spirits. This is something I also teach to my own children. The dead must always be respected.

RANGER ROBERT L. FRY'S STORY

Robert L. Fry.

My position at the park is Ranger Naturalist/Interpreter. I'm by profession an Ethnobiologist with a focus in the Native American use of plants. I've made bows, arrows, including nets, string and other plant fiber crafts. Some of my work is displayed in the museum. This year marks my 42nd year at the park, 13 years as a full-time employee. I came to Yosemite in 1960. Before being employed at the park, I was a high school science teacher. Most of the Native people whom I've talked to privately have describe seeing and hearing very unusual things. Without a doubt in their minds, they sincerely believe that spiritual beings do exist at the park.

A common belief, is that dead ancestors return to earth, and to Yosemite, in the physical form of a bear. Because bears have a heel with five toes facing front, a bear's footprint resembles a human's. When a Miwok happens to encountered a bear, they are taught to look directly at its eyes, and speak to it as normally, just as they would speak to another person. The Miwok never killed bears because they believed them to be sacred, or spiritually pure.

A Miwok female friend once described to me that not long after the well-known chief Lamee died in 1955, a bear began to visit not only her house, but the other Indian women's homes in the area. The bear would wonder around the houses, and scratch at their windows. During his life, the chief, although never married, was very fond of provoking laughter, and good-natured pranks on the women. My friend believed that the chief visited her, and other women, in the form of this bear. She said they were all a bit un-nerved by his visits.

I'm also aware that culturally, the Miwok have a great reverence, and sometimes fear of waterfalls. To the Miwok, all waterfalls held great power, and if not honored correctly could prove to be dangerous.

Children were never allowed to play or act disrespectfully when in the area of a waterfall. Pohono or Bridalveil Falls, is a waterfall which

'Pohono' or Bridalveil Falls.

is considered to be 'haunted' by the Miwok. I personally think it is a very spooky place. The Miwok name for the falls, 'Pohono' translates to 'bad puffing wind.' Pohono is in my opinion, one of the most beautiful waterfalls in the park. It's 620 feet high and unlike the other falls in the park, it never ceases to have water spilling over its rim. A common ritual when passing Pohono, is to lower one's voice, or cease to speak, until quite a distance away. Indians believe that spirits dwell at the base of the Pohono, and these spirits should not be disturbed.

The famous collector 'Ripley' once labeled Pohono, "The waterfall that flows uphill." He coined this phrase because, at times, usually in the month of September, there is a peculiar wind that hits the face of the waterfall with such force, that if the flow of water is low enough, it will push the water back, and cause it to stop flowing for a few seconds. Soon after, a huge amount of this restricted water will spill over the side in a gush.

The creek once flowed down an incline to join the Merced River. Ice Age glaciers filled and widened the main canyon, sheered its granite walls, and bulldozed away the lower stream channel. When the ice melt-ed, Bridalveil Creek was left hanging—with a 620-foot drop to the river. Around the Valley are similar glacier-chopped side streams such as Yosemite, Ribbon and Sentinel Falls.

I had an unusual experience with Pohono which took place at 2am. At the time, I was headed to a favorite fishing spot. The weather was calm, but as soon as I entered the area of the falls, I noticed that strangely, the trees were whipping wildly back and forth. Knowing what I did about the spiritual identity of the falls, I felt the strong urge to get out of my car, which I did, and said, "Oh, Pohono I honor you." Feeling personally convinced I did the right thing, I then drove away.

Another strange thing associated with Pohono, was described to me in 1973 by Dave Jarel, the Head of the Park's Heli-Attack crew. There had been a very heavy winter which dropped a lot of snow in the park. Badger Pass ski area which is located about five miles back from the fall's rim, is used by many skiers to reach Dewie Point. There were two skiers, a doctor and his son, who decided to also use this route. They got lost in a snow storm and the son decided to turn back, but the father chose to continue. The father got lost and somehow ended up at the lip of Bridaveil Falls. Obviously, there was no way down. Unable to locate him, his body was not discovered until the early spring thaw.

Dave said that as he was making a pass over the falls in his helicopter, he noticed a red patch of cloth at the rim. He swung the helicopter around for a closer look and recognized it to be the lost skier. As the ground crew approached the body, they noticed, he was frozen in a sitting position on a rock, with his chin in his hand blankly starring at the valley below. His skis were eventually located wedged among the boulders down below at the fall's base. He had apparently taken them off in frustration, and tossed them over the side. I say frustration, because the road down below is opened year-round, and he must have died watching the cars pass below, unaware of his grave situation up above.

One year, the skull of a young girl was found at Summit Meadow, again in the Badger Pass area. Many years after this girl was murdered in the park, the murderer was arrested in the state of Texas on another charge. I guess his conscious got the better of him, because he described in grim detail to the authorities, where and how he had committed the murder in Yosemite. I happened to be with the medical forensic examiner from Seattle, who was examining the skull's teeth. We searched for bones, and other evidence, but all we located was the skull. The examiner explained how animals will usually drag away most of the body's bones, except for the skull. Due to its round shape, the skull is difficult for animals to bite, or grasp a hold of. The skull is usually the only portion of the body that is left at the murder site.

I also know of a man who committed a gruesome suicide in 1958, by jumping off Half-Dome. He was staying at the Glacier Point Hotel, which in 1969 was consumed, and destroyed in a massive fire. He left a note in his room stating among other things, that he was going to hike the nine miles to Half Dome. Where he jumped, was found another note, which was folded in his coat pocket, stating his intentions. At the base of the rock, the search party located most of his body, minus one hind-quarter.

Glacier Point, also had an incident of a suicide/homicide. A disgruntled man apparently pushed the woman he was with, over the edge, then he followed her by jumping to his death.

Another sad case I'm aware of, is of an obese 350-pound man who committed suicide by jumping off Taft Point to his death. Taft Point is just west of Glacier Point. This man happened to be an employee of the park.

I know that each of us experiences paranormal events in our own way. And, I also think the human mind is flexible enough to believe whatever it wants. I believe, and 'feel' a parallel 'connection' to native people, and to the men from ancient times who fashioned arrowheads. These people didn't have much control over nature, and when you have very little control, you become very respectful of nature's power. To the native people of Yosemite, it was a given fact that the spiritual forces of coyote, frog, bear, lizard and all the rest, had their functions. Arching everything was the great Creator who lived beyond the setting sun. When the original inhabitants died, they're bodies were cremated, so to set the spirit free to join the Great One.

CRUZ GARCIA JR.'S STORY

I've been employed at the park for 30 years. I was born and raised in Bakersfield, California until the age of 22, attended the University of Fresno State for three years, then made the move to Yosemite. I've been at the park ever since. Currently my position is Head of Housekeeping.

Initially, employees were very open about discussing their experiences regarding encounters with ghosts at the park. So many strange things happen at Yosemite, I'm honestly surprised that more of the public aren't aware of just how much paranormal activity goes on here. Of course, some are simply rumors, but many of these "so-called" rumors have been confirmed by the park rangers. I have confirmed the truth of some of these stories, by tracking down former employees who worked here before I was employed at the park.

Cruz Garcia.

I have experienced spiritual manifestations, or ghosts. Because of my own family, and cultural upbringing, I am aware that these things do exist. As I said, Yosemite is filled with ghosts, and areas of tremendous spiritual energy.

Unfortunate as it is, Yosemite has also experienced a lot of deadly events. People have chosen to commit suicide by jumping off the falls, and there have even been several documented murders. And then there are the numerous deaths caused accidentally, from falls and drownings. From day one, I was told about different public buildings, and certain meadows that were known to be haunted, Leydig meadow, being one of the better known.

Leydig meadow is located directly behind our Housekeeping office, and has been the location for many strange occurrences. I've known of weird incidents of employees who have been "drawn" to sleep out in Leydig meadow, and the next day at work co-workers notice that the employee is missing, have searched the meadow, and not found the individual. Later in the day, when the "missing" person appeared their shift, surprised co-workers would ask for an explanation. The employee would answer that he, or she was unaware of losing track of time, even days.

Apparently, the meadow offers a sort of power to disguise, or hide people. I know that the persons it envelopes, are unable to see, or even hear the cries of others that are searching for them. It's a sort of "mesmerizing" of the senses that takes over the body. I've now heard of the meadow referred to as a 'power source.'

People have also told me that they've even seen people or "spirits" positioned in the tree branches that grown in the meadow. No one is abso-

Leydig Meadow has been the location for many strange occurrences.

lutely sure why, or how this power source came to be. I've been told that the National Park Service has records of strange occurrences taking place at the meadow that go back for many years, but they've never willing to disclose this information. It's extremely difficult to research this topic, unless you are able to get the cooperation of the Park Service.

As the Head of Housekeeping for the Yosemite Lodge, my staff have approached me several times with incidents of seeing faces reflected in mirrors of certain rooms, and lights that strangely begin to dim in rooms they start to enter. Mirrors have also disappeared from walls, and had later been found in unusual places, or tightly forced into drawers, to the point of getting stuck.

Maids have had numerous incidences. When entering rooms with unmade beds, they've turned their attention away for a few seconds, then turned around again, and the bed has been made! They've also seen the indentations of an invisible body lying on the mattress of a freshly made bed. I've personally been witness to several of these occurrences at the lodge. I had a maid so disturbed by the spirits, that she refused to clean one particular room, unless another maid was with her.

Maids cleaning supplies, bottles, brushes, etc., have been moved, and placed in areas where they shouldn't be. Further common experiences have been doors that are closed or opened, without a human presence. Maids have nervously reported being watched by an unseen presence, that follows them from room to room. I remember a maid who reported that three of her heavy linen bags, that she had filled with soiled sheets, towels, etc., were mysteriously removed from the first floor where she was working. She was alone at the time, and was unnerved when she discovered the bags mysteriously moved to the bottom floor of the lodge. The bags could only have been move by passing by her, and she never saw anyone physically move them.

One maid was so frightened by what had happened to her in one room, that her only means of escape, was to dash to the balcony and climb on to the roof on the second floor! I remember when she did this, and the ladders that were brought to the lodge. Eventually she was coaxed down. Following the incident, she was so terrified by what had happened to her in that room, she quit her job on the spot!

All these strange things took place in the older portion of the lodge which was damaged, then permanently dismantled and removed, in the immense Yosemite flood of 1997. The original lodge consisted of 16 rooms, and above that was the attic. which was built sometime in the early 1950's. One original staff member employed at the lodge, was a woman named Mildred. This information is important to the hauntings, because Mildred worked primarily in the original building as a maid. As I said, the original portion of the lodge is where all the spiritual occurrences were reported to have taken place.

This is how the story was told to me. One day Mildred was reported missing. After a search was begun, her lifeless body was eventually located hanging from a rope, attached to one of the rafters in the lodge's attic. The attic was built in such a manner, as to connect the two original lodge buildings. Now here is where the story gets interesting. It was reported that Mildred committed suicide, but a witness at the scene later stated that her hands were bound with a cord. Was it a suicide, or a murder?

Not long after, a curious employee came forward to say that she was so intrigued to actually see the attic where Mildred was found hanging, she took it upon herself to "borrow" the key to the attic's door, and view the area for herself. She told me that she happened to notice several mirrors lying against a wall. She glanced at one of the mirrors, and suddenly saw a woman's face staring back at her! She described the woman as being middle aged, and

My staff have approached me several times with incidents of seeing faces reflected in mirrors of certain rooms.

This author captured this orbs photo during an interview break while in Yosemite.

with somewhat greyish hair. Because of her startled fright, that was all the employee was able to remember before she rapidly exited the attic. Apparently when the original lodge was removed, Mildred ceased to want to hang around.

I've personally known several of the people that have reported these incidents to me. I knew them well enough to be able to say that they were credible, and sincere. I could see that they were visibly shaken by what they had experienced. As of today, I haven't heard of any further hauntings at the lodge.

Yosemite has attracted numerous types of individuals who have even attempted to misuse its spiritual areas for their own personal gain. I was aware of several staff members, who were employed several years ago at the park, that were involved in Satan worship. Employees reported seeing one of these employee's rooms filled, with lit black candles, and upturned crucifixes. On one wall of his room, he even had the lord's prayer written backwards, hung on his wall.

I want to make clear the distinction between Witchcraft and Satanism. Witchcraft, or 'Wicca' is historically a beneficial religion that benefits the person, or community. It's an earth based religion, however, Satanism is a totally different from what practicing Wiccans believe. Most people confuse Wicca with Satanism—they are not the same. This guy with the candles was a Satanist. He made no claims to hide this fact. He was also heavily into drugs. Eventually, he was fired. But what amazed me was why he wasn't fired any sooner. Again, this all took place many years ago.

Throughout the years, there have been other incidences of 'spiritual' power trips that I've heard of. I still hear the stories of people going to Yosemite's meadows and trails attempting to contact spirits, with Ouija boards, and fortune telling devices. I think these people are not capable of handling what the natural forces have to offer. I think they should leave the spirits, and power sources alone. The spirits have always been 'free floating' at the park. They should be left alone.

JULIA PARKER TRIBUTE

As far back as I can remember, I have had the exceptional honor and privilege of being welcomed, time and time again, by the native people living and working within Yosemite Valley and Yosemite National Park. I recall my very first trip into Yosemite, I was a young high school student and hitch-hiked from Los Angeles to Yosemite during a summer break with just a backpack, followed by numerous trips thereafter throughout my life.

On several of these visits I was permitted to stay overnight inside the Redwood "Bark House" (teepee structure) which are exhibit displays of traditional residential lodging of the Coast Miwok. During many of these stays, I found myself presented with profound moments of life altering knowledge and inspiration by remarkable individuals I've met here. One such person was exceptional basket weaver and American Indian spokeswoman, Julia Parker. I remain forever grateful for her grace, respect, encouragement and friendship over the years.

— Antonio

Julia Florence Parker is a Coast Miwok-Kashaya Pomo basket weaver, and long-time resident of Yosemite Valley. She was born in February 1928 in Marin County, California. Her father was Coast Miwok, and her mother was Kashaya Pomo. In 1945, when Julia was 17 years old, she married Ralph Parker. The couple moved to Yosemite, where

Garcez visiting Parker at her Yosemite Museum demonstration exhibit.

Garcez presenting Parker with an autographed copy of his 'Ghost Stories of California's Gold Rush Country and Yosemite National Park' book.

Julia began her studies of basketry.

At the Yosemite Museum, Julia proudly interpreted the history of regional American Indian tribes, masterfully demonstrated basket weaving and acorn processing to millions of park visitors. Julia remained a highly respected cultural specialist throughout her adult life in her beloved Yosemite Valley home.

In 2007, Parker was the recipient of a National Heritage Fellowship from the National Endowment for the Arts, the United States' highest honor in the folk and traditional arts.

Parker graciously accepts Garcez's generous labor of love gift.

NATIVE AMERICAN INDIANS

CHINLE, AZ - NAVAJO (DIN-NEH')

The name by which the Navajo are known is not so much the name of a people as the name of a place. The neighboring Pueblo people referred to the area of the Southwest that the Din-neh' occupied as Navajo. The Spanish later arrived referred to the Din-neh' as Apaches de Navajo. This label was in time shortened to simply Navajo. Given all this excess phraseology, the Navajo have always referred to themselves as Din-neh', which means 'the people,' and their homeland as Dinetah'. Current usage of either two nouns is acceptable. However, it is best to use the name that the Din-neh' have chosen for centuries.

Today the Din-neh' are the largest Indian nation in the United States. Presently they account for fifteen percent of the Native American population as reported in the 1990 U.S. census. Their tribal numbers are in excess of 250,000 members. Occupying a vast area of the Southwest, spreading across parts of Arizona, New Mexico, Colorado and Utah, Din-neh' land encompasses an area larger than the states of Connecticut, Rhode Island, Massachusetts, and New Jersey combined.

Chinle, near the geographic center of the Navajo Indian Reservation in northeastern Arizona, is at the entrance to Canyon de Chelly National Monument. Chinle became a center for population growth and trade after 1868 when the United States signed a treaty with the Navajos. The first trading post was established in 1882, the first mission in 1904, and the first government school in 1910.

Today the community, at an altitude of 5,082 feet, has been designated one of the major 'growth centers' on the Navajo Reservation by the tribal government. It is an important trade, administrative, and educational center within the Chinle Chapter (a local government unit) and is headquarters for the Chinle Agency, one of five Bureau of Indian Affairs administrative jurisdictions on the reservation.

JOSIE YELLOW GOURD'S (NAVAJO) STORY

I interviewed Josie on the Navajo Reservation not far from the town of Chinle, which is located in the northeast quadrant of the state. Josie is a 41-year-old widow and mother of twin daughters, aged 16. Our interview took place inside their mobile home, which is situated on deep red, rusty-colored desert land with wispy juniper trees growing in contorted shapes. Overhead is the endless vastness of the turquoise blue sky.

Within such beauty, this location would be complete if not for the reality of poverty that lingered all around. As with some Native Americans, Josie daily endures such inconveniences as living without modern plumbing, electricity or heating. The interview was conducted in Josie's kitchen. On the table were various small plastic tubes and glass jars containing a rainbow of assorted tiny, brightly colored glass beads. Josie and her daughters sew these beads onto leather and make hatbands, necklaces, earrings and bracelets. Once completed, they take these articles to local stores in town and either sell them or exchange them for personal items. Josie spoke in a calm, even tone when relating her personal experience with a witch and ghosts. Her daughters were in the adjoining living room and silently listened as their mother told me her story.

— Antonio

"My 70-year-old grandfather enjoys living in the traditional manner of us Navajos in a Navajo roundhouse or 'hogan,' which is right next to our mobile home. He also prefers to speak only our Native language. After my grandmother's death, he lived alone in his hogan for over twenty years. Both he and grandmother lived together in a previous hogan, but after she died, grandfather burned their original hogan, as is our tradition to do when the owner dies. A new hogan was built for grandfather a short time later, and this is where he now lives. About eight years ago, in the month of November, grandfather—who otherwise was in good health—began to suffer from headaches and body aches, which eventually caused him to be bedridden. When grandfather's condition worsened, he began to refuse food. After discussing his situation with my older brother, we both decided that it would be best to take him to a doctor in Window Rock. Grandfather was hesitant, but soon realized the logic in our decision to seek medical help. After being admitted into the clinic, he was taken through the long process of many blood tests and x-rays. My brother and I spent three days in Window Rock at a friend's house while grandfather was being cared for. When the results of the tests eventually came back from the lab, to our surprise and relief, they indicated that he only had a rise in blood sugar, which could be treated with drugs. Aside from this, his other tests were normal. Both my brother and I were still not totally convinced that all was well with him. We had seen the turn for the worse that our otherwise active and mentally alert grandfather had taken. His state of constant pain and fatigue was very unusual for him. The doctor prescribed pain medicine to help him sleep.

After filling the prescription, we returned home. On the drive home, grandfather stated that he wanted to seek the help of a local medicine man in Chinle. Grandfather wanted to have a 'Sing'. Among us Navajos, we have a curing ceremony, which we call a 'Sing'. The 'Sing' ceremony involves the participation of an elder medicine man or woman, special songs are sung, incense is burned, and a drum and other ritual items are used. It is a lengthy ceremony and highly respected among traditional Navajos. My brother and I assured my grandfather that we would honor his wishes and contact a medicine man back home. Arrangements were made with an elderly medicine man, and a date for the Sing was set.

Four nights before the ceremony, a strange thing happened to me. It had been snowing heavily during the day, and that evening, the moon was bright and full. At around 11 p.m. the barking of our dog, which we

471

keep chained to our porch, awakened me. Usually she barks at skunks that live under the mobile home, or in response to the yelping of coyotes that sometimes come around our property. This time her barking sounded different to me. It made me get out of my warm bed and walk to the window. As I parted the curtains on the front door, I saw the image of a woman I did not recognize walking about my grandfather's hogan. I reached for my jacket and boots, and walked outside. My dog was growling and barking. In the moonlit night, I followed this strange woman as she made her way to the rear of the hogan. When I yelled at her, 'What do you want?' she did not respond. I decided to confront her. With my dog still barking loudly, I quickly walked over to the hogan as my footsteps crunched noisily into the foot-deep snow. About twenty feet away from the woman, I saw that she was wrapped in a dark shawl from head to toe. Her face was hidden from my sight. Something inside me made me stop in my tracks.

As soon as I stopped, what happened next made my mouth open wide. The woman suddenly flew away and took off in a flash! She did not run, but seemed to "fly" over the snow-covered ground without leaving footsteps or tracks! My dog barked and barked even louder. I immediately turned and ran back to my trailer. I missed a step and remember taking a hard fall. Once I reached the trailer I rushed inside and locked the door! Both my daughters told me that they witnessed the whole shocking incident from inside the safety of the mobile home looking out the window. I was out of breath and shaking. I knew that I had seen something evil outside. My girls were also shaken, and that night we all slept together.

The next day I wasted no time in telling my brother everything. After hearing my story, he knew that what had taken place that night had to be witchcraft. A ghost or witch, had for some reason visited our property. My brother said, 'Who knows how long these evil visits have been going on without us being aware of them?' We all decided that it would be best not to tell our grandfather for fear of upsetting him, and we didn't want to risk him becoming even more ill. We also knew that this new information needed to be related to our medicine man.

My brother drove me to the medicine man's home, and we informed him of what I had seen. He was not surprised by my story. He said, 'Oh, I know who this is.' Then he explained to us that there was a Navajo medicine woman who lived not far from his house who wanted to gain a reputation in the Indian community as being a powerful spiritual person. After I heard the medicine man's description of who this woman was, I could recall her from a visit she made to my grandfather's hogan several weeks before grandfather became ill.

I remember grandfather telling me that this woman had visited him because she wanted him to be her boyfriend. When grandfather refused, she got very angry with him and yelled obscenities. She left our property in a rage! The medicine man further explained, 'It is difficult to gain power without earning it in the correct manner. This woman has decided to seek the help of certain animal spirits instead of asking the Creator for direction, and doing what is right.' He also said, 'You need to know that this woman wants to hurt your grandfather. Your grandfather refused to do what she demanded, so now she has taken revenge. She chose to make him ill, but she will not stop until he is dead.' My brother and I could not understand why this medicine woman would want to be so evil as to hurt our grandfather. Our concern now was for our grandfather to be healed. The medicine man said that he would be ready to confront this woman's witchcraft during grandfather's Sing.

The night of the ceremony came and we all gathered inside my grandfather's hogan. We used kerosene lamps for light and a fire was started in the wood stove. Soon the medicine man arrived and the ceremony began. Grandfather was seated on top of a blanket, which was placed on the dirt floor. In front of him the medicine man placed the items which would be used for the cleansing: a bowl of water, a leather bag of corn pollen, a basket with a beautiful eagle feather, and various other items. The medicine man began to drum and sing his songs, calling the positive forces of Mother Earth and the four directions. He sang towards the heavens and asked the Creator for vision, help, and power in defeating all evil.

His singing continued for about an hour or so. He reached for the basket, which held the eagle feather and grabbed hold of the feather's stem.

Saying a prayer, he passed the feather over grandfather's head and body. Then the medicine man returned the feather to the basket and closed his eyes. All our eyes were focused on the medicine man's face as it began to slowly change. His eyes closed tightly and his mouth began to display a severe expression of pain. His clenched teeth were very noticeable in the warm orange glow of the lanterns. I held onto my brother's arm so strongly that I knew I must have left bruise marks. I was scared from watching what was taking place before us. This small elderly old man seated on the ground before us was changing into something spiritual. A force had taken over him, and what we were seeing was scaring me.

Grandfather was so weak with illness that I had to brace his body with one hand so he wouldn't fall over. As grandfather closed his eyes and prayed to himself, he was unaware of the transformation which was taking place with the medicine man. With a quick motion, the medicine man turned over on all fours, and with the gestures of a determined dog or wolf, began to crawl around, sniffing the air and pawing at the ground. Then he crawled his way to a corner of the hogan, and began to dig vigorously with his bare hands at the dirt floor. His breathing became loud and filled with energy. He dug and dug with the force of a man much younger and stronger than he actually looked. I took a quick glance at my brother. His face showed that he was also in awe at what was taking place before us. I turned my eyes to the medicine man who had now dug a hole about a foot deep. Then he stopped his digging and seemed to recover from his trance. In a dazed voice, the medicine man asked my brother to bring a lamp over to him, which he quickly did.

Then the medicine man reached into the hole he had just dug, and to all our amazement, pulled out a soil-covered sweater, which belonged to my grandfather! The medicine man said, 'Here is what the witch used for her evil medicine against your grandfather, but now I will use it against her. She used this sweater as her only way to "witch" him. She will no longer be able to have control over him!' After saying this, he sang a song while placing the eagle feather and corn pollen over my grandfather's head and shoulders. My grandfather took a deep breath and fell to one side. My brother was ready to catch him as he fell. Grandfather said he was tired and wanted to sleep. We left him there in his hogan covered in warm wool blankets. The ceremony was over.

We followed the medicine man outside the hogan as he carried the sweater and placed it on the ground. He asked for a lamp, and emptied the kerosene from it over the sweater. He lit a match and tossed it on the sweater. The fire slowly began to burn and consume the sweater. Then, in the distance, we heard a piercing loud scream, a howl. We turned in the direction of the sound and spotted a ball of light, which rose up high into the sky, then bounced away and disappeared into the desert! The medicine man informed us that what we had just heard and seen was the witch. He said, 'She will never be able to recover her strength. I found her power and she will be eaten up by her own evil.'

After that night, grandfather returned to his former, healthy self. I am convinced of the powers which some bad people can use to harm others. So much jealously and evil exists in the world. However, it is good to know that in the end, the power of the Creator always wins. I have seen it."

HOPI (HOPITUH)

The Hopi Reservation lies within the larger Navajo Reservation in the northeast quadrant of Arizona. The nearest town of Tuba City is located to the west while the largest city of Flagstaff is located to the southwest. The Hopi area itself is quite isolated by many miles of desert and canyons. Highway 264 provides the major access to and from the reservation. When mentioning the Hopi or Hopituh Nation, it is difficult not to focus on such essential elements as farming and gardening. Existing and thriving in a desert environment is testament to the adaptive ability of these unique and deeply spiritual people. Hopi can trace their physical ancestral birth to their homeland as being approximately 1200 and earlier. Archaeologically, garden terraces at Third Mesa or Bacavi prove this. Farming methods used in times past are still in use to this day. Examples are the ingenious use of gardens located on mesa walls, which are irrigated terraces that are water-fed by the villages located above. Another method is 'dry farming.' This technique involves the planting of seed within arroyos (washes) and valleys located on the lower plateaus where seasonal rain produces the moisture necessary for their germination and growth.

The Hopi cosmology is composed of four worlds, or 'ways of life.' At the present time, the Hopi believe that they are in the fourth way. As they moved from the third way to the fourth way, they and other people were offered corn by the creator, or Ma'saw. Aside from the Hopi, all the other people eagerly and boldly took the largest of the corn that was offered. The Hopi in turn were left with the shortest and smallest blue corn. The Hopi immediately knew that this was symbolic of their life to come, as it too would be short and difficult. Thus, their response was to manifest the virtues of cooperation, humility and respect among themselves and others. They also knew that the earth was a wonderful and giving, living spirit and its health would depend on the Hopi people as its caretakers.

Today the Hopi live in three separate and autonomous mesas or villages, and within each village are sub-communities. First Mesa includes Waalpi (Walpi), Hanoki (Hano or Tewa), and Sitsomovi (Sichomovi). Second Mesa includes Songoopavi (Shongopavi), Musungnuvi (Mishongnovi) and Supawlavi (Shipaulovi). Third Mesa includes Hoatvela (Hotevilla), Paaqavi (Bacavi), Munqapi (Moencopi), Kiqotsmovi (Kykotsmovi), and Orayvi (Oraibi).

DONALD FIRST CRY'S (HOPI) STORY

Oh, boy! What a story you're about to read. As you might imagine, conducting the research for all my writing has always required me to travel about the Southwest. And because of this traveling I have had to spend many nights in hotels and out-of-the-way motels. Some of these establishments definitely have appealing qualities while others have me praying for the rescuing morning light to make my escape. Donald's story might prompt you to consider other 'issues' when picking a hotel room, 'extra' questions you might need to ask the front desk. His and his wife's encounter with the spiritual world in their hotel room might just also change your own thoughts regarding future vacation travel.

— *Antonio*

"My girlfriend Becky and I are both Hopi. I've spent most of my life on the reservation, except when I left to work for eight years in San Diego, California. My older brother and I were offered well-paying jobs as roofers in new home construction. Becky has worked at the reservation school cafeteria for just a couple of months, and we plan to get married next year. My experience with a ghost took place two years ago. Up to that time I had never had any kind of spooky stuff happen to me. I know that a lot of ghostly things do take place in the hills and mesas that surround our tribal lands, but I never really paid much attention to the stories. Anyway, two years ago Becky and I spent a summer weekend in the gambling town of Laughlin, Nevada. We never thought this short get-away was going to be anything but a fun time. We've driven together to Laughlin many times before without ever having encountered a ghost. So, this first weird experience shook us up for a long time afterwards.

Whenever we've driven to Laughlin, our normal routine is to arrive at a hotel, check into a room, then hit the 'one-arm bandits' downstairs. We've done this since we were in our early twenties. Sometimes we win big, and sometimes we lose, but we have a good time nonetheless. This time, we arrived at the hotel on a Friday evening at around 7 p.m. We checked into a room on the 14th floor with a view of the Colorado River below. We emptied our suitcases of clothes, which we hung on hangers in the closet. Then we decided to watch a little television before heading to the lobby downstairs for a bite to eat. As at other times, we knew we would spend most of the night gambling, so we were in no hurry.

As we were lying on the bed watching a comedy show, I felt an uneasy feeling strangely come over me, a feeling of depression that I had never experienced before. I thought that maybe I was getting the flu or had gotten food poisoning from lunch. I also felt a sort of a weird 'thickness' come over me. I know it sounds strange, but I felt something like a cold mud had covered me. I couldn't make sense of why I was suddenly feeling so bad. At one point, I looked away from the television and focused my eyes on the open window. Without being conscious of it, I started

477

thinking crazy thoughts of darkness coming over me like a cloud.

I began to shaking. My heart was throbbing and I was filled with a sense of dying. Becky must have noticed something was up, because I felt her hand touch my shoulder and say, 'Donald, Donald, what's the matter?' I answered, 'Nothing. I'm just not feeling too good. Maybe I'm getting a cold or the flu.' I told Becky that I needed to close my eyes and rest, but she looked at me funny and said, 'You're drenched in perspiration. Donald, just look at you.' I told her that I would be alright, but I needed to relax for a few minutes. Becky sat back on the bed, but kept an eye on me.

I turned my attention back to the television, and soon I began to feel better. Then that feeling of disaster, a sort of panic came slowly over me once again, and I glance out the window as before. I thought I was having an anxiety attack, because my hands began to shake and a feeling of fear began to take control of me. A friend of mine once had an anxiety attack when we were at a restaurant, so I am aware of the symptoms. I yelled to Becky, 'Look at me; something is happening to me!' Becky came to my side and said, 'Donald, what is it? What's going on?' After a few seconds, I decided to get up off the bed and walk to the bathroom and splash water on my face. Becky followed, and looking at me through my reflection in the mirror said, 'Donald, should we take you to a doctor? You might be having a heart attack.' I answered, 'No, no. Let's just go get something to eat.' As quickly as this thing came over me, it left. I soon regained my composure and told Becky that I was feeling much better. Whatever it was that had come over me was now gone. We decided to leave the room, go down to the lobby and get some dinner.

I began to feel much better and even got lucky when I won $800.00 playing the $1.00 slots! At about 2 a.m. we decided to call it a night, and took the elevator to our room on the 14th floor. Getting ready for bed, I brushed my teeth, then closed the drapes and got into bed. We both quickly fell asleep, but my sleep did not last for long. I was awakened a few hours later when Becky grabbed my arm and shook me hard. 'Donald, Donald, wake up, wake up, there is some guy in the room!' Becky said that she had awakened with the strong feeling of someone's eyes staring at her. When she opened her eyes, she saw the figure of a young man standing next to the bathroom door. Out of fear she grabbed my arm and woke me from my sleep. I watched as Becky pointed to look by the bathroom. At first I didn't see anyone and then I heard a loud 'thud!' It sounded like someone had fallen to the floor. I leaped out of bed and cautiously turned on the lights. As I looked around the room, I noticed there was nothing out of place.

As much as I could tell, we were alone in the room. I carefully walked to the closed bathroom door, reached for the knob, and opened it. I reached inside and felt for the light switch, then turned it on. There was no trace of anyone. Although we could easily explain away the figure of the guy Becky had seen as being a bad dream, we could not explain the falling thud sound we had both heard. Throughout the night, we would hear the thud sound again and again. Being too tired to stay up any longer and discuss it further, we returned to bed and fell asleep. The next morning Becky told me she was unable to sleep and was awake most of the night.

After breakfast, we walked to the parking lot, got into our car and drove to the local mall to do some shopping. We entered a dress shop where Becky began a conversation with a fellow customer, a woman who happened to work in the same hotel where we were staying. She introduced herself to us and said she was a prep-cook there. The woman was a Paiute Indian from California and she and Becky hit it off right away. I excused myself, and decided to wait outside the store on a bench, while Becky finished her conversation. When Becky caught up with me, she told me that the woman had given her some strange information about the hotel where we were staying. Apparently, three days before, there was a guy who had unintentionally killed himself on the 14th floor of the hotel. He was a drug addict who mixed a batch of heroin in the bathroom of his hotel room and died of an overdose. While doing her job, the maid found the body the next morning. The Paiute woman had informed Becky of this after Becky mentioned that we were staying on the 14th floor.

Although the woman was unaware of the dead man's room number, she told Becky it was a room that had a window that faced the river below. The cook also had Becky promise that she would not tell anyone at the hotel about what she had said, for fear that she would lose her job.

Well, this new information sure did give us a new perspective. Becky became very nervous and told me she did not want to worry or scare me, but that the figure she had seen in our room the night before appeared to her once again that night. She told me that she did not get much sleep because the ghost made a sound that caused her to look in the direction of the bathroom. Once again, she spotted the ghost standing against the wall, in a leaning position. His eyes were dark black, and opened wide, and even though his mouth moved to make words, no sound came out. Then the ghost suddenly disappeared. Becky said she closed her eyes and convinced herself that what she had seen was something her imagination had made up, but she spent the night drifting in and out of sleep.

With this new information, Becky and I returned to our hotel, requested and got us, a room change. Since that weekend, we've not had another experience with the supernatural. And I have not had another anxiety attack or anything like one."

SACRAMENTO, CA

CALIFORNIA STATE INDIAN MUSEUM

Shavehead, chief of the Hat Creek, Atsugewi people. The Atsugewi's homeland was in the area now known as Lassen National Park.

The museum is housed on the same two-block city location as Sutter's Fort. In the museum's collections is sheltered one of the finest collections of California Indian basketry. From cooking or boiling, to flawlessly beautiful and delicately decorated feather baskets, all regions of the state's Native American population is represented.

Other important displayed items are musical instruments and ceremonial dance regalia. There are exhibits that also highlight tools, hunting and gathering implements, and contemporary art. The spirituality of Californian's native peoples is a dominant theme throughout the displays. Outside demonstrations include the Gathering of Honored Elders (held in May), the Art Show and Acorn Day (both held in Autumn), and the Arts and Crafts Holiday Fair (held Fridays and Saturdays after the Thanksgiving holiday).

LINDA BLUE'S STORY

I'm Miwok/Maidu from the Wilton Rancheria on the Consumnes river, located about 38 miles southeast of Sacramento. This year marks my third season that I've been working at the State Indian Museum. My official title is 'on-call' Park Aid employee. I help out with the usual museum interpretation duties, such as describing to visitors the various rare California baskets, and other items of historical importance that are displayed.

Before beginning my employment at the museum, I was told by fellow Indians about the history of adjacent Sutter's Fort being built upon an Indian burial mound. I have knowledge of several burial sites that have been discovered and disturbed about the fort.

Our museum is housed in a building just a short walk behind the fort. And working at the Indian Museum has not been a "spiritual" problem for me. Anthropologist have also discovered Native American artifacts on the grounds surrounding the museum and fort. I know from working on archeological sites on my own reservation, that our ancestral spirits do care about their belongings. Fortunately, the state is now sensitive of our beliefs, because Native American employees are given the option of being re-assigned to other sites if they wish.

It's also well known that some Native Americans refuse to work at Sutter's Fort, because of sudden, and unusual illnesses that are reported by them, soon after entering the area. Because of this, today I can't name one Native American Indian who currently works at the Fort. Employees have mentioned to me that they have seen dark figures walking in the museum, and on the museum

Linda Blue.

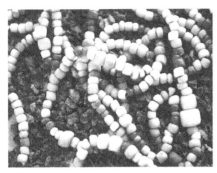

It was a common burial rite for Indian people to bury strings of hand-made shell beads with their dead. We call these burial beads, 'Cry Beads'.

grounds. Of course, I was hesitant at first to work so close to such a spiritual site. But, because I sincerely respect my ancestors, I know I'll be alright.

A very disturbing trend is when non-natives dig up Native Indian burial sites, and disrespectfully take the offerings, and jewelry that the dead person was lovingly buried with. For instance, it was a common burial rite for Indian people to bury strings of hand-made shell beads with their dead. We call these burial beads, 'Cry Beads." I've seen these funeral beads being displayed and sold at swap meets, auctions, etc. Non-Indians can't seem to relate, as we do, to the spiritual significance that these funeral items have to our culture. So, they take our burial offerings, restring and sell them. It's so disrespectful and terribly sad to see.

My own spirit or ghost experiences at the museum are not uncommon from others who have spent time, any long length of time there. For example, when I'm alone standing at the front desk, soon after closing the doors for the day, I'll sometimes hear the soft sound of older Indian women start a chanting song. Their songs are most evident in the rear of the building, where old baskets are displayed behind glass.

There are moments when I'll quietly walk to the rear of the museum, pause for a few seconds at the basket display then hear the spirit women singing in their native language. I don't recognize the language, but they're definitely Indian songs. The songs are not loud, but are more of a soothing, soft chanting. The chanting will continue without pause. As I walk, returning back to the front desk, I can still hear these women's voices chanting.

My explanation is that the chanting is due directly to the museum displays. Because the baskets being displayed have been collected from all over California, the singing spirit women could be from any one of the many Indian nations that existed in the state. Deep within my soul, I can 'feel' these spirit women's connection, and attachment to their baskets. I know they're overseeing that their work is being cared for, that it's being honored in the right way. It's almost as if they want their baskets to return home to their own people. Employees have also mentioned to me that they have seen dark figures, or shadows walking among the museum displays, and also on the museum grounds.

Other strange, but common occurrences are the various artifacts that move on their own, within the museum. These particular Indian displayed items are moved off shelves, as if the spirits are annoyed. Several times I've witnessed spoons, beads, and small baskets that I know have been securely attached to a pedestal, moved off the pedestal, and set on the bottom of the case.

Other things that has frightened employees, both Native and Anglo, have been the shaking of padlocks that hang on the cases. We've all seen this take place. We've stood by and watched as the mounted locks on the display cases, actually move as if some invisible hands were pulling, to forcibly open them. Our collective response has been "We've got to get out of here. Something is not right!" As recently as three weeks ago, some employees came to me and reported that the padlocks on the cases were once again moving. So, as I said, it's a common experience.

Not long ago, we had a group of about 100 gypsies visit the museum grounds. One gypsy woman came into the museum and engaged me in conversation about one of their family members who was being hospitalized in a local hospital. I immediately felt something come over me that was not right. This woman had a strong spiritual presence about her, and it was affecting me in a negative manner. As she spoke, I felt her energy, or power, pushing against me. I actually felt her energy pushing me away from her. This was very strange because it came over me without any warning. I moved several steps back away from her, when something unseen, and very powerful struck me from the side. Just then, another gypsy woman came to join her friend. Without them moving or saying a word, I was moved from side to side by these women's power.

Somehow I escaped this spiritual 'tug of war,' and walked over to a fellow ranger who was standing nearby. I asked the ranger to take over because I wasn't feeling well. I knew these women were trying to tap into my spirit, and take my Indian power from me. Their power was very strong and hard to break away from. It was a terrible and strange moment for me. An experience that I've never before had.

I'd hope the spirits who are attached to their baskets in our museum understand that we honor them, and their baskets. I think they do. Our people are very strong people. I enjoy being surrounded by my culture. We know how to identify and protect ourselves from bad spiritual things. We pray, and use sage to 'smoke' our homes, and to honor our families. The "Chaw'se,' or 'Big Time' gathering at Indian Grinding Rock State Park in the Sierra Nevada Foothills is also a special spiritual time for us. This gathering is attended by many Indian families from all areas of the state, and is primarily focused on unity and thanksgiving ceremonies.

SAN CARLOS APACHE (T'IIS-EBAH-NNEE)

The San Carlos Apache Indian Reservation is located east of Phoenix in southeastern Arizona and was established by Executive Order on November 9, 1871.

The total landmass of the reservation is just under 1,900,00 acres. The

reservation was reduced in size a total of five times for the benefit of copper and silver miners and land anxious Mormons whose demand for water surrounding the Gila Valley reduced it further. It is the seventh largest U.S. reservation, with over 7,100 people.

Within the reservation borders are forested alpine meadows and wooded mountains, as well as desert plains. Anthropologists speculate that the Apache nation entered this region around 1450. The San Carlos Apache call themselves "t'iis-ebah-nnee" or "grey cottonwood people" and their language is closely related to the Dineh' (Navajo).

The San Carlos Apache now consider themselves to be a unified people, even though their history shows they were originally several separate bands of the same Native nation. After his surrender in 1873, the great Apache chief Cochise, along with his followers was forcibly taken by the U.S. military to San Carlos.

Soon after, the famous medicine man Geronimo and his followers fled the oppression of the San Carlos Reservation. Presently, the reservation fights the continuous battle of arduous unemployment among its people, with the hope of further developing industry and tourism. Encouragingly, tourism is taking hold as a source of income and employment. The tribe is directly promoting its lakes and forests, focusing on campers and sportspeople. The cattle-ranching industry and the mining of Peridot, a semiprecious green stone found within the reservation, is also a source of employment. The largest nearby town of Globe provides needed medical and shopping facilities.

HENRY TALL HORSE'S STORY

As I turned off the main highway unto the roughly paved road that led to the center of the reservation, I was surprised by the starkness of the area. Given the extreme hot weather, there were no visible people anywhere to be seen outdoors. Slowly maneuvering my car through the dirt roads, I past a few humble homes, and the carcass of a dead calf laying aside the road. It struck me that the poverty of the area should be a wake-up call to the governmental department that oversees this reservation and its honorable people. This being said, I eventually met with Henry whereas he provided me with a very interesting story of which I know you'll appreciate.

— Antonio

"My mother died when I was two years old, and since that time, I've lived in San Carlos with my father. My experience was with two spirits. Everyone seems to think that ghosts only appear during the night, but in my case, I saw them during the day. These spirits didn't harm me, but

I still got pretty scared. My experience was a strange and powerful one that I know will stay with me for a long time.

One spring morning, when I was nineteen years old, a close friend and I decided to walk over to the nearby San Carlos River and fish for catfish. Before heading out, we found two metal beer can openers. We used two stones to pound them flat, and made them into spear points. We sharpened the metal points, grinding them against a large flat boulder. Then we wrapped each of these points with wire to the ends of long thin, but strong, poles. It was a primitive but effective tool in spearing fish. My friend and I went fishing like this many times before, so we were eager to catch a lot of fish. It was about 10 a.m. when we got to the river.

We followed the riverbed until we found a spot with a few trees to shade us from the sun, and a pool of water that we hoped had some fish. We each sat on the sand at opposite sides of the pool.

Because the pool of water was a short distance from the main river, the water was still. In this still water, it was easy to spot the movement of swimming fish. We fished for a few hours, and caught five fish. We decided to head home and fry the fish for lunch. Most Apache I know don't like to eat fish because of our traditional beliefs, but that is changing. My friend and I enjoy eating fish. After our catfish lunch, my friend went home to his house and I took a nap.

Around 6 p.m. I decided to walk back to the river, only this time I just wanted to walk and not fish. I followed the path back to the pool of water where my friend and I had been earlier. As I got closer, in the distance I heard a strange sound. The sound was a humming or buzzing noise that I couldn't identify. I decided to investigate by following the sounds up the riverbed ahead of me. The sun was starting to go down in the west, but there was still plenty of light. As I got closer, the noise seemed to change to something like the flapping wings of a large flock of birds. I decided to slow my pace in order not to surprise whatever might be making the noise. I walked as carefully as I could through the trees and spiny weeds. I had a feeling that animals might be nearby, so when I thought I was close enough, I stopped and got behind a large tree branch to hide myself. Flies were buzzing around my head, but I didn't want to make any noise by swatting them. I got down on my stomach and lay flat on the sand, so I wouldn't be seen.

In the distance, not far from me, I could see two large, dark shadow-like figures. They were about 70 yards away from me and I was unable to make out what they were. At first I thought they were two large dogs. They were about the same size as German shepherds. I strained my eyes to see the figures. Suddenly they changed into a shape that took on a human form! They were definitely not dogs, and I knew they were definitely not human either! As I said before, there was plenty of sunlight, so darkness was not a problem. Also, I noticed that something like a cloth, or maybe possibly animal skins, hung loose over their bodies. I couldn't tell what this stuff was.

The figures had arms and legs, hands and feet, and their faces were covered with this cloth like stuff. This covering made it impossible to a make out their faces. I saw them bent over on their hands and feet, walking just like a four-legged animal. While I was watching, coming from the direction of the figures, was the flapping wing noise that I had heard earlier. There were no birds anywhere and no wind blowing either! But I could hear the noise of what sounded to me like a tremendous flock of birds' wings flapping! These mysterious figures stood up, bowed down, turned around, and slowly moved away from each other. Several times they got down on all fours, and for many minutes, turned in complete circles. It seemed like they were dancing.

Something inside told me that these "things" were not normal, but in fact "spirits." I was scared. I tried my best to keep very still, but I was shaking all over.

After a few minutes, the spirits changed their steps and began to move from side to side. I know this might sound crazy, but the figures changed from animal to human to animal and back again. I couldn't believe what I was seeing! Suddenly, they did something that scared me even more: they stood upright on their feet, and leaped towards each other. I'm telling you, this really surprised me. I didn't expect them to do this, or to be so fast. I felt that if I moved, even a finger, they would discover me. Who knows what they would have done to me. Because they were moving all around the riverbed so much, I was afraid they would eventually spot me. I decided to keep lying flat on my stomach, hoping to camouflage, to blend into the background as much as possible. If they spotted me, I was ready to run for it. I kept quiet and watched them repeat their strange dance over and over again.

A few times one of them would jump about ten feet into the air. It was terrifying and, at the same time, fascinating to watch. I stayed hidden behind the branch for a few more minutes, until I felt a bug sting my leg. I felt it crawl into my pant leg and sting me on the ankle. It must have been a wasp because it hurt like heck! I didn't want to move, but knew I needed to get rid of it. I slowly sat up and stretched my arm over to scratch my leg. Through it all, I didn't take my focus off the spirits. Luckily, they didn't notice me. But when I turned my head, I hit it against a branch that was a few inches above me.

The sound of the moving branch gave me away! I saw the spirits freeze and immediately they turned their heads in my direction! I saw them crouch down and instantly disappear into thin air! That was all I needed.

I stood up and ran for my life, breaking branches as I ran through the bushes. Several times I lost my balance and fell to the ground. Each time I got up and ran back down the river retracing my steps, stumbling many more times before arriving at the road, which led back home. It's difficult for me to describe how absolutely terrified I was. I was shaking all over and a bit bloodied.

When I got home, my father saw me covered in sweat and dirt and asked me where I had been. I excitedly told him the story of what I had seen. He looked at me with a strange gaze that I had never seen before and shook his head saying, "Those were not things you should have been watching. You should not have been sneaking up on those spirits. They need to be left alone when they dance. You must not ever sneak up on spirits again." He also told me: "The spirits come down from the mountains from time to time." They have been doing this since Apaches first came to this area. The spirits live in the mountains and canyons. They follow the water because there is power in water. The river is like a big vein and water is the blood of life for spiritual beings.

You need to go back there to where you saw the spirits, and leave them an offering." I told my father that I would do as he said, but as of this day, I have not gone back to that spot. I don't want to see any more spirits. Knowing that the spirits did not wish to cause me any harm has changed my view of spiritual things, but I'm still not wanting to meet any more of them.

I was raised with the stories of spirits that lived in the nearby mountains around our reservation, and was always told of witches and ghosts that took many animal forms.

Years ago, it took my own experience with the dark, dancing spirits to prove to me that these were not just stories. I know these spirits are real because I have seen them."

TAOS PUEBLO, NM

Taos Pueblo, home of the Native American Taos-Tiwa, is the site of one of the oldest continually inhabited communities in the United States. Taos Pueblo is the most northern of New Mexico's 19 pueblos; it is located 70 miles north of Santa Fe, the state capital, two miles north of the world-famous art colony of Taos, and some 15 miles from the internationally renowned Taos Ski Valley. The pueblo is at an elevation of 7,000 feet.

The origin of the pueblo in its present form goes back many hundreds of years before the Spanish arrived in 1540. It goes back some 300 years before Marco Polo traveled to China in the 13th century. Had Columbus "stumbled" upon the "new" world even 500 years before he did, back when Europe as we know it was young and "America" was not even a vision, and had he proceeded immediately to the great Southwest after stepping ashore on a remote island off the Atlantic Coast, he would have found in place in Taos a vibrant and established culture. The pueblo

was here long before Europe emerged from the Dark Ages and made the transition from medieval to modern history.

A regiment of Spanish conquistadors from Coronado's 1540 expedition were the first Europeans to see Taos Pueblo. The Spaniards reportedly were on a quest for the Seven Cities of Cibola (the fabled cities of gold), and they believed they had finally found one of the cities of gold when they saw Taos Pueblo from afar, perhaps with the sun shining upon it. What the Spaniards saw was not a city of gold, but two massive, multi-storied structures made of mud and straw and with soft, flowing lines. This came to be the distinctive architectural style of the entire Southwest. Taos Pueblo then looked very similar to the way it does now, with houses to the north and south divided by the westerly flowing Rio Pueblo de Taos.

In 1680, a massive revolt against the Spanish was conceived in Taos and launched successfully by the united effort of all the pueblos. The Spanish were driven back into Mexico and all of the territory of New Mexico, including the Spanish capital of Santa Fe, was again in Native American hands. This was an event truly distinctive in the annals of Native American resistance to the spread of the "New World." It remains today the only instance where extensive territory was recovered and retained by Native Americans through force of arms.

TAOS

Population 3,369 · Elevation 6,983

The Spanish community of Taos developed two miles southwest of Taos Pueblo. It later served as a supply base for the "Mountain Men", and was the home of Kit Carson, who is buried here. Governor Charles Bent was killed here in the anti-U.S. insurrection of 1847. In the early 1900s, Taos developed as a colony for artists and writers.

Taos, the seat of the rebellion, returned to its traditional, full independence for a period of almost two decades. The Spanish returned in 1693 with a large army, but Taos itself remained the center of open rebellion for some five years after the southern pueblos were once again subjected to foreign control. This distinctive military success is especially noteworthy in light of the fact that it was achieved by the traditionally peaceful, agrarian-based pueblos, a tranquil society that initially welcomed the foreigners with open arms.

The pueblo's native religion and culture survived not only the turmoil of the last decade of the 17th century—a hundred years before the birth of the United States of America—but also the 1847 rebellion of the pueblo against the new American government that had replaced the Mexican, and other centuries of Spanish, Mexican, and American dominance. Taos Pueblo has retained its old ways to a remarkable degree. The rich cultural heritage of the pueblo is exemplified not only in the exquisite architecture, but also in the annual seasonal dances. Visitors to the pueblo are welcome to observe the dances, but are not allowed to take photographs of them.

The current reservation economy is primarily supported through the provision of government services, tourism, arts and crafts, ranching, and farming. In 1980, the tribal council established a Department of Economic Development to generate tribal revenue and job opportunities and to assist local Native American businesses. Many opportunities for development are available to the pueblo, some of which include increased capitalization of tourism, labor-intensive clean-industry plants, and office rentals.

ALFRED J. MONTOYA'S STORY

I was born on the Taos Pueblo Reservation in 1950. The beautiful mountains that surround the pueblo are the Sangre de Cristos (Blood of Christ). The Spanish gave them this name because, during some sunsets, the light that reflects from the sky onto these mountains colors the mountains red. These mountains are sacred to the pueblo people and are always honored in a very special way. I always enjoy hiking in the mountains and being at peace with our Mother Earth. I do some deer, elk, and bear hunting and a lot of fishing.

As a member of the pueblo, I don't need a hunting license to hunt these animals; however, outside of the pueblo land it's required. I prefer to stay here in our mountains where I feel free to do as I wish without restrictions. It was in these sacred mountains where I had my first experience with spirits.

Alfred J. Montoya.

In the fall of 1974, I was employed by the forest service. My job was to clean up areas where irresponsible hikers and campers had tossed papers, bottles, cans, and other trash in the forest. The crew I was with used horses to travel around the area. One day, we were instructed by our supervisor to ride up to Blue Lake, which lay deep within the mountains, and clean up the area. I was busy with some other work at the time and was not excused from heading out early. The others in my crew, including my supervisor, left in the morning. I was to meet up with them later in the afternoon.

At about 3:30 p.m. that afternoon, I eventually reached the lake. I scouted the area and spotted horse tracks and footprints all about the ground. I knew that the crew had done their job of cleaning up the area, so I decided to head out in the direction the crew might be in order to meet up with them. I had been instructed by my supervisor earlier that day to locate and follow an old, crude barbed-wire fence. By following the fence, I would travel in the direction the men would be going. This was a shortcut. I gazed above the mountaintops and noticed that the clouds were traveling fast. The cold night would soon come, so I attempted to hurry as best I could. Luckily, I had packed a few food supplies and a bedroll on my horse before leaving for the mountains. All I knew was that my destination, where I would meet the others, was what we called in our pueblo language, "place of the onion grass."

Ultimately, I did locate the barbed-wire fence. It branched out in two directions; one went East, the other, West. I sat on my horse for a few minutes, trying to decide which way to go. Trying to make sense of everything was difficult, especially since the forest was pretty thick with growth. I decided the best option was to follow my instincts and go in what I thought was North. I began to notice that things were not right. I knew I was getting lost because, after about five miles of riding, I began to travel down a ridge that was unfamiliar to me. To make matters worse, the sun would soon be giving way to the night, so I needed to locate my friends.

Before long, I reached an area that I recognized from other previous visits. Immediately I knew I had gone too far and had missed the trail. I reached a stream and followed it north; I needed to hurry, because the sun was now behind a ridge and a cool breeze was blowing.

Suddenly, I turned to my right and I saw a beautiful big buck, 10 points to his antlers! The buck had his head lowered and was drinking from the stream. My horse made a noise, and the buck raised his head. He faced my direction and I could see his big, dark eyes gazing at me. I always carried a pistol with me, so when I saw this buck out in the open, I knew the opportunity for fresh deer meat was just a few feet away from me.

I slowly reached for my gun, brought it into my line of sight, and had the buck in my view. Something inside me made me lower the pistol. I decided not to shoot. I put my pistol away and then looking right at those big black eyes, I held up my hand and in the Indian way said, "Good-bye, my brother. We will meet again someday." As I rode my horse away, I glanced behind me and noticed the buck just staring at me. I reached the meadow area known as "the place of the onion grass."

Since it was already dark, I thought it would be best to make camp for the night. I could join my buddies in the morning. It didn't take long for me to make a fire and roll out my sleeping bag. I led my horse a little way to a grassy area of the meadow and left him to graze for the night.

It was definitely a dark night. As I ate some of the food I had brought with me, I gazed up at the stars and felt at peace. I asked the Creator and Mother Earth to protect and watch over me. I threw more wood on the fire and listened to the cracking and snapping noises it produced as the wood was consumed. I rose from where I was seated, and went to get my horse. I returned to the camp and tied my horse close to where I could keep an eye on him. Throwing more wood onto the fire, I decided to make some coffee.

There I was in the cold darkness, with both hands wrapped around my coffee mug. Everything was peaceful, and soon I felt sleepy enough to climb into my sleeping bag for the night. I watched the fire dance before me and very soon my eyelids became heavy. Before I closed my eyes, I heard some noise to my right. I sat up within the sleeping bag and turned my head in the direction of the noise.

The flickering light of the fire illuminated the area I was looking at. There, from the forest came into view a man dressed in old, traditional-style Indian garments. He was dancing, but had his back towards me. He came closer and I kept still.

He had an odd manner of dancing that I was not familiar with. Soon, he was opposite the fire from me. Although I heard no music, no drumming sound, he danced and sang with a rhythm all his own. He danced in a backward motion. I was unable to make out his facial features because his head movements were so quick and sudden. I just saw a blur and very difficult to focus on his face. The song he sang was unrecognizable to me. Even the words he sang were strange. I was interested in knowing who this man was, but at the same time I was scared.

It was very odd to see this man out there in the forest before me. I knew he was from another time because of his clothes. As he danced, he raised his arms and soon began to motion towards the darkness. He motioned as if calling someone to join him in his dance. It was strange to see this faceless man dancing and motioning as he did.

Then, from the direction he was facing, came another figure, a woman.

She slowly entered the lit area and began to dance with the man. Unlike the man who sang throughout his dance, the woman remained silent. She danced in a forward direction, taking steps left then right, left then right. I was frozen with fear and amazement. I was as still as I could be.

She was also dressed in old-style clothes. She wore traditional leggings and moccasins, and her hair was in the traditional pueblo woman manner. Over her back she wore a manta (a shawl worn over the shoulders and back).

Although I was able to make out all the details of

her outfit, her face was a blur also, and she was not someone I recognized. I kept quiet as they both danced in unison. I was mesmerized.

Suddenly, they made their way away from my camp and fire and moved towards the stream. It was at this point that I heard them both laughing. They soon disappeared by the stream and into the darkness of the night. During this "spiritual performance," I was unable to move my arms, legs, or other parts of my body. My eyes saw the vision and my ears heard the sounds. My focus was centered in simply observing and nothing more.

After they had left me, I was alone with my thoughts. I knew what I had just witnessed was a spiritual sign. I was left mentally numb. I just sat there in a void.

Then again, I heard some sound coming from the north. I turned and saw what appeared to be flashlights coming my way through the forest.

Great! I thought, my buddies had seen my fire and had located my whereabouts! There were three lights and they moved around in the darkness, coming closer and closer towards me. I was so relieved and happy that they had found me. After what I had just seen, they couldn't have come at a better time. As the lights came closer, they suddenly stopped about 100 yards away. I threw more wood onto the fire and waited. Expecting to see my friends' faces any second, I sat back in my sleeping bag.

Out of the forest came three male figures, three men whom I did not recognize! As they got closer I saw that they had three horses with them. When they got to about 50 yards from me, I saw that they were Indians and were dressed in white man's clothes: Levi's jackets, jeans, etc.

Once they were close enough for me to hear their voices, I heard them speaking in mumbling tones. I was unable to make out what they were saying. As soon as they spotted me, they stood still. I don't know why or how, but immediately I knew I was being visited by more spirits once again. As soon as this thought came over me, I closed my eyes and prayed. When I opened my eyes, the men were opposite the campfire.

Then suddenly, in an instant, they had moved to another area of my camp, horses and all! Then, in a blink of an eye, they were back where they were before, all seated and gazing in my direction.

Together, they extended their fingers towards me, and pointed in a way that made me think I was something funny to them. They spoke, but all I could make out were mumbling sounds. At one point, one of the men bent forward to get a closer look at me. I looked at their horses and then at the fire that separated us. The man who had his eyes focused on me then let out a big laugh. I was scared. I must have passed out because when I came to, I found myself out of my sleeping bag, on the ground, several feet away from where I had been by the fire. I was on the cold ground, shivering. The last thing I remembered was being in my sleeping bag, and now here I was freezing on the open ground several feet away. I got up and walked over to where the fire was. It was out, but there were still some hot glowing coals in the pit. I threw in more wood on top of the coals and soon I had a fire going again. I took my loaded pistol in one hand and a flashlight in the other and walked around the area where I had seen the three men. There was no sign that the ground or grass had been disturbed. I noticed that the sun was lighting up the sky, before it came over the mountains.

As the light made the ground around me more visible, the only tracks I could find were the ones I had made coming into the meadow. There were no others. The grass was wet with dew and undisturbed. I packed up my horse, cleaned camp, and rode up the ridge away from the meadow. I couldn't erase from my memory what had happened to me just a few hours before. I was comforted by the morning sunlight that warmed my face and by the songs of the birds flying in and out of the trees.

Up in the distance I spotted my friends riding down the ridge. I heard them let out a yell and call out my name. I knew immediately these people were not spirits, but living human beings! As we met up with each other, my buddies had a shocked expression on each of their faces. "Hey, Alfred, you look pretty pale," one guy said. "What happened to you?" I began to describe the night before to them. They freaked out!

They were quiet throughout my story and when I was through, they began to tell me a story of their own. They said that at about the same time that the spirits had appeared to me, they had all seen two Indian spirits! At first, they had heard the sound of footsteps running over the forest ground among the trees.

Then, a strange sense of someone watching them from the darkness overwhelmed them all. As they all sat quietly before their campfire, looking at each other, suddenly two Indian men dressed in traditional style warrior outfits came out of the forest, running at full speed right by them.

Of course, they all knew something unusual and spiritual was taking place. The two warriors just raced by and disappeared into the forest, from where they had come. After discussing among ourselves the possible reasons for what we had all experienced, we were left with no answers and feeling perplexed. I was apparently the most puzzled of all.

I guess my friends saw this and decided that I needed to have a spiritual cleansing. My friends had me face North, and in the afternoon sunlight I was prayed over in the Indian way, in order to remove the bad energy I might have been exposed to. We headed home and did not ever speak about what we saw and experienced that night.

That evening, at my house, I did mention my experience to my grandmother. She looked at me and listened to each word as if I was telling her something very important, something sacred. Then, after I finished speaking, she held my hands and informed me that she had some sad news for me. I was told that my other grandmother had died the same night I had had my vision. My grandmother also told me that what I had experienced was my other grandmother's way of showing me that she was all right and was now passing into the other world, the spirit world. Grandmother further informed me that the dancing man and woman had headed in a southerly direction and disappeared because, "That's the spirits' way; they travel south. Where you were camped is where our Sacred Blue Lake is located. It's the spirits' way."

Grandmother then told me that the three men who had showed themselves to me, after the two dancing spirits had left, were very different from the man and woman. "You know, those three spirits were very powerful. It was a good thing you did not speak to them. Keeping quiet was the best thing for you to do. Otherwise, those spirits would have taken you away with them. You would have been left dead in the forest, your spirit would have been lifted away, and all we would have found would have been your body. We would not have known what caused Immediately your mysterious death. What saved you was the campfire that kept burning between where you were and where the spirits were. It was good that you asked the Creator for a blessing and for Mother Earth to protect you that night."

The story I have just told you is the truth. It is what I saw with my own eyes. There are people who do not believe in these things, but some do. I'm happy to know that my grandmother, who passed away, chose to let me know how she was and that she was heading to the spirit world. Because of the darkness that night, I could not recognize her. The dancing spirits were presented to me for a purpose; they were not bad or evil. But the other spirits, the three men . . . Well, I knew something was not right when I saw them.

You know, there are many other stories and incidents that have taken place in and around the pueblo. I have experienced some very strange things. There are such things as witches and evildoers, but I would rather not talk about them. To talk about them would only give them more strength and increase their power for doing bad things.

There are areas of power up here in the mountains, areas that feel negative to the soul. Indian people whom I've spoken to have told me that, as they travel through the forest, they can sometimes feel the presence of eyes gazing at them from between the trees. Some have even told me that they feel the presence of someone following them, something that moves from behind the trees, and hides among the shadows.

There are a lot of things that have happened to people around here. Most people prefer not to talk about them. Perhaps it's best not to. We'll leave it at that.

WHITE MOUNTAIN APACHE (NDE, INDEH OR TINNEH)

The White Mountain Apache have the notable history of being the direct descendants of the original Apache Tribes who settled the area many centuries ago. The ancestral homeland of the White Mountain Apache Nation is located in the east central region of Arizona. The Apache are now a nation comprised of several independent bands throughout the Southwest.

The reservation encompasses 1.6 million acres. It was established by Executive Order on November 9, 1891. Strongly traditional in culture and spirituality, the nation currently has over 12,000 members. Historically, they were hunters and raiders who did some farming, but in many cases carried out raids on neighboring agricultural-based villages for food that they were unable to obtain by hunting. The Apache consider the mountains that surround their lands to be sacred and the source of their spirituality. The Spaniards, Anglos and Mexicans were unsuccessful in their numerous attempts to subdue these true guerrilla warriors. As with almost everything ever written about the Apache, it is important for the reader to question the source of the written word, due in large part to a negatively skewed view regarding the Apache being linked to a vast amount of atrocities. In fact, this cautious approach should be taken when reading most anything printed about Native people—period.

Today a wide range of accommodations that include dining, shopping and gaming at the Hon-Dah Casino are available on the reservation.

CATHERINE TWO BEARS' (APACHE) STORY

Catherine and I sat under a traditional Ramada or patio that she herself constructed of pine poles and branches in her backyard. It so happened that at one particular point in our conversation, where she mentioned encountering an owl, a large yellow butterfly came fluttering about her head and landed on her wrist. Without flinching, she looked at me and said, "Antonio, I can see the spirits are with us. This sign is a message given to us of their presence. I honor them." After a few seconds of silence, we continued with the interview as the butterfly fluttered away. I'll leave this image with you to interpret, but personally I am convinced that Catherine and I were both honored with a simple and spiritual expression that day.

— Antonio

"In 1992, I was attending the University of Arizona in Phoenix. I was in my senior year and majoring in biology. During the summer of that same year, five seniors (including myself), four graduate students and a professor were conducting fieldwork at Theodore Roosevelt Lake. The lake is located in the Tonto National Forest, about a two-hour drive northeast of Phoenix. Our two-month study and research focused on native amphibians of the lake, specifically bullfrogs.

Throughout the years, this particular species of frog had begun to change the ecology of Arizona's lake and streams. Although the bullfrogs had increased in population, other smaller native populations of frogs were showing the beginning signs of extinction. Bullfrogs have a voracious appetite and will consume anything smaller than them, including snakes, other frogs, lizards and mice. Our focus of study was to specifically record data, and to ultimately discover a link to the bullfrog population explosion. Although I enjoyed the research fieldwork, it was wet, muddy, and smelly and I had to wade in waist-deep cold water. In order to catch the frogs, I had to dress in watertight rubber overalls. Another part of my uniform was a net laundry bag, which I tied to my belt, a pith helmet with a flashlight strapped on top, and of course a fish net attached to a six-foot pole.

My colleagues and I would get in the water at about eight in the evening and begin our 'hunt,' which would last until around ten or so at night. We initiated a process of surprise by which we would catch these fast and alert bullfrogs by slowly wading towards a floating mass of leaves or plants. Using the light strapped to my helmet, I would scan the area until I spotted the bright telltale sign of a bullfrog's reflecting eyes. Once spotted, I would make my way towards the frog, careful not to make any ripples and, using my fishing net, quickly catch it and place it inside the net bag tied to my belt. This system, although primitive, would bring in about ten to twenty frogs a night per student. Each pair of students had a section of lake in which to capture the frogs. After finishing our work for the night, we would drive back to the lab and place the frogs in a large stock-water tank for study the next day. Our evening captures took place three nights a week. Due to the many frogs in the area, we had enough specimens and paperwork to keep us very busy.

So, you may ask, what does capturing bullfrogs have to do with ghosts? Well, one evening during a night of bullfrog catching, something very, very strange happened to me. Another girl and I went off for the evening to do the night's frog gathering. We went into the water at about eight in the evening. The frogs were making their croaking sounds as usual, and we got right to work. But at about nine o'clock, I began to feel sick. My stomach was turning. I figured it was something I had eaten earlier at dinner. I decided to end the evening's hunt and get back to my warm bed. I informed my partner that I would be taking the truck, and for her to catch a return ride to the lab with the others. 'No problema,' she said. So off I drove. The road was dark. I had to drive slowly due to javelinas (wild desert pigs) and other small desert animals that were out and about. It was summer, so to get fresh air, I had both the windows in the truck lowered. Suddenly, I felt something come in through the passenger side window! Something hit the right side of my body and gave me a terrible scare! I quickly put on the brakes and nervously turned on the interior truck light. That's when I saw it—a small owl!

Apparently, the owl had flown across my path on the road, and mistakenly entered the truck through the open window. Well, there it was, on the floor of the truck flapping its wings with its beak wide open. I can look back now and say, that confused bird gave me a good scare! I opened my driver's side door and scrambled outside. I walked over to the passenger side door and opened it, to allow the owl a way out. But when I opened the door, the owl was gone! Where had it gone?

I carefully looked under and behind the truck seat, but there was no owl. If it had exited the truck on its own, I would have heard it, or even seen it because the dome light was still on inside the truck. This was definitely a strange thing that had just occurred. The owl in my truck simply disappeared! Knowing something about animal behavior, I knew that this was not normal. Also, being an Apache gave me a cultural knowledge about such things. Traditional Apache people do not consider owls to be positive animals to be associated with. I knew this owl was not a good omen. Owls to Apaches are messengers of bad news, and even death. My parents have told me that some medicine people who do evil use the owl's spirit in their witchcraft.

I quickly got back into the truck, rolled up both windows and drove at a fast speed to the cabin. I admit that at the time, I was scared being all by myself. When I entered the cabin, I went straight to the bathroom and showered. I still had the stomach-ache, but now I was more concerned about my recent owl incident. After making sure that all the doors in the cabin were locked, and the outside light was on, I got into bed and waited for the return of the others. After about twenty minutes, no one had returned, and I began to get worried. I got out of bed and looked out the window, and saw nothing but darkness. I thought it best to try and sleep, even though my stomach was a ball of nerves. As soon as I got back into bed, I heard footsteps in the front room. I knew there was no way someone could have entered the cabin without opening the locked door and making a sound. Something bad was definitely going on, and I was terrified!

As I gazed from my bed at the open doorway that led into the bedroom, the footsteps stopped. Then there was silence for a few seconds. Soon I heard the voice of what sounded like a small child speaking in my Apache language, 'Can I go see mama? I want to see mama. Can I go see mama?' I couldn't stop trembling. The words were very clear, and because they were spoken in Apache, that made them even more terrifying to me. I had had enough of this, so I jumped out of the bed and, in the darkness, scrambled for the light switch on the wall. Nervously, I tripped over my own shoes, smashed my big toe against the dresser and fell to the floor hitting my left shoulder. I was in such pain, and I figured my toe was broken. I managed to crawl across the floor, then find the wall with the light switch, turn it on, and crawl to the bathroom.

No sooner had I entered the bathroom, when I heard the sound of my fellow students' trucks returning to the lab. I was an emotional mess. I decided it would be best not to tell anyone about what had happened to me. After all, what could they say or offer me? One thing that I did need was to get some medical help for my toe. It was already swelling up when my roommate came in the door. I told her that I had fallen, and that was all. I was driven that night to the student university clinic in Phoenix, where an x-ray was taken. I was given the good news that the toe was not broken, but I eventually lost the nail. Still it hurt quite a lot and it was very bruised. Unable to do any more night wading for frogs in cold lake water, my research ended. I spent the remainder of the summer at home.

Once I arrived home, I told my parents all about the experience with the owl, and the child's ghostly voice. They told me to pray and to never again be out alone in that area. My parents could not offer an explanation regarding the owl that came into my truck, or the ghostly voice of the child. All I was told was that sometimes these 'things' are forces that foretell a future event. As of this date, I have not had anything happen to me that I can connect to that summer night in 1992. But that does not mean I won't. I'm hoping not to ever experience anything like that again. I'm not the type of person that goes looking for ghosts and things. Ghosts, and the thought of ghost's, really scare me."

YAQUI (YOEME)

Culturally, the Yaqui or Yoeme Nation is descended from the ancient Uto-Azteca, or Mexica people of Old Mexico. In 1533, the Spanish made contact with the Yaqui, and ultimately Christianity was introduced, which profoundly altered the Yaqui way of life. Interestingly, the Yaqui embraced Catholicism and the new Spanish system of government, but always kept an independent stance in this union. The Yaqui religious life of today is a result of this merger of ceremonies and cultural beliefs. San Ignacio Fiesta, Easter and Christmas are the most important ceremonies of the year for the modern Yaqui. The Yaqui have a history of being fiercely independent, and resisted Spanish colonialism until 1610, when a treaty was signed between the two. Originally they occupied eight villages in the state of Sonora, Mexico. Due to Mexican political changes, they migrated north to Arizona.

The U.S. Bureau of Indian Affairs did not recognize the Yaqui Nation as an 'historic tribe' until 1994. Their battle for such recognition was long and difficult. Considered political refugees because of their migration from Mexico, they were denied the services afforded to other American Indian Nations, and thus not recognized as an independent nation and reservation. Presently the population numbers just over 9,000. In Arizona, the Pascua Yaqui Indian Reservation was annexed into the city of Tucson in 1952. The tribal land, 222 acres, was established in 1964 by an Act of Congress and is surrounded by a desert landscape of scenic vistas, drives and trails. The San Ignacio Fiesta is observed at Old Pascua, a village located in Tucson that marks the annual fulfillment of the village's obligation to its patron saint, St. Ignatius of Loyola. The Yaqui also currently operate the successful Casino of the Sun. There is another group of Yaqui that resides close to Tempe and Phoenix in the town of Guadalupe. It is from this town that the following story was obtained.

BENJAMIN RED OWL'S (YAQUI) STORY

During our interview, I sat across from Benjamin in a humble and thankfully, very air conditioned neighborhood Mexican restaurant, located in Phoenix. Surprisingly, Benjamin's right arm was in a sling due to having been in a car accident just a few days prior. Benjamin was happy to know that I had contacted him for his personal story and stated: "It's great, it's all great. I've been wanting to tell my story for a long time, and you're just the guy I'm hoping will get it out there for others to know about." I assured him that I would do my best. I know you'll enjoy Benjamin's personal story for its emotionally inspired content and at times frightening character.

— Antonio

"My one and only experience with a ghost took place in the summer of 1991 when I was twenty-six years old. Up to that point, I can't remember ever having had any type of a paranormal experience. Of course, there have been times when I've overheard friends and family discuss such things as ghosts and haunted areas, but I've never paid much attention. All this changed for me during one summer night in Montana. I had completed four years of graduate work in Art History at the University of Colorado, and with a master's degree under my arm, I made plans to give myself a break from all my hours of study. I thought that rewarding myself with a trip to Canada would be a nice change. Also, I knew that once I entered the job market, it would be a long time before I would have the opportunity to travel for quite some time. In fact, I already had two job offers waiting for me once I returned home. Honestly, I was in no hurry to return to an office, so I was very eager to begin my trip.

My reason for driving all the way up to Canada was to visit Jerry, a Cree Indian friend, whom I met while attending school. Jerry lived in the province of Alberta, and was a real joker of a guy. Among us Indian students, Jerry was known for his wacky sense of humor. I couldn't wait to get on the road. I packed my small Toyota with all the necessary camping gear—tent and snacks—then got on the interstate heading north to Wyoming, Montana, and my ultimate destination, Canada. Along the way, I spent nights in public campgrounds, located in state and national parks. Before leaving the northern-most portion of the state of Wyoming, I spent six days in the town of Sheridan. Another friend from college, Tom, lived there. Tom is a Lakota Indian who graduated two years before me with a degree in Marketing Management. Tom told me about his friend, Joseph, who lived in the town of Billings, north of the Crow Indian Reservation. Tom gave Joseph a call and arranged for me to spend a couple of nights at Joseph's house. Joseph was known as a maker of award winning horse saddles. Tom and I said our good-byes, and off I left to continue my journey north.

I took my time, stopping frequently to take pictures and to observe the beautiful prairie landscape. Because of my many sightseeing stops, I arrived at the Crow Reservation late in the evening. I turned off the highway and found a rest stop where I made camp for the night. In the morning, I packed up my things and drove to the nearest restaurant, got breakfast, then drove to the Little Bighorn Battlefield Monument to have a look. Given its history, and I being Native American, the battlefield was an unsettling place to visit. The monument's visitor center was filled with historical paraphernalia. Being a history buff, I spent a good two hours reading the informational texts, and taking in all descriptions of the artifacts on display. Reading about the major battle that was fought and jointly won by the Sioux and Cheyenne against the invading General

Custer was fascinating. I felt proud to be Native American, and at the same time, saddened knowing the present social state that most Indians are locked into. After a few hours, I got in my car and drove on the two-lane road, which meandered through the battlefield itself.

At one point, I decided to park and go for a hike over the rolling hills and small valleys of the battle site. As I said earlier, I had an uneasy feeling about this place. Standing on the actual ground where the battle was fought many years ago gave me an eerie feeling. I didn't at all feel frightened, just uneasy. After spending several hours hiking about the area, evening was approaching and it began to get dark. I decided to head back to my car, where I had a quick dinner of warm coke, an apple and cookies. Billings was about an hour or two away, so I got back on the highway, anticipating that I'd have a bed at Joseph's house. This plan, as it turned out, was not to be.

After just a few miles on the highway, I noticed that my car started to somewhat stall and slightly jerk. I knew something was going to give out, and sure enough, just after getting on the interstate, my car stopped altogether. I got out and pushed it to the side of the road. Having been told by a mechanic back in Denver that the car's fuel line filter needed to be changed, I suspected this was the problem. I had the foresight to buy a new filter before I left on my trip. Because it was already too dark to get under the hood and replace it, I decided to tackle the problem the next morning. After all, it was not a very long, difficult job to change out the old filter for the new one—maybe a total of 30 minutes, max. Not far up the road, I noticed a flat area with tall trees. I decided to push my small car over to this area. I parked the car away from the highway traffic. It seemed like a safe camping site for the night.

All the hiking earlier in the day had tired me out. I couldn't wait to get into my sleeping bag and fall asleep. I opened the car's trunk, took out the sleeping bag, and lay it on the ground, with the car creating a buffer between the highway and me. I quickly fell asleep. Sometime during the night, I was awakened by the touch of someone stroking my neck. Because the strokes were gentle and soothing, I was not immediately frightened. Then the thought hit me that someone—a stranger was touching me! I opened my eyes and, still lying in my sleeping bag, I turned around. I gazed in the direction, which I imagined a person would be standing. At first I saw nothing in the darkness. Then I saw some movement to my left. My heart was beating hard and I was getting anxious.

I turned to look to my left and I saw the image of a small Indian woman. She startled me, and I let out a yell of surprise. I immediately knew this person was a spirit, because her image was vapor-like. She was the same luminous color as the moon, and I could see the trees right through her. I got scared and thought I was going to have a heart attack. I couldn't move. My body was trembling. I don't know why I couldn't find the strength to get up and run. My entire body was locked with fear.

The ghostly figure stood about five feet away from me and had a very sad look on her face. She was dressed in a dirty yellow-colored dress, and wore several necklaces made of big beads. She just stood there staring at me. I tried to speak, but my voice was weak and my throat was dry. One thing I do remember clearly was the strong scent of wet grass. It was a very earthy scent that I can remember to this day. It's difficult to explain, but I was able to smell and to "feel" the odor of mud, water and grass of a long time ago. It's weird, I know, but that's the best I can describe it.

Soon, and with much effort, I managed to get out a real yell. She then began to fade away, beginning at her feet and ending at her head. I yelled again, and soon it was all over. She was gone. Sweat was dripping down my face. My ghost encounter took place in what appeared to be all of about five minutes. I got out of the sleeping bag and jumped into the front seat of my car. I locked all the doors, turned on the radio, and after some nervously exhausting minutes passed, managed to fall asleep.

In the early morning, I was awakened when a large noisy semi-truck passing by on the highway. Inside the car, as I moved around, I felt something at the back of my neck. I reached my hand up to scratch, and was surprised when I felt a hardened substance which had attached itself to my hair. I pulled some of this off and looked at my hand. It was hardened mud! I pulled more of this hardened mud off of my neck and head, and then I carefully opened the car door, got out and shook the remainder of the dirt off me. I didn't know what to think. Did I have a bad dream during the night, and rolled about on the ground? Or, did the apparition of the ghost woman rub this mud on me? I didn't care to think any more about the mud. Frankly, I was eager to repair my car and get the heck out of there!

Now that there was plenty of morning sunlight, I replaced the fuel filter in my car, and after several false starts, got my car going again and hit the highway. Driving north on my way to Billings gave me a few hours to think about what I had experienced the night before. I couldn't believe that I had seen a real ghost just a few hours before. I had lots of questions, with no answers. But the most disturbing question of all was why did she cover my neck with mud? Was she trying to heal me of an injury? I soon arrived at Joseph's house. Joseph was not home, so I asked his whereabouts at a neighbor's house. After introducing myself to the older woman, she informed me that her neighbor, Joseph Dances Straight, was dead.

Apparently, two months prior, while visiting his sister in South Dakota, Joseph and two friends went hunting for deer. One of the shotguns accidentally went off, and the blast hit Joseph at the base of his skull, killing him instantly. I was in total shock and disbelief. The neighbor was not willing to give me any more information. I could tell that she and Joseph were close friends. I left her house filled with overwhelming sadness. Eventually, I arrived at my friend Jerry's house in Canada. I told him about what I had experienced during my short trip, describing the short ghost woman, and ultimately finding out about Joseph's death. Jerry got seriously quiet, and then told me that an Indian spirit messenger in the form of a woman had visited me. Also, because earlier in the day I had immersed myself in a powerful area—The Little Bighorn Battleground—I had "opened myself up" to this spiritual visitor. He went on to say that the messenger had rubbed "medicine" on my neck, which symbolized the manner of death which had taken Joseph.

After spending two weeks with Jerry, I returned to my home in Arizona. I'll never forget my experience with the native ghost woman or Jerry's explanations for this encounter. There are lots of things that us Indians need to be aware of. I know that modern society is a very powerful force, but we need to respect and honor our traditions from long ago. These are also very important, and necessary for our people."

LAW ENFORCEMENT

COULTERVILLE, CA

Located on Hwy 49, at the junction of Hwy 132, just a few miles north of Mariposa is the small community of Coulterville. Standing on main street with only the light from the crescent moon above, it isn't difficult to regress in time and imagine the shadowy figures of a mule pack train as it might have made its way down main street.

Named after founders George and Margaret Coulter, who began the first trading and retail shop in the area. Coulterville was initially named Maxwell's Creek, but in 1872 the U.S. post office officially changed the name from Maxwell's Creek to Coulterville.

The Coulters provided the local miners with needed supplies and a trading post all under a circular canvas blue roof. Because of their habit of flying a small Stars and Stripes flag at the entrance to their shop, it soon became known as a landmark for travelers, and was given the unofficial name "Banderita," or little flag by the Mexican miners.

Coulterville was not unlike most small gold rush towns, in that it had its share of disastrous fires. These fires took place at twenty year intervals: 1859, 1879, and 1899. Today, Coulterville is a State Historic Landmark with forty-seven designated historic buildings and sites, all located within the town limits. Surrounded by rugged, and steep terrain, the land is dotted with large native oaks which stand as rugged witnesses, guide posts to the towns history.

MICHAEL MARTINEZ'S STORY

My wife Juanita and I settled in Coulterville right after I retired from the Federal Prison system in 1994. I worked as a Correctional Officer in Lompoc California for fifteen years. I won't lie to you, working for that facility on a daily basis, was very intense and stressful. Although, I miss the friendships I made with my co-workers during all those fifteen years, I was very glad to leave when I did. I witnessed some terrible things that we as correctional officers have to confront as part of our jobs. Prisoners really don't give a damn about life, or anyone else's life, when they know they have to spend the rest of theirs within a concrete cell. It's pathetically sad.

During the last two years of my employment, I was assigned to work the Special Housing Unit or 'SHU'. This is an infamous area of the prison which isolates 'problem' inmates from the rest of the prison population. When taken outside of their cells, for their safety and ours, these inmates are always placed in handcuffs and leg shackles.

This unit also maintains a zero-tolerance policy for any misbehavior of any kind. The inmates know this, and the policy is enforced to the letter. Given this, we do have the occasional inmate that wants to physically challenge this policy, and this always turns into a 'no-win' situation for the inmate. Sure, some isolated abuses have taken place, and as we speak, those inmates have law suits pending in the courts, but I'm betting that the conditions at Lompoc are no different than those at other maximum facilities in the U.S. After all, these guys are not society's best, by any stretch.

My ghost story took place at the Lompoc facility. Looking back at my experience, it was one hell-of-a-thing to witness and something I will never ever forget. Not only did it change me in regards to how I used to view the after-life, it also changed my view of 'evil' as being something distant, or relegated to the Bible. I mean to say that if evil wishes to present itself, it can and is, from my experience, ready to do so at any time. All that is necessary for a person to allow evil to take over is their own desire and willingness. I know that there are individuals who have no problem in welcoming evil to do just that. My experience at Lompoc proved that to me.

Additionally, I still have reoccurring thoughts and sometimes, even nightmares about the experience. I know I'll never totally be able to forget what I saw. You need to understand that I've only spoken about this to my wife, and a handful of others who I trust.

Although my assigned permanent unit is the Special Housing Unit, my experience that night, didn't take place there, but instead at the Intake Unit. Transferring of prisoners at night is not unusual, and is in fact, preferred by the prison system due to light street and highway traffic, which lessens the possibility of a traffic accident. But more importantly the inmates at the prison are 'locked down' for the night, which alleviates the possibility, and obvious disruption that might be caused by an inmate spotting a fellow gang member, rival, etc. Boredom causes stress, and given any reason no matter how small, an inmate will focus all his attention on any miniscule disruption to elevate his daily routine. A much different world exists within the prison walls. A strange world indeed.

My story begins one Friday evening at the Intake Unit. The intake officers, including myself, were expecting an inmate prison transfer from Terminal Island, Long Beach California to arrive at 11 pm. I happened to be covering for an officer who was out ill at the time. The necessary paperwork and cell had been prepared ahead of time for the transfer, so we expected this everything to run smoothly without any problems. As is policy, our intake unit received the phone call advising us that the van had arrived at the prison grounds. Our unit's doors were opened, and the prisoner was escorted out of the van, into the facility, and into the intake area.

The prisoner, a middle aged, white man, was handcuffed and had his ankles in leg chains. As is customary, I and four other officers walked the prisoner to his isolation cell. He was also stripped searched for any contraband. During this phase of the intake, notes are taken to record any scars, or tattoos that can identify the prisoner. These notes are charted in the intake file and follow the inmate for the rest of his life. I was surprised by the number tattoos this guy had all about his body. Apparently, he belonged to a White Supremacist group, because of the usual insignias, and symbols. But his guy also had tattoos which were very malevolent. Tattoos of Satan, and numerous other symbols of pentagrams, daggers, skulls with bat wings, and so on.

New prisoners with a rap sheet history as brutal as this prisoner's, were kept isolated for a few hours, sometimes days, before being reassigned to their permanent cell, for reasons too numerous to mention here.

Aside from the inmate's weird body art, the transfer went smoothly, not much out of the ordinary took place except for one thing. The Hispanic officers who delivered the prisoner, kept referring to him as, "El Diablo" (The Devil), because of his tattoos. They informed us that this prisoner was a 'special' one. After reading his criminal record, 'horrible' and 'monstrous' are the only two words I can use to describe his heinous history of crime. The inmate was very violent, and if I described any of what was written in his file, I run the risk of having someone, who might read my story, possibly identify him. I'll just say this; he murdered three family members, not his own, through starvation. That's all I can say for now.

Well, after we contained the prisoner in his cell, the officers, myself included, walked back to our observation station and settled in for the night. Located at the observation station are video monitors which scan the halls, activity rooms and bathrooms every few seconds. There are also sensitive microphones that are placed in these areas. This is all state of the art equipment, and very necessary.

At 1:10 am, we heard a movement coming from one hall. We instantly studied the monitor and noticed that one of the doors to an inmate's cell was slowly opening! We prepared ourselves for a confrontation and rushed to the cell. As we arrived, we saw that the inmate was asleep in his bed and the door was opened about two feet. We woke up the inmate and asked him to explain how he unlocked his cell door. He was totally perplexed, and it was obvious our questioning had caught him by surprise. We 'shook down' his cell and clothing and found nothing, no key or homemade tool, nothing at all which he could have used to open the door.

Throughout the incident, the new inmate, "El Diablo" watched and occasionally made snickering noises. At one point, he said, "Azrael is walking the halls boys, better keep your eyes open. Azrael is making sure you guys treat me with respect." We told the 'jerk' to quiet down and mind his own business! He gave me a stupid smile, turned away and said nothing more. I re-checked the lock on the door and found it worked fine. We had no explanation and couldn't even guess how or why it had opened as it did. Perplexed by what had taken place we made a note in the log book and immediately had a technician attend to the problem.

While back at the observation station, I could clearly see the technician scratch his head in confusion. He was obviously also puzzled by the door. He said," Can't find a thing, it all checks out fine."

At 2:20 am the microphone picked up a noise coming from the same hall. I listened with the other officers and we all identified a 'moaning' sound. It is not unusual for inmates to have nightmares, so we listened without much concern. But suddenly the moaning became a series of screams. We turned on the main hall lights, and rushed to the cell. We approached the inmate's cell, and discovered him standing on his bed in the corner of the cell. He told us he had seen a black figure, "I saw the devil, you've got to believe me, I saw the devil standing right there. It was big and black and had a white face!" We told the inmate to be quiet and get over his nightmare.

The next night before starting my shift, as I checked the log book, I read that there had been problems with the new inmate speaking to an imaginary person, and yelling out the name "Azrael." "El Diablo" had been advised by the officer on duty to keep quiet, when the inmate refused, he was taken to the isolation cell. He was too remained in isolation for four days and nights. Because the inmate was away in isolation, I didn't expect any trouble to take place. But I was so very wrong to assume this.

At a 2 am the microphone picked up footsteps coming from the hall. I quickly looked at the video camera and noticed a grey image in the upper left corner of the hall, directly in front of El Diablo's cell! The grey image quickly became a large dark cloud and thinking we had a fire, the officers rushed to the hall. When we got to the hall, there was nothing burning, no smoke, or flames. Then the strangest thing happened, we felt a very cold chill come over us. It was an icy cold, bare-bone chill that I had never before experienced!

After returning to the observation station, we spoke about the incident among ourselves. No one had an explanation. I decided to keep the video monitor and microphone focused on the hall and every few minutes, I'd give a quick glance. To my surprise I heard the sound of something heavy, a rasping sound of something being dragged across the floor. I looked at the video screen and what I saw paralyzed me! There was a huge, I mean big, shadowy, black figure of a 'something' moving down the hall!

Before I had the chance to alert the other officers, it disappeared! I was sure the officers would think I was crazy if I told them what I had seen, so I decided to keep this to myself. I was shaking. This was something weird. Something not normal. I was not imagining it. I had just seen a ghost! The huge size of it was what I remember most, it was enormous! For the remainder of the night, I was torn between glancing at the screen, or avoid looking at it altogether. Whatever this thing was really terrified me.

I decided to give a call to the isolation unit where El Diablo was being kept. I was close to one of the officers who was stationed there, and ask to speak to him directly. When Peter answered the phone, he didn't give me the chance to tell him about my strange incident, instead he immediately asked, "Mike, what can you tell me about the new guy, we've been having some weird shit going on over here?" Peter told me he and another officer were hearing 'grinding noises' and footsteps coming from the new guy's cell. Of course, after investigating, there would not be anything unusual except for El Diablo stating, "Azrael is walking boys, he's walking the halls."

I didn't add much to what Peter said, but I did mention we were experiencing the same things at our unit. I didn't even want to elude that I had seen a ghost. The warden would have thrown me out of my chair and into the psych ward for sure! I can't say that I would have blamed him. If nothing else, my short conversation with Peter did comfort me to know I was not going totally crazy.

It was now confirmed to me that the paranormal activity was definitely associated with the new inmate. I was feeling uncomfortable knowing that in just one day, the inmate would once more be returning to my unit. My anxiety was growing as I thought about what other manifestations I might experience. Given everything, this murderer was not an ordinary criminal, he did some horrendous things. Bloody, "evil" things to his victims.

The next night prior to starting my shift, I was anticipating the worst. When I arrived at the unit, I was told that the inmate would not be returning to our unit because he had been transferred to the Medical Unit, at his release, he would be transferred to the Special Psychological Unit for evaluation. Apparently, he had gone "over the edge" the night before. He was observed tearing and swallowing pieces of his bed sheet, and swallowed enough fabric to cause a gastro impaction that required surgery. No problem, I thought to myself, the bastard would do us all some good if he were to just to die!

A couple of weeks after the inmate was sent to the Special Psychological Unit, he was transferred to another state, to stand trial for the murder of two children. I decided not to follow-up with his case after that. I was just grateful to know that he, and his "Azrael" ghost were sent far away from Lompoc.

I know many people do sincerely believe in such things as ghosts and the paranormal. I was never one of those types, until I witnessed unexplainable things upon the arrival of this inmate. Today I'm not the same person. I used to think all that talk about ghosts was for "kooks". I've changed my thoughts about that. That black thing I saw walking the hall convinced me that such things do exist. Evil really does live in the hearts of men, and I've seen it literally walk! Would I welcome another experience like that again? Absolutely no way in hell, no way!

Historical note-

Azrael is the name given to the Angel of Death in the Judeo-Christian-Islamic world. The name is of Hebrew derivation whose literal meaning is "whom God helps."

Islamic teachings describe that, "When the Angels Michael, Gabriel and Israfel failed to provide seven handfuls of earth for the creation of Adam, the 4th angel on this mission, Azrael, succeeded, and because of this feat, Azrael was appointed to separate body from soul."

The Koran also states that Azrael was given "all of the powers of the

heavens to enable him to master death." Further, "When a righteous person dies, Azrael comes with a host of divinity, carrying sweet odors of paradise and makes the soul leave the body like a drop taken out of a bucket of water. Though, when a wicked person dies, Azrael comes in the company of demons, who pull the soul out as with iron spits."

In Jewish literature, it is written that "When the soul sees Azrael, it 'falls in love', and thus is withdrawn from the body as if by a seduction."

LEADVILLE, CO

Situated at 10,152 feet, Leadville is said to be North America's highest incorporated city. The city, with its population of 3,000, is surrounded by the spectacular Rocky Mountains, and is home to six museums that include the National Mining Hall of Fame and Museum. In 1880, Leadville was noted to be the second-largest city in the state.

The town takes pride in its well preserved, 70 square city blocks of Victorian architecture. The citizens of Leadville worked hard to protect and to preserve its many Victorian-era buildings and historical sites. The town is, in fact, listed as a designated National Historic Landmark District. In addition, there are 20 additional square miles of a preserved mining district with 50 buildings that have been dated to the 1870s.

SHERIFF EDWARD HOLTE'S STORY

I met with Sheriff Holte in his office, within the courthouse where this interview was conducted. Surrounded by all manner of office paperwork, I was impressed with the sheriff's openness and understanding to the possibility that ghosts might indeed exist.

He didn't once laugh away the seriousness of my questioning, but instead gave concise, genuine, and sincere responses. He honestly left the possibility open to witnessing a ghost, and even mentioned he'd like to "analyze" one. Well, Sheriff, sometime in the future, I'd be more than happy to take you to just a few of the sites I've encountered during my research, areas where you'd have more than a few instances of "evidence" to analyze. You might be unusually surprised by what might present itself to you.

— Antonio

"I had lived in Leadville for 27 years prior, before taking my current position as Leadville's sheriff. I've now held this job for four years. Prior to that, I was employed with the Colorado State Police.

The jail is housed within the courthouse building. The original courthouse was built in the latter 1800s. A devastating fire burned the original building to the ground in the early 1900s, and this original site is where the current building now rests.

Prior to working at the jail, I heard the stories that are well known within the Leadville community of the town having several spirit or ghost sightings, specifically within the courthouse halls. I never gave these stories much thought, but not long after working at the jail, my own personal impressions of these "supposed" sightings were to change.

Last year at the jail, there were two trustees who were given the responsibility of doing a few jobs around the property. These trustees, or low security risk inmates, had served time within the county jail, and because of good behavior were placed in a trustee level status. Their supervised duty was to clean the jail and wash patrol cars. They were to account directly to the jailer. During one work period, they both mentioned to the jailer the strange activity that they had experienced in the rear of the jail. This unusual activity began with unexplained noises and hearing voices.

Sheriff Edward Holte.

The staff and myself didn't pay much at-

tention to their report, and simply "blew off" their weird accounts. We assumed that it was nothing more than their big imaginations working overtime. But strangely, our impressions started to change when one unusual incident after another "perked our ears up."

The point when we all started to take things more seriously started with incidences involving the television sets within prisoner's cells. One of the trustees stated that he had turned his television off, left his cell and then walked into the booking area. Upon returning to his cell, he noticed the television set he had turned off was now on. At first this incident was nothing dramatically out of order, but soon television sets turning themselves on and off had started becoming a common occurrence within the jail.

Prisoners, watching a program on their sets, began observing that the channels would start to switch stations on their own. Some reported that aside from channels being changed by unseen fingers, the television would sometimes go completely blank, with just a display of "white snow," or static. When they would physically reach for the knob to change the channel, the knob would be turned back once more on its own, displaying the white snow. Some reported the television would unexpectedly shut itself off. Others reported that the television would, on its own, turn itself on at any time of day, or night. The jail staff didn't give these unusual reports much thought. We assumed these reports were being caused by electrical interferences, causing the sets to malfunction.

This attitude began to change when one inmate reported that as he was watching his television, the set turned off. Nothing unusual about this, only this time the inmate visibly saw the television cord rise up from the floor and yanked from the wall outlet! Apparently, according to his report, an unseen hand had pulled the television's plug. He said he watched as it "popped" out from the wall socket. Not wanting to believe in such things as ghosts, he took hold of the plug that was lying on the floor, and personally re-plugged it back into the wall socket. Within just a few minutes later the plug was once again pulled away and out of the socket.

These ghostly experiences escalated to such a level other objects in the cells began to move about. In addition to these examples were reports of "cold spots" being felt, most notably, a large cold spot located towards the back of the jail's hallway. Again, we were unconvinced and considered the inmates reports to be imaginary and silly.

However, some of the staff investigated their concerns, and discovered that there were indeed areas, or spots, where they themselves could feel definite temperature changes. These areas were dramatically icy cold. The ghost of an elderly man has also been seen regularly.

Apparently, the unusual manifestations in our jail caught the ears of some media program executives. We had a major Denver television station, Channel 9 News, visit to the jail and film a report for a Halloween story. The jail was included in walking tours that were led by a local Leadville historian. He wrote follow-up articles to the ghost stories in our local newspapers that were very interesting to read.

This historian was so interested in our ghosts that he used his own money to purchase and lend to the inmates small, noise-activated tape recorders. He instructed the inmates to place the recorders in a central area of their cells, then to turn the recorders on whenever they left their cells. The purpose of doing this was to record the voices of any spirits that might be in their cells.

I had the opportunity to hear these tapes, and there are definitely sections in the recordings that appear to be sounds resembling human voices. Most of these recorded sounds are not easy, or clear, for my ears to make out, but once listening to them, I was able to make out the jumbled, low muttering sounds that somewhat resembled a male voice.

Aside from these experiences within the courthouse jail, I am also aware of other areas in town where locals have personally reported to me sightings of ghostly apparitions. Over on the east end of town, on 7th street, the ghost of an elderly man has been seen regularly. I'm further told that this is the ghost of an old Irish man who apparently died in a local mining accident some years ago, and he is readily identifiable as someone familiar to the town. They see his spirit walking the streets during the evening hours.

I find it surprising to hear them say that his facial features are very clear, not misty at all. His face is very identifiable. Now, I personally have never encountered or seen this spirit, but those witnesses who I've spoken to are very strong in their conviction that, yes, no doubt, they've actually seen this spirit.

Given all that I have experienced together with what the public has brought to my attention, I can say that I don't discount the possibility that ghosts do in fact exist. A lot of what I've already seen can be logically explained, however there are some things that cannot be so easily explained away.

I would like to have a ghost appear to me, so that I can analyze it, and definitely make up my mind. I think my initial reaction might be awe, but knowing myself as I do, the "cop" in me would kick in, force me to think rationally and ask, "How's this happening?" I don't think that I would be frightened, but I would be inquisitive. There are many stories of ghosts appearing in all of Colorado's mining districts, so much so that you have to ask yourself, "There must be more to all of these sightings and encounters!" As a matter of probability, not all of these stories are made up. They can't be. The best "proof" remains for me to have an actual sighting or encounter myself. Until that happens, I'll remain skeptical, but open to the possibility."

SANTA FE, NM

THE PENITENTIARY OF NEW MEXICO PRISON RIOT

The riot that took place on February 2nd and 3rd, 1980 in the state's maximum security prison south of Santa Fe, was one of the most violent prison riots in the history of the American correctional system: 33 inmates died and more than 200 inmates were treated for injuries.

None of the officers taken hostage were killed, but seven were treated for injuries caused by beatings and rapes. This was the third major riot at the New Mexico State Penitentiary, the first occurring on July 19, 1922 and the second on June 15, 1953. Author Roger Morris suggests the death toll may have been higher as a  number of bodies were incinerated or dismembered during the course of the mayhem.

The causes of the New Mexico Penitentiary riot are well documented. Author R. Morris wrote, "The riot was a predictable incident based on an assessment of prison conditions."

Prison overcrowding and inferior prison services, common problems in many correctional facilities, were major causes of the disturbance. On the night of the riot, there were 1,136 inmates in a prison designed for only 900. Prisoners were not adequately separated. Many were housed in communal dormitories that were unsanitary and served poor-quality food.

Another major cause of the riot was the cancellation of educational, recreational, and other rehabilitative programs that had operated from 1970 to 1975. In that five-year period, the prison had been described as relatively calm. When the educational and recreational programs were stopped in 1975, prisoners had to be locked down for long periods.

These conditions created strong feelings of deprivation and discontent in the inmate population that later lead to violence and disorder. Inconsistent policies and poor communications meant relations between officers and inmates were always in decline. These patterns have been described as paralleling trends in other U.S. prisons from the 1960s and 1970s, and as a factor that moved inmates away from solidarity in the 1960s to violence and fragmentation in the 1970s.

Due to a shortage of trained correctional staff, officers used a form of social manipulation called the "snitch game" to control uncooperative prisoners. Officers would simply label inmates who would not behave as

informers or as a snitch.

This tactic meant the named inmate would start being abused by fellow convicts. Often, prisoners would choose to become a snitch to get away from their tormentors. However, the practice hampered attempts to get accurate information from inmates. It also increased tensions within the prison, as inmates grew even more suspicious of the officers and each other.

Nevertheless, New Mexico's state Governor Bruce King, Director of Prisons Felix Rodriguez, and prison officials Robert Montoya and Manuel Koroneos tolerated conditions. Warnings of an imminent riot were not heeded.

In the early morning of Saturday, February 2, 1980, two prisoners in south-side Dormitory E-2 overpowered an officer who had caught them drinking homemade liquor. Within minutes, four more of the 15 officers in the dormitory were also taken hostage. At this point the riot might have been contained; however, a fleeing officer left a set of keys behind.

Soon, E-2 dormitory was in the inmates' control. Prisoners using the captured keys now seized more officers as hostages, before releasing other inmates from their cells. Eventually, they were able to break into the prison's master-control center, giving them access to lock and door controls, weapons and more key sets.

By mid-morning events had spiraled out of control within the cellblocks. Murder and violence had erupted. Gangs were fighting gangs, and a group of rioters led by some of the most dangerous inmates (who by now had been released from solitary confinement) decided to break into cellblock 4, which housed the protective-custody unit. This held the snitches and those labeled as informers. But it also housed inmates who were vulnerable, mentally ill or convicted of sex crimes. Initially, the plan was to take revenge on the snitches, but the violence soon became indiscriminate.

When the group reached cellblock 4, they found that they did not have keys to enter these cells. Unfortunately for the prisoners in protective custody, the rioters found blowtorches that had been brought into the prison as part of an ongoing construction project. They used these to cut through the bars over the next five hours. Locked in their cells, the segregated prisoners called to the State Police pleading for them to save them, but to no avail. Waiting officers could do nothing despite there being a back door to cellblock 4, which would have offered a way to free them. The inmates were not freed because State Police agreed to not enter the prison as long as Officers held hostage were kept alive.

Meanwhile the rioters taunted prison officials over the radio about what they were going to do to the men in cellblock 4. Still no action was taken. One official was heard to remark about the men in the segregation facility, "It's their ass." As dawn broke, an execution squad finally cut through the grille and entered the block. The security panel controlling the cell doors was burned off. Victims were pulled from their cells to be tortured, dismembered, decapitated or burned alive.

During an edition of BBC's Time Watch program, an eyewitness described the carnage in cellblock 4. They saw an inmate held up in front of a window; he was being tortured by using a blowtorch on his face. They then started using the torch on his eyes and then the inmate's head exploded.

Men were killed with piping, work tools and knives. One man was partially decapitated after being thrown over the second-tier balcony with a noose around his neck. The corpse was then dragged down and hacked up. Fires had also raged unchecked throughout several parts of the prison.

Talks to end the riot stalled throughout the first 24 hours because neither the inmates nor the state had a single spokesperson. Eventually, inmates made 11 general demands regarding basic prison conditions like overcrowding, inmate discipline, educational services, and the quality of food. The prisoners also demanded to talk to independent federal officials and members of the news media.

The officers who were held hostage were released after inmates met reporters. Inmates had protected some of the officers, but others had been brutally beaten and raped. Seven officers suffered severe injuries. One was tied to a chair. Another lay naked on a stretcher, blood pouring from a head wound.

Negotiations broke off again in the early morning hours of Sunday, February 3, 1980 with state officials insisting no concessions had been made.

However, eighty prisoners wanting no further part in the disturbances, fled to the baseball field seeking refuge at the fence where the National Guard had assembled.

Throughout Sunday morning, more inmates trickled out of the prison seeking refuge. Black inmates led the exodus from the smoldering cellblocks. These groups, large enough to defend themselves from other inmates, huddled together as smoke from the burned-out prison continued to drift across the recreation yard.

By mid-afternoon, 36 hours after the riot had begun, heavily armed State Police officers accompanied by National Guard servicemen entered the charred remains of the prison.

Official sources state that at least 33 inmates died. Some over dosed on drugs, but most were brutally murdered. Some sources cite a higher death toll. Twenty-three of the victims had been housed in the protective-custody unit. More than 200 inmates were treated for injuries sustained during the riot. After the surrender, it took days before order was maintained enough to fully ensure inmates could occupy the prison. National Guardsman over the next two nights threw lumber scraps from Santa Fe Lumber yards over the two-layered fence into the Prison Yard to make certain inmates who escaped into the yard would not freeze in the near zero temperatures. Nevertheless, rape, gang fights and racial conflict continued to break out among the inmates.

A few inmates were prosecuted for crimes committed during the uprising, but according to author Roger Morris, most crimes went unpunished. The longest additional sentence given to any convict was nine years. Nationally known criminal defense lawyer William L. Summers, led the defense team in defending dozens of inmates charged in the riot's aftermath. In 1982, Mr. Summers received the National Association of Criminal Defense Lawyers Robert C. Heeney award, the highest award available to a criminal defense lawyer for his work in defending the inmates prosecuted with regard to the riot.

After the riots, Governor King's administration resisted attempts to reform the prison. Actions were not settled until the administration of Governor Toney Anaya seven years later. Much of the evidence was lost or destroyed during and after the riot. One federal lawsuit that was filed by an inmate was held up in the New Mexico prison system for almost two decades.

However, systemic reforms after the riot were undertaken following the Duran v. King consent decree, which included implementation of the Bureau Classification System under Cabinet Secretary Joe Williams. This reform work has developed the modern correctional system in New Mexico. Situated within 20 feet of the main control center, the prison library and its law collection remained relatively untouched.

Today the older New Mexico State Penitentiary prison is rented out by the state for film crews, police training purposes, and even the occasional tour of ghost hunters.

DEPUTY WARDEN, LAWRENCE JARAMILLO'S STORY

I began my employment at the prison on April 3rd, 1991. Prior to that I was in the Marine Corps. I've been employed for over nineteen years and am currently the Deputy Warden of a super max prison. My goal is to advance to Chief Warden and to retire with that title. There were some that informed me, or even spoke in general terms directly to me of ghosts in the facility. It was only about three years into my employment that I had my own personal encounter with a ghost. After that time, individuals "opened up" even more and related their own experiences to me.

I know there exists unexplained presences or ghosts at the prison. I've seen them with my own eyes and that has made a believer out of me. Am I scared of the place? Well no, just a little leery.

At other times, I worked the graveyard shift and I had a female sergeant who would come across the radio in a very urgent and nervous voice, more like a panic. When the other officers or I would rush to where she was in the Control Center, we could clearly see on her face how traumatized she was. She would swear to us that there was another person or ghost in the room with her. By the time we'd reach her, the apparition would be gone. She was the only one allowed in the secured area and there was no possible way anyone could get inside the Control Center without her knowledge. We soon relieved her of that duty and she was placed at another post.

My first paranormal experience within the prison took place in the Chow Room at around 2:30 a.m. I was alone at the time and was in the process of eating my lunch. Suddenly, the cold-water faucet in the sink turned on. I rose off my chair, grabbed the handle, and turned it off. Before I could return to my chair, the hot water faucet was turned on! I looked around and was at a loss about what to think, but after I turned the water faucet off, I then sat back down to finish my lunch. Well, the faucets once more turned on! Now these faucets take some effort to turn so the ghost must have some degree of power to manage to do that. I decided to I speak out to the ghost, "Don't be a punk and show yourself to me!" Nothing happened.

An interesting side note is that during the riot, the Catholic chapel was left intact, however the interior of the Protestant chapel was totally destroyed by the inmates. Staff describes the prison as having "cold spots" and dark, shadowy figures moving about, and they particularly spoke of the laundry area. I did experience the cold spots, but nothing further.

Prior to the riot, I'm aware of one correctional officer, Officer Jewitt who was targeted by the inmates and was stabbed and killed here in cell block 4. During the take over the hash marks you see here made into the concrete floor in cell block 4 were apparently caused by an axe the inmates used as they chopped the head

off an inmate's body. Right over in this other area is a dark stain showing the spot where another inmate was tortured and burned to death. The body's fat, as it burned, must have seeped into the concrete as the fire's intense heat consumed it.

In another incident, the inmates stabbed another inmate who was in this cell for child sexual abuse. They stabbed him so brutally that I had never seen so much blood in one area before. The walls were marked with the victim's smeared bloody hand and fingerprints showing the effort he made to stand upright during the attack. There was so much blood it was ridiculous. A long stream of blood meandered out the cell and down the catwalk. The two inmates responsible for the murder were eventually convicted of homicide.

Both the laundry room and the gas chamber always gave me the creeps. Only one inmate was ever executed in the chamber, inmate Cooper. In what used to be the Captain's room, were two long rows of big windows. Each window was secured with a heavy latch. This was the pharmacy that during the riot was totally broken into and stripped of all its meds. The infirmary elevator was known to operate on its own, day or night. It was inspected many times but was never found by the mechanics to be broke.

When nursing staff from St. Vincent's hospital would visit, they always stated how uneasy they felt here. I was seated at the nurse's station one night within full view of the elevator and all the doors that opened into the hall. At the time, we had an inmate who was gravely ill in one of these rooms. A few days prior to this inmate being moved to his second and last cell, I caught him in the act of starting a fire while chanting satanic prayers only he knew the meaning of. The nurse from the hospital and I heard loud noises coming from this inmate's room at 4:30 a.m. and decided to investigate. When we unlocked the door, and walked to his bedside his eyes were rolling around in his head and he was making what I can only describe as animal noises. It was very scary to witness, but scarier still was that under his thin hospital gown, on his chest, was the movement of something large.

The nurse removed the gown and we saw what looked like a fist or a ball that moved from one side of his chest to the other. Then his eyes went completely white without any hint of a pupil. The nurse nervously checked his vitals and after which I locked the cell door and we returned to the nurses' station. We kept hearing the inmate making even louder growling sounds. We rose from our seats to check on him again and as we entered his cell, suddenly the closed two large windows flew opened in unison! As you can imagine, this startled us both, especially since we knew the windows are large, heavy-latched and take quite some effort to open. We returned to the nurse's station. The overwhelming sense of

unease between us was obviously marked on our faces and just a short time later, the inmate died.

Not long after his passing, the same nurse and I were in the infirmary once again. The time was 1 a.m. In the physical therapy room was an exercise bike. Suddenly, we both heard unusual noises coming from this locked room. As we reached the room, we immediately spotted the exercise bike's wheels turning as if someone was operating it! The nurse freaked out! I reached for my keys, opened the door, and stepped inside. I noticed how unusually freezing cold the room was. I took hold of the bike's handlebars and stopped the bike. Suddenly, behind us a patient's chart that was placed on top of the nurse's desk begins to rattle and shake and vibrate with enough force to loudly call attention to it. Just then, my focus was centered on the nurse who had fear written all over her face. After that night, she chose to quit working at the prison.

Recently, at around 2:30 in the morning, I was seated on the first floor of the cellblock known as cell block 6 or death row with a clear view of both the first and second floors. I was waiting to be relieved of my shift. Suddenly, my eyes caught the movement of a Chicano inmate with long frizzy hair wearing red canvas tennis shoes on the second-floor walkway about eight cells down from where I was seated. He had one foot resting on the railing as his upper body was bent over resting on top of the rail. He was leaning slightly over the railing and was smoking a cigarette. I yelled, "Hey what are you doing out of your cell?" He ignored my question. Then I yelled, "What cell are you in?"

Just then a correctional guard, Gonzales at the opposite end of the unit, radios me and asks, "What are you yelling for?" I responded, "We have an inmate out." He responded, "You must be high on something, everyone is locked down."

I answered, "Come on over to where I am. I want to show you something" So, he comes over to where I am and all the while I'm still keeping my eyes on the inmate. The guard arrives and asks, "So what's going on? Who the fucks out?"

I answer, "I don't know, but I'm going to call it in." On my radio, I say, "Unit 6, control center 1052, cell bock 6, unit 3 needs back up." So, I take off on foot and as I reach the area below the inmate, I watch as he takes a drag of the cigarette, exhales, then using his thumb and finger,

he flicks the cigarette over the railing, into the air and it sails in to the air then lands sparking on the concrete floor below. The inmate turned around, took a few steps, and faded away!

Guard Gonzales yelled out, "Did you see that? Where did he go?"

I answered, "I don't know. He just disappeared!" Then I looked to the floor at the cigarette and as I reached down to pick it up it was still lit and smoking. I said to myself, "Holy shit!" I radioed the Captain and he came over as we woke all the inmates up to account for their numbers. And even though Gonzales and I both witnessed the ghost, the Captain thought we were both crazy. Out of all the ghostly incidents I witnessed, this one for me was a game changer; I believe that ghost exists!

This latest sighting, the one with the cigarette, was so very different. If that doesn't make you believe then I don't know what would. These days, walking through the prison makes me hesitant, but frankly I'm not scared. Regarding the new prison, well as of this day, I've not heard of any such "going-ons." Would I welcome another experience? Sure, I'm up for the challenge, but I'm not going to seek it out by any means. I know there is a horrible history of violence and brutality associated with the facility and for lack of a better definition there have to be souls that still linger within these walls. There is evil and I do believe that's what you'll find here.

YUMA, AZ

HISTORY OF THE YUMA TERRITORIAL PRISON

On July 1,1876, the first seven inmates entered the Territorial Prison at Yuma and were locked into the new cells they had built themselves.

A total of 3,069 prisoners, including 29 women, lived within these walls during the prison's 33 years of operation. Their crimes ranged from murder to polygamy, with grand larceny being the most common. A majority served only portions of their sentences due to the ease with which paroles and pardons were obtained. 111 persons died while serving their sentences, most from tuberculosis, which was common throughout the territory. Of the many prisoners who attempted to escape, 26 were successful, but only two were from within the prison confines. No executions took place at the prison because the county government administered capital punishment.

Despite an infamous reputation, written evidence indicates that the prison was humanely administered and was a model institution for its time. The only punishments were the dark cell for inmates who broke prison regulations and the ball and chain for those who tried to escape. Prisoners had free time when they handcrafted many items to be sold at public 'markets' held at the prison on Sundays after church services. Prisoners also had regular medical attention and access to a good hospital.

Schooling was available for convicts, and many learned to read and write in prison. The prison housed one of the first "public" libraries in the territory, and visitor's fees for tours of the institution were used to purchase books. One of the early electrical generating plants in the West furnished power for the lights and ran a ventilation system in the cellblock.

By 1907, the prison was severely overcrowded, and there was no room on Prison Hill for expansion. The convicts constructed a new facility in Florence, Arizona. The last prisoner left Yuma on September 15,1909. The Yuma Union High School occupied the buildings from 1910 to 1914. Empty cells provided free lodging for hobos riding the freights in the 1920s and later sheltered many homeless families during the Depression. Townspeople considered the complex a source for free building material. This, plus fires, weathering, and railroad construction, destroyed the

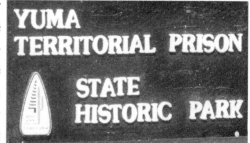

prison walls and all buildings except the cells, main gate and guard tower, but today these provide a glimpse of convict life a century ago.

LINDA D. OFFENEY'S STORY

My present position at the prison is as Park Ranger 2. My duties require me to be the curator, tour guide, and front desk clerk. I've worked at the prison as a ranger for over 14 years and have lived in Yuma for a total of 18 years.

Before working here, I never gave the matter of ghosts much thought. Now, my thoughts have changed, because I cannot explain the strange things that we have all witnessed.

One night, alone in the facility, I began my usual evening security check of the prison grounds. Walking outside the museum, I made my way toward an area of the prison known as the dark cell. Years ago, when the prison was in use, this particular cell was used as punishment for those prisoners who were not following the rules. It was solitary confinement. The dark cell to this day is not a pleasant area to visit. As the name implies, it is dark and very eerie.

As I continued with my security check, I walked over to the dark cell and proceeded to check the iron gate located at its entrance. Suddenly, I felt the presence of someone gazing at me from within the cell. I was overcome with fear. I had made the same check many times before, but this time something was different. This time, the hair on the back of my neck stood on end. I didn't actually see anything, but I sure did feel the horrible gaze of something staring back at me. I made sure that the gate was locked and hurried away from that area.

Officer Linda D. Offeney.

Returning to the comfort and safety of the museum, I thought about what had transpired and just could not shake the intense feeling of someone staring at me.

As a point of information, in our files is a picture that was taken in the late 1930s of a woman standing by the cellblock area near the dark cell. The woman is not the ghost, but in the background behind her is the figure of a ghostly man.

He appears to be outfitted in a World War I uniform. The soldier is standing in the archway to the left of the opening to the dark cell. The rangers who have seen the picture think that this room—which is now walled up—is where the insane prisoners were kept until they were transferred to an outside asylum. The woman is apparently unaware of the ghost standing just a few feet away behind her.

Another strange occurrence at the prison is when visitors report to me that they have been pinched while in the dark cell. I began to notice a pattern that these guests all shared; they all wore clothing where the dominant color was red. It made no difference if they were in the company of others or by themselves. They got pinched! Keep in mind that these were visitors who were unrelated and came to my desk at different times of the year. I can't explain it.

On another day, I took a tour of children into the dark cell. I gathered them all around and told them the history of the cell and, not wanting to frighten them, I kept the information as much as possible on a pleasant level. Well, in the middle of the tour I had a child that was wearing red clothing state to the group that someone had just pinched her! I tactfully ended my talk and escorted the children out the door.

Three years ago, we had a visiting staff writer from Arizona Highways magazine pay us a visit. She wanted to do a story about the prison and got the strange idea of spending two days and nights in the dark cell—alone. She wished to "experience" the isolation that a prisoner might have had in years gone by.

She even asked to be chained by her foot to the cell, as a prisoner would have been. We provided her with a jug of water and loaf of white bread and placed a heavy blanket over the entrance to the cell to keep out any sunlight. We also provided her with a makeshift toilet that brought a smile to her face. She had anticipated remaining in the dark cell much longer than she did, but she soon discovered that she was not welcome. As she described it, she began to sense the presence of someone else in the cell with her. She began to feel pinching or prickling sensations

In memory of the inmates, who lost their lives while serving their sentences, at the Arizona Territorial Prison at Yuma. Of the 3,069 convicts sentenced here, 111 died here of disease, accidents, murder, suicide and escape attempts. The remains of 104 unfortunate souls are interred in this cemetery.

all over her body. We heard her screams for us to get her out of the cell quickly, which we did.

Before I end my story, I do want to tell you about an unusual character that dwells inside the museum, which we all refer to as "Johnny." There were evenings when I was at the cash register totaling up the day's sales. A strange thing happened. As I had the register drawer open, suddenly, the coins jumped out! It was as if an invisible finger was flicking the coins out of the drawer compartments.

There were also other times when I was standing by the opened cash drawer with a hand full of coins. The coins suddenly jumped out of my hand and into the drawer! Now, is that strange or what? Other staff workers have also seen this happen. "Johnny" does not seem to be interested in paper money, just coins. We don't know who this playful ghost is, or why he is so interested in money. He still performs his antics every now and then with us.

There are other unusual things that have happened here. Local people have reported to us that they have seen lights from oil lanterns moving about the prison in the evening hours when it is closed. These lights have always been seen in the cellblock area of the prison. We have visitors and staff also reporting incidences of hearing voices of men in low conversation, usually heard in the museum area.

My own belief about ghosts in the prison is that they will not hurt me. I just know they won't. Of much more of a concern to me is encountering a rattlesnake or skunk that might have decided to venture into the facility. We have had such unwelcome visitors in the past. However, if I were to actually see the ghost of one of the prisoners, I would like to sit down and ask him a question or two about his experiences. I know it would scare me to death, but I would still be interested.

JESSE M. TORRES' STORY

Currently, I am the assistant park manager and have been employed at the prison for over 16 years. I was born and raised in Yuma, and because the prison is so familiar, I didn't really think much about it as a historic site. Little did I know that one day I would be responsible for its well-being.

Before working at the prison, I had heard stories in town about the place being haunted. I'm basically a skeptic, so I didn't pay these stories any mind. I used to think that if I ever felt or heard anything, which might be paranormal, it had to be my imagination. That's what I used to think.

My first experience with ghosts at the prison took place when I was about eight years old. I was brought to the prison during a school field trip. As our teacher led the school group through the grounds, we passed an area of the prison named the 'New Yard.'

The group was walking ahead of me as I lingered in front of cell number 7. Something drew me to this cell, and as I looked inside, I saw a man dressed in a striped prisoner uniform standing inside the closed iron door. At the time, I felt uneasy and quickly ran to keep up with my classmates. The museum staff has had visitors tell us that they have also seen a prisoner in that very same cell, dressed in prison-striped clothes!

Eight years after I began working at the prison, I had an experience I have never forgotten. The current storage

Officer Jesse M. Torres.

Outside Cell 14.

room in the museum used to be used as an office by the staff. One day, as I was in the museum cleaning the glass cases that hold artifacts of daily prison life, I heard voices coming from the office. Knowing I was alone in the building, I stood still and listened. The voices were the soft whispers of men in conversation. I clearly heard one or two words that I recognized, but I was unable to make a complete sentence out of them. Thinking that some unauthorized person was in the building, I quietly walked to the office door, took hold of the doorknob, and opened the door. Once I turned on the light, saw the room was completely empty; and the voices I had just heard a few seconds ago were now gone.

One early morning, alone in the museum, I clearly heard a voice ask, "Jesse, did you get it?" Startled by such a request, I turned around to face the person. I saw no one. I felt the hair on my neck stand right up!

Another experience in the prison happened in the old cellblock, directly outside cell number 14. One winter day, as I was walking down the cell block area, I walked past cell number 14. A movement in the cell caught my eye, and as I looked through the spaces of the iron door, I saw a ghostly figure moving about inside! Other staff members have also see this figure, and have heard its footsteps as it moves about the cell.

Visitors who know nothing about the history of cell number 14 have approached us to say that they have heard a noise and have felt the "heavy presence" of someone in the cell.

From old prison records, I discovered some information about a prisoner named John Ryan. As listed on the prison records, his was a "crime against nature." In early prison history, "crime against nature" was a label given to prisoners who had committed rape or other such acts of sexual deviation. The records also showed that Mr. Ryan did not get along well with the other prisoners and was placed alone in cell number 14! While in the cell, he committed suicide by hanging himself with a rope made from his blankets.

Description of Convict

Name: John Ryan
Number: 1660
Crime: Crime against nature
Sentence: 5 yrs. from 9/28/1900
County: Coconino
Nativity: Iowa
Legitimate Occupation: Miner/Cooking
Age: 31
Habits: Intemperate
Tobacco: Yes
Opium: No
Religion: Catholic
Size of Head: 7⅛
Size of Foot: 8
Color of Eyes: Gray
Color of Hair: Light Brown
Married: Yes
Children: 3
Can Read: Yes
Can Write: Yes
Where Educated: Iowa
When and How Discharged: May 6,1903 Committed suicide by hanging in cell 11:30 a.m.
Prison Record
NOV. 10, 1900: Solitary, 3 days for fighting
MAR.12, 1901: Solitary, 11 days for striking a fellow convict
MAY 27, 1902: Solitary, 4 days for Insubordination
SUPT.'S REPORT, MAR. 31, 1901: Report about his being temporarily demented.

In another area of the prison is a cell named the Dark Cell. The staff

*John Ryan photo curtesy of
Yuma Territorial Prison.*

has had several visitors narrate to us that when in the dark cell, an unseen entity—or ghost—pinches them. Some visitors feel such a negative presence that they have refused to enter the room during our ranger-guided tours. Once, a man stated that while visiting the dark cell, he saw moving and flashing lights. He said he was not about to stay in there another moment and quickly left.

When it was in use, the dark cell was a form of punishment to any prisoner who fought, was caught stealing, or tried to riot. Within the dark cell was a large iron cage with two iron rings at opposite corners. First, the prisoner was stripped down to his underwear. Next, the prisoner's legs were chained—one leg to each iron ring. His only food was plain bread and water. The prison records do not mention any prisoner ever dying while in the dark cell, but the records do state that at least two prisoners did leave the dark cell, only to be immediately transferred to an insane asylum in Phoenix.

I think that there are spirits trapped in the walls of the prison. But I find it interesting that the prison cemetery lacks any reports of ghostly sightings or activity. One would think that of all places on the grounds to be haunted, it would have to be the cemetery. I am not much for believing in ghosts or hauntings, but what we have seen here has really made me think more about this.

MEDICAL PROFESSIONALS

ABILENE, TX

FAMILY PRACTICE PHYSICIAN – ARMAND M. FAULKER'S STORY

"I've been in private practice now in Abilene, Texas, for over fifteen years and prefer it to working in a large, corporate-sponsored hospital environment. My patient call is not heavy, and I've found the community to be very well suited for my family's needs and for me. Speaking fluent Spanish is a plus in Abilene, and through the years, I've taken Spanish language courses for my work and Italian for the simple pleasure of it. My medical profession has prepared me for a lot of unusual situations, but never for what I experienced eight years ago on the paranormal level.

I remember the afternoon I had an older female patient come into my office complaining of a severe neck ache accompanied with ear aches. After examining her and taking blood vials for a comprehensive metabolic panel, I noticed three large red marks on both her upper right arm and abdomen. When I asked her how she acquired these obvious marks, she stated, "Doctor, I'm afraid to say, but sometimes a bad spirit comes to

me and attacks me." As you might imagine, her explanation left me puzzled. My facial reaction must have appeared obvious, because her next response was, "Oh, I can see you don't believe me." I told her I'd never heard this before and concluded the appointment by writing her a prescription for pain and scheduling a follow-up exam in two weeks.

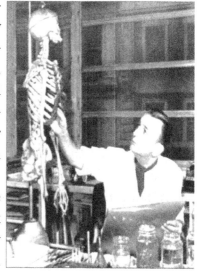

At her two-week follow-up exam, we discussed the results of her blood work that came back from the lab free of any pathological abnormalities. I mentioned that I was at a loss regarding the issues with her neck and ears that were still affecting her, but I referred her to a specialist and assured her that it was most likely a bad sprain and not much more to be concerned about.

When I asked her if the red marks had disappeared from her body, she responded, "Well, see for yourself." When I examined her, I could see that the marks had obviously increased, and numerous more had spread onto her abdomen. Concerned for her well-being, I was about to ask her once again about the marks when she stated, "I can't tell you how much I want the evil spirit to go away from my house. He comes up and yells vicious things at me."

He also knew I was coming to see you, and he screamed at me not to talk to you or he will hurt me in front of you." I attempted to reassure her that nothing like that was going to happen. I immediately knew this was a game changer. I knew right then that I was dealing with a woman displaying a psychological pathology I was not familiar with.

I mentioned to her that I was going to refer her to a therapist. She responded that she was okay with that. Before ending my examination, I asked her to open her mouth wide, and with a tongue depressor, I was about to look inside her throat when she unexpectedly pushed my arm away and cried out, "Doctor, he's here! He's here in the room with us!"

Before I could respond, I felt us both instantly wrapped within a sudden, unexplained, bone-chilling cold. Even more disturbing was witnessing skin on her neck depress down, forming red finger marks from some invisible hand!!

What I'm about to tell you next is equally more difficult to believe, but she appeared to be slapped violently from her right side and was knocked against the wall. She jumped up, stumbled to stand before me, and spit out two front teeth. She was struck violently by something invisible, right before my eyes. I was stunned and couldn't believe my eyes!

I yelled for my assistant to come help, and she quickly entered the room. Both the patient and I stood shaking with terror, staring at each other as blood slowly drooled out of her mouth. Using a paper towel, my assistant picked up the two teeth and then helped me sit the patient in a chair. My assistant couldn't believe what she was seeing, and I told her

I would tell her what happened later. I could see that the woman was in shock, and my first reaction was to call for an ambulance to take her to the nearby hospital, which we did. I removed my patient from the exam room and sat with her inside my office until the EMT crew arrived.

The last time I saw this patient, she told me that she would never see me again and was visibly terrified as she told me. She reminded me that the spirit warned her in her home not to see the doctor or something bad would happen. I never forgot this patient's words, symptoms or experience in my examination room. I don't know what happened to her or even if she is still alive. I think about her and regret that this was one area of my professional career that I had absolutely no knowledge of what to do or how to help.

To this day, I still cannot believe the description of these events coming out of me as I speak them. This one extreme paranormal experience—-terrifying, and unbelievable as it was—compels me to explore and investigate further claims of paranormal phenomenon.

ANCHORAGE, AK

SURGICAL SCRUB TECH – FRANCINE C. RAISOR'S STORY

I'm originally from Santa Maria, California. I moved to Anchorage twelve years ago to live with my girlfriend, Rachel, in her family's home of three generations. Rachel was also in the medical field and worked as a morticians' assistant in a different hospital than I did. We used to do quite a lot of outdoor activities before her untimely death. Rachel died of complications from hepatitis C. She contracted this disease from a deceased patient while assisting with an autopsy. So, I am left to manage alone on our property since her death two years ago.

I graduated from USC medical school in Southern California with a degree as a surgical tech. My job at Alaska Regional Hospital requires me to assist within the operating room during various invasive surgical procedures, especially open-heart operations. Because I've been at this job for so many years, I've become very friendly with my fellow co-workers. I know it might sound corny, but we genuinely regard each other as ex-

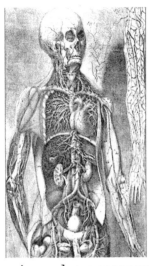

tended family members. We rely on each other for emotional support when a patient we're fond of dies while in our care.

My ghost story happened eight years ago in the hospital. We had an excellent female surgeon who worked at the hospital for just a few months. She died one Thanksgiving holiday in an auto accident while driving back home to Anchorage from Dawson City. Somehow she drove her car off the road, first hitting a tree and then coming to a stop in a shallow water channel. She sustained fatal injuries to both her skull and spine and was pronounced dead at the scene.

It was not long after her funeral that a few staff began to talk among themselves about seeing the doctor's shadow image standing at doorways and at one time even spotted by Arnold, our anesthesiologist, standing against a wall apparently observing everyone in the operating room.

Arnold once told me that during an operating procedure while he was adjusting the concentration of anesthetic vapor isoflurane for a patient, an unexpected movement caught his attention. He looked to see what moved and spotted the deceased surgeon standing about four feet away from the patient on the operating table.

He told me that he happened to glance about the room and noticed two other staff also witnessing the same paranormal image. Arnold said, "We elbowed each other to look in the direction of the ghostly figure. One nurse, a Catholic, made the sign of the cross and said in the direction of the spirit, 'Thank you for your assistance, Doctor.' As this was said, the surgeon's image gradually disappeared. Because we had a patient to tend to, we got back to the business at hand and only spoke of seeing the doctor's apparition later after completing the operation. We all agreed that the good doctor was continuing her involvement in the work she loved so much in life."

Aside from surgery room instruments being moved about, doors opening on their own, and footsteps being heard in empty halls, our job responsibilities continue as normal and as usual. I know the rational mind works to disprove, even deny what I'm describing, but eventually, even the most hardened minds can change with enough evidence. I sincerely believe this to my core.

ULTRASOUND TECHNOLOGIST – ROSALINDA C. TULL'S STORY

My job responsibilities include performing all small body part imaging, Doppler, arterial, and invasive imaging, including abdominal, obstetrical, gynecological, cranial, spinal, external and end cavity procedures, and prostates. I also do breast imaging as needed in the Breast Center, which includes diagnostic studies.

Once I completed my college work at the University of Washington in Seattle, I jumped right in for certification from the AMA school of ultrasonography. The story I'm about to tell you took place within the hospital and in a patient's room.

One late afternoon, as I was walking down one of our hospital's halls, I walked past a familiar patient's room—a young woman named Darla, who I remembered assisting in her admittance just a few days earlier. I knocked on her door and heard her respond, "Come in." As I entered, I could not help but notice how dark the room was. I asked her about this, and she said, "Oh, I hope I'm not offending your religious beliefs, but I was meditating with my Ouija board hoping to contact the spirits that are here in the hospital." Her response caught me totally off guard. She must have seen the surprised look on my face, because she immediately followed up by saying, "Don't worry, they won't hurt you. Come here. I'll show you."

As I approached her bedside, I noticed the Ouija board on her lap. Her fingertips were lightly resting on the device that points out each letter when a question is asked out loud of a spirit. She said, "Pull up a chair, and I'll show you how it's done." I pulled up a chair as she invited me to do, but admittedly, I was apprehensive.

Darla said, "I've already contacted the spirit of a fifty-six-year-old man who died in this very room fourteen months ago." Just as she finished speaking, I caught something move to the left of me, and as I turned to look, my eyes locked with the shadowy figure of a small statured man staring right back at me.

I froze with terror, but I somehow managed to say, "Darla, he's standing right here next to me—I'm scared!" I didn't wait to hear Darla's response and jumped off my seat and out of that room in a flash! There was no way I was ever going back in there again, and I kept this experience exclusively to myself.

Several days passed, and I was unable to erase that man's ghostly image from my memory. My nights were filled with anxiety to the point of insomnia. I knew that I needed to do something about this. Beyond my better judgment, I contacted Darla and described my disruptive situation. She agreed to meet with me outside in the hospital courtyard. Darla listened to my plight, but her response surprised me.

She said, "Rosa, that male spirit refuses to leave my room. I see him every day, and although he keeps his distance, I feel very uncomfortable with his presence. I don't want to scare you any further, but he's looking at us from over at that window [pointing].

"For some crazy reason, he's attached himself to me, and I don't like it. I'll have to figure out what to do about him. Thankfully, I don't think he means any harm to come to me, but I still don't appreciate his surprise visits, especially when he comes at night. I'll be abruptly awakened from sleep and open my eyes, and he'll be standing about ten feet away just staring at me. I don't like when he does that. Wait, I'm looking at the window, and he's staring at us right now. Turn around, Rosa. Look!"

The hair on my head stood up with fear. No way was I going to look again into those creepy ghost eyes. I yelled out to Darla as I started to walk away, "I've got to go now! I'll let you handle this on your own! My nerves can't take this anymore!"

As I approached the courtyard exit, I briefly glanced back over my shoulder to the window Darla pointed to, and sure enough, there it was, the ghostly face of that man just staring at us—that unmistakably creepy face, grinning back at me just as when I first saw it in Darla's room.

Since that scary episode, my idea of the afterlife has changed dramatically. I've read numerous books and have watched many documentaries that challenge society's skepticism on the subject. I've not reached out to

Darla since, and this is mostly due to my aversion to her use of the Ouija board and its potentially dangerous repercussions.

DALLAS, TX

MEDICAL TECHNOLOGIST – THOMAS D. SHARP'S STORY

I received my degree as a medical technologist from the University of North Texas–Dallas. I moved back to Dallas, Texas, going on seven years now and have been working for the VA Medical Center for about three years. Dallas is my hometown, and most of my family and close friends live here. My sister, Laura, worked at the hospital, and it was she who gave me the heads-up about the job opening. I immediately applied and was hired soon after.

My job requires me to conduct chemical analysis of body fluids, such as blood, urine, and spinal fluid to determine the presence of normal and abnormal components. I study blood cells, their numbers, and morphology. I also perform blood group, type, and compatibility tests for transfusion purposes. I work under the direct supervision of our chief medical technologist.

My paranormal experience took place in the fall of last year. My new wife, Connie, and I purchased our first home and immediately began purchasing several large pieces of furniture and a few decorative accessories. Because of our limited budget, we chose to first explore for bargains at our local flea market, numerous yard sales and thrift stores.

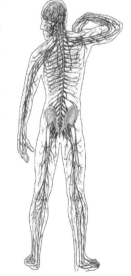

At one shop, I was instantly attracted to a large Victorian-style wall mirror on display and bought it on the spot.

On our return drive home from our day of shopping, I told Connie that I wanted to try the mirror in my office instead of our home. I faced a colorless wall and needed something interesting in order to improve the decor of my workspace. So, I took the mirror to my office and hung it above my computer.

Within a day after hanging the mirror in my office, I started to experience unusual things associated with it while working at my computer. I began to notice in the mirror's reflection fleeting images of a shadow figure either entering through my office door or walking past it. These unusual occurrences took place at all times of the day. I could never clearly make out if the shadow figure was male or female, because it would move extremely quickly. These distractions did not take place every day; sometimes a week would pass before I'd catch a momentary flash of movement in the mirror.

One afternoon, my office manager, Helen, approached me and explained in detail her experiences observing unexplained shadows similar to those I had seen near the new mirror. By the way, I never mentioned the mirror's shadows to anyone except to my wife. Helen reported to me the absolutely same sightings I had witnessed. Helen said, "I know a friend that is spiritually sensitive to these things. How would you feel if I approached him to come and investigate the mirror to see what he might pick up?" I told Helen that I didn't have a problem doing this and gave my permission as long as we kept it between ourselves.

The following afternoon, I received a call from a young man who introduced himself as Helen's friend Edward. He came over to my office within the hour, and I left him alone with the mirror for a few minutes. He didn't share exactly what he did in those few minutes, but he did say, "You have an interesting little problem. I communicated with the spirit in the mirror. The mirror belonged to a man named Austin. Austin tells me that he died of pneumonia many years ago. That mirror was hanging over his bed's headboard when he died. The shadow appearing here at the office is Austin's. He is unaware of his own passing and is looking for his bedroom."

Edward suggested I leave the mirror where it was in the office but to cover it with a dark-colored cotton cloth for two days and two nights. Then on the third day, we needed to take the still-covered mirror outdoors, place it directly facing the sun, and remove the cloth, saying, "Only light may enter. All else is now removed and forever gone."

I had nothing to lose at this point and did just as Edward instructed, and thankfully, I've not seen another shadow since.

SOCIAL WORKER – ALLAN C. SCOTT'S STORY

As a teenager, I was always getting into trouble with my family and the local authorities. The fact that I eventually got into the social work field is as much a surprise to me as to those who were aware of my early history. I imagine that the turning point for me was when I witnessed my best friend jump out of a three-story window during a drug-induced psychotic episode. That really changed the way I viewed my life and how I viewed my relationship with the "friends" I was associating with. Luckily, I sought help for my addiction to drugs before it was too late.

Today as a social worker, I perform substance abuse and mental health counseling to adult clients in an outpatient methadone treatment setting. I screen and assess individuals, facilitate group-counseling sessions, and arrange individual treatment planning. I'm responsible for a primary case load along with other clients as they are assigned to me. Additionally, I also evaluate, refer, and conduct client, family, and community education programs.

One morning while I was in my office setting up appointments for later that day, our supervisor called all the clinical staff together for a mandatory meeting in her office. At the conclusion of the meeting, we were each assigned additional new clients. I was assigned twin brothers, age twenty-two.

The family history recorded in their charts was very disturbing to read and not at all typical. They were raised in a family where both parents were addicted to drugs, and the two young boys were introduced to heroin at fourteen. The authorities eventually stepped in when the parents, during a drug-induced episode, abducted a man, imprisoned him in their home, killed him, and then proceeded to consume portions of his body.

The victim's friends, who reported seeing him last with the two murderers, raised suspicions, and partial body parts were discovered three days later. Both parents were tried, convicted, and sentenced. Their twin sons were placed in foster care and released when they reached their eighteenth birthdays, the legal age of emancipation.

Upon their release, both twins fell victim to negative influences and succumbed to heroin addiction and a criminal culture of illegal drug distribution. As a stipulation of parole, the court ordered them to enroll in our clinic's rehabilitation program.

When I first met with the brothers, I was struck by their odd appearances. They dressed in a style of clothes reminiscent of the 1940's; their shoes, hats, and even the three-pointed handkerchiefs in their sport coat pockets were straight out of a black-and-white movie. And when they spoke, they each had the usual twin trait of finishing each other's sentences. Not so impressive was their ever-present pungent body odor.

In the five month's they were enrolled in our program, I conducted both individual and joint counseling sessions with them. During that period, I also made two bi-monthly home visits. They moved back into their original family home, where their parents had committed the murder. I found this strange and creepy, but having regular access to the inside of their home, I was impressed with how neat and clean they kept it. I also couldn't help but notice how affectionate and caring both brothers acted toward their three very friendly live-in house pets—all black cats.

Well, as the last month of our series of counseling sessions was coming to an end, one of the brothers, Dean, lapsed back into using heroin. What was surprising is that he and another one of our methadone clients were discovered dead of an overdose in a parked car not far from the clinic. The remaining brother, Paul, took the death of his twin very hard, and I was deeply concerned for his mental state and safety.

The day following the funeral appeared to be the most difficult for Paul, so I, together with a team of mental health professionals from the clinic, thought it best to admit him for a week or two for observation to a rehab facility. He agreed without any resistance and was admitted the following day. Additionally, due to suicide concerns, it was also thought best to mildly sedate him. It was not until two whole days after Paul's admittance into the rehab facility that I remembered the three cats left alone in Paul's house without food or water.

I took it upon myself to volunteer to check on the pets and asked Paul for the house keys. Paul seemed slightly dazed and distant, but he freely signed his house keys over to me. I reassured him I would return with a full report on the cats. He seemed happy with this arrangement, and I planned to stop at his house after I got off work that day.

It was already dark when I arrived at Paul's front door; I turned the key in the lock, reached in, and felt around the wall for the light switch. As soon as I turned on the lights and stepped inside, I immediately sensed that something was not at all right. I looked about the living room before walking into the kitchen, when I spotted a few obvious droplets of fresh blood and a pair of scissors on the floor. I knew the blood was fresh, because I took my finger and moved it across one drop, and it smeared. I assumed the cats had gotten into a fight and scratched each other. I called to them, but there was no response.

After filling, each of the dishes with cat food and fresh water, I proceeded about the house searching everywhere, even under beds and furniture. I eventually found them huddled tightly together behind a huge pile of unwashed laundry near the back door.

As I approached them, they defensively hissed and swiped their claws out at me. It instantly became clear that no amount of softly spoken, reassuring words from me were going to calm them. As the three cats quickly broke away from their huddled position, I caught sight of several more unmistakable large blood spots on the floor. It was then that I noticed one of the cats' heads was covered in both dried and fresh blood! As I made a move toward them, the two uninjured cats darted away, while the obviously injured cat remained in place due to its weakened physical state. I reached down for the cat, and I was able to pick it up without resistance. As I placed it in my arms, I noticed that both of its ears had been cut right off—in fact, snipped off close to its skull.

I carried the injured cat to the kitchen and, with a wet dishcloth, wiped away most of the blood off its fur. I knew that whoever had done this must have used the scissors that I'd found lying on the floor earlier. After wrapping the cat in a bath towel and placing it on the living room sofa, I set about the house, searching for some evidence of how this happened and who might have done this.

I found not one open window or door—nothing at all. As I was standing alone in one of the back bedrooms, I heard the sudden loud sound of a door in the hallway slam shut. This scared me to the bone.

Before I could make a run for it, "something" invisible with a lot of strength pushed me back onto the bed and forcibly pinned me down! I fought and struggled to get up, but it was useless. When I gave up the struggle, immediately that's when I saw, right above me, the image of a middle-aged man with both of his extended arms on my shoulders! I screamed out for help, and after what seemed like an eternity, he slowly disappeared. As I felt the pressure of his large hands lift off me, I sat up and began to cry, first from terror and then from being overcome with pure and total relief.

I sat up slowly, stood up, stepped away from the bed, and walked in a complete daze to the front door. After stepping out onto the front porch, I sat on a garden chair and used my cell phone to call the police. I never mentioned to them about my paranormal assault in the bedroom, just the horrible condition of the cat. I was, however, interrogated at length before ultimately being released. The cats were rescued and handed over to the local animal shelter for adoption.

Following all this, and as I drove home mentally exhausted, I decided it would be best to distance myself from Paul and limit my contact with him to only occasional phone calls. After some time, our communication became less and less frequent to the point that our phone calls ended altogether. I intuitively knew this would be best for both of us.

At this point, it is my professional conclusion that without any doubt in my mind, I personally experienced something paranormal, dangerous, and evil within Paul's house and would never, ever want to again. Those cats must have been terrorized and so helpless trying to escape whatever that thing was.

DENVER, CO

GI SALES REPRESENTATIVE – ROBERT GUTMAN'S STORY

I've lived in Denver all my life, attending school and eventually graduating from Colorado State with a degree in biology. Four years ago, I returned to school and completed a master's program in clinical laboratory science, after which time I got a hospital job in Vermont. That job only lasted two months before I decided to return to Denver.

A week after my return, I was hired as a district sales manager for a pharmaceutical group that partners with a national health care company's district office located in the southwest.

My job includes working with a team of contracted professional sales representatives offering our client base current information pertaining to products and their approved indications. My team's sole purpose is to sell to the gastroenterology market by calling on gastroenterologists. I recruit, train, and evaluate performance management, operations, data/analytics, and compliance of individuals I supervise.

Well, one day, I was approached and asked by one of my sales staff, Nancy, if I could accompany her to a new account. Nancy was a new hire and did not yet feel altogether confident with approach such a large medical facility. I agreed to go along and to use the trip as a training session.

Arriving at the hospital, we walked up to the front desk and asked for directions to the doctor's office. I was not familiar with the hospital, so we both were unaccustomed to its surroundings. We were directed to the elevator, and after entering, I pushed the button to the fourth floor. After a few seconds, the doors opened. Stepping out onto the highly polished floor was like stepping back in time. The walls were painted an awful green, and the large, linoleum, square-tiled floor was a dismal blue color. The large, suspended, white glass globes that contained the dimly lit ceiling lights only added to the overall ominous feel of the place.

Strangely, we could hear activity taking place, but there was no one around to ask for further directions. I can simply try to explain it this way; it was as if we were in a "vacuum" of dead time. I walked ahead to what looked like a nurses' station while Nancy waited behind at the elevator.

I looked around and didn't spot anyone. But just then, I heard a voice call out to me, "Come here," from one of the rooms that had its door open wide. I turned around, and when I cautiously took two steps inside, I immediately spotted a patient, a very thin man sitting upright in his bed. Before I spoke a word, he looked at me with an angered gaze and began to scream.

I flew out of the room running to the elevator, and luckily, Nancy had held the door open for me. Once inside, we sent the elevator down to the ground floor, all the while hearing the man's screaming and mournful sobbing emanating from the floors above.

Arriving at the first floor, I informed the receptionist about our experience, and I didn't hold back a single detail. Surprisingly, she responded by saying, "You're lucky that's all that happened to you. In those rare times when staff report seeing the ghost of the 'skinny patient,' he tends to run right up to them! But what's most odd about your description of the fourth floor is that it's not at all painted in the color green and doesn't have a blue floor. The fourth floor is of the same decor as all the other floors of the hospital—that in itself is very weird!"

Walking across the parking lot back to our car, both Nancy and I were psychologically unnerved. After getting back on the road to my office, I said to her, "I know you also saw what I saw. Let's not ever talk to anyone about it, okay?"

She agreed and said, "I'm just glad I asked you to accompany me to this visit. I don't know what I would have done alone on that fourth floor by myself or, even worse, if that elevator would have stopped working!"

Although it was only 10:30 a.m., we both decided it would be best to call it a day and to go home. But just a few minutes after arriving at my house, my phone rang. It was Nancy informing me that she would never be returning to work.

I don't know what more I can add or even say to make sense of my experience. I do know I am quite positive I would never want another experience like that again. The new team salesperson I assigned to the hospital has never reported experiencing anything remotely close to what I did.

It's now been over five years since my brush with the ghost, and today, I live my life with the personal knowledge that indeed there is life beyond this one.

OR ANESTHESIOLOGIST – SUSAN HALUKA'S STORY

Originally, I'm from the Colorado town of Montrose. I arrived in Denver and attended college, graduating with my degree in anesthesiology in 2013. I currently live in Denver and plan to stay at my current job until my house in Montrose is completely built, and then I'll settle down with my husband to raise a family. I currently work part-time at two clinics six days a week and have been at this schedule for eighteen months now. I find my job to be very rewarding, and it gives me the opportunity to directly connect with each patient on a one-on-one basis.

My story took place about eight years ago. I was working at Denver Health Medical Center's operating room and, at the time, attending to a six-year-old female gunshot victim. Apparently, the little girl somehow got a hold of her parents' handgun and innocently dropped it, and it went off. The bullet entered her groin, traveled up through her torso, and exited out her lower jaw. Her injuries were so severe that there was no hope of her surviving.

A permanent vision that remains with me from that day is of her blood-soaked orange parka and underclothes that the EMTs had removed while preparing her for surgery. The bloodied clothes were quickly placed inside a large, clear plastic bag and removed from the room. I could still see her frail little body, lifeless and naked, lying on the operating table with a team of medical personnel all doing our best and hoping for a positive outcome. It was soon clear that the poor soul was not going to make it through. Ultimately, not long after initial intubation, she passed. Her death affected us all very deeply.

Now, here is where things get kind of strange. While I was undressing from my scrubs, I happened to glance over to the OR door, and I saw what looked to be the figure of an older, mustached man. He seemed to be in his late sixties and reaching out with one arm stretched toward the operating table where the girl's body lay. I also noticed that no one else in the room had noticed the man, whose image was clearly obvious to me. I couldn't take my eyes off him.

I froze immediately in place as an unseen force took over my body. I couldn't even speak as I witnessed the man move or float over to the little girl's side. This happened within a few seconds. As the man reached the table, I saw a smoke like mist moving up and out of the dead girl's stomach region. In a flash, both the mist and the man disappeared. As soon as these figure energies disappeared, I felt my entire body release tension. I looked around the room, and I was all alone.

That was eight years ago, and I'm still feeling the emotional impact of those few seconds. I can only assume the energy was a relative of the girl coming to guide her soul home. He didn't appear to be evil or even frightening, so I'm assuming he was someone familiar to her, perhaps even an angel.

I'm not sure about what people might think or how I might be judged, but I know what I saw that day was a special gift meant for me. And I'll totally accept it as that!

FRESNO, CA

BIOMEDICAL ENGINEERING TECHNICIAN – KUNAL PATEKAR'S STORY

I was born and raised in the Hindu religion in northwest India, and that is where I attended college at the University of the Punjab. One year after graduating, I studied two years of English and decided to move to the United States. I was hired at Fresno VA Medical Center in 1988 as a biomedical engineering technician. I've been employed here at the hospital since that time. My job entails quite an advanced degree of technical language, so I'll simplify and provide you as brief a description as possible.

Generally, I install, calibrate, and repair medical equipment. I teach clinical and technical staff troubleshooting and basic minor repair of a few pieces of equipment. I also provide information for the development of testing protocols, including software revisions and using data indicators in order to help identify system, safety, and quality problems. This is generally the scope of my position.

Today, as in the past, Hindus view death as an integral part of the living process as has been the case for thousands of years. Of course, we suffer the same human emotions of grief, pain, and loss as everyone does, but we find much comfort in the inherent knowledge of our spiritual path and instruction.

Back home in India, when a person dies, the body is dressed in white cotton cloth and laid out on a table under the cooling shade of a large tulsi bush. This particular plant is regarded to have properties that cleanse the person's soul, ridding the soul of humanity's impurities, frailties, and negativity. Both the immediate family and extended family are required to also wear white cotton clothes; however, a wife must continue to wear the color white for a total of one year after the death of her husband. The most important rule for widows is, although she may decide to wear another color, she must never, ever wear the color red again. Male members of the immediate family are also required to shave their heads each month for one year. Specific prayers and customary rituals described in the holy book Garuda Purana are traditionally offered to the loved one by a priest for a total of thirteen days.

Garuda Purana is one of the puranas that are part of the Hindu body of texts known as the Smriti. This scripture contains details of what happens after the person dies. This scripture also contains details of the various punishments given to a person after death for the sins committed in life. These include Khumbipakam (burned in oil) and Kirimibhojanam (given as prey to leeches). The scripture describes about twenty-four types of death. Some Western scholars see this script as analogous to the Judgment Day of Christianity.

Garuda Purana is in the form of instructions by Lord Maha Vishnu to Sri Garuda (the King of Birds—a vahana of Lord Vishnu). This purana deals with astronomy, medicine, grammar, and gemstone structure and qualities. In addition, the Garuda Purana is considered the authoritative Vedic reference volume describing the Nine Pearls, which includes not only the well-known Oyster Pearl but also the Conch Pearl, Cobra Pearl, Boar Pearl, Elephant Pearl, Bamboo Pearl, Whale Pearl, Fish Pearl, and

Cloud Pearl.

The latter half of this purana deals with life after death. The Hindus of northwest India generally read this purana while cremating the bodies of the dead. This has given great importance to the origin of Garuda. There are nineteen thousand verses describing the ways to the Lord.

On my very first day of employment, the human resources director took me on a personal tour through the various hospital departments that I would have close working interaction with. During this tour, I was introduced to a co-worker named Anita Muralidharan. Anita was a beautiful young woman and was, to my great surprise, originally from southern India. In just a few weeks, we both took a liking to each other, so much so that we scheduled our lunch breaks together. Not surprisingly, our friendly association quickly developed into a romance. Nine months later, in December of that year, we talked about marriage and mutual future plans together.

Anita's two girlfriends from college had planned a trip from the United States on a cruise ship to and from the Bahamas that month. Because I was a new employee, I had to stay behind and work before I'd accumulate enough vacation time, so Anita flew to Houston, Texas, on her own. She was having a great time and kept in contact with me by phone daily. On the morning of the fourth day of her vacation, as I was leaving my condo, I noticed a large black raven standing on my car's hood. Strange-

ly, as I got to about ten feet of it, it turned its head and faced me, and after a few seconds, it flew away.

I immediately took this as a symbolic omen that something terrible was about to take place. Being of the Hindu faith, we believe that crows and ravens are harbingers of death or, at the least, messengers of bad news. Think what you will, but I was raised in this belief, and because of it, I did not take this bird's appearance lightly. I got in my car and drove to work as usual.

I parked my car in my assigned parking space, not far from my office, in fact within a clear, direct view from my office window.

As expected, later that morning, I received a phone call from Anita at the lunch hour, detailing her day and what the girls had planned for the evening. As we ended the call, I turned around in my chair and glanced outside, and to my amazement, there it was again, the raven, again on the hood of my car! Concerned for Anita's well-being, I called her and described the two incidents with the bird. As I was sitting there talking on the phone, I kept my eyes on that black bird and watched as it seemed to tilt its head to look up at me. I froze with terror! When I realized my mistake of informing Anita, and not wanting to worry her any further, I lied and told her that I had just seen the raven fly off. In ending the phone call, I told her how much she meant to me and that I had a surprise waiting for her when she returned. I had decided I was going to ask her to be my wife.

I received a phone call later that same day from one of Anita's girlfriends, informing me that as Anita and two friends were strolling down a popular tourist street in downtown Nassau, a small truck drove unexpectedly onto the sidewalk, striking several people, including Anita. She survived the accident, but a portion of her left leg was permanently damaged.

Upon her return home, Anita and I flew to India, and we were married in a traditional Hindu ceremony. Approximately a year after marrying my new bride, she gave birth to our son. We named him Abnash, which means, "one that cannot be destroyed." Tragically, while giving birth to Abnash, Anita suffered a massive stroke and died less than five days later. I never expected this to happen, and I was shocked beyond belief.

For the past six years, my son, Abnash, and I have returned to India to traditionally honor Anita's soul with the Hindu rite of Pitrs. Pitrs is an elaborate ritual performed in the early morning, when specially made food is first offered to crows that are believed to be the departed souls in disguise. We do this to also ensure the passage during the soul's voyage to the other world. Together with this ritual, an eleven-day ritual called Shraddha is performed. It consists of daily offerings of rice balls called pindas, which provide a symbolic transitional body for the dead. During these days, the soul makes the journey to the heavens, or the world of their ancestors. On the twelfth day, the departed soul is said to reach its destination and be joined with its ancestors, a fact expressed symbolically by joining a small pinda to a much larger one. We believe that without these rites, the soul may never find its way to realm of Yama, the god of death.

In ending, I believe that omens such as the two ravens I saw and other unexplained messages are all around us. These omens are directly sent to present themselves to us. We simply have to adapt our thinking process, and open our hearts in order to tune in.

ANESTHESIA TECHNICIAN – FRANK RUSSO'S STORY

I was born in Ocala, Florida, and received my anesthesia technician, or PRN, degree at University of Florida– Gainesville. I worked as a paramedic for three years before attaining my PRN degree. I relocated to Fresno, California, in 2001 after a terribly bitter divorce. After arriving in Fresno, I applied for and was hired at Fresno VA Medical Center. I've had a few opportunities to change job locations, but I really do enjoy my co-workers and working for this VA facility overall.

As an anesthesia technician, my job requires me to prepare anesthesia instruments, equipment, supplies, and drugs for use throughout the Department of Surgery. I set up IV lines and equipment for surgical procedures, assist with insertion of lines, intubation, and pain blocks, and assist the medical team by doing whatever is needed to maintain efficient quality care to each patient.

I'm going to tell you what happened to me one night. It was an experience that I'll never forget. Although it scares me to even think about the details, I know it happened to me for a very good reason, if for nothing else than to teach me to be appreciative of what I have in this life.

On that particular evening, an eighty-five-year-old patient was rushed into the emergency room and was being prepped to undergo an operation to remove his infected gallbladder. I spoke to him, his wife, and his son while they were with him in the room. I attempted to offer some reassuring words by stating that everything possible would be done to help and that he would be fine. Conversely, I was inserting the usual IV line in his arm, beginning a slow drip to ease his distress. As we talked, he looked at me and stated how comfortable I made him feel and asked if I could feed his dog. I glanced over at his son and gave him a wink of understanding. Having experienced numerous similar patient reactions as the anesthesia begins taking its effect, I absolutely agreed to feed his dog. It took only a few more seconds for the anesthesia to fully take over. His eyes soon closed, and he was out. As the wife and son walked out of the room, I quickly prepared my surgical gown, booties, and mask and then wheeled him into the operating room for the doctor to begin the surgery.

The patient was undergoing a laparoscopic cholecystectomy (gallbladder removal). This is a minimally invasive surgery done under general anesthesia through a very small incision or two. With most of these now common surgeries, the patients usually return home the very same day and are back on a regular diet immediately.

After about an hour in surgery, the patient was taken to an adjacent room to recover before being discharged. I stayed with him and noticed that he was having trouble breathing. It soon became clear to me that this patient was going to require a doctor's immediately attention. As it turned out, he was having a not-so-uncommon episode, a postoperative complication resulting in respiratory failure, affected by a weakened state and his body's inability to tolerate the anesthesia. The medical team and I did what we could to save this man, but in the end, it became clear that he was too far gone. He never recovered consciousness, and all life support was ceased as he had requested in his medical directive. He passed two hours later with his family at his bedside.

Although I did not directly cause his death, I felt responsible for at least communicating to his family the sadness I felt for the patient's passing. But because of a string of emergencies that put me out of touch with scheduling the time to meet with them before they left the hospital, I was unable to do so.

Having arrived at my home that same night, I was in my kitchen fixing a snack when I unexpectedly began to smell the distinct odor of something burning. I stopped what I was doing and sniffed the air. I was sure there was a fire burning somewhere close by inside. Thinking something was on fire in my house, I ran throughout each room, hoping to spot the fire source, but I discovered nothing on fire. I opened both the back and front doors and stepped outside but didn't notice the odor any longer. The very strong odor had now disappeared. I walked back to the kitchen.

In less than thirty seconds, I felt the pressure of a hand on my right shoulder. I instantly turned around to see who was standing behind me. I didn't see anyone. I'm a bit embarrassed to also say that I had just finished showering, and I was in my kitchen totally naked. There was no doubt in my mind as I stood there that a ghostly hand had taken hold of my shoulder and given it a firm but gentle squeeze. I started to shake with fear and was so overcome with terror that I forgot about my sandwich.

I got a grip on my fear and decided to ease my mind by entering my living room to watch some television before heading off to bed. With the remote in hand, I tuned into a few minutes of a popular comedy series. Suddenly, the channels began to flip around on their own, ending on a news station covering a house fire. I thought, this is weird. The television has never done this before. I changed the channel back to the comedy, and as soon as I placed the remote back on the coffee table, I'll be damned if the channel didn't flip back over to the fire report. The channel flipping finally stopped on the fire story, but then an even stranger thing happened.

About one hour later, I was watching the local news, when I felt something brush along my arm. I can only best describe it as fingers gliding across my neck and down my outstretched arm. I jumped up off the couch and switched on the overhead light. Looking at every area of the couch, I didn't see anything at all. I was breathing fast with anxiety. I chose to leave the light on for a better sense of comfort and continued to watch the news station. Suddenly, a large shadow passed between the television and me, actually blocking my view. It only took place for one second, but there was no doubt in my mind that a shadow, possibly a spirit, large enough to block the entire screen had just walked by.

I had reached my breaking point and said to the ghost, "I don't know who you are or why you're here, but I've had enough! I want you to leave me alone. Get out of my house and leave me alone!" A silent stillness came over the whole room. I knew that whatever it was that had been bothering me was now gone. A short time later, I went to bed and had a very peaceful, uneventful night. I was grateful for that.

Two days later, I was back at work. As I was walking down a hallway on my way to my office, I entered the hospital patient discharge office to invite a co-worker for lunch. It so happened that the son of the patient who had died three-days prior, was picking up his father's personal items. I recognized him immediately. After I expressed my condolences, he invited me to a memorial service that a small group of his father's friends had planned that coming Friday evening at a fire station. Before I could ask about his father's memorial being held at a fire station, he mentioned that his father was a retired firefighter.

After hearing this information, the recent paranormal experiences that had taken place in my home a few nights before now made me wonder, if I was visited by that patient's ghost? If so, why me and what did this mean? I'll always wonder but find the unexplained activity an interesting connection.

I attended the memorial service that Friday and, on my return home, felt fully confident not only that I would no longer have another visitation but that encounter certainly re-confirmed my belief in a life-after-death.

HOBBS, NM

FUNERAL DIRECTOR – ANDREW SAMPRO'S STORY

"I was born in Wichita, Kansas and lived there until the age of 33 when in 1977, I married a New Mexico state employee, and moved to Hobbs. My wife and I have lived here in Hobbs ever since. My wife worked for the New Mexico Department of Agriculture and traveled about 30% of the time to neighboring states attending service trainings. It was during one of these trips to Kansas that she and I met, eventually fell in love, and married. My personal story with ghosts took place in Wichita, but ended in Hobbs.

My family's business was unique; a family owned and operated mortuary business. My Great Grandfather, Isadore Owen, who came to Kansas as a land surveyor with the federal government, married my Great Grandmother, Lilly, who happened to be the daughter of an undertaker. The term "undertaker" was changed years ago to "mortician" to sound less morbid and improve marketing for their professional, specialized care services. She and her family established their business along with many other entrepreneurs of the time.

After marring his wife, Great Grandfather Isadore made the decision to also work in his wife's family business and before long their funeral business became a very lucrative one. Many years later, as a young man, I personally I had my own unique position in the business. My specific job entailed that I assist grieving families with their selection of various coffins located in a room next-door to our main office. Our staff referred to his room as the display room. In this room were tastefully displayed between 10 to 12 caskets ranging in sizes that could accommodate newborns, young adults, adults and extra-large caskets for our obese clients. Vaults, markers, cremation jars, flowers, paper, and other memorialization products, or "tie-ins," were also displayed and very important options to offer the grieving family.

Adjacent to this display room was another room, a much smaller room, known to our staff as the economy or basic model room. This room held simple, basic wood caskets without much in the area of color and design. No frills, just caskets covered with simple fabric and little if any detail. It also helped to keep this economy room lit with low lighting. A dimmer switch kept the lights in the room a bit darker, giving the grieving clients an impression of "looming sadness". This was very effective in having them gravitate clients towards the 'brighter' showroom next-door, and the more expensive models and accessories. It didn't take a rocket scientist to decipher which of the two display rooms would offer the more positive atmosphere during an emotional period of grief—choosing the higher end, brighter lit room painted a calming powder blue over the economy room with the dim lighting and greyer colored walls. It was not uncommon for family members to say, when entering the economy room, "I get the willies in this room" or to weep and immediately ask to excuse themselves.

My job was to ascertain, by asking probing questions, the level of money a client would be able to spend, ensuring the right product—in this case a coffin or urn. If I performed my job correctly, having given the "right" presentation, I'd cleverly steer the client toward the more expensive products. Of course, we offered an extended payment plan, but this plan was fraught with a somewhat high interest rates and inserted additional fees. Tailoring the client's emotional needs was important, but always meeting the company's economic bottom line was, in reality, of most importance.

I want to make clear that the funeral business is just as the word implies—a "business," struggling against fellow competitors in the field. After all, in order to remain in business, sales must be tailored to meet the firm's objective and that is to make a profit. My experience working for the family business was almost fifty years ago. As of this date, things must have changed in many ways and in favor of the public. I am well aware that funeral directors go through years of schooling in order to learn their expertise through education and experience. It's really a very technical and skillful career to get into. Just imagine the psychological effort it takes as a funeral operator to deal with grief, not to mention all, and I do emphasis all stages of a decomposing cadaver. I sometimes think to myself, who would choose the funeral business as a career? Most likely not many. Since having been directly involved in the family business from birth, I have an appreciation for the vocation and for those who are employed as directors and staff.

They are a professional and a proud group of business owners, which add much to communities' resources and to the economy as a whole. Some other facts that your readers might find interesting about the funeral business that I'll disclose is that most wood coffins are not meant to seal permanently. If a client wishes one that seals "for all of eternity," they have to specify that when picking or ordering a coffin, which of course, will cost a bit more, quite a lot more. Coffins can be made from a variety of materials from compressed cardboard to particleboard. Most caskets these days are made from particleboard. However, still there remains a strong demand for caskets made from natural woods, such as oak, pine, maple, and such. There are even caskets that are made from stainless steel. These come in thickness or gages from 16, 18 and 20. The very costly caskets are made from stainless, copper, or bronze metals. These caskets can be quite expensive. When I was in the business, I recall only selling two of these expensive models. I attended a funeral trade show some years ago where a casket made entirely from stone was displayed. During the time my Great Grandfather was in the business, cast iron caskets had a built-in glass-viewing window to view the head and face of the deceased!

In my great-great-grandparents' days, viewing of the body was conducted at the family's home—in the living room or even the dining room. Flowers were very important because they were not only pretty, but if the body was exposed to the heat of the season, the natural perfume that the flowers aroma provided would mask a little of the odor of a decaying corpse. You've got to remember that perfecting the embalming process wasn't really accomplished until the 20th century. Sometimes the casket was placed within a zinc tub that had a compartment below the casket that held ice. Also, a drip tube that was connected to this tub ran below the tub and emptied into a bucket. This was meant to catch the liquid from the melting ice and even body fluids. Quite a change from what we do today.

I know that I might already be sounding a bit morbid, but these facts are the reality of the business, and the general public are not familiar with. Most everyone reading my story probably don't even know the color of embalming fluid. Well, the fluid's color contains a reddish-pink dye because after death, your skin will naturally lose its own natural color and will turn a yellowish white, sometimes gray. The pink dye helps to return the natural skin colors of the body to a somewhat more natural look. I imagine I've lost most of you by now, so I'll return to my story. I just thought you'd like to be a little bit informed of the industry. I'll move on.

As I stated earlier, my ghost experience took place in Wichita, but it eventually followed me all the way to Hobbs, New Mexico. I was in the economy room with the family of the deceased. Strangely, this family was unusually composed given they had just lost their son. The only visibly family member to showed any sign of sadness was the father who was especially heartbroken at the death of his 45-year-old son. Again, aside from the father, the mother and two daughters, were quite stoic and easy to communicate with. There was generally nothing to distinguish this family from any other, except for the unusual request they made—they wanted to have their son wrapped in a purple and orange colored cloth, which they had presented to me. The cloth had unusually embroidered hand-stitched symbols, which I had never seen before. They strongly requested, prior to being placed in the casket, that their son be wrapped in this cloth.

The other even stranger item they wanted to have placed in the casket was an iron horseshoe. The shoe was to be placed upon the deceased's stomach with his hands attached to this horseshoe as if grasping it from both ends! This particular family never did offer any indication of their religious orientation, but traditionally a Catholic rosary is given this placement of honor. None of my staff nor I had ever heard of such a request to use a horseshoe before. Nonetheless, our mortician did as was requested by the deceased's family.

The night of the viewing of the body took place without any problems, but something strange did take place. That night only the father of the deceased's family attended the wake. There was no priest or pastor to officiate during the viewing. The father remained seated alone at the front pew and after only about a half hour of meditation, he stepped up to the casket and, as I was observing him from behind a side door, unbeknownst to him, he reached into his coat, pulled out something and placed it within the casket. Then he turned away and left the room.

After the memorial viewing ended for the night, with no one else visiting the deceased, I proceeded to lock the doors. But before turning off the lights, I was curious to find out what the father had placed in his son's casket.

On the surface of the body there was nothing I could see, but after reaching a hand further down alongside the body, next to the right thigh, I felt what appeared to be a jar placed within a paper bag. I carefully removed the bag and opened it.

I almost dropped the jar when I saw what was sealed inside the jar. The jar was a glass, quart sized, old Mason pickling jar. Contained within the jar was the body of a small, what seemed to be a cat's embryo suspended in a clear liquid and to one side was a small dagger with a red handle.

I didn't understand what this was, but I assumed it might be related to some sort of spell or witchcraft. My being a Christian, compelled me to dispose of this bag and jar. I placing it in the trash dumpster outside that very night. If, by chance, the father asked about it the following day of the actual funeral, well, I'd think of some kind of deflecting response. This was so weird that I didn't care anymore what the family might do; I just wanted to get this body in the ground and be done with it.

The following day of the funeral, the only family member who attended the burial was the father who was lacking any words. Because there was not a priest or minister present, the casket was lowered into the ground quickly and without any last words of respect. Once completed, the father walked over to me and extended his hand. All, I could say was, "I'm sorry for your loss." He didn't even look at me, just turned, walked to his car, and drove away.

Earlier that morning I asked for the remainder of the day off, and drove from the cemetery straight home. I entered my home through the kitchen door in the back of the house. I changed out of my formal funeral service attire and put on my jeans and tee shirt, I walked outside to gather my mail, reentered the house, and sat at the kitchen table. As I was seated at one end of the table, I saw a movement of something. Then as I turned my head to look closer, it was gone. I thought about, but couldn't brush it off as being nothing more than the reflection of a passing car. However, I was in the rear of the house and I had never experienced any reflection from a passing car in my kitchen before.

This left me wondering what was going on because earlier, when I was walking up the stairs, I happened to glance up to the second story landing. There standing in full view was the image of a person surrounded in a foggy mist! It was a human shape and I was able to see right through the figure and could see the small-framed picture that was hanging on the wall directly behind it! After staring in disbelief for a few seconds, it disappeared!

What I also noticed, from about fifteen feet away, was that this ghostly figure wore a cloak with the faint pattern that was on the material that the family had me wrap and bury the body with earlier that day!

I ran back down the stairs, got into my car, and sat in my driveway until I could compose myself. I lived alone at the time so, even though the sun was shining, admittedly the experience I had terrified me quite a bit. Eventually, I returned to the house.

A few weeks following this, one evening over the phone, I described what I had experienced to my fiancé. She suggested I speak to my older brother and have him spend a few nights at my home. I did call him, but he was unable to get away from his family. So, I managed to tough it out alone, and thankfully, nothing in the manner of another ghost experience took place. But that would not be the case.

Less than two weeks later, I was at a local shopping mall. As I was walking among the shoppers on the second floor, I could not help but notice about twenty feet up ahead, starring directly at me was a young man who looked exactly like the person in the coffin! I was startled and froze in place. I didn't know whether to run or scream. After a few uncomfortable seconds that seemed to last hours, I walked up to and leaned my body against a store window. Not taking my eyes off this man, I noticed that passersby were simply walking past him, not noticing him at all. His eyes were locked on me and made me so uncomfortable.

Immediately, fear overcame me and I instinctively turned away from him. Then, in about a second or two, I looked back and he was gone! Keep in mind that I had just turned my head away from him for a split second. That was all it took for him to disappear into thin air. I looked down at my hands and they were trembling like leaves. I was so scared.

Somehow I managed to mentally break from my fear and continued on my walk through the mall. The public activity of the fellow shoppers gave me a sense of comfort, sort of safety in numbers. Eventually, I convinced myself that I had imagined all of it and soon a reassurance of peace came over me. I honestly thought, I imagined all of it.

When I got home, I was hesitant to enter my front door, but again, it was early in the day and I told myself, "I'm going to beat this." But no sooner had I placed my keys and shopping bag on the side table located at the entrance, did I spot movement to my left. Again, something like a large dark shadow appeared for a few seconds then disappeared!

As I turned my head to look—it was gone! Then, just a few seconds later, I heard a man's laughter! I yelled out, "What do you want? You're scaring me. What do you want from me?" I heard nothing. No response at all. That experience was so strange and eerie that, although I did not see or hear another thing that day, I was unable to sleep that night. I tried to convince myself I had imagined all of it and I must have been successful to some degree because, as I said, I did finally get to sleep.

The days that followed were uneasy ones for me. I felt as if an unusual and unfamiliar "energy" had taken over my thoughts and state of mind. By this I mean to say that I now had a constant feeling of not being myself. It's difficult to put into words, but my thoughts were hazy and unclear. I was preoccupied with thoughts of a terrible fire, depression and death. I had never in my life had such severe thoughts as these. I knew I needed to talk to someone at work about this. After I confided my ghostly experiences to a co-worker, also a close friend of mine, he advised me to seek professional help. He referred me to his therapist and the next week I was in the therapist's office telling him all about my experiences.

After a few days on medication followed by two counseling sessions, I did begin to notice a positive difference. The counseling sessions helped to clarify my thoughts and judgment in this regard. I was doing well for about a three-week period, but soon after I had another encounter with the ghost of the dead man.

I had just gotten off the phone with my fiancé and had walked into the kitchen, I reached for two cookies then walked into the living room and sat on the couch. As I reached for the television remote, I glanced down the hallway and spotted the same misty figure of the man I had seen weeks before at the top of my staircase! This time I took noticed that he was about six feet tall. I figured this out using one of the door jams as a reference. My eyes had enough time to assess this much. He must have stayed visible for about ten seconds. I kept blinking my eyes and thinking I couldn't possibly have seen what I just saw, but this time I knew I was not imagining him.

Suddenly I heard, "You did it. It was wrong?" I gasped! "What did I do? What did I do to you?" Then the ghost faded away. Stranger still, as it faded away, in its place was a pale bluish colored light that lit the hallway for about two to three seconds. Surprisingly, I was not in the bit scared, I was more startled and in awe of what I had just encountered. Now that this ghost had actually communicated with me that I had done something wrong, I was left needing and wanting to know more details.

Immediately, I knew that this had to do with that jar I removed from the casket, the one I tossed away in the dumpster. This had to be what the spirit was referring to. I guess I suspected all along that these visitations were tied to the jar and its contents, but I didn't want to admit to it.

After that day, a lot more "things" took place in the weeks that followed, but I did eventually speak with someone whom a friend referred me to. This man was a medium who informed me that what I needed to do was to go to the young man's gravesite and make an offering of wine and fresh sprigs of rosemary. I thought that this was too crazy to contemplate, but crazier still I followed the instructions.

I didn't tell anyone about this, except my friend who referred me to the medium. The instructions were for me to go to the man's grave during the day, and using the fresh rosemary sprigs as a brush, sprinkle the headstone with the wine. The medium stated that by doing this, I would show the spirit that my apology was sincere and I'd ritually "wash" my soul of the disrespect I displayed with my ignorance for removing and tossing the jar away.

I wasted no time and within a few hours I found myself at the gravesite, standing beside the headstone. I sprinkled the wine and rosemary leaves at the gravesite, rinsed my hands, and left the cemetery. So, now that you understand what took place all those years ago, I'll now tell you how it all relates to living in New Mexico.

After my wife and I were married, we moved to Hobbs and she continued to work for the state and I got a job as an insurance adjuster. During one of my field visits to assess the extensive damage caused to a garage and business by a fire, I came upon rubble of burnt wood planks and metal. I kicked around the small pile of debris and noticed the faint smell of something rotten. Using an unburned board of wood, I moved things around and found the remains of a foot! Given my years working at the funeral business, I was not repulsed, but I was shocked to find a human foot there among the rubble. I contacted the authorities and the insurance investigation I was working on was immediately halted. Law enforcement investigators replaced me and initiated a new homicide investigation of their own.

At the time, I was going through so much unexplainable experiences and remembered that just a few months before I was in the therapist office describing my thoughts of a fire and ghosts! Not much in that experience prepared me for such a gruesome discovery, but in some respect, I became more aware of a spiritual realm and how it can, in fact, impact the living."

LAS CRUCES, NM

RESPIRATORY THERAPIST – BRIAN G. SILVESTRE'S STORY,

I'm originally from Oklahoma and moved to New Mexico at the age of nineteen, in the spring of 1987. I enrolled at the University of New Mexico at Albuquerque and received my degree as a Respiratory Care Practitioner (RCP). Soon after I passed the RRT exam given by the National Board for Respiratory Care. After working for a few years at a major Albuquerque hospital, I moved south to Las Cruces and have been employed at Memorial Medical Center ever since.

My position responsibilities require providing respiratory care to patients in accordance with guidelines established by the American Association for Respiratory Care in association with other health care team members. I do this in a clinical/hospital setting or at a patient's home. Above all, it's my goal to practice safe and efficient treatment modalities.

About nine years ago I was on a home visit to a seventy-nine-year old female asthma patient, Ms. Yavari, originally from Iran. Her home was located in the southeast area of town, east of Interstate 25. Her home was located in a fairly upscale area and the interior was decorated with an obvious good eye for Persian and middle eastern art. Prior to my arrival, my instructions were that I was to let myself in the unlocked front door and that the patient would be waiting in a back bedroom. I followed the instructions and sure enough I found the woman sitting up in bed in one of the rear bedrooms.

Oddly her bedroom was unlike the rest of her elaborately decorated home because it was simply appointed with a bed, a night stand, a large red rug and a single chair. But most unusual were three of the bedroom's walls had floor to ceiling mirrors. It's not every day you see a room decorated in such an unusual manner. As much as I wanted to asked about the mirrored walls, I kept that question to myself.

I quickly assessed from the woman that her asthma problems occurred mainly during her sleeping, but despite medication, her breathing attacks had worsened to chronic level. Despite her doctor's advice she had chosen to remain living at home. Needless to say, I was to make frequent medication trips to her home both scheduled and on an emergency basis. The patient did not have health insurance and was placed on a 100% private payment

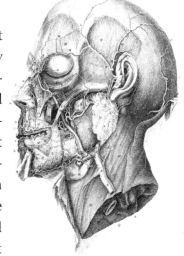

schedule. Her accountant always paid her medical bills in full at the end of each month.

Well, one evening I was called to her house for a routine Nebulized therapy often called a "breathing treatment." A nebulizer changes medication from liquid form into a mist so that it can be easily inhaled into the lungs. I was in the process of preparing the equipment for treatment when I noticed, reflected in one of the mirrored walls, the figure of a tall man dressed in a long coat. As soon as I turned my head to face him, he slowly disappeared before my eyes. I was shocked and could not believe my eyes! There was no doubt in my mind that I just saw the figure of a man appear and vanish in the mirrored wall. I would never, ever forget his image and felt terrified.

The woman was now laying on her back in bed and I'm sure noticed the fear on my face. My calm, focused demeanor had changed and she asked, "What did you see, tell me what you saw?" Without thinking I answered, "A man, a tall dark man wearing a long coat, over in that mirror." She said, "Oh, he's come for me. "Who?" I asked. "The Angel," she said. "He's been keeping his distance from me but now he's decided to release me from my torture. You can go now. I won't need any more asthma treatments." "Are you sure?" I said as my hands were obviously shaking. "Yes, yes you can leave, I'm feeling better now and you need to go," she said.

I didn't hesitate, packed up my things and as I sprinted for the front door, I said, "Well, Ms. Yavari feel free to call me again any time if you need me." In my mind, I knew I had no intention of ever returning to that home or to see that ghostly figure again! My footsteps were rapid all the way back to my truck. I have never in my life, seen anything so scary and drove all the way home completely terrified.

The following morning, I phoned Ms. Yavari to see how she was doing. She answered the phone in a pleasant voice and stated, "Oh, Brian everything is going to be fine with me, and just so you know my angel watched over me all night long. I'm going to be fine." I was surprised by her upbeat, positive attitude and lack of fear in her voice. But if knowing she believed she was "spiritually" being cared for gave her strength, well who could argue with that. Before I said my good-bye, I told her I'd call her visiting nurse, Patricia, who was scheduled to visit later that afternoon.

I mentioned to the nurse Patricia every detail of my visit and even added with apprehension my own experience having seen the dark, male ghost in the patient's bedroom mirror. I expected to hear laughter but instead the nurse stated, "Brian in my line of work I've encountered a lot of unusual, even strange unexplainable things, I'm not at all surprised by what you're telling me. I'll check on Ms. Yavari to find out how she's doing emotionally. But aside from this, you and I have got to get together so I can share my own similar experience I've had with patients. I'll call you later."

I received a call from nurse Patricia at 6:20 pm that evening informing me that Ms. Yavari had passed away earlier that day. The nurse had herself discovered the body sitting in a chair in her bedroom when she stopped by for her home visit. Nurse Patricia describe in detail how she found the body of Ms. Yavari. She said, "As I entered through the bedroom door I spotted Ms. Yavari seated in the chair, in a slouched position facing an opened window. She was dressed in her nightgown but had neatly placed an entire white outfit out on top of her bed. There was a white summer dress, stockings, flat slip-on shoes, a beaded pearl white purse and a white sun hat. She had prepared to dress for travel to some place special. The authorities removed Ms. Yavari's body and the coroner said died peacefully, most likely, while resting in the chair.

Several days later, both Nurse Patricia and I met one evening over dinner, where we fully discussed our personal thoughts regarding the afterlife. It's difficult to describe how spiritually enriched I was impacted by Nurse Patricia's personal stories. I do know that because of my own encounter with the spirit at Ms. Yavari's house and what I learned from nurse Patricia's encounters, I have a new, positive respect for dying and seek to live a more spiritually affirming lifestyle.

MIAMI, FL

SLEEP TECHNOLOGIST/RESPIRATORY THERAPY – CHET BENSON'S STORY

I've been employed at this facility going on five years this Christmas.

Originally, I'm from Montana, and after falling in love with a man from Sarasota, Florida, this is where we both ended up settling down and making a life for ourselves. My first partner of thirteen years, Daniel, was murdered in broad daylight during a hate crime at a supermarket parking lot in Missoula, Montana. His murder was extremely difficult to understand and ultimately accept. Adding to this horrific crime, Daniel was deaf since birth. We met while attending a deaf conference in Seattle. Like Daniel, my older brother was also born deaf, and because of this, my whole family and I are well versed in American Sign Language, or ASL. I knew I had to move away from Montana if I was going to ever find the necessary courage to move forward with my life.

I graduated with an AMA bachelor's degree in respiratory care seven years ago and am currently licensed to practice respiratory care in Florida. I am registered as a respiratory therapist with the National Board for Respiratory Care. Additionally, I am also certified with the Board of Registered Polysomnographic Technologists.

My current job involves my performing a variety of tests and studies related to the diagnosis and treatment of sleep-related breathing disorders. The facility has recently hired a new director who has been assigned to head the new sleep study research program. This particular program performs and evaluates the technical aspects of overnight sleep patterns and nocturnal pulse oximetry. Some of my responsibilities are to set up and apply polysomnographic monitoring devices, ensure patient safety with accurate test results, and provide summary analysis and reports of all studies for physician review.

Because of my skill in sign language, I'm at times called upon to assist deaf and hearing-impaired patients communicate with staff in other areas of the hospital. This being the case, one early morning around 3am, we had a middle-aged African American deaf woman brought into the hospital by ambulance who was being prepped for emergency surgery due to a terrible fall that resulted in internal bleeding. She was found semiconscious in her backyard by a neighbor hours after her fall. Her prognosis was not positive. When I arrived at her side, I could see she was in great pain, shocked and terrified. She definitely needed someone who could sign to offer reassurance and to walk her through the emergency room process she was about to experience. I introduced myself in sign language, and the tension in her face turned to relief.

Immediately, I could tell that her whole composure was beginning to change from dread to a more tranquil demeanor. Before long, she was sedated and taken into surgery. Just before she closed her eyes, I assured her in sign language that all would be well, and I promised her I would be at her side in the recovery room. I held her hand until she fell into controlled unconsciousness.

Sadly, the poor woman never made it out of surgery and died in the operating room. Her death affected me deeply. Having a deaf partner and now this deaf patient die hit an extremely sensitive nerve with me, and I fell emotionally apart.

Needing to recover and compose myself from this tragic event, I walked over and entered the brightly lit break room located just a few doors from surgery. I was exhausted. I reached for the light switch and turned off most of the overhead lights, leaving only one light on. I planned to sit quietly in the darkened room before returning back to my station.

As I was seated, I bent over the table, rested my head on my arms, and fell deep asleep. Suddenly, the loud voice of a co-worker shouting at me in the doorway woke me up. "Chet, Chet, quick, look!" He was pointing as I turned, and faced the deaf patient who had just expired! My co-worker said, "Do you see her, Chet? Tell me you see her too!" Yeah, there she was, clear as life.

I was dumfounded by the woman's apparition. I could see that a thin, blue, glowing light surrounded her, and the expression on her face was of peace and calm. Nothing in the least displayed any sense of pain, fear or panic as before.

Then in one smooth movement, she raised her right hand to her mouth, touched her fingertips to her lips, and extended her hand back toward me, giving me the universal deaf sign of "Thank you". I was completely unprepared for this and couldn't think of the proper "You're welcome" sign to acknowledge her. Apparently not bothered by my oversight, she smiled, turned, and walked right through the wall and vanished.

My co-worker looked at me and said, "What the hell was that? Did we just see a ghost?! I responded that we were just given an exceptional opportunity to witness something most people rarely do, to actually communicate with someone who has died and transitioned to a next life. I am convinced that not only do we, the living, have abilities to convey messages between each other while alive now, but clearly also when we transition over to the after-life.

SOCIAL WORKER – ARLAN E. DAVIDSON'S STORY

I was born in Racine, Wisconsin and at the age of 4-months my parents moved to Florida, where I was raised in Miami. After graduating high school, I was seriously considering entering the seminary to become a Catholic priest, but changed my mind after falling in love with a girl named "Obruni" from Nigeria. Our romance lasted just a few months but the break up seriously devastated me.

I chose to go into the social work field that Fall and entered the Florida University program at Miami. Six years later, I graduated with a Master's degree in Social Work (MSW). Today, I've been employed at the University of Miami Hospital, a statutory teaching hospital for a total of ten years.

My duties include providing psycho social assessments, crisis short-term counseling, community resources, group education and discharge planning for patients and families. I also serve as an administrative backup resource to physicians and staff at the hospital.

At the time of my ghost experience I was dating another black woman "Althea" who was as myself, employed by the hospital. Althea was born in the Caribbean island of the Dominican Republic. Our time together lead me down a path of discovery, as Althea disclosed to me that she was well versed in matters of voodoo and spiritualism. Her unique knowledge was attained from her grandparents on her mother's side, and as it turned out, her brother was a well-known voodoo priest back home in the Dominican Republic.

Once we decided to advance our relationship, we both thought it would be a good idea if I moved in to Althea's home to live as a couple. I moved in on a Thursday and all appeared to be going well, but by the third week after moving in, strange things started to happen in the house.

An eerie example of this began one morning around 9am. It was my day off and Althea was at work. I was lying in bed and, I might add fully awake at the time, thinking about how I would spend the day. Suddenly I heard the sound of footsteps coming down the hall and towards the opened bedroom door.

Knowing she was at work but now thinking she might have changed her mind to stay home, I called out her name, "Althea is that you? Why aren't you at work?" No response. I called out a second time, "Althea, what are you doing home?" Again, no response.

But just then I spotted movement at the door. I turned and was surprised to see the face of an older black man, in his 60's, peeking at me from behind the door frame! I could see his one hand grasping the frame for support while he stared at me flashing a disturbing, sinister grin.

Instantly I grabbed my pillow and flung it right at the man's head yelling, "You son of a bitch, get the f**k out of here!" Even though I was very shaken, I jumped off the bed and shot towards the figure in the door. I really expected to catch the intruder, because he was feet away from me but when I got to the hall, it was empty. In fact, except for the strong odor of cigar smoke, I was completely alone in the whole house.

I checked to make sure that all the doors were locked, I could see that absolutely nothing had been moved around or was missing. My experience with the male face left me stunned, but with full acceptance that what I saw was indeed a real ghost!

When Althea arrived home that evening I described everything to her in full detail. She shook her head and said, "I know who that ghost is, it's a 'Loa' an ancestral spirit. My mother told me about this Loa and to call him by his rightful name, "Samedi." Samedi dwell in cemeteries and offerings to him of cigars wrapped in black cloth are always placed at the entrance of crypts and tombs.

I also know why he's here. Althea said he was sent to our home because of my brother's wife who called two days ago demanding money from me. She did this knowing it was going to be a full moon last night.

I refused and she yelled to me, "You'll be sorry. You'll regret not helping us!" Samedi gets especially powerful when the moon is full and he can be quite dangerous if he chooses to be.

Without my having to ask, Althea stated, "Don't worry, I'll take care of us. That witch might be powerful but I know more about spirits than she realizes. I'll just have to send 'Papa Legba' to her home to teach her a lesson, a very hard lesson she won't forget. The nerve of her sending a dirty Samedi spirit to our home!"

Later that night, Althea performed a short ritual in our living room, invoking the voodoo god Papa Legba. Prior to the ceremony she instructed me to remain quiet and to listen for a dog or dogs barking. I had never heard any dogs barking in our neighborhood before and asked her the reason for this odd instruction. She answered, "No not now, I'll explain later. Just listen for it!"

Midpoint through the ritual Althea spoke, "Papa, grant my intentions tonight then remove the Samedi from our house and give me your sign." Then, as if scripted out of a Hollywood movie, a loud "bang" hit outside on our front door followed by the sound of a dog that barked five times! Althea spoke, "Five barks, did you hear that—a total of five barks! "Yes, what does that mean?" Adrian asked. It means that my sister-in-law is going to suffer five periods of physical pain and maybe even death—serves her right! I was left speechless by her callous attitude.

As predicted by Althea, my brother's wife mysteriously became sick with debilitating migraine headaches that lasted over five months. I couldn't help but wonder if Althea's spell really had anything to do with this. It was a few days later that I sought the advice of a Catholic priest, who expressed serious concern for someone practicing witchcraft and advised me to leave Althea as soon as possible for my own safety.

Because of all I experienced with Althea we parted company and I've not regretted a single minute since. I know that she returned to her home in the Dominican Republic and we've not communicated since. As for myself, I am today a very content man and happy to live alone with my three-year-old Siamese cat "Burtha" and pet iguana "Althea."

RALEIGH, NC

INFECTION CONTROL NURSE – DAVID R. SCROGGINS'S STORY

I'm from North Carolina and received my nursing degree from the University at East Carolina. After graduating, I enrolled at Fayetteville State University, where I graduated with a master's degree in public health. I am currently a state employee for Colorado Environmental Public Health Tracking, and although I live in Colorado, my experience with ghosts took place in 1987, when I was still living in North Carolina and was working at my first job at Central Prison.

The prison was completed in December 1884 and was the first prison built in North Carolina. The authorities at the time used a workforce of inmates to build it, and it took them a total of fourteen years to construct. It's located west of downtown Raleigh. The prison serves many functions. It houses the state's execution chamber, deathwatch area, and men's death row. The infirmary and mental health facility serve the needs of male inmates from around the state. It also serves as a diagnostic center, the point of entry into the prison system for male felons age twenty-two years or older with sentences greater than twenty years.

I was an infection control nurse. I was hired to investigate and monitor potential sources of suspected HIV infections in order to determine and ensure control. I counseled prisoners and staff on HIV infection control issues. I collaborated with other members of the team to follow up on exposure incidents, participated in multidisciplinary team treatment plans, and trained new staff regarding standard personal protective precautions using required equipment.

Personally, being an openly gay man, I was not always viewed positively by fellow employees—especially in a conservative, 'born-again' Christian state like this one. Given my level of education and connections within the medical community, I was respectfully treated and even honored, having been presented with two service awards. Surprisingly, I was asked to secretly assist in the HIV treatment of three separate, closeted gay family members of prominent conservative politicians—one woman and two men. Now if that is not the height of hypocrisy, then I don't know what is!

My ghostly experiences at the prison began late one Autumn morning as I was walking down a hallway within the prison's infirmary unit. I was on my way to the kitchen to make myself a hot cup of herbal tea before entering my office. I had overslept and missed our usual staff meeting that morning.

I walked past the closed door of one of our administrators' offices when I heard the retching sound of someone vomiting coming from within, even though I knew that the administrator was away on vacation in Europe. I immediately stopped and walked into the office, hoping to assist whoever the ill person might be. As I entered, I was overwhelmed by the strong, vile odor of fresh vomit, but when I looked around, I saw no one. I pinched closed my nostrils against the putrid odor and quickly looked about the office, but it was empty of any living soul. Perplexed, I walked out and continued walking toward the kitchen.

Once inside the kitchen, I met a fellow employee. We spoke briefly and I just had to tell him about my experience in the office. He responded, "Oh, David, if you had attended the staff meeting earlier, you would have known that one of the HIV patients died in Italy. He was discovered three days ago in his hotel room in Siena, dead from an apparent heart attack. He passed during the night in his sleep. It was reported his bed was covered in vomit and blood."

This was my first encounter with an unusual incident at the prison, and things progressed from that point—and not for the better.

About two weeks later, I was approached by an inmate, Jake, who served as our unit's janitor, regarding something strange he not only experienced but also visually witnessed while working in the women's restroom. "I saw the ghost of a prisoner who died here years ago," he said. "It was Artie M&M. I knew him; we were good buds. We all called him M&M because it was his favorite candy. I was on my knees, wiping the back of the sink, when I turned my head and saw M&M walking— no, floating—right past me, and he disappeared right into the door! I'm not afraid of his ghost, Mr. Scroggins. M&M was my friend, my buddy."

Five days later, approximately two hours after I returned from a lunch meeting in town, I was seated at my office desk going over my calendar, when I caught sight of someone standing at my opened door—a prisoner wearing a dirty T-shirt and his right arm completely covered in tattoos.

I asked the strange prisoner, "Can I help you?" He looked at me, smiled, and then moved away from the door, and I assumed he walked down the hall.

I immediately jumped out of my chair and ran to the door. Walking toward me were two women, who were about twenty feet away. I asked them about having seen the prisoner and where he went. They answered, "We've not seen anyone."

I was dumfounded. I contacted security, and after an intense search of the intake records facility followed by a head count, absolutely every prisoner and facility visitor was accounted for.

Of course, I approached Jake for some further information. I asked him to give me a few more details about M&M's physical appearance. Jake took a good look at my face and said, "Mr. Scroggins, you saw M&M, didn't you? He paid you a visit, didn't he? I can see it in your eyes."

I was caught off guard by Jake's question but responded truthfully by describing my encounter in full detail. Jake responded, "Well, his spirit must have a reason for returning back here. God knows once I'm released, I'm never setting foot in this place again, living or not!"

Jake also informed me of the manner of M&M's death. A few weeks after his release, he was crossing a street one night, struck and killed by an eighty-eight-year-old man driving drunk.

Initially, Jake never mentioned to me about M&M's tattoos on his right arm, but when I brought it up, sure enough, he confirmed to me that M&M indeed had his entire right arm covered in ink art. My suspicions were now confirmed—I actually had a spirit visit me—and in the middle of the afternoon.

I must confess I was not scared by this realization. I felt a sort of privilege to have been given the opportunity to experience just a fleeting glimpse of the after-life. For the last months that I worked at the prison, I kept a small candy dish filled with M&Ms on my desk, and I used to refer to it as "Artie's dish."

SANDIA "NA-FIAT" PUEBLO, NM

Sandia Pueblo is located in central New Mexico, adjacent to Albuquerque and covers a total of 22,877 acres on the east side of the Rio Grande Valley.

Interestingly, the people of Sandia are members of the pre-Columbian Tiwa language group who once dominated the Albuquerque area. They state that their lineage can be traced to the Aztec civilization of old Mexico. The Sandia people have cultivated the land and raised their families in the area since 1300 AD.

Of most importance is the Sandia Mountain, which dominates the panorama of Albuquerque to the east. This mountain range provides the source of the Sandia people's spirituality as well as offering valuable natural resources, which have been of significant historical importance to their survival. Historically, Sandia was at one time the largest pueblo in the area they had over 3000 people. Today they currently have approximately 500 enrolled members.

FUNERAL DIRECTOR – DOMINIC SANTIAGO'S STORY

Ever hear of a funeral worker who is American Indian? They're not very common, but they do exist, why wouldn't they? Today native people are found doing various types of work, from attorneys, administrators, astronauts, physicians and yes, even writers of ghost books! Sadly, the fearful, but ignorant stigma associated with the funeral industry still remains. But as Dominic stated during the interview, "It's changing. I tend to get strange looks from people and have interesting conversations when the subject of 'what type of work do you do?' arises at parties. First, they are surprised by my profession, then the usual follow-up question is asked, 'But you're Indian, doesn't that go against your culture?"

Presented here is the first recorded story that I am aware of which gives a personal ghost account from a mortician, but not your average mortician—an American Indian mortician.

— Antonio

"I've lived at the pueblo for most of my life. I joined the army right after graduating high school. I completed my degree in funeral science in the state of Kansas eight years ago, took a short break, then passed my board exam as a licensed Funeral Assistant. Following that, I worked for 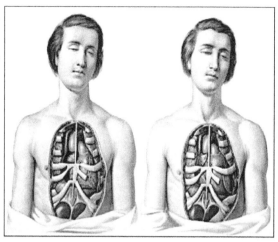 two years at a mortuary in Kansas City and after returning to the pueblo and spending three years at home, I moved away once again. Today, I live in Albuquerque with my cousin Ruth. I decided not to return to the pueblo because of personal reasons.

As I said, I'm a licensed funeral assistant. I served my apprenticeship for over a year before deciding on it as a career. So, today I am working my way up the corporate ladder to the position of Funeral Director. I plan to have a job at one of the major funeral offices in Albuquerque.

As it stands, my primary job is to take care of the deceased, assisting with the embalming, cremation and restorative work. I also get involved with arrangements and finalizing actual funerals, do some grief counseling and generally help the families through their bereavement process. It all might sound a bit odd to most people when I explain my job, especially to Indians, and especially when non-Indians figure out I'm native, but soon they come to realize that it's a job just like any other, well, maybe not like any other, but it pays the rent.

Having been raised from childhood within the pueblo's traditions, which included knowing that poking fun of the dead was a very serious offense, I honestly can say that I always take my work seriously, and always offer a prayer of reverence to each and every body that comes my way. I give them the respect they deserve and do my best to make their spirit content. I believe that in this way, I offer them a small blessing of peace.

Well, I guess I'll now get right to my story. At the time when I was working in Kansas, my office was located on the second floor of a well-known funeral home. The actual mortuary work was done at the first level and basement of the building. It was an older building but very suitable for the business end of the job I was involved with. The whole building had recently been remodeled and I was especially impressed by my work area's up-to-date equipment and the elevator that the owners had installed during the remodeling which made it a breeze to transfer bodies from the street level to the basement and back.

I was working on a woman's body one morning; her death caused by a combination of old age and lung cancer. This woman's body was particularly difficult given the large amount of restorative work needed. The family, against our better judgment, had requested an open viewing, they insisted on having an open casket and after I strongly advised against such an endeavor, they were still insistent. So, I was in the process of doing my best to comply with their needs; although given the severe degree of disfigurement, I knew I would at some point need the assistance of a superior's experience.

The poor woman's face was completely devoid of fatty tissue, so her skin was blotchy and discolored. Restoring this was not going to be a problem, but her lack of subcutaneous tissue was another matter altogether. Luckily for me I had a great director whose work had impressed me. Both he and I had worked on this woman's body for almost two hours; until we reached the result we were aiming for. I was left to dress the body after the embalming, restoration and make-up was accomplished. After this was completed I place her in her casket. The last step was for our resident beautician to do her hair.

I had finished putting on her dress, and was in the process of slipping on her stockings and shoes. Suddenly to my left, I noticed a figure, the figure of a woman standing close to me, observing my work. Holding one of the woman's lifeless legs in my left hand and her shoe in my right, I turned to face the person who was standing to my left. As I turned my face, I found myself facing directly into the eyes of this young woman's face! Startled I dropped the leg and shoe I was holding and admittedly, I let out a scream! Never taking my eyes off this ghost, I saw that she was not only related to the dead woman lying in the casket, but it was she, only a much younger version! The woman's form, or ghost, was giving off a type of amber light, which soon soothed my fear with a wonderful smile of kindness. I was a mixed bag of emotions at that point. Her spirit lingered for only a few seconds, but enough time to convey such a clear sense of approval, a message that I'll never forget.

In my people's language, I repeated a prayer in her honor and gave her my personal blessing. I didn't know what to think, but fear was no longer an issue for me. In fact, I absolutely had no fear at all. I completed my job, dressing the woman's body for the beautician and never mentioned my experience to anyone. I have nothing more to add to this story, only just to say that I hope someone takes from my experience something of value."

SANTA FE, NM

SPEECH LANGUAGE PATHOLOGIST – OWEN D. PETTIGREW'S STORY

"I was born and raised in Gatlinburg, Tennessee and relocated to Santa Fe in the winter of 1989. I attended college at The University of Tennessee at Knoxville, received my undergrad degree then transferred to graduate school at University New Mexico in Albuquerque for my Masters in Speech Language Pathology. Soon after I was licensed by the NM Speech-Language Pathology, Audiology, and Hearing Aid Dispensing Practices board. I waited one year before landing the job at St. Vincent Medical Center, renamed Christus St. Vincent Medical Center.

As of today, it's been eleven years that I've been employed at the hospital where I engage with patients of all ages having various disorders, including Asperger's and Autism. My goal is pragmatically instilling language and social communication skills.

My ghost story began when I lived in Tennessee. I was fourteen years old at the time and my family moved into a house that belonged to my aunt Rita. Aunt Rita was never one of my favorite relatives because as a child she once gave me a painfully hard spanking when she caught me throwing clumps of mud at her bee hives. Aunt Rita produced here own honey and sold it at Farmers Markets.

As I remember back now, I don't blame her much but those hand swats were unforgettably painful at the time. On Aunt Rita's property was a large, very old two-story barn. For some unknown reason after my aunt's death, I never felt good being inside that barn and avoided going anywhere near it and now, I'll tell you why.

Aunt Rita died at age 90 and had battled cancer for three years before succumbing to the disease. My mother discovered aunt Rita's body as it lay within the barn, outside on the ground for, she guessed, about 5 days. Mother said, "The odor of her body lying there in the high Tennessee humidity is something I'll never forget!"

We moved into my aunt's property in the spring of 1969 and wherever I walked on that property, I never feel totally comfortable. Strangely, I always felt her presence, even her now invisible eyes watching me. This uncomfortable feeling reached a high point when I began to experience disembodied footsteps at night coming down the short hall right outside my bedroom and into my room! I never saw a ghost or heard a voice just the sound of footsteps approaching. I never found out what caused the footsteps sounds and just accepted them, when I heard them.

One strange occurrence people would report to us seems to happen when we are not physically at home in the house. People tell us when they would call the house, an elderly female voice would pick up the receiver and answer, "Hello." Then silence and nothing else was said again, just the one word "hello."

One time while I was in the living room, the phone rang and when I lifted the receiver to my ear, I distinctly heard my aunt's voice speaking my name. I couldn't believe what I just heard and the hairs on the back of my neck stood up. I threw the receiver down and shouted, "Don't call me anymore, don't ever call again!" This time, when I put the receiver back up to my ear, all I heard was the busy tone.

As soon as I reached the age to move out of that house. I entered college and with my two roommates we rented a house near campus where I finally felt completely at ease.

As you can see, I have had my share of spiritual experiences as a young boy, but as an adult, I can also describe a significant level of spiritual experiences as well.

In June of 1999, I had been assigned a young 27-year-old man that had a problem speaking after undergoing surgery and radiation treatments on his throat. This young guy, named Thomas, was strikingly handsome and each time he came into our clinic the female employees just went into a flurry of excitement.

Thomas and I worked well together and with each of his clinic visits his speech was progressing at the expected level. I began to look forward to our therapy sessions not the least due to the fact that he and I were both gay men and could relate easily on our mutual orientation. Our association grew into a friendship, nothing romantic, simply a comfortable friendly relationship. I, myself, was already in a committed five-year relationship and Thomas and his partner had been together for nine years.

Well, one Friday afternoon on my day off, my partner Armando and I wondered into a local imported goods store. As we strolled down one isle, I just happened to look up at the far end of the isle and spotted Thomas unusually dressed wearing all white, white shirt, white pants and white shoes. It was without a doubt Thomas but something about him wasn't quite right.

As he slowly moved past a large antique blue cabinet. I called out, "Thomas, hey wait up!" Overall he appeared to be pre-occupied and not in the least listening to me. As I tugged on Armandos arm to look ahead at Thomas, Thomas seemed to briefly glance over at us, then instantly faded away into thin air! He absolutely dissolved into nothing right before both our eyes, just "poof" he was gone!

I asked Armando if he also just saw Thomas disappear? Armando responded saying, "What just happened, are we're seeing things? I quickly maneuvered around a large table display of glass Moroccan lamps and took no more than five seconds to reach the area where we had spotted Thomas. He was not anywhere. We searched all around the medium size store but never saw him. We also thought, perhaps it wasn't even Thomas at all.

The experience left us with a very odd feeling of unease. I assured Armando that I would be seeing Thomas on Monday when he came in for his therapy and I'd be sure to ask him about this.

At no time did either Armando or myself bring up the issue of Thomas's ghostly disappearance in the store. I imagine that to do so would open up the uncomfortable topics of death, etc. and we were just not ready to discuss this at that time.

Well, Monday early afternoon I received a phone call from the clinic director that he had been notified that Thomas had been shot to death outside a liquor store the night before Armando and I had spotted Thomas in that store!

The details were that he had been innocently caught between the cross fire of an armed robbery attempt. I was devastated and so depressed on hearing the sad news but I immediately knew there was so much more to his death. Thomas had appeared to both Armando and I the day after his death to acknowledge his passing and to left us with a vision of himself, dressed in pure white, perfectly prepared for his after-life journey.

Four nights later, Armando and I attended the funeral wake and were shocked upon viewing his body at it lay in the casket. Thomas was dressed in a white shirt, tie, jacket, slacks, belt and shoes-just as we had seen him when he appeared to us! His partner had also placed a beautiful rosary of white beads.

If there is a lesson to be learned in all this, I take from it that each one us is much too important to be taken for granted. We must honor the divine presence, the spiritual essence that makes us who we really are and not dwell on lifestyle differences but on our shared humanity."

ST. PETERSBURG, FL

HOME HEALTH CAREGIVER – JASPER HOWIE'S STORY

"In 1998, I was employed with Bayshore Home Care, a company located in Saint Petersburg that provides in-home health services. My job duties included personal care assistance to clients, such as helping them with grooming, dressing, and assisting with personal matters such as toileting. In a nutshell, I was generally responsible for the provision of personal care to patients in their homes and assisting them in meeting the everyday requirements of daily living. It was during this period of my life that I had a life changing ghost encounter that I'll never ever forget.

My story involved one of my patients, Mrs. Opperman, an eighty-seven-year-old retired Korean War veteran. Mrs. Opperman had served in the naval branch of the armed forces and was assigned to my care for about three months prior to when the incident took place at her home. She was typical of our clients needing assistance with personal care needs. I would characterize her personality as feisty and self-assured.

Mrs. Opperman had a well-appointed, attractive, upper-class three-bedroom condo two blocks from the beach. She lived alone, and on rare occasions, I'd find myself having to spend the night in a guest room at her home. Not being very stable on her feet, she was prone to falls, and one day while alone, she fell and nearly broke her nose. I arrived the next morning to discover the hallway carpet was stained with blood. Following that unfortunate episode, her medications were quickly adjusted, and her balance returned to normal. But nonetheless, I was required to spend a few overnight shifts simply to keep a close watch on her recovery progress.

Well, one afternoon as I was leaving her home for the day, Mrs. Opperman was seated in her living room, and she asked me to bring her a dozen red and white carnations when I returned the following morning. She handed me a twenty-dollar bill and said, "Good-bye." I answered, "Ok, see you tomorrow."

I arrived the next morning at 8:00, I opened the front door with a key the agency had assigned me, and as I walked inside, I spotted a green flower vase. I said, "Mrs. Opperman, good morning. I've got your flowers and I'll use this vase here if that's all right."

From the bedroom, I heard her respond, "Good morning. Yes, of course, use it." In a few minutes, I had finished filling the vase with water, cutting the flower stems, and arranging the carnations in the vase she left out. I said again, "Mrs. Opperman, where would you like me to place the vase?" She responded, "I'll be right there."

While I was standing next to the living room window and organizing my paperwork, I saw her shadow pass by the hallway entrance that led to her bedroom. She said, "Put them next to you on the table. Thank you." I heard movement away from the doorway and back toward the bedroom. As she seemed to have walked away, I said, "I'll have your coffee ready in a few minutes."

I placed her coffee cup and a cherry danish on her side of the kitchen table and then called to her, "Everything is ready for you, Mrs. O. Don't let the coffee get cold." Silence. I called again, and when she did not respond, I walked through the hallway and into her bedroom. She was not there.

I stepped past the open bathroom door and was shocked to discover her face down on the floor, her shoulders wedged between the toilet and the bathtub. I could see immediately that she had expired, and due to the cold temperature of her body, the stiff condition, and pooled blood-stains on the floor, she had obviously been dead since last night. I know I heard Mrs. Opperman's voice that morning responding to my greeting and questions. I even saw her shadow move in the hall. But how? This is the question I now live with every day.

After the authorities completed their work and Mrs. Opperman's body was removed, the coroner absolutely determined that she had died many hours before, prior to my arrival that morning. I knew better than to speak about what my arrival that morning and the communication I'd had with her spirit. What creeps me out is the thought that while I was talking to her spirit in the living room, her dead and bloody body was just a few feet away from me!

This experience was a life changer for me. It just makes me think that, without knowing, any one of us can also experience what I did. Who knows if the next person we come across is not simply what we think he or she is, but is instead a ghost? Like I said, I'll never forget this for as long as I live."

WARNINGS, REVELATIONS, AND MESSAGES

ALBUQUERQUE, NM

HOSPITAL CHAPLAIN – FATHER HENRY'S STORY

"Well, to begin with, I've been a Catholic priest for more than 40 years. I am now retired, and I have to say, I've lived a very active religious life. My faith has taken me to many parts of the world, including a 21-year spell in India where I worked as a missionary in the city of Bangalor. I belong to the Franciscan Order of priests and brothers, and have been retired for more than six years now. My provincial felt that it would be best for me to relax for the remainder of my life. I must admit, I also think this is best since I am losing my eyesight more and more.

You asked about my experience with ghosts. I have to laugh, because such things are difficult for many people to believe in, even priests. But, I'll tell you about something that happened to me many years ago. It doesn't have to do with ghosts, per se, but evil takes many forms. I believe what I experienced many years ago at the Veterans Hospital in Albuquerque will prove this.

It happened in August 1943. I had taken my final vows in July and was ordained to the priesthood. I was young and excited about my vocation as a pastoral minister. Among my first official duties as a priest was celebrating Mass for the patients and staff of the Veterans Hospital in Albuquerque. I offered Mass at 7 a.m., and then I made visits to the patients' rooms for personal counseling, confessions, etc. There was no set schedule of activities around the hospital and I often received late-night and early-morning emergency calls to perform last rites. I very quickly made good friends with several of the staff and patient families.

One afternoon, while at the hospital, I was summoned to the bedside of a 15-year-old female patient by her parents. A nurse informed me that the family was convinced their daughter was under the influence of an unseen evil force. The parents described in vivid detail several incidents that had occurred within a short time leading up to their daughter's hospitalization. According to the parents, they no longer recognized their daughter. Her personality had changed to such a degree that even her facial features had altered.

About seven weeks before, their daughter, Lisa, began to complain about hearing a small, whimpering puppy in her room. The sound was loud enough to wake her from sleep. Lisa would get out of bed, turn on the light, and search behind her dresser, under her bed, and was unable to find any evidence of a puppy. Eventually, the whimpering noise became so loud that poor Lisa would sit wide awake in bed with tears in her eyes concerned about the invisible, crying puppy.

The parents never heard the cries of the puppy and, as the weeks progressed, the nightly episodes of Lisa's fruitless searching escalated to the point that the poor girl was screaming for the dog. Her parents concluded that their daughter was imagining everything. Lisa became obsessed with locating the puppy. She refused to leave the house, and only walked out of her bedroom to use the bathroom. Her mother brought her food to her bed. Lisa became so preoccupied that she lost all interest in bathing and eating. Her parents sought the advice of several close friends but to no avail.

One night, Lisa's parents discovered her sleeping under her bed. Lisa told her parents that a man's voice had told her to crawl under the bed and that the puppy would come to her. Lisa did as she was instructed by the voice. The very same day her parents sought the help of a psychologist. They found a doctor who had a private practice in Albuquerque, but who also worked part-time for the Veteran's Hospital. The psychologist evaluated Lisa and diagnosed her as schizophrenic. Lisa was placed on medication, but the medicine caused her to remain drowsy most of the day.

After two weeks passed, poor Lisa worsened to the point of yelling obscenities at her parents and staring for hours at a time at her image reflected in a mirror. She also began to recite the Lord's Prayer, also known as the "Our Father," backwards! She began by yelling loudly, "Amen, evil from us deliver, etc." When she reached the first word, "Our," her father

592

took his daughter by the shoulders and shook her, pleading for her to stop. Lisa's reaction was to open her mouth wide and scream out a wild, explosive laugh. She was beyond the point of being reasoned with, and her parents could think of no other response but to take their daughter to the Veterans Hospital to visit the psychologist on an emergency basis. It was during this visit that I got to meet Lisa and her parents personally.

As I approached the hall where the hospital staff had restrained Lisa to the metal bed with thin leather straps, I could not help but notice the despair on her parents' faces. Lisa's arms and legs were tied firmly to the bed, as if she was a savage beast. Since the psychologist was unavailable, and Lisa's parents were Catholics, they asked for a priest. The parents asked me to bless their daughter with holy water.

Lisa had been given a shot of morphine and was quite tranquil in her bed. I assured her parents that everything would be fine. I went to my office and located a small bottle of holy water and then returned to Lisa's bedside. Arriving in the hall where I had seen her just a few minutes before, I saw Lisa moving hysterically and yelling, "Get away from me! Don't come any closer!"

Automatically I paused, but her parents begged me to approach their daughter. I must admit that I had mixed emotions about the situation before me. I decided to do a simple blessing over the child. I unscrewed the bottle containing the holy water and placed a few drops on my hand. Quickly, I recited a short prayer and placed my moist palm on Lisa's forehead. Immediately, Lisa yelled out the words, "Stop! You're killing me! You're killing me, you son of a bitch!" I backed away in shock! Then I immediately said, "Child, be at peace with your Savior who will deliver you."

She opened her eyes wide and stared at me with what appeared to be the eyes of the devil himself. Large grey pupils, surrounded by pitch black eyeballs-truly the most terrifying thing I've ever seen! At that point, there was no mistaking that I was in the presence of evil. I'll never forget the intense hatred directed at me in those large unnatural eyes. Being a young and inexperienced priest, I was shocked. Attempting to gain control of the situation before me I prayed aloud, "The love of our

Father in Heaven and of his son, Jesus Christ bless you!"

At that point Lisa went absolutely crazy! She broke away from the restraints, and we backed away as she sat up in bed. By this time, there must have been about five nurses looking on. No one made an attempt to intercede. Everything was happening so quickly and we did not have time to react.

Suddenly, Lisa reached past her extended legs with both hands, grabbed her left foot, and began to pull her foot back towards her chest as she repeated these words, again and again, "Jesus loves me, Jesus loves me."

I began to hear the bones in her foot dislocate and break. There was not one ounce of pain in her face, just a wild, unearthly smile. The sight of this poor girl doing such physical damage to her foot was horrible to watch. Both her father and I lunged towards her. We took hold of her arms and pulled with all our might. Her strength was unbelievable! Lisa's mother yelled for me to throw holy water on her daughter. I took the glass bottle out of my pocket as the nurses took my place holding her. I doused Lisa with the holy water.

Instantly she fell back on the bed and let out a terrible scream. It was awful. No one in Lisa's hospital room was prepared for what took place next.

As Lisa collapsed on her bed, we saw a large black dog crawl out from under the bed. Its ears were bent backwards; its long tail was curved tightly down between its legs and the hair on its back was standing straight up. As soon as it had cleared the bed frame, the dog growled, bolted out the door and down the hallway. Several courageous nurses went in pursuit of the animal, but amazingly it was never found.

There was no way for it to escape. The hall doors all had handles and latches, which needed to be turned in order to open them. The black dog had just vanished. None of us could ever say where this dog came from, how it got under the bed or where it went after running out of the room.

Lisa was shaking and crying in her mother's arms. After spending a night in another hospital under observation, Lisa regained her composure and was well enough to be released. Her foot was in a cast, but aside from that she looked fine.

I kept in touch with Lisa and her parents for a few years following the incident, and can give my personal assurance that she turned out to be as normal as can be. Lisa was unable to recall most of her brush with evil. Both her parents are now deceased, and Lisa is employed by the Albuquerque Public Schools.

Well, there you have it. I've not much more to add except please, let the readers of my story know that evil is very real and always ready to grab the opportunity to challenge God. May you all be blessed and protected."

ASPEN, CO

OPHELIA BAEZ'S STORY

Ophelia and I sat in her living room early one morning. She narrated the experience she had with an elderly couple that she had been caring for, and the unusual spiritual manifestation and expression of love, which in my experience, have never seen before. What follows here is her wonderful story and the unique bond of gratification that it would ultimately revealed to her.

—Antonio

"I was born in San Francisco California, and I've lived in Aspen, Colorado for more than nine years, but I consider San Diego, California to be my true home. In 1997, my husband Jerry and I moved to Crested Butte Colorado. At the time of our move, Jerry was a licensed electrician and was offered a nice paying job working at a newly approved Aspen subdivision. Admittedly, I was not as eager as Jerry to make the move to Colorado. I had to give it serious thought before making such a drastic move. Our future as a family was very important to me, and just the idea of having to leave my own family caused me to shed more than a few tears. After all, I would be moving several states away, leaving my own mother and two sisters. It was very difficult for me. My close friends were pulling me in the direction to stay in San Diego, and although the new environment, and the possibility to make a lot of money was potentially very real, it took me eight weeks to relent. However, in a short time Jerry and I made the drive to Colorado and within a week, were calling Crested Butte our home.

Jerry soon enrolled in, and after studying for many weeks completed, the State's electrician test in order to be licensed and work within Colorado. During this period, Jerry was working as an apprentice for a master electrician at a subdivision. A few months into Jerry's work, his employment with the contractor was complete. It was amazing how quickly, after completing his work and becoming a licensed tradesman, the number of job offers began to come his way. One of these offers involved working with a contractor who was building a very high-end condominium complex in Aspen. Through all these months, Jerry and I were saving our money while living in a comfortable trailer a few miles outside of Aspen's city limits.

Jerry was busy working, but I on the other hand was searching for productive ways to occupy my free time. I answered several employment notices in the Aspen newspaper and eventually settled on a job as a domestic with a family consisting of an elderly couple—the Taylors'. Basically, my job description was to care for Mrs. Taylor who was suffering from debilitating Parkinson's disease and was not in the best health. Taking Mrs. Taylor on trips to the hospital and to her other doctor appointments was a usual, run-of-the-mill scenario for me.

I enjoyed my job and was employed by the Taylors' for over a year when unexpectedly Mr. Taylor died in his sleep from a massive heart attack. I'd expected Mrs. Taylor, who was very feeble, to be the first to pass, but very surprised when she didn't.

Mr. Taylor was buried in The Aspen Grove cemetery, the oldest cemetery in Aspen. Her husband's passing was obviously very difficult for Mrs. Taylor. She missed her husband very much and

I could see how this was affecting her eating habits. It really took a lot of encouragement from me to have her eat more than a few mouthfuls at each meal.

An unvarying task Mrs. Taylor would request from me was to drive her, sometimes three times a week, to her husband's grave. She would place a fresh bouquet of flowers at the graveside and meditate in prayer for several minutes before we would finally leave. These short trips would bring her a few moments of relief, and I was happy to be of service. However, strangely, something unusual happened during one of these days that we visited the cemetery.

As we were walking along the footpath to Mr. Taylor's graveside, I noticed that nearby, someone had attached a wind chime high up in one of the branches of an aspen tree. Mrs. Taylor remarked, "What a lovely tribute. I think my husband would enjoy one of those wind chimes as well."

The following week, I drove Mrs. Taylor to a local garden supply store where she picked out a very nice sounding wind chime. My husband Jerry came along with us as we drove to the cemetery. With his help, we used a long pole to hook the new wind chime up on one of the highest branches of a tree. Although Mr. Taylor's grave was several feet away from where the chimes were suspended, Mrs. Taylor stated, "My husband will know that when those chimes make music, they'll be chiming just for him."

In the winter of that year, Mrs. Taylor's eldest daughter, Kate, came to visit her mother for the Christmas holiday. Kate thought it would be a good idea to take her mother to see a Christmas program being presented at a Presbyterian church in the town of Glenwood Springs. The roads were clear and plowed of any snow from the previous day's snowfall. While Kate and her mother were traveling to Glenwood Springs, Jerry and I were on the road traveling to Denver for a few days visit with two friends. Strangely, during the drive to Denver, I felt a strong urge to call Mrs. Taylor. I don't know what possessed me, but I couldn't shake the feeling to stop the car and get to a phone. Anyway, it wouldn't have done any good because I only had Mrs. Taylor's home phone and both she and her daughter were out of town attending the church function.

It wasn't until, after attempting to phone Mrs. Taylor without success, and after arriving in Aspen three days later that I found out that both Mrs. Taylor and her daughter never made it to Glenwood Springs. Tragically, the car Kate was driving that evening skidded on a patch of black ice, rolled over and landed, sandwiched between two large trees. Mrs. Taylor was badly injured, but her daughter died at the scene. Mrs. Taylor died five days later from internal bleeding. I was devastated!

During her hospital stay, Mrs. Taylor was never told about her daughter Kate's death. Although she was able to take liquids, before Mrs. Taylor died, she asked me to make her a bowl of soup. I told her that I would have a bowl of her favorite tomato soup for her when she returned to her home. But what was strange about her request, which she insisted, was that I have another bowl ready for her daughter. Mrs. Taylor firmly stated that her daughter Kate was present in the room with us, asking for something to eat. I was puzzled by Mrs. Taylor's request and by the fact that she kept stating over and over that her daughter had been visiting her constantly. As I said, no one ever mentioned to Mrs. Taylor that her daughter had passed away. I agreed to honor Mrs. Taylor's request but left the hospital perplexed.

Well, when Mrs. Taylor passed away, I was very upset. I was unable to attend the two memorial funerals, for both Mrs. Taylor and her daughter, which were held in Seattle, Washington. Both mother and daughter's remains were cremated in Aspen then sent to Seattle. I was very surprised at this. Mrs. Taylor never mentioned to me that that was her wish, but her family felt it was best to do this. I did not feel it was my place to interfere, or to cause any further emotional distress for the family, so I just accepted this as being best. But I could not help but imagine what Mrs. Taylor would have done differently, especially since her husband's body would remain in Colorado. I believe she would have wanted to be buried next to her husband. It just made sense to me, but the family obviously had the last say in this matter.

Just a few days after Mrs. Taylor's family bid me their last face-to-face goodbye, I was overcome by a strong feeling to visit Mr. Taylor's grave.

Perhaps it was a personal need to just offer my last goodbye. As I parked my car and began to walk through the snow-covered grounds, I glanced up and noticed that the wind chime had fallen from the tree branch where, for so many months before, it had hanged undisturbed. Now it was lying in a heap on the ground. It was so cold that I just left the chimes right where they lay, thinking I would ask Jerry to re-hang them when the weather was better. Just a couple of weeks later something very strange and unusual took place that would cause us all to wonder if the spirits of the Taylors' were  somehow offering me a message from beyond the grave.

Jerry had planned a surprise birthday party for me, and one of my sisters from California was planning to attend. Keep in mind that most everyone at the party was unaware of any of the details regarding the Taylors and my attachment to them.

My party went without a hitch, and I was totally caught by surprise. As the evening progressed, the moment came to open all my presents. I chose to first open my sister's present. When I opened her gift, I was so surprised and indeed shocked to discover that she had given me a wind chime! Even more shocking was the gift I was given from another friend. I opened her present next. She also, was unaware of the wind chime, and knew nothing of my experience at Mr. Taylor's graveside.

My husband Jerry was totally in awe when I opened her gift—it was another wind chime! When I opened another smaller box from an elderly couple who lived in the condominium complex next to ours, and who, I found out later, Jerry had invited on short notice, I discovered their gift was also a wind chime, only smaller and made of glass! I received a total of three wind chimes. This was all too much; I broke down and cried right in front of everyone.

When I regained my composure, I explained to all my friends why I

had reacted so emotionally. Jerry was surprised and very moved by the "coincidence" of these gifts. My sister explained that for some unknown reason she had had it in her head one day that I needed a wind chime. She explained to everyone that this urge was very strong, like a voice urging her to locate a wind chime for me. She decided to drive to several stores before she finally purchased the one she finally picked out for me. My friend added that his reason for also purchasing a wind chime for me was due to a very vivid dream he had had about seeing one chiming in the wind, high above in a tree.

Obviously, this caused the people that were gathered at the party to ask me personal questions regarding the paranormal, and how we might decipher whatever meaning was being presented to me, given the strange coincidence that had transpired before us all. We all had somewhat different answers, but shared the same conclusion, the Taylors were still with me, and wanted to send me a sign from beyond the grave.

After my birthday party ended and everyone had gone home, Jerry, my sister and I talked for a few more hours before going to bed about the unusually strange gifts I had received. To my own estimation, I believe that on some level Mrs. Taylor had something to do with this. The chance of three people giving me a similar gift was just too weird to disregard. I'll always remember my 31st birthday and the gifts that I know Mrs. Taylor helped personally pick for me.

When the spring weather finally arrived in Aspen, my husband and I drove to the cemetery. We hung the three wind chimes my sister and my two friends had given me as gifts up on the branches of the two aspen trees. Since then, I've only gone back once and noticed that others unbeknown to me, who have visited the graveyard, have also taken up the loving gesture of suspending wind chimes among the trees in the cemetery. It's a beautiful example of saying, "We love you, miss you, and present you with the gift of music to lull you to eternal sleep."

BLACK CANYON, CO

OLIVIA SAGEHORN'S STORY

Mrs. Sagehorn, who is 91 years old, and I discussed several things before her interview. She was very candid and direct about the experiences with spirits that both she and her family had had. On a personal level, what impressed me more was her insight into how society, so many years ago, dealt with the issue of a person's sexual orientation during Colorado's frontier era.

Clearly, not all communities handled such an issue in the same manner as Olivia's, but I believe that there were many who tolerated, if not embraced, gay and lesbians of past generations. There is direct anthropological documentation that proves not only Native Americans, but also many other pre-industrial peoples throughout the world held gay individuals in high regard and with cherished respect.

Olivia Sagehorn was a delight to speak with. I conducted the interview with her at a convalescent hospital in Grand Junction, within the facility's garden courtyard. Her detailed memory was always on point.

— Antonio

"I must tell you first of all, that I am one of a set of twin girls. My brother, Harold died after contracting polio in the late 1940's. The disease quickly traveled from his legs, to his lungs and spine. Immediately our family was quarantined by the government, and thankfully we were spared any more illness.

We buried my brother on a hillside just north of Gunnison, in the town of Almont. The twenty acres of land where he lies buried, belonged to my family. My great-grandfather, Walter McClain, along with his brother, William, homesteaded the land in 1877. Great-grandfather Walter married my great-grandmother Ophelia, who was from Orchard City, and

Olivia Sagehorn is seated while her sister Rosella stands beside her.

together had two boys and one daughter. My grandmother, Catherine, was their only girl.

In 1913, mother married and two years after gave birth to my eldest brother, Harold. Years later, mother gave birth to me and my twin sister, Rosella. So now that you have an idea of my family history, I'll get on with my story.

My older brother never married, but he did live with a man for most of his short life. His life partner's name was Clayton. Both of them lived in Orchard City for a few years, they moved to Grand Junction until Harold got sick. Clayton moved in with us and he cared for my brother in a room Father had converted from a goat house into a bedroom. During Harold's convalescence, Clayton also contracted polio, but he managed to survive the illness.

Homosexuality was not looked upon as negatively then, as it can be today. People knew about it, and just accepted two women or two men living together. Back then we had other more important things to concern ourselves with like making a living from the land. It was unusual to see two men living together as a couple, but I knew that there were other couples like my brother and Clayton who owned property in the area, because Clayton would tell us about them.

Our family lived acres away from most of our neighbors, separated by hills, and even mountains, so we didn't get to have much contact with each other. Our time was spent doing the usual chores that come with trying to make a living from the land. Most of us didn't have the time to spend gossiping about other families.

I remember, before Harold got the polio, when he and Clayton visited Denver for a few months. Clayton was an architect by trade, and helped design the Denver Club building in downtown Denver. With the money from this project they purchased a home in Grand Junction. After my brother's death, Clayton returned to Grand Junction and eventually sold their house, then moved to Denver.

During the time when my brother was ill in bed, I remember him telling us about the different people who he had seen standing by his bed. These people, he told us, were relatives of ours, who had passed away years before. He would point out to us where in the room they were standing, what they were wearing and some-times, what they would be saying. My mother and father knew, but didn't tell my sister and me until after my brother's death, that seeing the dead was a sign that he himself was not going to survive for much longer.

During his funeral, and after his burial, Clayton was very sad. Right before Clayton moved away, he gave my mother all of my brother's belongings and presented my father with Harold's rifle and belt buckle. A year after Clayton moved away to Denver, we received a few letters from Clayton, but eventually the letters stopped coming. I don't know what ever happened to him.

One day, while Rosella and I were outside washing clothes, Rosella came up to me and said, "Olivia, I heard Harold calling me last night." I answered, "What do you mean?" Then she told me that she had been see-ing our brother's spirit walking about the bedroom, and once even saw him staring at the front door. She was too upset to tell anyone, but she decided to confide in me because she felt it was time to do so.

I was caught by surprise by my sister's statements and I told her that I believed what she was saying, but I didn't think it was necessary for her to keep it to her-self. She needed to tell our parents about this. That evening, while the two of us with our parents were seated at the din-ner table, Rosella broke down and de-scribed to us what she had seen.

My father took this news the hardest.

Harold is seated while his partner Clayton stands beside.

He wept a little and then told us that he believed my sister, because he had also seen my brother's spirit standing a short distance away from where he was working, building a wall behind the house. Something caused my father to look in the direction of the yard, and there he spotted his son's spirit, standing and looking straight at my father.

"Harold didn't say anything, he just stood in place," father told us. Father asked him, "Son, is that you, is it you son?" Then, my brother's image slowly faded away. The only ones in our family who didn't get a visit from my brother were my mother and me. That would change a few years later, when I was in my twenties and was about to give birth to my only child, a daughter.

It was a difficult birth, and as soon as my daughter was born, I passed out from all the loss of blood and stress. It took me a long time to recover, but after I did, a few days later I landed back in bed with a terrible series of headaches. These headaches were the worst you could ever imagine. Day after day I'd suffer with migraines. They were terrible.

During one of these headaches, I was in so much pain that I remember crying out, "Lord, I can't take this any longer, take me with you!" After having said this, I remember laying on my right side in bed, staring with tear-filled eyes, at my infant daughter. Just then, I sensed a presence, hearing the footsteps of someone walking in the room. I turned my eyes to look at the door and I saw my brother slowly walking towards me! I was overcome, not with fear, but with joy. Even though I was unable to move, even a finger, I knew my brother was in the room with me.

As soon as he reached my bed, he held out his hand and placed it on my forehead. At first I felt coldness, then immediate warmth spread from my head to my shoulders. I closed my eyes and whispered, "Thank you Harold, my dear brother, thank you!" The terrible headache pain disappeared. I remember falling asleep and waking up when my husband came into the room and sat on the bed and called my name. Since that day, I haven't had another headache episode. I really haven't, the headaches have never returned.

As my daughter grew, I remember, at the age of six or seven that she once began talking and playing with an imaginary play-mate she named,

"Uncle man." Because she was so young and precocious I didn't think much of this, and I didn't question her regarding her playmate, until she reached her teen years, when she brought up the subject of her imaginary playmate once again.

She mentioned to me if I remembered the playmate she had had when she was younger, and I answered, "Yes, I do remember you telling me once or twice about him." She answered, "Well, Mother he told me he was your brother and that he was always going to be your brother." I answered, "Do you mean to say that you were talking with your Uncle Harold?" "Yes, yes Mother, that's who he was. It was Uncle Harold."

My immediate response was to not believe my daughter, but she was now old enough to know right from wrong, and she was very serious about this. I looked her straight in her eyes and asked, "You are not lying to me you actually were talking with my brother?" "Yes, yes I was, but somehow I knew, even as a little girl that I would have gotten into trouble if I were to keep bringing him up time after time. Anyway, he didn't visit me very often, just maybe two or three times total."

That conversation with my daughter took place many years ago, and in 1976, my daughter died of breast cancer. She was my only child. Before her death, during my prayers, I asked my brother's spirit to come and take my daughter, his niece's soul, with him to Heaven. My daughter died a peaceful death, and I would tell you more about this, but what happened was very personal and beautiful. I'll keep the rest between my daughter and me. My husband died eight years later in 1984.

Because of all the examples of love and the connection that I've seen in my life with my parents, my family and on a personal level, I have no doubt that the spirits of our family members will continue to help us when we need them the most. I'm aware that my time will not last too much more than a few more years, it might end earlier than that. I have a peace that has carried me throughout many years of hardship and even a few tragedies. My brother has made it known to me that life goes on after death. This is something wonderful to know. I know I have been blessed."

CAÑON CITY, CO

PAOLO PASCHAL'S STORY

I met with Paolo at the local senior center. Our interview lasted approximately two hours, but in this time, I was given a personal story of fear and faith. Paolo was very descriptive when mentioning periods of time in his life, and although these were helpful towards understanding who Paolo the man is today, I was most interested in his personal story of ghosts. Paolo was very aware of this, but as he stated, "I want you to know about my story growing up as a boy too!"

Having told his boyhood story, he began to describe his personal experiences with the paranormal. Our interview continued as I personally drove him to his house, along the way stopping at a grocery store where he had me pick up a phoned-in prescription order. Although I knew Paolo was using me as his personal taxi, to do a few "other" unrelated tasks, I felt very confident knowing this elderly man's story would be well worth my time. And worth my time it definitely was.

— Antonio

"My parents, along with my two uncles on my mother's side, moved to Cañon City in 1933. I was born three years later. My sister and I were the only children in my family—all Italian immigrants. When I was 10 years old, one of my uncles, Paolo who I was named after, died in a work accident when the large landscaping boulders that had been loaded upon a parked company truck gave way. Unfortunately, my uncle Paolo was crushed by one of the rocks, as it rolled across his chest. Although his fellow workers quickly assisted him, I was told he died within a few minutes after.

As much as I can remember of our relationship, my uncle never displayed much affection, or sentiment on any level, toward me. Although he never mistreated me, I regarded him as simply a distant person in our household. So, at the time of his death, when others around me were emotionally distraught, I personally was saddened, but did not display much grief for him.

I remember years earlier, my mother's words to me regarding her and her brother's relationship. Theirs was also a strangely

Uncle Paolo's funeral, 1946.

distant one, unlike the typical Italian family relationship where hugging and kissing played a major role—quite the opposite. There was even a time when he actually slapped her in the presence of a boyfriend she was dating. Apparently, he did not approve of their relationship. And he very obviously made it clear to both her and her boyfriend that the relationship was to end. My mother never forgot, or overcame, the embarrassment she felt that day. Times were different years ago as families were structured more clearly, and ideas of what was morally correct ruled with an iron fist. A lot different than how we behave in today's society.

Well, the day of my uncle's funeral arrived, and my uncle was laid to rest in Cañon City on March 31, 1943. Before being buried, a relative took a picture of him at the funeral home as he lay in his casket. I still have it, and can show it to you if you'd like to see it. Although I was only 10 years old, I have a very vivid memory of that day, and most of my years as a young child.

About five to seven days after he was buried, I began to have visions of my uncle walking about the house. At different times of the day, for no apparent reason, I'd begin to "feel" his presence in a room. About a week after he was buried, I spotted his figure sitting at the kitchen table! I just happened to walk into the kitchen and saw him seated at the table while no one else was in the room. His image lasted only for a few seconds, but I did see him. He just sat at the table looking straight ahead, then "poof" he was gone! I chose to keep this experience to myself. I didn't know how others in my family would react, and I didn't want to chance being verbally mistreated for having such a crazy imagination. So, I just kept quiet.

There was another incident where I witnessed seeing my uncle's ghost. It was just the following day after my first sighting. The day was a sunny one, about 2 or 3 p.m. in the afternoon. I was playing with my dog, and as I came running around to the front of the house, from the backyard, a movement caught my eye, and I glanced at the front porch. Seated on one of the chairs, this time staring directly at me was my uncle! I immediately stopped and froze in place. Not unlike before, his image lasted only but a few seconds, then disappeared! It was as if time stood still for me. I recall not even hearing the sounds of birds, traffic noise, or even the movement of the leaves of the trees moving in the breeze. Everything was deadly silent.

This time, being so startled by what I had seen, I ran around to the backyard and informed my mother. She stopped hanging clothes on the line and turned to face me. "What are you saying, you saw your uncle sitting on the porch?" I responded, "Yes, yes he was also sitting at the kitchen table yesterday!" Strangely, my mother's reaction was to take me into her arms, hold me tight, and weep. I thought this was strange because I assumed she would scold me, or take a belt to me for making up such a story, but instead she reacted with grief. I was so surprised by this that I too began to cry. I chose not to reveal any more to my mother about her brother's spiritual visits. I had mixed emotions and due to my young age, was in no position to mentally process what was going on. I began to feel a real fear that I had never felt before.

Later that night, I was awakened from my sleep by a loud sound in my bedroom. I opened my eyes and knew that my window was closed, but the curtains were moving as if from a light breeze. I focused my sight on the movement of the curtains, when I heard the sound of footsteps walking about the small room. I was so scared that I closed my eyes, threw the blanket over my head and somehow, eventually fell back to sleep. This same pattern continued for another two nights until the third night when a very scary incident took place.

Again, I was awakened as before from a sound sleep, only this time when I heard the noise, I felt an overpowering sense that something was in the room with me, something large and not very friendly. I tightly shut my eyes and before I could cover my head with my blanket, I felt the pressure of an unseen hand grasp my shoulder. It was a strong force that could only be that of a male hand that shook my shoulder. I was so scared that I couldn't yell or make a noise. I was frozen with fear! All I could do was to lay still in my bed hoping that whatever was grasping my shoulder would let me go. Suddenly, I felt a very cold hand take hold of my lower jaw and slowly begin to open it. I was ready to pass out from fear.

Somehow, I found the courage to open my eyes. I was very hesitant to do this, but when I did, I saw a male ghost, strangely not my uncle, standing next to my bed! I didn't recognize who it could be, but I'll never forget how deep and dark his eyes were. At first it was only a large silhouette against the darkness of my room, but that quickly changed. A recognizable form of a large man began to take shape, and I'll never forget his eyes. He was staring, fixated on me with those eyes, and before I could think of what to do next, he raised his left arm and slowly his hand came over my face, grasped my jaw, and opened my mouth. Then his index finger reached inside and came to rest on the top of my tongue. The finger was ice cold! I was overwhelmed by the sense that I was powerless to do anything to help myself get away from him. I could not move or speak. He opened my mouth wide. Once inside, I felt his fingernail make short little poking movements in my mouth, something like a dentist would do when exploring for cavities with a metal pick.

Suddenly, I saw another person in the room with us. I looked towards the window and spotted my uncle's spirit standing, and looking directly at me. His image was transparent, but without a doubt it was my uncle Paolo! I somehow gathered the strength to break away from the awful ghost's grasp. I rolled out of bed, fell onto the floor and yelled out to my mother. Immediately the ghost retreated into the darkness. Then I scrambled to the door and into my parents' bedroom. I attempted to explain to my parents every detail of what had happened but they would have none of it. I spent the remainder of the night sleeping in their bed with my head on my mother's lap.

Thereafter, because of the trauma and panic that was very evident on my face, even my father relented and moved my small bed into my parent's bedroom, where I spent several more nights. About a week after that, my cousin's family allowed me to stay with them for about another two weeks, until I was emotionally able to return to my own house and bedroom.

During my absence, my parents contacted a local Benedictine priest at the Holy Cross Abbey to perform a blessing and cleansing ceremony at my home. A special, personal blessing was also performed by that same priest over me. Within Catholicism the Benedictine Order is one of the oldest Catholic orders that was founded in the sixth century by St. Benedict. I've learned since then that the church employs St. Benedict's prayers and other protocols in its rituals of exorcism. Looking back, I was very fortunate to have been living within such close proximity of the abbey and its priests.

After having the blessings performed and returning home, I was not furthered bothered by ghosts. But many years after that experience the questions stayed with me as to why my uncle had appeared only to me, and who was the bothersome and terrifying ghost that had taken hold of my face, and most importantly, why didn't my uncle's spirit intervene when the evil presence came very close to actually causing me harm?

I have not been unable to fully understand why I was singled out for this physically dramatic and mental distress. I was only 10 years old. What or who could cause a young boy such emotional injury? Well, that incident took place many years ago. Today, I'm fortunate to be able to sit here and tell you my story. I hope there is someone who might read this and will recognize something in it that might help them."

HOLY CROSS ABBEY

The following text was reproduced here from the former Abbey's visitor brochure:

"Welcome to Holy Cross Abbey. The Monks (Priests and Brothers) wish to welcome you to the Holy Cross Abbey. As this is our home, we have living areas for the monks that are cloistered (private) and not available for public viewing. These areas include the second floor and above and many rooms on the first floor, some of which are offices. The simple Latin word PAX (Peace) is the Benedictine motto. The fundamental purpose of Benedictine monastic life is to seek God, "ut in omnibus glorificetur Deus": "That in all things God may be glorified."

We are of the ORDER OF ST. BENEDICT (O.S.B.), also known as Benedictines. The areas that are open for viewing include our chapel, parlor, gift shop and museum.

You will find us in Chapel six times a day for either mass or prayer. The public is always welcome to join us at these times. In the chapel, please do not enter the altar area. Silence is observed within the monastery at all times.

In the Chapel, you will notice the large wood crucifix that is suspended from the ceiling, it was carved in Oberammergau, Germany and given as a gift to the abbey in 1961.

Another statue, Our Lady of Montserrat, is mounted on the balcony just over the main entrance to the chapel. On the columns of the chapel stand the statues of the 12 Apostles. The stained-glass window was donated by the Simon P. Smith family. The Blessed Sacrament altar and the main altar are the work of monks of this Abbey.

The South Parlor of the Abbey has genuine, Victorian furniture that came to the Abbey following the closing of the Strathmore Hotel in Cañon City. The parlor is also used for wake services upon the death of a monk here at the Abbey.

The first Benedictine Priests came from St. Vincent's Archabbey in Latrobe, Pennsylvania, to Colorado in 1886, and settled in Breckenridge for two years. They moved to Boulder, then to Pueblo, and finally established themselves in Cañon City in 1924.

In 1925, the community of monks be-

came an abbey. The Abbey also developed a winery on the east end of the property.

Abbey — A monastery or convent governed by an Abbot or Abbess; also, the community of monks or nuns numbering at least twelve in a canonically erected monastery or convent. Generally, abbey refers to the entire group of buildings, but sometimes only to the church building.

Monastery — The place of residence of a group of monks; the building wherein monks live and carry on their religious life.

Monk — A name given to a member of a community of men living apart from the world under the vows of poverty, chastity, and obedience and according to some rule of religious order. In particular, it became associated with those following the Benedictine Rule.

Priest — One upon whom the sacrament of Holy Orders has been conferred and who is thereby a minster of divine worship; one upon whom the power of offering sacrifice, of blessing, of giving absolution, and of preaching has been conferred. The power to consecrate, thus to offer the Sacrifice of the Mass; the priesthood has the power to administer sacraments, forgive sins, and to bless.

Brothers — Members of a male religious community who have not taken priestly Holy Orders or who do not aspire to Holy Orders, but live a religious community life and devote themselves to various works of a religious nature.

As of this printing, the Abbey officials closed and sold the property due to the overwhelming costs of its up-keep and lack of new initiates to the Benedictine Order.

CARBONDALE, CO

FRANK CARTER'S STORY

When I entered Frank's home to conduct the following interview, he was exercising on his treadmill. His wife, Anita, provided me with a chair and from it, I asked my questions, as he continued exercising. Twice he stopped his walking to make clear to me how much he was emotionally affected by his ghost encounter. Eventually he found it difficult to continue exercising while recounting such a disturbing and personal experience. He turned off the machine, and pulled up a chair next to mine. What follows is Frank's very brave account of what occurred at his place of work, five years ago.

— Antonio

"I was raised in Albany, Georgia, by my father's sister, Jimette. My mother and father divorced when I was only 10 months old. After I graduated from high school, I attended a trade school in Georgia, and soon after I graduated, I joined the navy. After leaving the navy, I returned home in October of 1979, where I met my future wife, Anita, and we married. Roughly within two years, we moved to Colorado, where after completing the company's own training program, I was hired as a licensed Toyota mechanic. I was working at a Toyota dealership in Denver for four years, until my wife and I moved to Carbondale in 1992.

My ghost story took place close to five years ago, at the auto shop in Carbondale. I have never before had that type of experience like the one I had at the garage. The subject of ghosts never interested me and whenever I heard people talking about such things, I would think to myself that they were crazy. I was one of those who thought witchcraft, demons, and ghosts were all the same thing-nothing more than imaginary dreams. However, after having my own experience with a ghost, I've become an absolute true believer.

Before getting the job, and even after almost a year had past, no one ever mentioned to me about a guy that shot his brains out at the shop. When I eventually did find out that my co-workers knew about the suicide, I was a bit bothered, and I thought that it was unfair of them to have kept this tragic information to themselves. It didn't help that most of the guys didn't speak much English either. But they were cool. I had to find out about this guy the hard way, by encountering his ghost for myself!

The first time I began to suspect that there was something strange going on was when I was working in the back of the garage one morning, where we have a large metal barrel of solvent. I was cleaning off the oil from a few metal engine parts. I wasn't thinking about anything except getting these parts ready to replace into a car I was working on. My hands were covered with solvent and oil, when suddenly I heard the footsteps of someone walking on the gravel behind me. I thought it was a fellow worker, so without turning around I said, "Hey, can you hand me that rag that's hanging on the bar by the chair?"

Then I heard the sound of someone laughing. I turned around and saw no one. This kind of freaked me out at first, but I thought it must have been the radio that was playing in the garage. So, I didn't think any more about it. But with regularity, stranger things were beginning to take place. I was a new employee so I didn't want to give my boss the impression that I was already becoming a problem new hire. I kept these things to myself.

As I was walking back from selecting a part from our inventory, I noticed a very, and I mean a very, cold area, or spot in one of the aisles where the parts were stored. I remember that I even got goosebumps running up and down my arms. It was as if I had stepped inside a freezer. It was that cold.

I left the aisle and walked over to the front desk and asked the receptionists about the cold spot. She responded by saying, "Oh, yeah, I know what you're talking about, that area is always cold, but the coldness moves around the room. It could be a ghost. I think it's a ghost but can't mention it to the supervisor because he's a 'born-again' Christian. I asked him about it once and he told me I had to pray, etc. He said it all has to do with not believing in God and letting demons take control of my life. Then he started with passages from the Bible, boy was that a mistake." I then told the receptionist that I'd do as she advised. She responded, "But I know what you're saying, I feel the presence of someone's eyes following me all around the place. I know it's not evil, I think it's just a common, run-of-the-mill ghost.

As long as he or she lets me do my job I'm fine with it staying in the storage room, and not following me home." Thinking back to that time, I thought it was all interesting, but really just a bunch of crazy talk.

I began to notice that the cold spots were not only in the parts department, but also in the garage itself, and once in the back yard, where the cars needing repair were stored. It was strange to actually walk through a cold spot. In the back yard, there is just the outdoors, without a covering. So even on a bright and sunny day, when I'd walk through one of these cold spots, it would be a little bit of a shock.

The first real incident that got me thinking and even scared took place in the parts department's storage room. I remember I was searching for a gasket for a 1990 Four-Runner. As I was squatting down and reaching for a box on the lowest shelf, I distinctly heard a man's loud voice say, "I told you I'd get it for you!" I said, "What?" I quickly stood right up because I knew I was alone in the room. I turned around and looked between the aisles and spotted no one. I knew I was not imagining this, I actually heard a guy speak these forceful words to me.

The second time I experienced something that I can say was a ghost was when I was once again in the back yard. It was during the middle of the day. I had just finished cleaning off a timing chain and had draped it over a drip pan to dry. I noticed that someone, a man about in his early 50s, was standing 10 or 15 feet away from me against the cement wall of the building. Our eyes met and he just stood there glaring at me.

Since I didn't recognize him, I spoke, "Hey, you need something?" He took a puff of his cigarette, turned his head away from me and fell backward, disappearing right into the wall!

I dropped my towel and shot out of there, back inside the garage—I was so scared, I almost shit myself! I went up to the bathroom and splashed water on my face and when I came out, I approached a co-worker named Fernando, to tell him about what I had just seen. I couldn't keep this to myself, for my own sanity I had to share this with someone.

Fernando looked at me and I'm sure he could see that I was not joking and as serious as a heart attack. After I told him what I had seen he asked me to describe the ghost. I told him that his clothes were dirty and he was a small guy. His hair was combed back and greasy. He was smoking a cigarette and his eyes were totally black. I couldn't even tell if there was any white coloring around his pupils. They were totally dark and black. He just stood there staring at me, then turned away and disappeared.

Fernando said, "Hey Frank, don't worry, you've just been visited by Arnold. Sometimes he comes around the shop and visits us. Arnold's not going to do you any harm. I've never seen him, but a few of the office workers and some of the mechanics have mentioned seeing him. I've only smelled his cigarette around the shop, but I've never seen him. He must really like you if he actually appeared to you."

I was not comforted by his words in fact I was even more fearful to be standing in the shop knowing this was a ghost that others had seen. I asked, "So Fernando, who is this guy Arnold?" He said, "Arnold was a mechanic who worked here the year before I started working here, about eight years ago. I wasn't his friend; he was a quiet guy and for the most part always kept to himself. He was from Mexico and got involved with an Anglo woman in town who he was going to marry. He found out she was messing around with one of the guys who worked at the Baptist Church. It was a typical story of a woman seeing another guy on the side. Arnold took it pretty bad because one morning he was found dead from a self-inflicted shot to the head, he had committed suicide. He shot himself out back, sitting on a chair right against the wall where you actually saw his ghost. Scary stuff, huh?"

I was speechless. I decided I had seen enough of ghosts, and I spent the rest of the day thinking about what had happened and decided not to speak about this anymore. I asked Fernando if he could keep this information to himself. He said he would. And that was the last we ever spoke about Arnold, the ghost at the garage.

After the Christmas holidays, my wife and I decided to open a mountain bicycle repair shop so I quit my job at the garage. I haven't had any further ghost sightings and I'm glad for that. Just thinking right now about that experience causes the palms of my hands to sweat. You bet I believe in ghosts. I believe in ghosts after seeing Arnold's ghost at the garage. Oh, for sure, I believe cause I've seen it with my own eyes!"

GRAND RAPID, MI

SEBASTIAN LOFTENBERGER'S STORY

My ghost experience happened when I was 11 years old. My father moved our family to Grand Rapids, Michigan in the spring of 1963 from Glendale, California. Dad was offered an executive position with Crown Paper Industries and soon after my mother landed employment with the Grand Rapids school district as a French language teacher. Making the move were both my parents, my grandmother Mary Loftenberger, my baby brother Anthony and me. We settled into a house on Fuller Street and soon after our arrival I was enrolled into the nearby elementary school.

One Saturday morning my father asked me if I wanted to accompany him on a drive to run some quick errands before breakfast. I jumped onto the front seat of the car and off we went.

In route to our first stop, we drove through a nearby neighborhood and my father pointed out a hand painted tools for sale sign posted on one house's front lawn. Dad wasted no time in parking the car and we approached the owner to investigate.

A bald man that introduced himself as Eddie walked us into his garage where an array of hand tools was displayed. Eddie encouraged my father to have a look and to ask any questions he might have. As it turned out, Eddie happened to have worked at the same school district as my mother, but had retired for health reasons. Eddie was also now a deacon at the local Catholic church my family attended.

As my dad was engaged in conversation with Eddie, being ever the curious child, I wondered off to the back yard. It was there that I spotted a young boy staring directly at me from behind one of the windows. As our eyes met he waved his hand at me in a friendly greeting gesture. I remember smiling and returning a wave as well and just as I was about to take a few steps toward the boy, I heard my father call for me and I hurried back to where the two men were standing and exchanging money.

While standing back near the garage opening my eyes caught sight of a light blue bicycle the was leaning against a stack of plywood paneling. I walked over to the bike and with an excited voice asked, "Sir, is this bike for sale?" Eddie answered with a little hesitancy in his voice, "Well I wasn't planning on selling it, but since I can see that you like it so much, sure I'll let you have it for $5.00." Surprisingly my father quickly handed Eddie a five-dollar bill and quickly loaded the bike in our car's trunk, then we were off again to buy the signs.

On our drive, I mentioned the boy I saw in Eddie's window to my father. Dan asked me, "Did you ask him his name and does he go to the same school you do?" "I don't know, we didn't talk." I answered. That was the extent of our discussion.

In the weeks that followed my dad took the bicycle to a bike shop to purchase a replacement for a severely bent rear wheel and to take care of a few other needed updates. The day finally came when I had my bike at home, ready for me to ride. Of course, I had to learn how to ride it first, but after numerous falls I mastered the technique. Now, after Thanksgiving Day is when things with this bike begin to get strangely odd.

It was around 4 pm when I was riding my bike up and down my street's sidewalk. As I rode past a house that had a medium size, white dog, the dog began to bark then it ran after me. I had no other choice but to ride into the street and pedal as fast as I could to avoid getting bit.

I didn't see it coming at first, but I just happened to enter the street right in front of an oncoming car! The only thing I remember from that moment is the sound of the car's brakes and the impact. The next thing I remember is waking up in a hospital bed with a young boy sitting next to my bedside. It was the same boy I had seen a few months before at Eddie's house!

He smiled at me and spoke, "My name is Michael. The dog almost got you, but I got him first. You'll be alright. I got to go now, bye." I didn't speak a word, I just watched as he slowly faded away right in front of me into nothingness. Surprisingly I was not scared.

Then as if on que, a nurse entered the room, walked over to me, noticed I was awake and asked, "Who was in here with you? I just moved this chair by the door not more than three minutes ago, how did you get out of your bed? "Adam was here, he was sitting in the chair," I answered. "Well, I don't know who Michael is, but he couldn't have gotten past me since I was standing right outside your door. Something is very fishy here." she answered. The nurse then went about the room as if searching for someone hiding behind the drapery or in the closet, obviously, she discovered no one.

In the days that followed I was released from the hospital and aside from a broken collar bone, I was back to my normal self. But what we all found strange and oddly coincidental was that my bicycle received the same similar damage to both its frame and rear tire rim as it had when my father initially bought it. I also mentioned to my family about the little boy's visit but they regarded my story as having something to do with my accident, all with the exception of my grandmother that is.

My grandmother who was born and raised in a small village in France, she found this occurrence to be very troubling and stated to my parents in her native tongue, "Cela me semble être quelque chose de spirituel et pas une coïncidence." "This seems to me to be something spiritual and not a coincidence." She further asked my father to enquire from Eddie the bicycle's history, "J'ai le sentiment, quelque chose me dit qu'il n'y a où bien trouver la réponse à tout cela." "I have a feeling; something is telling me that this is where we'll find the answer to all this."

After lunch my father and I drove over to Eddie's house where we found him in his front yard doing some weeding. My dad wasted no time in recounting to Eddie all that had taken place with the bike, from the repairs to my accident. Throughout my father's account Eddie listened intensively and only spoke when it came my turn to describe the same boy I had seen by my hospital bedside and at Eddie's back window.

"So you saw my boy Michael, did you? You know it's been a long time since I last saw him. I'm sure happy to know he's still around and especially that he's looking after you. I miss him so much," Eddie said.

Eddie informed my father that Michael was the eldest of three sons, the other two boys had died together along with their mother in a traffic accident. But Michael was involved in an accident of his own just five days prior when a car hit him as he was crossing the street on the same bike you bought from me. Michael should have survived but passed from internal head injuries several days later. The damage to the rear tire was where the car struck the bike. "I've kept the bike in the garage ever since, that is until you came along. Somehow I 'felt' the bike belonged to you," Eddie said.

Well this new information gave us all something to think about. Information that has formed my thoughts and has influenced my spiritual life in a positive way. I never again received a visit from Michael, but I'm okay with that. I know that when my own time to depart this life happens, there will be loved ones waiting and welcoming me, easing my transition. I feel special knowing I had a little angel, Michael, looking out for me back then.

LEADVILLE, CO

THE CENTER/PITTS ELEMENTARY SCHOOL – RHIANNON BOYER'S STORY

I interviewed Rhiannon at her place of work—The Leadville Chronicle's office. As she described her experiences, a fellow employee was intently listening nearby to every word. Although he never did add any additional information, I could see he was very interested. Rhiannon was my first interview in Leadville, and after doing a bit more research, I discovered a few more individuals who could be interviewed. Therefore, I decided it would be best to spend the night in this historic town. As it was, this would prove to be a good move, because of the subsequent stories I would be able to include.

— Antonio

"Currently I am employed as the classified ad consultant, receptionist, and secretary for the town's local newspaper—The Leadville Chronicle. When I was a young child, my family moved from Greenriver, Wyoming, to Leadville in 1985. Both my parents operated a small gift shop in town, and as of this year, have been in business for 25 years.

My experience with a ghost in Leadville took place at what is now the Pitts Elementary school. Its full name is The Center/Pitts Elementary. When I worked at the building it was a day care center. Today it has been developed into an actu-

Rhiannon Boyer.

al public elementary school. My position at the day care center was that of childcare provider. I supervised and cared for the children throughout the week and also on many Saturdays.

My story begins one Saturday morning, as I was outside supervising the children during their play period. I remember feeling the need to use the bathroom, so I walked over to the main door and entered the school building. As I entered the hall, I began hearing the familiar sound of a ball being bounced. Knowing that all the children were outside with the other care providers, this sound caught my attention and struck me as strange. The sound was coming from the gymnasium, and sounded as if a game was being played, because I could hear the ball being bounced about and the squeaking of rubber-soled shoes running upon the highly polished gym floor.

As I said, this was very odd. I had not been told about any other children that were to be in the building that Saturday. Suddenly, before finishing my thought, I heard the distinct, clear sound of children's voices. This sound prompted my curiosity, and mentally putting aside my need to use the bathroom, I walked towards the gymnasium, wanting to know who might be in there. When I entered the gymnasium, it was silent and totally empty.

Thinking back, I don't know why I reacted as calmly as I did, but I thought it must have been sound from the playground kids somehow bouncing inside off the gymnasium walls. I turned around, walked to the restroom then returned outside to the playground.

Later that day, during lunch, as I and the other staff were escorting the children to the dining room, I heard the same sound of children playing in the gymnasium. Alone, I walked down the hall towards the gymnasium thinking I'd gather any children that might have wandered away from the group.

As I got closer to the gymnasium, I distinctly heard the sound of children running up and down the hall. When I reached the rear door of the gymnasium and opened it, the door suddenly pulled away from me and closed with a loud slam! I jumped back, the door just missing my face! There was no way without assistance from someone that door could have closed like that on its own. It was as if an invisible person wanted to hurt me. I was startled. Not bothering to reopen the door, I turned around and quickly returned to the dining room.

I walked up to another staff member and told everything that I had heard and now seen. She was concerned for what had occurred and decided to investigate the gymnasium for herself. I did not want to accompany her, so I chose to stay in the dining room with the children.

When she returned, she told me that as she was approaching the gymnasium, she also began to hear the very sound of a ball being bounced about—the same sound I had experienced. As she advanced toward the now-open door, it too came slamming shut, also almost hitting her in the face! We both got goosebumps and were shaken and scared. Scared enough to not ever want to work on a Saturday at the school again—and I never did.

I don't know what I would have done if I would have seen a ghost. If a ghost would have appeared to me, I think I would have screamed. It was a very scary time for me.

Historic, Victorian and quaint Leadville, CO.

I also need to tell you about other people who have had experiences with ghosts at the school. The reports about the school being haunted are pretty well known by staff members you choose to ask. Staff members know that spirits walk the halls within that school because most have encountered them.

One other experience that I remember being told about took place in a basement where the school supplies were stored. Whenever any staff member needed to enter the basement, we always made sure to take someone along as safe company. We knew that to go down there alone was not a good idea, because whenever a person would enter the basement alone, the door would always close and lock behind them. What is even stranger still about this is, the door to the basement has no lock! I know from speaking to current employees at the school this very day, this same activity takes place in the basement.

I've been told that historically many years ago, there was a devastating fire that burned down the original schoolhouse, which had stood on the same foundation as the current school. Whether children were burned to death, or anyone was killed in that fire, well, I don't know. But, some older residents of town have mention to me about the story of that fire. Maybe that might have something to do with all the ghostly activities."

TEACHER FELICIA'S & CUSTODIAN GERALDINE'S STORIES

I interviewed the following two staff members, Felicia and Geraldine, within the school's main building. Both described their personal encounters with ghosts, and even walked with me, describing the areas of the school where they had their personal ghostly encounters.

As I came to discover, the school is not a very large one. These women's experiences with ghosts are well known to fellow co-workers, and are not at all questioned regarding their authenticity.

Additionally, each woman was interview individually, unaware of the other's comments. I found it intriguing that each woman was so moved by recalling her experiences at the school, that she would rub her arms, as if to rub away the goosebumps that had formed in the process.

Do these occurrences still take place at the school? Well, I was recently informed by a staff member that the ghosts still walk the halls and gymnasium, only not as dramatically as in years past.

— *Antonio*

TEACHER FELICIA'S STORY

"I've lived in Leadville all my life, and have worked at the school for 17 years. I was hired as a pre-school teacher, and I still hold that position. My first experience with any ghostly type of activity at the school took place within my first year of employment. At that time the school was open 365 days of the year. This schedule required me to work quite a lot of weekends.

The ghostly experiences that I've had at the school began when I first started hearing the sounds of children playing within the school building. These sounds took place at the strangest times of the day or night. I was always alone during these experiences. Frequently, they took place in the early morning hours around 5:30 a.m. or so. Usually I thought that children were playing in the building, but realizing the time, this seemed very odd.

Several times after hearing these sounds, I would rise from my chair and walk out to the hall and have a look around. When I didn't spot anyone, I walked to the other adjacent rooms, where the sounds were projecting the loudest. Approaching a classroom, I'd open the door, and all at once the noise would cease.

One particular early morning, I heard loud noises coming from the gymnasium. Definitely these were the sounds of children bouncing balls and speaking very loudly. I thought perhaps a few parents had dropped these children off at the school without notifying the staff. I couldn't believe that these parents would be so irresponsible as to just leave their children unsupervised like that. So, I walked down the hall over to the gymnasium, to find out why these kids were in the building at such an early hour.

The noise was very loud as I approached the door, but as soon as I opened the door the noise immediately stopped! I looked inside and it was dark and empty. I was so surprised by this that I quickly, and very cautiously, went back to my room.

I've also heard, on several occasions, the sound of footsteps walking in the halls, and specifically on the long ramp located directly inside the main entrance to the school. These ghostly footsteps make a heavy walking, echoing sound. They resemble the footsteps that an adult walking with long strides would make. These are not the footsteps of a small

Felicia, pre-school teacher.

child. I can easily distinguish both sounds, because I work with children most every day.

Once, the school had a friendly resident cat that lived within the building. It would wander the halls at ease, and the children all enjoyed having it around. Another school pet that we maintained was a pot-bellied pig that the children named "Wilber." These pets were for the benefit of the children, and were well-behaved animals. The animals had full range of the building. My reason for mentioning them is because I witnessed these animals as they reacted, or were very visibly affected, by the spirits in the building.

I grew to expect to see paranormal activity take place, just by simply watching the animals' behavior. No doubt, it would. The cat would abruptly begin to hiss and meow nervously, and Wilber would squeal, as a pig is known to do when agitated. Loud noises might begin at one end of the building, and then, without warning, both of these animals would hiss, scream, and squeal, and run away in the opposite direction of the noise. This was really a strange, and very scary, thing to see take place in front of us.

One day, I was in one room of the school that was specially designated for our infant/toddler program. I was again, at the time of this experience, alone in the room caring for several infants. I was seated, feeding a young baby that I held in my arms, and listening to a radio that was sitting on top of a small table next to me. Suddenly, all by itself, it turned off. Not for a moment did I even imagine that a ghost might be behind this. So, I reached over and turned the knob to the 'on' position. But wouldn't you know, it turned itself off once again. It was then, right at that moment, that I felt something ghostly taking place. The atmosphere turned an icy cold, and I immediately felt that the babies and I were no longer alone in the room. I could somehow "sensed" the presence of an unseen person in the room with us. I still get chills just thinking about that.

I got quiet, when suddenly in an empty corner of the room I began to hear a little girl's voice speak. I distinctly heard her say, "Hi." My eyes scanned the room as I kept looking in the direction of the empty corner. Once again, I heard the voice say, "Hi." What really scared me was when two of the babies that were sitting in their small chairs, together, also visibly turned their heads in the direction of the voice. I knew then I was not imagining the voice, if the babies also heard the voice, then something had gotten their attention. Soon the voice stopped and the coldness in the room faded away. I'll never forget that experience.

On another night, sometime following that last experience with the little girl's voice, I needed to catch up on paperwork, so I decided to do this during the evening hours. I really hated being alone at night in the building, so I asked my sister to accompany me. I decided as a precaution to do a security check of the building by inspecting all the doors that lead outside. My sister followed right beside me, as did our resident cat.

We walked and talked among ourselves, as we went from hall to hall, and door to door. Well, behind the cafeteria is located a door, with a short flight of stairs that lead to the outside street level. Approaching the door, I reached out and held on to the knob. Suddenly, both of us, at that very same moment became overcome with the frightening feeling that something negative was in our immediate area. I could "feel" the presence of a person standing right beside us.

Pitts Elementary School.

We both looked at each other, with facial expressions that didn't need further explanations. My sister spoke saying, "Something does not feel right." I answered, "I don't think I like this either." Suddenly, we heard a very high-pitched scream! The cat hissed, and that was all we needed. I let go of the doorknob, and we shot down the hall! We had had enough. We decided to quickly leave the building, got in our car, and drive home.

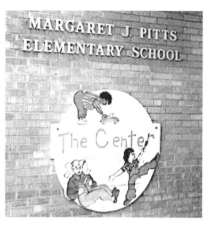

Now next, I'll try to describe to you my most horrific personal encounter in the school. This encounter was when I actually saw the ghost of a man! Again, I happened to be alone one early morning in the building. I was in one of the classrooms when I heard the school's front door open and slam shut. Immediately I heard the sounds of a man's footsteps walking down the hall. Thinking it might be staff, I waited for him to enter my room. The thought also crossed my mind that it might even be a parent wishing to speak to me. But strangely, after just a few moments, the footsteps stopped. I decided to walk into the hallway and meet this man.

After I opened my door and stepped into the hallway, I spotted a strange-looking man standing several feet away from me. He was unfamiliar to me, but I did get a very good look at him. He was average looking, in his 30s, wearing tan-colored pants, a vest, with short hair and looking not much out of the ordinary. I spoke to him saying, "Hi, can I help you?" He said nothing, but began to walk at a slow pace towards me. Again, I spoke to him, asking if he needed anything. He just looked straight ahead and kept walking. Just then a school phone located in the middle of the hallway began to ring. I moved in its direction to answer it, but I kept my eyes locked on the man in the hall. I noticed that he took a few more steps towards me, then instantly disappeared! I froze in place. I was so terrified. The phone just kept ringing but even though my hand was on top of the receiver, I could not bring myself to lift it to my ear. I was shaking, crying, and in shock. I could not move a finger.

What snapped me out of this shock was the sound of children playing in the nearby classroom. I rushed down the hallway to the classroom, opened the door, and saw that it was silently empty. Shaken even more, I returned to my room and stayed put. I couldn't wait until the parents and children arrived that morning to begin the day. I would very much hate to ever experience the spirit figure again. That really scared me quite a bit.

I refused to tell anyone at the school about what I had experienced. I waited until I arrived home and mentioned my experience to my family. Their response was to say, "You imagined it." But, eventually I finally did confide and mention my experience to the school's two custodians. They comforted me, and as it turns out, they themselves had had their own experiences with ghosts in the school. One, a male janitor, had experienced so many spiritual things in the building that he eventually quit his employment at the school. I was told that most of his experiences took place while he, like myself, was alone at night in the building.

I still find it difficult to repeat what happened to me at the school and especially that morning when I saw the ghostly male figure. I get shaky and get goosebumps all over. It's not a closely, guarded secret among the teaching staff that strange ghostly occurrences are common in the building. Doors slamming on their own, voices, footsteps, and the ghostly noise of children at play in empty rooms. It's all quite common. But lately, I've not heard about anyone having unexplained experiences at the school. I was told, when I first began working here, about a past principal who had died and who had very much loved working at the school. She genuinely loved the children and her job. Could she be one of the spirits?

From time to time, I still hear sounds of the children's ghosts in the building. Those voices do not bother me as much as they used to. It's the adults' spirits that cause me more concern."

CUSTODIAN GERALDINE C. RIVERA'S STORY

"I have lived in Leadville most of my life and have worked at the school

as a custodian for three years. I first need to say
that even though I do believe in spirits, I am not
afraid of them. I know they can't harm the living,
so I just respect and ignore them. Saying this,
my first experience took place as I was doing the
usual routine of cleaning classrooms. I remember hearing an unusual sound that caught my
attention. I thought I was hearing the children
playing in the gym. It was late in the evening,

and knew I was the only person in the building *Geraldine, school custodian.*
that night. I decided to investigate where the sounds were coming from.
When I got to the gym, it was dark and no one was in sight.

There have been other times in the school when I'll also hear the laughter of a small girl. I'll hear this girl's soft laughter from time to time. The
impression I receive from her is that she is somehow the main spirit that
is responsible for all the activity in the building.

Other common ghostly experiences that I have witnessed are the
sounds of bouncing balls, and children playing in the halls and gym. I
know these spirits exist in the school, and I want the spirit children to
be happy with me, because my work demands that I spend much time
alone at the school.

What I've started to do before I start my nighttime work routine, is after entering the building, I'll walk over to the gym, and I'll state out loud
to the spirit children, "I'm going to turn on the light for you kids, so that
you don't have to play in the dark. So, have a good time playing with your
ball. I'll come back later and turn off the light." I believe that by doing
this they'll know I don't mean them any disrespect, and they'll become
accustomed to my presence in the building by doing this little gesture.
I'd like to think that they have.

When I used to work in the area of the building where the library is
located, I'd sometimes "feel" the presence of someone watching me. As
I would go around the classroom and wipe off each table's top, I'd soon
sense the presence of someone's eyes watching me. As soon as I'd have
this sensation, I'd turn around and sometimes catch the shadow of a

man, or a dark misty male figure, walk past. The figure would travel right in front of me. I've never been able to make out his face, but I can tell that for sure, it is the shadow of a man.

A fellow custodian named Richard died two years ago. He used to work with me at the school. Since his death, I've experienced something else that's a little strange. I knew Richard well, as we spent many hours working alone together in the building. Well, since his death, there have been times when I'll be busy cleaning and doing my unusual tasks, when out of the blue, I'll catch the scent of Richard's cologne. I know what his cologne smelled like. As I said, we worked together and always complimented Richard on his colognes.

I'll be so busy at my work, that without thinking about him, I'll catch his scent. I know he's around watching me work, so I'll say, "Okay Richard, I know you are watching me. I know it's a mess in here, you know I'll clean it all up." Talking out loud to his spirit gives me comfort. I speak to him as I used to when we worked together.

One other thing that I need to mention is when I hear my name being called. I'll hear a woman's voice calling, "Gerie", or "Geraldine." A bit startled, I'll turn but not see anyone. Then I'll respond by saying, "Well, who's calling me?" But they never answer my question. The voice doesn't have the familiar sound of a male's voice—it belongs to a woman. I've told my family about these experiences, but they giggle and say that I'm crazy.

Out of the blue, a teacher asked me once if I had ever heard unusual things, or voices, in the school at night. I told her about the children's voices that I've heard coming from the gym and the classrooms. Her eyes lit up, and she said, "Yes, yes I've heard them too!" I'm also aware of the ghost of a man who is dressed in black. This ghost has been seen walking the halls.

There is another custodian who only speaks Spanish, who is employed here. Her name is Maria. I speak Spanish, and she and I talk all the time. Well, Maria reported to me once about the time she was working in a particular room, and had her own spirit encounter. She told me that in one of the classrooms she felt the presence of someone in the room, then

the spirit touched her. At which point, she immediately began to recite prayers, and the presence left the room. She has had many, many other experiences in this building. You ought to speak to her. I know she'll have a lot of stories to tell you.

I don't know much about the history of this building. I don't know what might be causing all the spiritual things. I only hope that I would not be afraid if any of the ghosts were to appear to me. I'd like to think that they would not do me any harm. As I said before, I do respect them. I've always believed that the living are the ones that should really be feared the most. The dead are dead. I don't believe they can do us any harm.

You know, something that I like to do is regularly visit the local cemetery and visit my twin brother's and a sister's graves. During my visits, I've passed the area of the cemetery that is reserved for the burial of babies. Their graves appear so sad to me. Because I don't like seeing how some of these children's graves have been neglected, I've taken it upon myself to straighten up the artificial flowers and toys that people have left. I also straighten up the fallen crosses, and I've even re-painted the cement borders that outline the little graves. I've painted the borders blue for the boys and pink for the girls. On some of those graves the headstones have words that are no longer possible to read. Since I can't make out if it's a girl or boy that's buried there, those head-stones I just paint them white.

I call all these children my "rainbow babies." Once, as I was doing this, a stranger came up to me and asked, "I was wondering who was painting the graves." I answered, "I wanted to do this because I felt no one was taking care of them."

LOS ANGELES, CA

HOSPITAL CHAPLAIN – FATHER DAVID M. EGGER'S STORY

The hospital was founded in 1878, and the Los Angeles County LAC+USC Medical Center (LAC+USC) is currently the nation's largest academic institution. It is one of the largest acute care hospitals in America and has been the primary teaching facility of the University of Southern California School of Medicine since 1885. Originally established as a 100-bed hospital with 47 patients, it is currently licensed for 600 beds and budgeted to staff 745 beds.

I'm gay and happen to be a Catholic priest in the Jesuit Order. My story took place in the winter of 1982. At the time, I had been one of four staff chaplains for the USC County Hospital. Prior to this position, I had cared for the spiritual needs of patients at Good Samaritan Hospital in Central Los Angeles. I received my master of divinity from Loyola Marymount University, and twelve months before my acceptance to Good Samaritan, I immediately undertook pastoral ministry within the Los Angeles Archdiocese. I stayed at this hospital for two years until eventually ending up at USC County Hospital.

The time period of my work at County Hospital coincided with the tragic beginning of the HIV/AIDS epidemic that was gripping the United States. UAC Hospital was mobilizing its staff to be at the forefront of treatment and caregiving to patients of this plague. As chaplain, I encountered many, many men and women, gay and straight, with various degrees of this condition. One man in particular, named Gustavio, remains in my memory still.

Gustavio was a twenty-two-year-old Hispanic man. When he arrived at the hospital, he stood five feet five inches tall, was very thin, and was prone to vomiting episodes. From his initial arrival to the day he passed away was not more than two weeks apart. But during that short time, he and I bonded as spiritual brothers. When Gustavio's family back in

Guatemala found out their son was gay, they gradually decreased regular phone correspondence with him to ultimately terminating all communication when he disclosed his AIDS diagnosis. They simply abandoned their son to face his health struggle alone. I found this heart wrenching and so un-Christ like. Sadly, this outcome was to become more the norm for thousands of affected AIDS patients rather than the exception. I experienced this to be so very tragically true with the patients I came into contact with on a daily basis.

Even though Gustavio was extremely weak and had lost so much weight his facial features resembled a mask of death, but he managed to hold on to what was encouraging about life, joking at times and always remaining so very positive.

One afternoon, as I sat by his bed, I noticed under his wisps of hair, several shiny metal ballpoint-looking dots jutting out from his scalp. I asked him about them, and he said, "Oh, I thought you knew about the probes the doctors implanted into my skull. I was told it's some type of experimental therapy they're trying out." I asked, "Do they hurt?" He said, "Yes, at times they do, when I forget they are there and touch one."

I was upset to hear him describe this as "experimental" and painful. Because of my rising outrage over this particular attempt at care, I decided to change the subject and not upset Gustavio.

The following weekend, I was called away to assist with a religious retreat in Santa Barbara. A new class of young postulants was visiting from Oklahoma, and I was asked to conduct the afternoon discussions. Everything went well, but on my last night, I had an unusual dream. I dreamed of Gustavio, surrounded with thousands of electric-blue butterflies beautifully fluttering in unison. "Gustavio, they are so beautiful," I said. He looked at me and simply smiled. He did not speak a word to me, but the impression I received was that he was in paradise.

That Monday morning as I made my rounds through the hospital, I entered Gustavio's eighth-floor room and found him standing at the window, gazing out at the sky. I stood at the door and said, "Good morning. How are you today?"

He turned, faced me, and said, "Oh, Father, I'm so happy." Just at that very moment, a loud commotion commenced behind me in the hallway. A nurse immediately approached me and screamed an order for me to follow her to the room where the commotion was happening. Upon arrival to that room, we encountered the aftermath of one patient's family member physically assaulting another patient's family member. It was clear that several people had already subdued the aggressor and were forcibly holding him down on the floor for hospital security personnel to arrive and take over.

Concerned with all that had just transpired in the hall and that it may have caused Gustavio undue alarm, I quickly walked back to his room. When I arrived at his room, I looked around and noticed he was gone. I checked the bathroom and found it empty. Then I noticed his bed and saw that it was completely made up and all his personal bedside table items were also gone. Unusual as this appeared, it was common practice to move patients as vacancies or hospital population needs require.

Eventually, I visited three more patients before opening the door to my office. On my desk were several patient files that the hospital social worker, Martha, left for me to look over. Social workers and hospital chaplains tend to work closely, sharing notes when appropriate to patients' well-being.

I quickly looked over the five files and pulled out Gustavio's familiar blue file. To say the least, I was shocked to spot the note stapled on the cover with the handwritten word deceased. While reading the social worker's notes, I discovered that Gustavo had passed away on Sunday morning, the day before. I thought, how could that be? I was just in his room three hours ago and had spoken directly to him and he to me!

I closed and locked my office door and then walked down to the hospital coroner's office. I was taken to the refrigerated holding area, where Gustavio's so very thin and deceased body was placed. I offered my personal prayers, all the while anointing him with holy oil and holy water.

Speaking for myself, I've never been the same since that day. My experience with Gustavio's spirit has forever positively added to my convictions and has immensely strengthened my faith in God's universal divine plan for us all, in Christ's name.

PUEBLO, CO

STEVEN KAKEMOTO'S STORY

Steven and I met for this interview within a hotel lobby in Pueblo. Currently retired from his archeological work, Steven is today working on completing his book entitled, "Pit House Fire Rings of the Eastern Colorado Plains."

Steven's face carries the lines of his profession, caused by years of working outdoors, among dirt, sunlight and wind. Steven joked about the number of added years the Colorado weather has forced on his "young" 67-year-old face. "Kind of sexy, I'm a magnet for senior Japanese ladies," he told me.

As I began to touch on his personal story that he experienced in Pueblo, he stopped me, then added, "This story I'm going to tell you is pretty interesting, but when you have more time, you should hear the stories I can tell you about what I saw when I spent a year in Peru. Now you talk about ghost stories! The supernatural things that I saw digging in those mountains would scare the living daylights out of you!"

I added, "Yeah, Steven I bet they might, but for the sake of argument, those mountains known as the Rockies, to the east of where we're sitting, also have a fair share of their own scary moments. When I begin my book of Peruvian Ghost Stories, I'll look you up."

After we toasted our wine glasses, Steven began his story.

— Antonio

"I'm a retired professor of biology, and I've lived in Pueblo all my life. Having now lived here for 67 years, I've heard lots of stories about ghosts and haunted areas from local people. My own personal experience with a ghost took place when doing archeological excavations at what remained at Fort Pueblo, which I soon discovered was not much.

Briefly, the fort was constructed of adobe brick and built in 1842 on the northern side of the Arkansas River. The fort was actually established by fur trappers. In 1854 the Utes attacked and completely killed everyone within its walls. My job was to excavate and record any artifacts that could be found at a circumscribed, designated area of the fort. I began with this work in the spring of 1987.

Beforehand, a graduate student related a story to me that the fort had a paranormal history of being haunted. That is to say, people reported such activity as a headless woman who is seen walking among the ruins. This story's legacy began at the time that the fort was actually inhabited. Whether true or not, as a historian, I took a mental note of this.

Well, beginning my work, I had a rotating staff of eight graduate students that I supervised at the site. The students would stake grid lines and take copious notes as instructed to do so, as dictated within the archeological process. This is very time consuming work, and I would be the first to agree that it is often boring, but very necessary.

About a week or so into our project, we began to uncover little objects of merit. Such artifacts were bottles, metal spoons, clay pipes, and bits of broken pottery, or shards. After a little more than a month of digging, we discovered the usual arrowhead or two, but soon we were filling a paper bag with numerous arrowheads. Given the history of the fort's demise, this was evidence of a major battle that had been fought against the trappers and other inhabitants. Well, about this time is when things started to get a bit uneasy, in terms of the supernatural.

Due to the warm spring weather, we were at times digging late into the night. Well, it was during one of these nights that two students began to report that they felt someone watching them as they did their work. One even reported that she had heard the disembodied, unmistakable voice of an elderly man say, "Leave us alone." Another student approached me to say that she at times was hearing a strange voice speaking in a language other than English, perhaps Ute.

One day, as I was alone in the excavation pit, I glanced to my right, and stretched out my arm reaching for my small hand pick. Spotting the pick, I noticed the pick made a quick half turn away from my reaching hand! As I turned completely around to face the pick, I heard a very low laughing voice! It was deep and haunting. This sent a shock of fear through me. Knowing I had just experienced something very unusual, something supernatural, I got out of the pit really quickly!

I decided to contact a friend of mine who worked as office secretary for the Catholic Pueblo diocese. I thought she might offer some insight, or explanation on some level, regarding the occurrences that I, and my students were experiencing. When I informed Patricia about this, she said she would inform a priest who she knew might have some answers, or at the least, be of some help.

Just a day later, I received a phone call from Father Tom. After introducing himself, he stated that he was also aware of the stories regarding the Fort grounds being inhabited by spirits. Further, that he would like to offer his services the following Tuesday morning to bless the area, if I would be open to it. At that split second, I was unsure as to my answer, but I found the words to say, "Yes, of course, Tuesday morning would be fine."

That following Tuesday found Father Tom, myself, and three students gathered together at the excavation pit. One of the students was the one that had first approached me and spoke to me about her experience.

The priest did his blessing rite and asked us to place a crucifix within the area where we would be working. Whether this blessing actually worked or not is difficult to prove, but since then we did not have any further unexplained issues or supernatural experience at the site, so I imagine it did."

STEAMBOAT SPRINGS, CO

CHARLES BATERNA'S STORY

There have been a few stories which I've written in past books that pertain to haunted businesses, here's one that I'm sure will cause you to think why the owners of this establishment would ever choose to stay in their building for as long as they did. The owners have now retired from their livelihood, and were quite assuredly pleased to discuss their experiences, but asked me not to disclose the name, or location of their former business, for the sake of the new owners. This story offers essential information regarding the

637

expressed nature of spiritual activity, but will leave the reader with a few questions that will pique your curiosity.

— Antonio

"My wife and I have lived in Steamboat Springs for 33 years. We moved here from Los Angeles, California, in 1973, and bought an existing restaurant that we redecorated and turned into a Mexican restaurant in 1974. We owned the building for several years before we retired. My story pertains to that original property which was raised to the ground and where a new building now stands in its place. I don't know if the new property owners have ever encountered any ghost activity, and I've not ever thought of following through and ask them. I'm sure that if I ever did, it would seem to them that I had lost my mind. My son's insurance agent told me not more than a year ago, of a customer who approached her, and informed her that she believed the old restaurant was haunted by an old man found dead many years ago on the grounds. However, we never researched this.

Curiously, staff used to report smelling a strong scent of something rotten, followed by headaches and nausea. Others used to report a feeling of being watched, a feeling of being unsafe and even threatened. Both my wife and I would come to work full of energy, but after having entered the restaurant would immediately become tired and out of breath. So much so that we'd even brought in a small lounge chair to relax on. We had the gas company check for natural gas leaks and measure carbon monoxide levels, but they did not find any leaks or other possible causes.

It was approximately 10 months after opening our doors that customers began to report unexplained experiences, such as intense cold spots throughout the building and customers being brushed-up against by unseen forces. Some recalled that after being physically shoved, they would turn around to look at who had bumped into them and no one would be there. The wait staff also had similar experiences, and their encounters were just as obvious. One waitress stated that she had felt unseen fingers stroke her right cheek, giving her the impression that she was being caressed. That same night a customer standing before the mirror in the women's restroom, reported being touched on the back of her neck. When she turned around, there was no one next to her, but said as she returned to look in the mirror, she saw the quickly fading image of a short man wearing a long white scarf around his neck!

These types of reports were common. But aside from the ones I already reported to you, the majority of these pranks by our resident spirits were so casual, that they would not frighten most of our patrons. Simple things such as napkins falling off tables, table settings getting rearranged and glasses of water tipping over on their own, were about the extent of these frequent incidents.

Employees also reported strange things in the kitchen where boxes and spices that had been placed within the kitchen pantry would turn up on the floor in other rooms the following morning. Once, a special long handled spatula that we use for making enchiladas was actually seen falling off a table, but right before it hit the floor, it rose up in the air and was placed back on the table by an unseen hand. Our cook, who was from old Mexico, also witnessed this take place, wanted no part of it, and resigned her position that very day!

Another interesting incident took place the evening before this last one. My wife and an employee were locking up the kitchen, getting ready to leave for the night when suddenly the water faucet in the main three bin sink turned on, then quickly turned off all by itself. My wife described to me how very quickly the water shot out in full force from the faucet, then just a few seconds later, the faucet knob turned itself off! My wife was standing just a few feet away from the sink, so she was obviously confident that no one else was in the kitchen but her and the employee in the next room. When she yelled to the other employee who was in the main dining room to come over, this time in the presence of two people, the water came on once again. It remained on, and it did not turn itself off until my wife took hold of the knob and physically turned it off herself. Was this coincidence, or was there an unseen force at work? There really was no explanation so I'll leave that up to you to decide.

Sometimes the toilets flushed by themselves when no one is inside. On another occasion when the restaurant was closed, my wife and I were stocking our refrigerator with chopped meat. Half-way through, we heard a pounding coming from the wall in the short hallway where the toilets are located. We both stopped what we were doing to listen. Then we heard the sound of a man's voice speaking words that we could not make out. The voice was loud, but that was the extent of it. The words resembled a muffled yelling. My wife walked over to the bathroom area, with me close behind. As we entered the hallway we heard the toilet in the men's bathroom flush. We knew that no one was in the building with us, but I yelled out, "Hey, who's in there? I'm coming in!" As soon as I said these words, the toilet in the woman's bathroom also flushed on its own. We walked into both restrooms to inspect the situation but were the only two people in the restrooms and entire building.

One very disturbing occurrence for my wife and I involved the phone. This would only take place when one of us would be alone in the building. The phone would ring, and after answering it by saying hello, the male voice at the other end would answer, "Are you the wife of Thomas?" That's all he would say, then he'd hang up. The voice was similar to the sound of what a person who was standing in another room far from the receiver might sound like. My wife was the first to experience this, then one evening I was alone in the restaurant and also picked up the phone and heard the same thing. Strangest of all was when we were both in the restaurant. The phone rang and the same familiar creepy voice spoke. I became very annoyed with this prank. My wife unplugged the phone jack from the wall, and in a few minutes, both of us heard the same voice repeating the words, "Are you the wife of Thomas!" This time the voice sounded as if the person was standing just a few feet away from us, in the same room. This un-godly voice ceased to call anymore, when I shouted, "No, I'm not Thomas's wife, and I don't know who Thomas is! Just go away, and don't talk to us anymore!" That sharp response must have worked because the calls and voice stopped right after this.

Our employees had always reported throughout the years of feeling chills on their arms and shoulders, and the sensation of someone's invisible fingers caressing their necks. Both men and women have reported this. A disembodied male voice in one of our larger rooms was also heard.

Sometimes after having the sensation that someone was following them about the room, the man's voice would begin to speak in sentences that were not clear to make out.

Some of our customers throughout the years had reported seeing a dark figure of a man that walked directly through the inside dining room wall of the restaurant. That wall shares the outside wall, which faces the rear alley. He'd be seen casually walking by a table and without slowing, would disappear into the wall! This ghost man's detached legs had also reported being seen by men using the bathroom. As they would enter the bathroom stall and take a seat upon the commode, they'd spot a pair of legs standing in the stall next to them facing the commode. For several customers, the feet of this figure just standing and facing the commode, made them take notice. In one minute the legs were there, then in a split second they were gone! The stall door was never opened, the sound of footsteps leaving were never heard. There is only one way in and out through the short hallway that leads to and from the bathroom, so who-ever would be in the bathroom could not escape being noticed. We had one man speak to me directly about seeing a man's face in the bathroom mirror. But he was convinced we were playing a trick on him by install-ing a two-way mirror. He was not amused, and threatened to report us for violating his privacy. We never heard from him again.

I admit that I myself saw a dark male figure that stood next to the bathroom hallway, years ago. The figure was very translucent almost fog like in appearance. He stood about 5'6" tall and remained motionless for a few seconds, then slowly disappeared! I've seen him three times, in different areas of the building. I didn't feel threatened by this ghost, I just hoped that he'd kept his distance from my customers and staff. I even spoke to him saying, "Go away, you're not wanted here!" Despite my pleading to leave, this spirit for some unknown reason seems very comfortable staying put.

I never thought about pursuing the cause for the hauntings. Many peo-ple have urged me to get a medium to channel the spirits, but I believe once you start doing this, it will open the door to even more, and potential-ly negative, spiritual activity. I also didn't want the reputation of owning a haunted Mexican restaurant in our small town—for obvious reasons."

SANTA FE, NM

SOFITA BECERA'S STORY

I conducted this interview with Sofita Becera at her home, in her living room, which also served as her bedroom. The simple items of decoration displayed about her home provided clues to Sofita's modest taste. Handcrafted, crocheted doilies and other needlework rested upon Sofita's well-worn furniture. Placed at the foot of her yellow/green sofa was an oblong rug that Sofita's best friend, Belinda Ortiz, had given to her as a wedding present many years before.

What remains dominant in my memory, however, was Sofita's religiosity. On a wooden table her deceased husband had made over 20 years ago, stood a statue of the Virgin Mary. In front of the statue was a small bouquet of plastic flowers and a votive candle that flickered continuously throughout the interview.

Born on August 12, 1899, Sofita was nearing 93 years of age, but had the spunk and vitality of a much younger woman. She wore thick-lensed glasses because of cataract surgery performed eight years earlier.

Sofita's story concerns a molcajete, a carved, stone kitchen tool developed by ancient indigenous peoples several hundred years ago in the valley of Mexico. It is shaped like an average sized melon, with the center hollowed out. A smaller stone is used inside the hollowed-out portion of the molcajete to crush or grind herbs and spices. This stone "mortar and pestle" was so useful that it remains a popular tool with people on both sides of the border dividing the United States and Mexico.

Unlike a metate—a long, flat stone used by Native Americans throughout the Southwest to grind corn into a flourlike powder—the molcajete is rounded and bowl-shaped.

— Antonio

In 1921, I was 22 and had just married Daniel the previous summer. We had a small house about two miles east of the Santa Fe Plaza. In those days, two to five miles was not considered very far to travel, and those of us without horses would walk, carrying supplies of food or firewood. It was not an easy life, but the good times made up for the bad.

My good friend since childhood, Belinda Ortiz, would join me at midday after I had done

Sofita Becera.

the cleaning and fed the all our animals. Belinda and I passed the time talking about what was going on in our neighborhood, things like who was romancing who.

During one of these afternoon visits, Belinda and I went outside to rid my yard of a stray dog that was barking and chasing my chickens. Three young neighborhood boys came by, saw our trouble, and started throwing stones at the mongrel.

Once rid of the dog, I asked the boys why they were covered in dirt. They explained that they had been exploring in the nearby hills, and had discovered a small cave behind a grove of trees, against the side of the mountain. They had gathered some sticks to enlarge the opening and peered inside. With the help of the afternoon sun, they had seen several pots and a quiver made out of fox pelts that contained arrows. I told them they must have uncovered a burial site, and should not have touched or taken anything because they must respect the dead. They listened with wide eyes, and then said they did not want to return but were afraid that others might disturb the cave. Belinda suggested they take us to the cave and we could help them seal it up. The boys agreed and off we went.

About six miles into the Sangre de Cristo Mountain Range, on the eastern edge of the city, we crossed a small stream and entered a grove of trees. There we found the cave. The opening was about four feet high and three feet wide. We peered inside and saw the small painted pots, a woven grass mat, and the quiver of arrows—just as the boys had described. In the back of the cave, I saw a large dark mass of fur and I

Sofita's primitive molcajete discovery.

knew this was a burial cave when I saw a bony foot protruding from underneath the fur. I realized that the corpse must have been a man and a hunter, because he was wrapped in a bear skin and had his hunting weapons with him, but I kept this knowledge to myself and made the sign of the cross.

I turned to Belinda and the boys and said, "We will have to seal this up, so go down to the stream and bring mud and stones."

While they were all busy at the stream, I looked inside the cave again. This time I noticed a roughly carved molcajete. I knew that taking anything from the dead or a burial is very wrong. I was raised knowing this, but mentally putting this knowledge aside, I nervously reached in and grabbed the molcajete and the small grinding stone that lay beside it. At the time, it didn't seem wrong to take the stone tool, and I thought this would fit in my kitchen perfectly, so I carried it some distance away and covered it with grass and leaves. I felt it was worthless compared to the pots or the fox quiver.

We diligently worked with our hastily gathered adobe building materials, and soon the sun had caused a thin crust to develop on the surface of the moistened mud. We placed large branches with lots of leaves in front of the sealed entrance. We all agreed that we had done a "good job."

I instructed the boys to return home on their own, but Belinda and I stayed behind. After they had gone, I told Belinda about the molcajate. She was not happy about what I had done, but after she had seen it, she agreed that it would do no harm to put it to use once in a while, after all those years lying in the cave.

I retrieved the tool and we went home. I scrubbed the molcajete clean of all mud and placed it on the kitchen table to surprise my husband. When Daniel saw it, he admired its beauty, but asked nothing about its origins. Instead, he suggested I grind some chile for the following day's dinner.

So, the next day I did as he had suggested and crushed some dried, red chile pods for dinner. The molcajete performed very nicely, but later that night, while I was sleeping, I was awakened by a loud banging sound. I shook my husband out of his sleep and told him to listen, but the sound had stopped. The next night, I was again awakened by the same sound, but this time I recognized it as the sound one rock makes as it is hit against another—a "click/click" sound. Immediately, I knew it was the molcajete. I got goosebumps on my goosebumps, but I kept still and eventually, after what seemed an eternity, the sound stopped.

The next morning, I told Belinda about the sounds in the night. She said it was my own fault for removing it from the gravesite and clearly taking what was not mine. I agreed, and asked her to return the molcajete to the cave. She refused and insisted I do it myself. But I was too frightened, so I carried the stone to the back of the house and left it outside beside the back door.

From time to time, I would hear the familiar clicking sound, but I dared not tell Daniel where the molcajete came from. I just endured the repetitive pounding and the guilt that had overcome me. Out of fear I could not bring myself to return the molcajete to its rightful resting place.

One November night, as a soft snow dusted everything, I heard the molcajete again. I got out of bed, went to the back door and carefully peered through the window. I saw the freshly fallen snow glistening in the bright light of a full moon. Then I looked down to where the molcajete stood and was surprised to see the imprints of a barefooted person in the snow. The footprints slowly moved away from the molcajete until they disappeared behind a large cottonwood tree. Although snow covered everything else in the yard, the exposed molcajete, which was being used as a doorstop, had been brushed clean, and fresh, human footprints surrounded the molcajete.

Modern day molcajete.

Since that night, I have heard the clicking sounds of the molcajete only twice:

on the day that my good friend Belinda died, and on the day that Daniel was laid to rest. But I am no longer afraid. I guess I've come to accept the spirit that dwells in or around the grinding stone as something that I will have to live with. I now consider the molcajete as if it were a chair or table, something to be taken for granted, but useful when needed. I believe this "stone friend" will stay with me and provide companionship until I leave this world.

Author's Note: *In September of 1991, Sofita suffered a massive heart attack and died at home, surrounded by her son and two neighbors. Later, her son contacted me and informed me that his mother had mentioned to him that she had wanted me to have the molcajete. I accepted the gift with nervous apprehension, and assured her son that I would take care of it and that eventually I would place it in a location that befits its history.*

POST-MORTEUM PHOTOGRAPHY

HISTORY AND POPULARITY

The invention of the daguerreotype in 1839 made portraiture much more commonplace, as many of those who were unable to afford the commission of a painted portrait could afford to sit for a photography session. This cheaper and quicker method also provided the middle class with a means for memorializing dead loved ones, and this was also an effective way of getting a person to "sit still" long enough for the extended exposure times of early photographs.

These photographs served less as a reminder of mortality than as a keepsake to remember the deceased. This was especially common with infants and young children. Victorian era childhood mortality rates were extremely high and a post-mortem photograph might be the only image of the child the family ever had. The later invention of the carte de visite, which allowed multiple prints to be made from a single negative, meant that copies of the image could be mailed to relatives.

Sadly, typical Victorian era photo showing a family posed with their now post mortem daughter. It was a custom in that era just before burial, and while it is sad, it is also understandable. This was a time before people could travel great distances in a quick or timely fashion to attend a funeral of loved ones. A well-posed, lifelike photograph was a way, for relatives from afar, to see the beloved one last time before burial.

The practice eventually peaked in popularity around the end of the 19th century and died out as "snapshot" photography became more commonplace, although a few examples of formal memorial portraits were still being produced well into the 20th century. This practice may have been somewhat more common in Europe, but was also popular in the USA.

EVOLVING STYLE

The earliest post-mortem photographs are usually close-ups of the face or shots of the full body and rarely include the coffin. The subject is usually depicted so as to seem in a deep sleep or else arranged to appear more life-like. Children were often shown in repose on a couch or in a crib, sometimes posed with a favorite toy or play thing. It was not uncommon to photograph very young children with a family member, most frequently the mother. Adults were more commonly posed in chairs or even braced on specially designed frames. Flowers were also common props in post-mortem photography of all types.

The effect of "life" was enhanced by either propping the subject's eyes open or by painting pupils onto the photographic print and many early images (especially tintypes and ambrotypes) have a rosy tint added to the cheeks of the corpse.

Later examples show less effort at a life-like appearance and often show the subject in a coffin. Some very late examples show the deceased in a coffin with a large group of funeral attendees. This type of photograph was especially popular in Europe and less common in the United States.

Circa 1860 post-mortem photograph of a deceased man in a chair with table.

The practice of post mortem photography is still found in some places such as in Eastern Europe and elsewhere. Photographs, especially depicting persons who were considered to be very holy lying in coffins are still circulated between faithful Eastern Orthodox and Oriental Orthodox Christians.

The End

AFTERWORD

Looking back on our remarkable 40-year life journey together, Antonio generously shared his tremendous gifts of spiritual awareness, his insights, knowledge, and experience. Only now, after his transition, I understand just how much he's prepared me for numerous signs of his continued presence. This beautiful soul has confirmed for me, beyond any doubt, that our love and life energy are continuing after his death!

I do not expect you to believe or accept this, nor do I feel it is my role to convince you. I am compelled to let those of you who may be curious to know that, YES, I have and do receive signs and messages from Antonio today!

I am excited to describe moments of communication and insights from Antonio that were delightfully unexpected and directly impacted me in completing this book for him. Some may question why or how this is possible, but with 40 years of life and paranormal investigations between us, I am in the extraordinarily unique position to provide for you my own, first-hand, experiences of Antonio's life-after-death existence and continued collaborations.

Antonio and I worked on this book, on and off for the last few years. Unfortunately, the complications of his Parkinson's disease prevented him from physically devoting the time or mental energy of sitting at his desk. His idea for this final book was to present a sampling of stories from each of his most popular books and include stories from interviews he had completed but never published. This book was to be a best of Antonio's ghost stories, with new unpublished interviews serving as an excellent introduction to Antonio for those who are not familiar with his exceptional talent for storytelling.

During the last few weeks of his life, our focus was on providing a peaceful transition and nothing more, least of all this book. Before he passed, I promised Antonio that I would complete and release this book for him in 2024. Fortunately, Antonio and I managed to set up the table of contents, with select story interviews he wanted included.

As soon as I sat down to begin organizing this book, I realized that many of the original interview recordings and photo files from previous books had been locked away in a storage unit for years. I was faced with the tremendous and challenging job of finding every one of these resources all by myself.

There were boxes of original interviews on cassette tapes, transcribed documents, and photos stored somewhere, and everywhere. I searched for hours, but found nothing. I was overwhelmed with frustration and panic because I could not find these original materials. I racked my brain trying to recall where we put these invaluable items; and all these years later, I opened box after box, file cabinet after cabinet, with no success. After several frustrating days of searching, I asked Antonio to please help me find these items.

Within a day or two, I suddenly remembered a large four-drawer file cabinet that we had placed in a closet at home that I had completely forgotten! As soon as I returned home from our storage units, I went to the closet, opened the middle drawer, and discovered a CD storage case folder with all the manuscripts and photo files for each of his original ghost books. For over 15 years we had not seen, used or opened this file cabinet, but there it all was! I was thrilled and so very, very relieved.

It had always been Antonio's plan to dedicate his *American Indian Ghost Stories of the West* book to Mrs. Julia Parker, a beloved Yosemite Museum & Indian Village spokeswoman, and world-renowned basket weaving artist. During one of many camping trips to Yosemite, we had the honor of meeting with Julia at the museum. Antonio asked me to photograph him presenting Julia with a copy of *Ghost Stories of California's Gold Rush Country & Yosemite National Park*. Soon after we returned to our campsite, Antonio wrote the dedication and photo captions he had intended to use.

When we returned to our home in New Mexico, these items were placed in files and stored. Approximately a year later, when we were completing the *American Indian Ghost Stories of the West*, we were unable to find these photos and dedication. After much searching, we remained unsuccessful so Julia's tribute was left out and Antonio composed a different one.

In February 2024, as I was organizing the Yosemite stories that Antonio had selected for this book, I recalled the importance and significance of this tribute to Julia he wanted to include in *American Indian Ghost Stories of the West*, all those years ago. So, while I was again searching though our storage unit, I asked Antonio again to help me find the tribute to Julia materials so I could include them in this book. During this same time, I was fulfilling a large book order of Antonio's other titles for a distributor which involved sorting, counting, packaging and preparing cases of books to ship out.

Sometime within an hour of making my plea to Antonio to and while I was sorting books for packaging, I noticed a medium-sized cardboard storage box sticking out above my head, situated on top of a tall metal shelf. I grabbed a step stool nearby, positioned it directly underneath the shelf and brought down the box. When I lifted the lid, I found a large zip-lock bag with all of Antonio's original photos from our Yosemite visits, including those with Julia at the museum and his dedication notes, on the original yellow notepad he used. I was so "over the moon" with joy to have finally found these for inclusion in this book. I genuinely believe, after all these years of our wondering about and searching for these items, Antonio was totally behind both these discoveries. I absolutely believe he was!

Over the years, Antonio and I discussed our desires to each be cremated and have our ashes scatter in significant locations that we experienced, enjoyed, and loved. Since we were both born and raised there, most of these locations are in California and include Malibu beach, Pacific Coast Highway, and Yosemite National Park.

About a month after Antonio transitioned, I was seated at my computer reading emails when suddenly I received an unexpected email from an author friend whom I had not been in touch with for over 25 years. Her message was announcing a writing workshop retreat that she would be facilitating in Big Sur, California. I had been feeling overwhelmed about all the work needed to complete this book, but instantly noticed that specific attention on tools for organizing and writing would be offered at this workshop. I was curious to learn more and clicked on the link for details.

Upon doing so, the web page opened with a beautiful, breathtaking photo of the coast of Big Sur. At once I recalled a road trip Antonio and I made from Los Angeles north on Pacific Coast Highway through Big Sur. It was my first time driving that unforgettable stretch of coastline, and one of many remarkable travel experiences Antonio and I shared.

As I read further details about the writing workshop, I felt moved, inspired and encouraged to register-and did! This trip from Central New Mexico to Big Sur, would be my first, cross-country, solo journey since Antonio's passing. I felt terrified, sad and excited at the thought of making this trip on my own. In my mind, this was an opportunity to get away, visit many of the beautiful locations that Antonio introduced me to, and scatter his ashes in significant locations we both loved. My hope was to also, somehow, find whatever comfort and relief for the overwhelming grief I carried.

I had already decided that I would scatter Antonio's ashes at Yosemite National Park, which he excitedly introduced me to early on in our relationship. Over the years, we often spoke of favorite memories from our multiple visits and vacation adventures in this magnificent park. The most significant place I released Antonio's ashes was at Malibu State beach, where on September 11, 1983, we first professed our love for each other.

Not surprising, as soon as I registered for the writing retreat, I felt Antonio behind it all; my seeing the writing workshop announcement email, the breath-taking Big Sur photo, and even the idea for me to include side trips to favorite locations to scatter his ashes. Ultimately, the entire trip, which I made two months after his passing, was filled with remarkable insights, personal growth, and healing.

Finally, throughout my entire life, I rarely recall my dreams, but several weeks after Antonio passed, I woke up remembering this one. In the dream, the plan was for Antonio and I to meet at a favorite restaurant for lunch. Upon entering the over-crowded dining area, I noticed Antonio sitting at a table on the opposite side of the dining room, holding on to the back of an empty chair, and waving for me to join him. His incredibly handsome smile, vibrant sparkle in his eyes and excitement for life had been completely restored. Antonio's entire physical appearance radiated health, confidence and joy; which I had not experienced in years since his debilitating Parkinson's disease diagnosis.

As I made my way up to his table, I sat down in the chair beside him, he leaned into me, placed his hand on my forearm, looked me directly in the eyes and said "It's AMAZING!" In that split second I understood, and knew, he was referring to his experiences on the other side. I also felt this was an incredible message of Antonio holding a place for me, when my own time to transition happens; a truly moving scenario that I am sincerely grateful for and look forward to. Believe me when I tell you, I am experiencing Antonio's loving life energy embracing me now, more than ever!

I am profoundly humbled, honored and very proud to have provided you here with Unforgettable Ghost Story Interviews by Antonio R. Garcez.

-Hank Estrada

ABOUT THE AUTHOR

Antonio R. Garcez is a renowned author known for his books on paranormal activities, based on first-hand interviews. Since 1989, he has conducted extensive research and interviews on real ghost encounters. His respectful and professional approach to life-after-death topics, along with his unique writing style, have made his ghost books exceptionally popular. His Otomi/Mescalero Apache heritage and loving childhood have shaped his sensitivity towards paranormal phenomena. A graduate from the University of California at Northridge, Garcez has been self-publishing his books while residing in Central New Mexico with his husband of 40 years, Hank Estrada.

On September 10, 2023, Antonio courageously and gracefully welcomed his own transition to a new "no limits" life in spirit.

ACKNOWLEDGEMENTS

To all the individuals whom I interviewed for this book, for generously sharing their courageous, unforgettable experiences I sincerely thank and wish you beauty of strength, beauty of patience, beauty of sacrifice, and the internal beauty that ultimately manifests with wisdom and humor. Some of the names and locations associated with the stories mentioned in this book may have been changed at the personal request of individuals to protect their identities and properties. Many of these individuals have moved on since the printing of this book, either within this world or into the next. Their stories appear here as they were directly recorded at the time they were interviewed.

--Antonio

"THANK YOU to Elaine Murphy, Dolores Cruz, Joey Cruz, Lisa Murray, David Murray, Merci Schon, Edward Schon, and John Gonzalez, to whom I am forever grateful to; for your invaluable support, feedback, and encouragement in helping me achieve my promise to complete Antonio's final book and gift to our world!"

--Hank Estrada

REFERENCES

ARIZONA

Arizona Department of Tourism

Arizona Department of Commerce

Arizona State Parks

Arizona State Archives

Infinity Horn Publishing, Chinle AZ

CALIFORNIA

California State Parks Magazine, 2001 tenth edition, Meredith Corporation.

California Native American Heritage Commission, "A Professional guide."

Tuolumne County Visitors Bureau, Sandy Esau and Patricia Newton "History of Tuolumne"

Sutter's Fort Visitors Center "History of Sutter's Fort"

Photo of Donner Doll courtesy of Bob Basura, Supervising State Park Ranger "Sutter's Fort State Park"

"The Old Sacramento News," Pub. by Capitol Weekly Corporation

Lassen Loomis Museum Assoc. "Baskets by Selena La Mare and "Atsugewi"

Leilah Wendell, 'Encounters with Death—History of Azrael'

Yosemite Association, "The Miwok In Yosemite"

California Native American Heritage Commission, "A Professional Gguide."

"Chief Shavehead of the Hat Creek Nation" — Lassen Loomis Museum Assoc.

COLORADO

"History of Sand Creek Massacre," and "Bent's Fort History"— National Park Service, U.S. Dept. of the Interior

History of Ludlow Massacre. (2005, December 10). Wikipedia

"The Updated Colorado Guide" by Bruce Caughey and Dean Winstanley

Buffalo Bill & Grave/ Koshare Indian Historical Information and Museum

U.S. Army Colonel John Chivington and Delegation of Cheyenne, Kiowa and Arapaho

Manitou Springs Visitor's Guide, Royal Gorge Country Visitor's Guide

History of Black Canyon of the Gunnison, Anasazi Historical Information

Colorado Vacation Planner

The Mile-High City, Denver Visitor Guide

History of Colorado Prisons provided by The Museum of Colorado

Mesa Verde Country Travel Planner

Four Corners Arts and Entertainment Magazine

The Leadville Herald Democrat Museum of Western Colorado

Ute Indian Museum

NEW MEXICO

IAIA-Institute of American Indian Arts, Santa Fe, New Mexico

Santa Fe Convention and Visitors Bureau

New Mexico Department of Tourism

Pueblo Cultural Center, Albuquerque, New Mexico

Photos of Zia Pueblo and Chaco Canyon provided by U.S. National Parks Dept.

Southwestern Indian Tribes, Tom and Mark Bahti, KC Publications, 1999

History of the Laboratory of Anthropology and the Museum of Indian Arts & Culture provided by David E. McNeece, Rights & Reproductions Manager Museum of Indian Arts & Culture/Laboratory of Anthropology Department of Cultural Affairs, State of New Mexico.

Photo of Alfred Kidder, University of Texas Austin

Teller, J. "The Navajo Skin-walker, Witchcraft, & Related Spiritual Phenomena: Spiritual Clues: Orientation to the Evolution of the Circle"

History of Gallup: "Find a County" National Association of Counties

"Plaques to be Guide to City's Past" Gallup Independent. "US Gazetteer files: 2000 and 1990".

Johnson, Judith R. (1994) "A Mighty Fortress is the Pen: Development of the New Mexico Penitentiary" pp. 119–132 In DeMark, Judith Boycw (editor) (1994) Essays in Twentieth-Century New Mexico History University of New Mexico Press, Albuquerque, New Mexico.

Morris, Roger (1983). The Devil's Butcher Shop: The New Mexico Prison Uprising. Albuquerque: University of New Mexico Press.

Mark Colvin The Penitentiary in Crisis: From Accommodation to Riot in New Mexico, SUNY Press (1992).

History of Franklin J. Tolby provided by Richard Melzer, Ph.D., from his book "Buried Treasures—Famous and Unusual Graves in New Mexico's History."

Histories of: Fort Union, Aztec Ruins, Pecos, Chaco Culture National Park Service, U.S. Department of the Interior

'Post-mortem photography: its History and Popularity' and photos of Dead Girl with Parents and Dead Man provided by Wikipedia the free encyclopedia.

OTHER BOOKS BY ANTONIO R. GARCEZ:

American Indian Ghost Stories of the West
ISBN 0-9740988-4-1

Arizona Ghost Stories
ISBN 0-9740988-0-9

Ghost Stories of California's Gold Rush Country and Yosemite National Park
ISBN 0-9634029-8-1

Colorado Ghost Stories
ISBN 0-9740988-1-4

Gay and Lesbian Ghost Stories
ISBN 0-989895-3-9

Ghost Stories of the Medical Profession
ISBN 0-989895-4-6

New Mexico Ghost Stories vol. 1
ISBN 0-9898985-2-2

New Mexico Ghost Stories vol. 2
ISBN 0-9898985-1-5